Adolescent Mental Health Care and the Law

Dr Camilla Parker is an independent legal and policy consultant, researcher and trainer specialising in the areas of mental health, disability and human rights. Much of her work focuses on the law and human rights relevant to the mental health care of adolescents, which was the subject of her PhD in Law (Cardiff University, 2017). Camilla was a member of the 'Children and Young People' and 'Maximising autonomy: consent to treatment' topic groups for the 2018 independent review of the Mental Health Act 1983. As a consultant for the Department of Health she led on the work to revise the children and young people's chapter in the Mental Health Act 1983 Code of Practice (2015). Camilla is a qualified (non-practising) solicitor, a member of the Law Society's Mental Health and Disability Committee and an Honorary Senior Lecturer at the Tizard Centre, University of Kent.

The Legal Action Group is a national, independent charity which campaigns for equal access to justice for all members of society. Legal Action Group:

- provides support to the practice of lawyers and advisers;
- inspires developments in that practice;
- campaigns for improvements in the law and the administration of justice;
- stimulates debate on how services should be delivered.

Adolescent Mental Health Care and the Law

Camilla Parker

LAG the access to justice charity
Legal Action Group
2020

This edition published in Great Britain 2020
by LAG Education and Service Trust Limited
c/o Oliver Fisher Solicitors, Royalty Studios
105-109 Lancaster Road
London W11 1QF
www.lag.org.uk

British Library Cataloguing in Publication Data
a CIP catalogue record for this book is available from the British Library.

FSC
www.fsc.org
MIX
Paper | Supporting responsible forestry
FSC® C020438

This book has been produced using Forest Stewardship Council (FSC) certified paper. The wood used to produce FSC certified products with a 'Mixed Sources' label comes from FSC certified well-managed forests, controlled sources and/or recycled material.

print ISBN 978 1 912273 20 1
ebook ISBN 978 1 912273 21 8
print / ebook bundle ISBN 978 1 912273 41 6

Typeset by Refinecatch Limited, Bungay, Suffolk
Printed in Great Britain by Hobbs the Printers, Totton, Hampshire

Preface

This book focuses on the law relating to children and young people aged under 18 (also referred to as adolescents[1]) whose mental health needs are such that they are considered to require a period of inpatient psychiatric care.

This is an area of law that is renowned for its complexity. This is unsurprising given that the law governing adolescents' admission to hospital and treatment for mental disorder engages points of uncertainty such as the limits of the decision-making powers between parents and their children and the developing law on deprivation of liberty. Furthermore, the provision of mental health services for this age group involves a range of differing agencies and engages a raft of legislation, case-law, regulations, codes of practice and policy guidance across the differing fields of law: mental health, mental capacity, community care, family and children's rights. That there is a potential problem with this crossover of specialisms was highlighted by Sir James Munby, former President of the Family Division, in his observation regarding the development of case law on the deprivation of liberty of under 18s:

> '. . .these cases lie at the intersection of three different bodies of domestic law – mental health law, mental capacity law and family law – where judicial decision-making is spread over a variety of courts and tribunals which, by and large, are served by different sections of the legal professions too few of whom are familiar with all three bodies of law.' (Speech to the LAG Community Care Law Conference, October 2018.)

Similarly, legal text books and policy guidance concerned with mental health and/or mental capacity law, tend to focus on adults whereas those concerned with children's services give little consideration to the specific issues for adolescents with mental

1 The reasons for using this term are explained in chapter 1.

health needs, or how legal frameworks, such as provisions for looked after children, interact with the Mental Health Act 1983. Moreover, while recent reports have highlighted the significant problems in the provision of children and young people's mental health services, most particularly that too few under 18s are receiving the specialist mental health services that they need, it is rare for such reports to provide an explanation of how the relevant legal frameworks operate or to consider the human rights implications of the problems raised.

Accordingly, the overarching aim of this book is to bridge a gap in the information currently available to legal advisers working with adolescents with mental health needs, such as those providing legal representation before the mental health tribunal, as well as non-lawyers, such as advocates and professionals working in children's services and mental health services (adult, as well as children and young people's services). It does so by drawing together the legal provisions relevant to the mental health care of adolescents and considering how they relate to one another. Consideration of such issues is particularly important given the events of 2020. As we all learn how to recalibrate our lives in this time of COVID-19, one of the emerging concerns is the adverse impact this pandemic is having on children and young people's mental health.

Although seeking to be as comprehensive as possible, regretfully, given the increasing differences in law between the two countries, this book covers the law relating to England but not Wales. Nor is youth justice and mental health covered (this subject probably meriting its own book).

In writing this book, I have received support and inspiration from many people. In particular, I would like to thank my family (Veronica, Lily, Sophie and John, Lucinda and Roger, Ed and Sujay), the three young people who kick-started my journey into this legal maze (Rebecca Collins, Lois Ward and Antonia Wilkinson) and the following friends and colleagues:

Paul Bacon, Tim and Amanda Barraclough, Francine Bates, Claire Bethel, Steve Broach, Russell Campbell, Jill Craigie, Suyog Dhakras, Kamena Dorling, Vicki Farrally, Phil Fennell, Stephen Gilmore, Richard Gordon QC, Daniel Hayes, Julie Hine, Jo Honigmann, Leigh Hogan (and colleagues: Holly Whitman, Michelle Sancho, Rashida Baig, Jane Seymour and Brenice Huntingdon), Richard Jones, Mat Kinton, Judith Laing, Penny Letts, (the late and much missed) Nick Lewis, Nicola Mackintosh QC (Hon), Mary Mitchell, Vicky Nicholls, Hugh Osmond, Kathryn Pugh, Moli Paul, Mary Purcell, Carlotta

Raby, Steven Richards, Kay Scorah, Lucy Series, Emma Silburn, Harriet Waldegrave, Jo White and Kathy Whitfield.

Especial thanks are due to Julie Beadle-Brown, Sarah Cannell, Luke Clements, Julie Doughty, Simon Foster, Anthony Harbour, Neil Hickman, John Horne, Christine Hutchison and Alex Ruck Keene who generously gave their time to read and comment on draft chapters. However, all mistakes in the text are mine.

I am indebted to the amazing Esther Pilger, LAG's publishing director, who has provided me with help, advice and encouragement throughout the long, and at times, difficult process of transforming the idea of a book into a reality. A second person who has been crucial to the delivery of this book is Robert Bellhouse. His unwavering support, willingness to comment on the clarity of tricky paragraphs at a moment's notice and patience when another weekend is taken up with 'the book' are just a few examples of the tasks undertaken by this one-man support team.

I have endeavoured to state the law as at 12 June 2020 and wherever possible have included developments since then up to 1 September 2020. Given the complexity of this area of law, there are bound to be gaps in points covered, differences in my interpretation of the law, and (despite my best efforts to avoid them) errors. I would welcome comments on the text and any other views on the issues raised. These can be sent to me at: camilla@justequality.co.uk

Finally, this book is dedicated to the wonderful adolescents in my life: Emma, Joe, Rosie, Rachel, Richard, Kate and of course Emilia and her little sister, Evelyn Sophie, who arrived today.

Camilla Parker
21 September 2020

Contents

APPENDICES

Table of cases

R (DA) v Secretary of State for Work and Pensions [2019] UKSC 21, [2019] 1 WLR 3289, [2020] 1 All ER 573, [2019] PTSR 1072, [2019] 5 WLUK 194, [2019] HRLR 12, [2019] HLR 31, (2019) *Times*, May 29	1.24
R (DPP) v Stratford Magistrates' Court [2017] EWHC 1794 (Admin), [2018] 4 WLR 47, [2017] 7 WLUK 342, [2017] 2 Cr App R 32, (2017) 181 JP 474, [2018] Crim LR 157, [2017] ACD 104	7.50
R (G) v Barnet LBC [2003] UKHL 57, [2004] 2 AC 208, [2003] 3 WLR 1194, [2004] 1 All ER 97, [2003] 10 WLUK 662, [2004] 1 FLR 454, [2003] 3 FCR 419, [2004] HRLR 4, [2004] HLR 10, [2003] BLGR 569, (2003) 6 CCLR 500, [2004] Fam Law 21, (2003) 100(45) LSG 29, [2003] NPC 123, (2003) *Times*, October 24, (2003) *Independent*, October 29	9.25
R (G) v Nottingham City Council [2008] EWHC 152 (Admin), [2008] 2 WLUK 6, [2008] 1 FLR 1660, (2008) 11 CCLR 273, [2008] Fam Law 410	3.94, 4.74, 7.54, 9.34
R (G) v Nottingham City Council [2008] EWHC 400 (Admin), [2008] 3 WLUK 67, [2008] 1 FLR 1668, [2008] 3 FCR 568, (2008) 11 CCLR 280, [2008] Fam Law 630	4.74, 9.34
R (G) v Southwark LBC [2009] UKHL 26, [2009] 1 WLR 1299, [2009] 3 All ER 189, [2009] PTSR 1080, [2009] 5 WLUK 474, [2009] 2 FLR 380, [2009] 2 FCR 459, [2009] BLGR 673, (2009) 12 CCLR 437, [2009] Fam Law 668, (2009) 159 NLJ 791, (2009) 153(20) SJLB 42, [2009] NPC 73, (2009) *Times*, June 4	2.41, 9.31, 9.37, 9.85
R (HP and KP) v Islington LBC [2004] EWHC 7 (Admin), [2004] 1 WLUK 63, (2005) 82 BMLR 113	9.42
R (Hertfordshire CC) v Hammersmith and Fulham LBC and JM [2011] EWCA Civ 77, [2011] PTSR 1623, [2011] 2 WLUK 512, [2011] BLGR 536, (2011) 14 CCLR 224, [2011] Med LR 181, (2011) 119 BMLR 27, [2011] MHLR 76, [2011] ACD 60	9.92, 9.93
R (IH) v Secretary of State for the Home Department and others [2003] UKHL 59, [2004] 2 AC 253, [2003] 3 WLR 1278, [2004] 1 All ER 412, [2003] 11 WLUK 313, [2004] HRLR 5, [2004] UKHRR 115, 15 BHRC 571, (2004) 7 CCLR 147, (2004) 76 BMLR 179, [2004] MHLR 51, (2004) 101(2) LSG 30, (2003) 147 SJLB 1365, (2003) *Times*, November 14, (2003) *Independent*, November 18	9.52

Table of statutes

Table of statutory instruments

Table of European and international legislation

Abbreviations

AC	approved clinician
ACA 2002	Adoption and Children Act 2002
ASD	autistic spectrum disorders
AMCP	approved mental capacity professional
AMHP	approved mental health professional
AWOL	absent without leave
BDRA 1953	Births, Deaths and Registration Act 1953
CA 1989	Children Act 1989
CA 2004	Children Act 2004
CAMHS	Child and Adolescent Mental Health Services
CAO	child arrangement order
Care Planning Guidance	*Children Act 1989 guidance and regulations. Volume 2: care planning, placement and case review,* Department for Education, June 2015
Care Planning Regs	Care Planning, Placement and Case Review (England) Regulations 2010 SI No 959
CCG	clinical commissioning group
CETR	Care, Education and Treatment Review
CETR Code and Toolkit	*Care, Education and Treatment Reviews for children and young people: Code and Toolkit. A guide for commissioners, panel members and people who provide support,* NHS England, April 2017
CETR Policy	*Care and Treatment Reviews (CTRs): Policy and Guidance. Including policy and guidance on Care, Education and Treatment Reviews (CETRs) for children and young people,* NHS England, March 2017
CFA 2014	Children and Families Act 2014
CoP	Court of Protection
COVID-19 Legal Guidance	*Legal guidance for mental health, learning disability and autism, and specialised commissioning services supporting people of all ages during the coronavirus pandemic,* NHS (Publications approval reference: 001559), 19 May 2020 version 2

CPA	Care Programme Approach
CPA Guidance	*Refocusing the Care Programme Approach: policy and positive practice guidance*, Department of Health, March 2008
CQC	Care Quality Commission
CRG	Clinical Reference Group
C(R&S)A 1995	Carers (Recognition and Services) Act 1995
CSDPA 1970	Chronically Sick and Disabled Persons Act 1970
CTO	community treatment order
CYPMHS	Children and Young People's Mental Health Services
DfE	Department for Education
DHSC	Department of Health and Social Care (formerly the Department of Health until 2018)
DoH	Department of Health (renamed the Department of Health and Social Care in 2018)
DoLS	Deprivation of Liberty Safeguards
DP(SCR)A 1986	Disabled Persons (Services, Consultation and Representation) Act 1986
ECHR	European Convention on Human Rights
ECT	electro-convulsive therapy
ECtHR	European Court of Human Rights
EHC	education, health and care
EHRC	Equality and Human Rights Commission
EPO	emergency protection order
EqA 2010	Equality Act 2010
FLRA 1969	Family Law Reform Act 1969
FOI	freedom of information
GP	general practitioner
HA 1996	Housing Act 1996
HESC	Health, Education and Social Care
HFEA 2008	Human Fertilisation and Embryology Act 2008
Housing Guidance	*Prevention of homelessness and provision of accommodation for 16 and 17 year old young people who may be homeless and/or require accommodation. Guidance to children's services authorities and local housing authorities about their duties under Part 3 of the Children Act 1989 and Part 7 of the Housing Act 1996 to secure or provide accommodation for homeless 16 and 17 year old young people*, Ministry of Housing, Communities and Local Government and Department for Education, 2018
HRA 1998	Human Rights Act 1998

ICO	interim care order
IMCA	independent mental capacity advocate
IRO	independent reviewing officer
JCHR	Joint Committee on Human Rights
LASSA 1970	Local Authority Social Services Act 1970
LHB	Local Health Board
LPA	lasting powers of attorney
LPS	Liberty Protection Safeguards
LTP	local transformation plan
MCA 2005	Mental Capacity Act 2005
MCA Code	*Mental Capacity Act 2005: Code of Practice,* Department for Constitutional Affairs, July 2007
MC(A)A 2019	Mental Capacity (Amendment) Act 2019
MHA 1983	Mental Health Act 1983
MHA 2007	Mental Health Act 2007
MHA Code	*Mental Health Act 1983: Code of Practice,* Department of Health, 2015
MHA Reference Guide	*Reference guide to the Mental Health Act 1983,* Department of Health, 2015
MHA Review	*Modernising the Mental Health Act: Increasing choice, reducing compulsion,* Final report of the Independent Review of the Mental Health Act 1983, December 2018
MHRT Wales	Mental Health Review Tribunal for Wales
NAO	National Audit Office
NHS	National Health Service
NHS CCG Regulations	National Health Service Commissioning Board and Clinical Commissioning Groups (Responsibilities and Standing Rules) Regulations 2012 SI No 2996
NHSCCA 1990	National Health Service and Community Care Act 1990
NICE	National Institute for Health and Care Excellence
NR	nearest relative
NYAS	National Youth Advocacy Service
PHE	pre-hearing examination
PICU	psychiatric intensive care unit
PR	parental responsibility
PSED	public sector equality duty
PTSD	post-traumatic stress disorder
RB	responsible body
RC	responsible clinician

Restrictive Intervention Guidance	*Reducing the need for restraint and restrictive intervention: Children and young people with learning disabilities, autistic spectrum conditions and mental health difficulties in health and social care services and special education settings*, HM Government, June 2019
SCR	social circumstances report
SEN	special educational needs
SEND	special educational needs and disability
SEND Code	*Special educational needs and disability code of practice: 0 to 25 years. Statutory guidance for organisations which work with and support children and young people who have special educational needs or disabilities*, Department for Education and Department of Health, January 2015
SGO	special guardianship order
SOAD	second opinion appointed doctor
SoS	secretary of state
STAMP	Supporting Treatment and Appropriate Medication in Paediatrics
Statutory Visits Guidance	*Statutory visits to children with special educational needs and disabilities or health conditions in long-term residential settings: Statutory guidance for local authorities, health bodies and health or educational establishments*, Department for Education and the Department of Health, November 2017
STOMP	Stopping over-medication of people with a learning disability autism or both
TCEA 2007	Tribunals, Courts and Enforcement Act 2007
Tribunal Procedure Rules	Tribunal Procedure (First-tier Tribunal) (Health, Education and Social Care Chamber) Rules 2008 SI No 2699
UNCRC	UN Convention on the Rights of the Child
UNCRPD	UN Convention on the Rights of Persons with Disabilities
Visits Regs	Visits to Children in Long-Term Residential Care Regulations 2011 SI No 1010
WHO	World Health Organization
Working together	*Working Together to Safeguard Children: A guide to inter-agency working to safeguard and promote the welfare of children*, HM Government, July 2018

CHAPTER 1

Introduction to adolescent mental health care and the law

Introduction

1.1 One of the many challenges facing anyone with an interest in understanding the situation of children and young people aged under 18 ('adolescents')[1] with mental health needs in England is the dearth of information. In 2014, the House of Commons' Health Committee reported that the lack of 'reliable and up to date information' meant that those planning and running children and young people's services 'have been operating in a "fog"'.[2] Since then steps have been taken to address this information gap. For example, the long awaited survey of children and young people's mental health was published in 2018[3] (the previous survey having been published over a decade before (2004[4])), which found that in 2017 one in eight (12.8 per cent) five to 19 year olds have a mental health disorder. Furthermore, emotional disorders have become more common in five to 15-year olds (rising from 3.9 per cent in 2004 to 5.8 per cent in 2017). Nonetheless, the lack of information remains a concern. While welcoming the government's focus on improving NHS services for children and young people, the House of Commons Public Accounts Committee's 2019 report, *Mental health services for children and young people* (the PAC report), highlighted the 'significant gaps in the data to monitor progress'.[5]

1.2 Another significant problem raised by the PAC report is the 'treatment gap', meaning that services for children and young people with mental health needs 'will not reach most of those who need help'.[6] Noting that the government's target is to 'increase the proportion of children and young people with a diagnosable mental health condition who receive NHS-funded treatment, from 25% in 2016–17 to

1 The reasons for using this term are explained at para 1.9 below.

2 *Children's and adolescents' mental health and CAMHS*, House of Commons Health Committee (2014–2015 HC 342) summary, see also paras 23–24. See also *Future in mind: promoting, protecting and improving our children and young people's mental health and wellbeing*, DoH and NHS England, 2015, paras 2.16, 3.25, 5.15, 7.15, 9.3 and 10.5.

3 *Mental Health of Children and Young People in England: Summary of key findings*, NHS Digital, 2017, pp6–8.

4 H Green H, A McGinnity, H Meltzer, T Ford, R Goodman, *Mental health of children and young people in Great Britain 2004*, Palgrave Macmillan, 2005 – a survey carried out by the Office for National Statistics on behalf of the DoH and the Scottish Executive.

5 *Mental Health Services for Children and Young People*, House of Commons Committee of Public Accounts (2017–2019 HC 1593), ('the PAC Report') paras 11 and 18–21.

6 PAC report, para 4.

35% by 2020–21', the PAC report observes: 'even if the 2020–21 target is reached, two-thirds of children will not have access to such treatment'.[7] Its conclusion is stark:

> Most young people with a mental health condition do not get the treatment they need, and under current NHS plans this will still be true for years to come, while many face unacceptably long waits for treatment. . .There is a clear risk that young people reach crisis point if they do not get help but the NHS has limited sight on what happens to children and young people turned away from NHS services.[8]

1.3 In relation to those under 18s who do receive help, it is estimated that in 2018/2019, nearly 380,000 children and young people were treated by NHS-funded community services ('approximately 36.1% of children and young people with a diagnosable mental health condition').[9] A much smaller number of this age group (less than 5,000[10]) are admitted to children and young people's inpatient mental health services.

1.4 This book is concerned with the adolescents falling within this small group of children and young people whose mental health needs are such that they are considered to require a period of inpatient psychiatric care. It focuses on the law governing decisions about their admission to hospital and treatment for mental disorder. Again, efforts to understand their situation is thwarted by the paucity of information. It is only since January 2016 that the number of under-18s admitted to hospital under the Mental Health Act (MHA) 1983 has been published.[11] For the years 2017/2018 and 2018/2019 such information has been disaggregated by gender and ethnicity, but other important points, such as how many of such adolescents were looked after by local authorities prior to their admission to hospital or the length of their stay is not readily available.[12] Moreover, while the

7 PAC report para 5. The *NHS long term plan*, January 2019 states (para 3.25): 'Over the coming decade the goal is to ensure that 100% of children and young people who need specialist care can access it.'

8 PAC report, Conclusions and recommendations, para 1.

9 This figure is given at: www.england.nhs.uk/mental-health/cyp/. See also *NHS long term plan*, January 2019 para 3.23.

10 See Report by the Comptroller and Auditor General *Improving children and young people's mental health services* National Audit Office (NAO), October 2018, figure 9. The latest year covered in figure 9 shows that in 2017/2018 there were 4,705 inpatient admissions.

11 NHS Digital: https://digital.nhs.uk/data-and-information/publications/statistical/mental-health-services-monthly-statistics. The information is described as 'experimental'.

12 Concerns about out of area placements and admissions to adult wards are discussed in chapter 6 below.

available information suggests that the majority (at least two thirds) of under 18s are admitted to hospital and treated for their mental disorder 'informally' (ie not detained in hospital under the MHA 1983),[13] the legal basis on which adolescents are receiving such informal inpatient psychiatric care is not published.

1.5 The rest of chapter is divided into two parts. First, it first provides an overview of the book (its scope and purpose, an explanation of the terms used and a note on codes of practice and statutory guidance). Secondly, reflecting the overarching importance of human rights to the issues examined in subsequent chapters, an outline of the Human Rights Act (HRA) 1998 is provided together with a note on additional human rights standards relevant to adolescents' mental health care.

Overview

Scope and purpose

1.6 In focusing on the law, as applied in England, relevant to adolescents who, due to their complex mental health needs are considered to require a period of inpatient psychiatric care, this book is concerned with the following two broad areas:

1) *Adolescents admission to hospital and treatment for mental disorder:* First and foremost, this book provides a detailed examination of the legal framework for adolescents' admission to hospital and treatment for mental disorder. This is an area of law that has long been renowned for its complexity. It was described by the 1999 the review of the Mental Health Act (MHA) 1983 as being 'in need of clarification' and creating 'a climate of uncertainty'.[14] Nearly 20 years later, a similar conclusion was reached by the MHA review of 2018. It noted the 'legal complexities and ambiguities surrounding admission and consent to treatment, including the role of parental responsibility' and the need to consider the interaction

13 In its report *Monitoring the Mental Health Act* in 2015/16 at 29, the Care Quality Commission (CQC) noted that its 'snapshot' in October 2016 showed that of the 1,320 under 18s receiving inpatient psychiatric care, a third had been admitted under the MHA 1983. A comparison with the total number of admissions for 2017/2018 stated to be 4,705 (see *Improving children and young people's mental health services* (NAO) 2018, figure 9) with the number of detentions under the MHA 1983 in 2017/2018 stated to be 1,177 (see NHS Digital *Mental Health Statistics, Annual Figures 2017-18*) suggests an even lower percentage (25 per cent).

14 *Report of the Expert Committee, Review of the Mental Health Act 1983*, Department of Health (DoH), November 1999, para 13.1.

between the MHA 1983 and legal frameworks such as the Children Act (CA) 1989 and the Mental Capacity Act (MCA) 2005 (for those aged over 16).[15]

2) *Services and support for adolescents and their families:* Reflecting that decisions about adolescents' inpatient psychiatric care are not made in a vacuum, this book also provides an overview of the various legal frameworks that might apply to adolescents with complex needs, given that they may be 'children in need', 'looked after children' or have special educational needs.[16] Such legal frameworks will be of particular relevance when considering whether an adolescent requires in-patient psychiatric care (as noted by the Health Select Committee, timely support to under-18s may help to avoid the need for admission to in-patient services),[17] when planning an adolescent's after-care on leaving hospital, as well as when considering local authorities on-going responsibilities to adolescents who are receiving inpatient care.

1.7 These two areas are considered in subsequent chapters as follows:

- overview of law and policy underpinning the range of services and agencies that together form children and young peoples' mental health services (often referred to as 'CAMHS' – children and adolescent mental health services) (chapter 2);
- overview of the legal framework for adolescents' admission to hospital and treatment for mental disorder (chapter 3);
- the MCA 2005 and its relevance to adolescents aged 16 and 17 (chapter 4);
- the rules for identifying who has parental responsibility for the adolescent and who is the 'nearest relative' for the purpose of the MHA 1983 (chapter 5);
- admission to hospital, including an explanation of the criteria and procedures for admission to hospital under the MHA 1983 (chapter 6);
- treatment and care in hospital, including the rules governing treatment under Part 4 of the MHA 1983 (chapter 7);

15 The Independent Review of the Mental Health Act, Interim Report, May 2018. See also, *Modernising the Mental Health Act: Increasing choice, reducing compulsion* ('MHA Review'), Final Report of the Independent Review of the Mental Health Act 1983, December 2018.

16 These terms are explained in chapter 2.

17 *Children's and adolescents' mental health and CAMHS*, House of Commons Health Committee (2014–2015 HC 342, para 33.

- the rules governing discharge from detention under the MHA 1983, including the procedures before the Mental Health Tribunal (chapter 8);
- the range of legal frameworks relevant to planning adolescents' discharge from hospital: after-care planning (chapter 9); and
- community powers, including community treatment orders and police powers (chapter 10).

1.8 By drawing together the differing legal frameworks that might apply to adolescents with mental health needs, this book seeks to assist in generating a better understanding of this complex area of law. In addition to providing a resource for legal advisers, this book seeks to be accessible to non-lawyers, including professionals working in children's services and mental health services (adult as well as children and young people's mental health services).

Terminology

1.9 Key terms are explained in each chapter and a glossary of terms at appendix D to this book. The box below provides an explanation of terms used throughout this book.

Box 1.1: Terms used in this book

- '*Adolescent*': Means any person who is aged under 18. Whereas the term 'adolescent' is usually applied to older children (from 10 onwards),[18] for the purpose of this book, it also includes children under 10, reflecting that in some cases younger children may require in-patient psychiatric care.[19] The reason for using this term is because, whereas for the purpose of the CA 1989, '"child" means . . . a person under the age of eighteen', in this area of law, important distinctions are made between those aged under 16 and those aged 16 and 17[20] while in some legislation the term 'young person' includes people older than 18.[21]

18 *Adolescent Friendly Health Services: An Agenda for Change*, World Health Organization (WHO), 2003, p5 refers to adolescents as spanning the age range from 10–19 years.

19 See V Thomas and others, 'The application of mental health legislation in younger children' (2015) BJPsy Bulletin 39, 302 in which the authors discuss a case in which an eight-year-old boy was detained under the MHA 1983.

20 Where these are discussed the term 'child' will be used for those aged under 16 and 'young person' for those aged 16 and 17.

21 For example, under the Children and Families Act (CFA) 2014 s83(2) a young person can be anyone up to the age of 25.

- '*Complex mental health needs*'. This term is used in relation to adolescents who are considered to require specialised mental health care, which may necessitate their admission to hospital and treatment for mental disorder ('in-patient psychiatric care').
- '*Mental health care*': A diverse range of terms are often used, such as 'mental health needs', 'mental health problems' and 'emotional and psychological problems'. In addition to such generic terms, this book refers to 'mental disorder', which is defined in the MHA 1983 as 'any disorder or disability of the mind'.[22] This broad definition can cover a range of conditions, such as anxiety, depression, eating disorders, learning disabilities and autistic spectrum disorders, which can affect adolescents as well as adults.[23] The MHA Code includes 'behavioural and emotional disorders of children and young people' in the list of 'clinically recognised conditions' which could fall within the definition of 'mental disorder'.[24]
- *Patients:* While seeking to avoid using this term wherever possible, reference is made to 'patient(s)' when citing relevant parts of the MHA 1983 and the MHA Code.

Codes of practice and statutory guidance

1.10 Throughout this book, reference is made to 'codes of practice' and 'statutory guidance'.

- *Codes of practice:* three codes are of particular relevance:
  - the *Mental Health Act 1983: Code of Practice* ('MHA Code') is of key importance when considering the legal framework for adolescents' admission to hospital and treatment for mental disorder. As explained in more detail in chapter 2, the MHA Code was issued under the MHA 1983, which requires mental health professionals to 'have regard to the code'.[25]
  - the *Mental Capacity Act 2005: Code of Practice* ('MCA Code'), which is issued under the MCA 2005[26] and the *Special*

22 MHA 1983 s1(2).

23 See S Bailey and M Shooter (eds), *The young mind: an essential guide to mental health for young adults, parents and teachers*, Bantam Press, 2009; and M Mitchell 'The Diagnosis and Management of Complex Mental Illness in Young People' 150, in A Harbour, *Children with mental disorder and the law: a guide to law and practice*, Jessica Kingsley Publishers, 2008.

24 *Mental Health Act 1983: Code of Practice*, DoH, 2015, para 2.5.

25 MHA 1983 s118(2D).

26 MCA 2005 s42.

educational needs and disability code of practice: 0 to 25 years ('SEND Code') which was issued under the Children and Families Act (CFA) 2014.[27] Although the wording is not identical, just like the MHA 1983 (in relation to the MHA Code), the MCA 2005 (in relation to the MCA Code)[28] and the CFA 2005 (in relation to the SEND Code),[29] require that specified individuals and organisations 'have regard' to the code of practice when exercising their statutory functions.

- *Statutory guidance:* various guidance relevant to the provision of services and support to children and young people are referred to as 'statutory guidance', such as *Working Together to Safeguard Children: A guide to inter-agency working to safeguard and promote the welfare of children;*[30] and *The Children Act 1989 guidance and regulations – Volume 2: care planning, placement and case review.*[31] This is because they have been issued under Local Authority Social Services Act (LASSA) 1970 s7,[32] which requires local authorities, when exercising their social services functions, to act under the general guidance of the Secretary of State. The courts have held that a departure from such guidance 'would be unlawful unless there is cogent reason for it'.[33]

Coronavirus Act 2020

1.11 In response to the coronavirus (COVID 19) pandemic, the government introduced the Coronavirus Act 2020. This includes a wide range of measures with the potential to affect adolescents with mental health needs. Unsurprisingly, given the fast-changing situation and the breadth of law and policy relevant to addressing the

27 CFA 2014 s77.
28 MCA 2005 s42(4).
29 CFA 2014 s77(4).
30 HM Government, July 2018.
31 DFE June 2015.
32 LASSA 1970 s7 is not unique. See, for example, the list of legislation requiring compliance with guidance listed in HM Government, *Working Together to Safeguard Children: A guide to inter-agency working to safeguard and promote the welfare of children,* July 2018, p7. See also Care Act 2014 s78; and see guidance to assist local authorities to carry out the implementation of the Care Act 2014: *Care and support statutory guidance,* Department of Health and Social Care (DHSC), regularly updated and available online at: www.gov.uk/government/publications/care-act-statutory-guidance/care-and-support-statutory-guidance.
33 *R (X) v Tower Hamlets LBC* [2013] EWCA Civ 904 at [28]. See also *R(TG) v Lambeth LBC* [2011] EWCA Civ 526 at [17].

impact of this disease, law and guidance is constantly being updated. Accordingly, subsequent chapters highlight relevant provisions of this Act and include suggested resources on where information on the current situation can be obtained.

Adolescent health care and human rights

Introduction

1.12 Although restrictions on the rights and freedoms of individuals with mental health problems are permitted under mental health law in certain circumstances, as Lady Hale has emphasised:

> People suffering from mental disorders have the same human rights as everyone else and are entitled to enjoy those rights without discrimination on account of their mental status. So we must start from the proposition that they are entitled to the same freedom and autonomy as everyone else, unless there is some justification within the scheme of the Convention for interfering in this.[34]

Within the United Kingdom (UK), the Human Rights Act (HRA) 1998 forms the basis of the human rights framework within which decisions about adolescents' mental health care are made.[35] The HRA 1998 incorporates the European Convention on Human Rights (ECHR) into UK law and requires public authorities, such as NHS bodies and local authorities, to act compatibly with the ECHR unless an Act of Parliament prevents them from doing so (see para 1.16 below).

An overview of the HRA 1998 is set out below. This is followed by, first, a summary of human rights standards that are of particular relevance to adolescent mental health care and, secondly, examples of the provision of mental health care of adolescents that have raised significant human rights concerns.

Human Rights Act 1998

Overview

1.13 A significant effect of the HRA 1998 is that those making decisions in relation to adolescents' mental health care must consider the

34 *Rabone v Pennine Care NHS Foundation Trust* [2012] UKSC 2.

35 The UK's withdrawal from the European Union (EU) will not affect the application of the HRA 1998, which will remain in force unless and until it is abolished by an Act of Parliament.

human rights implications of their decisions: how these impact on the ECHR rights of both the adolescents concerned and on the adolescents' family, in particular their parents.

1.14 Under the HRA 1998, it is unlawful for a 'public authority' (defined below) to act in a way that is incompatible with ECHR rights,[36] unless it is required to do so by primary legislation.[37] Nor can public authorities fail to act if compliance with the ECHR requires action on their part.[38]

1.15 Individuals who consider that their rights under the ECHR have been infringed by a public authority can pursue a claim against that public authority.[39] However, to do so they must be '(or would be) a victim of the unlawful act',[40] which means that they must be able to show that they have been '"directly affected" by the measure complained of'.[41] In certain circumstances, others can pursue a claim on behalf of the victim, for example, a relative or representative where the victim is unable to do so due to their age or disability.[42] Parents can make claims on behalf of their children aged under 18.[43] Where the court upholds the complaint, it may grant whatever remedy within its powers that it considers just and appropriate, which may include damages.[44]

36 The ECHR rights falling within the HRA 1998 (referred to as 'Convention rights' in s1(1)) are set out in Sch 1.

37 In other words, an Act of Parliament: see HRA 1998 s6(2). So far as it is possible to do so, legislation must be interpreted in a way that is compatible with ECHR rights (HRA 1998 s3). Where this is not possible, certain courts, such as the High Court, Court of Appeal and the Supreme Court, can issue a 'declaration of incompatibility' (HRA 1998 s4), which is intended to act as a prompt to government on the need to amend the relevant law so that it is compatible with the ECHR.

38 HRA 1998 s6(6).

39 HRA 1998 s7(1): they may '(a)bring proceedings against the authority under this Act in the appropriate court or tribunal, or (b) rely on the Convention right or rights concerned in any legal proceedings'.

40 HRA 1998 s7(1); see also s7(7) which links the meaning of 'victim' under the HRA 1998 to victim for the purposes of ECHR Article 34.

41 *Centre for Legal Resources on behalf of Valentin Câmpeanu v Romania* [2014] ECHR 789 at [96]. See also [97]–[103] for discussion on when individuals other than the 'victim' can pursue a claim.

42 *European Court of Human Rights Practical Guide on Admissibility Criteria*, Council of Europe, updated 31 August 2019, para 51.

43 See, for example, *Glass v UK* [2004] ECHR 102; and *MAK v UK* [2010] ECHR 363.

44 HRA 1998 s8.

Public authorities under HRA 1998

1.16 The term 'public authority' includes courts and tribunals as well as 'any person certain of whose functions are functions of a public nature'[45] which therefore includes a wide range of bodies such as local authorities and NHS bodies. It also covers individuals carrying out statutory functions, so will include mental health professionals undertaking functions under MHA 1983, for example assessing whether a person should be admitted to hospital under the MHA 1983. Accordingly, even where they have statutory powers to place restrictions on the rights and freedoms of individuals, mental health professionals must ensure that they not only act in accordance with the relevant legislation, case-law and codes of practice, but also that their actions comply with their obligations to ensure that they protect and secure the ECHR rights of everyone who uses services.[46]

Depending on the circumstances, private organisations, such as independent hospitals, will be a 'public authority' for the purpose of the HRA 1998.[47] For example:

> The Government's position has been that all providers of publicly arranged health and social care services, including those in the private and voluntary sectors, should consider themselves to be bound by the duty imposed by section 6 of the Human Rights Act 1998 not to act in a way that is incompatible with a Convention right.[48]

45 HRA 1998 s6(3)(b).

46 MHA Code para 3.3. The Care Quality Commission (CQC) incorporates a human rights approach to its regulation and inspection of health and social care; see, for example, *Human rights approach for our regulation of health and social care services*, 2014; and *Monitoring the Mental Health Act in 2018/19*, 2020, p5: 'We intend to focus more clearly on the human rights aspects of the working of the MHA during MHA monitoring visits, particularly in services where there is a risk of a closed culture developing'.

47 *R (Weaver) v London and Quadrant Housing Trust* [2009] EWCA Civ 587, in particular [35]. In *R (A) v Partnership in Care Ltd* [2002] EWHC 529, the court held that in making decisions about the care and treatment of detained patients, an independent hospital was a public authority under HRA 1998 s6.

48 *The Care Bill explained Including a response to consultation and pre-legislative scrutiny on the Draft Care and Support Bill*, HM Government, May 2013, Cm 8627, para 129. Nonetheless, the government was persuaded to introduce a provision in the Care Act 2014 that made this clear in relation to adult social care. See Care Act 2014 s73, which (Care Act 2014 Explanatory Note para 425):

> . . . makes explicit that registered care providers, when providing adults with either personal care in their home or accommodation with nursing or personal care, which has been arranged or funded by a public authority pursuant to specific duties and powers, are exercising a function of a public nature for the purposes of the Human Rights Act 1998.

Overview of ECHR rights

1.17 Essentially, the rights under the ECHR are 'negative' in nature, in that their primary purpose is to protect individuals from arbitrary interference by the state. They do so by placing limits on the circumstances in which rights and freedoms can be restricted – 'negative obligations'.

1.18 Save for the few 'absolute rights' – for example, ECHR Article 3, which prohibits torture, inhuman or degrading treatment or punishment – the rights under the ECHR can be restricted, but only in certain circumstances:

- 'Limited rights' specify the circumstances in which restrictions on that right are permitted. For example, whereas it protects the right to liberty, ECHR Article 5 sets out six exceptions to this right, which include 'the lawful detention . . . of persons of unsound mind'.[49]
- In addition, there are 'qualified rights'. These set out the general circumstances or conditions in which it would be permissible to interfere with an individual's rights. They are: Article 8 (respect for private and family life, home and correspondence), Article 9 (freedom of thought, belief and religion), Article 10 (freedom of expression) and Article 11 (freedom of assembly and association) are examples of such qualified rights. These rights can only be restricted if it is lawful, 'necessary in a democratic society' and for a legitimate aim.

1.19 A violation of a person's ECHR rights will arise where that person's rights have been restricted without justification. As the HRA 1998 protects the ECHR rights of individuals of all ages, any interference with an adolescent's ECHR right(s) must be justified, otherwise there will be a violation of the adolescent's ECHR right(s).

1.20 The question whether a restriction of an ECHR right is justified will depend on the particular circumstances of the case and the extent to which (if at all) the ECHR right in question permits an interference. However, in all cases, the restriction must be lawful under national law (eg the law that applies in England). It must also comply with the 'principle of proportionality', which in essence, means that 'even where it is clear that there is a legitimate purpose for restricting a Convention right, the authorities must show that the actual restriction employed does not go beyond what is strictly necessary to

49 Article 5(1)(e).

achieve that purpose'.[50] Key to the concept of proportionality is the aim of achieving a balance between protecting the interests of society and respecting individuals' fundamental rights and freedoms.[51]

1.21 Whereas the ECHR rights are framed as imposing 'negative obligations' (in other words, limiting interferences with individual's rights), in some circumstances public authorities will be under a 'positive obligation' to take action to protect individuals' ECHR rights – for example, putting in place measures to protect individuals who are vulnerable to physical, sexual or financial abuse.

1.22 The box at the end of this chapter summarises the ECHR rights that are likely to be of particular importance to adolescents' mental health care.

Human rights: the wider landscape

1.23 Increasingly, the importance of additional European and international human rights standards are recognised by the national courts and policy-makers, the UN Convention on the Rights of Persons with Disabilities (UNCRPD)[52] and the UN Convention on the Rights of the Child (UNCRC)[53] are recognised as being of particular importance. This accords with the approach of the European Court of Human Rights (ECtHR), which has stated that the ECHR 'cannot be interpreted in a vacuum but must be interpreted in harmony with the general principles of international law'.[54] In relation to mental health law reform, the Independent Review of the Mental Health Act 1983 noted that in addition to the obligation to comply with the

50 K Starmer, *European human rights law: The Human Rights Act 1998 and the European Convention on Human Rights*, LAG, 1999, para 4.38. As noted by the Court of Appeal, there is now 'a substantial jurisprudence on the concept of proportionality and its application in domestic, EU and ECHR law' (*Re B (secure accommodation order)* [2019] EWCA Civ 2025 at [83]).

51 For a summary of the concept of proportionality, see Lord Reed, *Bank Mellat v HM Treasury (No 2)* [2013] UKSC 39, [2014] AC 700, at [68]–[76].

52 See, for example, *P v Cheshire West and Chester Council; P and Q v Surrey CC* [2014] UKSC 19 at [36].

53 See, for example, *R (SG) v Secretary of State for Work and Pensions* [2015] UKSC 16 at [82]–[86]; and *ZH (Tanzania) v Secretary of State for the Home Department* [2011] UKSC 4 at [23].

54 *Neulinger v Switzerland* [2010] ECHR 1053 para 131 as noted in *ZH (Tanzania) v Secretary of State for the Home Department* [2011] UKSC 4 at [22].

ECHR, they were 'also required to take into account other international conventions ratified by the UK', in particular, the UNCRPD.[55]

1.24 Government guidance concerning children and young people aged under 18 highlights the importance of the UNCRC.[56] UNCRC Article 12 emphasises the importance of seeking and taking into account the views of the 'child' (individuals aged under 18[57]), such views 'being given due weight in accordance with the age and maturity of the child'. Whereas UNCRC Article 3 provides that in all actions concerning children 'the best interests of the child shall be a primary consideration', the Committee on the Rights of the Child's 'authoritative guidance'[58] on this article emphasises that the views of the child is a key factor in determining that child's best interests.[59] The 'evolving capacities of the child'[60] is also relevant to

55 Modernising the Mental Health Act: Increasing choice, reducing compulsion, December 2018 (MHA Review) p19. Individuals (of any age) fall within the UNCRPD if they 'have long-term physical, mental, intellectual or sensory impairments which in interaction with various barriers may hinder their full and effective participation in society on an equal basis with others' (Article 2).

56 See for example, *The Children Act 1989 guidance and regulations Volume 2: care planning, placement and case review*, Department for Education (DfE), 2015, para 1.8; and *Working Together to Safeguard Children: A guide to inter-agency working to safeguard and promote the welfare of children*, HM Government, 2018.

57 UNCRC Article 1: 'a child means every human being below the age of 18 years unless, under the law applicable to the child, majority is attained earlier'.

58 Albeit not binding, this general comment is 'authoritative guidance' on the scope of Article 3(1) (*R (DA) v Secretary of State for Work and Pensions* [2019] UKSC 21 at [69] (Lord Wilson JSC)); so 'it may "influence" but never "drive" a conclusion that the [UN]CRC has been breached' (*R (McConnell and another) v Register General for England and Wales* [2020] EWCA Civ 559 at [85]).

59 Committee on the Rights of the Child, General Comment 14 (2013) on the right of the child to have his or her best interests taken as a primary consideration (Art 3 para 1) CRC/C/GC/14 para 43 includes the statement: 'Assessment of a child's best interests must include respect for the child's right to express his or her views freely and due weight given to said views in all matters affecting the child'.

60 For explanation of this term, see Committee on the Rights of the Child, General comment No 20 (2016) on the implementation of the rights of the child during adolescence, CRC/C/GC/20 para 18:

> . . . an enabling principle that addresses the process of maturation and learning through which children progressively acquire competencies, understanding and increasing levels of agency to take responsibility and exercise their rights . . . the more a child knows and understands, the more his or her parents will have to transform direction and guidance into reminders and gradually to an exchange on an equal footing'.

Article 5 provides that parents exercise their rights and responsibilities 'in a manner consistent with the evolving capacities of the child'. See also G Lansdowne, *The evolving capacities of the child*, Save the Children and UNICEF, 2005.

the determination of bests interests in that 'as the child matures, his or her views shall have increasing weight in the assessment of his or her best interests'.[61]

Concerns about the mental health care of adolescents

1.25 The imperative to keep under close scrutiny the human rights implications of the provision of mental health care on adolescents (and the lack of appropriate mental health care) was highlighted by Sir James Munby, President of the Family Division of the High Court in *Re X (a child) (No 3)*.[62] The case concerned a 17-year-old young woman ('X') who had significant mental health problems and had made numerous and determined attempts to kill herself, but despite this no appropriate placement in a psychiatric facility could be found. In addition to his strong condemnation of the 'well-known scandal' of 'the disgraceful and utterly shaming lack of proper provision' for services 'so desperately needed by the increasing numbers of children and young people with the same kind of difficulties as X is burdened with',[63] the President expressed his concern on the impact of the lack of proper provision for X.

1.26 While accepting that the actions taken were focused on preserving X's life, the President raised concerns about the regime which meant that X was confined to her bedroom, which was stripped of all personal effects to make it secure, under constant and close supervision, isolated from her peers, receiving no education and subject to frequent restraint.

> It is no criticism whatever of the devoted staff at ZX, who are doing their very best for X in what they recognise is not the right kind of placement for her, but I am bound to question whether these conditions, particularly when imposed upon a profoundly damaged and vulnerable young woman, can really be thought to meet the requirements imposed upon us by Article 3 of the European Convention – which, without qualification, prohibits subjecting anyone to 'inhuman or degrading treatment' – let alone the more demanding obligation under Article 8 to 'respect' X's 'private and family life.' And, lest it be thought that I have overlooked the point, given the by now well documented and repeated attempts by X to take her own life, the State's positive obligations under Article 2 of the Convention are plainly

61 CRC/C/GC/14 para 44.

62 [2017] EWHC 2036 (Fam).

63 [2017] EWHC 2036 (Fam) at [37].

engaged . . . I remind every agent of the State involved with her of the duties owed to X under Articles 2, 3 and 8 of the Convention.[64]

1.27 In a similar vein, the Joint Committee on Human Rights (JCHR) has raised a series of significant concerns in relation to young people with learning disabilities and/or autism who are placed in in-patient psychiatric facilities. Following its inquiry into the situation of this group of young people, the JCHR concluded that 'the human rights of many of those with a learning disability and/ or autism are being breached in mental health hospitals'. In particular, the JCHR considered that detaining such young people without providing them with individualised, therapeutic treatment risks violating their right to liberty under ECHR Article 5 and in some cases 'may even reach the threshold of degrading treatment contrary to Article 3'.[65]

Box 1.2: Key ECHR rights for mental health care[66]

Article 2: right to life

Article 2 requires that people's lives are protected by law.[67] In addition to the duty not to unlawfully take people's lives, Article 2 establishes positive obligations in two areas:

- *Duty to take measures to protect individuals' right to life:* This includes a general requirement that hospitals employ competent and properly trained staff, as well having proper systems in place to 'protect the lives of patients', including the supervision of individuals receiving in-patient psychiatric care to prevent suicide.[68] In addition, an 'operational duty' arises requiring staff to take reasonable steps to prevent a real and immediate risk to the life of a particular individual from materialising where they

64 [2017] EWHC 2036 (Fam) at [36].

65 House of Commons House of Lords Joint Committee on Human Rights *The detention of young people with learning disabilities and/or autism*, HC 121, HL paper 10, 1 November 2019, at para 87.

66 The Council of Europe has produced a series of guides, one for each ECHR article. These are available at: www.echr.coe.int/Pages/home.aspx?p=caselaw/analysis/guides&c=#.

67 It does not establish a 'right to die': see *Pretty v UK* (2002) 35 EHRR 1 at [39].

68 *Savage v South Essex Partnership NHS Foundation Trust* [2008] UKHL 74 at [69].

know or ought to know of that risk.[69] Such an operational duty can arise in relation to informal patients as well as individuals who have been detained under the MHA 1983.[70] However, measures taken to protect a person 'must be compatible with the rights and freedoms of the individual concerned',[71] so there is 'a difficult balance to be struck between the right of the individual patient to freedom and self-determination and her right to be prevented from taking her own life'.[72] The positive duty to protect the life is relevant to decisions about overriding an under 18's refusal of life-saving treatment (see paras 3.94–3.99).[73]

- *Duty to investigate deaths of individuals for which the state may have some responsibility:* Where a person has died while detained (for example, under the MHA 1983) or in circumstances where the operational duty noted above was engaged, a coroner's inquest must be held.[74] Where the coroner believes that action should be taken to prevent future deaths the coroner must send a report outlining the concerns to the person, organisation, local authority or government department or agency with the power to take such preventative action.[75]

69 *Savage v South Essex Partnership NHS Foundation Trust* [2008] UKHL 74 at [72].

70 *Rabone v Pennine Care NHS Foundation Trust* [2012] UKSC 2 at [104] Lady Hale notes:

> The State does have a positive obligation to protect children and vulnerable adults from the real and immediate risk of serious abuse or threats to their lives of which the authorities are or ought to be aware and which it is within their power to prevent.

See also *Fernandes de Oliveira v Portugal* [2019] ECHR 106; and discussion in *R (Parkinson) v HM Senior Coroner for Kent* [2018] EWHC 1501 (Admin) at [50]–[81].

71 *Keenan v UK* (2001) 33 EHRR para 92.

72 *Rabone* at [107].

73 *Re P (a child)* [2014] EWHC 1650 (Fam) at [15]; citing *Rabone v Pennine Care NHS Foundation Trust* [2012] UKSC 2 and *Osman v UK* [1998] 29 EHRR 245.

74 See Coroners and Justice Act 2009 ss1–6; *Article 2 of the European Convention on Human Rights and the investigation of serious incidents in mental health services*, DoH, 2015.

75 Coroners and Justice Act 2009 Sch 5 para 7; and Coroners (Investigations) Regulations 2013 SI No1629 reg 28 (report on action to prevent other deaths).

Article 3: freedom from torture, inhuman or degrading treatment or punishment

Article 3 'prohibits in absolute terms torture[76] or inhuman or degrading treatment or punishment,[77] irrespective of the circumstances and the victim's behaviour'.[78] A violation of Article 3 can arise even if there was no intention to humiliate or debase the victim.[79] For ill-treatment to fall within Article 3, it 'must attain a minimum level of severity', but in determining whether the minimum level has been reached will depend on the circumstances of the case. Relevant factors include the duration of the treatment, its physical and mental effects, and in some cases the sex, age and state of health of the victim.[80] The ECtHR takes into account the 'special vulnerability of mentally ill persons' when assessing whether the treatment or punishment concerned breaches Article 3.[81]

The 'detention of a person who is ill in inappropriate physical and medical conditions may in principle amount to treatment contrary to Article 3'.[82]

Treatment without consent, seclusion and restraint do not in themselves amount to a violation of Article 3 given that 'as a general rule, a measure which is of therapeutic necessity cannot be regarded as inhuman or degrading'.[83] However, they must be shown to be 'necessary and proportionate in the circumstances'.[84]

76 The intentional infliction of severe pain and suffering; see *El-Masri v The Former Yugoslav Republic of Macedonia* (App No 39630/09) 13 December 2012, para 197.

77 Treatment has been held to be 'inhuman' where it 'was premeditated, was applied for hours at a stretch and caused either actual bodily injury or intense physical or mental suffering'. Degrading treatment covers action that arouses feelings of fear, anguish and inferiority capable of humiliating or debasing the person concerned. See: *Stanev v Bulgaria* [2012] ECHR 46 (App No 36760/06) para 210.

78 *Stanev v Bulgaria* [2012] ECHR 46 (App No 36760/06) para 210.

79 *Price v UK* [2002] ECHR 453 para 30.

80 *MS v UK* [2012] ECHR 804 para 38.

81 *MS v UK* [2012] ECHR 804 para 96; and *Keenan v UK* para 111.

82 *Rooman v Belgium* [2019] ECHR 105, para 144 (paras 145–148 for discussion of Article 3 and the treatment of detainees).

83 *MS v UK* [2012] ECHR 804.

84 *MS v Croatia (No 2)* (App No 75450/12) 19 February 2015, [2015] MHLR 226, para 110. See also *Bureš v Czech Republic* (App No 37679/08) 18 October 2012 [2013] MHLR 126; *Nevmerzhitsky v Ukraine* (2006) 43 EHRR 32 para 94; *Fyodorov and Fyodorova v Ukraine* (App No 39229/03) 7 July 2011, para 62; *Gorobet v Moldova* (App No 30951/10) 11 October 2011, para 51.

The ECtHR scrutinises the circumstances in which such non-consensual interventions took place to satisfy itself that the medical necessity has been 'convincingly be shown to exist, 'taking into account the current legal and medical standards on the issue'.[85]

In the ECtHR's view 'the developments in contemporary legal standards on seclusion and other forms of coercive and non-consensual measures' in relation to individuals with mental disorders who are deprived of their liberty 'require that such measures be employed as a matter of last resort and when their application is the only means available to prevent immediate or imminent harm to the patient or others'.[86] Furthermore, there must be adequate safeguards from abuse that demonstrate that the measures are necessary and proportionate, 'that all other reasonable options failed to satisfactorily contain the risk of harm to the patient or others' and the measures were used for no longer than 'strictly necessary'.[87]

In addition to the duty not to inflict ill-treatment (torture, inhuman or degrading treatment or punishment) on individuals, Article 3 establishes positive obligations in two areas:

- *Duty to take measures to protect individuals from ill-treatment (whether by the state or by private individuals)*: These measures should provide effective protection, in particular, of children and other vulnerable persons and include reasonable steps to prevent ill-treatment of which the authorities had or ought to have had knowledge'.[88]
- *Duty to investigate undertake credible allegations of ill-treatment:* This requires a thorough and effective investigation capable of leading to the identification and punishment of those responsible where are made. In *MS v Croatia (No 2)*,[89] the ECtHR held that this principle applies to 'allegations of ill-treatment in the context of psychiatric internment where physical restraint has been used against the applicant'. Such investigations 'must be started if

85 *MS v Croatia (No 2)* (n84) paras 96 and 103; *Herczegfalvy v Austria* (1993) 14 EHHR 437 para 83.

86 *MS v Croatia (No 2)* (n84) para 104.

87 *MS v Croatia (No 2)* (n84) para 105.

88 *Z v UK* [2001] ECHR 29392/95 para 73. See also *Dordevic v Croatia* (App No 41526/10) [2012] ECHR 41526/10 para 138 (in relation to measures to protect a disabled man from harassment). In *Rabone v Pennine Care NHS Foundation Trust* [2012] UKSC 2 para 104, Lady Hale noted that 'the operational duties under both Article 2 and Article 3 are similar if not identical'.

89 App No 75450/12.

there are if there are sufficiently clear indications that ill-treatment might have occurred' and this applies even if no complaint has been made, given that those who have been subjected to serious ill-treatment will often be less ready or willing to make a complaint. There is also a need for particular vigilance to ensure compliance with the ECHR in relation to 'patients confined in psychiatric hospitals' given their 'position of inferiority and powerlessness'.[90]

Article 5: right to liberty

This right protects all individuals (including under-18s[91]) from arbitrary detention.[92] Under Article 5(1), everyone 'has the right to liberty and security of person',[93] no one can be deprived of their liberty save for the limited circumstances specified by Article 5 (which includes on grounds of mental disorder[94]). Any such deprivation of liberty must be 'in accordance with a procedure prescribed by law' and subject to strict procedural safeguards, including the right to be given reasons for their detention (Article 5(2)) and a periodic review of the lawfulness of the detention (Article 5(4)).[95]

- *Article 5 and the MHA 1983:* The right to liberty under Article 5 is of major significance given that the MHA 1983 permits individuals to be deprived of their liberty on grounds of mental disorder.[96] Subsequent chapters consider the circumstances in which adolescents are found to be deprived of their liberty (chapter 3),

90 *MS v Croatia (No 2)* [2015] ECHR 196, para 74. See also *Rooman v Belgium* [2019] ECHR 105, para 155.

91 *Nielsen v Denmark* (1988) 11 EHHR 175, para 72; *Re D (a child)* [2019] UKSC 42 at [30] and [31].

92 See, for example, *Austin v UK* [2012] ECHR 459, para 60.

93 The ECtHR regards 'security' to be concerned with protecting individuals from arbitrary interference with their liberty. See *Bozano v France* (1987) 9 EHHR 287, para 54.

94 Article 5(1)(e) refers to 'the lawful detention of . . . persons of unsound mind'.

95 See discussion of the principle of proportionality and its relevance to Article 5: *Re B (secure accommodation order)* [2019] EWCA Civ 2025 (Baker LJ at [83] and Green LJ at [115]–[121]).

96 In contrast, the Committee on the Rights of Persons with Disabilities considers that UNCRPD Article 14 prohibits detention on the grounds of disability (which includes a mental disorder), see *Guidelines on Article 14 of the Convention on the Rights of Persons with Disabilities: The right to liberty and security of persons with disabilities,* Committee on the Rights of Persons with Disabilities, 2015.

the procedures for their detention in hospital under the MHA 1983 (chapter 6) and the review of their detention in hospital (chapter 8).

- *Scrutiny of reasons for restricting individuals' right to liberty:* Since the introduction of the UNCRPD, the ECtHR has demonstrated an increased scrutiny of the circumstances in which individuals are deprived of their liberty under Article 5(1)(e). The ECtHR requires 'very weighty reasons' for involuntary admissions to hospital for psychiatric care.[97] It also considers there to be a close link between the lawfulness of the detention and the appropriateness of the treatment provided. In *Roomen v Belgium*,[98] the ECtHR stated that it was necessary 'to recognise explicitly that there exists an obligation on the authorities to ensure appropriate and individualised therapy'. This includes the provision of a suitable medical environment and individualised care plans that have the therapeutic purpose of curing or alleviating the person's mental health conditions as well as preparing them for future reintegration into society.[99]

Article 8: right to respect for private and family life, home and correspondence

A wide range of diverse matters fall within this right, such as sexual orientation, choice of where to live, contact with family and the development of relationship with others.

- *Scope of Article 8:* This right is intricately linked to mental health care, for example, it will be engaged where non-consensual interventions are applied, (such as medical treatment, seclusion and restraint), confidential information is disclosed without the person's consent, personal searches are made and restrictions placed on communication with family and friends. The rights of adolescents' parents can also be engaged. For example, where adolescents are detained in hospital under the MHA 1983 this will be an interference with both adolescents and their parents' right to respect for family life.[100] In relation to younger children

97 *MS v Croatia (No 2)* [2015] ECHR 196, para 147.

98 *Rooman v Belgium* [2019] ECHR 105.

99 *Rooman v Belgium* [2019] ECHR 105, at paras 205–211 the ECtHR explains its 'refinement' of principles established in previous case-law 'and clarification of the meaning of the obligation on the authorities to provide treatment'. For link between Article 5 and Article 3 see paras 212–214.

100 *Hillingdon LBC v Neary* [2011] EWHC 1377 (COP).

unable to make such decisions for themselves, the ECtHR has held that giving treatment without their parents' consent breached both the child's and the parents' Article 8 rights.[101]

- *Circumstances in which interferences with Article 8 rights might be justified:* Restrictions of rights protected by Article 8 are only permitted if they are justified under Article 8(2). This requires that where a public body is responsible for an interference with a person's Article 8 rights it must show that such an interference was lawful ('in accordance with the law') and had a legitimate aim, meaning that the reason for the interference was to protect at least one of the exhaustive, but extremely broad, set of interests of 'national security, public safety, economic well-being of the country, prevention of disorder or crime, protection of health or morals and the protection of the rights and freedoms of others'. In addition, the interference must be 'necessary in a democratic society', which requires that the action taken is a proportionate response to the legitimate aim pursued.[102] Key questions are therefore whether the interference is lawful, has a legitimate aim and is 'necessary and proportionate'.[103]
- *Positive duty under Article 8:* In certain circumstances authorities are required to take measures to secure respect for individuals' private and family life. For example, in *Kutzner v Germany*,[104] the ECtHR upheld the complaint of parents with mild learning disabilities that their children had been taken into care in breach of their Article 8 rights. In reaching this decision, the ECtHR questioned whether the authorities had given sufficient consideration to providing additional educational support to the parents rather than removing their children and also noted that the authorities had failed to comply with their positive duty to take measures to facilitate the family's reunion.
- *Procedural rights:* Although, not an explicit requirement of Article 8, the ECtHR places great emphasis on the importance of ensuring that the decision-making process in relation to

101 *Glass v UK* [2004] ECHR 102; and *MAK v UK* [2010] ECHR 363.

102 See, for example, *McDonald v UK* [2014] ECHR 492 at [53].

103 See, for example, *K v LBX and others* [2012] EWCA Civ 79; *Re C (a child)* [2019] EWCA Civ 1998 at [2](3).

104 *Kutzner v Germany* (App No 46544/99) 26 February 2002. See also *Saviny v Ukraine* (2010) 51 EHRR 33 in which the ECtHR refers to the 'Convention obligation to promote family unity' and whether the authorities 'had sufficiently explored the effectiveness of less far-reaching alternatives before seeking to separate the children from their parents'.

individuals' Article 8 rights must be fair, in particular that it sufficiently involves the person(s) whose rights are to be affected.[105] For example, it has been suggested that the failure to give parents the opportunity of being involved in the decision-making process prior to making an application for an adolescent's detention under the MHA 1983 would give rise to a violation of this right.[106]

Article 14: prohibition of discrimination

This right protects individuals from discrimination in relation to the exercise of other rights guaranteed under the ECHR. It does so by prohibiting different treatment of individuals without justification. Key points are as follows:

- Article 14 has no independent existence given that it is concerned with 'the enjoyment of the rights and freedoms' under the ECHR. To make a claim under Article 14, it is therefore necessary to show that the discrimination complained of relates to another ECHR right. However, it is not necessary for the other ECHR right to be violated. All that is required is for the facts of the case to fall 'within the ambit' of one or more of the ECHR rights.[107]
- Although Article 14 sets out a list of specific grounds on which discrimination is prohibited – sex, race, colour, language, religion, political or other opinion, national or social origin, association with a national minority, property or birth – it also has a broad category of 'any other status', which includes disability[108] and age.[109]
- A difference in treatment is discriminatory under Article 14 if:

  > . . . it has no objective and reasonable justification in other words, if it does not pursue a legitimate aim or if there is not a reasonable relationship of proportionality between the means employed and the aim sought to be realised.[110]

- As with Articles 2, 3, 5, and 8, Article 14 may give rise to positive obligations in certain circumstances. For example, the ECtHR considers that 'the authorities must use all available means to

105 *Re S (minors) (care order: implementation of care plan); Re W (minors) (care order: adequacy of care plan)* [2002] UKHL 10 at [99], citing *TP and KM v UK* [2001] ECHR 332, at para 326.

106 R Jones, *Mental Health Act Manual*, 23rd edn, Sweet & Maxwell, 2020, p1015.

107 *Botta v Italy* [1998] ECHR 12, para 39.

108 *Glor v Switzerland* (App 13444/04) 30 April 2009.

109 *Khamtokhu v Russia* (2017) 65 EHRR 6, para 62.

110 *Stec and others v UK* [GC] no 65731/01, para 51.

combat racism, thereby reinforcing democracy's vision of a society in which diversity is not perceived as a threat but as a source of enrichment'.[111]

- When considering Article 14, the following questions are engaged:

  (1) Do the circumstances 'fall within the ambit' of one or more of the Convention rights? (2) Has there been a difference of treatment between two persons who are in an analogous situation? (3) Is that difference of treatment on the ground of one of the characteristics listed or 'other status'? (4) Is there an objective justification for that difference in treatment?[112]

111 *DH and others v Czech Republic* (2008) 47 EHRR 3, para 176; and *Timishev v Russia* (2007) 44 EHRR 37, para 58.

112 *Re an application by Siobhan McLuaglin for Judicial Review (Northern Ireland)* [2018] UKSC 48, Lady Hale at [15].

CHAPTER 2

Mental health care for under-18s: the legal and policy landscape

continued

Introduction

2.1 There is no one organisation or legal framework governing the provision of mental health care for children and young people aged under 18 ('adolescents') in England. In a system described by the Care Quality Commission (CQC)[1] as 'complex and fragmented', many different organisations and services are involved in identifying under-18s' mental health needs, helping them to access care, and providing care and treatment. The range of services involved, collectively known as Child and Adolescent Mental Health Services (CAMHS) or Children and Young People's Mental Health Services (CYPMHS) engage differing and sometimes overlapping legal frameworks. In-patient psychiatric care forms just a small, albeit important, part of this wider network of services and support.

2.2 While other agencies, such as schools, play an important role within CAMHS, for adolescents who develop complex mental health needs, the two agencies with core responsible for their care and support are 1) the NHS (providers and commissioners) and 2) local authorities, in particular children's services departments. Specialist mental health care professionals, such CAMHS consultant psychiatrists and clinical psychologists, fall within the remit of the NHS. As discussed below, local authorities are responsible for the provision of services for 'children in need', 'looked after children' and children and young people with special educational needs (SEN) and/or disabilities, any of which might apply to adolescents with complex mental health needs (whether for reasons related to their mental health needs or otherwise).[2]

2.3 This chapter sets out an overview of the law and policy underpinning the provision of NHS-funded and local authority services relevant to adolescents with mental health needs.[3] It covers the following areas:

- mental health care for under-18s (the range of services falling within CAMHS);

1 The independent regulator for health and adult social care. See Glossary.

2 Detailed information on the provision of services for disabled children can be found in S Broach and L Clements, *Disabled children: a legal handbook*, 3rd edn, LAG, 2020.

3 As this topic is covered extensively elsewhere, this chapter does not cover the various statutory complaints procedures relating to health, social care and education and other mechanisms for challenging decisions by relevant public bodies, see for example chapter 11 ('Remedies') in S Broach and L Clements, *Disabled children: a legal handbook*, 3rd edn, LAG, 2020.

- local authority support – including children's social care; care leavers; SEN and disability; transition at age 18; and joint working;
- key guidance for adolescent mental health care – including the *Mental Health Act 1983 Code of Practice* ('the MHA Code'); and
- confidentiality and sharing information.

Mental health care for under-18s

Introduction

2.4 Mental health services for children and young people aged under 18 (CAMHS), cover a wide spectrum of care, ranging from general advice and support given by general practitioners (GPs) and health visitors to specialist care, including the provision of in-patient psychiatric care. As such, the delivery of CAMHS is not the responsibility for any one organisation and depends upon the input from specialists from differing professions.

2.5 The network of services forming CAMHS is often described as being structured across four levels – Tier 1 to Tier 4. These tiers are used to distinguish between the differing levels of support and types of intervention offered, which are commissioned and provided by a range of agencies. Although the use of such a tiered model is considered by some to be unhelpful because it creates 'barriers between services, embedding service divisions and fragmentation of care',[4] the four tiers are set out below to illustrate the wide spectrum of care and the differing agencies that may be involved in providing support to under 18s.[5] Identifying the multi-agency nature of the services and the complex commissioning arrangements also highlights the 'potential for a lack of integration between agencies, particularly at a time of shrinking resources'.[6]

4 *Future in mind: promoting, protecting and improving our children and young people's mental health and wellbeing*, Department of Health (DoH) and NHS England, 2015, p41. House of Commons Health Committee *Children's and adolescents' mental health* and CAMHS Third Report of Session 2014–15, para 26.

5 This list is drawn from the information provided in Joint Commissioning Panel for Mental Health, *Guidance for commissioners of child and adolescent mental health services*, 2013, pp5–6; *Child and Adolescent Mental Health Services (CAMHS) Report*, NHS England, July 2014, pp10–11; and the report of the National Audit Office (NAO) *Improving children and young people's mental health services*, October 2018, p17.

6 *Child and Adolescent Mental Health Services (CAMHS) Report*, NHS England, July 2014, 14.

2.6 The tiers are as follows:

- *Tier 1 – universal services*: Support to under 18s from practitioners such as:
  - GPs;
  - health visitors;
  - school nurses;
  - teachers; and
  - social workers.

  Such practitioners can promote mental well-being, identify problems early and refer to more specialist services (these services are commissioned by clinical commissioning groups (CCGs),[7] local authorities and schools);
- *Tier 2 – targeted services*: Services provided to under 18s with mild to moderate mental health problems which may be delivered by
  - specialist CAMHS professionals based in schools;
  - school counsellors; and
  - voluntary sector youth counselling

  These services (which are commissioned by CCGs, local authorities and schools), can act as effective early intervention, as well as identifying more severe and complex needs requiring more specialist intervention;
- *Tier 3 – specialist community multi-disciplinary teams of specialist CAMHS professionals*: Services for under 18s with mild to moderate mental health problems that are causing significant impairments in their day-to-day lives, can be provided by practitioners such as:
  - child and adolescent psychiatrists;
  - social workers; and
  - clinical psychologists, and
  - community psychiatric nurses.

  These services include crisis/home treatment teams working intensively to prevent admission to hospital and are commissioned by CCGs, possibly with a contribution from local authorities;
- *Tier 4 – highly specialist services*: Such services include:
  - in-patient services (see further at para 2.10 below);
  - some highly specialist outpatient services; and
  - services such as crisis/ home treatment services which provide an alternative to admission.

7 CCGs are responsible for commissioning NHS services. See Glossary for further information.

2.7 The above four-tier model shows that specialist CAMHS can be provided as part of targeted services in non-health settings, such as schools[8] (Tier 2); through community CAMHS (which can include CAMHS learning disability teams and home treatment teams working intensively to prevent admission to hospital) (Tier 3); or as highly specialised CAMHS (Tier 4).

2.8 The term 'specialist CAMHS' is used to describe 'services with a core remit and responsibility to provide specialist mental healthcare'.[9] Such services will be typically provided by a multi-disciplinary team made up of a range of professionals, for example: child and adolescent psychiatrists, social workers, clinical psychologists, community psychiatric nurses and other therapists, working in a community mental health clinic or child psychiatry outpatient service.[10]

2.9 The Department of Health and Social Care (DHSC) is responsible for mental health policy (for all ages) and NHS England[11] oversees the commissioning of NHS-funded services, either directly or through local CCGs. Such NHS-funded health care can be provided by NHS bodies (for example NHS trusts) as well as by the independent sector.[12] The National Audit Office (NAO) reports that 'NHS England and CCGs collectively spent £1,042 million on children and young people's services in 2017–18 (around 1% of their total expenditure)'.[13]

8 The government has taken a range of initiatives to increase the support available in schools. See: *Government response to the consultation on transforming children and young people's mental health provision: a green paper and next steps*, Department of Health and Social Care (DHSC) and Department for Education (DfE), July 2018 Cm 9626.

9 This is the definition adopted in *Building and sustaining specialist CAMHS to improve outcomes for children and young people Update of guidance on workforce, capacity and functions of CAMHS in the UK*, Royal College of Psychiatrists, November 2013.

10 *Improving children and young people's mental health services*, NAO, October 2018, p17.

11 The legal title of NHS England is 'the National Health Service Commissioning Board'. It was established in April 2013 under the Health and Social Care Act 2012.

12 The law relating to the planning, commissioning of NHS-funded care is beyond the scope of this book. For an extensive analysis of this area of law, see David Lock QC and Hannah Gibbs, *NHS Law and Practice*, LAG, 2018. See also S Broach and L Clements, *Disabled Children: a legal handbook*, 3rd edn, LAG chapter 5 ('Health') which provides an overview of key issues, including the structure of the NHS and the importance of the NHS Constitution (paras 5.11–5.18).

13 *Improving children and young people's mental health services*, NAO, October 2018, p5.

2.10 Tier 4 in-patient care services include:

- general services – children's units (for those aged under 13) and adolescent units (for those aged 13–18);
- specialist units for different groups, such as eating disorders and learning disabilities;
- specialist units for differing levels of need, such as psychiatric intensive care units (PICUs), low secure units and medium secure units; and
- adolescent forensic units.[14]

Since April 2013, NHS England has been responsible for commissioning Tier 4 services.[15] However, the way in which Tier 4 services are commissioned is due to change. As from April 2020 local service providers are able to form 'NHS-led Provider Collaboratives' that are 'responsible for managing the budget and patient pathway for specialised mental health, learning disability and autism care for people who need it in their local area'. These collaboratives, which will cover CAMHS Tier 4 services, are intended to 'seek to avoid inpatient admissions and provide high quality alternatives to admission'.[16]

2.11 The following service specifications for Tier 4 CAMHS set out the standards of care NHS England expects from the organisations it funds:[17]

14 *Child and Adolescent Mental Health Services (CAMHS) Report*, NHS England, July 2014, describes the range of Tier 4 services (pp11–12).

15 NHS Commissioning Board and Clinical Commissioning Groups (Responsibilities and Standing Rules) Regulations 2012 SI No 2996 reg 11 and Sch 4 sets out the services for which NHS England has responsibility for arranging, Tier 4 CAMHS are listed at 33.

16 NHS England, *NHS Operational Planning and Contracting Guidance 2020/21 – Annex G: Planning Guidance for NHS Led Provider Collaboratives*, (Publishing Approval Reference 001300) *Annex G*, February 2020. This document notes that the collaboratives will not include CAMHS for under 13-year olds (p8). It also notes that 'commissioning responsibility remains with NHS England' (p9). See also *NHS Long Term Plan Implementation Framework*, NHS England and NHS Improvement, June 2019, para 2.31. The policy background to this initiative is explained in Centre for Mental Health, *Evaluating the New Care Models for children and young people's mental health*, March 2020, pp5–6.

17 These are available at: www.england.nhs.uk/commissioning/spec-services/npc-crg/group-c/c03/. NHS England explains that the service specifications are important because they define 'the standards of care expected from organisations funded by NHS England to provide specialised care' and : 'have been developed by specialised clinicians, commissioners, expert patients and public health representatives to describe both core and developmental service standards.'

- *Tier 4 Child and Adolescent Mental Health Services (CAMHS) (General Adolescent Services)* (updated 26 February 2018);
- *Tier 4 Child and Adolescent Mental Health Services (CAMHS) (Children's Services)* (2013);
- *Tier 4 Child and Adolescent Mental Health Services (CAMHS) (Specialist Autism Spectrum Disorder)* (2013);
- *Community Forensic Child and Adolescent Mental Health Service* (2017);
- *Child and Adolescent Mental Health Services (CAMHS) – Psychiatric Intensive Care Unit* (updated 26 February 2018);
- *Child and Adolescent Mental Health Services (CAMHS) – Low Secure* (updated 26 February 2018);
- *Child and Adolescent Mental Health Services (CAMHS) – Medium Secure* (updated 26 February 2018).

2.12 The report of the NAO *Improving children and young people's mental health services,* published in October 2018 ('NAO report') noted that NHS England planned to increase the number of in-patient beds by 150–180 beds to around 1,630 beds by March 2019, 'as part of a separate plan to open beds in underserved areas of the country and close beds in overserved areas'.[18] However, as at 2 June 2020 the number of in-patient beds was 1,456.[19]

Under-18s' mental health services: areas of concern

2.13 In its 2017 report, *Review of children and young people's mental health services: Phase one report,* the CQC concluded:

> Mental health care is planned funded, commissioned provided and overseen by many different organisations, that do not always work well together in a joined-up way. Poor collaboration and communication between agencies can lead to fragmented care, create inefficiencies in the system, and impede efforts to improve the quality of care.
>
> As a result, too many children and young people have a poor experience of care and some are simply unable to access timely and appropriate support.[20]

18 *Improving children and young people's mental health services,* NAO, October 2018, p24.

19 Response to freedom of information request (submitted to NHS England by the author), July 2020.

20 *Review of children and young people's mental health services: Phase one report,* CQC, October 2017, pp4–5.

Moreover, there is no specific legislative framework, nor national guidance, for the assessment of needs and provision of specialist CAMHS.[21] The CQC's review of CAMHS found that the level of provision and threshold for acceptance (eligibility criteria) is decided locally[22] and raised concerns about the 'excessively restrictive eligibility criteria, confusing referral routes, and gaps in the availability of services'.[23]

2.14 The CQC's report is one of many that have raised significant concerns about the provision of mental health care for under-18s in recent years. For example:

- NHS England's July 2014 detailed national review of Tier 4 services, *Child and Adolescent Mental Health Services (CAMHS) Tier 4 Report*, highlighted a range of concerns in relation to the arrangements for in-patient care, such as:
  - the inequity of provision across the country;
  - problems in accessing beds when needed; and
  - under-18s having to travel long distances to access a bed.
- The House of Commons Health Committee's 2014 report, *Children's and adolescents' mental health and CAMHS*, concluded that there were 'serious and deeply ingrained problems with the commissioning and provision of Children's and adolescents' mental health services', affecting the 'whole system from prevention and early intervention through to in-patient services for the most vulnerable young people'.[24] The Committee noted that throughout its inquiry, 'witnesses have emphasised the crucial role played by early intervention services in preventing mental health problems from escalating, minimising the need for in-patient care'.[25]
- *Future in mind: Promoting, protecting and improving our children and young people's mental health and wellbeing*, the 2015 report of

21 The general provisions governing NHS bodies under the NHS Act 2006 will apply.

22 *Review of children and young people's mental health services: Phase one report*, CQC, October 2017, pp15–16. As noted at para 2.10, Tier 4 services are different in that they are commissioned by NHS England.

23 See *Are we listening? Review of children and young people's mental health services*, CQC, March 2018, p17. S Broach and L Clements, *Disabled children: a legal handbook*, 3rd edn, LAG, 2020, paras 3.59–3.61 in which they highlight principles for the use of eligibility criteria in relation to children's services, including compliance with human rights standards.

24 House of Commons Health Committee Children's and adolescents' mental health and CAMHS Third Report of Session 2014–15, para 7.

25 House of Commons Health Committee Children's and adolescents' mental health and CAMHS Third Report of Session 2014–15, para 27.

the Children and Young People's Mental Health and Wellbeing Taskforce, raised concerns about:

- gaps in data;
- the 'treatment gap' (too few under-18s receiving support);
- increased waiting times;
- lack of crisis services;
- complexity of commissioning arrangements; and
- concerns about vulnerable groups, for example, 'looked after' children.[26]

• Subsequent reports[27] have similarly highlighted a range of serious concerns, such as:
  - 'unacceptably long waits for treatment';[28]
  - the lack of crisis services;[29]
  - most children and young people not getting the mental health treatment that they need;[30]
  - poor data;[31]
  - insufficient funding;[32]

26 *Future in mind: promoting, protecting and improving our children and young people's mental health and wellbeing*, DoH and NHS England, 2015.

27 For an overview of policy developments in CAMHS since 2010, see House of Commons Briefing Paper, Number 07196, *Children and young people's mental health – policy services, funding and education*, January 2020.

28 House of Commons Committee of Public Accounts Mental health services for children and young people Seventy-Second Report of Session 2017–19, January 2019 HC 1593, p3.

29 Mental Health Task Force, *The five year forward view for mental health*, NHS England, 2016, p30: 'Less than half (48 per cent) of children and young people's services have a crisis intervention team'. Recommendation 17 states that community-based mental health crisis response services should be in place by 2020/21.

30 House of Commons Committee of Public Accounts Mental health services for children and young people Seventy-Second Report of Session 2017–19, January 2019 HC 1593, p5. See also W Crenna-Jennings and J Hutchinson, *Access to children and young people's mental health services – 2018*, Education Policy Institute, October 2018, pp24–26 and W Crenna-Jennings and J Hutchinson, *Access to children and young people's mental health services in 2019*, Education Policy Institute, January 2020, pp18–21.

31 House of Commons Committee of Public Accounts, *Mental health services for children and young people*, Seventy-Second Report of Session 2017–19, January 2019 HC 1593; and CQC *Are we listening? Review of children and young people's mental health services. Phase Two supporting documentation. Quantitative analysis*, March 2018, p8.

32 *Lost in transit*, British Medical Association (BMA), 2018, pp6–10. *Children's mental health briefing: A briefing by the Office of the Children's Commissioner for England*, Children's Commissioner, November 2018.

- out-of-area placements;[33]
- admissions to adult wards,[34] and
- the complexity of the current commissioning arrangements.[35]

2.15 In line with a recommendation of *Future in mind*, CCGs are required by NHS England to develop 'local transformation plans' (LTPs) in collaboration with local partners that provide a clear description of what the local area offers, covering:

> ... the whole spectrum of services for children and young people's mental health and wellbeing from prevention to interventions, for existing or emerging mental health problems, including in patient care and transitions between services.[36]

The first LTPs were published in 2015 and should be updated annually. However, no national review of these plans has been published since 2015.[37] The CQC has recommended that that statutory guidance is issued to local authorities and health service providers to ensure that LTPs 'explicitly set out a local offer for children and young people's mental health and wellbeing'.[38]

2.16 Since 2014, considerable investments have been made to improve children and young people's mental health services. For example, in 2017 the Department of Health (DoH) and the Department for Education (DfE) published *Transforming children and young people's mental health provision: a green paper*, which set out a raft of measures such as introducing mental health support teams in schools to provide early intervention services and act as a link to local children

33 *Improving children and young people's mental health services*, NAO, October 2018, p27 and figure 9, p30.

34 E Frith, *Inpatient provision for children and young people with mental health problems*, Education Policy Institute, July 2017.

35 Health Committee Oral evidence: *Child and adolescent mental health services: access and funding*, HC 522, November 2017.

36 *Local transformation plans for children and young people's mental health and wellbeing: guidance and support for local areas*, NHS England, 2015.

37 *Children and young people's mental health services baselining report: local transformation plans review 2015*, NHS England, January 2016 Gateway Ref: 04894; *Children and young people's mental health. local transformation plans – a summary of key themes*, NHS England, August 2016. The NAO raised concerns about the limited national oversight of LTPs, NAO report para 3.6.

38 *Are we listening?* CQC, p46.

and young people's mental health services.[39] In its 2018 report *Improving children and young people's mental health services*, the NAO notes that the government committed to providing an additional £1.4 billion of funding specifically for transforming children and young people's mental health services in the 2014 Autumn Statement and the 2015 Budget, with the commitment of an additional £300 million to deliver the proposals set out in the 2017 green paper.[40]

2.17 However, there has been an 'historic under-investment' in this area. In the NAO's 2018 report, its review of the government's progress towards meeting the 'laudable ambitions to improve mental health services for children and young people' concluded that there is 'still has a long way to go'.[41] The NAO was particularly concerned that even if the government achieved its targets there would remain a significant unmet need for mental health services.[42] The government has since published its *NHS Long Term Plan* in 2019 (see below) in which it has committed to make further investments in children and young people's mental health in the coming years.[43] In her January 2020 report, *The state of children's mental health services*, which provides an overview of the situation of CAMHS community services, the Children's Commissioner for England welcomed the significant progress in the development of NHS services but also notes that there 'remains a chasm between what children need and what is being provided'.[44]

CAMHS: mental health policy and the *NHS Long Term Plan*

2.18 The need to improve the provision of mental health care for under-18s has been recognised by successive governments.

39 However, these measures were criticised for their lack of ambition: House of Commons Education and Health and Social Care Committees, *The government's green paper on mental health: failing a generation*, 9 May 2018 (Cm 9627). See also *Government response to the consultation on transforming children and young people's mental health provision: a green paper and next steps*, DHSC and DfE, July 2018 Cm 9626.

40 *Improving children and young people's mental health services*, NAO, October 2018, p18.

41 *Improving children and young people's mental health services*, NAO, October 2018, p53.

42 *Improving children and young people's mental health services*, NAO, October 2018, p6.

43 *Improving children and young people's mental health services*, NAO, October 2018, pp6–7.

44 Children's Commissioner for England, p2.

2.19 The 2003 green paper, *Every child matters*, set the expectation that the NHS and social care work together 'so that all areas are delivering a comprehensive Child and Adolescent Mental Health Service (CAMHS) by 2006', meaning that there is 'a diverse range of services appropriate to the age and circumstances of children and young people, and to their different levels of need'.[45]

2.20 This was followed in 2004 by the publication *The mental health and psychological well-being of children and young people*,[46] ('the CAMHS standard'), which formed part of the government's 10-year plan for children's health and social care.[47] The CAMHS standard set out the range of actions and 'markers of good practice' to meet the expectation that all under-18s with mental health needs 'have access to timely, integrated, high quality, multi-disciplinary mental health services to ensure effective assessment, treatment and support, for them and their families'.[48] Well over a decade after the 2006 target, a comprehensive CAMHS has yet to be achieved.

2.21 The *NHS Long Term Plan*, published in January 2019, sets out a range of proposals for both children and young people's mental health and for people with learning disabilities and/or autism (including under-18s).[49] For mental health generally, there is 'a renewed commitment that mental health services will grow faster than the overall NHS budget, creating a new ring-fenced local investment fund worth at least £2.3 billion a year by 2023/24'.[50] For children and young people's mental health, funding 'will grow faster than both overall NHS funding and total mental health spending' to meet the commitments to expand mental health services for under 18s.[51]

45 Paras 2.28–2.31.

46 Standard 9 of the *National service framework for children, young people and maternity services* ('CAMHS Standard'), Department of Education and Skills and DoH, 2004.

47 Core Document, *National service framework for children, young people and maternity services*, Department of Education and Skills and DoH.

48 CAMHS Standard p4. Annex A gives more detail on what a comprehensive CAMHS should entail.

49 *NHS long term plan* paras 3.22–3.30. *The NHS long term plan implementation framework*, June 2019 sets out further details on how these initiatives are to be taken forward (see below at paras 2.22–2.24).

50 *NHS long term plan*, January 2019, version 1.2, with corrections, August 2019, 8.

51 *NHS long term plan* para 3.24. See also *NHS Long Term Plan Implementation Framework*, June 2019, paras 5.5–5.7 and for people with learning disabilities and autism see paras 5.8–5.14.

2.22 The commitments for children and young people's mental health in the *NHS Long Term Plan*[52] include:

- extending NHS-funded mental health services in schools and colleges;[53]
- improving access to mental health services for university students (including focusing on suicide reduction);
- improving access to eating disorder services, crisis services, transition services; as well as
- the development of new services for under-18s with complex needs, including those who have been subject to sexual assault.[54]

In a statement that underlines the current 'treatment gap', the plan also states that '[o]ver the coming decade the goal is to ensure that 100% of children and young people who need specialist care can access it'.[55]

2.23 These commitments build upon the various priorities set and investments made since the government's 2011 mental health strategy, *No health without mental health: a cross-government mental health outcomes strategy for people of all ages*, which recognised that action was required to achieve 'parity of esteem' between mental health and physical health care.[56] NHS England's *Five year forward view for mental health*, which set out objectives to improve children and young people's mental health services has been particularly influential.[57] In turn, these

52 *NHS long term plan* paras 3.22–3.30.

53 *NHS long term plan* para 3.28. See also *Transforming children and young people's mental health provision: a green paper*, DoH and DfE, December 2017, Cm 9523.

54 In October 2019, NHS England established a taskforce 'to improve current specialist children and young people's inpatient mental health, autism and learning disability services in England' alongside an independent oversight board to scrutinise and support this work (chaired by Anne Longfield, Children's Commissioner for England); see: https://www.england.nhs.uk/mental-health/cyp/children-and-adolescent-mental-health-service-inpatient-services/improvement-taskforce-children-young-people/

55 *NHS long term plan* para 3.27.

56 See NAO report (at p5) which notes that this term means 'that mental health is valued as much as physical health: an expert group' and includes 'equal access to care and an allocation of resources in proportion to need'. See also the NHS Constitution 2015, Principle 1: 'The NHS provides a comprehensive service, available to all . . . The service is designed to improve, prevent, diagnose and treat both physical and mental health problems with equal regard'.

57 *The five year forward view for mental health: a report from the independent mental health taskforce to the NHS in England*, Mental Health Taskforce, February 2016; and *Implementing the five year forward view for mental health*, NHS England, July 2016. The taskforce's report was recognised in full by the government: *The government's response to the five year forward view for mental health*, HM Government, January 2017.

objectives were based on the recommendations of the 2015 report *Future in mind: Promoting, protecting and improving our children and young people's mental health and wellbeing*[58] which set out a series of detailed recommendations on action to improve how children and young people's mental health services are organised, commissioned and provided.[59]

2.24 In relation to people with learning disabilities, autism or both,[60] the *NHS Long Term Plan*'s commitments include expanding programmes to stop their overmedication,[61] providing NHS staff with information and training on supporting them, improving the quality of in-patient care across the NHS and independent sector,[62] and reducing the length of in-patient care settings (with 'a "12-point discharge plan" to ensure discharges are timely and effective'). Specific action in relation to children and young people includes working with the DfE and local authorities to improve their awareness of, and support for, this age group, ensuring that by 2023/24 children and young people with a learning disability, autism or both with the most complex needs will have a designated key worker and develop specialist community teams for children and young people. In relation to the reduction of in-patient provision, the target is that by March 2023/24, no more than 12–15 children with a learning disability, autism or both per million, will be cared for in an in-patient facility.[63]

58 The report was published jointly by the DoH and NHS England in May 2015.

59 See the NAO report for an analysis of the development of mental health policy in relation to children and young people since 2011.

60 Paras 3.31–3.36. See also *NHS long term plan implementation framework*, June 2019, paras 5.8–5.14.

61 Stopping over-medication of people with a learning disability autism or both and Supporting Treatment and Appropriate Medication in Paediatrics (STOMP-STAMP).

62 By 2023/24, all care commissioned by the NHS will need to meet the Learning Disability Improvement Standards: see *The learning disability improvement standards for NHS trusts*, NHS Improvement, June 2018.

63 *NHS long term plan* para. 3.34. However, note Joint Committee on Human Rights *The detention of young people with learning disabilities and/or autism*, Second report of session 2019, HC 121 HL Paper 10 at p51, para 1: 'Given the limited progress to date, we have no confidence that the target to reduce the numbers of people with learning disabilities and/or autism in mental health hospitals, set out in the NHS Long Term plan, will be met.'

Local authority support

Introduction

2.25 The powers and duties of local authorities to provide services and support to under 18s may be engaged in relation to adolescents with complex mental health needs[64] for a variety of reasons. For example, due to their mental health needs, some adolescents might be a 'child in need', while the support provided to others may mean that they are a 'looked after child'. Some adolescents may have additional needs, such as SEN. Importantly, consideration of the role of local authorities will be relevant across the whole spectrum of mental health care for under-18s, including where adolescents are receiving in-patient psychiatric care.

2.26 An overview of the various legal and policy frameworks is set out below, with links to where further details are provided in subsequent chapters. Provisions for assessing carers' support needs are summarised in chapter 9.[65]

Children's social care

Overview

2.27 The provision of services and support by children's services is centred on local authorities' duties to safeguard and promote the welfare of those aged under 18 who are living in their area.[66] Such duties are set out in the Children Act (CA) 1989: Part 3 provides for local authority support to children, young people and their families; while Parts 4 and 5 set out local authorities' duties and powers to take action where child protection concerns are raised. These duties are enhanced by provisions for joint working between the local authority and partner agencies, such as NHS bodies and the police. For example, the Children Act (CA) 2004 s11 places a general duty on local authorities and other organisations (including NHS England, CCGs and NHS

64 This term is explained at para 1.9.

65 See also chapter 8 'Carers' in S Broach and L Clements, *Disabled children: a legal handbook*, 3rd edn, LAG, 2020.

66 For an overview of the key challenges facing local authority children's social care services, see: House of Commons Briefing Paper, *Children's social care services in England*, Number 08543, 28 June 2019. The House of Commons Briefing Paper, *Local authority support for children in need (England)*, Number 7730, 10 October 2016, considers the term 'child in need', the assessment process and the services available to children in need and their families.

trusts) to ensure their functions, and any services that they contract out to others, are discharged having regard to the need to safeguard and promote the welfare of children.[67]

2.28 Like CAMHS, children's social care services cover a wide spectrum of needs, with interventions ranging from 'early help'[68] for children, young people and their families to child protection:

> Where a child's need is relatively low level, individual services and universal[69] services may be able to take swift action. Where there are more complex needs, help may be provided under section 17 of the Children Act 1989 (children in need). Where there are child protection concerns (reasonable cause to suspect a child is suffering or likely to suffer significant harm) local authority social care services must make enquiries and decide if any action must be taken under section 47 of the Children Act 1989.[70]

2.29 The Department for Education (DfE), which is responsible for the legal and policy framework in which children's services are expected to operate, has issued a range of guidance in relation to children's services responsibilities under the CA 1989. One of the DfE's key documents is *Working together to safeguard children: a guide to inter-agency working to safeguard and promote the welfare of children*, July 2018 ('*Working together*'), which has been issued as statutory guidance[71] for a range of organisations in addition to local authorities, including NHS bodies, such as CCGs, NHS trusts and NHS England.

Working together to safeguard children: guidance

2.30 *Working Together* sets out the procedures to be followed by practitioners in assessing if action is needed to safeguard and promote the welfare of children and young people aged under 18.[72]

2.31 *Working together* summarises the safeguarding duties of local authorities and other agencies in relation to under-18s as follows:

67 *Working Together to Safeguard Children. A guide to inter-agency working to safeguard and promote the welfare of children* ('Working Together' Chapter 2).

68 This term is used to describe services that are intended to 'provide support as soon as the problem emerges'. It will include services such as 'family and parenting programmes, assistance with health issues, including mental health, responses to emerging thematic concerns in extra-familial contexts, and help for emerging problems relating to domestic abuse, drug or alcohol misuse by an adult or a child'. See *Working together* paras 13–17.

69 These services include schools and health visiting.

70 *Working together* para 16.

71 The implications of this are explained at para 1.10.

72 *Working together* chapter 1 'Assessing need and providing help'.

> Whilst it is parents and carers who have primary care for their children, local authorities, working with partner organisations and agencies, have specific duties to safeguard and promote the welfare of all children in their area. The Children Acts of 1989 and 2004 set out specific duties: section 17 of the Children Act 1989 puts a duty on the local authority to provide services to children in need in their area, regardless of where they are found; section 47 of the same Act requires local authorities to undertake enquiries if they believe a child has suffered or is likely to suffer significant harm. . . .
>
> These duties placed on the local authority can only be discharged with the full co-operation of other partners, many of whom have individual duties when carrying out their functions under section 11 of the Children Act 2004 (see chapter 2). Under section 10 of the same Act, the local authority is under a duty to make arrangements to promote co-operation between itself and organisations and agencies to improve the wellbeing of local children (see chapter 1). This co-operation should exist and be effective at all levels of an organisation, from strategic level through to operational delivery.
>
> The Children Act 2004, as amended by the Children and Social Work Act 2017, strengthens this already important relationship by placing new duties on key agencies in a local area. Specifically the police, clinical commissioning groups and the local authority are under a duty to make arrangements to work together, and with other partners locally, to safeguard and promote the welfare of all children in their area.
>
> Everyone who comes into contact with children and families has a role to play.[73]

2.32 *Working together* states that anyone who has 'concerns about a child's welfare should make a referral to local authority children's social care'. Moreover, they 'should do so immediately if there is a concern that the child is suffering significant harm or is likely to do so'.[74] Where such a referral is made, a local authority social worker should acknowledge receipt of the referral within one working day and make a decision on the steps that should be taken. The action taken will depend on the circumstances. The local authority will determine whether immediate protection is required or whether an assessment should be undertaken to determine whether the under-18-year-old is a child in need of services under the CA 1989 and/or is in need of protection following investigations under the CA 1989 s47.[75] Reasons for the action taken should be recorded.[76]

73 *Working together* Introduction.

74 *Working together* p16 para 17.

75 *Working together* pp30–31.

76 *Court orders and pre-proceedings: for local authorities*, DfE, April 2014, 13, para 11.

2.33 Local authorities, with their partners, are expected to develop and publish local protocols for assessment, which 'set out clear arrangements for how cases will be managed once a child is referred into local authority children's social care'.[77] Such protocols should reflect where assessments will require particular care, for example, young carers and under 18s with SEN (see below at para 2.57). They should set out the process for challenge by under-18s and their families by publishing the complaints procedures.[78] Highlighting the importance of co-ordinating assessments, *Working together* states that there should be 'clear procedures for how these organisations and agencies will communicate with the child and family' and that 'the local protocol for assessment should clarify how organisations and agencies and practitioners undertaking assessments and providing services can make contributions'.[79]

Box 2.1: Action following a referral to children's services

- *Acknowledgement of the referral:* A local authority social worker should acknowledge receipt of the referral within one working day and make a decision on the steps that should be taken.[80]
- *Procedures following the referral:* The procedures to be followed by practitioners when assessing an adolescent who may be in need, including those suffering harm and deciding upon the action to be taken are set out in *Working together*.[81]
- *Decisions to be taken:* The local authority will determine whether the adolescent requires immediate protection; or whether an assessment should be undertaken to determine whether the adolescent is a child is in need of services under CA 1989 s17 and/or is in need of protection following investigations under CA 1989 s47.[82]

77 Local protocols for assessment' in *Working together* pp23–24. See also p15 para 16 which states that a 'threshold document' should be published which sets out the local criteria for action which should include 'the criteria, including the level of need, for when a case should be referred to local authority children's social care for assessment and for statutory services under [CA 1989 s17] . . . disabled children'.

78 CA 1989 s26(3); and Children Act 1989 Representations Procedure (England) Regulations 2006 SI 2006 No 1738.

79 *Working together* p24 para 42.

80 *Working together* p30 para 71

81 *Working together* pp32–55.

82 See *Working together* flowchart, p32.

- *Reasons for action to be recorded:* 'It is important that when acting under sections 17 or 47 there is a clear rationale for the local authority taking action and providing help, with reasons recorded'.[83]

2.34 *Working together* highlights the importance of advocacy, listing 'to be provided with advocacy to assist them in putting forward their views' as one of the points that children want from an effective safeguarding system.[84]

Services for 'children in need'

2.35 Under CA 1989 s17, local authorities are under a general duty to 'safeguard and promote the welfare of children within their area who are in need' and to do so 'by providing a range and level of services appropriate to those children's needs'.[85]

2.36 Services falling under CA 1989 s17 are wide-ranging.[86] They include:

- provision for children living with their families[87] (such as advice, guidance and counselling; occupational, social, cultural or recreational activities and home help);
- 'giving assistance in kind or in cash';[88] as well as
- specific services for disabled children and young people aged under 18.[89]

Although services under CA 1989 s17 include accommodation,[90] for the reasons discussed at paras 9.30–9.37, save for 'short-term breaks',[91]

83 *Court orders and pre-proceedings: for local authorities*, DfE, April 2014, 13, para 11.
84 *Working together* p9 para 13.
85 CA 1989 s17(1). See *R (Sanneh) v Secretary for Work and Pensions* [2013] EWHC 793 (Admin) at [43]–[45].
86 CA 1989 s17 and Sch 2.
87 CA 1989 Sch 2 Part 1 para 8.
88 CA 1989 s17(6).
89 CA 1989 Sch 2 Part 1 para 6 'Provision for disabled children'.
90 CA 1989 s17(6).
91 This is where the adolescent is accommodated away from the family home for a short period of time, such as an overnight stay or weekend. In some cases, it may be considered appropriate for such accommodation to be provided under CA 1989 s17(6). See *Short breaks – statutory guidance on how to safeguard and promote the welfare of disabled children using short breaks*, Department for Children Schools and Families, 2010. See also *Short breaks for disabled children – a legal guide for local authorities*, S Broach and Council for Disabled Children, 2017.

it is more usual for this to be provided under the local authority's powers, or duties, to accommodate under CA 1989 s20.

2.37 Local authorities' duties under CA 1989 s17 are likely to be relevant to adolescents in need of specialist mental health care. Furthermore, when undertaking an assessment of an adolescent who is a 'disabled child' (the definition of which includes 'mental disorder of any kind'[92]), the local authority must also consider whether it is necessary to provide services under Chronically Sick and Disabled Persons Act (CSDPA) 1970 s2.[93] Further details on the assessment of a 'child in need', including determining whether the adolescent is a 'child in need', the relevance of the CSDPA 1970 and the provision of services to children in need, are provided in chapter 9 in the context of after-care planning for adolescents leaving hospital (paras 9.20–9.38).

2.38 Adolescents who are receiving services as a 'child in need' should have 'a multi-agency child in need plan' in place which sets out which organisations and agencies will provide which services to the adolescent and the adolescent's family.[94]

Welfare services under the Chronically Sick and Disabled Persons Act 1970[95]

2.39 Assessments for welfare services under CSDPA 1970 s2 will be relevant to adolescents with SEN (see discussion of education, health and care (EHC) plans below),[96] children in need (see paras 9.21–9.25) and to those adolescents who are entitled to after-care services under the Mental Health Act 1983 s117 (see paras 9.39–9.55). Assessments under CSDPA 1970 s2 are discussed further at paras 9.26–9.29.

The provision of accommodation

2.40 Accommodation falls within the range of services that children's social care services can, and in some cases must, provide to

92 CA 1989 s17(11). For further discussion on 'children in need' see below paras 9.21–9.25

93 *Working together* p21 para 28. See also CA 1989 Sch 2 para 3.

94 *Working Together* p35.

95 See Broach et al, paras 3.66–3.78 for discussion on services provided under the CSDPA 1970.

96 See *Special educational needs and disability code of practice 0–25 years: Statutory guidance for organisations which work with and support children and young people who have special educational needs or disabilities* ('SEND Code'), DfE and DoH, January 2015, paras 10.13–10.20.

adolescents who are a child in need. The type and duration of the accommodation provided will depend on the adolescent's particular circumstances. For example, it might be a placement with foster carers (on a short- or long-term basis) or a 52-week placement in residential care.

2.41 Whereas local authorities can provide accommodation under CA 1989 s17, in cases where the duty to provide accommodation under section 20 arises, the adolescent must be accommodated under section 20, not section 17.[97] Local authorities' duty to accommodate a child in need under section 20 also takes precedence over the local authority duties under the Housing Act 1996.[98] This is relevant because adolescents accommodated under section 17 are not included in the definition of a 'looked after child' and therefore not entitled to the range of services and support that local authorities are required to provide to those adolescents who are looked after children (see below). As noted in *R (M) v Hammersmith and Fulham LBC*:

> Once a child is 'looked after' by a local authority, a great many other duties arise. These include, crucially, the duty to safeguard and promote her welfare and to maintain her in other respects apart from providing accommodation for her: 1989 Act, sections 22(3) and 23(1)(b).[99]

2.42 Further details on local authorities' responsibilities for the provision of accommodation are given at paras 9.30–9.38.

Direct payments and personal budgets

2.43 Direct payments can be made in lieu of services provided under the CA 1989 and the CSDPA 1970.[100] Direct payments and personal budgets can be arranged as part of EHC plans.[101]

97 *R (G) v Southwark LBC* [2009] UKHL 26.

98 *R (G) v Southwark LBC* [2009] UKHL 26; and *R (M) v Hammersmith and Fulham LBC* [2008] UKHL 14.

99 [2008] UKHL 14 at [20].

100 CA 1989 s17A; and Community Care, Services for Carers and Children's Services (Direct Payments) (England) Regulations 2009 SI No 1887. Note that services provided under the CSDPA 1970 are provided in the 'exercise of . . . functions' under CA 1989 Part 3 – see CSDPA 1970 s2(4). See S Broach and L Clements, *Disabled children: a legal handbook*, 3rd edn, LAG, 2020, paras 3.103–3.107 ('Personal budgets and personalisation').

101 CFA 2014, s49. See also SEND Code paras 9.95–9.124.

Child protection plan

2.44 A 'child protection plan' will be in place if the adolescent has been assessed by the children's social care team as being at risk of significant harm.[102] The plan will set out what action is being taken to ensure that the adolescent is safe from harm, prevent the adolescent from suffering further harm and promote the adolescent's health and development.[103] Such adolescents will be 'a child in need' and may become a 'looked after child' (see below).

'Looked after children'

2.45 Local authorities have specific responsibilities for 'looked after children',[104] including the provision of accommodation[105] (which might be placements with foster carers or residential care settings such as children's homes[106]) and maintenance.[107] Crucially, they must 'safeguard and promote the welfare of the looked after child and to act as good corporate parents to enable each looked after child to achieve his/her full potential in life'.[108] *Transforming children and young people's mental health provision: a green paper* notes that studies estimate 'that 45% of looked after children have a diagnosable mental disorder (compared to 10% of all children)'.[109]

2.46 The term 'looked after child' covers adolescents who are either in the local authority's care (under a care order,[110] or interim care order[111])[112] or have been provided with accommodation by the local

102 CA 1989 s47. A duty to investigate will arise where a the local authority has 'reasonable cause to suspect that a child who lives in or is found in their area is suffering, or is likely to suffer, significant harm or if they are informed that a child who lives or who has been found in their area is subject to an emergency protection order or is in police protection'. *Working together* states (p21) that in some cases, it might be necessary to take 'immediate protection whilst the assessment is carried out'. See also *Court orders and pre-proceedings* p59.

103 *Working together* p48.

104 CA 1989 s22.

105 CA 1989 s22A.

106 As noted by *Children's services: spending and delivery*, DfE, Research report by Aldaba and the Early Intervention Foundation, July 2016.

107 CA 1989 s22B.

108 Vol 2, para 1.2, paraphrasing CA 1989 s22(3). See also the 'corporate parenting principles', Children and Social Work Act 2017 s1.

109 DoH and DfE, 2017, p7.

110 CA 1989 s31.

111 CA 1989 s38.

112 See C*ourt orders and pre-proceedings* para 4, p23 for effect of a care order.

authority under CA 1989 s20 for a continuous period of more than 24 hours.[113]

2.47 The court can only make a care order if it is satisfied that the criteria under CA 1989 s31 are met and having considered the welfare checklist,[114] and the 'no order' principle,[115] it is appropriate to make the order.[116] Such orders continue up until an adolescent's 18th birthday (unless discharged by the court beforehand[117]). However, neither a care order nor an interim care order can be made if the adolescent is seventeen (or 16, if married or in a civil partnership).[118] In contrast, local authorities can accommodate adolescents aged 16 and 17 under CA 1989 s20.[119]

2.48 Examples of where a local authority might accommodate adolescents under CA 1989 s20 include where this has been requested by their parents because of the adolescent's 'behavioural problems' and 'where the parents and social services are working co-operatively together to resolve the issues and to secure a return home in early course' and where the adolescent has 'a medical condition or disability and the parent or parents seek(s) respite care for a short period of time'.[120]

113 CA 1989 s22. Adolescents will also be a looked after child if they are accommodated by, or on behalf of the local authority by virtue of an emergency protection order (EPO) under CA 1989 (ss44–45) or in certain cases where they are accommodated by the local authority at the request of the police, see CA 1989 s21. See *The Children Act 1989 guidance and regulations. Volume 2: care planning, placement and case review June 2015* ('Care Planning Guidance') DfE, paras 1.21–1.23.

114 CA 1989 s1(3).

115 CA 1989 s1(5).

116 *Court orders and pre-proceedings* p24. Courts can also make 'supervision orders' under CA 1989 s31. However, unlike a care order, being subject to a supervision order does not mean that the adolescent is a looked after child. For a discussion on the differences between a care order and a supervision order see: *Re O (a child)* [2001] 1 FLR 923; and *RW v Neath Port Talbot CBC* [2013] EWCA Civ 1227.

117 An application for the order to be discharged can be made by the adolescent, a person with parental responsibility or the local authority. See *Court orders and pre-proceedings* paras 39–43on discharge and revocation of orders.

118 CA 1989 s31(3). This provision applies to interim care orders, see: *Re Q (child: interim care order: jurisdiction)* [2019] EWHC 512 (Fam) [2019] All ER (D) 46 (Mar). For age restriction of 16 applying to those in a civil partnership, see *Court orders and pre-proceedings* p23.

119 See *Williams and another v Hackney LBC* [2018] UKSC 37 concerning the powers of s20 and its relationship to decisions by those with parental responsibility at [38]–[49].

120 *A local authority v AA (a child though his children's guardian)* [2019] EWHC 1855 (Fam).

2.49 If an adolescent is subject to a care order or interim care order, the local authority has parental responsibility for that adolescent (shared with others who have parental responsibility). Although the local authority will not have parental responsibility for adolescents who are accommodated under CA 1989 s20 'they are nevertheless replacing to some extent the role played by a parent in the child's life, and are expected to look after the child in all the ways that a good parent would'.[121]

2.50 Detailed guidance on local authorities' extensive responsibilities in relation to care planning, placement and case review for looked after children are set out in regulations[122] and *The Children Act 1989 guidance and regulations, Volume 2: care planning, placement and case review June 2015* ('Care Planning Guidance').[123]

Care leavers

2.51 Adolescents who have been 'looked after' for a total of at least 13 weeks (this period having begun after their 14th birthday and ended after their 16th birthday) are entitled to support from local authorities in preparing to leave care and making the transition into adulthood.

2.52 The support provided to adolescents falling within this category entails the preparation, and regular review, of a 'pathway plan' (which sets out the support the adolescent needs for a successful move into adulthood)[124] and the appointment of a personal adviser whose role includes providing the adolescent with advice and support and liaising with the local authority on the provision of services).[125] Such support should start once the adolescent reaches the age of 16. The type of 'leaving care' support local authorities are required to provide will depend on whether the adolescent is aged 16 or 17 and continues to be looked after (an 'eligible child') or is 16 or 17 but is no longer looked after (a 'relevant child'). Local authorities are under a duty to

121 *R (M) v Hammersmith and Fulham LBC* [2008] UKHL 14 at [20]. For further information on parental responsibility, see chapter 5.

122 Care Planning, Placement and Case Review (England) Regulations 2010 SI No 959 (as amended).

123 See also Applying corporate parenting principles to looked-after children and care leavers: statutory guidance for local authorities, DfE, February 2018 which concerns the 'corporate parenting principles as set out in section 1 of the Children and Social Work Act 2017'.

124 CA 1989 s23B(3)(b) and Sch 2 para 19B(4).

125 CA 1989 s23D and Sch 2 para 19C; Vol 2 5.18.

continue to support those aged over 18 who were an eligible child or a relevant child (these young adults are referred to as 'former relevant child') until they reach the age of 21, or beyond that if the care leaver is in an approved programme of education or training.

2.53 Guidance on the support to be provided for an eligible child is set out in the Care Planning Guidance. Guidance in relation to those who are no longer looked after children is set out in DfE's 2015 guidance *Children Act 1989 guidance and regulations, Volume 3: planning transition to adulthood for care leavers.*

Special educational needs and disability[126]

Introduction

2.54 Children and Families Act (CFA) 2014 Part 3 makes provision for children and young people with SEN and/or disabilities.[127]

2.55 A raft of guidance on relevant law and policy is available on the government's website.[128] This includes the *Special educational needs and disability code of practice: 0 to 25 years. Statutory guidance for organisations which work with and support children and young people who*

126 It should be noted that in response to the COVID-19 pandemic, the government introduced changes relevant to the provisions noted below. These fall into the following categories: a) enactment of the Special Educational Needs and Disability (Coronavirus) (Amendment) Regulations 2020 to temporarily amend the Special Educational Needs and Disability Regulations 2014, by relaxing various time limits for the completion of steps to be taken in the preparation of Education, Health and Care (EHC) assessments and plans (which will cease to have effect on 25 September 2020); and b) issue of statutory notices modifying the duty to secure the provision specified in EHC plans under Children and Families Act (CFA) 2014 s42 (pursuant to powers conferred by the Coronavirus Act 2020 s38 Sch 17 with the effect that the duty to secure the making of the provision specified in an EHC plan was replaced for three months by a duty to use 'reasonable endeavours' to secure the provision (as from 1 August 2020 the duty to secure the provision in an EHC plan has returned to normal). These changes were unsuccessfully challenged: see *R (Shaw) v Secretary of State for Education* [2020] EWHC 2216 (Admin). It is understood that this decision is to be appealed. See also *Education, health and care needs assessments and plans: guidance on temporary legislative changes relating to coronavirus (COVID-19)* DfE, updated 26 August 2020.

127 For further information on this area of law, see S Hannett, A McColgan and E Prochaska, *Special educational needs and disability discrimination in schools: a legal handbook*, LAG, 2017; and S Broach and L Clements, *Disabled children: a legal handbook*, 3rd edn, LAG, 2020, chapter 4 'Education'.

128 See: www.gov.uk/topic/schools-colleges-childrens-services/special-educational-needs-disabilities.

have special educational needs or disabilities ('SEND Code'), issued jointly by the DfE and DoH in January 2015.

The SEND Code

2.56 The SEND Code applies to a range of organisations – including local authorities, NHS England, CCGs, NHS trusts and NHS foundation trusts – who are required 'to demonstrate in their arrangements for children and young people with SEN or disabilities that they are fulfilling their statutory duty to have regard to the Code'.[129] Its scope is wide, and covers issues such as:

- the role of schools;
- undertaking assessments for EHC plans;
- preparing children and young people with SEN and/or disabilities for the transition into adulthood; and
- supporting particular groups of children and young people with SEN and/or disabilities – such as looked after children, children in need and children and young people in hospital.

Education, health and care plans

2.57 Some adolescents with complex mental health needs are likely to have SEN ('having a learning difficulty or disability which calls for special educational provision to be made for him or her'[130]) and may therefore have an EHC plan, the purpose of which is to:

> . . . make special educational provision to meet the special educational needs of the child or young person, to secure the best possible outcomes for them across education, health and social care and, as they get older, prepare them for adulthood.[131]

2.58 Local authorities' 'local offer' (see below) must include how parents and young people can request an assessment for an EHC plan[132] and arrangements for identifying and assessing children

129 SEND Code p12.

130 CFA 2014 s20(1). For children of 'compulsory school age' or young person (under the age of 25) this means that they have 'a significantly greater difficulty in learning than the majority of others of the same age' or 'has a disability which prevents or hinders him or her from making use of facilities of a kind generally provided for others of the same age in mainstream schools or mainstream post-16 institutions' (s2(2)).

131 SEND Code para 9.2.

132 CFA 2014 s36.

and young people's SEN, including arrangements for EHC needs assessments.[133]

2.59 In addition to provision for the adolescent's SEN, the EHC plan, which must be reviewed every 12 months,[134] must include provision for both health and social care:[135]

- *Health care:* 'any health care provision reasonably required by the learning difficulties or disabilities which result in him or her having special educational needs'[136] (which could include the involvement of CAMHS[137]).
- *Social care:* The EHC plan must include (for under-18s) any social care provision which must be made for the adolescent under CSDPA 1970 s2[138] and any other social care provision reasonably required by the learning difficulties or disabilities which result in the adolescent having SEN.[139] The duty to undertake an assessment under CSDPA 1970 s2 is underlined:

  > If a local authority determines that a disabled child needs support under Section 17, it *must* consider whether such support is of the type outlined in Section 2 of the Chronically Sick and Disabled Persons Act (CSDPA) 1970. Where it is, the local authority *must* provide that support[140] [emphasis in original].

2.60 The SEND Code emphasises the importance of involving children, young people and parents in the process of assessing, developing and reviewing EHC plans and highlights the need for local

133 SEND Code para 4.30.

134 CFA 2014 s44. See SEND Code paras 9.166–9.155.

135 CFA 2014 s42 requires the local authority maintaining the EHC plan to secure the specified special educational provision (s42(1) and (2); and SEND Code paras 9.131–9.136) and if the plan specifies health care provision, the responsible commissioning body (likely to be a CCG) must arrange for its provision (s42(3) and (4) and SEND Code para 9.141). However, note the temporary modifications to s42; see: www.gov.uk/government/publications/modification-notice-ehc-plans-legislation-changes.

136 CFA 2014 s37(2)(d).

137 The role of health services care is noted in the SEND Code paras 3.59–3.63. See also *Quick guide: guidance for health services for children and young people with special educational needs and disability (SEND)*, NHS England, July 2018.

138 CFA 2014 s37(2)(e). For the duty to provide the social provision specified in the plan, see SEND Code paras 9.137–9.141; see also paras 3.45–3.50 and 10.13–10.20.

139 CFA 2014 s37(2)(f).

140 SEND Code para 10.13.

authorities to ensure that children and young people have access to advocacy where necessary.[141]

EHC plans and looked after children

2.61 Where their placement includes the provision of social care, this is likely to mean that adolescents become a looked after child, or if they were already a looked after child, will continue to be so.[142] The SEND Code highlights the importance of co-ordinating social care provision for children in need and looked after children with the assessment and review of EHC plans.[143] The SEND Code notes that this will mean 'that a considerable amount of planning will be done around the care, health and education needs of looked after children'.[144]

2.62 Guidance has been published by NHS England for health commissioners: *Quick Guide: Guidance for health services for children and young people with special educational needs and disability*[145]; and by the DfE for social care professionals on their statutory duties under the CFA 2014: *Social care: guide to the 0 to 25 SEND code of practice. Advice for social care practitioners and commissioners*[146] (September 2014)).

Disability and the Equality Act 2010

2.63 The term 'disability' under CFA 2014 s83(6) shares the same definition as that set out in the Equality Act (EqA) 2010. This means that under both Acts, disability means:

> . . . a physical or mental impairment which has a long-term and substantial adverse effect on their ability to carry out normal day-to-day activities.[147]

141 SEND Code paras 9.21–9.26 and 9.168. CFA 2014 s36 ('Assessment of education, health and care needs') and s44 ('Reviews and reassessments') require local authorities to consult children's parents and young people aged 16 on these matters. The SEND Code (para 9.21) states that they should also involve children 'as far as possible in this process'.

142 *R (O) v East Riding of Yorkshire CC* [2011] EWCA Civ 196.

143 SEND Code, paras 3.49 and 3.50. See also paras 10.1–10.12 which concern looked after children and care leavers.

144 SEND Code para 10.6.

145 NHS England, 2018.

146 DfE, 2014.

147 EqA 2010 s6(1). CFA 2014 s83(3): 'A child or young person has a disability for the purposes of this Part if he or she has a disability for the purpose of the Equality Act 2010'. The relevant 'Part' is Part 3 of the CFA 2014.

2.64 The EqA 2010 makes it unlawful to discriminate (directly, or indirectly) against individuals on the basis of a 'protected characteristic', which includes age; disability; gender reassignment; marriage and civil partnership; pregnancy and maternity; race; religion or belief; sex; and sexual orientation.[148]

2.65 The SEND Code notes that the definition of disability 'provides a relatively low threshold and includes more children than many realise: "long-term" is defined as "a year or more" and "substantial" is defined as "more than minor or trivial"'.[149] Guidance issued by the governmental Office for Disability Issues, *Equality Act 2010. Guidance. Guidance on matters to be taken into account in determining questions relating to the definition of disability* (May 2011), provides a non-exhaustive list of impairments that can give rise to a disability, which include:

- autistic spectrum disorders (ASD);
- learning disabilities;
- mental health conditions 'with symptoms such as anxiety, low mood, panic attacks, phobias, or unshared perceptions; eating disorders; bipolar affective disorders; obsessive compulsive disorders; personality disorders; post traumatic stress disorder, and some self-harming behaviour';[150] and
- 'mental illnesses, such as depression and schizophrenia'.[151]

2.66 Accordingly, although the EqA 2010's definition of 'disability' is narrower than the definition under the CA 1989 (which includes 'mental disorder of any kind'[152]), it has the potential to include adolescents with complex mental health needs, as well as those with learning disabilities and/or autism.

2.67 The *Mental Health Act 1983: Code of Practice*[153] ('MHA Code') notes that the EqA 2010 places a duty on providers of services to the public and those exercising public functions, including NHS services, to make reasonable adjustments for people with a disability and gives examples of reasonable adjustments, such as providing

148 EqA 2010 s4. See also EqA 2010 s149 (public sector equality duty). For further information on the EqA see chapter 9 (Equality and non-discrimination) in S Broach and L Clements, *Disabled children: a legal handbook*, 3rd edn, LAG, 2020.

149 SEND Code p16.

150 Para A5.

151 Para A5.

152 CA 1989 s17(11).

153 DoH, 2015.

information in an accessible format and ensuring that there are adequate numbers of staff with the appropriate skills and experience to respond to patient's individual needs.[154]

Information and advice

2.68 Local authorities are required to arrange for information and advice to be provided to under-18s with SEN or disabilities and their parents about matters relating to their SEN or disabilities.[155] The SEND Code states that when carrying out their duties under CFA 2014 Part 3, 'local authorities *must* have regard to the importance of providing children and their parents and young people with the information and support necessary to participate in decisions' (emphasis in original).[156]

The 'local offer'

2.69 Local authorities are required to publish and keep under review, a 'local offer' which sets out the support they expect to be available across education, health and social care for children and young people who have SEN or are disabled.[157]

2.70 The planning and development of the local offer must involve children with SEN or disabilities as well as their parents, and young people with SEN or disabilities.[158] A range of bodies, including NHS bodies and NHS England, are required to co-operate in the preparation of the local offer.[159]

154 MHA Code paras 3.11–3.13.

155 The local offer must include details of how information, advice and support related to SEN and disabilities can be accessed and how it is resourced (see SEND Code para 2.3). For information on the 'local offer' see paras 2.69–2.72.

156 SEND Code para 2.1, albeit this falls short of advocacy. By way of comparison, see House of Lords House of Commons Joint Committee on the Draft Care and Support Bill, *Draft Care and Support Bill Report, Session 2012–13,* paras 94–99 on the importance of advocacy.

157 CFA 2014 s30. This covers provision in the local authority's area as well as outside its area for children and young people for whom it is responsible and those who are in its area and have a disability (s30(1)(b)). SEND Code chapter 4 provides guidance on how local authorities are to meet this duty.

158 CFA 2014 s30(8); and Special Educational Needs and Disability Regulations 2014 SI No 1530 reg 55. See also SEND Code paras 4.8–4.13.

159 CFA 2014 s31.

2.71 The local offer must include:

- information about special educational, health and social care provision for children and young people with SEN or disabilities;
- how parents and young people can request an assessment for an EHC plan; and
- arrangements for identifying and assessing children and young people's SEN, including arrangements for EHC needs assessments.[160]

2.72 The local offer should cover 'specialist services for children and young people with SEN or disabilities who require specialised, longer term support'[161] and should also include information about services relating to mental health.[162] CAMHS are included in the range of services that must be included in the joint commissioning arrangements 'for 0–25 year old children and young people with SEN or disabilities, both with and without EHC plans' that local authorities are required to make with CCGs and NHS England.[163] These services must be set out in the local offer.[164]

Transition to age 18

2.73 For adolescents who are nearing the age of 18, consideration will need to be given as to what, if any, care and support they will need from adult social care services and/or adult mental health services. For adolescents with EHC plans, consideration of what is needed to prepare them for 'adulthood and independent living' must start from Year 9.[165]

2.74 This stage, often referred to as 'transition', has long been recognised as problematic for both for disabled young people generally[166] and for those with mental health problems in particular.[167] NHS England reported to the Health Committee's 2014 inquiry into chil-

160 SEND Code para 4.30.

161 SEND Code para 4.31.

162 SEND Code para 4.40.

163 CFA 2014 s26.

164 SEND Code paras 3.9–3.12; see also paras 3.35–3.37.

165 Special Educational Needs and Disability Regulations 2014 SI No 1530 regs 20(6) and 21(6). See SEND Code chapter 8 'Preparing for adulthood from the earliest years'.

166 See for example, DfE, *Support and aspiration: A new approach to special educational needs and disability A consultation* Cm 8027 March 2011.

167 *Closing the gap: priorities for essential change in mental health*, DoH 2014, p26.

dren and young people's mental health that 'transition from child centred to adult services is currently poorly planned, poorly executed, and poorly experienced'.[168]

2.75 The SEND Code states that CCGs and local authorities 'should have regard to any published service specification for transition from CAMHS' and that they 'should use the specification to build person-centred services that take into account the developmental needs of the young person as well as the need for age-appropriate services'.[169] Recognising that the structure of mental health services often creates gaps for young people making the transition from children and young people's mental health services, the *NHS Long Term Plan* aims to develop an integrated model (health, social care, education and the voluntary sector) of mental health services for 0–25 year olds.[170]

2.76 The legal provisions under the Care Act 2014 and the CA 1989 which aim to facilitate transition are considered in chapter 9.

Joint working

2.77 The requirement for NHS bodies and local authorities to co-operate is included in differing legislation. For example:

- *CA 1989:* s27 (duty on local authorities and NHS bodies (NHS England, CCGs and NHS trusts) to co-operate with each other);[171]
- *NHS Act 2006:* s82 (duty of co-operation between NHS bodies and local authorities);

168 House of Commons Health Committee Children's and adolescents' mental health and CAMHS Third Report of Session 2014–15, para para 104. See also Quick *guide: commissioning for transition to adult services for young people with special educational needs and disability* (SEND), NHS England, 2018; and general guidance issued by the National Institute for Health and Care Excellence (NICE): *Transition from children's to adults' services for young people using health or social care services* ('NICE guidelines'), 2016.

169 SEND Code para 8.56. See also *Model specification for transitions from Child and Adolescent Mental Health Services*, NHS England, 2015.

170 *NHS long term plan* para 3.30.

171 *Working together* p31 para 72:

> Where requested to do so by local authority children's social care, practitioners from other parts of the local authority such as housing and those in health organisations have a duty to co-operate under section 27 of the Children Act 1989 by assisting the local authority in carrying out its children's social care functions.

- *CA 2004:* s10 (duty on local authorities to make arrangements to promote co-operation with their relevant partners to improve the well-being of children in their area);[172] and s16E (local arrangements for safeguarding and promoting welfare of children);[173]
- *CFA 2014:* s25 (promoting integration); s26 (joint commissioning arrangements) and s28 (duty of co-operation between local authorities and their local partners);[174]
- *CA 2014:* s3 (promoting integration of care and support with health services); s6 (duty of co-operation between local authorities and their relevant partners) and s7 (duty of co-operation in specific cases).[175]

Key guidance for adolescent mental health care

Overview

2.78 Adolescents requiring specialist mental health support may receive this under the system known as 'the Care Programme Approach' (CPA). For those with learning disabilities and/or autism, NHS England's policy on Care, Education and Treatment Reviews (CETRs) may be relevant. However, the guidance that is of central importance to the legal framework for the care and treatment of individuals with a mental disorder, including those aged under 18, is the *Mental Health Act 1983: Code of Practice* ('MHA Code'). Each of these are summarised below, starting with the MHA Code.

172 *Working together* highlights the importance of co-operation between agencies; eg in relation to CA 2004 s10 (p5):

> Under section 10 of the same Act, the local authority is under a duty to make arrangements to promote cooperation between itself and organisations and agencies to improve the wellbeing of local children (see chapter 1). This co-operation should exist and be effective at all levels of an organisation, from strategic level through to operational delivery.

173 *Working together* (p5) states:

> The Children Act 2004, as amended by the Children and Social Work Act 2017, strengthens this already important relationship by placing new duties on key agencies in a local area. Specifically the police, clinical commissioning groups and the local authority are under a duty to make arrangements to work together, and with other partners locally, to safeguard and promote the welfare of all children in their area.

174 See SEND Code chapter 3. The importance of co-operation is highlighted throughout the Code, see for example, paras 1.22, 4.14–4.17 and 8.55.

175 See *Care and support statutory guidance* chapter 15.

Mental Health Act 1983: Code of Practice

Status of the MHA Code

2.79 The MHA Code was published by the Department of Health (DoH) in 2015 in accordance with section 118 of the MHA 1983 which requires the secretary of state to prepare such a code as guidance for a range of mental health professionals on how they perform their functions under this Act.[176] The MHA 1983 requires such professionals to 'have regard to the code'.[177]

2.80 The MHA Code explains that for these professionals the MHA Code is 'statutory guidance' and as their failure to comply with it may lead to a legal challenge, they would need to have convincing reasons for this.[178] Such advice reflects the House of Lords decision in *R (Munjaz) v Mersey Care NHS Trust*[179] which concerned an earlier version of the MHA Code. The House of Lords noted that although only guidance, the MHA Code should be given great weight and should only be departed from if there are 'cogent reasons for doing so'.[180]

2.81 Such 'cogent reasons' would include where the courts have held the guidance to be wrong or it is clearly incorrect (for example, because it misstates a provision of the MHA 1983); compliance would give rise to a breach of the ECHR or it has been made redundant by subsequent case-law or legislation.[181]

2.82 The MHA Code has also been issued under LASSA 1970 s7, which places a duty on local authorities to 'act under general guidance of the Secretary of State' when exercising their social services functions. Such functions include the provision of services and accommodation under Part 3 of the CA 1989 and the provision of after-care under MHA 1983 s117.[182] The 'relevant legal principles' in

176 MHA 1983 s118(1).

177 MHA 1983 s118(2D). A similar provision applies to the MCA Code – see s42(4).

178 MHA Code p12.

179 [2005] UKHL 58.

180 [2005] UKHL 58 at [21].

181 These points are made by Richard Jones in his analysis of the MHA Code. See R Jones, *Mental Health Act Manual*, 23rd edn, Sweet & Maxwell, 2020, para 1–1237, p577.

182 Local Authority Social Services Act 1970 s1A defines 'social services functions' by referring to relevant legislation listed in Sch 1, which includes the Chronically Sick and Disabled Person Act 1970 ss2 and 2A; and Children Act 2004 ss9A and 16A–16Q and 'children in transition to adult care and support' under the Care Act 2014.

relation to guidance issued under LASSA 19970 s7 were noted by the Court of Appeal in *R (X) v Tower Hamlets LBC*:[183]

> ... the guidance does not have the binding effect of secondary legislation and a local authority is free to depart from it, even 'substantially'. But a departure from the guidance would be unlawful unless there is cogent reason for it, and the greater the departure, the more compelling must that reason be. Conversely a minor departure from the letter of the guidance while remaining true to its spirit may well be easy to justify or may not even be regarded as a departure at all. The court will scrutinise carefully the reason given by the authority for departing from the guidance. Freedom to depart is not necessarily limited to reasons resulting from 'local circumstances' ... although if there are particular local circumstances which suggest that some aspect of the guidance ought not to apply, that may constitute a cogent reason for departure. However, except perhaps in the case of a minor departure, it is difficult to envisage circumstances in which mere disagreement with the guidance could amount to a cogent reason for departing from it.'[184]

Reach of the MHA Code

2.83 The MHA Code can extend beyond the use of the compulsory powers of the MHA 1983. In *C v A Local Authority*,[185] Mr Justice Ryder stated:

> The purpose of the *MHA 1983 Code of Practice* and its enabling section is to protect those who have mental disorders as defined in the 1983 Act by making provision for their reception, care and treatment whether or not the Act's compulsory measures have been engaged. In my judgement, in the absence of any corresponding guidance that is applicable to a severely learning disabled child who is resident in a special school and whose condition *prima facie* falls within the definition of a mental disorder, the guidance applies.[186]

183 [2013] EWCA Civ 904.

184 [2013] EWCA Civ 904 at [28], see also [39]. The court noted (at [28]) two key authorities for such legal principles: *R v Islington LBC ex p Rixon* (1997–98) 1 CCLR 119; and *R (Munjaz) v Mersey Care NHS Trust* [2006] 2 AC 148.

185 [2011] EWHC 1539 (Admin).

186 [2011] EWHC 1539 (Admin) at [69]. Whereas MHA 1983 s118(1)(a) does not apply to a children's home, 'there is nothing in the scheme of the 1983 Act or its application to children in the community who are incapacitated within the meaning of the MCA 2005 which prevents section 118(1)(b) from applying.'

Limits to the authority of the MHA Code

2.84 The MHA Code provides detailed guidance on the implementation of the MHA 1983 (and in some chapters wider aspects of law such as the MCA 2005 and limits of decision-making by those with parental responsibility). However, its purpose is to reflect the law (which might be sourced from legislation or case-law (judgments made by the national and the European Court of Human Rights (ECtHR)), not create it. As made clear by the Supreme Court in *An NHS Trust v Y*,[187] codes such as the MHA Code cannot create legal obligations. A similar point is made in the introduction to the MHA Code, which notes that it 'describes legislative functions and duties and provides guidance'. It adds that while the whole of the code should be followed, the term 'must' is used where this reflects legal obligations in legislation and case-law and 'must be followed', as opposed to 'should' ('departures should be documented and recorded') and 'may', 'can' or 'could' (guidance 'is to be followed wherever possible').[188]

2.85 In addition, the MHA Code, like other codes and guidance, cannot be used to interpret legislation, unless 'they were contemporaneously prepared, so that the draft regulations formed part of the background against which Parliament was legislating'.[189]

Principles of the MHA Code

2.86 Chapter 1 of the MHA Code sets out five overarching principles (see box 2.2 below) that are expected to inform decision-making under the Act and which should be considered when making decisions under the MHA 1983.

187 [2018] UKSC 46 at [97].

188 MHA Code p13. The MHA Code has been criticised for 'creating ambiguities over which standards to be applied' (P Bartlett and R Sandland, *Mental health law policy and practice*, 3rd edn, OUP, 2007). See also P Fennell, 'Mental health law: history, policy and regulation' in L Gostin, P Bartlett, P Fennell, J McHale and R Mackay (eds) *Principles of mental health law and policy*, OUP, 2010 para 1.164: 'Some of the most invasive interventions, seclusion, restraint, and forcible feeding are not subject to direct legal regulation but are dealt with in the Code of Practice.'

189 *R (CXF) v Central Bedfordshire Council* [2018] EWCA Civ 2852 at [23]–[25].

Box 2.2: MHA Code guiding principles[190]

Least restrictive option and maximising independence

Where it is possible to treat a patient safely and lawfully without detaining them under the Act, the patient should not be detained. Wherever possible a patient's independence should be encouraged and supported with a focus on promoting recovery wherever possible.

Empowerment and involvement

Patients should be fully involved in decisions about care, support and treatment. The views of families, carers and others, if appropriate, should be fully considered when taking decisions. Where decisions are taken which are contradictory to views expressed, professionals should explain the reasons for this.

Respect and dignity

Patients, their families and carers should be treated with respect and dignity and listened to by professionals.

Purpose and effectiveness

Decisions about care and treatment should be appropriate to the patient, with clear therapeutic aims, promote recovery and should be performed to current national guidelines and/or current, available best practice guidelines.

Efficiency and equity

Providers, commissioners and other relevant organisations should work together to ensure that the quality of commissioning and provision of mental healthcare services are of high quality and are given equal priority to physical health and social care services. All relevant services should work together to facilitate timely, safe and supportive discharge from detention.

The Care Programme Approach

2.87 Chapter 34 of the MHA Code provides guidance on the CPA – the name given to multi-agency and multi-disciplinary process for assessing, planning and reviewing the care and support of individu-

190 MHA Code para 1.1.

als (of any age) with complex mental health needs who are in contact with secondary mental health services. It 'requires close engagement with service users and their carers'.[191]

2.88 NHS England's specifications for Tier 4 services require that under-18s' mental health care is planned in accordance with the CPA.[192]

2.89 Although health led, the MHA Code emphasises that care planning under the CPA 'requires a thorough assessment of the patient's needs and wishes', which includes an assessment of the person's wider needs, involving consideration of accommodation, specific needs arising from learning disability or autistic spectrum disorder, social, cultural or spiritual needs and personal support.[193] The DoH's 2008 guidance on the CPA, *Refocusing the Care Programme Approach: policy and positive practice guidance* lists an assessment of social care needs under the heading 'What the service user should expect'.[194] In relation to under-18s, it states:

> CPA needs to be seen in the context of other planning mechanisms for children with complex needs and agreement must be made locally on how to co-ordinate multi-agency care planning.[195]

2.90 Further information on the application of the CPA to adolescents with complex needs is provided in subsequent chapters.

Care, education and treatment reviews (CETRs)

2.91 CETRs will be relevant to adolescents who have a learning disability, autism or both these conditions. They 'are focused on those children and young people who either have been, or may be about to be admitted to a specialist mental health / learning disability hospital either in the NHS or the independent sector'.[196] CETRs should be held when the admission of an adolescent with learning disabilities and/or

191 MHA Code para 34.8.

192 See, for example, *Child and Adolescent Mental Health Services Tier 4 (CAMHS T4): general adolescent services including specialist eating disorder services,* 5.2.1. The services specifications can be found at: www.england.nhs.uk/commissioning/spec-services/npc-crg/group-c/c03/.

193 MHA Code para 34.19.

194 2008 Guidance, Table 3, p16.

195 2008 Guidance, p48. Annex B of the CPA guidance considers how the CPA can be adapted to apply to CAMHS – this is included at appendix C below.

196 *Care, Education and Treatment Reviews for children and young people. Code and Toolkit: A guide for commissioners, panel members and people who provide support* ('CETR Code and Toolkit'), NHS England, April 2017, p6.

autism for psychiatric care is being considered, during that adolescent's stay in hospital and when planning the adolescent's discharge and aftercare. The review panel is made up of three people and will include: a Chair (the person's commissioner); and two independent advisers – an expert by experience and a clinical expert.

2.92 The policy to hold such care and treatment reviews, which for children and young people will include education, has been developed by NHS England as part of its 'transforming care' programme to develop community services as alternatives to in-patient provision for people with learning disabilities and/or autism.[197] Their aim is to reduce the numbers of people with learning disabilities and/or autism being admitted to hospital and reduce the length of stays in hospital.

2.93 NHS England has published a range of resources to support these reviews.[198] Two key documents are:

- *Care and Treatment Reviews (CTRs): Policy and Guidance. Including policy and guidance on Care, Education and Treatment Reviews (CETRs) for children and young people* (March 2017) ('CETR Policy'); and
- *Care, Education and Treatment Reviews for children and young people: Code and Toolkit. A guide for commissioners, panel members and people who provide support* (April 2017) ('CETR Code and Toolkit').

Together they provide detailed guidance on how CETRs should be conducted.[199]

2.94 The Joint Committee on Human Right's report *The detention of young people with learning disabilities and/or autism* concluded that 'when done well' CETRs 'can provide a crucial opportunity to develop viable alternatives to inpatient care' and recommended that CETRs

197 See *Building the right support A national plan to develop community services and close inpatient facilities for people with a learning disability and/or autism who display behaviour that challenges, including those with a mental health condition*, Association of Directors of Adult Social Services, Local Government Association and NHS England, 2015. Such work follows the exposure of the abuse of people with learning disabilities and autism by staff at Winterbourne View, an independent hospital. See *Transforming care: a national response to Winterbourne View Hospital: Department of Health Review Final Report*, DoH, 2012.

198 See: www.england.nhs.uk/learning-disabilities/care/ctr/.

199 Standard 5.1 of Principle 5 (Open, independent and challenging) (CETR Policy p85) states: 'The review panel is made up of three people and will include: Chair – the person's commissioner; and two independent advisers – an expert by experience and a clinical expert'.

'should be put on a statutory footing to strengthen their ability to perform this role'.[200]

2.95 Key points on CETRs and their application to adolescents are set out in the box below.

Box 2.3: Care, Education and Treatment Reviews – key points

Comprehensive review

- CETRs aim to 'bring a person-centred and individualised approach to ensuring that the care and treatment and differing support needs of the person and their families are met, and that barriers to progress are challenged and overcome.[201]
- They consider twelve areas, covering issues such as whether in-patient care is needed and whether the right care, education and treatment is being provided.[202]
- The initial CETR is anticipated to take the equivalent of a day.[203]

Participation

- Adolescents and their parents should be at the centre of the review.[204]
- The CETR is based on a set of 'principles of human rights, child and young person-centredness and co-production' that emphasise this approach.[205]
- The CETR Policy highlights the need to facilitate and support such participation and to consider 'the need for, and access to, advocacy'.[206]

200 Second report of session 2019, HC 121 HL Paper 10, para 57.

201 CETR Policy p50.

202 The CETR Policy (p7 explains that the CETR is to use 'key lines of inquiry (KLOE)' to guide and structure the review process. Each KLOE 'consists of a key question followed by examples of probe questions that reviewers can use to explore and gather information on the issue under discussion'

203 CETR Policy p25.

204 CETR Policy p52; referring to the MHA Code's statements on the importance of participation and the duties on local authorities to support and involve children and young people under Children and Families Act (CFA) 2014 s19.

205 See CETR Code and Toolkit pp7–9.

206 The CETR Policy p71; referring to the right to advocacy under the MHA 1983 (explained in paras 6.63–6.65) and local authorities' duties to make arrangements for advocacy services under the CA 1989.

Trigger for a CETR

- In addition to where admission to hospital is being considered, CETRs may also be required if the adolescent's education or care provision has changed.[207]

Regular review

- Adolescents who are in hospital should have a CETR on a regular basis (within two weeks of admission[208] and every three months[209]).

Consent

- The review can only be undertaken with the adolescent's consent, the consent of a person with parental responsibility or in accordance with the Mental Capacity Act (MCA) 2005 (where the adolescent is aged 16 or 17 and lacks capacity as defined under the MCA 2005).[210]
- Assessing an adolescent's ability to make decisions (capacity and competence) is considered in chapter 3.

Multidisciplinary approach

- The involvement of local authorities and education services is regarded as integral to the CETR.
- It is essential that all agencies who are involved with the adolescent's care are invited, such as the SEN team if the adolescent as an EHC plan; children's social care services; and all those involved from children and young people's mental health services.[211]

Link to the CPA

- The CETR is expected to complement the CPA with the outcome of the CETR feeding into the CPA process which will 'lead to a revised CPA plan that will be the responsibility of the CPA care co-ordinator to complete and share with others including the individual and their family'.[212]

207 CETR Policy p51.

208 CETR Policy p35.

209 CETR Policy p72. The policy suggests that more regular reviews might be required for under-13s.

210 CETR Policy p55. The MHA Code provides guidance on assessing 'Gillick competence' at paras 19.36–19.37.

211 For a list of who should be invited to the CETR, see CETR Policy pp58–60.

212 CETR Policy p22.

Confidentiality and sharing information

Overview

2.96 Adolescents, like adults, have a right to have their personal information kept confidential. However, as with adults, adolescents' right to confidentiality may be qualified or limited in certain circumstances, for example if there is reasonable cause to believe that they are suffering, or at risk of suffering significant harm.[213]

2.97 MHA Code chapter 10 provides guidance on confidentiality and sharing information. It explains that the duty of confidentiality:[214]

> . . . arises when one person discloses information to another in circumstances where it is reasonable to expect that the information will be held in confidence. Certain situations, such as discussions with a health professional or social worker, are generally presumed to be confidential.

Disclosure of confidential information

2.98 The MHA Code notes that there are 'circumstances in which it is both justifiable and important to share otherwise confidential patient information with people outside the immediate team treating a patient'.[215] In such circumstances the person's consent should be sought before disclosing their personal information. However, where the person lacks the capacity to make such decisions 'it may be acceptable and appropriate to disclose the information in the person's best interests'.[216] The MHA Code adds:

> Otherwise, confidential patient information should be disclosed outside the team only:
>
> - with the patient's consent (where the patient has capacity to consent)
> - if there is a specific legal obligation or authority to do so, or
> - where there is an overriding public interest in disclosing the information.[217]

213 MHA Code para 19.14. See also *Information sharing: Advice for practitioners providing safeguarding services to children, young people, parents and carers*, HM Government, July 2018.

214 MHA Code para 10.3.

215 MHA Code para 10.3.

216 MHA Code para 10.3 p78.

217 MHA Code para 10.3 p79.

2.99 Although the above points focus on adults, the position is the same for adolescents. Where they have the competence (if aged under 16) or have the capacity (if aged 16 or 17) to make decisions about the use and disclosure of information they have provided in confidence, their views should be respected.[218] This means that their confidential information may not be disclosed without their consent unless it falls under one of the two lawful justifications for disclosure noted above.

Confidentiality and sharing information with parents

2.100 The principles of confidentiality also apply to the sharing of information with parents.[219] As they develop and mature, it is common for adolescents to prefer to discuss personal matters with health, social care and other professionals without their parents being present.

2.101 The MHA Code advises that practitioners should encourage adolescents to involve their parents (unless this would not be in the best interests of that child or young person). However, where adolescents have the competence or capacity to make such decisions and do not want their parents (or others with parental responsibility) to be involved in discussions about their care and treatment, the adolescents' decisions should be respected unless the disclosure can be justified. The MHA Code emphasises the importance of discussing with the adolescent the consequences of their decision and whether their concerns could be addressed – for example, by providing general information to parents but not disclosing information about specific aspects of their care.[220] Furthermore:

> Where a child or young person does not wish their parent(s) to be involved, every effort should be made to understand the child or young person's reasons and with a view to establishing whether the child or young person's concerns can be addressed.[221]

2.102 It is suggested that if parents and other carers are concerned that the lack of certain information will prevent them from providing adequate care, they should inform the adolescent's care team

218 MHA Code para 19.14.

219 Concerns about information sharing and who is involved in decision making were raised by young people and their families during the course of the independent review of the MHA 1983 but no specific recommendations on this point were made in the review's final report.

220 MHA Code paras 19.15–19.16.

221 MHA Code para 19.16.

and ask that the care plan be reviewed to take account of these concerns.

2.103 Further information is provided in the document *Information sharing: Advice for practitioners providing safeguarding services to children, young people, parents and carers.*[222]

222 HM Government, July 2018, available at: https://assets.publishing.service.gov.uk/government/uploads/system/uploads/attachment_data/file/721581/Information_sharing_advice_practitioners_safeguarding_services.pdf. See for example, 'Flowchart of when and how to share information' p12.

CHAPTER 3

The legal framework for adolescent inpatient psychiatric care: admission to hospital and medical treatment

continued

Introduction

3.1 Where children and young people aged under 18 ('adolescents') are considered to require a period of inpatient psychiatric care, it will be necessary to determine the legal authority for their admission to hospital and treatment while in hospital. This chapter focuses on the decision-making process for determining whether adolescents can be admitted and treated informally, or whether formal procedures, such as the compulsory powers of the Mental Health Act (MHA) 1983, must be engaged to authorise their inpatient psychiatric care.

3.2 Although the MHA 1983 provides for the circumstances in which individuals (of any age) can be admitted to hospital and treated for 'mental disorder'[1] without their consent, such compulsory powers are intended to be measures of last resort.[2] MHA 1983 s131 provides for 'Informal admission to hospital',[3] which means that individuals can be admitted 'without the formalities and procedures for admission necessary for detention under the Act'.[4] In addition, the *Mental Health Act 1983: Code of Practice* ('MHA Code') states that when practitioners are considering whether detention under the Act (commonly referred to as being 'sectioned') is necessary, they 'must

1 Mental Health Act (MHA) 1983 s1(2) defines this as 'any disorder or disability of the mind'.

2 As noted by Lord Steyn in *R v Bournewood Community and Mental Health NHS Trust, ex p L* [1999] AC 458 at 496; [1998] 3 All ER 289 at 306, this was the intention of the *Report of the Royal Commission on the Law Relating to Mental Illness and Mental Deficiency* (1954–1957) (Cmnd 169) (para 291) when recommending that mental health legislation should permit admission without the use of compulsory powers.

3 MHA 1983 s131(1):

> Nothing in this Act shall be construed as preventing a patient who requires treatment for mental disorder from being admitted to any hospital or [registered establishment] in pursuance of arrangements made in that behalf and without any application, order or direction rendering him liable to be detained under this Act, or from remaining in any hospital or [registered establishment] in pursuance of such arrangements after he has ceased to be so liable to be detained.

4 *R v Bournewood Community and Mental Health NHS Trust, ex p L* [1999] AC 458; [1998] 3 All ER 289, at p295 (Lord Goff of Chieveley).

always consider the alternative way of providing treatment and care', such as informal admission.[5]

3.3 Guidance on the informal admission and treatment of under-18s is provided in MHA Code chapter 19. It should be noted, however, that this guidance predates the cases on deprivation of liberty considered below. Furthermore, as noted in chapter 2 above, the MHA Code is merely guidance and cannot create legal obligations.

3.4 Given the complexity of this area of law, this chapter seeks to provide a step by step examination of the decision-making process. It breaks down the relevant issues into the following parts:

- an overview of the legal framework for adolescent inpatient care: identifying the potential 'legal routes' for admission to hospital and treatment for mental disorder;
- key pointers to help identify the relevant legal route;
- four legal 'milestones' in the decision-making process: a) adolescents' ability to make decisions for themselves ('capacity' and 'competence'); b) consent to admission and treatment; c) deprivation of liberty; and d) parental consent and the scope of parental responsibility;
- informal admission and treatment of under 18s; and
- overriding adolescents' refusal of treatment (including the MHA Code's approach to the provision of emergency (life-saving) treatment).

3.5 The rules governing the admission and treatment differs as between adolescents aged under 16, and those aged 16 or 17. Accordingly, where these differences apply, this chapter adopts the approach taken by the MHA Code, distinguishing between the two age groups by using the term 'child' or 'children' when referring to under-16s, and 'young person' or 'young people' when referring to 16- and 17-year-olds.[6]

5 Department of Health (DoH), 2015, para 14.11; see also para 19.51 in relation to under-18s. See *AM v South London and Maudsley NHS Foundation Trust* [2013] UKUT 365 (AAC) at [36]:

> . . . a first stage for decision makers responsible for making decisions about a person's assessment or treatment for mental disorder (or other health problems) is to consider whether the admission of that person to hospital, as opposed to treatment or assessment in the community or as a day patient, is warranted.

6 For the purposes of the Children Act (CA) 1989 all under-18s are 'children' (see CA 1989 s105).

Legal framework for adolescent inpatient care: overview

Introduction

3.6 Just as with adults, the legal authority for an adolescent's admission to hospital and treatment for mental disorder must be identified. Adolescents can be admitted to hospital and given medical treatment (including treatment for mental disorder) informally via one of the following three 'legal routes':

1) the adolescent's consent;
2) 'parental consent' – meaning the consent of the adolescent's parents, or others with 'parental responsibility';[7] or
3) the Mental Capacity Act (MCA) 2005 – if the adolescent is aged 16 or 17 and lacks capacity (as defined by this Act) to make decisions about the admission and/or treatment.[8]

3.7 Which (if any) of these legal routes apply depends on the circumstances of the adolescent's case at the time it is proposed that the adolescent should receive inpatient psychiatric care. If none of these legal routes apply, it will not be possible to admit or treat the adolescent informally.

3.8 Under current law, the formal legal routes are the MHA 1983 or court authorisation. However, when in force (April 2022), the 'Liberty Protection Safeguards' (LPS)[9] may provide an alternative legal mechanism for authorising the deprivation of liberty of 16- and 17-year-olds who lack capacity to make decisions about their care arrangements.[10]

3.9 Table 3.1 below summarises the differing legal routes for an adolescent's admission to hospital and treatment for mental disorder.

7 Unless otherwise stated, the term 'parent' is used to refer to those individuals with 'parental responsibility' (defined in CA 1989 s3(1)). This will usually, but not always, be the parents of the adolescent. See chapter 5 for identifying who has parental responsibility.

8 See MHA Code paras 19.50 and 19.51.

9 See paras 4.53–4.77 below.

10 The provisions are considered in chapter 4.

Table 3.1: The 'legal routes' for admission and treatment

Informal admission / treatment	Formal admission / treatment
• Adolescent's consent	• Mental Health Act 1983
• Parental consent	• Court order
• Mental Capacity Act 2005 (16-17 year olds)	• Liberty Protection Safeguards (16-17 year olds, from April 2022)

The exception to the above legal routes is where the adolescent is considered to require emergency treatment. This is considered below at paras 3.91–3.93.

Legal capacity and decisional capacity

3.10 A useful starting point when considering this area of law is to distinguish between two core aspects of decision-making: 1) 'legal capacity' and 2) 'decisional capacity'. In this chapter, the term 'legal capacity' is used where a person is recognised in law as having the authority (in other words, the right) to make a particular decision; and the term 'decisional capacity' is used where the person has the actual ability to make the particular decision.

3.11 The difference between the two can be illustrated by the right to vote in a general election. Irrespective of their ability to make a decision about who to vote for (decisional capacity), under 18s cannot vote because the franchise is limited to those aged 18 and over.[11] Under 18s therefore do not have the right (legal capacity) to vote.

Admission and treatment: three core questions

3.12 Determining the legal authority for an adolescent's proposed admission and treatment requires consideration of the following three sequential questions (each of which is considered in more detail below). The terms 'young person' and 'young people' refer to adolescents aged 16 and 17 and the term 'child' and 'children' refer to adolescents aged under 16.

11 Representation of the People Act 1983 s1(d).

1) Is the adolescent able to decide about the proposed hospital admission or treatment?	*• Together with the adolescent's age, this will detemine which group the adolescent falls within: a) young person able to decide; b) young person unable to decide; c) child able to decide; or d) child not able to decide.*
2) Which, if any of the legal routes for informal admission apply to the adolescent?	*• This will determine whether the adolescent can be admitted informally: on the basis of the adolescent's consent, parental consent or the MCA 2005).*
3) If it is not possible to admit or treat informally, is admission to hospital under the MHA 1983 the appropriate course of action?	*• It will be necessary to consider the criteria for admission under the MHA 1983; if they are not met court authorisation will be required. (Note: as from April 2022 the Liberty Protection Safeguards may be relevant for 16 and 17 year olds).*

1) Is the adolescent able to decide about the proposed hospital admission or treatment?

3.13 The decision-making process starts by assessing the adolescent's ability to make the relevant decision(s): admission or treatment, or both. Ascertaining whether the adolescent is able to make the decision in question (ie the adolescent's decisional capacity) is pivotal to the process of identifying the legal basis on which the adolescent can be admitted to hospital and treated for mental disorder.

The law's approach to adolescent decision-making

3.14 The law's approach to under-18s differs as between those who are aged 16 or 17 ('young people') and those who are aged under 16 ('children').

- *Adolescents aged 16 and 17 (young people):* this age group has the legal capacity to make decisions about both their admission to hospital and medical treatment (including treatment for mental disorder). This is because MHA 1983 s131 makes specific provision for young people to decide about their admission to hospital and the Family Law Reform Act (FLRA) 1969 s8[12] provides that young people can consent to their own medical treatment.[13] In addition, by virtue of MCA 2005 s1(2), young people are assumed to have the mental capacity to make decisions about their admission and treatment unless evidence shows otherwise.[14] If there are doubts about this, the young person's capacity must be assessed in accordance with the MCA 2005.

- *Adolescents aged under 16 (children):* In contrast to young people, the starting point for children is that they do not have the legal capacity to make decisions for themselves and they are presumed to lack decisional capacity. However, case-law has established that under-16s can make decisions for themselves if they are assessed as being 'Gillick competent' to make the relevant decision.[15] The term 'Gillick competent' derives from the House of Lord's decision in *Gillick v West Norfolk and Wisbech Area Health Authority* ('Gillick'),[16] which held that a child with sufficient understanding and intelligence to make the decision can consent to medical

12 FLRA 1969 s8:

> The consent of a minor who has attained the age of sixteen years to any surgical, medical or dental treatment which, in the absence of consent, would constitute a trespass to his person, shall be as effective as it would be if he were of full age; and where a minor has by virtue of this section given an effective consent to any treatment it shall not be necessary to obtain any consent for it from his parent or guardian.

13 Young people are therefore recognised in law as having the right, or 'legal capacity', to make decisions about their admission to hospital and treatment for mental disorder.

14 MCA 2005 s1(2).

15 See, for example, *Re JA (medical treatment: child diagnosed with HIV)* [2014] EWHC 1135 (Fam), [2015] 2 FLR 1030, [2015] Fam Law 139 at [68]: 'A child under the age of 16 is deemed to have legal capacity to consent to medical examination and treatment if he or she has sufficient maturity and intelligence to understand the nature and implications of the proposed treatment'.

16 *Gillick v West Norfolk and Wisbech Area Health Authority* [1986] AC 112, [1985] 3 WLR 830, HL. [1986] AC 112. The term 'Gillick competent' was coined during the legal arguments before the Court of Appeal in *Re R (a minor) (wardship: consent to treatment)* [1992] Fam 11, [1991] All ER 177, CA, 23. How to assess whether a child is competent (which was not considered by the House of Lords) is considered at para 3.31–3.34.

treatment.[17] This principle now extends to a wide range of decisions made by under-16s. Accordingly, under-16s can consent to their admission to hospital and medical treatment but only if those seeking to rely on such consent are satisfied that the child is able to make the particular decision at the time that it needs to be made.[18]

- The legal tests for adolescents' ability to decide are considered below (see 'Assessing adolescents' ability to decide (decisional capacity)').

The importance of participation

3.15 Whether or not they have been assessed to be able to make the decision in question, adolescents' views will be a crucial factor in determining the legal basis for their admission and/or treatment. Their participation in the decision-making process should be encouraged and supported.[19] Similarly, even if parents are not the decision-makers, unless there are grounds for not doing so,[20] they should be involved in the discussions about their child's admission to hospital and treatment for mental disorder.

2) Which, if any, of the legal routes for informal admission apply to the adolescent?

3.16 The key factors for determining whether an adolescent can be admitted to hospital and treated informally are summarised in table 3.2 below.

17 MHA Code para 19.34 describes the 'Gillick competent child' as understanding 'fully what is involved'. This is based on a comment made by Lord Scarman in *Gillick*. However Lord Fraser of Tullybelton's judgment (with which Lord Scarman agreed) does not have such a high threshold, referring to a child with 'sufficient understanding and intelligence' to know what the medical examination and treatment involves (see *Gillick v West Norfolk and Wisbech Area Health Authority* [1986] AC 112 p170).

18 MHA Code para 19.65.

19 MHA Code para 19.5. See also UN Convention on the Rights of the Child (UNCRC) Article 12. Albeit in non-mental health care cases, the importance of the views of the child have been highlighted by the courts eg *Mabon v Mabon* [2005] EWCA Civ 634; and *R (Axon) v Secretary of State for Health and the Family Planning Association* [2006] EWHC 37 (Admin).

20 MHA Code para 19.15 See paras 2.96–2.103 on confidentiality and sharing information.

Table 3.2: Identifying the legal routes for informal admission/treatment

Legal Route	When Applicable	Further Information
Consent	Just like adults, adolescents can consent to their admission and treatment if they are able and willing to do so.	Determining whether an adolescent can consent requires consideration of i) the rules governing adolescents' ability to decide (paras 3.23–3.37) and ii) what constitutes valid consent (paras 3.38–3.46).
Parental consent	The consent of the adolescent's parents, or others with parental responsibility may be sufficient authority for an adolescent's admission to hospital and treatment for mental disorder, but only if the decision falls within their decision-making powers.	Parental consent requires consideration of the 'scope of parental responsibility' (paras 3.62–3.65), 'deprivation of liberty' (paras 3.47–3.61) and how they relate to one another (paras 3.66–3.67).
Mental Capacity Act (MCA) 2005	The MCA 2005 may provide authority for the admission and treatment of 16 and 17 year olds who lack capacity (as defined by this Act)[21] but cannot do so if the proposed admission or treatment gives rise to a 'deprivation of liberty'.[22]	This requires consideration of when the MCA 2005 might apply. Chapter 4 below provides an overview of the MCA 2005 and its application to young people. The MCA 2005's relevance to young people's informal admission and treatment is considered at paras 3.73–3.79 below.

3.17 As the above summary shows, differing rules apply to each of the potential 'legal routes' for informal admission (consent; parental consent; and the MCA 2005).

The importance of determining if there is a deprivation of liberty

3.18 A crucial question for adolescents who are unable to make their own decisions about their admission to hospital or medical treatment is

21 MCA 2005 s5.

22 MCA 2005 s4A provides that individuals can only be deprived of their liberty under this Act in limited circumstances (court order (s16(2)(a)), life-saving or other emergency treatment (s4B) or (for those aged 18 or over) 'deprivation of liberty safeguards' (s21A and Sch A1).

whether such interventions give rise to a deprivation of liberty. If they do, informal admission and treatment is not possible. A general overview of 'deprivation of liberty' and its application to under 18s is provided at paras 3.47–3.61. Specific considerations for under-18s' inpatient psychiatric care are set out below (paras 3.72 and 3.76–3.77 for 16-17s and paras 3.88–3.91 for under-16s).

3) If it is not possible to admit or treat informally, is admission to hospital under the MHA 1983 the appropriate course of action?

3.19 Where it is concluded that it is not possible to admit and treat a child or young person informally, formal procedures will be needed to authorise the proposed inpatient psychiatric care.[23]

3.20 Under current law, this is likely to mean that the adolescent is admitted to hospital and treated under the MHA 1983, provided that the relevant criteria are met. However, in some cases alternative legal mechanisms may be more appropriate.[24] The potential 'formal' legal routes are summarised in the table below.

23 MHA Code paras 19.51 and 19.52.

24 See for example, *Re D (A Child)*, also known as *Trust A v X and others* [2015] EWHC 922 (Fam), in which an application was made to the High Court to determine whether a 15 year old was deprived of his liberty and if so whether this was lawful. The judgment notes that the child's psychiatrist considered that the MHA was not applicable.

Table 3.3: Identifying the legal routes for formal admission/ treatment

Legal Route	When applicable	Further information
MHA 1983	If the criteria for admission under the MHA 1983 are met. (See below, potential relevance of LPS as from April 2022.)	The criteria and procedures for admission to hospital under the MHA 1983 are explained in chapter 6 below. The provisions governing treatment for mental disorder of those detained under the MHA 1983 are considered in chapter 7 below.
Alternatives to admission under the MHA 1983 (court authorisation)	If, for whatever reason, the MHA 1983 is not applicable, it will be necessary to seek a court authorisation.	Depending on the circumstances this is most likely to be either the High Court exercising powers under its inherent jurisdiction[25] or (in relation to 16 and 17 year olds who lack capacity as defined by the MCA 2005 to make decisions about the proposed admission and/or treatment), the Court of Protection.[26]
Liberty Protection Safeguards (LPS) (due to come into force April 2022)	When in force the LPS[27] may provide an alternative legal mechanism for authorising the deprivation of liberty of 16 and 17 year olds who lack capacity (as defined under the MCA 2005) to decide about their care arrangements.	A summary of the LPS scheme is provided in Chapter 4 below (paras 4.53–4.77).

Emergency treatment

3.21 The exception to the requirement for formal procedures is where the adolescent requires emergency treatment to prevent death or severe permanent injury and there is no time to admit the adolescent under the MHA 1983 or seek a court order (see paras 3.91–3.97).[28]

25 See *Re A-F (Children)* [2018] EWHC 138 (Fam) in which the (then) President of the Family Division set out the procedures to be followed where an application to authorise a deprivation of liberty is required.

26 MHA Code para 19.52.

27 See the Mental Capacity (Amendment) Act 2019. These provisions are due to come into force in April 2022.

28 MHA Code paras 19.71–19.72.

Secure accommodation orders[29]

3.22 Although in the past, 'secure accommodation orders' under the Children Act (CA) 1989 s25[30] were considered to be an alternative to the MHA 1983 for under 18s,[31] current law suggests that this is no longer a viable option. In *Re C (detention: medical treatment)* (1997)[32] Wall J held that a psychiatric hospital was not 'secure accommodation' under CA 1989 s25 because its primary purpose was 'to achieve treatment', with the restriction on the adolescent's liberty being incidental to the treatment. The requirement for 'secure accommodation' to have the restriction of liberty as its 'primary purpose' was confirmed by the Court of Appeal in *Re B (secure accommodation order)*.[33] Furthermore, there are no powers to treat adolescents without their consent under CA 1989 s25[34] and as noted when discussing the 'scope of parental responsibility', there are limits to the circumstances in which parents can consent to treatment on behalf of their child.[35]

29 It should be noted that given the lack of placements in secure children's homes in England, an increasing number of applications are being made to the courts to authorise under 18s' placement in other settings, including unregulated settings (see for example *Z (A Child: DOLS Lack of secure placement* [2020] EWHC 1827) and see also: the President of the Family Division, Sir Andrew MacFarlane's *Practice Guidance Placements in unregistered children's homes in England or unregistered care homes in Wales*, November 2019.

30 CA 1989 s25(1) sets out the criteria such an order. An application for a secure accommodation order can only be made by a local authority in respect of certain 'looked after children' or by a health body that is accommodating a child or young person who is not a looked after child: Children (Secure Accommodation) Regulations 1991 SI No 1505 regs 7 and 8.

31 *Re K, W and H (minors) (medical treatment)* [1993] 1 FCR 240, [1993] 1 FLR 854, CA. For commentary on this case, see P Bates 'Children in secure psychiatric units: Re K, W, and H – out of sight, out of mind?' (1994) *Journal of Child Law* 6(3) 131.

32 *Re C (detention: medical treatment)* [1997] 3 FCR 49, [1997] 2 FLR 180. See also *Re X (a child), Re Y (a child)* [2016] EWHC 2271 (Fam), [2017] Fam 80, [2016] 3 WLR 1718 at [33].

33 [2019] EWCA Civ 2025 at [59]. See also Lady Black's (obiter) observations in *Re D (a child)* UKSC 42 at [115].

34 Another limitation is that by virtue of Children (Secure Accommodation) Regulations 1991 SI No 1505 reg 5(2); CA 1989 s 25 cannot be applied to 16- to 21-year-olds accommodated under local authorities' discretionary powers under CA 1989 s 20(5). However, *Re W (a child)* [2016] EWCA Civ 804, [2016] 4 WLR 159 confirms that 16- and 17-year-olds accommodated under CA 1989 s20(3) (which places a duty on local authorities to accommodate) are not excluded from the ambit of CA 1983 s25).

35 See paras 3.62–3.65.

Assessing adolescents' ability to decide (decisional capacity)

Overview

3.23 As noted at para 3.10 above, the term, 'decisional capacity' is used to describe an adolescent's ability to make the decision in question. The rules governing adolescents' ability to make decisions about their admission to hospital or medical treatment (including treatment for mental disorder) differ depending on the age of the adolescent. The test for capacity under the MCA 2005 will be relevant to adolescents aged 16- and 17-year-olds, whereas the question for under-16s will be whether they are 'competent' (applying the 'Gillick competence' test).

3.24 Whichever legal test is applied, the assessment of decisional capacity is both decision-specific and adolescent-specific. In other words, the assessment must focus on the ability of the adolescent to make the relevant decision at the time that decision needs to be made. This means that although in practice the two decisions are closely linked, an adolescent's ability to decide about admission to hospital is separate to that adolescent's ability to make decisions about medical treatment and therefore requires separate consideration.

Adolescents aged 16 and 17 (young people)

Overview

3.25 Like adults, the starting point for young people is that they can make decisions about their medical treatment and admission to hospital unless evidence shows that they are unable to do so.

Young people: assessing capacity under MCA 2005

3.26 Young people are assumed to have the mental capacity to make decisions about their inpatient psychiatric care unless evidence shows otherwise.[36] However, if there are concerns that the young person is not able to make the decision in question, the adolescent's capacity must be assessed in accordance with the MCA 2005[37] and its code of practice (*Mental Capacity Act 2005: Code of Practice* ('MCA Code')).[38]

36 MCA 2005 s1(2): 'A person must be assumed to have capacity unless it is established that he lacks capacity'.

37 MCA 2005 ss2 and 3.

38 Department for Constitutional Affairs, 2007.

3.27 To lack capacity under the MCA 2005, a young person must be unable to make the particular decision (often referred to as the 'functional element') and this inability to decide must be 'because of an impairment of, or a disturbance in the functioning of the mind or brain' (often referred to as the 'diagnostic element').[39] To be unable to make the decision (the 'functional element'), MCA 2005 s3 provides that the young person must be unable:

(a) to understand the information relevant to the decision,
(b) to retain that information,
(c) to use or weigh that information as part of the process of making the decision, or
(d) to communicate his decision (whether by talking, using sign language or any other means).

3.28 The assessment of capacity under the MCA 2005 is considered in more detail in chapter 4.

Young people unable to decide, but not lacking mental capacity

3.29 Both the MHA Code[40] and the MCA Code[41] envisage that in some cases young people may be unable to make a decision for a reason other than because of an impairment of, or a disturbance in the functioning of the mind or brain (the diagnostic element). The MHA Code suggests that such (rare) cases might arise because the young person is 'in an unfamiliar and novel situation', being asked to absorb a type and quantity of information that is new to them, or worrying about the implications of making the decision one way or the other.[42] It advises that the young person be given information and support, as well as time to make the decision.[43]

3.30 The likelihood of such cases arising is not clear, but if they do, the young person concerned will not lack capacity as defined by the MCA 2005 (because the diagnostic element under MCA 2005 s2 is not met). This is significant because it means that the MCA 2005 does not apply and therefore cannot provide the authority for the decision in question, such as the young person's admission to hospital or treatment for mental disorder, or both.[44] The relevance of such a finding is considered at tables 3.4 and 3.5.

39 MCA 2005 s2.
40 MHA Code para 19.31.
41 MCA Code para 12.13.
42 MHA Code para 19.31.
43 MHA Code paras 19.31–19.33.
44 For further discussion see paras 4.32–4.33.

Adolescents aged under 16 (children)

3.31 Before they reach the age of 16, children are presumed to be unable to make decisions for themselves. However, this presumption can be rebutted if they are found to be 'Gillick competent' to make the decision in question.[45] In *Re S (child as parent: adoption: consent)*[46] (which concerned the question whether an adolescent aged under 16 could consent to the adoption of her baby) Mr Justice Cobb noted:

> . . . in applying the *Gillick* test in the context of determining the competence of a child to make decisions, I regard it as appropriate, and indeed helpful, to read across to, and borrow from, the relevant concepts and language of the [MCA 2005].[47]

3.32 The judge considered that for a child to be Gillick competent:

> . . . the child should be of sufficient intelligence and maturity to:
>
> i) Understand the nature and implications of the decision and the process of implementing the decision;
> ii) Understand the implications of not pursuing the decision;
> iii) Retain the information long enough for the decision-making process to take place;
> iv) Weigh up the information and arrive at a decision;
> v) Communicate this decision.[48]

3.33 Although published before this decision, the guidance in the MHA Code on assessing competence (see box 3.1) reflects a similar approach to that adopted in *Re S*. The MHA Code sets out questions for practitioners to consider when assessing an under 16's competence to make a particular decision. This guidance draws from the wording of MCA 2005 s3 (inability to make decisions). However, whereas the test under the MCA 2005 focuses on whether the person *is unable* to make the relevant decision,[49] the MHA Code's questions on competence focus on whether the child has demonstrated that they *are able* to make the decision in question.

45 *Gillick v West Norfolk and Wisbech Area Health Authority* [1986] AC 112, [1985] 3 WLR 830, HL.

46 [2017] EWHC 2729 (Fam).

47 [2017] EWHC 2729 (Fam) at [15].

48 *Re S (child as parent: adoption: consent)* at [18].

49 MHA Code paras 19.34–19.37.

Box 3.1: Assessing 'Gillick competence'

19.36 When considering whether a child has the competence to decide about the proposed intervention, practitioners may find it helpful to consider the following questions.

- Does the child understand the information that is relevant to the decision that needs to be made?
- Can the child hold the information in their mind long enough so that they can use it to make the decision?
- Is the child able to weigh up that information and use it to arrive at a decision?
- Is the child able to communicate their decision (by talking, using sign language or any other means)?

19.37 A child may lack the competence to make the decision in question either because they have not as yet developed the necessary intelligence and understanding to make that particular decision; or for another reason, such as because their mental disorder adversely affects their ability to make the decision. In either case, the child will be considered to lack Gillick competence.

Mental Health Act 1983: Code of Practice, Department of Health (DoH), 2015

3.34 When considering the assessment of an under-16's competence, both *Re S* and the MHA Code make the following points:

- *The assessment of competence is decision-specific:* An under-16's competence must be assessed in relation to the decision in question.
- *There is no presumption of capacity:* It must be established that the child is able to make the decision.
- *A lack of competence does not require a 'diagnostic element':* Whereas individuals can only lack mental capacity within the meaning of the MCA 2005 if their inability to decide is due to 'an impairment of, or a disturbance in the functioning of the mind or brain' (the 'diagnostic' element), this is not required to lack Gillick competence. While a child might not be competent for a reason that would fall within the MCA 2005's diagnostic element, there could be another reason, such as the child not yet having developed the necessary understanding and intelligence to make the particular decision.[50]

50 *Re S (child as parent: adoption: consent)* [16]–[17]. See also MHA Code paras 19.34–19.37.

Supporting adolescents' decision-making

3.35 The MHA Code highlights the importance of ensuring that adolescents (including those aged under 16) are given relevant information in an appropriate manner and to consider what kind of support is needed.[51] For example, it states that it is 'essential that steps are taken to enable a person to understand information, such as using simple language and visual aids'.[52] Furthermore, 'children and young people should always be kept as fully informed as possible' and that they should receive clear and detailed information concerning their care and treatment, in an age appropriate format and that their views, wishes and feelings should always be sought and their views taken seriously.[53]

3.36 The questions in box 3.2 below are taken from the MHA Code's guidance on assessing whether an adolescent is able to make the relevant decision.

Box 3.2: Practical steps to support adolescents' decision-making

Practitioners should consider the following three questions:

- has the child or young person been given the relevant information in an appropriate manner (such as age appropriate language)?
- have all practicable steps been taken to help the child or young person make the decision? The kind of support that might help the decision-making will vary, depending on the child or young person's circumstances. Examples include:
  - steps to help the child or young person feel at ease
  - ensuring that those with parental responsibility are available to support their child (if that is what the child or young person would like)
  - giving the child or young person time to absorb information at their own pace, and
  - considering whether the child or young person has any specific communication needs (and if so, adapting accordingly).
- can the child or young person decide whether to consent, or not to consent, to the proposed intervention?

Mental Health Act 1983: Code of Practice, DoH, 2015, para 19.25

51 MHA Code paras 19.5, 19.25 and 19.32.

52 MHA Code para 19.28.

53 MHA Code para 19.5.

3.37 Further points on supporting under-18s in making decisions for themselves is given in chapter 4.

Consent to admission and treatment

Overview

3.38 Like adults, adolescents can be admitted to hospital and treated for their mental disorder on the basis of their consent, if they are able and willing to give such consent.[54] In such cases their consent 'will be sufficient authority for their admission to hospital and/or treatment for mental disorder'.[55] Their parents' additional consent is not required (although it is good practice to involve them in the decision-making process unless there is a good reason for not doing so).[56]

3.39 Consent should be sought for each aspect of the adolescent's admission, care and treatment as it arises[57] and those seeking to rely on the adolescent's consent must be satisfied that the adolescent's consent is valid.[58]

The requirements for consent

3.40 To give consent, adolescents must:

a) have sufficient information to make the decision;
b) have made the decision without any undue pressure being placed on them; and
c) have the mental capacity (if aged 16 or 17) or 'Gillick competence' (if aged under 16) to make the decision in question.

3.41 The importance of ensuring that all three requirements for consent are met is illustrated by the National Institute for Health and Care Excellence (NICE) guidance which describes consent as follows:

54 The MHA Code notes (para 14.16) that notwithstanding a person's consent, compulsory admission under the MHA 1983 should be considered where there are there is 'a strong likelihood that they will have a change of mind about informal admission either before, or after they are admitted, with a resulting risk to their health or safety or to the safety of other people'.

55 MHA Code para 19.21.

56 MHA Code para 19.21. Confidentiality and sharing information is discussed at paras 2.96–2.103.

57 MHA Code para 19.22, which adds: ' "Blanket" consent forms (ie forms that purport to give consent to any proposed treatment) are not acceptable and should not be used.'

58 MHA Code para 19.24.

> The voluntary and continuing permission of the person to receive particular treatment or care and support, based on an adequate knowledge of the purpose, nature, likely effects and risks including the likelihood of success, any alternatives to it and what will happen if the treatment does not go ahead. Permission given under any unfair or undue pressure is not consent. By definition, a person who lacks capacity to consent cannot consent to treatment or care and support, even if they cooperate with the treatment or actively seek it.[59]

3.42 Whereas the NICE guidance refers to 'capacity', as discussed above, for adolescents aged under 16 the question will be whether they are Gillick competent to make the particular decision.

Information: admission

3.43 In relation to the information relevant to the admission, it is suggested that when deciding whether they wish to consent to their admission to hospital, adolescents will need to be told:

- the reason for their admission to hospital (why they need inpatient psychiatric care);
- what (if any) medical treatment it is proposed they should have while an inpatient;
- where the hospital is located; and
- whether it is known how long they might be away from home.

Other points might include information about arrangements for visits from family and friends.

3.44 In addition, adolescents will need to be informed of the type of restrictions that will be placed on them – for example, that the doors to the psychiatric unit will be locked and they will need to ask for permission to leave (which at certain times, such as after dark, will not be given).[60] They should also be told that if they do consent to

59 See NICE (National Institute for Health and Care Excellence, *Decision-making and mental capacity* NICE guideline October 2018, pp31-32. See also MHA Code para 24.34.

60 See the observation by Charles J in *AM v South London and Maudsley NHS Foundation Trust* [2014] AACR 13, [2013] UKUT 365 (AAC) at [40] on the question whether an adult has the capacity to consent to admission to hospital for the purpose of MHA 1983 s131: That question will be likely to include consideration of the person's capacity to agree (a) to the relevant admission to hospital for the relevant purpose, (b) to stay in hospital whilst its purpose is carried out and (c) to the circumstances relating to a possible deprivation of liberty that will prevail during that admission.

their admission to hospital, they can change their mind – although this may lead to their detention under the MHA 1983.[61]

Information: treatment

3.45 In relation to treatment, the MHA Code emphasises that is the duty of everyone seeking consent to use reasonable care and skill, in giving information prior to seeking consent and also to meet the continuing obligation in providing 'the patient with sufficient information about the proposed treatment and alternatives to it.'[62]

3.46 Sufficient information should be given to the adolescent so that the adolescent understands 'in broad terms the nature, likely effects and all significant possible adverse outcomes of that treatment, including the likelihood of its success and any alternatives to it'.[63] They should be 'invited to ask questions and professionals should answer fully, frankly and truthfully'[64] and should be told that their consent to treatment can be withdrawn at any time and given a clear explanation of the likely consequences of not receiving the treatment.[65]

Deprivation of liberty

Introduction

3.47 The question of whether an adolescent's admission or treatment amounts to a deprivation of liberty is key to determining the legal basis for authorising the adolescent's inpatient psychiatric care.

61 More detailed (and stringent criteria) were applied in *A primary care trust v LDV* [2013] EWHC 272 (Fam) but Baker J explicitly stated that these were not intended to set a precedent. R Jones, *Mental Health Act Manual*, 23rd edn, Sweet & Maxwell, 2020 at 1-1356, (p616) suggests that information relevant to the assessment of capacity under MCA 2005:

> . . . might be: can the patient understand, retain and weigh the information that he is being admitted to hospital informally and that this means, subject to s.5 [of the MHA 1983], he can leave whenever he wants, that the purpose of the admission is to treat his mental disorder, that such treatment might involve the administration of medication, that during his stay he will be subject to hospital rules, and that the rules might involve placing restrictions on him.

62 MHA Code para 24.36. See also *Montgomery v Lanarkshire Health Board* [2015] UKSC 11. Although this case concerned adults, its emphasis on the provision of appropriate information and including the patient in the decision-making process about the treatment would also be relevant to under-18s.

63 MHA Code para 24.37.

64 MHA Code para 24.28

65 MHA Code para 24.29.

3.48 As noted in chapter 1 above, Article 5 of the European Convention on Human Rights (ECHR), requires any deprivation of liberty to be in accordance with strict procedural safeguards, including a periodic review of the lawfulness of the detention.[66] Accordingly, if the proposed admission and/or treatment gives rise to deprivation of liberty it will not be possible for the adolescent to be admitted and treated informally (it cannot be authorised by either parental consent[67] or the MCA 2005[68]). In such circumstances, it may be possible for the adolescent to be detained in hospital under the MHA 1983. If the criteria for admission under the MHA 1983 are not met a court authorisation would be required (which court will depend on the circumstances of the case).

Meaning of 'deprivation of liberty'

3.49 In *Re D (a child)*, the Supreme Court confirmed that, irrespective of the person's age, for a deprivation of liberty to arise, the following three conditions must be met:

(a) the objective component of confinement in a particular restricted place for a not negligible length of time;
(b) the subjective component of lack of valid consent; and
(c) the attribution of responsibility to the state.[69]

3.50 This tripartite test was first articulated by the ECtHR in *Storck v Gernany*[70] which is why the national courts sometimes refer to these conditions as the 'Storck components' or 'Storck limbs'. Each component, or 'limb' must be considered to establish whether a deprivation of liberty has arisen, thereby engaging the safeguards under ECHR Article 5. Accordingly, the following three questions must be considered:

1) *'The confinement question':* The first question to consider is whether the person's situation means that the person is confined

66 Article 5(4). The mental health tribunal performs the function required under Article 5(4) in relation to individuals detained under the MHA 1983 – see chapter 8.

67 *Re D (a child)* [2019] UKSC 42 at [49].

68 MCA s4A provides that individuals can only be deprived of their liberty under this Act in limited circumstances (court order (s16(2)(a)), life-saving or other emergency treatment (s4B) or 'deprivation of liberty safeguards' (s21A and Sch A1) which do not apply to under-18s.

69 [2019] UKSC 42 at [1]. Confirming the approach adopted in *P v Cheshire West and Chester Council; P and Q v Surrey County Council* [2014] UKSC 19, [2014] 2 All ER 585 at [37].

70 *Storck v Germany* (2006) 43 EHHR 6.

'in a particular restricted place for a not negligible length of time' (*Storck limb (a)*).

2) *'The no consent question'*: If the person *is* confined, the second question is whether valid consent has been given for that confinement (*Storck limb (b)*). If consent has been given, there is no deprivation of liberty; whereas the person's situation will amount to a deprivation of liberty if there is no consent for the confinement.
3) *'The state responsibility question'*: Article 5 will be only be engaged if the state is responsible for the person's confinement (*Storck limb (c)*).

3.51 Although these questions apply to everyone, whatever their age, there is a significant difference between adults and adolescents, in that for under-18s a conundrum for the courts has been the extent to which (if at all) the decision-making role of those with parental responsibility is relevant, in particular in relation to the confinement question and the no consent question.

Deprivation of liberty: children and young people

3.52 Each of the three questions concerning a deprivation of liberty (the confinement question, the no consent question and the state responsibility question) are considered below.

1) Is the adolescent confined?

3.53 In determining *the confinement question*, the Supreme Court confirmed in *Re D* that whereas for adults the question is whether they are 'under continuous supervision and control and was not free to leave' (commonly referred to as the 'acid test'[71]), for under-18s a comparison is to be made between the restrictions placed on them with the restrictions that fall within 'the normal parental control for a child of that age'.[72] Lady Hale considered that 'the crux of the matter' is whether 'the restrictions fall within normal parental control for a

71 The test established by Lady Hale in *Cheshire West* [2014] UKSC 19, [2014] 2 All ER 585 at [48] and [49].

72 [2019] UKSC 42 at [39].

child of this age or do they not?'[73] This means that 'a mentally disabled child who is subject to a level of control beyond that which is normal for a child of his age has been confined within the meaning of Article 5'.[74]

3.54 While such a modification of the 'acid test' recognises the need to take into account restrictions that parents will need to place on their child as part of their normal responsibilities, this raises two potential areas of uncertainty, in particular in relation to under-16s. The first is that it leaves room for interpretation on what restrictions are normal parenting restrictions and what are not. Second, to date the courts have given no firm upper age limit at which an under 18-year-old would not be confined even though the acid test is met. Munby P declined to do so when highlighting the need for a similar comparator approach in *Re A-F (children)*,[75] a decision preceding *Re D*, albeit expressing the view that the constant supervision of a 12-year-old might give rise to a confinement. However, when the President's approach was adopted in a subsequent case in relation to a 14-and-a-half-year-old girl, the court found that 'on balance' she was not confined.[76]

3.55 In relation to young people, the decision in *Re D* is a strong indication that 16- and 17-year-olds will be confined if the acid test is met, given that none of the parties before the Supreme Court disputed the first instance judge's finding, based on the acid test, that the adolescent concerned (then aged 16) was confined.[77] Moreover, 16- and 17-year-olds are not generally kept under 'consent supervision and control' and are 'free to leave'.

3.56 When considering whether an adolescent's admission to hospital for inpatient psychiatric care gives rise to a deprivation of liberty it will be necessary to determine the level of restrictions placed on the adolescent and how this compares with the parental restrictions usually

73 [2019] UKSC 42 at [39]; having noted (at [38]) that in *Nielsen v Denmark* (1989) 11 EHRR 175, the majority decision of the ECtHR 'clearly turned on the comparative normality of the restrictions place on the freedom of a 12-year-old boy'. Lady Hale also noted the comments made by Lord Kerr in *Cheshire West* ([77]–[78]). See also the discussion in *Re A-F (children)*, [2018] EWHC 138 (Fam), in particular [33] and [43]; and *Re RD (deprivation or restriction of liberty)* [2018] EWFC 47.

74 [2019] UKSC 42 at [42].

75 [2018] EWHC 138 (Fam).

76 *Re RD (deprivation or restriction of liberty)* [2018] EWFC 47. See also *Hertfordshire CC v NK and AK (by his children's guardian)* [2020] EWHC 139 (Fam).

77 [2019] UKSC 42 at [9].

placed on an adolescent of the same age. Whether an adolescent is confined will depend on the particular facts of each individual case. However, as noted at para 3.72 below, the care regime of a psychiatric ward is likely to entail restrictions that exceed those usually placed on older adolescents, in particular young people aged 16 and 17.

2) *Is there consent to the confinement?*

3.57 Like adults, adolescents with decisional capacity can consent to their confinement so that no deprivation of liberty arises.[78] However, in relation to adolescents who lack decisional capacity, *the no consent question* has given rise to a controversial issue, which would not be relevant to adults: whether their parents (or others with parental responsibility)[79] can consent to the confinement on their behalf.

3.58 The extent of the decision-making role of parents is another area in which there is a sharp difference in how the law applies to under 16s (children) as compared to adolescents aged 16 or 17 (young people).

- *Young people:* The Supreme Court held in *Re D (a child)* that parents of adolescents aged 16 or 17 may not consent to their child's confinement.[80] This means that where young people are confined and do not consent to their confinement (whether because they have capacity and do not agree to their confinement, or they lack the capacity to make such decisions) they will be deprived of their liberty.
- *Children:* As the Supreme Court's decision in *Re D (a child)* was concerned with 16- and 17-year-olds, not under-16s, the case of *Re D (a child: deprivation of liberty)* (also known as *Trust A v X and others*)[81] still applies to children. Accordingly, it may be possible for parents to consent to the confinement of under-16s who lack

78 *Local authority v D* [2016] EWHC 3473 (Fam). Compare with discussion on consent and secure accommodation orders under CA 1989 s25 in *T (a child)* [2018] EWCA Civ 2136.

79 Unless stated otherwise 'parents' includes others who have parental responsibility for the adolescent.

80 [2019] UKSC 42. This decision upheld the appeal against the Court of Appeal's decision in *Re D (a child)* [2017] EWCA Civ 1695.

81 [2015] EWHC 922 (Fam), [2015] Fam Law 636. For commentary on this case see A Ruck Keene, 'Baby Bournewood'?, *Mental Capacity and Policy*, April 2015; B Dolan and S Simlock, 'When is a DOL not a DOL? When parents of a 15 year old agree to it – Re D (A child: Deprivation of liberty) [2015] EWHC 922 (Fam)', Serjeants' Inn Chambers, September 2015; and C Parker (2016) 'Trust A v X and others: The Ghost of Nielsen returns?', *Medical Law Review*, 24(2) 268.

Gillick competence to make such decisions for themselves (discussed further at paras 3.83–3.90 below). An important caveat is that neither the parents nor the responsible local authority can consent to the confinement of adolescents who are subject to a care order.[82]

3) When is the state responsible for the deprivation of liberty?

3.59 The threshold for the engagement of state responsibility is low. The state will be responsible for a deprivation of liberty where a public body has been directly involved.

3.60 In *Re D (a child)*, Lady Hale noted that the local authority was 'involved in making and funding the arrangements' for the adolescent's care and had assumed statutory responsibilities for him under the CA 1989 s20, 'thereby making him a "looked after child"'. In the case of an adolescent's inpatient psychiatric care, the state will be involved because such services are arranged and funded by the NHS.[83]

3.61 Lady Hale also made clear that state responsibility may also be engaged because a public body knows, or ought to know of a deprivation of liberty due to the positive obligation on the state to protect individual's right to liberty under ECHR Article 5: [84]

> . . . it is clear that the first sentence of Article 5 imposes a positive obligation on the State to protect a person from interferences with liberty carried out by private persons, at least if it knew or ought to have known of this'.[85]

Accordingly, in relation to adolescent psychiatric inpatient care, the state will be responsible for any deprivation of liberty that arises[86] so the key considerations will be whether the adolescent is confined and if so, whether there is any consent for that confinement.

82 *Re AB (a child) (deprivation of liberty: consent)* [2015] EWHC 3125 (Fam) at [29] (considered in *Re D (a child)* [2017] EWCA Civ 1695 at [31]).

83 See discussion on Tier 4 CAMHS in chapter 2.

84 *Re D (a child)* [2019] UKSC 42 at [43]. See also *Secretary of State for Justice v Staffordshire CC and others* [2016] EWCA Civ 1317 at [78].

85 *Re D (a child)* [2019] UKSC 42 at [43].

86 There may be cases where an adolescent's admission is arranged and funded privately and delivered in an independent hospital. However, even then, the positive obligation under Article 5 is likely to be relevant.

Parental consent and 'the scope of parental responsibility'

Introduction

3.62 The 'scope of parental responsibility' is a term used in the MHA Code to highlight that before relying on parental consent to authorise an adolescent's admission to hospital or treatment for mental disorder, practitioners will need to establish that the decision in question is one that it is possible for the parent to make.[87]

Limits to parental decision-making powers

3.63 Although the MHA Code is concerned with mental health care, the recognition that there are limits to the decision-making powers of parents (or others with parental responsibility) is not unique to mental health law. The principle that there are limits to the type of decisions that parents can make in relation to their child applies to general health care decisions as well.[88] More widely, within criminal law there are restrictions on parents' control over their children (the extent to which corporal punishment can be used),[89] while the state can intervene in cases where the adolescent is 'suffering or is at risk of suffering significant harm attributable to lack of reasonable care'.[90] Both the national courts[91] and the ECtHR[92] have emphasised that there are limits to parents' decision-making powers. The difficulty is that to date, there has been little guidance on where those limits lie.

87 MHA Code paras 19.40–19.41. The MHA Code 2008 use of the term 'the zone of parental responsibility; but this was criticised by legal commentators and practitioners as being vague and unhelpful; eg see: J Watts and R Mackenzie, 'The Zone of Parental Control: a reasonable idea or an unusable concept?' (1996) 18(1) *Tizard Learning Disability Review*, pp38–44; R Sandland, 'Children, Mental Disorder, and the Law' in *Principles of Mental Health Law and Policy* (eds L Gostin, P Bartlett, P Fennell, J McHale and R MacKay), OUP, 2010. See also *Stronger Code: better care, consultation on the proposed changes to the Code of Practice: Mental Health Act 1983*, DoH, July 2014, at para 7.2.

88 *Reference guide to consent for examination or treatment*, 2nd edn, DoH, 2009, p35, para 19.

89 Children and Young Persons Act 1933 s1(7).

90 CA 1989 s31. See discussion in S Gilmore and L Glennon, *Hayes and Williams family law*, 6th edn, OUP, pp428–429.

91 See, for example, *Gillick v West Norfolk and Wisbech Area Health Authority* [1986] AC 112; *Hewer v Bryant* [1970] 1 QB 357 at 369. See also discussion in *Re D (a child)* [2017] EWCA Civ 1695; and *Re D (a child)* [2019] UKSC 42.

92 *Nielsen v Denmark* (10929/84) (1989) 11 EHRR 175 at [72].

3.64 The MHA Code sets out a range of factors to consider when determining whether the decision in question is one that the parent has authority to make. It also notes:

> If the decision is not one that a parent would reasonably be expected to make, or there are concerns about the validity of the consent of the person with parental responsibility, it will not be appropriate to rely on parental consent.[93]

3.65 Box 3.3 below sets out key areas to consider when determining whether parental consent can be relied upon to authorise the adolescent's admission to hospital and/or or medical treatment.

Box 3.3: Determining the scope of parental responsibility – key points

1) *Parental responsibility:* The person whose consent is being sought must have parental responsibility for the adolescent.[94]
2) *Decisional capacity:* As noted above (para 3.14) MHA 1983 s131 provides that where 16- and 17-year-olds have the capacity to make such decisions, parental consent cannot override their refusal of admission to hospital[95] and the MHA Code advises that parental consent 'should not be relied upon when the child is competent or the young person has capacity to make the particular decision'.[96] The MHA Code summarises the position as follows:

> The effect of section 131(4) of the Act in relation to the informal admission to hospital of a 16 or 17 year old, who has capacity, is that parental consent cannot be relied upon to override that young person's decision about their admission. In relation to decisions about such a young person's treatment, it is inadvisable to rely on the consent of a person with parental responsibility to treat a young person who has capacity to make the decision and has refused the treatment. Similarly, in relation to children, it is not advisable to rely on

93 MHA Code para 19.42.

94 CA 1989 s3; *Re A (children) (conjoined twins: surgical separation)* [2001] Fam 147, 178: 'the right and the duty to give consent to medical treatment is an incident of parental responsibility vested in the parent.' MHA Code paras 19.6–19.8. See also chapter 5.

95 MHA 1983 s131(4) provides that parental consent cannot override the views of a young person who has capacity to decide about admission to hospital for treatment for mental disorder; see MHA Code para 19.39, in relation to treatment.

96 MHA Code para 19.39.

the consent of a parent with parental responsibility to admit or treat a child who is competent to make the decision and does not consent to it.[97]

3) *Questions to determine the 'scope of parental responsibility'*: Where adolescents lack decisional capacity to make the relevant decision, the question whether their parents can consent to that decision on the adolescent's behalf 'will need to be assessed in the light of the particular circumstances of the case', taking a range of factors into consideration.[98] These fall under two broad questions:
   a) *Is this a decision that a parent 'should reasonably be expected to make'?* If the decision goes beyond the kind of decisions parents 'routinely' make about their child's medical care, then 'clear reasons' for relying on parental consent are required'. The issues noted by the MHA Code cover points such as the type and invasiveness of the proposed intervention, the age maturity and understanding of the adolescent, the extent to which the decision accords with the adolescent's wishes and whether the adolescent is resisting the decision. The MHA Code explains:

      > Relying on parental consent to authorise an intrusive form of treatment might be justified because it is necessary to prevent a serious deterioration of the child or young person's health, but this would need to be balanced against other factors such as whether the child or young person is resisting the treatment; whether the specific form of treatment is particularly invasive and/or controversial (eg careful consideration should be given to the appropriateness of relying on parental consent to authorise electro-convulsive therapy (ECT).[99]

   b) *Are there any factors that might undermine the validity of parental consent?* This covers points such as whether the parent(s) lack capacity to make the decision or are unable to focus on what course of action is in the best interests of their child. It also notes that whereas the consent of one person with parental responsibility is usually sufficient,[100] it may not be appropriate to rely on parental consent where there is a disagreement between the parents (one parent agreeing with

97 MHA Code para 19.39. The reasons for this advice is considered at paras 3.98–3.99 below.

98 MHA Code para 19.41.

99 MHA Code para 19.41. See chapter 7 for information on the provision of ECT

100 CA 1989 s2(7).

the proposed decision but the other objecting to it and likely to take preventative action, 'such as removing the child from hospital or challenging the decision in court).[101]

4) *Adolescents' wishes:* the views of adolescents will be of central importance to the question whether parental consent can authorise the adolescent's admission to hospital and/or treatment for mental disorder.[102] This is because:
   a) The importance of taking under 18s' views into account has been highlighted by the national courts[103] and the European Court of Human Rights (ECtHR).[104] In addition, both the UN Convention on the Rights of the Child (UNCRC) and the UN Convention on the Rights of Persons with Disabilities (UNCRPD) emphasise the importance of taking into account the 'evolving capacities of the child'.[105]
   b) As noted in point 3a above, a key factor is whether the adolescent is resisting the decision.
   c) In addition, the adolescent's age, maturity and understanding must be considered. Reflecting the view of the courts, the MHA Code states that the parents' decision-making role 'should diminish as their child develops greater

101 MHA Code para 19.41. See *An NHS trust v SR* [2012] EWHC 3842 (Fam) in which the mother of a young child withheld her consent to her son receiving treatment following brain surgery for a malignant brain tumour (radiotherapy and chemotherapy). Mr Justice Bodey noted at [2] that although generally medical professionals can act on the consent of either parent, 'when the matter is a very serious one and the parents cannot agree, it is accepted that an application will or may need to be made to the court for a declaration that the procedure in question is lawful'. See also *Re H (a child) (parental responsibility: vaccination)* [2020] EWCA Civ 664 at [94].

102 In non-mental health cases, the importance of the views of the child have been highlighted, see for example, *R (Axon) v Secretary of State for Health* [2006] EWHC 37 (Admin); *Mabon v Mabon* [2005] EWCA Civ 634; *Re Roddy (a child) (identification: restrictions on publication)* [2003] EWHC 2927 (Fam). See also UNCRC Article 12 ('Respect for the views of the child').

103 See for example, *R (Axon) v Secretary of State for Health* [2006] EWHC 37 (Admin); *Mabon v Mabon* [2005] EWCA Civ 634; *Re Roddy (A Child) (Identification: Restrictions on Publication)* [2003] EWHC 2927 (Fam).

104 *M and M v Croatia* [2015] ECHR 759, paras 184–186 and *Pini v Romania* [2004] ECHR 275 para 164.

105 See UNCRPD Article 3(h) and UNCRC Articles 5 and 12 (Respect for the views of the child). See also Committee on the Rights of the Child, General Comment 14 (2013) on the right of the child to have his or her best interests taken as a primary consideration (Art 3 para 1), CRC/C/CG/14.

independence, with accordingly greater weight given to the views of the child or young person'.[106]

d) Furthermore, even though under-18s cannot make legally binding advance refusals under the MCA 2005,[107] the MHA Code highlights the importance of considering any views expressed by the adolescent in relation to the proposed intervention when able to make such decisions. It notes that if the adolescent 'had expressed a willingness to receive one form of treatment but not another, it might not be appropriate to rely on parental consent to give the treatment that they had previously refused'.[108]

Parental consent and deprivation of liberty

3.66 The scope of parental responsibility is relevant to decisions that might give rise to an adolescent's deprivation of liberty. The question for the courts has been whether, and if so, in what circumstances, parents can consent to the confinement of their child so that no deprivation of liberty arises.[109]

3.67 Although the Supreme Court's decision in *Re D (a child)* (para 3.58 above) is crystal clear that consenting to a 16- or 17-year-old's confinement is outside the scope of parental responsibility, this decision explicitly leaves open the role of parental consent in relation to the deprivation of liberty of under-16s. The situation of under-16s and the relevance of the scope of responsibility when determining if they are deprived of their liberty is considered at box 3.4 below.

A point at which to recap: seven decision-making principles

3.68 Reflecting on the areas considered above, seven principles for determining the legal authority for an adolescents' admission to hospital and/or treatment for mental disorder can be identified. These are set out in box 3.4 below.

106 See *Hewer v Bryant* [1970] 1 QB 357; and *Nielsen v Denmark* (1988) 11 EHHR 175, para 72: 'the rights of the holder of parental authority cannot be unlimited'.

107 MCA 2005 s24.

108 MHA Code para 19.41.

109 As noted above (para 3.58), if parents can give valid consent to their child's confinement, one of the conditions for a deprivation of liberty (lack of valid consent) is not met.

Box 3.4: Adolescents' admission to hospital and treatment for mental disorder: seven decision-making principles

1) While there are various 'legal routes' for adolescents' admission to hospital and treatment for mental disorder: adolescent's consent, parental consent or the MCA 2005, each is subject to differing rules governing their application;
2) The age of the adolescent is important because there are differences between the law's approach to under 16s as compared to adolescents aged 16 and 17;
3) Determining whether the adolescent has decisional capacity is key to identifying which legal route might apply;
4) Adolescents can only be admitted and/or treated on the basis of their consent if they are able (have decisional capacity) and willing to give their consent;
5) It will not be possible to admit or treat adolescents informally if the admission or treatment gives rise to the adolescent's deprivation of liberty;
6) If there is no deprivation of liberty it may be possible to informally admit or treat adolescents who lack decisional capacity on the basis of parental consent (subject to the scope of parental responsibility) or (in the case of 16- and 17-year-olds) in accordance with the MCA 2005; and
7) Where informal admission is not possible, formal procedures will need to be engaged: MHA 1983 (if the criteria are met) or court authorisation, while (as from April 2022) a potential alternative route for 16- and 17-year-olds will be the Liberty Protection Safeguards (if the criteria are met).

Informal admission and treatment of under-18s

Introduction

3.69 Depending on their age and decisional capacity (see paras 3.23–3.37 above), adolescents will fall within one of the following four groups:

1) young people who are able to decide about admission and treatment;
2) young people who are *not* able to decide about admission and treatment;
3) children who are able to decide about admission and treatment; and

4) children who are *not* able to decide about admission and treatment.[110]

The rules governing the admission to hospital and treatment for mental disorder of each of these four groups of under-18s are considered below. In all cases it will be important to keep adolescents ability to make decisions about their admission and on-going in-patient care under regular review.

Admission and treatment of young people: overview

3.70 The situation for young people can be summarised as follows:

- *Young people who are able to make such decisions:* can be admitted to hospital and treated for their mental disorder informally on the basis of their consent. Without their consent, it will not be possible to admit or treat them informally.[111]
- *Young people unable to decide (admission and treatment):* the question whether they can be admitted and/or treated informally depends upon whether or not the proposed admission or treatment gives rise to a deprivation of liberty. Where it does, the MHA 1983 will be needed to authorise the young person's in-patient psychiatric care (or a court order obtained if the criteria for admission under the MHA 1983 is not met).

Reflecting that there are some differences between the law's approach to young people's admission and their treatment, the legal authority for their admission is considered first, followed by their treatment.

Young peoples' admission to hospital

Admission to hospital: young people able to decide

3.71 MHA 1983 s131 makes specific provision for 16- and 17-year-olds to have 'capacity to consent'[112] to the arrangements for their admission. It provides that such young people can:

110 This is the approach adopted by the MHA Code, see paras 19.49–19.70.

111 This is the effect of the MHA 1883 s131 in relation to their admission (preventing parental consent from overriding the young person's refusal) and the MHA Code in relation to the treatment of 16- and 17-year-olds (see paras 3.71 and 3.75).

112 MHA 1983 s131(5) states 'the reference to a patient who has capacity is to be read in accordance with the [MCA] 2005'.

- *Consent to admission to hospital:* Young people with the capacity to do so[113] can consent to their admission to hospital (MHA 1983s131(3)).[114] Where they give their consent, young people 'can be admitted, irrespective of the views of persons with parental responsibility (who cannot prevent the admission)'.[115]
- *Refusal of admission to hospital:* Where young people with the capacity to make such decisions do not consent to their admission to hospital, the MHA 1983 states that parents cannot consent to informal admission on the young person's behalf (MHA 1983s131(4)).[116] Informal admission will not possible, so if the young person requires inpatient psychiatric care formal procedures for admission will need to be considered (subject to the criteria being met, this is likely to be detention under the MHA 1983).

Admission to hospital: young people unable to decide

3.72 Following the Supreme Court's decision in *Re D (A Child)*[117] (discussed at para 3.58 above), it is difficult to envisage a situation where the admission to hospital for psychiatric care of a young person who is unable to make such decisions will not amount to a deprivation of liberty. Where a deprivation of liberty arises, young people cannot be admitted informally. A deprivation of liberty is likely to arise because:

- the question whether such young people are deprived of their liberty, turns upon whether they are confined 'in a particular restricted place for a not negligible length of time'.[118] Where they are so confined, the two other components for a deprivation of liberty (discussed at paras 3.49–3.51 above) will be met. There will be no 'valid consent' (the young person is unable to consent and parents cannot give 'valid consent'[119]) and where the inpatient care is funded by the NHS, the State will be responsible for the confinement.[120]

113 MHA 1983 s131(2) refers to 'the case of a patient aged 16 or 17 years who has capacity to consent' to their admission.

114 MHA 1983 ss131(2), (3) and (4). MHA 1983 s131(5)(2) provides that 'the reference to a patient who has capacity is to be read in accordance with the Mental Capacity Act 2005'.

115 MHA Code para 19.53.

116 See also MHA Code para 19.53. The statutory recognition of a young person's refusal was introduced as part of the reforms under the Mental Health Act (MHA) 2007.

117 *Re D (a child)* [2019] UKSC 42.

118 See para 3.50 above.

119 *Re D (a child)* [2019] UKSC 42.

120 If cases arise in which parents make private arrangements with an independent hospital for the admission of their child, the question would be whether the state knows, or ought to know, about the deprivation of liberty (see para 3.61).

- while every case must be decided upon its own facts, young people are likely to be confined because the level of restrictions placed on them during their stay on a psychiatric ward will in most cases exceed those usually placed on 16 and 17 year olds in their normal day to day life. For example, doors to Child and Adolescent Mental Health Services (CAMHS) units are usually locked and patients only able to leave with the permission of staff, while the level of control and supervision will be higher than normally placed on this age group by their parents.[121]

Young peoples' admission to hospital: flowchart

3.73 The flowchart below summarises the key points for determining the legal basis on which young people can be admitted to hospital for inpatient psychiatric care. Additional notes are set out in the table 3.5. Albeit (as noted above), such cases are unlikely, theoretically it is possible for a young person's admission to hospital not to give rise to a deprivation of liberty, in which case it might be possible to admit the young person on the basis of parental consent or the MCA 2005. It is for this reason that these potential legal routes are included in the flow chart. However, it must be (re)emphasised that whether this would happen in practice is highly questionable.

Admission to Hospital and Young People (YP)

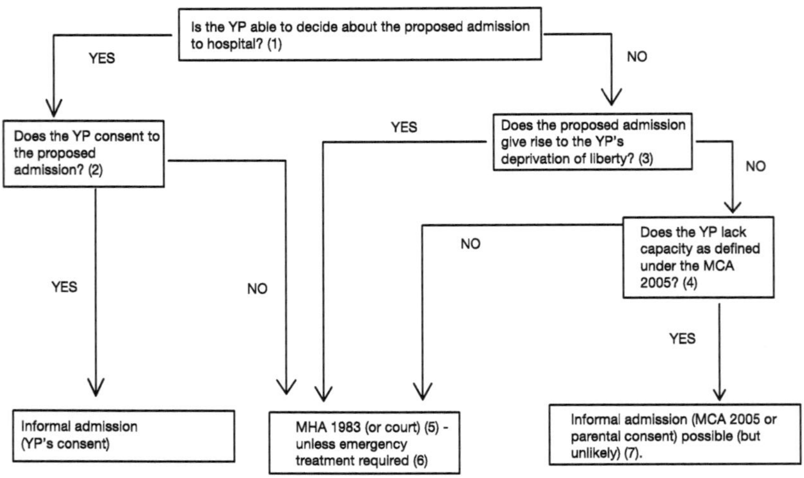

121 Similarly, under 18s admitted to adult wards are likely to be under close supervision and not free to leave, which would be far higher restrictions normally placed on adolescents of this age.

Table 3.5: Notes to flowchart (admission to hospital and young people)

Notes	Comments and cross-references
1)	The starting point for young people is that they are assumed to be able to make decisions for themselves unless evidence shows otherwise (see paras 3.23–3.37 above for assessing a young person's ability to decide).
2)	For consent to admission see paras 3.47–3.61.
3)	As noted at para 3.72 above, the answer to this question is most likely to be 'yes'. Where young people are deprived of their liberty it will not be possible to admit them to hospital informally (see determining a deprivation of liberty (paras 3.25–3.30 above)).
4)	The assessment of capacity under the MCA 2005 is considered at paras 3.26–3.28 above and paras 4.20–4.33
5)	For further information see: chapter 6 below (procedures for admission under the MHA 1983) and paras 3.19–3.22 above for alternatives to detention under the MHA 1983. Chapter 4 below summarises the circumstances in which, when in force (expected date April 2022), the Liberty Protection Safeguards may apply).
6)	Emergency treatment is considered at paras 3.91–3.101.
7)	In the unlikely event that a young person's admission to hospital does not give rise to a deprivation of liberty, the following points would be relevant to determining whether the young person can be admitted informally: • *MCA 2005:* may be able to authorise the admission of young people who lack capacity (as defined by the MCA 2005)[122] to make decisions about the arrangements for their admission.[123] A key consideration will be whether the proposed admission is in the young person's best interests.[124] Decision-making under the MCA 2005 is considered below (chapter 4). • *Parental consent:* if the decision falls within the 'scope of parental responsibility' (see paras 3.62–3.67), parental consent may provide the requisite legal authority for the young person's admission to hospital as an alternative legal route to the MCA 2005.[125] However, MHA 1983

122 MCA 2005 s2 and s3.

123 MCA 2005 s5. See also MHA Code para 19.57.

124 If decisions are made in accordance with the MCA 2005, parental consent is not required but the young person's parents must be consulted about the relevant decision(s) unless this is not 'practicable and appropriate' (see MCA 2005 s4(7)(b)).

125 This not referred to in the MHA Code but the MCA Code para 12.16 states: 'Under the common law, a person with parental responsibility for the young person is generally able to consent to the young person receiving care or treatment where they lack capacity under section 2(1) of the Act.' See also *Re D (A Child)* [2019] UKSC 42 (comments made by Lady Black (at [71]) and Lord Carnwarth (at [145])) to the effect that the MCA 2005 does not oust the decision-making role of those with parental responsibility.

s131 'only allows informal admission on the basis of parental consent if the young person lacks capacity within the meaning of the MCA'.[126]

- *Young people unable to decide but not for reasons falling within the MCA 2005:* as noted at paras 3.29–3.30, the MHA and MCA Codes envisage that some young people may be found to be unable to make the relevant decision but for reasons that fall outside the remit of the MCA 2005.[127] How often such cases occur is unclear. In any event, in such cases, it will not be possible to admit informally because the MCA 2005 will not apply, nor (as noted above) can the admission be authorised by parental consent.

Young peoples' treatment for mental disorder

Overview

3.74 Consideration of the basis on which the legal authority for their treatment will be relevant to the following young people:

- Young people admitted to hospital informally (see paras 3.70–3.73 above)
- Young people who have been detained in hospital under the MHA 1983 under the short-term detention powers (sections 4, 5, 135 and s136)[128]
- Young people receiving treatment in the community, eg as an out-patient.

As with their admission to hospital, differing rules apply to the treatment of young people, depending on their ability to make the treatment decision in question.

Treatment for mental disorder: young people able to decide

3.75 Decisions about young people's treatment for mental disorder are governed by FLRA 1969 s8 and guidance in the MHA Code:

- *Consent to treatment for mental disorder:* 16- and 17-year-olds can consent to their own medical treatment (FLRA 1969 s8). This means that young people can be treated for their mental disorder

126 MHA Code para 19.54. See MHA 1983 ss131(2) and (5)(a).

127 See MHA Code para 19.31 and MCA Code para 12.13.

128 The provisions governing treatment without consent under MHA 1983 part 4 (considered in chapter 7) which will apply to young people who have been admitted to hospital under MHA 1983 ss2 and 3, do not apply to those who are detained under these shorter term detention provisions of the MHA 1983.

informally, on the basis of their consent, where they are able and willing to give such consent.[129]

- *Refusal of treatment for mental disorder:* Unlike admission to hospital, there is no legislative bar on relying on parental consent to override a 16- or 17-year-old's refusal of medical treatment. However, the MHA Code's advice is that in such cases informal treatment is not possible and consideration should be given to whether admission under the MHA 1983 is necessary and if so, whether the criteria are met (but see 'emergency treatment' at para 3.95–3.97).[130] The MHA Code's reason for advising against relying on parental consent in such cases is discussed below at para 3.98.

Treatment for mental disorder: young people unable to decide

3.76 As with their admission to hospital, the first consideration when determining the legal authority for treating young people who are unable to make such decisions is whether the proposed treatment is likely to give rise to a deprivation of liberty. Provided that no deprivation of liberty arises, it may be possible for the treatment to be authorised either by the MCA 2005 (if the young person lacks capacity[131] to make decisions about such treatment[132]) or by parental consent (if the young person is unable to make the treatment decision(s) for him or herself and the decision falls within the scope of parental responsibility).[133]

3.77 For the reasons noted above, it is doubtful that young people who lack capacity to make such decisions for themselves can be admitted informally given that their admission to a psychiatric ward is likely to give rise to a deprivation of liberty. If young people have been admitted informally, it will be necessary to determine the legal authority for their treatment.

3.78 In theory it is also possible for young people to be willing and able to consent to their admission to hospital (and therefore admitted informally on the basis of their consent), but unable to make decisions about their treatment. In practice, such cases are unlikely given the

129 MHA Code para 19.58. Although FLRA 1969 s8 is silent on this point, given that it states that 16- and 17-year-olds' consent 'shall be as effective as it would be if he were of full age', it is suggested that the effect of this provision is that, like adults 16- and 17-year-olds will be assumed to have capacity unless evidence shows otherwise MCA 2005 s1(1).

130 MHA Code paras 19.59 and 19.66.

131 MCA 2005 ss2 and 3 (see para 4.16–4.33).

132 MHA Code para 19.59.

133 See table 3.5 and footnote135 below.

close connection between the two decisions (decisions about admission to, and on-going stay in, hospital will require an understanding of the purpose of hospital admission, ie to receive medical treatment).[134] However, if such cases arise, provided that the treatment does not give rise to a deprivation of liberty, it might be possible for a young person to be given treatment informally in accordance with the MCA 2005 or on the basis of parental consent (subject to the points noted in para 3.65).

Young peoples' treatment for mental disorder: flowchart

3.79 The flow chart below summarises the key points for determining the legal basis on which young people can be treated for mental disorder. Additional notes are set out in the table 3.6.

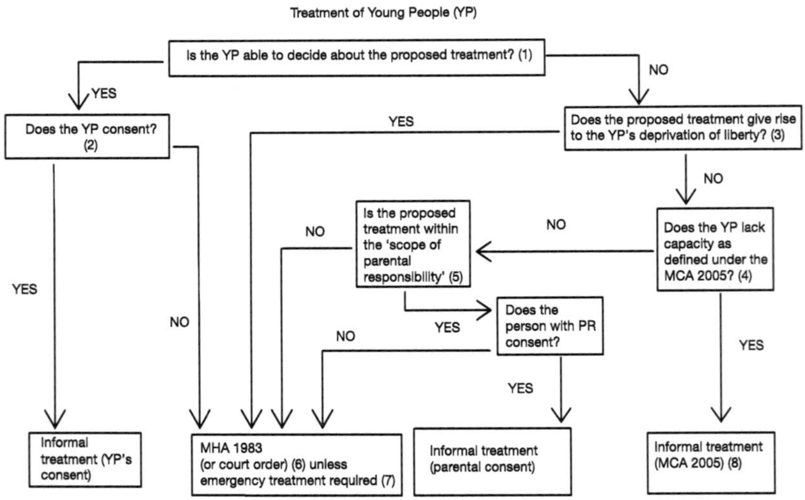

134 See comment by Charles J in *AM v South London and Maudsley NHS Foundation Trust* [2014] AACR 13, [2013] UKUT 365 (AAC) at [41]: 'Also, it seems to me that it may well be difficult to assert that the person does not have the capacity to consent to the assessment or treatment but does have the capacity to agree to be admitted to and remain in hospital in the relevant circumstances and for the relevant period, and so whilst the assessment is carried out or the treatment is given that requires the person to be an in-patient.'

Table 3.6: Notes to flow chart (treatment of young people)

Notes	Comments and cross-references
1)	As noted at para 3.25, the starting point for young people is that they are assumed to be able to make decisions for themselves unless evidence shows otherwise (see paras 3.26–3.30 above for assessing a young person's ability to decide).
2)	For consent to treatment see paras 3.38–3.46.
3)	If the proposed treatment gives rise to the young person's deprivation of liberty it will not be possible to treat informally (see determining a deprivation of liberty (paras 3.52–3.61 above)).
4)	The assessment of capacity under the MCA 2005 is considered at paras 4.20–4.30.
5)	Provided that the treatment does not give rise to a deprivation of liberty, parental consent may be able to authorise the treatment of young people who are unable to make such decisions for themselves,[135] if this is within the 'scope of parental responsibility' (see paras 3.62–3.66).
6)	For further information see: chapter 6 below (procedures for admission under the MHA 1983) and paras 3.19–3.22 above for alternatives to detention under the MHA 1983. Chapter 7 below considers treatment under MHA 1983 Part 4 and chapter 4 below summarises the circumstances in which, when in force (expected date April 2022), the Liberty Protection Safeguards may apply.
7)	Emergency treatment is considered at paras 3.91–3.101.
8)	Provided that the treatment does not give rise to a deprivation of liberty, the MCA 2005 may be able to authorise the medical treatment of young people who lack capacity (as defined by the MCA 2005)[136] to make decisions about such treatment.[137] Decision-making under the MCA 2005 is considered in chapter 4.[138] A key consideration will be whether the proposed admission is in the young person's best interests.[139]

135 As noted in the flow chart, it might be possible for parental consent to authorise a young person's treatment in circumstances where the young person does not lack capacity as defined by the MCA 2005 (see MHA Code 19.63). It may also be possible for parental consent to provide the requisite legal authority for the young person's medical treatment where the MCA 2005 applies; see *Re D (A Child)* [2019] UKSC 42, in which (at [50]), Lady Hale declined to 'express any view on the extent of parental responsibility in relation to other matters, such as serious and irreversible medical treatment, which do not entail a deprivation of liberty'; see also Lady Black (at [90]) and Lady Arden (at 117]).

136 MCA 2005 s2 and s3.

137 MCA 2005 s5. See also MHA Code para 19.59

138 Although the MHA Code (para 19.60) states that the MCA 2005 will apply in the same way as it does to adults it should be noted that there are some differences as between adults and young people, e.g. under 18s cannot make advance refusals of medical treatment (MCA 2005 s24(1)).

139 If decisions are made in accordance with the MCA 2005, parental consent is not required but the young person's parents must be consulted about the relevant decision(s) unless this is not 'practicable and appropriate' (see MCA 2005 s4(7)(b)).

Children able to decide about admission and treatment

Overview

3.80 Children who are assessed as being able to make such decisions (and are therefore regarded as 'Gillick competent') can be admitted to hospital and treated for mental disorder informally with their consent.[140] The MHA Code advises against overriding their refusal of admission to hospital or treatment for mental disorder.[141] These points are considered further below.

Consent to admission and treatment: the Gillick competent child

3.81 Where adolescents aged under 16 are able to decide about the proposed admission to hospital and treatment for mental disorder and they consent to such interventions, such consent will be sufficient authority for their informal admission and treatment.[142] However, those seeking to rely on the consent to admission to hospital or treatment for mental disorder must establish whether the child is able to make the particular decision at the time it needs to be made.[143] The MHA Code (para 19.65) states:

> Where a child who is Gillick competent to decide about their admission to hospital for assessment and/or treatment of their mental disorder consents to this, they may be admitted to hospital as an informal patient. A child who is Gillick competent and has consented to being admitted informally, may also be given treatment if they are competent to consent to the proposed treatment, and do consent. Consent will be required for each aspect of the child's care and treatment as it arises. This will involve an assessment of the child's competence to make the particular decision and, where the child is competent to do so, confirmation that they have given their consent.

Refusal of admission or treatment: the Gillick competent child

3.82 If a child is Gillick competent and refuses to be admitted to hospital or treated for mental disorder, the MHA Code states that consideration should be given to whether admission under the MHA 1983 is

140 MHA Code para 19.65.

141 MHA Code para 19.66.

142 It should be noted however that under the MHA 1983 certain treatments for mental disorder such as ECT for under-18s and psychosurgery can only be given if specific procedures are followed. These are discussed in chapter 7.

143 MHA Code para 19.34.

necessary, and if so, whether the criteria are met.[144] The MHA Code's reason for advising against relying on parental consent to override a competent child's refusal is because of developments of case-law since the introduction of the Human Rights Act (HRA) 1998.[145] This advice, which is discussed at para 3.98, is subject to cases where 'emergency treatment' is required (see paras 3.91–3.101).

Children unable to decide about admission and treatment

Overview

3.83 Children who lack Gillick competence to make such decisions can be admitted to hospital and treated for their mental disorder informally on the basis of their parents' consent, provided that this is within 'the scope of parental responsibility'.[146] This entails consideration of whether the proposed admission and/or treatment gives rise to the child's deprivation of liberty.

Children's inpatient psychiatric care and deprivation of liberty

3.84 As noted at para 3.16 above, it may be possible for parents of children who are not Gillick competent to consent to their child's confinement, so that no deprivation of liberty arises.

3.85 This means that for under-16s, the question whether a deprivation of liberty arises is connected to parental consent, which in turn hinges upon the extent of parental decision-making powers (the scope of parental responsibility). To date the courts have provided little clarity on this issue. For this reason, the circumstances in which parents can consent to the admission to hospital and treatment for mental disorder of adolescents aged under 16 is one of the most difficult and contentious issues in this area of law.

Determining if parental consent can authorise admission or treatment

3.86 There are two key considerations when determining whether a child who lacks Gillick competence can be admitted and treated informally:

144 MHA Code para 19.66.

145 MHA Code para 19.39. For further discussion on refusal of treatment see paras 3.98–3.100 below.

146 MHA Code paras 19.70 and 19.40–19.41.

1) *Deprivation of liberty:* This is the first consideration (see box 3.4 below). If there is a deprivation of liberty, the child cannot be admitted informally. It will be necessary to consider admission to hospital under the MHA 1983 (or seek a court authorisation if the criteria for admission under the Act are not met).
2) *Parental consent and the scope of parental responsibility:* If there is no deprivation of liberty[147] the second consideration is whether the decision to consent to the child's admission or treatment is one that the child's parents can make. The MHA Code's guidance on the scope of parental responsibility will therefore need to be considered (see paras 3.64–3.65 above).

Children's admission to hospital and treatment: flowchart

3.87 The flow chart below, summarises the suggested key points for determining whether a child can be admitted to hospital and treated informally (on the basis of the child's consent, or parental consent) or whether formal procedures, such as admission under the MHA 1983 need to be engaged.

In relation to treatment, consideration of the legal authority for their treatment will be relevant to the following children:

- Children admitted to hospital informally
- Children who have been detained in hospital under the MHA 1983 under the short-term detention powers (sections 4, 5, 135 and s136)[148]
- Children receiving treatment in the community, eg as an out-patient.

For the reasons noted in relation to young people (paras 3.78) while in theory it is possible that a child is willing and able to consent to their admission to hospital (and therefore admitted informally on the basis of their consent), but unable to make decisions about their treatment, in practice this is unlikely. However, if such cases arise, provided that the treatment does not give rise to a deprivation of liberty, it might be possible for the child to be given treatment informally on the basis of parental consent.

147 This could be either because the child was not confined; or that there was no deprivation of liberty because the second *Storck* limb was not met because the parent(s) consented to the confinement.

148 The provisions governing treatment without consent under MHA 1983 part 4 (considered in chapter 7) do not apply in such cases.

Readers should note that the extent of parental decision-making powers, particularly in relation to the determination of their child's deprivation of liberty is a developing area of law. For the reasons noted below, the current position (that it is possible for parents to consent to their under 16-year-old child's confinement) may change.

Admission and Treatment: Under 16s

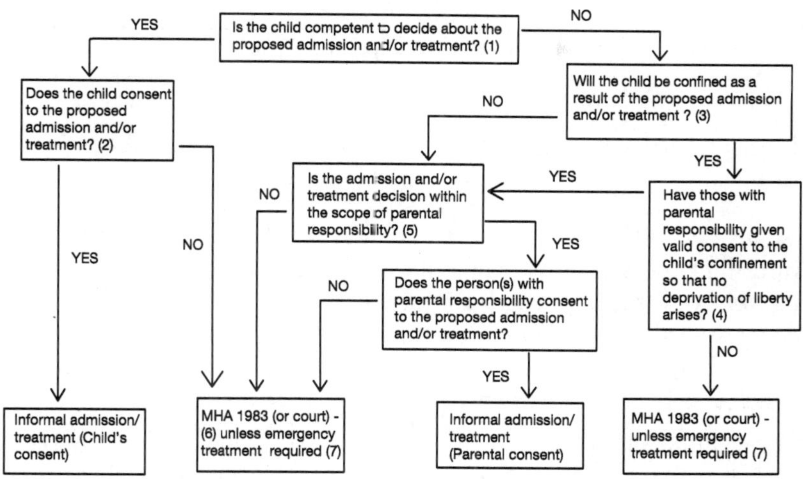

Table 3.7: Notes to flow chart (admissions and treatment of children)

Notes	Comments and cross-references
1)	As noted at para 3.31, under 16s are presumed to be unable to make decisions for themselves unless they are assessed as being 'Gillick competent' (see paras 3.31–3.37 above for assessing a child's ability to decide).
2)	For consent to admission and treatment, see paras 3.38–3.46.
3)	See paras 3.49–3.61 for the test for determining a deprivation of liberty, the first consideration being whether the child is confined 'in a particular restricted place for a not negligible length of time'.
4)	See box 3.4 'Deprivation of liberty and children lacking Gillick competence' below, which explains the relevance of parental consent to determining whether a deprivation of liberty has arisen.[149] If the child is subject to a care order or interim care order (ICO), neither the parents, nor the local authority maintaining the care order or ICO can consent to the child's confinement (see box 3.4).

149 As noted in box 3.4, it is suggested that the scope of parental responsibility is relevant when determining whether parents can consent to their child's confinement so that no deprivation of liberty arises.

5)	As noted above (para 3.86) in cases where it is established that there is no deprivation of liberty, the next question is whether the parent(s) can authorise their child's admission to hospital or treatment for mental disorder; i.e. whether the decision is within the 'scope of parental responsibility'. The scope of parental responsibility is considered at paras3.62–3.65.
6)	See chapter 6 for the procedures for admission under the MHA 1983 and paras 3.19–3.22 above for alternatives to detention under the MHA 1983. See also chapter 7 for consideration of treatment under MHA 1983 Part 4.
7)	Emergency treatment is considered at paras 3.91–3.101.

Keeping informal admission and treatment under review

3.88 Where it has been decided that a child can be admitted and treated informally because this does not give rise to a deprivation of liberty (either because there is no confinement, or the child's parents can consent to the confinement so that no deprivation of liberty arises) the appropriateness of such informal inpatient psychiatric care will need to be kept under review. The MHA Code notes:

> . . . although initially informal admission might be appropriate because the child or young person's care plan involves only restrictions of liberty, a change in circumstances may mean that the restrictions placed upon the child or young person amount to a deprivation of liberty for which lawful authority will be needed.[150]

Deprivation of liberty and children unable to decide

Box 3.4 considers the relationship between deprivation of liberty and parental consent.

Box 3.4: Deprivation of liberty and children lacking Gillick competence

Whether a child's inpatient psychiatric care gives rise to a deprivation of liberty will depend on whether the *Storck* tripartite test is met. As discussed at paras 3.49–3.61 above, this requires consideration of three questions (the confinement question, the no consent question and the state responsibility question).

150 MHA Code para 19.46.

For under-16s who lack Gillick competence, the two key questions to consider are the confinement question and the no consent question (the state will be responsible for any deprivation of liberty that arises from an adolescent's inpatient psychiatric care). The no consent question is relevant to children who are unable to make such decisions for themselves because, whereas this is not possible for young people, in some circumstances an under-16s' parents may consent to the confinement on their child's behalf.

If parental consent can be given, and the parents give their consent, there will be no deprivation of liberty. On the other hand, if the decision is considered to fall outside the type of decisions parents can make, parental consent cannot be given for the confinement, in which case there is no consent and the child will be deprived of their liberty.

Parental consent and the scope of parental responsibility

The leading case in relation to under-16s and deprivation of liberty is *Re D (a child: deprivation of liberty)*, which concerned D, a 15-year-old with autism who had been placed in a locked CAMHS unit but was not Gillick competent to make decisions about his residence or care arrangements. Mr Justice Keehan held that although the conditions in which D lived meant that he was confined,[151] he was not deprived of his liberty because his parents consented to his confinement on his behalf and their decision was within 'the proper exercise of parental responsibility'.[152] The parents were making decisions 'of which he is incapable, in the welfare best interests of their son'.[153] To date the courts have given little guidance on how to determine whether parents can consent to their child's confinement. Both the courts[154] and the MHA Code[155] emphasise the importance of considering each case on its specific circumstances. In *Re D* Keehan J, emphasised that his decision was based on the particular facts and declined to give wider guidance on the approach to be taken in such cases, noting that such cases 'are invariably fact

151 Although applying the *Cheshire West* acid test, Keehan J also (at [57]) compared the level of control and supervision placed on D with those of a 15-year-old without D's diagnosed conditions, commenting that this 'would undoubtedly be considered as an inappropriate exercise of parental responsibility and probably amount to ill-treatment'.

152 *Re D (a child: deprivation of liberty)* [2015] EWHC 922 (Fam) at [57].

153 *Re D (a child: deprivation of liberty)* [2015] EWHC 922 (Fam) at [58].

154 *Re D (a child: deprivation of liberty)* [2015] EWHC 922 (Fam) at [68].

155 MHA Code para 19.46.

specific and require a close examination of the "concrete" situation on the ground'.[156]

Given the emphasis the courts have given to whether parents' consent to their child's confinement falls within the 'zone' or 'scope' of parental responsibility,[157] it is suggested that when determining whether parents can consent to their child's confinement, practitioners should consider the MHA Code's guidance on the scope of parental responsibility. Whereas the key issue for Keehan J in *Re D* was that D's parents were acting in his best interests, the MHA Code's guidance highlights the importance of considering additional factors: the age and maturity of the adolescent, the wishes of the adolescent and whether restraint is required. It also sets out questions to consider in relation to the validity of parental consent, for example 'where one parent agrees to the proposed decision but the other is opposed to it'.[158]

Parental consent and children subject to a care order

The courts have held that neither the parents nor the responsible local authority can consent to the confinement of adolescents who are subject to a care order.[159] If therefore, their inpatient psychiatric care means that such children are confined, they will be deprived of their liberty because there is no consent to the confinement. While not relevant to the case, all the parties agreed with this approach in the Supreme Court's decision in *Re D* (albeit Lady Hale – without expressing any firm view – questioned the basis for this limitation on the role of parental consent).[160]

Parental consent, deprivation of liberty and human rights

3.89 The law, as it stands, has serious implications for under-16s who require inpatient psychiatric care. If parents can consent to their

156 *Re D (a child: deprivation of liberty)* [2015] EWHC 922 (Fam) at [68].

157 See *Re D (a child: deprivation of liberty)* [2015] EWHC 922 (Fam) at [66]; and *Re D (a child)* [2017] EWCA Civ 1695 at [144].

158 MHA Code para 19.41.

159 *Re AB (a child) (deprivation of liberty: consent)* [2015] EWHC 3125 (Fam) at [29] (considered in *Re D (a child)* [2017] EWCA Civ 1695 at [31]).

160 *Re D (a child)* [2019] UKSC 42 at [18] By way of comparison, see *R v Kirklees MBC ex p C (a minor)* [1992] 2 FCR 321, [1992] 2 FLR 117, [1993] Fam Law 455 (CA), which concerned a child's informal admission on the basis of the local authority's consent, the child being in the local authority's care under s10(2) of the Child Care Act 1980.

child's confinement, there will be no deprivation of liberty so that unless there are any other reasons for not relying on parental consent, the child can be informally admitted and treated. As discussed in subsequent chapters 6, 7 and 8, there are a range of safeguards that apply to people who are detained under the MHA 1983, but will not apply to these children, even though the level of restrictions may be the same.

3.90 Although the Justices in *Re D*, including Lady Hale, made clear that their decision did not extend to under-16s, there are strong grounds for arguing that the basis on which the majority view that parents cannot consent to a young person's confinement should also apply to children.[161] In Lady Hale's analysis, with which Lady Black and Lady Arden agreed, there is no principle of substituted consent under ECHR jurisprudence,[162] meaning that parental consent 'cannot substitute for the subjective element in limb (b) of *Storck*'.[163] While acknowledging that this was not relevant to the case in hand, Lady Hale commented that 'logically' her conclusion 'would also apply to a younger child whose liberty was restricted to an extent which was not normal for a child of his age'. Lady Hale added:

> The common law may draw a sharp distinction, in relation to the deprivation of liberty, between those who have reached the age of 16 and those who have not, but the extent to which that affects the analysis under the Human Rights Act is not clear to me and we have heard no argument upon it. I therefore prefer to express no view upon the question.[164]

Adolescent's refusal of treatment

Emergency treatment

3.91 The MHA Code notes that in exceptional cases, emergency treatment can be given to adolescents. It states:

> If the failure to provide such treatment is likely to lead to their death or to severe permanent injury, treatment may be given without their consent even if this means overriding their refusal when they have the competence (children) or the capacity (young people and those

161 Note, however, Lord Carnwarth's dissenting judgment.

162 *Re D (a child)* [2019] UKSC 42 at [42] (per Lady Hale); [51] (per Lady Black) and 116] (per Lady Arden).

163 *Re D (a child)* [2019] UKSC 42 at [42].

164 *Re D (a child)* [2019] UKSC 42 at [50].

with parental responsibility), to make this treatment decision. In such cases the courts have stated that doubt should be resolved in favour of the preservation of life, and it will be acceptable to undertake treatment to preserve life or prevent irreversible serious deterioration of the child or young person's condition.[165]

3.92 The MHA Code envisages that such action will only arise in limited circumstances, where there is no time to detain and treat the adolescent under the MHA 1983 or seek a court declaration.[166] When such emergency treatment is given, it 'must be no more than necessary and in the best interests of the child or young person'. Furthermore, once the situation is stabilised the 'legal authority for on-going treatment must be established'[167] (meaning that it must be decided whether the treatment can be give on an informal basis, or whether the MHA 1983 or a court order is needed to authorise the provision of the treatment).

3.93 Although not cited in the MHA Code, this advice would seem to be based on comments made by Munby J (as he then was) in *R (G) v Nottingham City Council*.[168] In that case the judge noted that CA 1989 s3(5) (which permits individuals who do not have parental responsibility, but do have 'care of the child', to 'do what is reasonable in all the circumstances of the case for the purpose of safeguarding or promoting the child's welfare') would in some circumstances allow action to be taken without parental consent or a court order:

> For instance, medical intervention might be required in order to preserve the child's life or to protect a child from irreversible harm in circumstances of such urgency that there is not even time to make an urgent telephone application to a judge. In such a situation of emergency a doctor can act without parental or judicial consent and, if parents are acting unreasonably or contrary to the child's best interests, even despite a parental refusal of consent: see Grubb, *Principles of Medical Law*, ed 2, para 4.21.[169]

165 MHA Code para 19.71. Similar guidance is provided in *Reference guide to consent for examination or treatment*, 2nd edn, DoH, 2009 p35. Neither cite relevant case-law in support of this advice. See discussion at paras 3.94–3.101 below.

166 MHA Code para 19.71.

167 MHA Code para 19.72.

168 [2008] EWHC 152 (Admin).

169 [2008] EWHC 152 (Admin) at [24]–[25]. The author of the chapter quoted is Sir James Munby.

Adolescents and the refusal of treatment: commentary

Introduction

3.94 The consequences of a refusal of treatment is an area in which there is a marked difference between the law's approach to adults as compared to under-18s. Whereas adults with capacity to make such decision for themselves cannot be treated without their consent unless they are detained under the MHA 1983, as noted above, the MHA Code's guidance on emergency treatment makes clear that under-18s' refusal can be overridden even if they have decisional capacity. This reflects case-law from the 1990s.

3.95 The Court of Appeal decided first, in relation to a 15-year-old in *Re R*[170] and subsequently in relation to a 16-year-old in *Re W*,[171] that irrespective of their ability to make such decisions for themselves, adolescents' refusal of treatment can be overridden if this is in the adolescent's best interests. In doing so, the Court of Appeal countered the widespread view that following the decision of the House of Lords in *Gillick*, adolescents who are able to make decisions about their medical treatment could not only consent to such treatment but also refuse it, regardless of the outcome.[172]

3.96 In one of the few decisions that has considered this issue from a human rights perspective, *An NHS Foundation Trust Hospital v P*,[173] held that the wishes of an adolescent aged 17-and-a-half years ('P') who was refusing life-saving treatment following an overdose should be overridden. While recognising that P's wishes were important and 'are of course, entitled to be taken into account as part of her article 8

170 *Re R (a minor) (wardship: consent to treatment)* [1992] Fam 11, [1991] 4 All ER 177. See also *Re E (a minor) (wardship: medical treatment)* [1992] 2 FCR 219, [1993] 1 FLR 386.

171 *Re W (a minor) (medical treatment: court's jurisdiction)* [1993] Fam 64.

172 These decisions were subject to widespread criticism. See for example: G Douglas 'The Retreat from Gillick', (1992) 55 MLR 569; A Bainham 'The Judge and the Competent Minor' (1992) 108 LQR 194. For a contrary view, see N Lowe and S Juss, 'Medical Treatment Pragmatism and the Search for Principle' (1993) 56 MLR 865; LF Ross 'Against the Tide: Arguments against Respecting a Minor's Refusal of Efficacious Life-Saving Treatment' (2009) Camb Q Health Ethics 18, 302.

173 [2014] EWHC 1650 (Admin). For other such cases post the HRA 1998, see: *University Hospitals Plymouth NHS Trust v B (a minor) (urgent medical treatment)* [2019] EWHC 1670 (Fam) (21 June 2019). *F (mother) v F (father)* [2013] EWHC 2683, [2014] 1 FLR 1328 and *Re P (medical treatment: best interests)* [2003] EWHC 2327 (Fam).

rights' (right to respect for private and family life), the court considered that these rights were 'not absolute' and were 'outweighed by her rights under Article 2' (the right to life). The court was under a 'heavy duty' to protect P's life and it was in her best interests to be treated notwithstanding her refusal of treatment.[174]

3.97 The question of whether, and if so in what circumstances, the refusal of medical treatment by adolescents with decisional capacity can be overridden has been the focus of long-standing debate.[175] An area of particular controversy[176] and uncertainty is the role of parental consent.[177] Although not relevant to the issue before the court in either case, in *Re W*, Lord Donaldson MR repeated the view he had expressed in *Re R*[178] that parental consent could override the wishes of minors.[179]

Overriding adolescent's refusal of treatment: human rights implications

3.98 In the mental health context, as explained above, by virtue of MHA 1983 s131[180] (in relation to young people's admission to hospital) and

174 For commentary on this case, see M Brazier and E Cave, *Medicine, patients and the law*, 6th edn, Manchester University Press, 2016, para 14.21. See also C Parker 'Treatment without consent' in M Shaw and S Bailey, *Justice for children and families*, Cambridge University Press, 2018.

175 S Gilmore and J Herring, '"No" is the hardest word: consent and children's autonomy' (2011) CFLQ 23(1), 3; and E Cave and J Wallbank 'Minors' capacity to refuse treatment: a reply to Gilmore and Herring' (2012) MedLRev 20 (3), 423; S Gilmore and J Herring, 'Children's refusal of treatment: the debate continues' [2012] Fam Law 973.

176 Lady Hale noted that this is a 'controversial question' in *Re D* [2018] UKSC 42 at [26(i)].

177 See, for example, J Fortin, *Children's rights and the developing law*, 3rd edn, Cambridge University Press, 2009, pp158–163; and S Fovargue and S Ost, 'Does the theoretical framework change the legal end result for mature minors refusing medical treatment or creating self-generated pornography?' (2013) *Medical Law International* 13(1) 6.

178 *Re R* [1992] Fam 11; [1991] 4 All ER 177; however, Staughton LJ at [29] indicated that he did not agree with this interpretation. In *Re W* Nolan LJ commented (at [94]) that, save for emergencies, an application to the court should be made.

179 Similar obiter remarks were made in *K, W and H (minors) (consent to treatment)* [1993] 1FLR 854 at 859 and more recently in *University Hospitals Plymouth NHS Trust v B (a minor) (urgent medical treatment)* [2019] EWHC 1670 (Fam) (21 June 2019) at [12].

180 The statutory recognition of a young person's refusal was introduced as part of the reforms under the MHA 2007. See C Parker, 'Children and Young People and the Mental Health Act 2007' (Nov 2007) 16 JMHL 174.

the guidance in the MHA Code on the 'scope of parental responsibility', the circumstances in which parental consent can be relied upon to authorise adolescents' admission and treatment are limited to cases in which adolescents are unable to make such decisions for themselves.[181] The MHA Code's reason for doing so is that the Court of Appeal's decisions on adolescents' refusal of treatment were made prior to the introduction of the HRA 1998 'and since then court decisions concerning children and young people have given greater weight to their views'.[182]

3.99 However, as noted above, the MHA Code envisages that in cases of life-threatening emergencies, treatment can be given despite an adolescent's refusal. Jane Fortin questions both the legal basis for this 'significant qualification' and whether it is compatible with the ECHR.[183] Surmising that the MHA Code's wording is in anticipation of the courts holding that the wishes of adolescents with decisional capacity will only be overridden where this is to avoid death or severe permanent injury,[184] Fortin considers that notwithstanding the positive obligation under ECHR Article 2 to safeguard life:

> It would involve the courts promoting the dubious proposition that by overriding an adolescent's autonomy rights, through enforced medical treatment involving bodily restraint, they are in fact safeguarding his

181 MHA Code paras 19.39, 1959 and 19.66.

182 MHA Code para 19.39.

183 J Fortin, *Children's rights and the developing law*, 3rd edn, Cambridge University Press 2009, 162–163. Fortin notes that if this exception is based on the doctrine of necessity this is 'normally reserved for the treatment of unconscious patients' and refers to relevant case-law: *Sidaway v Board of Governors of the Bethlem Royal Hospital and the Maudsley Hospital* [1985] AC 871 *per* Lord Scarman p882; and (in relation to children) *Gillick v West Norfolk and Wisbech Area Health Authority* [1986] AC 112 [1985] 3 WLR 830 HL [1986] AC 112, per Lord Scarman p189 (see also in *Gillick*, Lord Scarman (p182) and at Lord Templeman (p200). See also R White et al in *White, Carr and Lowe, The Children Act in Practice*, 4th edn, Lexis Nexis, 2008, para 3.26, (fn3) note: 'Medical practitioners have long been advised that on the basis of the common law defence of necessity emergency treatment may be given if the well-being of the child could suffer by delay caused by obtaining consents' and refer to *F v West Berkshire Health Authority and another (Mental Health Act Commission intervening)* [1989] 2 All ER 545 and *Re A (conjoined twins: surgical separation)* [2001] Fam 147, [2000] 4 All ER 961.

184 The MHA Code's reference to taking action to prevent death or severe permanent injury reflects the view of Balcombe LJ in *Re W* (p88) that in such circumstances the court should override the adolescent's wishes 'if the court's powers are to be meaningful'.

> or her future to self-fulfilment . . . hopefully a test case will soon provide a suitable vehicle for reviewing this area of law. [185]

Adolescents' refusal of admission and treatment: the role of parental consent

3.100 The need for clarity on circumstances in which parents might override their child's refusal of admission or treatment was highlighted by the Independent Review of the Mental Health Act 1983, *Modernising the Mental Health Act: Increasing choice, reducing compulsion* (December 2018) ('MHA Review'). The MHA Review's recommendations reflect and reinforce the law's growing divide between young people and children:

- *16- and 17-year-olds with the capacity to make decisions for themselves:* The provision under MHA 1983 s131 should be retained and be extended to treatment, thereby putting 'beyond doubt that a parent cannot consent on their behalf if they refuse treatment'.[186]
- *Under-16s who are competent to make decisions for themselves:* 'Government should consult on the ability of parents to consent to admission and treatment for those under 16'.[187] The MHA review comments:

  > The MHA Code of Practice is clear that it is 'inadvisable' to rely on parental consent to admit or treat a competent child under 16 who is objecting to either the admission or treatment (para 19.39). We don't want to undermine this but we think a consultation will enable the government to see how this is currently working in practice, and understand the complexities of and range of views on the issue, before considering whether legislation or further guidance is necessary. We also think a consultation will help the government decide whether there needs to be further clarification in relation to the position for

185 Fortin, J, *Children's rights and the developing law*, 3rd edn, Cambridge University Press 2009, 162–163. Fortin's remarks predate the decision in *An NHS Foundation Trust Hospital v P* (see para 3.96).

186 Independent Review of the Mental Health Act 1983, *Modernising the Mental Health Act: increasing choice, reducing compulsion* ('MHA Review'), December 2018, p177.

187 MHA Review p182.

under 16s who lack competence who are objecting to their admission or treatment.[188]

3.101 It is not known whether the government will accept these recommendations (the white paper on the reform of the MHA 1983 is awaited). If a consultation on the situation for under-16s is issued, a crucial consideration will be the human rights implications of parental consent overriding the objections of under-16s who are competent to decide about their psychiatric care. As Fortin and the case of *An NHS Foundation Trust Hospital v P*[189] highlight, ECHR rights will be engaged where it is proposed to treat adolescents without their consent. Moreover, decisions about admission are likely to engage the right to liberty under ECHR Article 5 (which may also be the case for some treatment). Whereas *Re D* (2015)[190] held that it is possible for parents to consent to their child's confinement if this is a proper exercise of parental responsibility, this case concerned a child who lacked Gillick competence and there is no authority for holding that parents can consent to their child's confinement when that child is Gillick competent to make such decisions for themself.

188 MHA Review pp177–178. The Children and Young People's Topic Group established under this review suggested a different approach:

> . . . that neither admission, remaining in hospital or treatment should be imposed in reliance on PR on any CYP [child or young person] with the ability to decide who is not consenting (the MHA should be used in these circumstances). The current exception to this, where failure to treat would lead to death or serious permanent injury, should stand (para 19.71–19.72 of the MHA Code of Practice).

See Independent Review of the Mental Health Act 1983: supporting documents, February 2019, p295.

189 [2014] EWHC 1650.

190 [2015] EWHC 922 (Fam).

CHAPTER 4

Mental Capacity Act 2005[1]

continued

1 Parts of this chapter derive from S Broach and L Clements, *Disabled Children: a legal handbook*, 3rd edn, LAG 2020, chapter 3 'Decision-making: the legal framework' (written by the author). The author is grateful to the editors of that work for permitting its reuse in this publication.

Introduction

4.1 The Mental Capacity Act (MCA) 2005 sets out the circumstances in which decisions can be taken on behalf of individuals aged 16 or over who lack capacity to make such decisions for themselves.[2] In summary:

> The MCA empowers individuals to make their own decisions where possible and protects the rights of those who lack capacity. Where an individual lacks capacity to make a specific decision at a particular time, the MCA provides a legal framework for others to act and make that decision on their behalf, in their best interests, including where the decision is about care and/or treatment.[3]

4.2 The MCA 2005 forms a major part of the legal framework for the care and treatment of 16- and 17-year-olds who lack capacity to make decisions about the services that they need for mental health care and other support needs. As noted in chapter 3 above, in some circumstances the MCA 2005 may authorise the admission to hospital and treatment for mental disorder. It will also be relevant to the provision of 16- and 17-year-olds' care and treatment in the community and non-hospital settings, such as children's homes and residential schools. In addition, the assessment of capacity under the MCA 2005 is relevant to the provision of treatment to 16- and 17-year-olds detained in hospital under the Mental Health Act (MHA) 1983[4] and those who are subject to community treatment orders (CTOs).[5]

4.3 Accordingly, this chapter provides an overview of the MCA 2005, focusing on its application to adolescents aged 16 and 17 – referred to as 'young people'[6] in this chapter.

4.4 It should be noted that the provisions under the MCA 2005 concerning individuals who lack capacity and who are deprived of

2 A detailed analysis of the MCA 2005 is beyond the scope of this book. More detailed guidance can be found in : A Ruck Keene, K Edwards, Professor A Eldergill, N Mackintosh QC (Hon) and S Miles, *Court of Protection handbook: a user's guide*, 3rd edn, LAG, 2019; and R Jones, *Mental Capacity Act Manual*, 8th edn, Sweet & Maxwell, 2018.

3 *Mental Health Act 1983: Code of Practice* ('MHA Code'), Department of Health (DoH), 2015, para 13.9.

4 See MHA Code paras 24.31–24.32. Treatment under the MHA 1983 is discussed in chapter 7.

5 See MHA 1983 Part 4A (discussed in chapter 10).

6 The terms 'young person' and 'young people' are used to distinguish 16- and 17-year-olds from under-16s. However, these terms are not used in the MCA 2005 itself.

their liberty[7] – known as the 'Deprivation of Liberty Safeguards' (DoLS) – do not apply to under-18s.[8] However, as discussed below, when the Mental Capacity (Amendment) Act (MC(A)A) 2019 comes into force,[9] DoLS will be replaced by a new administrative scheme, known as the 'Liberty Protection Safeguards' (LPS), which will apply to 16- and 17-year-olds as well as to adults.[10]

4.5 Despite its importance, it seems that the MCA 2005 has yet to be fully embedded in practice. Although regarding it as 'a visionary piece of legislation for its time', the 2014 report by the House of Lords Select Committee on the Mental Capacity Act 2005 found that the MCA 2005 'has suffered from a lack of awareness and a lack of understanding'.[11] In relation to its application to 16- and 17-year-olds, the Law Commission's 2017 report, *Mental capacity and deprivation of liberty* states that it had 'received some evidence of poor knowledge amongst health and social care professionals about how the Mental Capacity Act applies to young people'.[12] The Care Quality Commission (CQC) raised similar concerns in relation to staff working in Child and Adolescent Mental Health Services (CAMHS). In its 2017 report, *Review of children and young people's mental health services: Phase one report*, the CQC notes that 'staff did not always have an adequate understanding' of this Act or 'what it meant for their role as a mental health professional'.[13]

7 The circumstances in which a deprivation of liberty arises is discussed in paras 3.47–3.61.

8 MHA Code chapter 13 provides an overview of the MCA 2005, including the deprivation of liberty safeguards (DoLS).

9 The anticipated date was October 2020. However, on 16 July 2020 the government announced that the LPS would be in force by April 2022. See https://www.parliament.uk/business/publications/written-questions-answers-statements/written-statement/Commons/2020-07-16/HCWS377/

10 See MC(A)A 2019 Sch 1. This will be inserted as Sch AA1 to the MCA 2005.

11 House of Lords, Select Committee on the Mental Capacity Act 2005, *Mental Capacity Act: post legislative scrutiny* (2013–14) HL Paper 139, 7–8. A similar concern was raised in *Somerset CC v MK (deprivation of liberty: best interests decisions: conduct of a local authority)* [2014] EWCOP B25.

12 Law Commission Mental Capacity and Deprivation of Liberty (Law Com No 372, 2017) para 7.38.

13 *Review of children and young people's mental health services, Phase One Report*, Care Quality Commission (CQC), October 2017, 21. See also *Review of children and young people's mental health services, Phase One supporting documentation: Inspection report analysis*, CQC, October 2017, 28.

4.6 The *Mental Capacity Act 2005: Code of Practice* ('MCA Code') provides guidance on the implementation of the MCA 2005[14] and those acting 'in a professional capacity' or 'for remuneration' must have regard to the MCA Code.[15] MCA Code chapter 12 considers how the MCA 2005 applies to under 18s. At the time of writing (September 2020), the MCA Code is currently being revised.[16] Given the significant development in case-law under the MCA 2005 since the MCA Code's publication in 2007, the revisions are likely to be substantial.

4.7 The following areas are considered below:

- MCA 2005 principles;
- supporting people to make decisions for themselves;
- capacity and the MCA 2005;
- decision-making for people who lack capacity;
- determining best interests;
- independent mental capacity advocates (IMCAs);
- the Court of Protection and the appointment of deputies;
- specific issues for children and young people; and
- deprivation of liberty and the Liberty Protection Safeguards (LPS).

Mental Capacity Act 2005 principles

4.8 The implementation of the MCA 2005 is underpinned by the principles, which are set out in MCA 2005 s1 (see box 4.1 below).

Box 4.1: The Mental Capacity Act 2005 principles[17]

1) *Presumption of capacity*: A person must be assumed to have capacity unless it is established that they lack capacity.
2) *Provision of support to assist in decision-making*: A person is not to be treated as unable to make a decision unless all practicable steps to help them to do so have been taken without success.

14 *Mental Capacity Act 2005: Code of Practice*, Department for Constitutional Affairs (now Ministry of Justice), 2007: www.gov.uk/government/publications/mental-capacity-act-code-of-practice. See also MHA Code chapter 13.

15 MCA 2005 s42(4). The MCA Code (at p2) states that those who are subject to this duty must be aware of the code and 'should be able to explain how they have had regard to the Code when acting or making decisions'. See also discussion on the status of the MHA Code at paras 2.79–2.82.

16 See Ministry of Justice: https://consult.justice.gov.uk/digital-communications/revising-the-mca-2005-code-of-practice/.

17 See MCA 2005 s1; and MCA Code chapter 2.

3) *Right to make unwise decisions:* A person is not to be treated as unable to make a decision merely because they make an unwise decision.
4) *Act in person's best interests:* An act done, or decision made, under the MCA 2005 for or on behalf of a person who lacks capacity must be done, or made, in their best interests.
5) *Consider less restrictive option:* Before the act is done, or the decision made, regard must be had to whether the purpose for which it is needed can be as effectively achieved in a way that is less restrictive of their rights and freedom of action.

4.9 The principles guide all actions and decisions under the MCA 2005: the first three principles are key to the assessment of capacity; the fourth principle requires that acts or decisions taken on behalf of someone who lacks capacity are undertaken in that person's best interests; and the fifth principle requires those making decisions on a person's behalf to consider whether there is a less restrictive way of achieving the same purpose.

Supporting people to make decisions for themselves

4.10 The MCA 2005, in particular through principle 2 (provision of support to assist in decision-making), emphasises the importance of encouraging and supporting people to make decisions for themselves. MCA Code chapter 3 provides detailed guidance on how this can be done, emphasising the importance of:

- providing information relevant to the decision;
- communicating with the person in an appropriate way;
- making the person feel at ease; and
- considering whether others might be able to support the person in making choices or expressing a view.

4.11 Such support in decision-making should be part of the care planning process.[18] The *Mental Health Act 1983: Code of Practice* ('MHA Code') states that the MCA 2005 'should be central to the approach

18 MCA Code para 3.5.

professionals take to patients who lack capacity in all health and care settings (including psychiatric and general hospitals)'.[19]

4.12 There is a range of ways that can be taken to help young people make decisions for themselves. The manner in which they can be helped to do so 'will vary depending on the decision to be made, the time-scale for making the decision and the individual circumstances of the person making it'.[20] The support that might be provided includes choosing where and when is best to talk to the young person and ensuring that the information is provided (orally and in writing) in a manner that is appropriate (taking into account the young person's age and any communication needs). In addition, family members and others who know the young person could be asked about the best form of communication; for example, whether help is available from people the young person trusts (subject to the young person's right to confidentiality)[21] and if an advocate might improve communication.[22]

4.13 Those supporting the young person in making decisions should ensure that they provide appropriate advice and information but not pressurise the young person into making a decision or seek to influence the decision.[23]

Capacity and the Mental Capacity Act 2005

Overview

4.14 The starting point for young people is that, like adults, they are to be regarded as having the mental capacity to make the decision in question (principle 1: presumption of capacity).[24] However, if a young person's capacity to make the relevant decision(s), such as admission to hospital, or treatment for mental disorder, is in doubt, an assessment of that young person's capacity should be undertaken in accordance with the MCA 2005 and the MCA Code.

19 MHA Code para 13.11.
20 MCA Code para 3.1.
21 See paras 2.96–2.103.
22 MCA Code para 3.10; see also paras 15.4–15.6.
23 MCA Code para 2.8.
24 MCA 2005 s1(2): 'A person must be assumed to have capacity unless it is established that he lacks capacity'.

4.15 As with adults, the question whether the young person lacks capacity will be decided on the balance of probabilities,[25] which 'means being able to show that it is more likely than not that the person lacks capacity to make the decision in question'.[26] It will be for those asserting that the young person lacks capacity to establish this.[27]

Lacking capacity under the MCA 2005

Overview

4.16 The MCA 2005's provisions permitting actions to be undertaken, or decisions made, on behalf of others are only engaged if the person concerned lacks capacity as defined by the MCA 2005. Accordingly, the 'gateway' to the application of the MCA 2005 is the determination of a lack of capacity. It is therefore essential that those seeking to rely on the MCA 2005 when making decisions on behalf of a young person have established that the young person lacks capacity as defined under this Act.

Meaning of lacking capacity (MCA 2005 s2)

4.17 The test for lacking mental capacity under the MCA 2005 is set out in s2(1),[28] which states:

> For the purposes of this Act, a person lacks capacity in relation to a matter if at the material time he is unable to make a decision for himself in relation to the matter because of an impairment of, or a disturbance in the functioning of, the mind or brain.

This makes clear that the assessment of capacity is decision-specific and time-specific. Accordingly, those assessing a young person's capacity must focus on whether the young person is able to make the particular decision at the time it needs to be made. It is essential that both elements of the test set out under MCA 2005 s2 are met.[29] These

25 MCA 2005 s2(4).

26 MCA Code para 4.10.

27 *King's College NHS Foundation Trust v C* [2015] EWCOP 80 at [25]:

> The burden of proof lies on the person asserting a lack of capacity and the standard of proof is the balance of probabilities (Mental Capacity Act 2005 s 2(4) and see *KK v STC and others* [2012] EWHC 2136 (COP) at [18]).

See also the MCA Code para 4.10.

28 For a useful summary of the 'cardinal principles' for assessing capacity see *King's College NHS Foundation Trust v C* [2015] EWCOP 80 at [25]–[34].

29 *PC v City of York* [2013] EWCA Civ 478, [2014] Fam 10.

are often described as the 'functional element' and the 'diagnostic element':

1) *Functional element:* Requires that evidence establishes that the person is unable to decide at the material time. MCA 2005 s3(1) provides that:

   > . . . a person is unable to make a decision for himself if he is unable–
   > (a) to understand the information relevant to the decision,
   > (b) to retain that information,
   > (c) to use or weigh that information as part of the process of making the decision, or
   > (d) to communicate his or her decision (by talking, using sign language or any other means).[30]

2) *Diagnostic element:* The person's inability to decide is 'because of an impairment of, or disturbance in the functioning of, the mind or brain'.[31] Although it does not matter whether the impairment or disturbance is permanent or temporary,[32] if the impairment or disturbance is temporary, the person wishing to make the decision 'should justify why the decision cannot wait until the circumstances change'.[33] Conditions covered by the diagnostic element could include 'physical or medical conditions that cause drowsiness or loss of consciousness', 'concussion following a head injury' and 'the symptoms of alcohol or drug use'.[34]

Undertaking the assessment

4.18 Who undertakes the assessment will depend on the type of decision being made. For example, in relation to medical treatment, this will be the doctor or other health care professional (such as a nurse) who

30 MCA 2005 s3(1). A failure to meet any one of these aspects of the decision-making process is sufficient: *NHS Trust v JP* [2019] EWCOP 23 at [16]. See also *RT and LT v A local authority* [2010] EWHC 1910 (Fam) at [40].

31 MCA 2005 s2(1). See *NHS Trust v JP* [2019] EWCOP 23 at [16]:

> It is important to note that the question for the court is not whether the person's ability to take the decision is impaired by the impairment of, or disturbance in the functioning of, the mind or brain but rather whether the person is rendered unable to make the decision by reason thereof.

32 MCA 2005 s2(2).

33 MHA Code para 13.18.

34 MCA Code para 4.12. See also Mental Capacity Act 2005 Explanatory Notes para 22.

is proposing to give medical treatment.[35] Where the decisions concern daily care and support, those providing such care (whether they are paid carers or the young person's parents, or other relatives) will need to assess the young person's capacity to make such decisions.[36]

4.19 There may be cases where a professional is asked to undertake the assessment of capacity, for example because of the serious consequences of the decision, or there is a disagreement as to whether or not the young person lacks capacity. However, the final decision on capacity rests with the person who is proposing to make the decision in question.[37]

Assessing a young person's capacity

Relevant points

4.20 The MCA Code emphasises the importance of ensuring that the person's capacity is assessed correctly.[38] It must be based on the person's ability to make a particular decision at a particular time.

4.21 The following points will be relevant to the assessment of a young person's capacity (explained below):

1) presumption of capacity (principle 1);
2) non-discrimination and the assessment of capacity;
3) provision of support to assist in decision-making (principle 2);
4) right to make unwise decisions (principle 3); and
5) establishing reasons for inability to decide.

1) Presumption of capacity (principle 1)

4.22 The young person must be assumed to have capacity unless it is established that the person lacks capacity.

35 MCA Code para 4.40, which notes that although the assessment of capacity can involve the multi-disciplinary team 'ultimately it is up to the professional responsible for the person's treatment to make sure that capacity has been assessed'.

36 MCA Code para 4.38. This highlights the need for significant public education about the MCA 2005 as it is likely that many family carers are unaware of such requirements.

37 MCA Code paras 4.38–4.43, 4.51–4.54.

38 MCA Code paras 4.34–4.37. See *King's College Hospital NHS Foundation Trust v C* [2015] EWCOP 80 at [25]–[39] for the 'cardinal principles' for assessing whether a person lacks capacity.

2) Non-discrimination and the assessment of capacity

4.23 MCA 2005 s2(3) states that a lack of capacity cannot be established merely by reference to the person's age or appearance; or to the person's condition (such as a disability) or behaviour 'which might lead others to make unjustified assumptions' about the person's capacity.

4.24 For example, the fact that a young person has a learning disability is not a basis for concluding that the young person lacks capacity to make decisions about admission to hospital or medical treatment. To hold that the young person lacks the capacity to make such a decision, it must be shown that the learning disability affects the young person's ability to make the decision in question at the time it needs to be made.[39]

3) Provision of support to assist in decision-making (principle 2

4.25 The MCA 2005 and the MCA Code emphasise the importance of encouraging and supporting people to make decisions for themselves.[40] Box 4.2 below identifies some points to consider when considering whether young people are able to make the relevant decision. These points might also be of assistance when considering whether a child is Gillick competent (see paras 3.31–3.34).

4) Right to make unwise decisions (principle 3)

4.26 The principle that a 'person is not to be treated as unable to make a decision merely because he makes an unwise decision'[41] is as important to the assessment of a young person's capacity as it is for an adult. There is a difference between an 'unwise' decision and a decision that is 'based on a lack of understanding of risks or inability to weigh up the information about a decision'.[42] Furthermore, while young people may take risks that are unwise (this being 'an inherent, inevitable, and perhaps necessary part of adolescence and early adulthood experience'), the question will be whether their decisions represent 'unwise' decision-making, or evidence of their lack of capacity.[43] Points to consider are whether they are easily influenced

39 MCA Code para 4.48.

40 See MCA Code chapter 3.

41 MCA 2005 s1(4).

42 *YLA v PM* [2013] EWHC 4020 (COP) at [43](e).

43 *WBC v Z* [2016] EWCOP 4 at [1].

by undue pressure and whether they need more information to help them understand the consequences of the decision they are making.[44]

4.27 Accordingly, whereas an unwise decision in itself is not a reason for suggesting that a young person lacks capacity, further investigation may be required where young people are repeatedly making decisions that put them at significant risk of harm or exploitation'.[45] In *WBC v Z*, Cobb J stated:

> In dealing with risk issues in relation to a young person in the context of assessment under the *MCA 2005*, it is necessary to separate out as far as is possible the evidence which indicates that second category of risk taking (unhealthy, dangerous, unwise) from that which reveals or may reveal a lack of capacity.[46]

5) Establishing reasons for inability to decide

4.28 If the young person is unable to decide, it will be necessary to consider whether this is 'because of an impairment of, or a disturbance in the functioning of the mind or brain' ('the diagnostic element'). If the connection between the inability to decide and the diagnostic element is established, the young person will lack capacity for the purpose of MCA 2005 s2, but as noted at para 4.32 below there may be cases in which the young person's inability to decide is for reason falling outside the diagnostic element, in which case the young person will not lack capacity as defined by the MCA 2005 and, therefore, this Act will not apply.[47]

Fluctuating capacity

4.29 In some cases, adolescents' capacity to make decisions may vary from time to time. For example, when considering capacity to make treatment decisions, the MHA Code notes that 'capacity in an individual with mental disorder may vary over time' and that where a person's capacity fluctuates in this way and the decision is not urgently required, consideration should be given to delaying the decision until the person has regained capacity.[48] The MHA Code also highlights the importance of care teams encouraging their patients to express their preference for future care and treatment,

44 MCA Code para 2.11. These points apply to people of all ages, not just young people.

45 MCA Code para 2.11.

46 *WBC v Z* [2016] EWCOP 4 at [67].

47 MCA Code para 12.13.

48 MHA Code para 24.32.

noting that this 'is often a helpful therapeutic tool, encouraging collaboration and trust between patients and professionals'.[49]

Adolescents' advance decisions

4.30 The MHA Code also notes that advance decisions to refuse treatment should be recorded, as should reasons for making a decision which is contrary to the person's expressed wish.[50] Although under-18s are not able to make advance decisions to refuse treatment under the MCA 2005 ensuring that their views are sought and recorded will help to ensure that the adolescent's wishes and preferences are taken into account even during periods in which the adolescent may not be able to express them.[51]

Box 4.2: Assessing a young person's ability to decide – points to consider

- *Adequacy of the information:* In all cases, the provision of relevant information will be essential.[52] Relevant information will include the nature of the decision, the reason why the decision is needed and the reasonably foreseeable consequences of deciding one way or another, or not making the decision.[53] While the provision of a broad explanation, in simple language, may be enough in some cases, in others the nature of the decision (for example, if it could have serious consequences) may require more detailed information or access to advice.[54]
- *Effective communication:* The information needs to be presented in a way that is appropriate to the young person's needs and circumstances 'using simple language, visual aids or any other means'.[55] For young people, it will important that the information is provided in an age appropriate manner, as well as being in the

49 MHA Code para 9.15.

50 MHA Code paras 9.19–9.23.

51 MCA 2005 s4(6)(a) emphasises the importance of considering relevant written statements. See also MCA Code paras 5.41–5.45 on the importance of taking into account the person's previously expressed views, in particular, written statements.

52 MCA 2005 s3(1).

53 MCA 2005 s3(4); and MCA Code para 4.19.

54 MCA Code para 4.19.

55 MCA 2005 s3(2) and MCA Code para 4.17 Individuals are not to be regarded as unable to understand the relevant information if they are able to understand an explanation that is presented to in a manner appropriate for them.

most effective form of communication for that adolescent, which might require the use of sign language, visual representations and computer support.[56]

- *Assistance in retaining the relevant information:* It should not be assumed that the fact that a person cannot retain the information for very long means that the person is unable to make the decision. What will need to be assessed is whether the person is able to hold the information in their mind long enough to make an effective decision – and this will depend on the particular circumstances of the case. People can be helped to retain information, by for example, photographs, posters videos and voice recorders.[57]
- *Assistance in using or weighing information as part of the decision-making process:* Individuals must not only be able to understand the information but be able to weigh it up and use this to make a decision. People can be supported in doing so, by for example, family members and professional advisers.[58]
- *Assistance in communicating a decision:* Before deciding that a young person cannot communicate their decision, 'it is important to make all practicable and appropriate efforts to help them communicate', which might require the involvement of professionals such as speech and language therapists or specialists in non-verbal communication.[59]
- *Seeking the views of family members and others:* People close to the young person may be able to provide valuable information, such as the types of decisions the person is able to make (although their views on what they want for the person must not influence the outcome of the assessment).[60]

Young people lacking capacity

4.31 MHA Code chapter 19 provides examples of where a young person will lack capacity as defined by the MCA 2005. It explains that the

56 MCA 2005 s3(2) and MCA Code paras 4.16–4.19. See also MHA Code 3.12 and figure 3.

57 MCA 2015 S3(3): 'The fact that a person is unable to retain the information for a short period only does not prevent him from being regarded as unable to make the decision'. MCA Code para 4.20.

58 *V v R* [2011] EWHC 822 (QB), noted in G Ashton (ed), *Court of Protection practice*, Jordan Publishing, 2015, para 2.82.

59 MCA Code para 4.24.

60 MCA Code para 4.52.

reason for a young person's inability to make the decision might be because of their mental disorder, or it might arise from a temporary 'impairment of, or disturbance in, the functioning of, their mind or brain' that does not amount to a mental disorder, for example it is caused by the distress related to the proposed admission or treatment.[61] In either case, the young person's inability to decide will be 'because of an impairment of, or a disturbance in the functioning of the mind or brain' so that the young person lacks capacity for the purposes of the MCA 2005.[62]

4.32 It should be noted that both the MCA Code[63] and the MHA Code[64] suggest that there may be cases in which a young person is unable to decide, but for reasons that do not fall within the 'diagnostic element' of the test for lacking incapacity under MCA 2005 s2. Given the wide range of circumstances in which the diagnostic test can be satisfied (see para 4.17 above), the extent to which such cases are likely to arise is not clear.[65] However, if they do, the consequence is significant because the young person will not lack capacity as defined by the MCA 2005 and therefore this Act does not apply.[66] This is considered further in box 4.3 below.

Box 4.3: Young people unable to decide but not lacking capacity

- If the young person is unable to decide but this is due to something other than 'an impairment of, or a disturbance in the

61 MHA Code para 19.30.

62 MHA Code para 19.31.

63 MCA Code para 12.13

64 MHA Code para 19.31

65 In relation to adults see the developing case-law on 'vulnerable adults' in which the courts have noted that there may be circumstances where adults' 'ability to make decisions for themselves has been compromised by matters other than those covered by the MCA 2005'. This might be because they are under constraint, subject to coercion or undue influence, or '[f]or some other reason deprived of the capacity to make the relevant decision or disabled from making a free choice, or incapacitated or disabled from giving or expressing a real and genuine consent'. *DL v Local Authority* [2012] EWCA Civ 253, [2013] Fam 1 [53]–[54].

66 That young people may be unable to decide but for reasons falling outside the MCA 2005 is also noted by the Law Commission in *Mental Capacity and Deprivation of Liberty*, Law Com No 372, March 2017. At para 7.35 the report refers to young people who are not Gillick competent, explaining 'they do not have sufficient maturity and intelligence to understand the nature and implications of the proposed decision'.

functioning of the mind or brain' that young person will not lack capacity for the purposes of the MCA 2005 so this Act will not apply.

- The MCA Code anticipates that such cases may arise, referring to such young people as being 'overwhelmed by the implications of the decision'.[67] The MHA Code suggests that this might arise because the young person is 'in an unfamiliar and novel situation', for example, this might be the first time they have had to make such a decision they are worrying about the implications of deciding one way or the other.[68]

4.33 The Independent Review of the Mental Health Act 1983 considered the notion that a 'young person has mental capacity but nonetheless lacks competence' to be 'unhelpful and confusing' and recommended that the MHA 1983 should make clear that 'the only test that should be applied when deciding whether the young person can consent to admission or treatment, should be that set down in the MCA'.[69] While further guidance on this issue would be helpful, it is suggested that the MCA and MHA Codes do not set an additional test before young people can consent to their admission or treatment, rather they highlight two important points. The first is that to lack capacity under the MCA 2005 both the functional and diagnostic elements of s2 must be met (see para 4.17 above). The second is the importance of ensuring that the young person concerned is in fact consenting to the proposed intervention. As noted in chapter 3, para 3.40, this requires that the young person has sufficient information to make the decision and any consent is given voluntarily. The MHA Code states that in the rare cases in which this situation arises 'every effort should be made to ensure that the young person is supported in making the decision'.[70]

67 MHA Code 12.13.

68 MHA Code para 19.31.

69 *Modernising the Mental Health Act: increasing choice, reducing compulsion*, Final report of the Independent Review of the Mental Health Act 1983, December 2018 ('MHA Review'), p175 and fn189.

70 MHA Code 19.32.

Decision-making for people who lack capacity

Overview

4.34 Where a person lacks capacity as defined by the MCA 2005, others (such as health care and social care professionals and family members providing day-to-day care) can take action and make decisions on behalf of that person, provided that they do so in accordance with the MCA 2005. Two key provisions are MCA 2005 ss5 and 6, which are summarised below.[71]

Acts in connection with care or treatment (MCA 2005 s5)

4.35 Individuals can undertake certain acts 'in connection with the care and treatment' of a person who lacks capacity. Those undertaking such acts must reasonably believe that the person lacks capacity (and have taken reasonable steps to establish whether or not the person does lack capacity) and that it is in the person's best interests to undertake that act. They must also follow the principles set out in MCA 2005 s1 (see box 4.1 above).

4.36 Provided that individuals taking action for a person who lacks capacity have complied with these requirements, they will not incur liability (ie there will not be any civil or criminal penalties) for doing so without the person's consent, so long as the act taken is something that the person could have consented to if the person had capacity.[72] This means, for example, that young people who lack capacity to consent to treatment can be given that treatment by health professionals, or if young people lack capacity to feed or dress themselves, their carers can help them do so, relying on MCA 2005 s5. However, section 5 would not provide a defence to a claim that the person undertaking the act had done so negligently.[73]

Limitations on use of restraint (MCA 2005 s6)

4.37 Restraint cannot be used when undertaking 'acts in connection with care or treatment' under MCA 2005 s5 unless the conditions specified by section 6 are met.

71 See MCA Code chapter 6 for further guidance.

72 MCA 2005 s5(2).

73 MCA 2005 s5(3).

4.38 The term 'restraint' is broadly defined. It covers the use, or threat to use, force to make a person do something that they are resisting, or restricting a person's liberty of movement, whether or not they are resisting.[74] An individual can only use restraint if this is reasonably believed to be necessary to prevent harm to the person who lacks capacity and is a proportionate response to likelihood of the person suffering harm, and the seriousness of that harm.[75]

4.39 Crucially, acts under MCA 2005 s5 cannot authorise actions that amount to a deprivation of liberty (see paras 3.16–3.18). Where young people are deprived of their liberty, legal authority for this must be sought. As discussed at paras 3.19–3.20, under current law, this will be by either a court order or detention under the MHA 1983, but when they come into force the Liberty Protection Safeguards will provide an administrative mechanism for authorising a deprivation of liberty (discussed below).[76]

Conflicts with other decision-makers (MCA 2005 s6)

4.40 Acts cannot be undertaken under MCA 2005 s5 if they conflict with a decision made by an individual authorised under the MCA 2005 to make decisions for the person who lacks capacity.[77] In the case of a young person, this might be a deputy appointed by the Court of Protection to make personal welfare and/or financial decisions on behalf of the young person.[78]

Determining best interests

Overview

4.41 MCA 2005 s1(5) provides that anything done for, and any decision made on behalf of, a person without capacity must be done or made in the 'best interests' of that person (principle 4: act in person's best interests).[79] It is important to note that this principle of 'best interests'

74 MCA 2005 s6(4).

75 See MCA Code paras 6.40–6.46 for further information.

76 The Liberty Protection Safeguards are due to come into force in April 2022.

77 MCA 2005 s6(6); but see s6(7) in relation to life-sustaining treatment.

78 MCA 2005 s16 and chapter 8. See also *Re L, Re M, Re H* [2019] EWCOP 22 for discussion on principles for the practice and procedure in the appointment of personal welfare deputies.

79 MCA 2005 s1(5).

in decision-making under the MCA 2005 only applies where people lack capacity to make decisions for themselves. People who have capacity are free to make decisions for any reason and are not required to do what is 'best' for them.

4.42 The requirement to act in the best interests of the person who lacks capacity to make the decision in question applies to anyone making decisions or acting under the MCA 2005. It does not matter what decision is being made (whether in relation to financial, personal welfare or healthcare decisions) or who is making the decision(s) (whether family members, health or social care professionals or individuals appointed to act as the person's deputy).[80]

4.43 The MCA 2005 does not define 'best interests', rather it sets out a range of factors that must be considered when seeking to determine what is in the person's best interests. Decision-makers 'must take into account all relevant factors that it would be reasonable to consider, not just those that are important' and they must not make the decision based on what they would do.[81] The Supreme Court has emphasised the importance of the person's own views, wishes and feelings in determining what is in their best interests.[82]

Relevant points in determining best interests

4.44 Where a young person lacks capacity, the following points will be relevant to determining what is in their interests:

- *Non-discrimination:* The determination of best interests must not be based on assumptions about the young person's age or appearance; or their disability or other condition; or an aspect of their behaviour.[83]
- *Encouraging participation:* Wherever possible the young person should be encouraged to be involved in the decision-making process and give their views on matters relevant to the decision

80 MCA Code para 5.2. The two exceptions to this concern advance decisions to refuse medical treatment (which do not apply to under-18s – see s24(1)) and research. See MCA Code para 5 4.

81 MCA Code para 5.7.

82 *Aintree University Hospitals NHS Foundation Trust v James* [2013] UKSC 67, [2014] AC 591, see Lady Hale at [24]: 'the preferences of the person concerned are an important component in deciding where his best interests lie'. For consideration of best interests in the context of a young woman with learning disabilities and who lacked capacity to decide about the termination of her pregnancy, see M Welstead, *Mental capacity and abortion: Re AB (termination of pregnancy)* [2019] EWCA Civ 1215, November [2019] Fam Law 1343–1248.

83 MCA 2005 s4(1).

and what outcome they would like.[84] Thus, steps will need to be taken to help the young person participate, for example using simple language and/or visual aids to help the young person understand the options and asking the young person about the decision at a time and location where the person feels the most relaxed and at ease.[85]

- *Considering if the decision can be delayed until the young person has capacity:* Although it may not be possible to do so because the decision needs to be made as a matter of urgency, if it is possible to put off the decision until the young person regains capacity, then the decision should be deferred until that time.[86]
- *Considering the young person's wishes and feelings: so far as reasonably ascertainable,* to consider the following:
  - the young person's past and present wishes, in particular, any advance statement made when the young person had capacity;
  - the beliefs and values that would be likely to influence the young person if they had capacity;
  - the other factors the young person would be likely to consider if they had capacity, such as the effect of the decision on other people, providing or gaining emotional support from people close to the young person.[87]
- *Consulting other people close to the young person:* The views of anyone involved in caring for, or interested in the welfare of, the young person, must be taken into account if it is practicable and appropriate to consult them.[88]
  - In most cases, this will include the young person's parents (unless there are good reasons for not doing so).[89] Even if they are not 'engaged in caring' for their child (because their child is a 'looked after child'[90]) it will be necessary to consult parents who are 'interested' in their child's welfare.
  - If a deputy has been appointed for the young person (see paras 4.48–4.51 below), that person should also be consulted (in addition, a deputy will be entitled to take the relevant decision

84 MCA 2005 s4(4); and MCA Code para 5.22.
85 MCA Code para 5.24.
86 MCA 2005 s4(3); and MCA Code paras 5.25–5.28.
87 MCA 2005 s4(6); and MCA Code paras 5.37–5.46.
88 MCA 2005 s4(7).
89 See paras 2.96–2.103 on confidentiality and sharing information.
90 See glossary for explanation of a 'looked after child'.

themselves if it comes within the scope of their powers conferred by the Court of Protection order).

- Those consulted should be asked their views on what they think is in the young person's best interests and if they can give any information on the young person's wishes and feelings, beliefs and values.[91]

- *Special consideration for life-sustaining treatment:* When considering whether such treatment is in the young person's best interests, the decision-maker must not be motivated by a desire to bring about that young person's death. Where there is any doubt as to what is in the young person's best interests, an application should be made to the Court of Protection.[92]
- *Considering less restrictive principle (principle 5):* Before an action or decision is taken on behalf of a young person who lacks capacity, consideration must be given as to whether there is an alternative approach that would interfere less with that young person's basic rights and freedoms.[93] However, 'it may be necessary to choose an option that is not the least restrictive alternative if that option is in the person's best interests'.[94]

Independent mental capacity advocates

4.45 Although the MCA 2005 makes provision for people to be supported by IMCAs, the circumstances in which they must be engaged are limited.[95] IMCAs must be available to people who lack capacity to make certain decisions (concerning 'serious medical treatment'[96] or a long-term change in accommodation[97]) and the person has no suitable family or friends who could be consulted on their best interests.

4.46 The role of the IMCA is to represent and support the person who lacks capacity to make the relevant decisions. Support from an IMCA must be made available in the following cases:

91 MCA 2005 s4(7); and MCA Code paras 5.49–5.54.

92 MCA 2005 s4(5); and MCA Code paras 5.29–5.38.

93 MCA Code para 2.14. The courts have also taken this approach. See, for example, *FP v GM and a Health Board* [2011] EWHC 2778 (Fam), [2011] 2 FLR 1375, in which Hedley J at [18], stated that this principle 'in effect, is a principle of minimum intervention consistent with best interests'.

94 MCA Code para 2.16.

95 The provisions concerning IMCAs are set out in ss35-41.

96 MCA 2005 s37.

97 MCA 2005 ss38 and 39.

- *'Serious medical treatment'*: This is 'treatment which involves providing, withholding or withdrawing treatment' which is further described in regulations.[98] The MCA Code notes that it is impossible to set out all types of procedures that may amount to serious medical treatment but suggests that they will include chemotherapy and surgery for cancer, therapeutic sterilisation and major surgery, such as open-heart surgery.[99]
- *Change in accommodation:* This includes a placement in hospital for longer than 28 days[100] or in a social care setting (eg a care home) for what is likely to be longer than eight weeks.[101]

4.47 As noted in chapter 9 (paras 9.80–9.81), the Care Act 2014 includes a right to advocacy in the assessment and support planning process for adults and young people in transition to adulthood.[102] The statutory guidance to the Care Act 2014 makes clear that the same person can be an IMCA and a Care Act advocate, as long as they are suitably qualified for each role.[103] The provisions for IMCAs under the Liberty Protection Safeguards are noted in box 4.4 below.

The Court of Protection and the appointment of deputies[104]

4.48 The Court of Protection has a range of powers, which include deciding on whether a person has capacity to make a particular decision and making declarations, decisions or orders in relation to financial

98 MCA 2005 s37(6) and the Mental Capacity Act 2005 (Independent Mental Capacity Advocates) (General) Regulations 2006 SI No 1832, as amended. This section does not apply to treatments given under MHA 1983 Part 4 (see paras 7.7–7.36) or Part 4A (see paras 10.35–10.41).

99 MCA Code para 10.45.

100 MCA 2005 s38.

101 MCA 2005 s39; see s39(1B) for accommodation falling within this provision: accommodation provided under Care Act 2014 Part 1 or MHA 1983 s117 (for after-care services under s117 see paras 9.39–9.56).

102 Care Act 2014 s67.

103 *Care and support statutory guidance*, DHSC, issued under the Care Act 2014, para 7.9.

104 See MCA 2005 ss15–21A; and MCA Code chapter 8. For a detailed analysis of the role of the Court of Protection, see A Ruck Keene, K Edwards, Professor A Eldergill and S Miles, *Court of Protection handbook: a user's guide*, 3rd edn, LAG, 2019.

or welfare matters affecting those lacking the capacity to make such decisions.[105]

4.49 The Court of Protection can also appoint deputies to make decisions on welfare (including educational or healthcare) decisions as well as property and financial matters on behalf of a person who lacks capacity. The deputy is likely to be a family member or someone who knows the person well, but this will not always be the case – for example, the Court of Protection may decide to appoint a professional deputy, such as a solicitor to deal with the person's property or affairs.[106] A representative of the local authority, for example the Director of Adult Services, can also be appointed as a deputy if the Court of Protection considers this to be appropriate but the court will need to be satisfied that the authority has arrangements to avoid possible conflict of interest.[107]

4.50 MCA 2005 s16(4) states that in deciding whether it is in the best interests of the person lacking capacity to appoint a deputy, in addition to the factors set out in section 4 (best interests), the Court of Protection must have regard to the following two principles:

1) a decision by the court is to be preferred to the appointment of a deputy to make a decision; and
2) the powers conferred on a deputy should be as limited in scope and duration as is practicably reasonable in the circumstances.

4.51 In *Re Lawson, Mottram and Hopton (appointment of personal welfare deputies)*,[108] Hayden J set out principles for practice and procedure in the appointment of personal welfare deputies and in doing considered para 8.38 of the MCA Code. This paragraph anticipates that personal welfare deputies 'will only be required in the most difficult cases', where 'important and necessary actions cannot be carried out without the court's authority', or 'there is no other way of settling the matter

105 See MCA 2005 s16 for the power for the court to make decisions on P's behalf and appoint deputies.

106 MCA Code para 8.33. See *Re P* [2010] EWHC 1592 (Fam) at [9]:

> . . . the court ought to start from the position that, where family members offer themselves as deputies, then, in the absence of family dispute or other evidence that raises queries as to their willingness or capacity to carry out those functions, the court ought to approach such an application with considerable openness and sympathy.

See also *Re GMP* [2015] EWCOP 67 at [33]–[35] in which the court gave examples of when a family member would not be appointed as a deputy, such as where 'the proposed deputy has physically, emotionally or financially abused' the person who lacks capacity. For a discussion on conflicts of interests, see *Re JW* [2015] EWCOP 82 at [28]–[49].

107 MCA Code paras 8.41 and 8.60.

108 [2019] EWCOP 22.

in the best interests of the person who lacks capacity to make particular welfare decisions'. [109] However, Hayden J concluded that this paragraph 'is reflective of likely outcome and should not be regarded as the starting point' and added that 'This paragraph of the Code, in particular, requires to be revisited'.[110]

Specific issues for children and young people

4.52 Although the main provisions of the MCA 2005 apply to individuals aged 16 and over, some provisions distinguish between adults and young people aged 16 and 17. Furthermore, in some circumstances, the MCA 2005 can cover those aged under 16. Chapter 12 of the MCA Code provides guidance on how the MCA 2005 applies to under-18s. The key points are summarised as follows:

- *Planning for possible future incapacity – MCA 2005 ss9–14 and 24–26:* Unlike adults, young people cannot appoint an attorney under the LPA provisions,[111] nor can they make an advance refusal of treatment under the MCA 2005 (the minimum age for both being 18 and over).[112]
- *Young people with special needs and/or disabilities – MCA 2005 and Children and Families (CFA) Act 2014:* The 2014 Act includes special provisions concerning decision-making where individuals aged 16–25 years lack capacity to make decisions in relation to matters governed by Part 3 of that Act, for example their education, health and care (EHC) plan or an appeal to the tribunal in relation to such a plan.[113]

109 See discussion in A Ruck Keene, K Edwards, Professor A Eldergill and S Miles, *Court of Protection handbook: a user's guide*, 3rd edn, LAG, 2019 on the appointment of personal welfare deputies at paras 3.126–3.138.

110 [2019] EWCOP 22 at [53(k)].

111 Provisions for lasting powers of attorney (LPA), which allow adults to appoint another adult to make decisions on their behalf should they lack the capacity to make such decisions for themselves, are set out in MCA 2005 ss9–14. LPAs can cover decisions concerning finance and welfare (including healthcare). MCA 2005 s9(2)(c) provides that individuals must be aged 18 or over to make a LPA.

112 MCA 2005 ss24-26 covers advance refusals. MCA 2005 s24(1) provides that to make an advance refusal the person must be aged 18 or over. In addition, the Court of Protection's power to make a will does not apply to those aged under 18; see MCA 2005 s18(2).

113 CFA 2014 s80 and the SEND Regs 2014 SI No 1530 regs 63–64. For further information, see S Broach and L Clements, *Disabled children: a legal handbook*, 3rd edn, LAG, 2020, paras 11.83–11.91.

- *Children and property and affairs – MCA 2005 s18(3):* The Court of Protection can make decisions in relation to a child's property and affairs if the court thinks it likely that the child will still lack capacity to make financial decisions after reaching the age of 18.[114] For example, this would allow the court to make an order concerning the investment of an award for compensation for the child and/or appoint a deputy to manage the child's property and affairs.[115]
- *Transferring proceedings between a court with jurisdiction under the Children Act (CA) 1989 and the Court of Protection – MCA 2005 s21:* Regulations set out a range of considerations to be taken as to which court (ie the Court of Protection or the Family Court) should hear a particular case.[116] The MCA Code notes that a case involving a young person who lacks mental capacity to make a specific decision could be heard in the family courts or in the Court of Protection. It adds:

  > If the case might require an ongoing order (because the young person is likely to still lack capacity when they are 18), it may be more appropriate for the Court of Protection to hear the case. For one-off cases not involving property or finances, the Family Division may be more appropriate.[117]

- In *Re A-F (children) (No 2)*, which concerned young people who were subject to care orders under CA 1989 s31 and whose care arrangements gave rise to a deprivation of their liberty, Sir James Munby (sitting as a Judge of the High Court) held that their cases should not be transferred to the Court of Protection.[118] This was because the benefits weighed 'heavily in favour' of maintaining the care orders whereas there were 'no reasons for thinking that . . . the children's welfare will be better safeguarded within the Court of Protection'.[119]

114 MCA 2005 ss2(6) and 18(3).

115 See MCA Code paras 12.3–12.4.

116 Mental Capacity Act 2005 (Transfer of Proceedings) Order 2007 SI No 1899 art 3(3)(c).

117 MCA Code paras 12.24; see also para 12.7.

118 [2018] EWHC 2129 (Fam).

119 *Re A-F (children) (No 2)* [2018] EWHC 2129 (Fam) at [12 (vi)]. The points to be considered by the court when deciding if an application for a care order should be transferred to the Court of Protection to be dealt with under the MCA 2005 instead were set out in *B (a local authority) v RM and others* [2010] EWHC 3802 (Fam). These were endorsed by Sir James Munby, President of the Family Division in *Re A-F (children) (No 2)*; see [9]–[11]. The importance of taking action to assess a young person's capacity when this is in doubt was highlighted in *Re M (children)* [2016] EWCA Civ 937.

- *Criminal offence (Ill-treatment or neglect – MCA s44):* There appears to be no age limit to this provision which makes it a criminal offence for an individual who is caring for a person who lacks capacity (to make decisions concerning their care[120]) to ill-treat or wilfully neglect that person. The provision could, therefore, apply to a child provided that they lacked capacity under MCA 2005 s2, albeit other criminal offences are likely to be applicable whether or not the child lacks capacity, such as offences of child cruelty or neglect.[121]

Deprivation of liberty and the Liberty Protection Safeguards

Overview

4.53 As discussed in chapter 3 above, a crucial factor in determining whether or not adolescents can be admitted to hospital and treated for mental disorder informally is whether such admission or treatment gives rise to a deprivation of liberty. Those working with under-18s who are being provided with care in community settings such as residential schools or children's homes will also need to consider carefully whether the care regime amounts to a deprivation of liberty. This is because wherever a deprivation of liberty arises, legal authority for this must be obtained. Under current law, under-18s' deprivation of liberty can be authorised either by a court order or (which is more likely in relation to adolescent inpatient psychiatric care) by admission under the MHA 1983.[122]

4.54 In cases where an application to a court is required, for 16- and 17-year-olds who lack capacity to make decisions about their care arrangements, the appropriate court is likely to be the Court of Protection.[123] However, when the MC(A)A 2019 comes into force, it will introduce a new administrative scheme for authorising a deprivation of liberty. Although this term is not used in the legislation, the

120 *R v Dunn* [2010] EWCA Crim 2935, see also *R v Hopkins* [2011] EWCA Crim 1513 at [43].

121 MCA Code, para 12.5.

122 The criteria for admission under the MHA 1983 is considered in chapter 6.

123 *Trust A v X and others* [2015] EWHC 922 (Fam) at [51]. However, see para 4.52 above on transferring proceedings between courts.

scheme is known as the 'Liberty Protection Safeguards' (LPS) and will replace the 'Deprivation of Liberty Safeguards' ('DoLS').[124]

4.55 Whereas DoLS do not apply to individuals under the age of 18,[125] the LPS scheme applies to individuals aged 16 and over.[126] Furthermore, whereas the scope of DoLS is limited to care homes and hospitals, the LPS scheme covers any setting. It is therefore likely to be relevant to young people who lack capacity to make decisions about their care or treatment (their 'care arrangements') and who are deprived of their liberty in placements such as residential schools, children's homes and psychiatric units (both private and NHS hospitals). It may also apply to such young people who are living in the family home.

4.56 The LPS scheme will operate in addition to the existing mechanisms for authorising a young person's deprivation of liberty noted in chapter 3. In some cases, the LPS scheme may provide an alternative means of authorising a young person's admission to hospital and treatment for mental disorder to that of the MHA 1983. It will therefore be necessary for those considering the legal basis for a young person's in-patient psychiatric care to determine whether the LPS scheme is applicable, and if so whether it should be applied.

4.57 Information on the background to the LPS scheme and an overview of how it will impact on young people, including the interface of LPS and the MHA 1983, are set out below. Regulations and a code of practice which will provide more detail on how the LPS is intended to operate are expected, however at the time of writing (September 2020) are yet to be published.[127]

4.58 It is understood that the code will include a chapter focused on the LPS scheme's application to young people, as well as a chapter explaining the interface between the LPS scheme and the MHA 1983. In addition to guidance on how the LPS scheme will impact on the legal framework for adolescents' inpatient psychiatric care, clarification is required on the interplay between the LPS and existing legal frameworks relevant to young people, in particular: the application of the LPS scheme to young people with education, health and care (EHC) plans and to those who are looked after children (whether subject to a care order or accommodated under CA 1989 s20).

124 MCA 2005 Sch A1.

125 See MCA 2005 Sch A1.

126 MC(A)A 2019 Sch 1. This will be inserted as Sch AA1 to the MCA 2005.

127 It is understood that draft regulations and code of practice will be issued for public consultation.

Another area requiring clarification is the relationship between the LPS scheme and secure accommodation orders under CA 1989 s25.

Background

4.59 The provisions of the MC(A)A 2019 are broadly based on the Law Commission's 2017 report, *Mental capacity and deprivation of liberty*[128] which concluded that there was a 'compelling case for replacing the DoLS' and recommended that this should happen as 'a matter of pressing urgency'.[129] The recommendations and a draft bill for the introduction of an new administrative scheme, referred to as 'the Liberty Protection Safeguards', included the extension of the new scheme to include young people as well as adults.[130] Initially this recommendation was not reflected in the government's parliamentary bill. However, 16- and 17-year-olds were subsequently included in the LPS scheme following government amendments at the report stage of the House of Lords' consideration of the MC(A) Bill in November 2018.[131]

4.60 The inclusion of young people in the LPS scheme was in response to concerns that the current system is not working for this age group. This was the conclusion of the Law Commission, which noted that the need to go to court (where the MHA 1983 is not engaged) entails a process that is 'unnecessarily onerous and expensive' for NHS bodies and local authorities and 'potentially distressing for the young person and family concerned.[132]

4.61 Another significant concern raised by the Law Commission was that 'public authorities are not currently taking cases to court when they should'.[133] A similar point was made by the Department of Health and Social Care (DHSC) in its analysis of the potential equality impact of the MC(A) Bill ('the equality analysis report'). Having noted that local authorities are required to apply to the Court of

128 Law Com No 372.

129 Law Com No 372, recommendation 1.

130 Law Com No 372, recommendation 5.

131 HL Deb 21 November 2018 Vol 794 cols 260–262. As a consequence, the Joint Committee of Human Rights' scrutiny of the government's proposals did not include the application of the LPS system to this age group (see: Joint Committee of Human Rights *Legislative Scrutiny of the Mental Capacity (Amendment) Bill* (2017–19 HL 208, HC 1662).

132 Law Commission, March 2017, para 7.28. See also *Equality analysis Liberty Protection Safeguards – Mental Capacity (Amendment) Bill*, DHSC, December 2018.

133 See Law Com No 372, paras 7.20–7.41.

Protection to sanction the deprivation of liberty of young people 'formally in care', the equality analysis report stated that 'on average there are only between four and twelve applications made by local authorities each year'.[134] This is clearly a low figure. However, it is difficult to gauge the extent of the problem given that the numbers of young people the government estimate to be deprived of their liberty, thereby requiring a court authorisation, was not included in this analysis.

4.62 The lack of information about under-18s deprived of their liberty was highlighted by the Children's Commissioner's report *Who are they? Where are they? Children locked up* (May 2019), which draws together information on the numbers of under-18s who are detained in different settings in England. In relation to applications to the Court of Protection, the Children's Commissioner noted that the information received from the Ministry of Justice was that 'there were 89 children on applications related to deprivation of liberty' (but it was not known how many applications were granted or where these young people were placed).[135] As the Children's Commissioner notes, there is a significant discrepancy between the number of applications to the Court of Protection provided by the Ministry of Justice (89) as compared to the number given in the DHSC's equality analysis (4–12) noted above. However, her office was unable to ascertain the reason for this.[136]

4.63 Steps to ensure that both young people who lack capacity to make decisions for their care arrangements and their families have easy access to safeguards when such arrangements give rise to the young person's deprivation of liberty are much needed. However, as acknowledged by the DHSC's equality analysis report, the LPS provides weaker safeguards than the existing legal mechanisms:

> . . . it is worth noting that the Court of Protection, as a highly diligent judicial authority, has very high standards for the protection of both younger groups (16 and 17- year olds, and those in community settings): a guarantee lost in the Liberty Protection Safeguards system. This is also the case for young people detained under the Mental Health Act (if they are in a psychiatric unit) who now could possibly fall under LPS. Government will need to work with stakeholders

134 *Equality analysis Liberty Protection Safeguards – Mental Capacity (Amendment) Bill*, DHSC, December 2018 p12.

135 Children's Commissioner, May 2019, p34.

136 Children's Commissioner, May 2019, p35.

including Children's services to ensure that safeguards are not lost through being excluded from these robust systems.'[137]

4.64 Significant concerns have been raised about the LPS, in particular questioning the adequacy of the safeguards for individuals subject to the LPS and the need for further consultation on the impact of these provisions.[138] Furthermore, as noted above, questions remain on how the LPS scheme will apply to young people.

Liberty Protection Safeguards and young people

4.65 An overview of the LPS scheme, which focuses on its application to young people is set out in box 4.4 below.

Box 4.4: Liberty Protection Safeguards[139] and young people – overview

Application of LPS

- The LPS apply (in any setting) to individuals who are a) aged 16 or over; b) lack capacity to consent to the arrangements (that enable their 'care or treatment'[140] and which give rise to their deprivation of liberty); and c) have a mental disorder.[141] The MC(A)A 2019 refers to these individuals as the 'cared-for person'.

137 DHSC *Equality analysis Liberty Protection Safeguards – Mental Capacity (Amendment) Bill*, December 2018 p12.

138 See, for example, Mental Capacity (Amendment) Bill [Lords] 18 December 2018 vol 651 cols 731–732 and the Law Society Parliamentary Brief: Mental Capacity (Amendment) Bill, December 2018.

139 Note that when in force, MC(A)A 2019 Sch 1 will be inserted as Sch AA1 into the MCA 2005. It will replace Schs A1 and 1A to the MCA 2005. As the LPS forms part of the MCA 2005 the principles under s1 (see para 4.8) will apply. See also Mental Capacity (Amendment) Bill, 15 January 2019, vol 652, col 46 in which Caroline Dineage, Minister for Care stated that: '. . . it is worth reminding hon. Members that the Bill will not replace the current Mental Capacity Act 2005, but amend it. Best interest decision making remains fundamental to the existing Act, within which the liberty protection safeguards will sit. Before a liberty protection safeguards authorisation is considered, it will need to be decided that the arrangements are in a person's best interests. That is included in section 4 of the 2005 Act.'

140 MC(A)A 2019 Sch 1 para 2(1) refers to arrangements 'for enabling the care or treatment of a person (the "cared-for person")' that give rise to the cared for person's deprivation of liberty and exclude arrangements under Part 7 (certain arrangements for the person's mental health care).

141 MC(A)A 2019 Sch 1 para 2(2).

- The arrangements, or proposed arrangements, can cover the following areas: where the cared-for person is to reside; for the cared-for person to receive care or treatment at a particular place; or for transporting the cared-for person to, from, or between particular places.[142]

Authorisation of the young person's deprivation of liberty

- The LPS provisions set out the procedures to be followed by a 'responsible body' when determining whether to authorise the deprivation of liberty (such a deprivation of liberty having arisen from the arrangements for the care or treatment of a person who lacks capacity to consent to such arrangements).[143]

Responsible body (RB)

- Depending on the circumstances of the case, the RB will either be an NHS body or a local authority.[144]
- For young people it is likely that the RB will be a local authority, save where the deprivation of liberty arises in an NHS hospital, in which case the RB will be the hospital managers.[145] Where they are admitted to an independent hospital, the RB will be a local authority (see para 4.77 below).[146]

Conditions for authorisation

- The RB must be satisfied that three conditions are met: a) the cared-for person lacks the capacity to consent to the arrangements; b) the cared-for person has a mental disorder[147] and c) the arrangements are both necessary to prevent harm to the cared-for person and 'proportionate in relation to the likelihood and seriousness of harm to the cared-for person'.[148]

142 MC(A)A 2019 Sch 1 para 2(3) and (4).

143 MC(A)A 2019 Sch 1 para 2(1). It excludes arrangements set out under MC(A)A 2019 Sch 1 Part 7 (mental health arrangements).

144 MC(A)A 2019 Sch 1 paras 6–12. Para 6(d) refers to the responsible body where a person is receiving 'NHS continuing healthcare'. It is not clear whether this provision is intended to apply to under 18s given that this term usually applies to adults only; see: DoH, *National framework for children and young people's continuing care* 2016, para 5.

145 MC(A)A 2019 Sch 1 para 6(1)(a). See para 7 for definition of 'hospital manager'.

146 MC(A) A 2019 Sch 1 para 6(1)(b).

147 As defined under MHA 1983 s1(2), namely: 'any disorder or disability of the mind'.

148 MC(A)A 2019 Sch 1 para 13.

- Each of these conditions must be determined on the basis of an assessment.[149]

Right to information

- Hospital managers, clinical commissioning groups (CCGs), and local authorities must publish information about the LPS, including: the effect of an authorisation under the LPS scheme; when IMCAs should be appointed (see below); the right to apply to the Court of Protection; and rights to request a review.
- Such information must be made available to individuals where arrangements falling within the LPS are proposed and also when they are authorised.[150]

Pre-authorisation review

- The RB must arrange for a pre-authorisation review to be carried out by a person who is not involved in the cared-for person's day-to-day care or providing any treatment to the cared-for person to ensure that the conditions for authorisation are met.[151]

Consultation

- As part of the process for determining whether it can authorise the arrangements, the RB must consult various people, including the cared-for person, to ascertain the cared-for person's wishes and feelings about the care arrangements.[152]
- Although parents are not referred to specifically, the list of people who must be consulted includes those 'engaged in caring for the cared-for person or interested in the cared-for person's welfare').[153] Accordingly, parents must be consulted unless 'it is not practicable or appropriate' to do so.[154]
- The list of consultees also includes anyone named by the young person as someone to be consulted about such arrangements; a deputy appointed by the Court of Protection; any 'appropriate

149 MC(A)A 2019 Sch 1 paras 21–22.

150 MC(A)A 2019 Sch 1 paras 14–16.

151 MC(A)A 2019 Sch 1 paras 18(e) and 24.

152 MC(A)A 2019 Sch 1 para 23; para 23(3) states that the 'main purpose' of the consultation 'is to try to ascertain the cared-for person's wishes or feelings in relation to the arrangements'.

153 MC(A)A 2019 Sch 1 para 23; para 23(2)(c).

154 MC(A)A 2019 Sch 1 para 23(4).

person' (a person who is a suitable person to represent and support the cared-for person, who consents to undertaking this role and is not a professional carer);[155] and the young person's IMCA (if one has been appointed – see below).[156]

Approved mental capacity professional (AMCP)

- The AMCP will be a health or social care professional with specialist training.[157] They will be required to carry out the pre-authorisation review in cases where the arrangements are for the cared-for person to reside in a particular place, or to receive care or treatment at a particular place and it is reasonable to believe that the cared-for person does not wish to reside there, or to receive care or treatment at that place.[158]
- In determining the cared-for person's wishes, the views of those engaged in caring for, or with an interest in the welfare of, the cared-for person must be considered.[159] Accordingly, in relation to young people, this will include their parents.
- An AMCP's involvement will also be required where the arrangements are for the young person to receive care or treatment mainly in an independent hospital.[160]

155 MC(A)A 2019 Sch 1 para 42(5). See also para 42(6) which provides that in relation to a person who lacks capacity, a person is not be regarded as suitable unless the responsible body 'is satisfied that being represented and supported by that person is in the cared-for person's best interests'.

156 MC(A)A 2019 Sch 1 para 23(2)(b), (e) and (f).

157 MC(A)A 2019 Sch 1 Part 4 (paras 39–40) covers AMCPs. Further detail on how they will operate is awaited. Regulations will prescribe for training and criteria for approval for AMCPs (whose professional backgrounds are likely to include Approved Mental Health Professionals, registered social workers and first level nurses; see *Mental Capacity (Amendment) Bill Memorandum from the Department of Health and Social Care to the Delegated Powers and Regulatory Reform Committee*, July 2018. See also Lord O'Shaughnessy HL Deb Vol 794 col 565:

> They will be qualified, knowledgeable and experienced professionals. It is intended that they will act independently, both of the care provider and the responsible body, and that they will make a determination on proposed arrangements after meeting the person and reviewing relevant information.

158 MC(A)A 2019 Sch 1 paras 24–25.

159 MC(A)A 2019 Sch 1 para 24(2)–(4).

160 MC(A)A 2019 Sch 1 para 24(2)(d).

IMCAs

- The provisions concerning the appointment of IMCAs are excessively complex.[161] In summary, the RB 'must take all reasonable steps to appoint an IMCA to represent the cared-for person' save for certain circumstances. For example, the RB does not have to do so where satisfied that there is an 'appropriate person' (a 'suitable person' to represent and support the cared-for person, who consents to undertaking this role and is not a professional carer).[162]
- Although a young person's parents could undertake the role of the 'appropriate person', they do not have to do so and may prefer to request that an IMCA is appointed given that IMCAs are expected to have knowledge and expertise on the operation of the LPS scheme which parents are unlikely to have.[163]
- An IMCA should be appointed at the request of a young person who has capacity to consent to being represented and supported by an IMCA.[164] Likewise, save for where an 'appropriate person' takes on this role[165] an IMCA should be appointed where a young person lacks capacity to decide about receiving help from an IMCA, unless the RB 'is satisfied that being represented and supported by an IMCA would not be in the cared-for person's best interests'.[166]

Duration, renewal and review

- The RB's authorisation can last for up to 12 months which can then be renewed for another year and thereafter every three years.[167]
- Challenges to the authorisation are heard by the Court of Protection.[168]

161 MC(A)A 2019 Sch 1 Part 5 paras 41–43.

162 MC(A)A 2019 Sch 1 para 42(5). See also para 42(6) which provides that in relation to a person who lacks capacity, a person is not be regarded as suitable unless the responsible body 'is satisfied that being represented and supported by that person is in the cared-for person's best interests'.

163 MC(A)A 2019 Sch 1 para 43.

164 MC(A)A 2019 Sch 1 para 43(2).

165 MC(A)A 2019 Sch 1 para 43(5).

166 MC(A)A 2019 Sch 1 para 42(3). It is difficult to envisage when representation by an IMCA would not be in a cared-for person's best interests.

167 MC(A)A 2019 Sch 1 paras 28–36. See also variation (para 37), reviews (para 38) and monitoring (Part 6 para 44). There must be a record of the authorisation (see para 27).

168 MC(A)A 2019 s3 (when in force, will be inserted as MCA 2005 s21ZA).

Liberty Protection Safeguards in context

Overview

4.66 When considering the provisions governing LPS, it is crucial to keep their purpose and context in mind. The purpose of the LPS scheme is to provide an administrative mechanism for authorising a deprivation of liberty. It will do so by replacing the DoLS. Accordingly, when in force, the LPS will be included in the MCA 2005's framework of decision-making for people who lack capacity to make decisions for themselves.

4.67 Under the MCA 2005, a deprivation of liberty is only permitted in the circumstances set out in MCA 2005 s4A (restriction on deprivation of liberty). It states that the MCA 2005 'does not authorise any person ("D") to deprive any other person ("P") of his liberty' (s4A(1)) save for the circumstances set out in this section.' When in force, MC(A)A 2019 s1 (Deprivation of Liberty: authorisation of arrangements enabling care and treatment) will amend MCA 2005 s4A(5) and will provide one of the situations in which a deprivation of liberty is permitted under the MCA 2005.[169] It states:

> D may deprive P of liberty if, by doing so, D is carrying out arrangements authorised under Schedule AA1 (arrangements enabling the care and treatment of persons who lack capacity).

4.68 Schedule AA1 is where the LPS scheme sits, the 'Liberty Protection Safeguards' being the term given to the provisions contained in this schedule.[170] Accordingly, if the arrangements that give rise to the person's deprivation of liberty are authorised in accordance with the LPS scheme, the deprivation of liberty is permitted under the MCA 2005. Furthermore, those carrying out such arrangements gain protection from liability for the actions they have taken

169 The other circumstances are: where a court order 'under section 16(2)(a) in relation to a matter concerning P's welfare' and where it is authorised under s4B (a new s4B will be inserted by MC(A)A 2019 s2 ('Deprivation of liberty: authorisation of steps necessary for life-sustaining treatment or vital acts').

170 When it comes into force, MC(A)A 2019 Sch 1 will be inserted as Sch AA1 into the MCA 2005). See MC(A)A 2019 s1(4). The Explanatory Note to the MC(A)A 2019 states (at para 15) that Sch AA1: contains the new administrative scheme for authorising arrangements enabling the care and treatment of persons who lack capacity to consent to those arrangements, which give rise to a deprivation of liberty (referred to in these Notes as the Liberty Protection Safeguards).

(although this does not protect them from liability for negligent acts).[171]

4.69 In effect, like the DoLS, the LPS scheme is a 'bolt-on' to the MCA 2005. They do ***not*** provide the legal authority for the provision of care and treatment. This point was emphasised by the Law Commission's report, *Mental Capacity and Deprivation of Liberty*. When discussing how the proposed LPS scheme was intended to operate, the report noted that the LPS:

> . . . cannot be used to authorise the actual delivery of care or treatment to the person. Whilst the arrangements which can be authorised include that the person 'is to receive care or treatment at one or more particular places', the delivery of that care or treatment would continue to be governed by the statutory defence in section 5 of the Mental Capacity Act.[172]

4.70 It might be helpful to consider the decision-making process in two stages – in that *stage 1* is to identify the legal authority for the proposed care and treatment arrangements; and *stage 2* is to authorise any deprivation of liberty that arises from such arrangements. The LPS scheme is concerned with the second stage, not the first. This separation of the decision-making process stage 1 (legal authority for the provision of care and treatment) and stage 2 (authorising the deprivation of liberty) will be relevant when considering the role of parents.

Role of parents

4.71 Whereas the absence of any reference to parents in the provisions for authorising a deprivation of liberty under the LPS scheme may give rise to the perception that their views are not relevant, this is not the case. For the reasons explained further below, it is argued that parents will continue to have a crucial role given that their views will be relevant to establishing the legal authority for the provision of care and treatment (stage 1). In some circumstances parental consent can provide the legal authority for a young person's care and treatment. Moreover, if parents object to such arrangements, it will be necessary to seek a court order (or in relation to inpatient psychiatric care),

171 See (when inserted by MC(A)A 2019 s1(3)) MCA 2005 4C(2), which provides that no liability is incurred where such acts could have been made if the person had capacity and had consented to them and MCA 2005 4C(3) which provides that this is subject to civil or criminal liability arising from negligence.

172 Law Com No 372, para 17.16. See also para 11.19: 'The draft Bill does not provide any protection for the provision of medical treatment or restricting contact with third parties, since "arrangements" cannot extend to these matters'.

consider whether the criteria for admission under the MHA 1983 are met.[173]

Parental consent and the legal authority for the care and treatment arrangements

4.72 Whereas, like adults young peoples' care and treatment can be authorised in accordance with MCA 2005 s5, unlike adults, it may be also possible for such arrangements to be authorised by their parents' consent (or the consent of others who have parental responsibility). For example, parents might agree to the local authority accommodating their child in a residential school under CA 1989 s20, or a local authority arranging such placement for a young person who is subject to a care order. In such cases, the decision of those exercising parental responsibility provides the legal authority for the delivery of the care and treatment (stage 1). If such arrangements give rise to a deprivation of liberty, it will be necessary to consider how this can be authorised (stage 2). Whether LPS can be engaged will depend on whether the criteria are met (the key issues are summarised in box 4.4 above).

Parents' objection to care and treatment arrangements

4.73 An area of potential confusion is the relevance of parents' objection to proposed care and treatment arrangements for their child. Here it is important to note that there is nothing to indicate that the LPS scheme affects parents' current powers to veto proposed arrangements such as their child's placement away from home (whether in a children's home, residential school, hospital or any other setting). Moreover, during the parliamentary debates the government confirmed that there was no conflict between the provisions of the MCA(A) Bill and the CA 1989 'or indeed with any other existing legislation'.[174] On this basis, depending on the circumstances of the case, where parents object to their child's care and treatment arrangements, it will be necessary to seek a court order (or in relation to psychiatric inpatient care, consider admission under the MHA 1983).

173 Given its significance to the operation of the LPS scheme, it is hoped that the code of practice will provide guidance on the relevance of parents' decision-making powers. The government plans to issue a draft Code for public consultation (see written statement Helen Whately (Minister of State (Minister for Care)) 16 July 2020 HCWS377).

174 Caroline Dinenage, Minister for Care, Mental Capacity (Amendment) Bill, 17 January 2019, vol 652, col 84. In *Re D (a child)* [2019] UKSC 42 both Lady Black (at [71]) and Lord Carnwath (at [145]) in his dissenting judgment (and with whom Lord Lloyd-Jones agreed) considered that the MCA 2005 does not exclude common law powers and other statutory provisions.

4.74 That the courts must be involved where parents do not agree to their children being removed from their care,[175] (save where immediate action to prevent significant harm is required)[176] was emphasised by Lady Hale when considering the application of CA 1989 s20 in *Williams v Hackney LBC*. In addition to stating that 'no local authority have the right or the power to remove a child from a parent who is looking after the child and wants to go on doing so without a court order',[177] Lady Hale endorsed the view expressed by Munby J (as he then was) in *R (G) v Nottingham City Council*[178] that health bodies do not have such powers either.[179]

Similarly, in cases concerning the application of the MCA 2005, the courts have made clear that disputes that engage the right to respect for private and family life under the European Convention on Human Rights (ECHR) Article 8 should be resolved by the Court of Protection.[180] In *Hillingdon LBC v Neary*, in which a young (adult)

175 *Re A (child), Re C (adult)* [2010] EWHC 978 (Fam) at [61]: 'unless clothed with the authority of either an emergency protection order or a care order, a local authority has no power to remove a child from its parent'. See also *R (G) v Nottingham City Council* [2008] EWHC 152 (Admin) [15]–[26].

176 In *R (G) v Nottingham City Council* [2008] EWHC 152 (Admin) the court noted (at [21]–[26]) that action can be taken to protect individuals (of any age) from criminal assault and under CA 1989 s3(5) those who have care of a 'child' can 'do what is reasonable in all the circumstances of the case for the purpose of safeguarding or promoting the child's welfare'.

177 [2018] UKSC 37 at [38]. See CA 1989 s20(7) and (8). As noted by Lady Hale (at [48]) this is subject to CA 1989 s20(11), which provides that 16- and 17-year-olds may agree to being accommodated by a local authority under CA 1998 s20 even if their parents do not. However, it is difficult to see how this provision would apply to young people who lack capacity to make decisions about their living arrangements.

178 [2008] EWHC 152 (Admin) at [17]: 'Only if a court has authorised that step, whether by making an emergency protection order or by making a care order or an interim care order or in some other way, can a local authority or a social worker remove a child from a parent. And the same goes, of course, for a hospital and its medical staff.' In relation to actions by medical staff see *R (G) v Nottingham City Council* [2008] EWHC 400 (Admin).

179 [2018] UKSC 37 at [38].

180 See *Hillingdon LBC v Neary* [2011] EWHC 1377 (COP) at [33]; *C v Darwen BC* [2011] EWHC 3321 (COP) at [37]. See also *J Council v GU* [2012] EWHC 3531 (COP). Note also the discussion in A Ruck Keene, K Edwards, Professor A Eldergill, N Mackintosh QC (Hon) and S Miles, *Court of Protection Handbook: a user's guide*, 3rd edn, LAG, 2019 para 24.12 in which the authors state: 'it is clear that any decision by a public body to remove a person from their own home, especially in the face of their objections, and/or to restrict their contact with others, will undoubtedly engage the person's rights to private and family life under Article 8 ECHR (and quite possibly those of others), and that proceeding without the sanction of the court may well give rise to a breach of the implied procedural safeguards that accompany Article 8.

man had been kept in a residential home against his father's wishes, Mr Justice Peter Jackson stated that DoLS 'is not to be used by a local authority as a means of getting its own way on the question of whether it is in the person's best interests to be in the place at all'.[181]

Liberty Protection Safeguards and the MHA 1983

Overview

4.75 The interrelationship between the LPS scheme and the MHA 1983 is set out in MC(A)A 2019 Sch 1 Part 7. When in force, these complex provisions will be relevant to adolescents' psychiatric care given that the LPS may provide an alternative legal mechanism for authorising a young person's deprivation of liberty to that of the MHA 1983.[182]

The LPS as an alternative to detention under the MHA 1983

4.76 The circumstances in which the LPS scheme provides an appropriate alternative to admission under the MHA 1983 for young people is an area in which further detail on how the LPS will operate is required. For example:

- *Objection and the MCA 2005 / MHA 1983 interface:* As with adults, the LPS scheme cannot be applied if the young person objects to being accommodated in hospital or 'to being given some or all' of the treatment for mental disorder.[183] As no definition is included in the MC(A)A 2019, such guidance on what constitutes an 'objection' is needed. By way of comparison, the MHA Code's guidance on a similar provision in relation to DoLS states:

  > Whether a patient is objecting has to be considered in the round, taking into account all the circumstances, so far as they are reasonably ascertainable. The decision to be made is whether the patient objects, the reasonableness of that objection is not the issue. In many cases the patient will be perfectly able to state their objection. In other cases the relevant person will need to consider the patient's

181 [2011] EWHC 1377 (COP) at [33]. See also [151]: 'the issue that arises under Article 8 represents the nub of the matter . . . they apply directly to cases where the legitimacy of the removal of a person from a family is in question'.

182 The LPS cannot apply if the young person is already detained under the MHA 1983 (MC(A)A 2019 Sch 1 para 47).

183 MC(A)A 2019 Sch 1 para 51(5). In relation to young people, there is one exception to this which is if a deputy, with the authority to do so, consents to the arrangements on the young person's behalf; see MC(A)A 2019 Sch 1 paras 51(5). For the principles governing the appointment of deputies (MCA 2005 s16(4) see paras 4.48–4.51 above.

behaviour, wishes, feelings, views, beliefs and values, both present and past, so far as they can be ascertained. In deciding whether a patient objects to being admitted to hospital, or to some or all of the treatment they will receive there for mental disorder, decision-makers should err on the side of caution and, where in doubt, take the position that a patient is objecting.[184]

- *Relevance of the views of parents:* For the reasons set out at paras 4.71–4.74 above, it is suggested that the LPS cannot be applied in cases where the parents of young people who lack capacity to make such decisions object to their child's admission to hospital. In such cases, it seems likely that it would be necessary for an application for admission to hospital under the MHA 1983 to be made, or a court authorisation sought, if the criteria for such admission under the MHA 1983 was not met.[185]

Admission to independent hospitals

4.77 Where it is proposed that the young person is to be admitted and treated in an independent hospital under the LPS scheme, there are two important differences to admissions to NHS hospitals:

1) *The involvement of an AMCP:* The pre-authorisation review must be undertaken by an AMCP.
2) *The responsible body (RB) will be a local authority:* Which local authority is to undertake the role of the responsible body will depend on the young person's circumstances:
   a) *Where the young person has an EHC (education, health and care) plan:* The RB is the local authority responsible for maintaining that plan.[186]
   b) *If there is no EHC plan but the young person is accommodated under CA 1989 s20:* The RB is the local authority providing that accommodation.

184 MHA Code para 13.51. MC(A)A 2019 Sch 1 para 52 states that in determining whether the person objects, 'regard must be had to all the circumstances (so far as they are reasonably ascertainable)', including the person's behaviour, wishes and feelings and 'views, beliefs and values'.

185 It should be noted that there are powers to intervene where urgent action is needed to safeguard under-18s; see for example, emergency treatment in para 3.95–3.97, police powers under CA 1989 s46 (paras 10.100–10.103). See also MCA 2005 s4B. When MC(A)A 2019 s2 comes into force, it will insert a new MCA 2005 s4B: 'Deprivation of liberty necessary for life-sustaining treatment or vital act'. In addition, CA 1989 ss44–45 provides for the circumstances in which an application can be made to a court for an emergency protection order under (see box 5.2).

186 MC(A)A 2019 Sch 1 paras 6(b) and 9(3)(a).

c) *If neither a) nor b) apply and the young person is subject to a care order (CA 1989 s31) or interim care order (CA 1989 s38) for which a local authority in England is responsible:* The RB is that responsible local authority.

d) *If none of the above apply:* The RB is the local authority for the area in which the independent hospital is situated.[187]

187 These are to be considered in sequence. See MC(A)A 2019 Sch1 paras 6(1)(b) and 9(3)(b)–(d) and 9(4); see also para 9(5).

CHAPTER 5

Parental responsibility and the nearest relative

Introduction

5.1 People with parental responsibility (PR) for children and young people aged under 18 ('adolescents')[1] have an important role in the decision-making process for adolescents' psychiatric care. In some circumstances, those with PR for an under 18-year-old can consent to interventions, such as admission to hospital and treatment for mental disorder on behalf of their child. Even if not the decision-makers, those with PR will need to be involved in the planning and delivery of care to adolescents, before, during and after their admission to hospital (unless there is a good reason for not doing so).

5.2 In addition, adolescents who are admitted to hospital under the Mental Health Act (MHA) 1983 will have a 'nearest relative' (NR), who has a significant role in relation to the application of the MHA 1983.[2] The role of the adolescent's NR is in addition to, and separate from, the role of those who have PR for the adolescent.

5.3 This chapter focuses on these two legal entities: PR and the NR. PR is a creation of the Children Act (CA) 1989 and it is this Act that sets out the rules for identifying who has PR. The NR's role and function is determined by the MHA 1983, which sets out the rules for identifying who is the NR. Accordingly, this chapter is divided into the following two parts:

- *parental responsibility:* covering the meaning, identification and delegation of PR; and
- *nearest relative:* covering the identification, delegation and displacement of the NR; confidentiality and the NR; and wardship and the NR.

Parental responsibility

Overview

5.4 The legal concept of PR and who has PR is set out under the CA 1989. However, as noted below, the definition of PR is broad and the powers that it confers ill-defined. To some extent this is understandable. As PR spans from birth up to 18, the decision-making powers of those who hold PR will need to adapt in accordance with the child's

1 For reasons explained at para 1.9, this term is used to cover all under-18s.

2 *R (M) v Secretary of State for Health* [2003] EWHC 1094 (Admin) at [4]–[6]. See also *TW v Enfield LBC* [2014] EWCA Civ 362, [2014] 1 WLR 3665 at [49].

developing maturity and ability to make decisions for themselves. Such a shift in the role of parents in the decision-making process in relation to their child was described by Lord Denning in *Hewer v Bryant* as a 'dwindling right' which 'starts with a right of control and ends with little more than advice'.[3] It is also is reflected in the UN Convention on the Rights of the Child (UNCRC), which recognises the rights of parents to make decisions on behalf of their child 'in a manner consistent with the evolving capacities of the child' (UNCRC Article 5).

Parental consent and the scope of parental responsibility

5.5 The dynamic relationship between the decision-making powers of parents (and others with PR) and those of their child is highlighted by the *Mental Health Act 1983: Code of Practice* ('MHA Code').[4] While recognising that those with PR 'have a central role in relation to decisions about the admission and treatment of their child', the MHA Code also advises that before relying on parental consent to authorise a particular intervention, it will be necessary 'to establish whether the particular decision can be authorised by parental consent or not'.[5] The MHA Code provides guidance on the factors to consider when determining whether the decision in question falls within 'the scope of parental responsibility' and can therefore be made by the parent(s).[6]

Involving those with parental responsibility in the decision-making process

5.6 Although the MHA 1983 makes no specific provision for involving parents in either the procedures for the admission to hospital, or for compulsory treatment, the importance of doing so is emphasised by the MHA Code. It states that those with PR should be identified and consulted about the proposed admission to hospital or medical treatment (subject to the adolescent's right to confidentiality).[7]

3 [1970] 1 QB 357 at 369. See also discussion in *Re D (a child)* [2019] UKSC 42 at [19]–[24] (Lady Hale) and at [69]–[72] (Lady Black).

4 Department of Health (DoH), 2015.

5 MHA Code para 19.40.

6 MHA Code paras 19.40–19.41. The scope of parental responsibility is discussed in chapter 3, paras 3.62–3.67.

7 MHA Code para 19.38. See paras 2.96–2.103.

5.7 Although CA 1989 s2(7) makes clear that one person with PR can make decisions about their child without the need to seek the agreement of others with PR,[8] the MHA Code advises:

> It is good practice to involve the child or young person's parents and/or others involved in their care in the decision-making process, if the child or young person consents to information about their care and treatment being shared.[9]

5.8 The MHA Code also states that where both parents have PR they should both be involved in making decisions about an adolescent's psychiatric care, even if the adolescent 'is living with one parent in accordance with a child arrangements order'[10] (child arrangement orders are explained below).

5.9 The MHA Code's guidance reflects the courts' view that those with PR have 'the right to be consulted on schooling, serious medical problems, and other important occurrences in a child's life',[11] while for certain medical interventions such as immunisation, authorisation by the court is required if one parent disagrees with it.[12]

8 CA 1989 s2(7):

> Where more than one person has parental responsibility for a child, each of them may act alone and without the other (or others) in meeting that responsibility; but nothing in this Part shall be taken to affect the operation of any enactment which requires the consent of more than one person in a matter affecting the child.

9 MHA Code para 19.21.

10 MHA Code para 19.9. See *R v E* [2016] EWHC 3113 (Fam) at [27]–[28] (parents having 'joint and equal parental responsibility' in relation to their child's treatment (lumbar puncture) and comments made by King LJ in *Re H (a child) (parental responsibility: vaccination)* [2020] EWCA Civ 664 at [94].

11 *Re H (parental responsibility)* [1998] 1 FLR 855 at 859, *Re G (a minor) (parental responsibility: education)* [1995] 2 FCR 53, [119] 2 FLR 964, CA; and *Re C (minors) (change of name)* [1997] 2 FLR 730 [1997] 3 FCR 310. The CA 1989 also sets limits on the types of decisions that parents can make on their own, see for example s13 (change of child's surname or removal from the UK).

12 *Re C (welfare of child: immunisation)* [2003] 2 FLR 1095; affirmed in *Re B (a child) (immunisation)* [2003] EWCA Civ 1148 at [16]–[17]. See also *Re J (specific issue orders: child's religious upbringing and circumcision)* [2000] 1 FLR 571 (CA) at 577D:

> . . . a small group of important decisions made on behalf of a child which, in the absence of agreement of those with parental responsibility, ought not to be carried out or arranged by a one-parent carer although she has parental responsibility under s 2(7) of the Children Act 1989.

And see also *Re H (a child) (parental responsibility: vaccination)* [2020] EWCA Civ 664 at [94].

The meaning of parental responsibility

5.10 The term 'parental responsibility' is defined in CA 1989 s3(1) as:

> . . . all the rights, duties, powers, responsibilities and authority which by law a parent of a child has in relation to the child and his property.[13]

5.11 This broad definition leaves the detail of what falls within parental decision-making powers to an examination of 'common law' (in other words laws developed by the courts in deciding individual cases) and any other statutes that give rights to parents.[14] As noted by the Court of Appeal in *Re G (children)*:

> Although the Act gives little further assistance as to the attributes of parental responsibility', it is clear that it includes taking decisions about aspects of the child's upbringing such as education, religion, medical treatment, and holidays abroad . . .[15]

5.12 Accordingly, the MHA Code's advice (that it is 'essential that those proposing the admission and/or treatment identify who has parental responsibility'[16]) reflects the position that the legal authority for making decisions in relation to an under-18's care and upbringing derives from holding PR, not the fact of being a parent. Furthermore, the 'concept of parental responsibility describes an adult's responsibility to secure the welfare of their child which is to be exercised for the benefit of the child not the adult'.[17]

13 CA 1989 s3(1). For the purpose of the CA 1989 a child is 'a person under the age of eighteen' (CA 1989 s105).

14 In *Re D (a child)* [2019] UKSC 42, at [20] Lady Hale stated:

> 'By law' obviously refers to the common law, but also includes those statutory provisions which give rights etc to parents, such as the Marriage Act 1949, which gives them the right to withhold consent to the marriage of a 16 or 17-year-old child (section 3).

Another example is Children and Young Persons Act 1933 s1, the effect of which is that parents will be guilty of neglect if they fail to ensure that their child aged under 16 has adequate food, clothing, medical care and accommodation.

15 *Re G (children)* [2014] EWCA Civ 336 at [32]. For discussion on the role of parental responsibility in the context of arrangements for an under-18's care arrangements see: McFarlane LJ in *Re W (children)* [2012] EWCA Civ 999 at [47] 'where two parents share parental responsibility, it will be the duty of one parent to ensure that the rights of the other parent are respected, and vice versa, for the benefit of the child'.

16 MHA Code para 19. 6.

17 *Re D (a child)* [2014] EWCA Civ 315 at [11].

Identifying who has parental responsibility

5.13 Being a parent and having PR are not synonymous. In many cases, both parents will have PR, but this will not always be so. In addition, in some circumstances, individuals who are not the parents will have PR. Box 5.1 below sets out key points to note.

Box 5.1: Parental responsibility – key points

1) Where the parents are not married to each other, it will be necessary to establish whether the father has acquired PR.
2) Step-parents will also need to take steps to acquire PR.
3) Where a care order, or interim care order, is in place, the local authority will share PR with the parents (if they both have PR (and see 6) below).
4) Individuals who have been appointed as 'guardians', or 'special guardians' under the CA 1989 will have PR.
5) Individuals who are named in a 'child arrangements order' under CA 1989 s8, as being the person(s) with whom the adolescent is living (known as a 'lived with order') will have PR.
6) Save for adoption orders, the fact that a person acquires PR does not remove PR from others.

5.14 The MHA Code advises practitioners to ascertain whether any relevant orders or agreements are in place, such as care orders, child arrangement orders (CAOs), special guardianship orders (SGOs) or parental responsibility agreements.[18] The table below provides an overview of who can have PR and how PR is acquired. Box 5.2 below summarises the key orders and powers relevant to identifying those with PR. It also highlights which of these are relevant to identifying the adolescent's NR.

18 MHA Code para 19.8.

Table 5.1: Parental responsibility	
For ease of reference, the table below uses the term 'child' to mean a person aged under 18 years (adopting the same definition as the CA 1989).	
Mother	Has PR for her child[19] unless *she loses PR through*: • adoption;[20] or • a parental order (concerning surrogacy arrangements).[21]
Father	• Has PR if he was married to, or in a civil partnership with his child's mother when his child was born[22] (and will gain PR if the parents marry or enter a civil partnership after their child's birth[23]); • Unmarried fathers *acquire PR through*: – registering the birth with his child's mother on or after 1 December 2003;[24] – obtaining a PR order from the court[25] (this will be automatic if the father is named on a CAO as being a person with whom the child will be living,[26] or if appointed as the child's guardian[27]);

19 CA 1989 s2(1)-(2A). *Whittington Hospital NHS Trust v XX* [2020] UKSC 14 at [10]:

> The starting point is that the woman who bears the child is always the child's legal mother when the child is born (Human Fertilisation and Embryology Act 1990, section 27 Human Fertilisation and Embryology Act 2008, section 33).

20 Adoption and Children Act (ACA) 2002 s46(2) and Human Fertilisation and Embryology Act (HFEA) 2008 s33.

21 Through a parental order, the birth mother passes parental responsibility to the 'commissioning parents'. See Human Fertilisation and Embryology Act (HFEA) 1990 s54; and *A and another v P and others* [2011] EWHC 1738 (Fam) at [24]: 'the effect of the order is that the child is treated as though born to the applicants'. See also *Whittington Hospital NHS Trust v XX* [2020] UKSC 14.

22 CA 1989 s2(1). As amended by Civil Partnership (Opposite-sex Couples) Regulations 2019 SI 2019 No 4158 regs 1(2), 15(2).

23 Family Law Reform Act 1987 s1(2) and 1(3) (as amended by SI 2019 No 4158 reg 15) read with the Legitimacy Act 1976 ss2 and 10.

24 CA 1989 s4(1)(a), (1A); and Births, Deaths and Registration Act (BDRA)1953 s10. BDRA 1953 s10A sets out the circumstances in which unmarried parents can re-register the birth of their child and by doing so the father can acquire parental responsibility under CA 1989 s4(1)(a).

25 CA 1989 s4(1)(c).

26 CA 1989 s12(1).

27 CA 1989 s5(6). He could be appointed as a guardian either by the court (where 'the child has no parent with parental responsibility' (CA 1989 s5(1)(a)) or by the child's mother, guardian or special guardian (which can only take effect following the death of the appointee (see CA 1989 s5(3)–(9)).

	– making a PR agreement with the child's mother and registering this with the court.[28]
Mother's civil partner / wife	• The mother's civil partner / wife will have PR of the child if at the time the mother conceived her child (by assisted reproduction or artificial insemination) the women were in a civil partnership / married and the mother's civil partner / wife had given her consent to this procedure (consent is assumed unless shown otherwise).[29] • The mother's civil partner / wife will have PR of her child if at the time the mother conceived her child (by assisted reproduction or artificial insemination) she had agreed to be the second female parent in accordance with the 'agreed female parenthood conditions' under the Human Fertilisation and Embryology Act (HFEA) 2008[30] and she and the child's mother were in a civil partnership / married at the time of the child's birth.[31]
Second female parent	• A woman who consented to be the second parent for a child in accordance with the 'agreed female parenthood conditions' under the HFEA 2008,[32] but has not entered into a civil partnership / marriage with the mother of the child, may acquire PR for the child by similar routes to that of the unmarried father (registering the birth of the child with the mother; obtaining a court order; or entering into a parental responsibility agreement with the mother).[33]
Step-parents	May acquire PR for a child if they are married to, or the civil partner of, a person with PR for the child. They can do so either: • by agreement with the parent (and with the other parent if they have PR);[34] • by court order;[35] or • through adoption.[36]

28 CA 1989 s4(1)(b) and (2). The procedures for doing so are set out in Parental Responsibility Agreement Regulations 1991 SI No 1478, as amended by SI 2005 No 2808 and SI 2009 No 2026. Two copies of the agreement must be lodged with the Principal Registry of the Family Division.

29 CA 1989 s2(1A)(a); HFEA 2008 s42. Note: Marriage (Same-Sex Couples) Act 2013 Sch 4 Part 2 para 2 provides that the 'common law presumption of legitimacy' (that a child born to a woman during her marriage is also the child of her husband) does not apply to same-sex couples.

30 HFEA 2008 s43.

31 CA 1989 s2(1A)(b): HFEA 2008 ss43 and 44; Family Law Reform Act (FLRA) 1987 s1(3)(bb)(i). The provisions also cover cases where the marriage/civil partnership has ended, see FLRA 1987 s1(3)(bb)(ii).

32 HFEA 2008 s43.

33CA 1989 s4ZA. See also CA 1989 s12(1) and s12(1A) in relation to PR and CAOs.

34 CA 1989 s4A.

35 CA 1989 s4A.

36 ACA 2002 s46(1).

Adoption	The person(s) adopting the child will have PR.[37]
Placement order	PR is shared between the local authority and the birth parents and, where the looked after child is living with prospective adopters, the prospective adopters.[38]
Person(s) named on child arrangement orders (CAOs)	• Will have PR if named as a person with whom the child lives.[39] • Courts also have the power to award PR to a person named in a CAO as a person with whom a child spends time or otherwise has contact.[40]
Special guardian(s)	• Will have PR.[41] • The special guardian must be aged 18 or over and cannot be the child's birth parent.[42]
Guardian(s) (appointed under CA 1989 s5)	Will have PR when the appointment takes effect[43] (eg on appointment by the court where no one has PR for the child[44] or on the death of the child's parent(s) or the person named in a CAO as the person with whom a child is to live.[45])
Care orders and interim care orders	A local authorityacquires PR where a care order or interim care order is made.[46]
Emergency protection (EPO)	The applicant for the EPO (usually a local authority) has PR but must only take action that 'is reasonably required to order safeguard or promote the welfare of the child'.[47]

Box 5.2: Parental responsibility and the nearest relative – relevant orders and powers

Child arrangements order (CAO) – CA 1989 s8

- A CAO is 'an order regulating arrangements concerning with whom a child is to live, spend time or otherwise have contact and when a child is to live, spend time or otherwise have contact with any

37 ACA 2002 s46(1).
38 ACA 2002 s25. See also Vol 1, 25.
39 CA 1989 s12. Note: for those other than parents or guardians of the child, 'shall have parental responsibility for the child while the order remains in force so far as providing for the child to live with that person' (s12(2)).
40 CA 1989 s12(2A). See also s12(1A) regarding parents who do not have PR.
41 CA 1989 s14C(1).
42 CA 1989 s14A(2).
43 CA 1989 s5(6).
44 CA 1989 s5(1)(a).
45 CA 1989 s5(1)(b) and s5(6).
46 CA 1989 s33(1) and s31(11).
47 CA 1989 s44(4)(c) and s44(5)(b).

person'.[48] Usually these orders do not extend beyond the child's 16th birthday and cannot continue beyond the child's 18th birthday.[49]

- Where the CAO concerns contact arrangements (previously known as a 'contact order', now known as a 'time spent order') the court may provide for the person(s) named as having contact with the adolescent to have PR for the duration of the order.[50]
- Where the CAO concerns the adolescent's living arrangements (previously known as a 'residence order', now referred to has a 'lived with order'), the person(s) named as the person(s) with whom the adolescent is to live will have PR.[51] They will also be the adolescent's NR.[52]

Special guardianship order (SGO) – CA 1989 ss14A–14F

- The court may appointone or more individuals to act as 'special guardian' for an under-18-year-old. The special guardian (who must be aged 18 or over and cannot be the under-18-year-old's parent), will have PR for the duration of the SGO.[53] The SGO has 'clear responsibility for all the day to day decisions about caring for the child or young person and his upbringing'.
- Subject to any other order in force under the CA 1989, special guardians 'may exercise parental responsibility to the exclusion of all others with parental responsibility, apart from another special guardian'.[54]
- Although the parents do not lose their PR and their consent is required in relation to certain decisions (such as their child's

48 *Court orders and pre-proceedings: for local authorities*, DfE, April 2014, para 6, p7. In *L v L (child arrangements following treatment)* [2017] EWHC 1212 (Fam) the court made a CAO in favour of the father of a 14-year-old who was detained under MHA 1983 s3, providing that the adolescent would live with him on her discharge from hospital.

49 CA 1989 ss9(6), (7) (6A) and 91(11).

50 CA 1989 s12(2A).

51 CA 1989 s12(1) and (2). If the father gains PR by virtue of a CAO stating that his child is to live with him, his PR will continue beyond the CAO (s12(1)).

52 MHA 1983 s28. It is possible for more than one person to be the NR (s28(1)).

53 CA 1989 s14C.

54 CA 1989 s14C. There are some limits to special guardians powers, eg changing the child's surname requires the consent of all those with PR (s14C(3)). For discussion on special guardianship see: *Re S (a child)* 2007 EWCA Civ 54 at [41]–[49]. See also: *Special guardianship guidance: Statutory guidance for local authorities on the Special Guardianship Regulations 2005 (as amended by the Special Guardianship (Amendment) Regulations 2016)*, January 2017, para 12.

adoption[55] and decisions requiring the consent or more than one person with PR)[56] the status of an SGO 'effectively prevents the exercise of parental responsibility on the part of the child's natural parents'.[57] This means that in most cases (including decisions about an adolescent's admission to hospital and treatment for mental disorder) special guardians 'can trump the exercise of parental responsibility by a parent'.[58]

- SGOs will have PR. They will also be the adolescent's NR.[59]

Guardianship – CA 1989 s5

- Guardianship provides for the circumstances in whichindividuals can be appointed to act as the guardian for under-18-year-olds.
- For example, the court can appoint a person to be an adolescent's guardian in circumstances such as where no one has PR for the adolescent,[60] or a parent with PR has appointed a person to be their child's guardian in the event of the parent's death.[61]
- Those appointed as guardians under CA 1989 s5 will have PR[62] for the adolescent. They will also be the adolescent's NR.[63]

Placement orders – Adoption and Children Act 2002 s21

- A placement order provides for the circumstances in which the court may authorise the local authority to place a looked after child for adoption with any prospective adopters who may be chosen by the local authority.[64]
- Where a placement order is made, PR is shared between the local authority and the birth parents and, where the looked after child is living with prospective adopters, the prospective adopters.[65]

55 See CA 1989 s14C(2) and (3).

56 CA 1989 s14C(2)(a). Other decisions requiring the parent's consent include changing their child's surname and removing their child from the UK. See *Statutory guidance for local authorities on the Special Guardianship Regulations 2005 (as amended by the Special Guardianship (Amendment) Regulations 2016)* January 2017, p8.

57 *Birmingham City Council v LR and others* [2006] EWCA Civ 1748 at [78].

58 *L (a child)* [2007] EWCA Civ 196 at [33].

59 MHA 1983 s28. Subject to the exceptions in s28(2) (but cases in which these are relevant are likely to be rare).

60 CA 1989 s5(1).

61 CA 1989 s5(3).

62 CA 1989 s5(6).

63 MHA 1983 s28.

64 *Court orders and pre-proceedings* pp24–25.

65 ACA 2002 s25. See also Vol 1, 25.

Emergency protection orders (EPOs) – CA 1989 ss44–45

- EPOs authorise the removal of under-18s to alternative accommodation or require them to be kept in the place in which they are being accommodated.
- EPOs are intended to apply only in genuine emergencies, and only if 'this is necessary to provide immediate short-term protection'.[66] 'The courts have emphasised that using the powers under an EPO to remove a children from their parents is a "draconian" and "extremely harsh" measure, requiring "exceptional justification" and "extraordinarily compelling reasons"'.[67]
- Any person can apply for an EPO (although it is usually a local authority[68]) but the court can only make an EPO if it is satisfied that there is reasonable cause to believe that such powers are necessary to protect the under-18-year-old from significant harm.[69] The maximum period for an EPO is eight days and it can only be extended once (for seven days).
- While it is in force, the person in whose favour (usually the local authority) has PR, but this is limited to taking such action as is 'reasonably required to safeguard or promote the welfare of the child'.[70] On this basis, legal commentators suggest that the PR conferred under EPOs 'would not give the applicant power to authorise any major medical or psychiatric treatment without the agreement of a parent or other person with parental responsibility, unless the child is in urgent need of such treatment'.[71]

Care order – CA 1989 s31

- The court will only make a care order if it is satisfied that the threshold criteria set out under CA 1989 s31(2) are met and

66 *Re X (Emergency Protection Orders)* [2006] EWHC 510 (Fam) at [63]. See *Court orders and pre-proceedings* (pp37–40) which states (p38) that applications for an EPO 'are a very serious step and the court must be satisfied that the EPO is both necessary and proportionate and that there is "no less radical form of order available"'.

67 *X Council v B* [2004] EWHC 2015 (Fam) at [34]. In this case, Munby J set out (at [57]) a list of factors to be considered by the court before making an EPO, which were adopted by McFarlane J in *Re X (Emergency Protection Orders)* [2006] EWHC 510 (Fam) at [65], considering these factors to be '"required reading" for every magistrate and justices clerk involved in any EPO application'.

68 *Court orders and pre-proceedings* 37, para 13.

69 CA 1989 s44(1).

70 CA 1989 s44(4) and (5).

71 S Gilmore and L Glennon, *Hayes and Williams' family law*, 6th edn, OUP, 640.

having considered that welfare checklist (CA 1989 s1(3)) and the 'no order' principle (CA 1989 s1(5)) it is appropriate to make the order.[72]

- Adolescents who are subject to a care order (or interim care order (ICO)), are in the care of the local authority. This means that the local authority is required to provide accommodation for them, maintain and safeguard them, to promote their welfare.[73]
- The local authority will have PR for the adolescent, which it shares with the parents. While parents may continue to exercise their PR, provided that their actions are not incompatible with the care order,[74] the local authority can limit parents' powers to make major decisions about their child, if 'they are satisfied that it is necessary to do so in order to safeguard or promote the child's welfare'.[75]
- Accordingly, the local authority 'effectively holds a "trump" card, which it can choose to play, in the decision-making process in relation to a child in care'[76] (for example, deciding where that adolescent is to live). Notwithstanding such powers, the courts have recognised that in some cases where the local authority and parents disagree, the matter should be determined by the court.[77] Such cases 'chiefly concern decisions with profound or enduring consequences for the child',[78] which in relation to medical

72 Detailed guidance on the proceedings involved in seeking such orders provided in the DfE's *Court orders and pre-proceedings: for local authorities*. The guidance notes (at p23) that a) a care order automatically discharges a CAO (or any other order made under CA 1989 s8), a supervision order, and education supervision order or a school attendance order and brings wardship to an end; and b) a care order is automatically discharged by the making of a SGO or a CAO dealing with the living arrangements of a child and is suspended by the making of a placement order and will be revived if the placement order is revoked.

73 CA 1989 s22. See also *Court orders and pre-proceedings* p23.

74 *The Children Act 1989 guidance and regulations Volume 2: care planning, placement and case review* ('Care Planning Guidance'), June 2015, para 1.22; referring to CA 1989 ss2(8) and 33(3)(b).

75 CA 1989 s33(4).

76 *Re C (children) (child in care: choice of forename)* [2016] EWCA Civ 374 at [59]. See CA 1989 s33(3), (4) and (5). See also *Court orders and pre-proceedings* p23. See CA 1989 s33(6) and (7) for limits to the decision-making powers of local authorities.

77 *Re C (children) (child in care: choice of forename)* [2016] EWCA Civ 374 at [104]. The court considered that there will also be issues that represent a 'serious invasion' of the parent's rights under the right to private and family life under Article 8 of the European Convention on Human Rights (ECHR).

78 *Re H (a child) (parental responsibility: vaccination* [2020] EWCA Civ 664 at [27].

treatment 'may well be a matter of life and death'.[79] While there are no set criteria for such cases, the Court of Appeal's decision in *Re H (a child) (parental responsibility: vaccination)* makes clear that they do not include disagreements about *any* medical treatment.[80] Whereas Sir James Munby, President of the Family Division observed that local authorities would 'usually be ill-advised' to rely on CA 1989 s33 to authorise medical treatment that is opposed by parents with PR,[81] in *Re H*, Lady Justice King (giving judgment for the court) thought it likely that the President was referring to cases concerning 'desperately ill' children adding that if such comments related to *any* medical treatment, 'with the greatest of respect, I would disagree'.[82]

- The local authority will be the adolescent's NR (unless the adolescent is married or in a civil partnership, in which case the NR will be the adolescent's spouse / civil partner).[83]

Delegation of parental responsibility

5.15 Although those with PR may not 'surrender' or transfer any part of their PR to someone else, they can delegate their responsibilities to others.[84]

5.16 The Department for Education (DfE) 2015 guidance *The Children Act 1989 guidance and regulations. Volume 2: care planning, placement and case review* ('Care Planning Guidance') includes guidance to local

79 *Re C (children) (child in care: choice of forename)* [2016] EWCA Civ 374 at [98]. The court also noted that the issues in dispute are likely to engage parents' rights under the right to private and family life under ECHR Article 8 – see discussion at [72]–[77].

80 In relation to vaccinations, the Court of Appeal held that unless there are concerns that it is not in the child's best interests to do so it is 'neither necessary nor appropriate' for a local authority to apply to court where the child's parents object to their child's immunisation.

81 *AB (a child)* [2018] EWFC 3 at [24(iii)]; referring to *Barnet LBC v AL and others* [2017] EWHC 125 (Fam), [2017] 4 WLR 53, at [32], and the discussion in *Re C (children: power to choose forenames)* [2016] EWCA Civ 374, [2017] 1 FLR 487, at [92]–[95].

82 *Re H* at [67].

83 MHA 1983 s27.

84 CA 1989 s2(10).

authorities on delegation in relation to looked after children.[85] It divides decisions into three categories:

1) The first concern day-to-day parenting, eg routine decisions about health/hygiene, education or leisure activities (which should in most cases[86] be delegated to the child's carer (and/or the child if they can take any of these decisions themselves)).
2) The second concerns routine but longer-term decisions, such as school choice (the involvement of parents and others will depend on the circumstances).
3) The third category of decisions are described as being:

   > . . . likely to be more serious and far reaching. Where the child is voluntarily accommodated the child's birth parents or others with PR should make these decisions. Where the child is under a care order or emergency protection order, decisions may be made by the birth parents or others with PR, which includes the local authority, depending on the decision and the circumstances. Such decisions should, however, always take account of the wishes and feelings of the child and their carer.[87]

   It is suggested that the admission of an adolescent to hospital for mental health care is likely to fall within this third category.[88] The involvement of parents of adolescents who are subject to care orders in the assessment procedures for admission under the MHA 1983 is considered at para 6.43.

85 Care Planning Guidance paras 3.196–3.215. In *Williams v Hackney* [2018] UKSC 37 when considering CA 1989 s20, Lady Hale noted at [39]:

> . . . it may be confusing to talk of parental 'consent' to the removal (or accommodation) of her child. If a parent does agree to this, she is simply delegating the exercise of her parental responsibility for the time being to the local authority. Any such delegation must be real and voluntary.

86 See Care Planning Guidance para 3.209 for when decisions might not be delegated to the carer.

87 Care Planning Guidance para 3.211.

88 In relation to medical treatment, the Care Planning Guidance (at para 3.215) refers to *Reference guide to consent for examination or treatment*, second edition, DoH, 2009. The decision-making role of parents in relation to admission to hospital and treatment for mental disorder are discussed in chapter 3.

Nearest relative

Overview

5.17 The person identified as the adolescent's NR has a significant role in relation to the application of the MHA 1983.[89] For example:

- An adolescent's NR must be informed if the adolescent is admitted to hospital under MHA 1983 s2.[90]
- The approved mental health professional (AMHP) must consult an adolescent's NR before making an application for the adolescent's admission to hospital under MHA 1983 s3[91] and if the NR objects, the application for admission cannot go ahead unless the NR is displaced.[92]
- The NR can seek to discharge the adolescent from hospital[93] (albeit the adolescent's 'responsible clinician' can prevent this by issuing a 'barring certificate'[94]).
- Unless the adolescent requests otherwise, the NR must be given information about the adolescent's rights, such as the right to apply to the Mental Health Tribunal to be discharged from detention.[95]

Identifying the nearest relative

Overview

5.18 For many adolescents, the NR will be one of their parents. However, this should not be assumed. The MHA 1983 sets out a complex array of rules for identifying the NR which are linked to the individual's

89 *R (M) v Secretary of State for Health* [2003] EWHC 1094 (Admin) at [4]–[6]. See also *TW v Enfield LBC* [2014] EWCA Civ 362, [2014] 1 WLR 3665 at [49]. See *Reference guide to the Mental Health Act 1983* (MHA Reference Guide'), DoH, 2015, Table 5: The rights of the nearest relative, pp22 and 23. The functions of the NR are considered in subsequent chapters.

90 The approved mental health professional (AMHP) must inform the NR 'within a reasonable time after the application' (see MHA 1983 s11(3)).

91 MHA 1983 s11(4). See paras 6.36–6.43 for further information on the role of the AMHP

92 MHA 1983 s29 The court will only do so if the grounds under MHA 1983 s29(3)(c) are met.

93 MHA 1983 s23.

94 MHA 1983 s25 (stating that if discharged the patient 'would be likely to act in a manner dangerous to other persons or himself').

95 MHA 1983 s132(4). The role of the mental health tribunal is discussed in chapter 8.

personal circumstances. As these are likely to change over time, the identity of the adolescent's NR may also change and must be determined by considering the adolescent's current situation.

5.19 Whereas for adults MHA 1983 s26 governs the identification of the NR, for those aged under 18 additional provisions are set out in MHA 1983 ss27 and 28. Significantly, the provisions for determining an adolescent's NR under MHA 1983 s26 will only be relevant if neither s27 (where a care order is in place) nor s28 (court orders concerning private law arrangements) do not apply.

The nearest relative and 'relatives': MHA 1983 s26

5.20 MHA 1983 s26(1) sets out a hierarchy of relatives who might be the patient's NR, depending on a range of factors specified in MHA 1983 s26(2)–(7). The list is as follows:

- 'husband or wife, or civil partner';
- 'son or daughter';
- 'father or mother';
- 'brother or sister';
- 'grandparent';
- 'grandchild';
- 'uncle or aunt';
- 'nephew or niece'.

5.21 The NR will be the person who is highest up in the list, and if there are two or more people in the same category, it will be the eldest person. For example, unless the adolescent is married or in a civil partnership, the next relevant category will be 'father or mother'[96] and the NR will be the elder of the two. However, as explained below, if the adolescent's parents are not married, the father must have acquired PR if he is to be included in the list as 'father'.[97]

5.22 The provisions set out in MHA 1983 s26(2)-(7) must also be considered, as these may affect who is the NR. These include factors such as who the adolescent is living with (and how long for) and which, if any of the relatives on the section 26(1) list of relatives is providing care for the adolescent.

96 The category of 'son or daughter' would not be relevant because even if the adolescent had a child, that child would be aged under 18 and therefore could not be the nearest relative – see MHA 1983 s26(5).

97 MHA 1983 s26(2).

The unmarried father and the nearest relative: MHA 1983 s26(2)

5.23 If the adolescent's parents are not married to each other, the father will need to have acquired PR in order to be included as 'father' in the list of relatives set out in section 26(1). Table 5.1 above sets out the various ways in which unmarried fathers may gain PR.

5.24 It is possible for unmarried fathers who do not have PR to become the NR. This is either by:

- the NR delegating the power to him (see paras 5.29–5.31 below);
- being appointed by the court as acting NR under MHA 1983 s29; or
- the 'five-year rule' under MHA 1983 s26(7) (see below).

5.25 The 'five-year rule' (MHA 1983 s26(7)) provides that individuals who do not fall within any of the categories of relatives listed under MHA 1983 s26(1) can be added to that list if they have been 'ordinarily residing' with the patient 'for a period of not less than five years'.[98] It is possible, therefore, for a father to become the adolescent's NR even though he does not have PR. This could happen, for example, where the adolescent's mother has died and the adolescent has been living with the adolescent's father for over five years.[99]

Determining an adolescent's nearest relative

5.26 The table below considers some common scenarios and the relevance of the MHA 1983 provisions for determining an adolescent's nearest relative.

98 MHA 1983 s26(7).

99 This is by virtue of the operation of MHA 1983 s26(7) (which places the person at the bottom of the list of relatives) and (4) (which give preference to relatives who 'ordinarily reside with' or 'care for' the patient). In cases where the adolescent's mother is also living with the adolescent, the mother would be the NR because she is higher up the list than the father (s26(7)).

Table 5.2

Scenario	MHA 1983	Who is the adolescent's nearest relative?
The adolescent is subject to a care order, or interim care order[100]	MHA 1983 s27	The local authority responsible for the care order/ interim care order will be the NR *unless* the adolescent is married or in a civil partnership. • The local authority can delegate the functions of the NR to a member of staff.[101] • It will therefore be necessary to ascertain the details of the person who is undertaking the NR's role on behalf of the local authority.
A guardian or special guardian has been appointed under the CA 1989[104]	MHA 1983 s28	The guardian(s)[102] or the special guardian(s) will be the NR.[103] • Where there is more than one guardian or special guardian each of them will be deemed to be the NR.[105] • Note: the term 'guardian' under MHA 1983 s28 does not include a guardian appointed under MHA 1983 s7.[106]
A child arrangements order states that the adolescent is to live with the person(s) named in that order	MHA 1983 s28	The person(s) named in the child arrangements order will be the adolescent's NR.[107] • Such orders were previously referred to as 'residence orders', but now are sometimes referred to as 'lived with orders'. • Where there is more than person named in the child arrangements order, each person will be deemed to be adolescent's NR.[108]

100 See CA 1989 s31(11).

101 Mental Health (Hospital) (England) Regulations 2008 SI No 1184 reg 21 and Local Government Act 1972 s101 permit the local authority to arrange for the discharge of its functions to be undertaken by an officer of the local authority. Usually the Director of Children's services will undertake the role of the NR and if necessary, delegate this to another member of staff.

102 Appointed under CA 1989 s5.

103 Appointed under CA 1989 s14A.

104 MHA 1983 s28(2) provides that this is subject to MHA s26(3) which excludes certain individuals from being the NR, for example individuals aged under 18. It is difficult to see how any of these exceptions would be relevant to a person appointed to act as a guardian or special guardian.

105 MHA 1983 s28(1).

106 MHA 1983 s28(3).

107 MHA 1983 s28(2) provides that this is subject to MHA s26(3) which excludes certain individuals from being the NR. These exceptions are unlikely to be relevant where a CAO has been made.

108 MHA 1983 s28(1).

The adolescent is married or in a civil partnership	MHA 1983 s26(1)(a)	The adolescent's spouse or civil partner will be the NR. • The exception to this is if the adolescent is permanently separated from their spouse / civil partner (or one has deserted the other).[109] • Whereas in other cases the NR must be aged 18 or over, the adolescent's spouse / civil partner may be aged under 18.[110]
The adolescent's parents are not married who is the NR:	MHA 1983 ss26(1)(b) and 26(2)	Further information will be required to ascertain • If MHA 1983 s27 or s28 apply, they will determine who is the NR. • If the NR is either the mother or the father, determining which one is the NR will depend on: – whether the father has PR (see para 5.23 above); – (if the father has PR) who is the eldest as between the father and mother[111] (in contrast to MHA 1983 s28, under s26 there is only one NR at any given time).
The adolescent is living with one parent and a step-parent the NR:		Further information will be required to ascertain who is • Step-parents are not included in the list of relatives in MHA 1983 s26(1) so further inquiry would need to be made to determine whether the step-parent might be the adolescent's NR, for example, whether the step-parent has adopted the adolescent.[112]

Nearest relatives and MHA 1983 s28

5.27 Individuals who have been appointed to act as the adolescent's guardian appointed under the CA 1989 (ie guardians appointed under section 5 or 'special guardians' appointed under s14A[113]) or are named in a child arrangement order[114] will be the adolescent's NR.

5.28 Whereas the effect of the provisions in MHA 1983 s26 is that there can only be one NR for the patient at any one time, under MHA 1983 s28, two or more people can be the NR. For example, if the

109 MHA 1983 s26(5)(b).
110 MHA 1983 s26(5)(c).
111 MHA 1983 s26(3).
112 See ACA 2002 s46(1) and the MHA Reference Guide para 2.8.
113 CA 1989 s14A–14G. See box 5.2.
114 CA 1989 s8. See box 5.2.

adolescent is living with his grandparents in accordance with a child arrangement order, both being named on the order as the people with whom he is living, both will have PR and both will be his NR. In contrast, where an adolescent is living with her parents, both of whom have PR, only one (the eldest of the two) will be the NR.

Delegating the role of the nearest relative

5.29 The person who is identified as the NR under the MHA 1983 can delegate this role to somebody else but must do so in accordance with the procedures set out in Mental Health (Hospital, Guardianship and Treatment) (England) Regulations 2008 reg 24.[115] The role *cannot*be delegated to the following people:

- 'the patient';[116]
- a person deemed not to be the NR under MHA 1983 s26(5) (for example, a person aged under 18 years); or
- a person who has been displaced as the NR by the court under MHA 1983 s29.[117]

5.30 The delegation must be in writing[118] and the NR must 'immediately notify the patient' that another person has been authorised to undertake the NR's[119] as well as the hospital managers (if the patient is detained in hospital or subject to a community treatment order (CTO)), or the local authority and private guardian (if any) (if the patient is subject to guardianship).[120] The NR can revoke the delegation at any time but this must be in writing and the NR must inform the patient of this as well as the hospital managers (if the patient is detained in hospital or subject to a community treatment order (CTO)), or the local authority and private guardian (if any) (if the patient is subject to guardianship).[121]

115 SI 2008 No 1184.

116 This will be the adolescent: 'patient' is the term used in the MHA 1983 for individuals who are subject to the powers of the Act.

117 SI 2008 No 1184 reg 24(1)(a)–(c).

118 The MHA Reference Guide (p23) states that the authorisation must be signed and dated, must address whether it is time limited or until further notice and will not be completed until received and accepted by the new person.

119 SI 2008 No 1184 reg 24(7)(a).

120 SI 2008 No 1184 reg 24(7). It also provides that the hospital managers of the responsible hospital should be informed if the person is on a CTO, or the relevant local authority and private guardian (if any) if the person is subject to guardianship.

121 SI 2008 No 1184 reg 24(5), (6) and (7).

5.31 Although there is no statutory form for the delegation of the NR, the Department of Health's (DoH) 2015 *Reference guide to the Mental Health Act 1983* ('MHA Reference Guide') suggests the following form of wording:

> I [insert name] of [insert address] being the nearest relative of [insert patient's name and address] for the purposes of the Mental Health Act 1983, hereby delegate my powers of nearest relative to [insert name] of [insert address]. I confirm that [insert name] has consented to act as the nearest relative of [insert patient's name].[122]

Displacement of the nearest relative

5.32 MHA 1983 s29 sets out the circumstances in which the county court can displace the NR and appoint someone else to act as the NR, or appoint a person to act when there is no known NR.[123] The application to the court can be made by the 'the patient', 'any relative of the patient', 'any other person with whom the patient is residing' (or was residing before being admitted to hospital) or an AMHP.[124]

5.33 The grounds on which a NR can be displaced are set out in MHA 1983 s29(3) as follows:

> (a) that the patient has no nearest relative within the meaning of this Act, or that it is not reasonably practicable to ascertain whether he has such a relative, or who that relative is;
> (b) that the nearest relative of the patient is incapable of acting as such by reason of mental disorder or other illness;
> (c) that the nearest relative of the patient unreasonably objects to the making of an application for admission for treatment or a guardianship application in respect of the patient; . . .
> (d) that the nearest relative of the patient has exercised without due regard to the welfare of the patient or the interests of the public his power to discharge the patient . . . under this Part of this Act, or is likely to do so; or
> (e) that the nearest relative of the patient is otherwise not a suitable person to act as such.

122 DoH, 2015, Figure 5 p23.

123 MHA 1983 s29(2) lists who can make the application, which includes the patient, any relative of the patient and an approved mental health professional (AMHP). The MHA Code para 5.17 states that local authorities should have 'clear practical guidance to help AMHPs decide whether to make an application and how to proceed.

124 For role of the AMHP see chapter 6.

5.34 The MHA Code (paras 5.7–5.24) provides guidance on making an application to the court for the displacement of the NR and the appointment of another person to be NR, including the circumstances in which it might be appropriate for an AMHP to make an application to the court.[125] It should be noted that displacing a parent as the NR has no effect on that parent's PR.

Confidentiality and the nearest relative

5.35 Although various provisions of the MHA 1983 and regulations require information to be given to the NR, in most cases the disclosure of such information is subject to the patient's objection. The MHA Code states:

> 4.32 When a patient detained under the Act or subject to a CTO is given information, they should be told that the written information will also be supplied to their nearest relative, so that they can discuss their views about sharing this information and following this discussion, raise any concerns or object to the sharing of some or all of this information. There should be discussion with the patient at the earliest possible time as to what information they are happy to share and what they would like to be kept private.
>
> ...
>
> 4.35 These duties to inform nearest relatives are not absolute. In almost all cases, information is not to be shared if the patient objects.[126]

5.36 Such an approach is equally applicable to under-18s, given that the MHA 1983 makes no specific provisions for under-18s and the sharing of information with their NR.[127]

Wardship and the nearest relative

5.37 Although rare, wardship orders can be made by the High Court under its inherent jurisdiction. The effect of wardship was explained in *Re A (ward of court)*:

> Once a child is a ward of court, that child is under the continuous protection of the court, even after a final order has been made determining the issues in respect of that child. Once a child is a ward of court

125 See also the MHA Reference Guide paras 2.48–2.61.

126 See also MHA Code para 4.36 for the human rights implications for disclosing information to the NR without the patient's consent.

127 Confidentiality and sharing information with parents are considered at paras 2.96–2.103.

that child's place or country of residence or school cannot be changed without court order. The court can make various orders providing for the care of the child and access/contact and orders for the protection of the child. The court can order the return of the child to this jurisdiction.[128]

5.38 MHA 1983 s33 makes specific provision for under-18s who are subject to wardship, which include limitations on the role of the NR. AMHPs are not required to consult the NR prior to making an application for admission under MHA 1983 s3, nor can the NR object to such an application being made.[129] In addition:

> Where a ward is liable to be detained in hospital on the basis of an application for admission, or is a patient on a community treatment order (CTO), the powers of the nearest relative to discharge the patient, or to apply to the Tribunal (where applicable) may only be exercised with the leave of the court. They may also be exercised by the court itself.[130]

128 [2017] EWHC 1022 at [51].

129 MHA 1983 s33(1) Applications for admission under MHA 1983 s3 are discussed at paras 6.13–6.26.

130 MHA 1983 s33(2) as summarised by the MHA Reference Guide para 12.14. See subsequent chapters for the procedures for admission (chapter 6), discharge from detention (chapter 8) and community treatment orders (chapter 10).

CHAPTER 6

Admission to hospital and the Mental Health Act 1983

continued

Introduction

6.1 The Mental Health Act (MHA) 1983 sets out the circumstances in which individuals, of any age,[1] can be detained in hospital for assessment and/or treatment for 'mental disorder' without their consent. Such powers will be relevant where children and young people aged under 18 ('adolescents') require in-patient psychiatric care and (for whatever reason) this cannot be authorised by any of the 'informal' legal routes discussed in chapter 3 above.

6.2 Another crucially important feature of adolescent in-patient psychiatric care is the type and location of the services that will be provided. This will be of relevance to adolescents who are admitted to hospital informally, as well as those detained under the MHA 1983.

6.3 Accordingly, this chapter covers the following two broad areas:

- *admission to hospital under MHA 1983 Part 2:*[2] setting out the process for determining whether the criteria for admission to hospital under the MHA 1983 are met; and
- *provision of in-patient psychiatric care:* providing an overview of Child and Adolescent Mental Health Services (CAMHS) in-patient provision; the age-appropriate environment duty under MHA 1983 s131A; and out-of-area placements.

6.4 Guidance on the application of the MHA 1983 is provided by the *Mental Health Act 1983: Code of Practice* ('MHA Code').[3] Chapter 14 (Applications for detention in hospital) and chapter 19 (Children and young people under the age of 18) of the MHA Code are of particular relevance to the procedures for the adolescents' admission to hospital under the MHA 1983.

1 See V Thomas and others, 'The application of mental health legislation in younger children' (2015) BJPsy Bulletin 39 302 in which the authors discuss a case in which an eight-year-old boy was detained under the MHA 1983.

2 The powers of the courts to order the admission to hospital of those involved in criminal proceedings under MHA 1983 Part 3 are not covered in this book. For the relationship between the MHA 1983 and court orders under Children Act 1989 s25, see para 3.22.

3 *Mental Health Act 1983: Code of Practice,* Department of Health (DoH), 2015('MHA Code').

Admission to hospital under MHA 1983 Part 2[4]

Introduction

6.5 For the past three years, figures provided by NHS Digital in its annual reports on the use of the MHA 1983[5] show an increase in the numbers of detentions of under-18s. For the years 2017/18 and 2018/19 these figures have been disaggregated by gender and ethnicity. In relation to gender, as noted in table 6.1, the figures show that for each of these years nearly two-thirds of the detentions of under-18s relate to girls or young women.[6]

Table 6.1: Detentions of under-18s

	2016/17	2017/18	2018/19
Under-18s	1,044	1,177 (male: 384; female: 746)	1,241 (male: 356; female: 764)
16–17s	722	799 (male: 273; female: 494)	808 (male: 248; female: 479)
Under-16s	322	378 (male: 111; female: 252)	433 (male: 108; female: 285)

6.6 Given that individuals will only fall within the scope of the MHA 1983 if they are considered to have a 'mental disorder', the definition

4 Coronavirus Act 2020 s10 and Sch 8 make provisions for modifications to these procedures (see para 3 'Applications for compulsory admission to hospital for assessment or treatment' and para 4 'Applications for compulsory admission of patients already in hospital'). However, as at September 2020 these are not in force. Guidance on the implications of the coronavirus (COVID-19) on the legal framework for the mental health care of people receiving mental health services is provided in NHS (Publications approval reference: 001559) *Legal guidance for mental health, learning disability and autism, and specialised commissioning services supporting people of all ages during the coronavirus pandemic* 19 May 2020 version 2 ('the COVID-19 legal guidance).

5 *Mental Health Act statistics: annual figures,* available from NHS Digital's website: https://digital.nhs.uk/data-and-information/publications/statistical/mental-health-act-statistics-annual-figures. The data collected on detentions is incomplete (so the true figures may be higher).

6 There appears to be no commentary or explanation for this significant difference between genders. For the breakdown of ethnicity see Table 1e in NHS Digital, Mental Health Statistics 2017-18 and NHS Digital, Mental Health Statistics 2018-19 (https://digital.nhs.uk/data-and-information/publications/statistical/mental-health-act-statistics-annual-figures).

of this term is considered first,[7] followed by the procedures for determining whether the relevant criteria are met and an application for the adolescent's admission under the MHA 1983 should be made, and if so, under which section of the MHA 1983.

Mental disorder: the gateway to the Mental Health Act 1983

Definition of 'mental disorder'

6.7 The MHA 1983 defines 'mental disorder' as 'any disorder or disability of the mind' (MHA 1983 s1(2)). Accordingly, its potential application is extremely broad. However, as discussed below (paras 6.13–6.16), determining that an adolescent has a mental disorder will not in itself be sufficient to justify that adolescent's detention under the Act, as this requires further criteria to be met.

6.8 Furthermore, the expansive definition of 'mental disorder' is narrowed somewhat as follows (explained below):

1) exclusion of dependence on alcohol or drugs from the definition of mental disorder (MHA 1983 s1(3));
2) the 'learning disability qualification' (MHA 1983 s1(2A) and (2B)); and
3) mental disorder to be a 'clinically recognised condition' (MHA Code paras 2.4–2.8, figure 1).

Exclusion of dependence on alcohol or drugs from the definition of mental disorder (MHA 1983 s1(3))

6.9 The effect of this exclusion is that no one can be detained under the MHA 1983 on the basis of their alcohol or drug dependence alone. However, this would not prevent adolescents (or adults) being detained under the MHA 1983 in cases where their drug or alcohol dependence is 'accompanied by, or associated with a mental disorder' or related to their use, such as associated psychotic disorder or acute intoxication.[8]

7 MHA 1983 s1: 'The provisions of this Act shall have effect with respect to the reception, care and treatment of mentally disordered patients, the management of their property and other related matters'. However, the management of property and affairs of patients (MHA 1983, Part 7) was repealed by the Mental Capacity Act (MCA) 2005.

8 See MHA Code paras 2.9–2.13.

The 'learning disability qualification' (MHA 1983 s1(2A) and (2B))

6.10 The effect of this provision (referred to as the 'learning disability qualification'), is that no one with a learning disability (whatever their age) can be detained under s3[9] unless their learning disability 'is associated with abnormally aggressive or seriously irresponsible conduct on his part'.[10] This means:

- Adolescents who have a learning disability (defined as 'a state of arrested or incomplete development of the mind which includes significant impairment of intelligence and social functioning'[11]) will fall within the MHA 1983 definition of mental disorder. Whereas this is sufficient for their admission under MHA 1983 section 2 (if the other section 2 criteria are met), they can only be admitted under section 3 if the learning disability qualification is met. MHA Code chapter 2, which provides guidance on the definition of mental disorder, explains:

  > Someone with a learning disability and no other form of mental disorder may not be detained for treatment or made subject to guardianship or a community treatment order (CTO) unless their learning disability is accompanied by abnormally aggressive or seriously irresponsible conduct on their part.[12]

- It is possible for adolescents with autistic spectrum disorders to meet the criteria for detention under the MHA 1983 s3 'without having any other form or mental disorder, even if the autism is not associated with abnormally aggressive or seriously irresponsible conduct'. This is because the learning disability qualification does not apply to individuals with Autistic spectrum disorders (including Asperger's syndrome).[13] However, the MHA Code considers that compulsory treatment in a hospital setting 'is rarely likely to be helpful' to people with autism and that less restrictive means of providing care should be found.[14]

9 The learning disability qualification also applies to guardianship under MHA 1983 s7 (see paras 10.82–10.85) and certain patients covered by Part 3.

10 MHA 1983 ss2A and 2B.

11 MHA 1983 s1(4). See also the MHA Code paras 20.4–20.6.

12 MHA Code para 2.15.

13 MHA Code para 2.17.

14 MHA Code para 20.19. See Joint Committee on Human Rights *The detention of young people with learning disabilities and/or autism*, Second report of session 2019, HC 121 HL Paper 10 p52. para 9 for concerns about the application of the MHA 1983 to young people with learning disabilities and/or autism.

6.11 Guidance on determining whether a person's learning disability is associated with abnormally aggressive behaviour or seriously irresponsible conduct, is provided in MHA Code chapter 20 (paras 20.7–20.17).

Mental disorder to be a 'clinically recognised condition' (MHA Code paras 2.4–2.8, figure 1)

6.12 The presence of mental disorder should be determined 'in accordance with good clinical practice and accepted standards of what constitutes such a disorder or disability'.[15] The non-exhaustive list of 'Clinically recognised conditions which could fall within the definition of mental disorder' includes conditions that may affect adolescents, for example:

- depression, anxiety; phobic disorders; obsessive compulsive disorders; post-traumatic stress disorder (PTSD); personality disorders;[16] mental and behavioural disorders caused by psychoactive substance use; eating disorders; and autistic spectrum disorders (ASD); and
- the broad category of 'behavioural and emotional disorders of children and young people' is also listed.[17]

Admission to hospital under MHA 1983 ss2 and 3

Overview

6.13 There are no age-related criteria for the compulsory admission to hospital under MHA 1983 Part 2 – commonly known as 'sectioning'. Like adults, an application for an adolescent's detention under the MHA 1983 can only be made if the criteria under sections 2 or 3 are met. The MHA 1983 also provides for the 'admission for assessment in cases of emergency' (under s4) and the 'holding powers' of doctors (under s5(2)) and of nurses (under s5(4)).

15 MHA Code para 2.4

16 MHA Code chapter 21 provides guidance on the assessment and treatment of people with personality disorders.

17 MHA Code para 2.5, Figure 1. See also M Mitchell, 'The Diagnosis and Management of Complex Mental Illness in Young People' 150, in A Harbour *Children with mental disorder and the law: a guide to law and practice*, Jessica Kingsley Publishers, 2008; and S Bailey and M Shooter, *The young mind: an essential guide to mental health for young adults, parents and teachers*, Bantam Press, 2009, Part 5 'Serious disorders: context, causes and effects'.

Criteria for admission

6.14 The criteria for 'admission for assessment' under MHA 1983 s2 and for admission for treatment under section 3 are set out in box 6.1 below. For the reasons explained at para 6.30 above, an adolescent's first compulsory admission to hospital for psychiatric care is likely to be under MHA 1983 s2.

> **Box 6.1: Criteria for admission under MHA 1983 ss2 and 3**
>
> *MHA 1983 s2 ('admission for assessment'):* For an adolescent to be admitted under s2, it must be determined that the following criteria set out under s2(2) are met:
>
> (2) An application for admission for assessment may be made in respect of a patient on the grounds that–
> (a) he is suffering from mental disorder of a nature or degree which warrants the detention of the patient in a hospital for assessment (or for assessment followed by medical treatment) for at least a limited period; and
> (b) he ought to be so detained in the interests of his own health or safety or with a view to the protection of other persons.
>
> Detention under s2 lasts for up to 28 days.[18] This cannot be renewed although the period of detention can be extended in certain cases concerning patients absent without leave (AWOL)[19] and the displacement of the nearest relative.[20]
>
> *MHA 1983 s3 ('admission for treatment'):* For an adolescent to be admitted under s3, it must be determined that that the following criteria set out under s3(2) are met:
>
> An application for admission for treatment may be made in respect of a patient on the grounds that–
> (a) he is suffering from mental disorder of a nature or degree which makes it appropriate for him to receive medical treatment in a hospital; and
> (b) [repealed]

18 MHA 1983 s2(4).

19 MHA 1983 ss18 and 21(1) (the patient returns to hospital within the final week of the s2 detention).

20 MHA 1983 s29(4). The two cases are: s29(3)(c) (the nearest relative has unreasonably objected to the admission under s3) and s29(3)(d) (the nearest relative has sought to discharge the patient under MHA 1983 s23 'without due regard to the welfare of the patient or the interests of the public').

(c) it is necessary[21] for the health or safety of the patient or for the protection of other persons that he should receive such treatment and it cannot be provided unless he is detained under this section; and
(d) appropriate medical treatment[22] is available for him.

Detention under MHA 1983 s3 can be for a period of up to six months. It can be renewed for another six months, and thereafter for a year at a time, in accordance with section 20 (see paras 6.51–6.53 below).[23]

Nature and degree

6.15 Both MHA 1989 ss2 and 3 refer to the 'nature' and 'degree' of the person's mental disorder. The MHA Code states that both 'nature' (chronicity and prognosis of the mental disorder, as well as the patient's response to receiving treatment for that disorder) and 'degree' (current manifestation of the disorder) require consideration.[24]

Learning disability qualification

6.16 In relation to the criteria for admission under s3, the learning disability qualification noted above (para 6.10) applies.[25]

Procedures for admission to hospital under MHA 1983 ss2 and 3

Overview

6.17 In cases where it has been determined that an adolescent requires admission to hospital under MHA 1983 s2 or s3, an application,

21 The use of the word 'necessary' in s3, is regarded as a higher threshold than 'ought' in s2. See S Johnston, S Miles and Dr C Royston, *Mental Health Tribunal Handbook*, LAG, 2015, paras 20.20 and 20.24; and R Jones, *Mental Health Act Manual*, 23rd edn, Sweet & Maxwell, 2020 para 1-073.

22 Defined in MHA 1983 s3(4) as 'medical treatment which is appropriate in his case, taking into account the nature and degree of the mental disorder and all other circumstances of his case'. R Jones *Mental Health Act Manual*, 23rd edn, Sweet & Maxwell, 2020, para 1-080 notes the 'circularity' of this definition. Similarly, P Bartlett and R Sandland, *Mental health law: policy and practice*, 4th edn, OUP, 2014, p254 note that the effect of this provision is that 'appropriate treatment is appropriate if it is appropriate'.

23 MHA 1983 s20.

24 MHA Code para 14.6, reflecting *R v Mental Health Review Tribunal for the South Thames Region ex p Smith* 47 (1999) BMLR 104 at 109.

25 MHA 1983 s1(2A).

which must be supported by two medical recommendations,[26] will be made to the managers of the hospital in which the adolescent is to be detained.[27]

The applicant

6.18 Usually, the applicant will be an approved mental health professional (AMHP).[28] Although it would also be possible for the adolescent's 'nearest relative' (NR) (see paras 5.17–5.28) to make the application,[29] it is rare for this to happen. It is considered more appropriate for AMHPs to be the applicant given their professional training and knowledge of the legislation and local resources.[30] Whoever makes the application (whether it is the AMHP or the NR), that person must have personally seen the adolescent within the period of 14 days ending on the date of the application.[31]

The Mental Health Act assessment

6.19 The objective of the MHA assessment is 'to determine whether the criteria for detention are met and, if so, whether an application for detention should be made'.[32]

6.20 Unless there is good reason for undertaking separate assessments 'patients, where possible should be seen jointly by the AMHP and at least one of the two doctors involved in the assessment'.[33] Both doctors should discuss the patient's case with the AMHP.[34] The specific responsibilities of the AMHP are explained at paras 6.36–6.43 below.

26 The application and the supporting medical recommendations must all be completed in the prescribed form, see the Mental Health (Hospital, Guardianship and Treatment) (England) Regulations 2008 SI No 1184 reg 4(1).

27 MHA 1983 s11(2).

28 An AMHP is a professional (usually a social worker but could also be a nurse, occupational therapist or psychologist) who has been approved by a local social services authority as having 'appropriate competence in dealing with persons suffering from mental disorder' (MHA 1983 s114(3)).

29 MHA 1983 s11(1).

30 MHA Code para 14.30.

31 MHA 1983 s11(5).

32 MHA Code para 14.33.

33 MHA Code para 14.45. See the COVID-19 Legal Guidance on conducting assessments through the use of video pp20–32 (including with under-18s (pp29–30) and those with learning disability and autism (pp30–31).

34 MHA Code para 14.46.

Medical recommendations

6.21 The application must be based on the written recommendations of two doctors.[35] One of the doctors must be approved under MHA 1983 s12 as having 'special experience in the diagnosis or treatment of mental disorder' and one of the doctors must 'if practicable', have previous acquaintance of the patient.[36]

6.22 The medical recommendations (which can be joint or separate[37]) must be signed on, or before the date of the application and be given by doctors who have 'personally examined' the adolescent 'either together or separately'.[38] If the doctors examined the person separately, no more than five days must have elapsed between the days on which these examinations took place.[39]

Importance of ensuring specialist input

6.23 At least one of the assessors (either one of the doctors or the AMHP) should be a CAMHS professional. Where this is not possible, the AMHP should have access to an AMHP with experience of working in CAMHS and the doctors 'should consult a CAMHS clinician as soon as possible and involve them as closely as the circumstances of the case allows'.[40] Specialist clinicians may need to be involved if adolescents have additional needs, for example, learning disabilities.[41]

Consideration of potential alternatives to detention under the MHA 1983

6.24 The adolescent should only be admitted to hospital under the MHA 1983 if this is the least restrictive option.[42] The MHA Code states that in determining 'whether it is necessary to detain patients, doctors and AMHPs must always consider the alternative ways of providing

35 MHA 1983 ss2(3) and 3(3).
36 MHA 1893 s12(2). See also MHA Code para 14.73.
37 MHA 1983 s11(7).
38 MHA 1983 s12(1).
39 MHA 1983 s12(1).
40 MHA Code para 19.73.
41 MHA Code para 19.73.
42 MHA Code para 14.7 states that consideration 'must be given to whether there are alternative means of providing the care and treatment which the patient requires'. See also *AM v South London and Maudsley NHS Foundation Trust and Secretary of State for Health* [2013] UKUT 0365 at [15].

the treatment or care they need'.[43] It also notes that 'a proper assessment cannot be done without considering alternative means of providing care and treatment' and that 'AMHPs and doctors should, as far as possible in the circumstances, identify and liaise with services which may potentially be able to provide alternatives to admission to hospital, such as crisis and home treatment teams'.[44]

6.25 AMHPs can only make the application if satisfied 'that detention in a hospital is in all the circumstances of the case the most appropriate way of providing the care and medical treatment of which the patient stands in need'.[45] Regulations under the MHA 1983 require the medical recommendations to state 'why informal treatment is not appropriate'.[46]

6.26 For MHA 1983 s3, the doctors must also 'say whether other methods of treatment or care (eg out-patient treatment or social services) are available and, if so, why they are not appropriate'.[47] Accordingly, it will be necessary to consider whether the adolescent could be supported by the provision of community-based services, such as crisis services,[48] as well as whether (if hospital admission is required) the adolescent can be admitted informally, for example, on the basis of the adolescent's consent.[49]

The nearest relative and applications for admission

6.27 The MHA Code notes that if the NR approaches doctors about the possibility of an application being made, they 'should advise the NR of their right to require a local authority to arrange for an AMHP to consider the patient's case'.[50] If the NR makes such a request but the

43 MHA Code para 14.11; see also para 14.7.

44 MHA Code para 14.34. These points are underpinned by the principle of proportionality (see para 1.20).

45 MHA 1983 s13(2).

46 See Mental Health (Hospital, Guardianship and Treatment) (England) Regulations 2008 SI No 1184 reg 4(1)(b)(ii) and Sch 1 (forms A3, A4, A7 and A8).

47 SI 2008 No 1184 (n127) reg 4(1)(b)(ii) and Sch 1 (forms A7 and A8). This reflects MHA 1983 s3(3)(b) which requires the medical recommendations to specify 'whether other methods of dealing with the patient are available and, if so, why they are not appropriate'.

48 MHA Code para 14.11.

49 Informal admission is considered in chapter 3.

50 MHA Code para 14.32.

AMHP decides not to make such an application, the AMHP must give the NR written reasons for this decision.[51]

Care, Education and Treatment Reviews

6.28 NHS England's policy on Care, Education and Treatment Reviews (CETRs) (see paras 2.91–2.95) will be relevant to adolescents who have a learning disability or autism, or both. One of the criteria for Standard 6.3 of the *Care, Education and Treatment Reviews for children and young people: code and toolkit* (which concerns the accessibility and availability of the report of the review)[52] states:

> When a child or young person has had a community CETR, that report will always be provided to doctors making a decision about any admission and/or detention to hospital and the Approved Mental Health Professional in the case of a detention.[53]

Determining whether MHA 1983 s2 or s3 should be applied

Introduction

6.29 In addition to considering the relevant criteria noted in box 6.1, the AMHP and doctors undertaking the assessment must have regard to the MHA Code, which provides advice on how to determine whether to use MHA 1983 s2 or s3.[54]

Admission under MHA 1983 s2

6.30 While subject to the particular circumstances of the case, it is likely that an adolescent's first admission to hospital under the MHA 1983 will be under section 2 (assessment, or assessment followed by treatment) given the advice in the MHA Code on the factors to consider when deciding between section 2 and section 3. The first two of the MHA Code's pointers for the appropriate use of section 2 are as follows:

51 MHA 1983 s13(4).

52 It states: 'Following the CETR, the commissioner will write a report about the review in words that all involved can understand. The commissioner will make sure the child or young person, their parent carers and others who need a copy get the report within two weeks.'

53 NHS England, April 2017, p26, para 6.3.6.

54 MHA 1983 s18(2D).

- 'the full extent of the nature and degree of the patient's condition is unclear'; and
- 'there is a need to carry out an initial assessment in order to formulate a treatment plan or to reach a judgment about whether the patient will accept treatment on a voluntary basis following admission'.[55]

6.31 For adolescents who have had previous admissions, the third scenario might also be relevant given that it refers to cases where:

> . . . there is a need to carry out a new in-patient assessment in order to re-formulate a treatment plan, or to reach a judgement about whether the patient will accept treatment on a voluntary basis.[56]

Admission under MHA 1983 s3

6.32 In line with the MHA Code's guidance, adolescents should be admitted under MHA 1983 s3 in two sets of circumstances.

6.33 The first is where the adolescent is already detained under MHA 1983 s2. As noted below, it is not possible to renew detention under section 2.[57]

6.34 The second type of case in which MHA 1983 s3 should be used is where:

> . . . the nature and current degree of the patient's mental disorder, the essential elements of the treatment plan to be followed and the likelihood of the patient accepting treatment as an informal patient are already sufficiently established to make it unnecessary to undertake a new assessment under section 2.[58]

6.35 Although the wording used by the MHA Code is not as explicit, it would appear therefore that MHA 1983 s3 should be used in cases where there is a clear treatment plan and it is also clear that the adolescent will not agree to the treatment being proposed. Whichever section is decided upon, the rationale for the decision 'should be clearly recorded'.[59]

55 MHA Code para 14.27.
56 MHA Code para 14.27.
57 MHA 1983 s2 cannot be renewed.
58 MHA Code para 14.28.
59 MHA Code para 14.29.

The role of the approved mental health professional

Overview

6.36 Before applying for an adolescent's admission to hospital under the MHA 1983, the AMHP must:

- interview the adolescent in a suitable manner;
- be satisfied that the criteria for detention under the MHA 1983 are met; and
- be satisfied that 'detention in hospital is in all the circumstances of the case the most appropriate way of providing the care and medical treatment of which the patient stands in need'.[60]

6.37 Unless local arrangements state otherwise, the AMHP will be responsible for the co-ordination of the adolescent's MHA assessment.[61] In doing so the AMHP will need to consider matters such as the adolescent's age, sex, disability and ethnicity and take steps to meet any communication needs, such as a signer or professional interpreter,[62] as well as assisting in securing the attendance of the person the adolescent wants to be present during the assessment.[63]

Duty to inform or consult the adolescent's nearest relative

6.38 The AMHP has significant duties in relation to the adolescent's NR and will therefore, as a first step, need to identify who that person is,[64] applying the relevant provisions of the MHA 1983. The rules for identifying the NR are set out in chapter 5.

6.39 Where the AMHP makes an application for an adolescent's admission to hospital under MHA 1983 s2, the AMHP must 'take such steps that are practicable' to inform the adolescent's NR that the application has been, or will be, made.[65] The AMHP must also inform the NR of their power to discharge the adolescent.[66] Similarly, where

60 MHA 1983 s13(2); and MHA Code para 14.49.

61 MHA Code para 14.41.

62 MHA Code paras 14.41–14.42.

63 MHA Code para 14.53.

64 MHA Code para 14.57.

65 MHA 1983 s11(3).

66 MHA 1983 s11(3). MHA Code para 14.58 notes that if different the carer should be informed that the application is to be (or has been made). For under-18s, this is likely to be the second parent. See also MHA Code para 19.38 which notes that those with parental responsibility 'should be consulted about the proposed decision concerning their child'.

an application under section 4 (admission for assessment in cases of emergency – see below) has been made, the AMHP should inform the NR of this at the time, or within a reasonable time afterwards.[67]

6.40 In practice, an adolescent's NR is likely to have been involved in the discussions prior to the decision to make an application for admission under the MHA 1983.

6.41 Where consideration is being given to detaining an adolescent under MHA 1983 s3, the AMHP must consult with the adolescent's NR before making the application unless such consultation 'is not reasonably practicable, or would cause unreasonable delay'.[68] If the NR objects, the admission under MHA 1983 s3 cannot go ahead unless the NR is displaced by the county court.[69] While such applications can be made in relation to under 18s, it is suggested that such action should be considered very carefully and only after every effort has been made to reach an agreement on the course of action with the NR. This is because, as discussed in chapter 5, the 'NR' is a different legal entity to that of 'parental responsibility': even if a parent is displaced as the NR, that parent will not lose the status of having 'parental responsibility'. Unless there are specific reasons for not doing so,[70] that parent will therefore need to be involved in the adolescent's ongoing in-patient care and after-care.

6.42 The MHA Code provides guidance to AMHPs on the factors to consider when determining whether or not to notify or consult with the NR notwithstanding the patient's request that they do not do so, which would need to be considered if an adolescent made such a request. The duties to consult and notify the NR are regarded as significant safeguards for patients[71] and decisions not to do so 'should not be taken lightly'.[72]

Liaising with local authority children's services

6.43 An important part of the AMHPs preparation for an adolescent's mental health assessment should be liaison with the local authority

67 MHA 1983 s11(3). MHA Code para 15.4. If the adolescent does not wish the nearest relative to be informed the points set out in the MHA Code at para 14.62 should be considered.

68 MHA 1983 s11(4). See MHA Code paras 14.59–14.62.

69 MHA 1983 s29(3)(c). See MHA Code paras 5.7–5.24 for guidance on making an application for the nearest relative's displacement.

70 Confidentiality is considered at paras 2.96–2.103. If there are safeguarding concerns this should be raised with the local authority's children's services.

71 *TW v Enfield LBC* [2014] EWCA Civ 362.

72 MHA Code para 14.62.

children's services.[73] While unfortunately this does not always happen in practice, the points listed in box 6.2 below highlight the potential benefits of such collaboration.

Box 6.2: Liaising with local authority children's services departments

Gathering information

In addition to providing general information about local services for children and young people, local authority children's services will be able to inform the AMHP the extent to which, if at all, they have had previous involvement with the adolescent. For example, children's services will be able to inform the AMHP if the adolescent:

- is a 'child in need';
- is subject to a 'child protection plan';
- is a 'looked after child';
- has special educational needs (SEN) and whether an education, health and care (EHC) plan is in place.

Children's services may also have information on whether a special guardianship order (SGO) or child arrangements order (CAO) has been made in relation to the adolescent, which will be relevant to identifying the NR. Further information on these arrangements is given at box 5.2.

Identifying who has parental responsibility and who is the nearest relative[74]

Information from children's services may help AMHPs in performing this task, specifically whether MHA 1983 s27 or s28 applies to the adolescent (see paras 5.26–5.28).

Consider with children's services whether they should attend the assessment[75]

This will be particularly important where the adolescent is subject to a care order given that the local authority will share parental responsibility with the adolescent's parent(s).

73 Anecdotally there are barriers to such liaison, most notably due to misunderstandings about rules on data protection. For guidance on information sharing (including a 'myth-busting guide') see *Information sharing Advice for practitioners providing safeguarding services to children, young people, parents and carers*, HM Government, July 2018.

74 MHA Code para 19.74.

75 MHA Code para 19.74.

Where adolescents are subject to a care order, the local authority responsible for that care order has the power to limit the extent of the parents' decision-making powers.[76] The MHA Code states that the local authority and those with parental responsibility 'should negotiate and agree who should be consulted about admission and/or treatment decisions'.[77] It is important to note that this statement is concerned with discussions that will need to be held with those individuals who have parental responsibility. This is a separate issue to that of the involvement of the NR.

The identification of the NR, the provision of information to the NR and the consultation with the NR where admission to hospital under MHA 1983 s3 is being considered are all governed by the MHA 1983. As such, they are not a matter of negotiation (see paras 6.38–6.42).

Where an adolescent is subject to a care order, the local authority will be the NR unless that adolescent is married or in a civil partnership.[78]

Notifications to local authorities

6.44 The MHA Code states that where a decision has been made to admit a looked after child to hospital under the MHA 1983, the AMHP should inform the responsible local authority as soon as possible[79] (albeit as noted above, where the adolescent is subject to a care order or interim care order, children's services should have been involved in making this decision). In addition, if the looked after child is placed out of area (see below) 'AMHPs should inform children's services in both the responsible authority and the local authority in which the child is placed'.[80]

6.45 In relation to adolescents with an EHC plan,[81] the MHA Code states that the local authority who maintains the plan should be informed, so that they can ensure that educational support continues to be provided'.[82] Although the MHA Code does not specify who

76 CA 1989 s33.
77 MHA Code para 19.13.
78 MHA 1983 s27.
79 MHA Code para 14.97.
80 MHA Code para 14.97.
81 Information on EHC plans are provided at paras 2.54–2.72.
82 MHA Code para 19.118.

should notify the relevant authority, presumably the hospital managers should do so.[83] NHS England includes the following statement in its specifications for CAMHS in-patient services:

> Where a young person has an EHC plan or statement of special educational needs, the education provider should contact the local authority responsible for drawing up the plan or statement to establish both the provision required whilst the young person is in the Tier 4 CAMHS and any additional funding available.[84]

Follow up where an application for admission to hospital is not made

6.46 The MHA Code notes that AMHPs 'should decide how to pursue any actions which their assessment indicates are necessary to meet the needs of the patient', adding that this might include 'referring the patient to social, health or other services'.[85] In relation to adolescents, this may lead to a referral to children's services and/or the local CAMHS.

Admission for assessment in cases of emergency: MHA 1983 s4

6.47 MHA 1983 s4 applies where the criteria for admission under s2 are met but 'the patient's need for urgent assessment outweighs the desirability of waiting for a second doctor'.[86] It should only be used in 'a genuine emergency'.[87] The MHA Code states that there should be evidence of 'immediate and significant risk of mental or physical harm to the patient or to others'; 'danger of serious harm to property', or 'a need for the use of restrictive interventions on a patient'.[88]

6.48 Both the application (made by either an AMHP or the adolescent's NR who must have seen the adolescent personally within the

83 Notifications under CA 1989 ss85 and 86 are discussed at paras 7.78–7.86. See also *Statutory visits to children with special educational needs and disabilities or health conditions in long-term residential settings – statutory guidance for local authorities, health bodies and health or educational establishments*, Department for Education (DfE) and DoH, November 2017, p12.

84 This para is included in the specifications that were updated in 2018, available at: www.england.nhs.uk/commissioning/spec-services/npc-crg/group-c/c03/.

85 MHA Code para 14.104.

86 MHA Code para 15.6.

87 MHA Code para 15.6.

88 MHA Code para 15.8.

previous 24 hours[89]) and the medical recommendation must state that:

- 'it is of urgent necessity for the patient to be admitted and detained under section 2'; and
- obtaining a second medical recommendation, as required by MHA 1983 s2, 'would involve undesirable delay'.[90]

6.49 The period of detention is for up to 72 hours. However, if a second medical recommendation is obtained within that time, the MHA 1983 s4 detention is 'converted' into detention under section 2, meaning that the patient may be detained for up to 28 days from the day they were admitted under section 4.[91]

6.50 If practicable, the medical recommendation is to be given by a doctor with previous acquaintance of the patient. Although there is no need for the first medical recommendation to be MHA 1983 s12 approved, if that doctor is not so approved, the doctor providing the second medical recommendation must be section 12 approved.[92]

Renewal of detention: MHA 1983 s20

6.51 Provided that the relevant criteria are met, an adolescents' detention in hospital under section 3 can be renewed for further 6 months and thereafter can be further renewed on a yearly basis under MHA 1983 s20,

6.52 The criteria for detention (MHA 1983 s20(4)) is the same as for s3 save that rather than the provision in s3(2)(c) (that the treatment cannot be provided unless the person 'is detained under this section'), s20(4)(c) requires that the treatment cannot be provided unless the person 'continues to be detained'. The procedure for renewal under MHA 1983 s20 is as follows:

- Two months before the adolescent's detention under MHA 1983 s3 is due to expire, the adolescent's responsible clinician (RC) must examine the adolescent to decide whether the criteria for renewal are met.

89 MHA 1983 s4(5).

90 MHA 1983 s4(2) and (3). See Forms A9–A11 (SI 2008/1184 regs 4(1)(e)(i) and (ii) and (f)).

91 *Reference guide to the Mental Health Act 1983*, DoH, 2015 ('MHA Reference Guide'), para 8.52.

92 MHA 1983 s4(4).

- If the RC considers that the criteria under MHA 1983 s20(4) are met, the RC must make a report to the hospital managers.[93] However, before doing so, the RC must consult one or more people who have been professionally concerned with the adolescent's medical treatment[94] and may not make the report to the hospital managers unless a person who has been professionally concerned with the adolescent's medical treatment (and who has a different profession to that of the RC), agrees with the RC that the criteria for renewal under MHA 1983 s20 are met and states this in writing.[95]

6.53 The MHA Reference Guide (at para 25.34) explains:

> Unless the managers decide to discharge the patient . . ., they must arrange for the patient to be told about the renewal. They must also take whatever steps are reasonably practicable to arrange for the person they think is the nearest relative to be informed, unless the patient has requested otherwise, or the patient does not have a nearest relative. They must do this as soon as practicable after the decision is made not to discharge the patient. Information given to nearest relatives must be in writing, but may be communicated by electronic means (eg email) if the nearest relative agrees.

Procedures for detention of patients already in hospital

6.54 Adolescents already receiving in-patient care can be detained in hospital for a limited period under the 'holding powers' under MHA 1983 s5 as set out below.

'Doctors' holding powers' (MHA 1983 s5(2))

6.55 MHA 1983 s5(2) applies to individuals who are receiving in-patient treatment (whether or not this is for mental disorder). They may be detained for up to 72 hours where the doctor or approved clinician in charge of their treatment (or the nominated deputy[96]) submits

93 The report is made on Form H5 (see SI 2008 No 1184 reg 13(1), (2) and (3)). For meaning of 'hospital managers' see 'the managers' under MHA 1983 s145. The MHA Code glossary (annex A) describes the 'hospital managers' as: 'The organisation (or individual) responsible for the operation of the Act in a particular hospital'. See also MHA Code paras 37.2–37.6.

94 MHA 1983 s20(5).

95 MHA 1983 s20(5A).

96 MHA 1983 s5(3) provides that the doctor or approved clinician 'may nominate one (but not more than one) person' to act on their behalf.

a report (Form H1[97]) to the hospital managers stating that an application for their admission to hospital under the MHA 1983 ought to be made.

Nurses holding powers (section 5(4))

6.56 MHA 1983 s5(4) applies to individuals who are receiving in-patient treatment for mental disorder. They may be detained in hospital for up to six hours if a nurse within the 'prescribed class'[98] authorises their detention on the grounds for doing so are that:

- 'the patient is suffering from mental disorder to such a degree that it is necessary for his health or safety or for the protection of others for him to be immediately restrained from leaving the hospital' and
- '. . . it is not practicable to secure the immediate attendance' of a doctor or approved clinician who can submit a report under MHA 1983 s5(2).

6.57 Guidance on these powers is provided in chapter 18 of the MHA Code.

Wards of court and applications for admission under the MHA 1983

6.58 Although such powers are used infrequently, under-18s may be made wards of court,[99] in which case MHA 1983 s33 will apply. This means:

- The leave of the High Court must be obtained before an application for admission to hospital under the MHA 1983 is made.
- The role of the NR is limited in that neither the AMHP's duty to consult the NR in relation to MHA 1983 s3, nor the NR's power to object to detention under s3 applies. The NR's powers under the MHA 1983 are exercised either by the court or with its leave.[100]

97 SI 2008 No 1184 Sch 1 reg 4(1)(g).

98 This means a nurse who is included in the Nursing and Midwifery Council's register of qualified nurses and is registered as practicing in field of mental health or learning disability (levels 1 or 2). See Mental Health (Nurses) (England) Order 2008SI No 1207 reg 2.

99 *Inherent jurisdiction (including wardship) proceedings*,Ministry of Justice Practice Direction 12D, January 2018.

100 Additional provisions are made in relation to guardianship under MHA 1983 s7 (MHA 1983 s33(3)) and community treatment orders (s33(4)).

Rights under the MHA 1983

6.59 Adolescents who have been detained under the MHA 1983 will have the following rights (explained below):

- information (MHA 1983 s132 'Duty of managers of hospitals to give information to detained patients);
- advocacy – independent mental health advocates (IMHAs) (MHA 1983 ss130A–130L);
- review of the decision to detain;
- treatment for mental disorder;
- monitoring the use of the MHA 1983 (s120); and
- complaints.

Information (MHA 1983 s132 'Duty of managers of hospitals to give information to detained patients)

6.60 The right to information under MHA s132 includes information (which must be given orally and in writing) about:

- the section of the MHA 1983 under which the adolescent is detained;
- their rights to apply to the First-tier (Mental Health) Tribunal ('the tribunal') and other powers of discharge (see chapter 8);
- treatment provisions under the Act (see chapter 7); and
- the role of the Care Quality Commission (CQC) (see below).

6.61 MHA Code chapter 4 provides further detail on the information to be given. Importantly, it also states that the reasons for the detention should be given ('the essential legal and factual grounds'), noting that this is necessary for 'the patient to be able to adequately and effectively challenge the grounds for their detention'.[101]

6.62 MHA Code chapter 19 highlights the importance of ensuring that under-18s are 'kept as fully informed as possible', receive 'clear and detailed information about their care' provided in an age-appropriate format.[102] It also notes that the views of under-18s should always be sought and taken seriously.[103]

101 MHA Code para 4.15. See also European Convention on Human Rights (ECHR) Article 5(2).

102 MHA Code para 19.5.

103 MHA Code para 19.5.

Advocacy – independent mental health advocates (MHA 1983 ss130A–130L)

6.63 The right to the support of an IMHA is available to 'qualifying patients'.[104] This term covers those detained under MHA 1983 s2 and s3, but not those detained under the shorter term sections (s4 and s5) noted above, nor those detained in a place of safety under s135(1) and s136 (see paras 10.92–10.99). Those who are subject to community treatment orders (CTOs) and guardianship (see chapter 10) are also 'qualifying patients'.[105]

6.64 IMHAs are 'specialist advocates who are trained specially to work within the framework of the Act and enable patients to participate in decision-making'.[106] Those entitled to the support of an IMHA must be informed of this right and how to get the help of an IMHA.[107]

6.65 MHA Code chapter 6 provides further information on the role of IMHAs. It emphasises that the involvement of an IMHA does not affect the right of the patient or the NR to seek legal advice, nor any entitlement to legal aid.[108]

Review of the decision to detain

6.66 Individuals who are detained under MHA 1983 ss2, 3 and 4[109] have the right to apply to the tribunal (an independent judicial body) and the hospital managers to seek their discharge from detention. Both have the power to discharge detained patients if they consider this appropriate to do so. Detained patients may apply to either one, or both.

6.67 The MHA Code provides information on the role of the tribunal (chapter 6) and the power of hospital managers to discharge detained patients (chapter 38). The powers of discharge and their application to adolescents is considered in chapter 8. The MHA Code states that patients and their NRs should be made aware that they may ask to be

104 MHA 1983 s130C(2)(a).

105 MHA 1983 s130C(2)(b) and (c).

106 Specialist IMHA services for under-18s are provided by organisations such as National Youth Advocacy Service (NYAS) and Coram Voice.

107 MHA 1983 s130D.

108 MHA Code para 6.14.

109 MHA 1983 s66(1) (a) and (b). Those detained under s4 are included under s661(a) as they are, like s2, 'an application for admission for assessment'. The tribunal and hospital managers' power of discharge do not apply to individuals detained under s5, s135 or s136.

discharged by the hospital managers and of the distinction between this right and the right to apply to a tribunal.[110]

Treatment for mental disorder

6.68 MHA 1983 Part 4 sets out the circumstances in which detained patients may be given treatment for mental disorder, including the provision of treatment without consent. These powers are considered in chapter 7.

Monitoring the use of the MHA 1983 (s120)

6.69 The CQC monitors the use of the powers under the MHA 1983. Individuals who are detained under the Act have the right to meet with representatives of the CQC in private[111] and may make a complaint to the CQC in relation to their care and treatment.[112]

Complaints

6.70 MHA Code chapter 4 includes guidance on complaints (see paras 4.53–4.68). It states that patients and anyone providing them with support 'must be supported to make a complaint if they think the safeguards of the Act are not being appropriately applied or they have concerns about the care and treatment being provided'.[113] Moreover: 'All providers should have clear complaints policies and procedures',[114] with information on how to make a complaint being readily available[115] and that qualifying patients may request the support of an IMHA in pursuing their complaint.[116]

6.71 As noted above, detained patients have the right to make a complaint about their treatment and care under the MHA 1983 to the CQC.

110 MHA Code para 38.11.

111 MHA 1983 s120(3).

112 MHA 1983 s120(4). See: information provided by the CQC ('Complain about the use of the Mental Health Act'): www.cqc.org.uk/contact-us/how-complain/complain-about-use-mental-health-act

113 MHA Code para 4.56.

114 MHA Code para 4.55.

115 MHA Code para 4.63.

116 MHA Code para 4.66.

The nearest relative: rights on admission

6.72 In relation to the adolescent's admission to hospital, the adolescent's NR has the following rights (explained below):

- right to request MHA assessment;
- right to make an application for admission;
- right to be informed if the adolescent is detained under MHA 1983 s2;
- right to be consulted prior to the AMHP making an application for the adolescent's admission under MHA 1983 s3 and to object to the admission;
- right to information about the adolescent's rights;
- right to be informed about the role of IMHAs;
- right to seek the adolescent's discharge from detention in hospital; and
- right to be given notice of the adolescent's discharge from detention.

Right to request MHA assessment

6.73 The local authority in which the adolescent is living must make arrangements for an AMHP to consider whether an application for the adolescent's admission to hospital should be made if requested to do so by the adolescent's NR, whether verbally or in writing. Although the NR cannot require such an application to be made, if the AMHP decides not to do so, the AMHP must give the NR written reasons for this decision.[117]

Right to make an application for admission

6.74 The NR could make an application for the adolescent's admission to hospital under the MHA 1983 (ss2, 3 and 4) and guardianship under s7.[118] However, such applications are rare[119] and the MHA Code advises that AMHPs are 'usually the more appropriate applicant'.[120]

117 MHA 1983 s13(4); and MHA Code paras 14.36 and 14.102.

118 Note that guardianship only applies to individuals aged 16 and over – see MHA 1983 s7(1).

119 MHA 1983 s11(1). This is of course subject to other requirements, including the need for two medical recommendations (s11(7)).

120 MHA Code para 14.30.

Right to be informed if the adolescent is detained under MHA 1983 s2

6.75 The AMHP must 'take such steps as are practicable' (see below) to inform the NR both of the adolescent's detention under MHA 1983 s2 and of the NR's power to seek the adolescent's discharge from detention.[121]

Right to be consulted prior to the AMHP making an application for the adolescent's admission under MHA 1983 s3 and to object to the admission:

6.76 The AMHP must consult with the NR unless it 'is not reasonably practicable or would cause unreasonable delay'.[122] Such consultation is regarded as a significant safeguard in the process for determining whether a person should be detained under the MHA 1983.[123] If the NR objects, the admission cannot go ahead unless the NR is displaced by the court under MHA 1983 s29.[124]

6.77 It is important to note that the NR's right to be informed (MHA 1983 s2) and consulted (s3) is subject to whether it is reasonably practicable to do so. The MHA Code notes:

> There may be cases where, although physically possible, it would not be reasonably practicable to inform or consult the nearest relative because the detrimental impact of this on the patient would interfere with the patient's right to respect for private and family life under article 8 of the European Convention on Human Rights to an extent that would not be justified and proportionate in the particular circumstances of the case.[125]

6.78 The MHA Code provides guidance for AMHPs in determining whether to inform or consult in cases where there are concerns that doing so would have such an impact, for example where this is likely to cause emotional distress or a deterioration in the persons' mental health.[126]

121 MHA 1983 s11(3); and MHA Code para 14.58.

122 MHA 1983 s11(4); and MHA Code paras 14.59–14.65 (see paras 6.38–6.42 above)

123 *TW v Enfield LBC* [2014] EWCA Civ 362.

124 MHA 1983 s29(3)(c).

125 MHA Code para 14.61.

126 MHA Code paras 14.60–14.63; see also para 4.36.

Right to information about the adolescent's rights

6.79 Unless the adolescent requests otherwise, the NR has the right to be given certain information in writing, including information about the adolescent's rights (such as the right to apply to the tribunal to be discharged from detention[127]), if the adolescent is transferred to another hospital under MHA 1983 s19[128] and if the adolescent's detention has been renewed under s20.[129]

Right to be informed about the role of IMHAs

6.80 Unless the adolescent requests otherwise, the hospital managers must 'take such steps as are practicable' to provide the adolescent's NR with a copy of the information provided to the adolescent about the help that is available from an IMHA and how to obtain such help.[130]

Right to seek the adolescent's discharge from detention in hospital

6.81 The adolescent's NR can seek to discharge the adolescent from hospital, if the adolescent is detained under MHA 1983 s2 or s3, although this can be blocked by the adolescent's responsible clinician (the clinician with overall responsibility for the adolescent's case).[131] The NR's power of discharge is discussed at paras 8.9–8.12. The NR can authorise a doctor or approved clinician to visit and examine the adolescent for the purpose of advising the NR on whether to order the adolescent's discharge.[132] The AMHP must inform the NR of this power of discharge.[133]

Right to be given notice of the adolescent's discharge from detention

6.82 Unless the adolescent has requested that such information should not be given, the hospital should, if practicable, give the adolescent's

127 MHA 1983 s134((4).

128 SI 2008 No 1184 reg 26(1)(a).

129 MHA 1983 s132(4); and SI 2008 No 1184 reg 26(1)(b); see also reg 26(1)(c) and (d).

130 MHA 1983 s130D(5).

131 MHA 1983 ss23(2)(a) and 25.

132 MHA 1983 s24. The doctor or approved clinician will have the right to inspect any records relating to the adolescent's detention or treatment (s24(2).) A person who refuses, without reasonable cause, to allow the doctor or approved clinician to carry out an examination or inspect records under this provision, will be an offence under MHA 1983 s129.

133 MHA 1983 s11(3).

NR seven days' notice before the adolescent is discharged from detention under MHA 1983 s2 or s3.[134]

Provision of in-patient psychiatric care

Introduction

6.83 Whether or not they are to be detained in hospital under the MHA 1983, a key question for all adolescents who require in-patient psychiatric care, as well their families, will be the nature of the in-patient provision and its whereabouts, most importantly, its distance from the family home. The differing types of CAMHS provision are noted below. This is followed by consideration of two areas of concern: out-of-area placements for adolescents in need of in-patient psychiatric care and admissions to adult psychiatric wards. Both fall within NHS England's objectives for children and young people's mental health care:

> By 2020/21, in-patient stays for children and young people will only take place where clinically appropriate, will have the minimum possible length of stay, and will be as close to home as possible to avoid inappropriate out of area placements. Inappropriate use of beds in paediatric and adult wards will be eliminated.[135]

6.84 As noted below, from the information available, significant progress will need to be made if these objectives are to be met.

In-patient provision: Tier 4 CAMHS units

6.85 NHS England is responsible for commissioning Tier 4 in-patient services.[136] These services fall within four levels 'to support the effective management of differing nature of risk presented by children and young people who are under 18 years', which NHS England describes as:

- *Medium secure services:* These accommodate young people with mental and neurodevelopmental disorders (including learning disability and autism) who present with the highest levels of risk

134 MHA 1983 s133.

135 *Implementing the five year forward view for mental health*, NHS England, July 2016, p7.

136 The NHS Implementation plan includes plans to modify this arrangement (see para 2.10).

of harm to others including those who have committed grave crimes.

- *Low secure services:* These accommodate young people with mental and neurodevelopmental disorders at lower but significant levels of physical, relational and procedural security. Young people may belong to one of two groups:
  - those with 'forensic' presentations involving significant risk of harm to others; and
  - those with 'complex non-forensic' presentations principally associated with behaviour that challenges, self-harm and vulnerability.
- *Psychiatric intensive care units (PICU):* These manage short-term behavioural disturbances which cannot be contained within a Tier 4 CAMHS general adolescent service. Behaviour will include serious risk of either suicide; absconding with a significant threat to safety; aggression; or vulnerability due to agitation or sexual disinhibition. Levels of physical, relational and procedural security should be similar to those in low security.
- *General adolescent services:* These provide in-patient care without the need for enhanced physical or procedural security measures.[137]

6.86 NHS England's service specifications require that adolescents admitted to PICU, low or medium Tier 4 in-patient units are detained under the MHA 1983.[138] The general adolescent services, which do not require those admitted to be detained under the MHA 1983, include units for children aged under 12 years.[139]

6.87 The number of Tier 4 CAMHS beds fluctuates. As noted at para 2.12, NHS England planned to increase the number of in-patient beds by 150–180 beds to around 1,630 beds by March 2019. However, in July 2019 there were 1,558 in-patient beds and 51 providers (NHS trusts and independent hospitals)[140] whereas as at 2 June 2020,

137 *Child and Adolescent Mental Health Services (CAMHS) Tier 4: General adolescent services including specialist eating disorder services*, NHS England, updated February 2018.

138 The specifications are available at: www.england.nhs.uk/commissioning/spec-services/npc-crg/group-c/c03/.

139 See Tier 4 Child and Adolescent Mental Health Services (CAMHS) (Children's Services)at:www.england.nhs.uk/commissioning/spec-services/npc-crg/group-c/c03/

140 NHS England, response to request for information by the author under the Freedom of Information Act 2000, ('FoI request'), August 2019.

there were 1,456 'specialised Mental Health Child and Adolescent beds directly commissioned by NHS England'.[141]

The 'age-appropriate environment duty': MHA 1983 s131A

Overview

6.88 MHA 1983 s131A ('the age appropriate environment duty'), is one of the few provisions under the MHA 1983 that considers the specific needs of under-18s. It provides that where under-18s are admitted to hospital (whether or not they are detained under the Act), the managers of that hospital must 'ensure that the patient's environment in hospital is suitable having regard to his age (subject to his needs)'.[142]

6.89 This duty was introduced by the Mental Health Act (MHA) 2007 as a means of preventing the inappropriate placement of under-18s on adult psychiatric wards, the government having been persuaded by organisations with an interest in children's rights (with the close involvement of young people who had been placed on adult wards) that such a statutory duty was necessary.[143] The need for such a provision was highlighted by the Office of the Children's Commissioner's 2007 report, Pushed into the Shadows: young people's experience of adult mental health facilities, which identified that the issues of concern were not just about unsuitable environments and staff lacking the requisite skills to care for young people, but also that young people felt very unsafe, for example due to harassment (verbal or sexual) by patients or intimidation by staff.[144]

141 NHS England, response to author's FoI request, July 2020.

142 MHA 1983 s131A(2). Section 131A(3) provides that in determining the suitability of the in-patient environment, the hospital managers must consult with a person with relevant knowledge or experience, which the MHA Code (para 19.92) notes 'will usually be a CAMHS professional'. See also MHA 1983 s140 (notification of hospitals which can provide 'accommodation of facilities designed so as to be specially suitable for patients who have not attained the age of 18 years').

143 A raft of measures and guidance were issued to support this objective. See *Working together to provide age-appropriate environments and services for mental health patients aged under 18*, National Mental Health Development Unit, June 2009; *Safe and appropriate care for young people on adult mental health wards pilot programme report*, Royal College of Psychiatrists CCQI, July 2009; and *Safe and appropriate care for young people on adult mental health wards* (AIMS-SC4Y) Royal College of Psychiatrists CCQI, 2009.

144 Office of the Children's Commissioner, 2007, pp66–67.

Application of the 'age-appropriate environment' duty

6.90 The age-appropriate environment duty applies to all in-patient mental health services, including eating disorder units and learning disability services.[145] It also applies to under-18s who are detained in a hospital-based 'place of safety' under MHA 1983 ss135 and 136.[146] In relation to under-16s, the MHA Code states (at para 19.97):

> In the case of children aged under 16, it is Government policy that they should not be admitted to an adult ward. If this occurs or if the child is treated in any other inappropriate setting due to lack of appropriate CAMHS beds, the commissioner of the CAMHS inpatient services should be notified. The commissioner should report it as a serious incident and investigate it in accordance with the NHS Serious Incident Framework.

6.91 Although the precise numbers are not known, it is clear from information provided by the CQC and data published by NHS Digital[147] and NHS England that under 18s continue to be placed on adult psychiatric wards with recent figures showing an increase in the numbers of such admissions. For example, data published by NHS England in the *Mental Health Five Year Forward View Dashboard*[148] for the financial year 2019/20 shows that 133 under-18s were admitted to adult wards in the second quarter of this year as compared to 182 in the third quarter and 205 in the fourth quarter. However, information on the circumstances in which such admissions are made and therefore whether any (and if so, how many) admissions are inappropriate is not provided. Nor is it clear how long

145 MHA Code paras 19.92.

146 MHA Code para 19.104. It notes that under-18s may be detained in places of safety that are not specifically designed for this age group if this is assessed as suitable for that under-18-year-old at that time, given the particular circumstances. However, police stations cannot be used as a place of safety for under-18s (MHA 1983 s136A(1)). For information on a 'place of safety' (defined under MHA 1983 s135(6) and (7)) see para 10.97.

147 NHS Digital includes information on under-18s' admission to adult psychiatric wards in its monthly mental health bulletins (bed days and number of under-18s, providing separate information on under-16s, 16-year-olds and 17-year-olds). See: https://digital.nhs.uk/data-and-information/publications/statistical/mental-health-services-monthly-statistics.

148 See: www.england.nhs.uk/publication/mental-health-five-year-forward-view-dashboard/.

under-18s stay on adult wards.[149] Information provided by the CQC is considered below.

MHA Code: Guidance on the 'age-appropriate environment' duty

6.92 The MHA Code (paras 19.90–19.104) provides guidance on the age-appropriate environment duty. Key aspects of the duty are set out in box 6.3.

Box 6.3: Key aspects of age-appropriate provision

An age-appropriate environment

The MHA Code states that all under-18s admitted to hospital for mental health care 'should have:

- appropriate physical facilities;
- staff with the right training, skills and knowledge to understand and address their specific needs;
- a hospital routine that will allow their personal, social and educational development to continue as normally as possible;
- equal access to educational opportunities as their peers, in so far as that is consistent with their ability to make use of them, considering their mental state.'[150]

Admissions to adult psychiatric wards

Although MHA 1983 s131A does not prohibit all admissions of under-18s to adult wards, such admissions 'are permissible only in exceptional circumstances, where this is considered to be the most suitable place for an under 18 year old' and must be 'suitable for that particular individual at the time that the admission is being considered.[151] This might happen in two types of cases:

- *The 'atypical' case:* (Thought likely to be rare) in which despite being under 18, the adult ward is considered to be the best option, even if a CAMHS bed was available, such as the admission of a young mother to a mother and baby unit, thereby allowing her child to remain with her.[152]

149 *Child and Adolescent Mental Health Services (CAMHS) Tier 4 Report*, NHS England, July 2014. Recommendation 15 states: 'A consistent process should be established by NHS England to notify CAMHS case managers when a young person from their area is admitted to an adult ward. All children and young people should have access to age-appropriate services'.

150 MHA Code para 19.91.

151 MHA Code paras 19.94–19.95.

152 MHA Code para 19.100.

- *Emergency situations:* Such as a crisis in which 'the first imperative is to ensure that the child or young person is in a safe place' and waiting for a bed to become available on a CAMHS unit is not an acceptable option.[153]

Concerns that an adolescent's placement on a CAMHS ward might have a detrimental effect on other children and young people on that ward is not an acceptable reason for transferring that adolescent to an adult ward.[154]

Recording reasons for admissions

Where such an admission is made, the reasons for this should be recorded, 'including an explanation as to why this is considered to be suitable having regard to their age and why other options were not available and/or suitable'.[155]

Provision of care during placement on an adult ward

Arrangements to safeguard under-18s during their time on adult wards must be put in place:

> Discrete accommodation in an adult ward, with facilities, security and staffing appropriate to the needs of that young person, might provide the most satisfactory solution; for example, young female patients should be placed in single sex accommodation. Wherever possible all those involved in the care and treatment of children and young people should be CAMHS specialists. Anyone who looks after them must always have enhanced disclosure clearance from the disclosure and barring service (DBS), including a barred list check, and that clearance must be kept up-to-date.[156]

Monitoring by the Care Quality Commission

6.93 Regulations require hospital managers to inform the CQC if an under-18-year-old's placement on an adult ward 'has lasted for longer

153 MHA Code para 19.99.

154 MHA Code para 19.102.

155 MHA Code para 19.96, which goes on to state: 'Details of whether action will be necessary to rectify the situation, and what action taken by whom, and when, should also be recorded.'

156 MHA Code para 19.102. As noted in the first bullet point of this box, the MHA Code highlights (at para 19.91) the importance of equal access to education.

than a continuous period of 48 hours' (whether or not they are detained under the MHA 1983).[157]

6.94 The CQC's report, *Monitoring the Mental Health Act in 2018/19* shows that for each of the last five financial years, the CQC has been notified of between 152 and 260 of such admissions.[158] Although these figures might appear low, this suggests that on average between two and five under-18s are placed on an adult psychiatric ward every week. Even if the CQC is being informed about every admission (not just those under-18s who have been placed on the ward for 48 hours or more) this is of concern, particularly given that on the limited information that is currently available, the lack of CAMHS provision would seem to be a significant reason for under-18s' placement on adult wards.

6.95 The CQC does not routinely analyse the reasons given for the admissions of under-18s to adult wards.[159] However, in response to a request for information under the Freedom of Information Act 2000 (FoI request), the CQC kindly provided information which showed that 45 of the 49 notifications it received in the last quarter of 2017/18 stated that the admissions were emergencies and 31 included 'no alternative CAMH inpatient or outreach service is available' as a reason for the admission.[160] This accords with the CQC's observation in its *Monitoring the Mental Health Act in 2017/18* report. While noting that there may be clinical and other reasons for such admissions, the CQC added:

> . . . it is also likely that some placements are simply due to problems in accessing appropriate services. In our 2017 review of children's mental health services, we found a lack of access was identified as a

157 Care Quality Commission (Registration) Regulations 2009 SI No 3112 reg 18(2)(h) (as amended by Care Quality Commission (Registration) and (Additional Functions) and Health and Social Care Act 2008 (Regulated Activities) (Amendment) Regulations 2012 SI No 921 regs 2, 5(b)).

158 CQC, 2020, p41 (233 (2014/15); 241 (2015/16); 260 (2016/17); 200 (2017/18) and 152 (2018/19). These figures do not quite tally with the figures given the year before: *Monitoring the Mental Health Act in 2017/18* (at p28): 237 (2015/16); 256 (2016/17) and 199 (2017/18).

159 The CQC's notification form (*Statutory notification Regulation 18(2)(h) Care Quality Commission Registration) Regulations 2009: Admission of a child or a young person to an adult ward*) is available at: www.cqc.org.uk/guidance-providers/registration-notifications/mental-health-notifications.

160 CQC, response to FoI request by the author, August 2019.

problem, as this led to children and young people being supported by adult mental health services teams.[161]

6.96 Similarly, the CQC's CAMHS review noted that in some parts of the country, the 'demand for inpatient beds outstrips availability' and that:

> As a result, some children and young people are being admitted to adult wards as there are no beds available in wards for people their age.[162]

Out-of-area placements

Overview

6.97 An issue of concern in relation to the provision of in-patient psychiatric care for adolescents, whether or not they are detained under the MHA 1983, is the number of under-18s who are placed in CAMHS units out-of-area, often at great distances (in some cases hundreds of miles) away from their home.[163]

6.98 The MHA 1983 is silent on the question of where individuals are detained. It simply requires that applications for admission under MHA 1983 ss2, 3 and 4 are made to a named hospital.[164] Although the MHA Code does not provide specific guidance on decisions about out-of-area placements, it highlights the following points:

- The hospital in which a person is detained should be 'as close as reasonably possible to a location that the patient identifies they would like to be close to (eg their home or close to a family member or carer)'[165]

161 CQC, 2019, p28. As the CQC noted in its report *Mental Health Act Monitoring in 2013/14* (p52) 'these types of admission could be an important indication of systemic issues in providing appropriate mental health crisis services to children and young people'.

162 CQC, *Review of children and young people's mental health services, Phase One Report*, October 2017, p18.

163 E Frith, *Centre Forum Commission on Children and Young People's Mental Health: state of the nation* (Centre Forum 2016) 24; *Review of children and young people's mental health services: Phase one report*, CQC, October 2017, p16, citing Faculty of Child and Adolescent Psychiatry, *Survey of in-patient admissions for children and young people with mental health problems*, Royal College of Psychiatrists, 2015. One of the objectives of the NHS 'Provider-Collaboratives' noted at para 2.12 is to address the problem of under 18s being placed out-of area (see Centre for Mental Health, *Evaluating the New Care Models for children and young people's mental health*, March 2020, p4).

164 MHA 1983 s140 places a duty on clinical commissioning groups to provide details of hospitals in their area that provide for under-18s.

165 MHA Code para 1.4.

- 'In order to promote a patient's recovery, NHS Commissioners and providers should work together to take steps, appropriate help from section 12 doctors and AMHPs and, should work together' to place individuals as close as possible to the place they would like to be near.[166]
- Local policies should be in place for 'the safe and appropriate admission of people in their local area'.[167]
- 'Commissioners should have in place a policy so that the patient and/or the patient's carers are able to challenge a decision' concerning the location of the hospital to which the patient is admitted.[168]
- 'The location of the placement and considerations relevant to that decision should be monitored and reviewed regularly'.[169]

6.99 Guidance on the Care Programme Approach (CPA) states that out-of-area placements can lead to service users' care planning becoming detached from any local co-ordination arrangements and that:

> Where commissioners agree to out of area placements, they must make sure that such care packages adequately take account of the resources required to ensure care co-ordination is carried out effectively.[170]

Information provided by NHS England

6.100 The National Audit Office's (NAO) report *Improving children and young people's mental health services* of October 2018 ('NAO report') noted:

> Data from NHS England suggest that since 2015-16, the total number of in-patient admissions of children and young people has remained steady, while the numbers of total, and 'inappropriate', out-of-area admissions have fallen . . . NHS England has not yet formally defined an 'inappropriate' placement, and currently uses a working definition based on whether the needs of the particular child or young person can be met by the most local in-patient unit, taking into account their clinical need, individual preference and any special circumstances. This is distinct from distance from a patient's home because more

166 MHA Code para 14.81.
167 MHA Code para 14.80.
168 MHA Code para 14. 84.
169 MHA Code para 14.81.
170 *Refocusing the Care Programme Approach Policy and Positive Practice Guidance*, DoH, March 2008, p28.

specialised in-patient services would normally serve a larger geographical area.[171]

6.101 Figure 9 of the NAO report shows that in 2017/18 there were 1,255 out-of-area admissions, of which 518 were considered to be 'inappropriate'.

6.102 The NAO report notes that NHS England's working definition of 'inappropriate' is based on whether the under 18's needs 'can be met by the most local in-patient unit, taking into account their clinical need, individual preference and any special circumstances'.[172]

Admission to adult psychiatric wards and out-of-area placements: human rights implications

6.103 While such matters will depend on the circumstances, in particular the length of stay and the reason for the admission, cases in which under-18s are placed in adult psychiatric wards or are placed out-of-area may have significant human rights implications. Either might raise concerns about compliance with the right to respect for private and family life under ECHR Article 8 (in particular, whether the placement was necessary and proportionate).

6.104 The placement on an adult ward may also engage the right to liberty under ECHR Article 5 (whether the adolescent received 'appropriate and individualised treatment'[173]) while Article 37(c) of the UN Convention on the Rights of the Child (UNCRC) states that 'every child deprived of liberty shall be separated from adults unless it is considered in the child's best interest not to do so'.[174]

6.105 Out-of-area placements are likely to engage ECHR Article 8 given that placing under-18s a long distance from home will restrict their contact with family and friends significantly. In this regard, it is noteworthy that although interferences with Article 8 rights must be 'in accordance with the law', there are no set procedures for out of area placements for inpatient psychiatric care. This is in stark contrast to

171 NAO Report para 2.10.

172 NAO Report p27. The report then makes the point that this definition is distinct from distance from the person's home 'because more specialised in-patient services would normally serve a larger geographical area'.

173 See *Rooman v Belgium* [2019] ECHR 105 paras 205–211.

174 This Article was referred to in *Nart v Turkey* (2008) (App No 20817/07) 6 May 2008 para 31, which held that a 17-year-old's remand in a prison for adults (for 48 days) amounted to a breach of ECHR Article 5(3).

the regulations[175] and guidance[176] that detail the procedures to be followed by local authorities where it is proposed to place a looked after child out of area. These provisions emphasise the importance of seeking and taking into account the views of looked after children and their families:[177] even where an emergency placement is necessary, the under-18's wishes and feelings must be ascertained and given due consideration,[178] and the under-18's relatives consulted within five working days.[179]

175 Care Planning, Placement and Case Review Regulations (England) 2010 SI No 959 reg 11.

176 *The Children Act 1989 guidance and regulations. Volume 2: care planning, placement and case review*, DfE, June 2015, paras 3.33–3.63.

177 SI 2010 No 959 reg 11(2)(a) and (c).

178 SI 2010 No 959 reg 11(3)(a).

179 SI 2010 No 959 reg 11(3)(b).

CHAPTER 7

Adolescents' treatment and care in hospital

continued

Introduction

7.1 This chapter is concerned with the treatment and care of children and young people aged under 18 ('adolescents') who are admitted to hospital for the purpose of either assessing their mental health needs, or treating such needs, or both. It explains the provisions of the Mental Health Act (MHA) 1983 which are relevant to adolescents who are detained under this Act, in particular, Part 4 of the MHA 1983 which governs treatment for mental disorder and includes powers to treat without the person's consent. It also considers areas that will be of relevance to all adolescents, whether or not they are detained under the MHA 1983.

7.2 The chapter therefore focuses on the following four areas:

- *adolescents' in-patient psychiatric care:* the planning and provision of care for adolescents during their stay in hospital;
- *treatment under MHA 1983 Part 4:* the rules governing treatment for mental disorder;
- *seclusion and restraint:* the use of 'restrictive interventions'; and
- *local authority responsibilities:* the powers and duties of local authorities in relation to adolescents who are receiving in-patient psychiatric care.

Adolescents' in-patient psychiatric care: overview

Introduction

7.3 A range of issues will be relevant to the care and treatment of all adolescents who have been admitted for in-patient psychiatric care, whether or they have been admitted informally or are detained under the MHA 1983. These general points are noted below. Provisions specific to adolescents detained under the MHA 1983 are set out in box 7.1.

The Care Programme Approach

7.4 Adolescents' in-patient psychiatric care should be underpinned by the Care Programme Approach (CPA), which as noted at para 2.87 is guidance setting out the process for planning the provision of mental health care for people with complex mental health needs.[1] NHS England's specifications for Tier 4 services states that the CPA 'must underpin the structure of care in the service' and expects the CPA process to be age appropriate, with adolescents being involved in their care planning and given a copy of the plan.[2]

Care, Education and Treatment Reviews

7.5 As noted at para 2.91, Care, Education and Treatment Reviews (CETRs) are relevant to adolescents who have a learning disability, autism or both of these conditions. NHS England's policy guidance *Care and Treatment Reviews (CTRs) – Policy and Guidance. Including policy and guidance on Care, Education and Treatment Reviews (CETRs) for children and young people* (March 2017), states that where no previous CETR has taken place, under-18s should have a CETR within two weeks of their admission.[3] The purpose of this CETR is to review whether in-patient care is the most appropriate solution and to 'establish a clear idea of the purpose of admission, the expected outcomes, timescales and to ensure that planning is already underway for discharge with preliminary timescales'. Ongoing reviews should take place every three months and should focus on 'the reasons for extended hospital stay, barriers to progression and discharge and whether the correct or most effective treatments are being provided'.[4]

1 Further information is provided at paras 9.19.

2 See, for example, *Child and Adolescent Mental Health Services Tier 4 (CAMHS T4): General Adolescent Services*, para 5.2.1. The services specifications can be found at: www.england.nhs.uk/commissioning/spec-services/npc-crg/group-c/c03/.

3 NHS England, March 2017, p35. See pp18–19 on the CETR links with the CPA. It should also be noted that CETRs require either the consent of the individual concerned (in the case of under 18s), those with parental responsibility) or (where this Act is relevant) in accordance with the Mental Capacity Act (MCA) 2005, see pp21–22 and Annex A p55. See paras 3.25–3.30 (for assessment of capacity) and paras 3.31–3.34 (assessment of competence) and see Chapter 4 for overview of the MCA 2005.

4 *Care (Education) and Treatment Review – policy and guidance*, NHS England, March 2017, p36.

Box 7.1: Adolescents' in-patient psychiatric care and the MHA 1983

Appointment of a 'responsible clinician' (RC)

- An RC is the 'approved clinician with overall responsibility for the patient's case'.[5] The RC should be allocated 'promptly on the patient's detention in hospital'.[6]
- Guidance on appointing the RC is set out in *Mental Health Act 1983: Code of Practice*[7] ('MHA Code') chapter 36, which notes that an adolescent's RC should be a Child and Adolescent Mental Health Services (CAMHS) specialist.[8]

Leaving hospital

- Adolescents who are detained under the MHA 1983 can only leave hospital if they are given leave of absence by their RC (MHA 1983 s17).
- Adolescents who leave hospital without their RC's agreement will be 'absent without leave' (AWOL). They can be taken into custody and returned to hospital under MHA 1983 s18.[9]

Independent mental health advocates (IMHAs)

- IMHAs are specialist advocates who 'support patients to exercise their rights and ensure that they can participate in the decisions that are made about their care and treatment'.[10]
- Adolescents who are detained under MHA 1983 s2 or s3 are entitled to help from an IMHA as they fall within the category of 'qualifying patients' for the purpose of MHA 1983 s130C. Adolescents who are detained under the shorter-term sections (MHA 1983 ss4, 5, 135 and 136) are not 'qualifying patients' but those who are on leave under s17, subject to a community

5 MHA 1983 s34(1). MHA 1983 s145: an approved clinician (AC) is a mental health professional (medical registered practitioner, chartered psychologist, nurse (with relevant qualifications), occupational therapist or social worker) who has been approved by, or on behalf, of the secretary of state to act as an AC for the purposes of the MHA 1983. RCs will in most cases be a psychiatrist.

6 *Mental Health Act 1983: Code of Practice*, DoH, 2015, para 36.7.

7 DoH, 2015.

8 MHA Code para 36.6. In cases where adolescents are admitted to an adult psychiatric ward (see paras 6.88–6.96) clinical staff 'should have regular access to, and make use of, a CAMHS specialist for advice and consultation' (MHA Code para 19.106).

9 MHA 1983 s18(1). See also MHA Code chapter 28.

10 MHA Code 6.1.

treatment order (CTO) or guardianship (see chapter 10) are entitled to help from an IMHA.
- IMHA services do not replace any other advocacy and support available to adolescents.[11] MHA Code chapter 6 provides guidance on the role IMHAs.[12]

Care Quality Commission (CQC)
- The CQC reviews and, where appropriate, investigates the exercise of powers and the discharge of duties in relation to individuals' detention in hospital under the MHA 1983, as well as those subject to CTOs and guardianship. The CQC is also responsible for the appointment of second opinion appointed doctors (SOADs) and arranging their visits for the purpose of determining whether to approve the provision of treatment for mental disorder under MHA 1983 Part 4 (see below).
- The CQC reports each year on its findings – see for example, *Monitoring the Mental Health Act in 2018/19*.[13]

Treatment for mental disorder

7.6 Medical treatment (including treatment for mental disorder) can only be given if there is the legal authority to do so. The legal basis for an adolescent's treatment for mental disorder will depend on that adolescent's status (whether an informal patient or detained under the MHA 1983 (and if detained, under which section) and the type of treatment being proposed. This is summarised in the box 7.2 below.

11 MHA Code 6.4. A helpful summary of under-18's entitlement to advocacy is provided in 'Appendix – legal framework for advocacy for children' of *Advocacy for children: Children and young people's advocacy in England*, Children's Commissioner for England, June 2019.

12 The role and function of IMHAs, which are set out under the MHA 1983, should not be confused with the role of functions of IMCAs (independent mental capacity advocates) under the MCA 2005 (see paras 4.45–4.47).

13 The CQC's reports are available at: www.cqc.org.uk.

Box 7.2: Treatment for mental disorder – overview of the legal framework

Adolescents admitted to hospital under MHA 1983 ss2[14] and 3

- Such adolescents will be subject to the provisions of MHA 1983 Part 4 which authorises treatment without consent in certain circumstances.[15] These provisions, (referred to as the 'compulsory treatment provisions'), are considered below (paras 7.7–7.36).

Adolescents detained under short-term detention powers

- The compulsory treatment provisions under MHA 1983 Part 4 do not apply to individuals who are detained under MHA 1983 s4 (admission for assessment in cases of emergency), the holding powers under s5 (doctor's holding power (s5(2)) and the nurse's holding power s5(4)) or those held in a 'place of safety'[16] under s135 or s136.[17]
- Adolescents subject to these shorter-term detention powers are in the same position as adolescents who have been admitted to hospital informally.

Adolescents admitted to hospital informally

- Depending on the circumstances, they can be treated on the basis of their consent, parental consent or (for 16- and 17-year-olds) in accordance with the MCA 2005 (see paras 3.74–3.90). Otherwise, treatment can only be given in cases where emergency life-sustaining treatment is needed (see paras 3.95–3.97) or a court order is obtained.
- If the adolescent's circumstances change in that they are detained under MHA 1983 s2 or s3, the provisions of MHA 1983 Part 4 will then apply.

Specific safeguards for certain treatments for mental disorder

- Electro-convulsive therapy (ECT) for under-18s (MHA 1983 s58A) and other treatments for individuals of any age, such as

14 Although the heading for s2 is 'Admission for assessment', it also covers 'assessment followed by medical treatment' (s2(2)(a)).

15 The compulsory treatment provisions under MHA 1983 Part 4 also apply to some individuals detained in hospital under Part 3. However, these are not covered in this book.

16 See paras 10.92–10.99.

17 MHA 1983 s56(3).

neurosurgery[18] (s57) can only be provided if certain procedures are followed. These requirements apply to all adolescents, whether not they are detained under the MHA 1983.

- ECT is rarely proposed for under-18s (in 2019/ 2020 the provision of ECT was approved for eight under 18s) while neurosurgery (rarely proposed as treatment for mental disorder for anyone of whatever age[19]), is not given to under 18s.[20]

Treatment under MHA 1983 Part 4

Introduction

7.7 MHA 1983 Part 4 includes provisions that only apply to certain detained patients ('the compulsory treatment provisions') and provisions that apply to certain treatments for mental disorder, whether or not the person concerned is detained under the MHA 1983 ('the specific safeguards provisions'). Although potentially all these provisions could apply to under-18s, in practice the compulsory treatment provisions will be the most relevant given that, as noted above, the treatments covered by the specific safeguards provisions (ECT and neurosurgery) are rarely proposed for under-18s.

7.8 Accordingly, the compulsory treatment provisions are considered first (MHA 1983 s63 (treatments not requiring consent); s58 (treatment requiring consent or a second opinion); and s62 (urgent treat-

18 The other treatments under s57 is the surgical implantation of hormones to reduce male sex drive (SI 2008 No 1184 reg 27(1)(a)). To the extent that either of these two interventions are likely to be proposed for under-18s, neurosurgery is the most likely so this will be the treatment referred to when considering s57.

19 In *Mental Health Act monitoring report 2018/19* the CQC reported (p39) that it had received three referrals for s57 treatment (one not authorised and the two others still being considered).

20 Of the eight under '18' for whom ECT was approved six were females and two were male (one request for ECT was not approved). In 2018/19 provision of ECT was approved for seven females. For this financial year, as of 29 June 2020, no requests for approval of ECT for under 18s had been made. This information was kindly provided by Mat Kinton, Mental Health Act Policy Advisor, Care Quality Commission, who also confirmed that the CQC has received no requests for s57 treatments (personal communication). The procedures to be followed where ECT is proposed for under 18s are explained at paras 7.31–7.34.

ment)); followed by the specific safeguards provisions relevant to ECT (s58A) and neurosurgery (s57).

7.9 MHA Code chapter 24 provides general guidance on consent to treatment under the MHA 1983, and chapter 25 gives guidance on special rules and procedures in relation to treatments given under MHA 1983 ss57, 58 and 58A.[21] MHA Code chapter 19 includes guidance on the provision of ECT in relation to under-18s. Further information is provided in *Reference guide to the Mental Health Act 1983* ('MHA Reference Guide') chapter 23.[22]

7.10 The treatment provisions for individuals (including under-18s) who are subject to CTOs and have not been recalled to hospital, which are governed by MHA 1983 Part 4A are discussed in chapter 10.

Treatment without consent under the MHA 1983

7.11 Adolescents who have been admitted to hospital under MHA 1983 s2 or s3 will, like adults, be subject to the compulsory treatment provisions of the MHA 1983. How these provisions will apply to this group of under-18s are summarised below.[23] The general points are set out in box 7.3.

Box 7.3: Treatment under the MHA 1983 – general points

- *The definition of mental treatment is broad:* It 'includes nursing, psychological intervention and specialist mental health habilitation, rehabilitation and care'.[24] The provision of medical treatment for mental disorder must be 'for the purpose of alleviating or preventing a worsening of a mental disorder or one or more of its symptoms or manifestations'.[25]
- *Approved clinician in charge of the treatment:* This term is used in the MHA 1983 to mean 'the clinician in charge of the particular

21 See also MHA Code chapter 23 'The appropriate medical treatment test'.

22 DoH, 2015.

23 The compulsory treatment provisions under MHA 1983 Part 4 apply to individuals of all ages who are detained under MHA 1983 ss2 or 3 as well as those detained under certain provisions of MHA 1983 Part 3 (concerning individuals involved in criminal proceedings) eg MHA 1983 s37 (hospital order). See figure 68 of the MHA Reference Guide for details of those detained patients who are subject to Part 4 compulsory treatment provisions and those who are not.

24 MHA 1983 s145(1).

25 MHA 1983 s145(4).

treatment in question for the patient'.[26] This is not necessarily the same person as the responsible clinician (RC) (who as noted in box 7.1 will have the overall responsibility for the adolescent's case).[27]

- *The role of the SOAD:* The main safeguard under the MHA 1983 is the requirement that a SOAD[28] certifies that the treatment can be provided. SOADs are appointed by the CQC, which is responsible for administration of the SOAD service.[29] However, 'SOADs are independent and reach their own conclusions by using their clinical judgment'.[30]
- *Limited role of parents where MHA 1983 Part 4 applies:* Where the provision of treatment is governed by MHA 1983 Part 4, parents cannot give consent on behalf of their child, even if the adolescent lacks the competence or capacity (see below) to make such decisions. However, parents should be involved in discussions about their child's treatment (unless there are good reasons not to do so).[31]
- *Consent and the assessment of ability to decide:* Provisions under MHA 1983 Part 4 requiring consideration of the patient's ability to consent or refuse the proposed treatment, refer to whether the person is 'capable of understanding the nature, purpose and likely effects'[32] of the treatment. The MHA Code advises that the rules for answering questions as to whether a patient has the capacity to consent or refuse treatment and whether the patient

26 MHA Code para 25.4.

27 MHA 1983 s34(1)). In some cases different clinicians may be in charge of different forms of treatment (see the MHA Reference Guide paras 23.9–23.11). See MHA Code chapter 36 on allocating and changing the responsible clinician, including for under-18s (para 36.7).

28 The MHA Code refers to 'second opinion approved doctors' at paras 25.2 and 25.3 but the glossary at annex A and the CQC refer to 'second opinion appointed doctors'.

29 For procedure for remote working of SOADs because of the COVID-19 pandemic, see CQC, *Letter to providers: Interim methodology for second opinions (COVID-19) 20 March 2020.* Guidance on the implications of the coronavirus (COVID-19) on the legal framework for the mental health care of people receiving mental health services is provided in NHS (Publications approval reference: 001559) *Legal guidance for mental health, learning disability and autism, and specialised commissioning services supporting people of all ages during the coronavirus pandemic,* 19 May 2020 version 2 ('COVID-19 Legal Guidance') p45 (H. Second Opinion Appointed Doctors).

30 *Monitoring the Mental Health Act in 2018/19,* CQC, 35. See also MHA Code para 25.60; and *R (B) v S (Responsible Medical Officer, Broadmoor Hospital)* [2006] EWCA Civ 28.

31 MHA Code paras 24.50–24.52.

32 See MHA 1983 ss57, 58 and 58A.

'does in fact consent' are 'the same as for any other patients'.[33] It refers to the test for capacity under the MCA 2005 (in relation to individuals aged 16 and over) and the test of Gillick competence for those aged under 16 (paras 24.31–2433). These tests are considered at paras 3.23–3.27.[34]

- *Poor recording of discussion on treatment:* The insufficient recording of capacity and consent in relation to treatment decisions has been a long-standing concern, having been highlighted by the CQC in its Mental Health Act Monitoring reports, since the first such report was published in 2009.[35] *Monitoring the Mental Health Act in 2017/18* notes that although the MHA 1983 permits treatment without consent, a person-centred plan should be adopted so that:

  > . . . individuals are fully supported to be involved in decision-making as much as is appropriate. Patients' views on proposed treatment should be considered and fully documented in care plans, as well as the reasons why professionals take any decision that is contrary to the patient's preferences.[36]

- *Leave from hospital under MHA 1983 s17:* The compulsory treatment provisions of MHA 1983 Part 4 apply to individuals who are 'liable to be detained', which means that they will apply to adolescents who have been given leave from hospital under MHA 1983 s17.[37]

MHA 1983 s63

Overview

7.12 Adolescents detained under MHA 1983 ss2 and 3 can be given a wide range of treatment for mental disorder with, or without, their

33 MHA Code paras 24.34–24.39 consider consent.

34 See MHA Code para 24.54 and figure 12 for information on interface between MHA 1983 Part 4 and the MCA 2005.

35 See, for example, *Monitoring the use of the Mental Health Act in 2009/10: The Care Quality Commission's first report on the exercise of its functions in keeping under review the operation of the Mental Health Act 1983*, 79–81. *Monitoring the use of the Mental Health Act in 2014/15*, 51, noted 'some problems relating to assessment and understanding of consent to treatment and care for children'. In *Monitoring the use of the Mental Health Act in 2016/17* at 13, the CQC noted that in previous reports they had 'highlighted that clinicians do not always make sure safeguards are in place when they treat patients without consent'.

36 *Monitoring the Mental Health Act in 2017/18*, CQC, 2019, 15.

37 MHA 1983 s17 leave is explained at paras 10.4–10.6.

consent provided that it is 'given by or under the direction of the approved clinician in charge of the treatment' (MHA 1983 s63).[38] Treatment under MHA 1983 s63 includes psychiatric medication for up to three months (see the 'three-month rule' below at para 7.17). Section 63 states:

> The consent of a patient shall not be required for any medical treatment given to him for mental disorder from which he suffering, not being a form of treatment to which section 57, 58 or 58A applies if the treatment is given by or under the direction of the approved clinician in charge of the treatment.

7.13 Even though MHA 1983 s63 permits treatment without consent, the adolescent's consent to the proposed treatment should be sought 'wherever practicable' and if the adolescent is able to make the decision but either does not give, or withdraws consent, 'the clinician in charge of the treatment must consider carefully whether to proceed in the absence of consent, to give alternative treatment or stop treatment.[39]

Range of treatments authorised under MHA 1983 s63

7.14 Although the stated purpose of MHA 1983 s63 was to authorise 'perfectly routine, sensible treatment',[40] in practice its scope is far wider than this. As noted above, the broad definition of 'medical treatment' includes 'medical treatment the purpose of which is to alleviate, or prevent a worsening of, the disorder or one or more of its symptoms or manifestations'. This means that while the MHA 1983 does not regulate medical treatment for physical health problems,[41] section 63 can authorise treatments that are 'part of, or ancillary to, treatment for mental disorder', such as 'treating wounds self-inflicted as a result of mental disorder'[42] and naso-gastric tube feeding.[43]

7.15 Such treatments can therefore be given to adolescents without their consent, provided that the treatment 'is given by, or under the direction of the approved clinician in charge of the treatment' (which is likely to be the consultant psychiatric who is the adolescent's RC).

38 See box 7.3 for note on the 'approved clinician'.

39 MHA Code para 24.41.

40 Lord Elton Hansard HL 25th February 1982 vol 426, col 1071.

41 See MHA Code paras 24.57–24.58 for guidance on 'Promoting good physical health'.

42 MHA Code paras 24.4–24.5. See also *Nottinghamshire Healthcare NHS Trust v RC* [2014] EWCOP 1317 at [31].

43 *B v Croydon Health Authority* [1995] Fam 133, [1995] 1 All ER 683.

7.16 Crucially, MHA 1983 s63 only applies where the procedures for the treatments governed by sections 57, 58 and 58A (explained below) do not apply.

Psychiatric medication and MHA 9183 s63: the 'three-month rule'

7.17 MHA 983 s63 provides the legal authority for the provision of psychiatric medication for an initial three-month period.[44] This is because MHA 1983 s58 (see below), which concerns the provision of medication for mental disorder is only triggered where medication is to be given beyond the first three months. This 'three-month rule' is calculated from the day on which the person is first given medication when subject to the compulsory treatment provisions. For example, if an adolescent is detained under MHA 9183 s2 and is given psychiatric medication on the second day of detention, the three-month period will start on the second day.

Human rights and MHA 1983 s63

7.18 Given the extent of the powers under MHA 1983 s63, combined with its lack of safeguards, it is questionable whether this provision is compatible with the European Convention on Human Rights (ECHR).[45] This point has been raised by both the CQC[46] and the Independent Review of the Mental Health Act 1983[47] in the light of *X v Finland*.[48] In that case, the European Court of Human Rights (ECtHR) upheld the applicant's complaint that her compulsory treatment under the Finnish mental health legislation violated her rights to respect for private and family life under ECHR Article 8. Holding that 'the forced administration of medication represents a serious interference with a person's physical integrity', the ECtHR concluded that there was a breach of this right because the decision to detain included 'an automatic authorisation to treat the patient, even against her will' without any independent scrutiny of the treating doctor's

44 MHA Code para 24.40 states that this is to 'give time to develop a treatment programme suitable for the patient's needs'.

45 The human rights implications of non-consensual treatment are acknowledged in the MHA Code at paras 24.43–24.44.

46 *Monitoring the use of the Mental Health Act in 2016/17*, CQC, 13–14.

47 *Modernising the Mental Health Act: Increasing choice, reducing compulsion. Final report of the Independent Review of the Mental Health Act 1983*, December 2018, p75 and Annex B, p244.

48 [2012] ECHR 1371.

decision. The same criticism could also be applied to treatment under MHA 1983 s63.

MHA 1983 s58: treatment for mental disorder (medication)

7.19 MHA 1983 s58 governs the provision of medication for mental disorder beyond the initial three-month period discussed above (para 7.17).[49]

7.20 The effect of MHA 1983 s58 is that adolescents who are detained under the MHA 1983 and are not willing, or are unable, to give consent to their psychiatric medication, cannot be given medication beyond the initial three-month period unless a SOAD[50] certifies that the treatment can be provided ('the SOAD certification requirement').[51] The only exception to this requirement is if it is necessary to give urgent treatment under MHA 1983 s62 (see paras 7.23–7.28 below).

7.21 Where MHA 1983 s58 is engaged, medication for mental disorder can only be given to an adolescent in the following circumstances:

- *where the adolescent consents*: either the approved clinician in charge of the treatment or the SOAD certifies in writing[52] that the adolescent is 'capable of understanding its nature, purpose and likely effects and has consented to it';[53] or

49 See also MHA Code paras 25.11–25.12; and the MHA Reference Guide paras 23.26–23.30. The Coronavirus Act 2020 s10 and Sch 8 para 9 makes provisions for modifications to these procedures. At the time of writing (September 2020) these are not in force.

50 See box 7.3 above.

51 MHA Code para 25.3 explains that the SOAD is appointed by the CQC to approve certain forms of treatment; and at para 25.43 that it is the responsibility of the clinician in charge of the treatment to arrange for a request to be made to the CQC for a SOAD to visit. See also the MHA Reference Guide paras 23.12–23.14.

52 Form T2. Reg 27(2). MHA Code para 25.17 notes that a record of the discussion, 'including any capacity assessment' should be included in the patient's notes. MHA Code para 25.18 sets out the what information should be included about the authorised treatment.

53 MHA 1983 s58(3)(a). If the adolescent withdraws such consent, or no longer has the capacity or competence to make the relevant treatment decision a SOAD certificate will be required (s60). The adolescent's treatment can continue pending compliance with the SOAD certificate requirement if the approved clinician in charge of the treatment considers that stopping the treatment will cause the adolescent serious suffering (s62(2)).

- *where the adolescent has not consented:* the SOAD certifies in writing[54] either that the adolescent 'is not capable of understanding the nature, purpose and likely effects of that treatment' or being so capable has not consented to it but that it is appropriate for the treatment to be given'.[55]

7.22 In determining whether it is appropriate for the treatment to be given, the SOAD must consult with two professionals concerned with the adolescent's care (the 'statutory consultees').[56] Guidance on the role of the SOAD and the statutory consultees is provided by the MHA Code (paras 25.43–25.71).

Urgent treatment: MHA 1983 s62

7.23 MHA 1983 s62 concerns urgent cases where treatment is 'immediately necessary'. Where it applies, the procedures governing the provision of treatment as set out under MHA 1983 s57 (treatments such as neurosurgery), s58 (medication beyond the initial three months) and s58A (ECT) do not.

7.24 In relation to medication for mental disorder, the effect of MHA 1983 s62 is that like adults, adolescents can be given such treatment without following the procedures under s58 noted at paras 7.19–7.22 above (certifying their consent or a SOAD having certified that it is appropriate for the treatment to be given). Such urgent treatment can only be given to the adolescent if it is immediately necessary either to:

1) save the adolescent's life;
2) prevent a serious deterioration of the adolescent's condition (if the treatment is not irreversible[57]);

54 Form T3. Reg 27(2). See also MHA Code para 25.18.

55 MHA 1983 s58(3)(b). If the adolescent 'becomes capable of understanding' the nature, purpose and likely effects of the treatment before it is completed, the SOAD's certificate will cease to apply so that the remaining treatment is regarded as a separate form of treatment (see s60(1C) and 1(D)). However, the adolescent's treatment can continue pending compliance with the SOAD certificate requirement if the approved clinician in charge of the treatment considers that stopping the treatment will cause the adolescent serious suffering (s62(2)).

56 One of whom must be a nurse and the other must be neither a nurse nor a medical doctor: MHA 1983 s58(4). See also MHA Code paras 25.53–25.69.

57 This means 'if it has unfavourable irreversible physical or psychological consequences' (s62(3)).

3) alleviate the adolescent's serious suffering (if the treatment is neither irreversible nor hazardous[58]); or
4) prevent the adolescent from behaving violently or being a danger to themself or others (if the treatment represents the minimum interference for that purpose and is neither irreversible consequences nor hazardous).[59]

7.25 The same points apply in relation to treatments under MHA 1983 s57, albeit it is difficult to envisage when such treatments could appropriately be given under s62.[60] If the treatment in question is ECT, such treatment can only be given if it is immediately necessary to save the adolescent's life (point 1) above) or to prevent a serious deterioration of the adolescent's condition (point 2) above).[61]

7.26 It is important to note the effect of MHA 1983 s62. It disapplies, the procedural requirements that would otherwise be required under sections 57, 58 and 58A in circumstances where the treatment is 'immediately necessary' (as defined above at para 7.24). However, it does not provide the legal authority for the treatment.[62] For example, in relation to the treatment of medication for an adolescent detained under MHA 1983 s2 or s3, the legal authority will be provided by s63 if the treatment is given by or under the direction of an approved clinician (see para 7.12 above). Furthermore, MHA 1983 s62 only applies to treatments falling under ss57, 58 and 58A. This means that it is not applicable to adolescents who have been admitted informally or those who are detained under the short-term detention powers, such as s4.

7.27 Where adolescents have previously given their consent to treatment, for example medication, but then change their mind, MHA 1983 s62(2) permits the approved clinical in change of their treatment to continue with the treatment if that clinician considers that discontinuing the treatment 'would cause serious suffering to the

58 This means 'it entails significant physical hazard' (s62(3)).

59 MHA 1983 s62(1) and (3); see also MHA Code paras 25.37–25.42.

60 See R Jones, *Mental Health Act Manual*, 23rd edn, Sweet & Maxwell, 2020, para 1-847. As neurosurgery is likely to be irreversible it will only fall within s62 if it is 'immediately necessary' to save the person's life. The legal authority for the provision of the treatment would also need to be established.

61 MHA 1983 s62(1A).

62 MHA Reference Guide paras 23.60–23.61. See also MHA Code para 25.41. MHA 1983 s62 only applies to treatments under ss57, 58 and 58A – ie it is not relevant to informal patients and those detained under the shorter-term provisions of the MHA 1983 such as s4.

patient'. However, the clinician 'should immediately take steps to ask for a SOAD visit'.[63]

7.28 Treatment can only be given under MHA 1983 s62 for so long as it remains 'immediately necessary' (after which the SOAD certification requirement will apply).[64]

Special provisions under MHA 1983 Part 4

Overview

7.29 MHA 1983 Part 4 includes safeguards that apply where certain treatments are proposed. These will be relevant to adolescents whether or not they are detained under the MHA 1983. They concern the following treatments:

- ECT where this is proposed for under-18s (s58A); and
- treatments specified under MHA 1983 s57 (primarily neurosurgery[65]) for individuals of any age.

7.30 As noted above it is rare for either types of treatment to be proposed for under-18s, but if such cases arise, the adolescent is eligible for assistance from an IMHA[66] and must be informed of this right.[67]

ECT: treatment under MHA 1983 s58A

7.31 MHA 1983 s58A provides that ECT can only be given to under-18s if a SOAD certifies that such treatment is appropriate (there is no 'three-month' rule for the administration of ECT). This requirement applies to all under-18s, whether or not they consent to the ECT and whether or not they are detained under the MHA 1983. Guidance on the provision of ECT to under-18s is given in the MHA Code at paras 19.80–19.88.

7.32 The effect of MHA 1983 s58A is that (save for cases where urgent treatment under s62 is required (see paras 7.23–7.28 above)), ECT cannot be given to adolescents unless the following applies:

- *Where the adolescent consents to ECT:* The SOAD certifies in writing that the adolescent 'is capable of understanding the

63 MHA Code para 25.81.

64 MHA Code para 25.41.

65 MHA 1983 s57 also covers the surgical implantation of hormones to reduce male sex drive; see MHA Code para 25.7.

66 MHA 1983 s130C(3)(a) and (b) and (4).

67 MHA 1983 s130D(1)(e).

nature, purpose and likely effects of the treatment and has consented to it' and that it is appropriate for the ECT to be given.[68]

- *Where the adolescent is not capable of consenting to ECT:* The SOAD certifies in writing that the adolescent 'is not capable of understanding the nature, purpose and likely effects' of the ECT but that it is appropriate for the ECT to be given.[69] In addition, for 16- and 17-year-olds who lack capacity to consent to the ECT, the SOAD must certify that giving the adolescent ECT does not conflict with a decision made either by a deputy (appointed by the Court of Protection) or the Court of Protection.[70]

7.33 It is important to note that for adolescents who are not subject to the compulsory treatment provisions of MHA 1983 Part 4, it will be necessary to establish the legal basis on which ECT can be given where the adolescent lacks the competence (under-16s) or capacity (16 and 17s) to make this decision.[71] The MHA Code cautions that 'careful consideration should be given as to whether to rely on parental consent', noting that although there is no case law on this point, 'given the nature and invasiveness of ECT, it may lie outside the types of decision that parents can make on behalf of their child'.[72] For young people aged 16 and 17 who lack capacity to decide about the proposed ECT, it may be possible that this treatment can be given under the MCA 2005, provided that the procedures for administering ECT do not give rise to a deprivation of liberty.[73]

7.34 In cases where it is not possible to rely on parental consent or the MCA 2005 to give ECT, alternative legal routes would need to be considered, such as detention under the MHA 1983 (if the criteria are met), or a court order.[74]

68 MHA 1983 s58A(4). See Form T 5 reg 27(3)(b).

69 MHA 1983 s58A(5). See Form T 6 reg 27(3)(b).

70 Section 58A(5)(c)) refers to advance decisions and decisions by a 'donee' (see also s58A(8)), but these relate to powers under the MCA 2005 that do not apply to under-18s.

71 MHA 1983 s58A(7).

72 MHA Code 2015 para 19.85. See discussion on the scope of parental responsibility at paras 3.62–3.67. As noted in chapter 3, the MHA Code advises against relying on parental consent to override the refusal of an adolescent with the capacity or competence to make their own treatment decisions.

73 Deprivation of liberty is considered at paras 3.47–3.61. The question whether the procedures entailed in the provision of ECT would give rise to a deprivation of liberty also applies to under-16s.

74 MHA Code para 19.87.

Neurosurgery: treatment under MHA 1983 s57

7.35 Reflecting the seriousness of such interventions, whether or not they are detained under the MHA 1983, treatments under s57 (primarily neurosurgery for mental disorder) can only be given if three conditions are met:

- the individual has consented to the treatment;
- a SOAD and two other people appointed by the CQC certify that the person 'is capable of understanding the nature, purpose and likely effect of the treatment' and has given such consent; and
- the SOAD has certified that it is appropriate for the treatment to be given.[75]

7.36 In practice such s57 treatments are not given to this age group.[76] In theory, treatments under MHA 1983 s57 can be given to under-18s but only if they have the competence or capacity to consent to such interventions and they give their consent. As emphasised by the MHA Code, MHA 1983 s57 treatments cannot be given to 'any young person or child who does not have the competence or capacity to consent, even if a person with parental responsibility consents'.[77] Further guidance on the safeguards under MHA 1983 s57 is given in MHA Code chapter 25 (paras 25.7–25.10).

Seclusion and restraint

Introduction

7.37 During their time in hospital, some adolescents may be subject to restraint and possibly seclusion. This is an area that is fraught with difficulties both in relation to law and practice.

7.38 The law in this area is obscure, being based on an assortment of common law principles (law developed from decisions made by judges) and legislation.[78] It is important to note that there is no explicit provision for either restraint or seclusion under the MHA 1983. However, detailed guidance on their use is set out in MHA Code

75 MHA 1983 s57(2)(a) and (b).

76 See footnote 20 above.

77 MHA Code para 19.79.

78 Restraint and seclusion are discussed in P Bartlett and R Sandland, *Mental Health Law: policy and practice* 4th edn, OUP, 2014, pp84–98. See also B Hale, *Mental Health Law*, 6th edn, Sweet & Maxwell, 2017, pp229–236; and R Jones, *Mental Health Act Manual*, 23rd edn, Sweet & Maxwell, 2020, appendix A.

chapter 26 'Safe and therapeutic responses to disturbed behaviour'. Whereas the MHA Code makes clear that seclusion should only be used for individuals who are detained under the MHA 1983, it anticipates that restraint can be used for informal patients, albeit noting that in relation to under 18s this should be with 'great caution'.[79] These points are considered further below. Further (non-statutory) guidance is provided in the HM Government report *Reducing the need for restraint and restrictive intervention: Children and young people with learning disabilities, autistic spectrum conditions and mental health difficulties in health and social care services and special education settings* ('Restrictive Intervention Guidance') published in June 2019.[80]

7.39 In relation to practice, as noted below, the Joint Committee on Human Rights (JCHR) and the CQC have raised significant concerns about the use of seclusion and restraint for under-18s receiving in-patient psychiatric care, in particular those with learning disabilities or autism or both.

Concerns about the use of seclusion and restraint

7.40 Having received evidence from young people with learning disabilities and/or autism about their experience of the use of restraint and 'solitary confinement' (the JCHR considered this a more accurate term than 'seclusion'), the JCHR's report *The detention of young people with learning disabilities and/or autism* (October 2019), concluded:

> . . . the brutal truth is that we are failing to protect some of the most vulnerable young people – those with learning disabilities and/or autism. And indeed, we are inflicting terrible suffering on those detained in mental health hospitals and causing anguish to their distraught families.[81]

79 MHA Code para 26.59.

80 *Violence and aggression: short-term management in mental health, health and community settings*, National Institute for Health and Care Excellence (NICE) ('NICE Guideline'), published: 28 May 2015 (NICE Guideline NG10), available at: www.nice.org.uk/guidance/ng10. This guidance is due to be revised – as proposed in NICE's *2019 surveillance of violence and aggression: short-term management in mental health, health and community settings (NICE guideline NG10)*, 18 December 2019.

81 Second report of session 2019, HC 121 HL Paper 10 Summary p3.

7.41 The JCHR noted that in June 2019 of those subject to restrictive interventions, 26 per cent were aged under 18.[82] The JCHR's conclusion on the failure to respect the human rights of these adolescents was stark:

> 87. We consider that the human rights of many of those with a learning disability and/ or autism are being breached in mental health hospitals. The detention of individuals in the absence of individualised, therapeutic treatment risks violating an individual's Article 5 right to liberty and security. In some cases, detention may even reach the threshold of degrading treatment contrary to Article 3.
>
> 88. The current legislation governing admission, treatment, and discharge from mental health hospitals is failing to protect the Article 5 rights of those with learning disabilities and/or autism.

7.42 Although welcoming the Mental Health Units (Use of Force) Act 2018, which when in force[83] will require in-patient mental health units to keep a record (for three years) of any use of force by staff which is more than 'negligible', the JCHR recommended 'on every occasion that anyone is restrained or kept in conditions amounting to solitary confinement their families must be automatically informed'.[84]

7.43 In November 2018 the CQC was asked by the Secretary of State for Health and Social Care to undertake a review of 'the use of restrictive interventions in settings that provide in-patient and residential care for people with or who might have mental health problems, learning disabilities and/or autism'.[85] The CQC's May 2019 *Interim report: Review of restraint, prolonged seclusion and segregation for people with a mental health problem, a learning disability or autism. Segregation in mental health wards for children and young people and in wards for people with a learning disability or autism*, found, from information received from 89 providers, that 62 people were in segregation and of these 16 had been in segregation for a year or more. Having considered 39 of these cases in greater detail, the CQC concluded

82 JCHR para 104, which also noted: 'In June 2019 a total of 3,565 restrictive interventions were carried out, 1,190 of them on under 18 year-olds and 1,120 on those age 18–24.' This information is from NHS Digital, *Learning disability and autism monthly statistics from Mental Health Services Dataset June 2019*. Reference Tables 1 and 17 (19 September 2019).

83 At the time of writing (June 2020) the main provisions of this Act have yet to come into force.

84 JCHR, *The detention of young people with learning disabilities and/or autism*, para 115.

85 *Thematic review of the use of restraint, prolonged seclusion and segregation for people with mental health problems, learning disabilities and/or autism*, Terms of Reference, 26 November 2018.

that 'the "current system of care" . . . is not fit for purpose'.[86] At the time of writing (September 2020), the CQC's final report is awaited.

Legal and policy framework: overview

7.44 As noted above, whereas the MHA 1983 makes no explicit provision for either restraint or seclusion, MHA Code chapter 26 provides guidance on their use.[87] The chapter refers to the use of 'restrictive interventions' (such as enhanced observation, physical restraint, mechanical restraint, rapid tranquillisation, seclusion and long-term segregation). The MHA Code uses the following definition:

> Restrictive interventions are deliberate acts on the part of other person(s) that restrict a patient's movement, liberty and/or freedom to act independently in order to:
> - take immediate control of a dangerous situation where there is a real possibility of harm to the person or others if no action is undertaken, and
> - end or reduce significantly the danger to the patient or others.
>
> Restrictive interventions should not be used to punish or for the sole intention of inflicting pain, suffering or humiliation.[88]

7.45 Although both the MHA Code and the Restrictive Intervention Guidance emphasise the importance of ensuring that restrictive interventions are lawful, reasonable and proportionate as well as being complaint with the Human Rights Act (HRA) 1998, neither make explicit the legal justification for the use of such interventions in mental health settings.[89] The MHA Code highlights the human

86 CQC, Interim report: review of restraint, prolonged seclusion and segregation for people with a mental health problem, a learning disability or autism, May 2019, p6.

87 See also COVID-19 Legal Guidance p43 'E. Medical Reviews when a patient is placed in seclusion'.

88 MHA Code para 26.36. In comparison, the definition of restraint under MCA 2005 s6 focuses on two aspects: a) the use, or threat to use force 'to secure the doing of an act' which the person who lacks capacity to agree to such interventions, resists; or b) the restriction of the liberty of movement of the person who lacks capacity, whether or not that person resists.

89 HM Government's Restrictive Intervention Guidance notes (at para 1.17): 'The use of all forms of physical intervention and physical contact, or even imminent threat of force, are governed by criminal and civil law'. Annex A of this guidance (Legal duties and relevant guidance) provides 'a summary of the purposes for which restraint or force may be used lawfully and the legislation relevant' but makes clear that it is not comprehensive and notes that 'a precise statement of the law . . . can only be found in the legislation and case law'. The use of restraint in relation to under-18s is set out in the Education and Inspections Act 2006 s93 (for schools) and Children's Homes (England) Regulations 2015 SI No 541 reg 20 (for children's homes).

rights implications of restrictive interventions focusing on three Articles of the ECHR (which the HRA 1998 incorporates into UK law). It notes that:

- unless such interventions are 'medically necessary' they may breach ECHR Article 3 (freedom from torture, inhuman or degrading treatment or punishment);[90]
- they may breach ECHR Article 8 (right to respect for private and family life)[91] if they have 'a sufficiently adverse effect on the patient's private life'; and
- if they 'deprive a patient of their liberty without lawful authority' this will breach ECHR Article 5(right to liberty).[92]

7.46 The MHA Code states:[93]

> Where a person restricts a patient's movement, or uses (or threatens to use) force then that should:
> - be used for no longer than necessary to prevent harm to the person or to others
> - be a proportionate response to that harm, and
> - be the least restrictive option.

7.47 These points reflect the principles of necessity and proportionality, which are common to case-law, relevant legislation and human rights. The MHA Code also states that when restrictive interventions are required, 'they are required, they should be planned, evidence based, lawful, in the patient's interests, proportionate and dignified.'[94]

Detention under the MHA 1983: seclusion and restraint

7.48 Although not specifically provided for by the MHA 1983, seclusion and restraint are considered to fall within the implied powers of the

90 The MHA Code notes (para 26.107) that seclusion 'should not be used as a punishment or a threat, or because of a shortage of staff', nor should it form part of a treatment programme.

91 P Fennell, *Mental health: law and practice*, 2nd edn, Jordans, 2011, p41 notes: 'seclusion and restraint provide an important example of interventions which potentially breach the right of physical integrity in [ECHR] Art 8'. The author also notes that the MHA Code (referring to the MHA Code 2008) 'provides guidance on interventions which find no mention in the legislation'.

92 MHA Code paras 26.45–26.51. See also *Human rights framework for restraint: principles for the lawful use of physical, chemical, mechanical and coercive restrictive interventions*, Equality and Human Rights Commission (EHRC), March 2019.

93 MHA Code para 26.37.

94 MHA Code para 26.7.

control and discipline of those detained under the MHA 1983.[95] In *R (Munjaz) v Mersey Care NHS Trust*, Hale LJ (giving judgment for the court), identified three potential grounds for the use of seclusion:

- an implied power, being 'necessary ingredient flowing from a power of detention for treatment';[96]
- treatment which may be authorised under MHA 1983 s63;[97] and
- 'a general power to take such steps as are reasonably necessary and proportionate to protect others from the immediate risk of significant harm' (which applies irrespective of the person's decisional capacity).[98]

Informal patients: seclusion and restraint

7.49 Whereas seclusion should only be used for individuals detained under the MHA 1983[99] (its use for informal patients should lead to an assessment for their detention under the Act[100]), the MHA Code envisages that in some circumstances restraint may be used for informal patients of whatever age.[101] Where individuals are not detained under the MHA 1983 but physical restraint (of any form) is necessary, the MHA Code states that consideration should be given to whether restraint can be given in accordance with the MCA 2005 (ss5 and 6) or whether detention under the MHA 1983 is appropriate.[102]

95 *Pountney v Griffiths* [1976] AC 314.

96 *R (Munjaz) v Mersey Care NHS Trust* [2003] EWCA Civ 1036 at [40], citing Auld LJ in *R v Broadmoor Special Hospital Authority, ex p S, H and D*, unreported, 5 February 1998.

97 *R (Munjaz) v Mersey Care NHS Trust* [2003] EWCA Civ 1036 at [41]–[45]. That seclusion falls within the definition of 'medical treatment' under the MHA 1983 was also confirmed by Lord Bingham in the House of Lords, *R (Munjaz) v Mersey Care NHS Trust* [2005] UKHL 58 at [19] ('even though seclusion cannot properly form part of a treatment programme').

98 Hale LJ, *R (Munjaz) v Mersey Care NHS Trust and others; R (S) v Airedale NHS trust and others* [2003] EWCA Civ 1036, [2003] 3 WLR 1505 at [46]. It is suggested that this general power is based on the points noted in relation to the justification for action to prevent harm to others noted at para 7.50 below.

99 MHA Code para 26.106 notes:

> If an emergency situation arises involving an informal patient and, as a last resort, seclusion is necessary to prevent harm to others, then an assessment for an emergency application for detention under the Act should be undertaken immediately.

100 MHA Code para 26.106. See also Restrictive Intervention Guidance para 5.25.

101 MHA Code para 26.3.

102 MHA Code para 26.73.

7.50 Depending on the circumstances, the use of restraint may be lawful where it is needed to prevent the person concerned (whatever their age) from harming themselves or others. In summary:

- *Preventing harm to others:* Where the action taken is to prevent harm to others, the criminal law provides 'a right to restrain a patient who is doing, or is about to do, physical harm to another person or to property'.[103] This is based on the common law power to take action to prevent a breach of the peace,[104] to use reasonable force in self-defence[105] and Criminal Law Act 1967 s3(1) (which permits a person to use reasonable force to prevent a crime).[106]
- *Preventing self-harm:* In relation to individuals aged 16 and over who lack capacity to make relevant decisions about their care and treatment, the use of restraint may be authorised under the MCA 2005 ss5 and 6. However, such action must be in the person's best interests[107] and is limited to preventing harm to the person concerned (not others) and the action must be a proportionate response to the likelihood of the person suffering harm and the seriousness of that harm.[108] For individuals who have capacity, Brenda Hale suggests that it 'is probably always lawful to prevent someone committing suicide', noting the positive obligation to protect life under ECHR Article 2 (the right to life) and the duty of care under common law. However, there are limits to what can be done to control individuals who are not detained under the MHA 1983; any action taken 'would have to be proportionate to the likelihood and severity of the possible harm' and '[i]f there is any doubt, it is safer to section the patient under the MHA'.[109]

103 B Hale, *Mental Health Law*, 6th edn, Sweet & Maxwell, 2017, p230.

104 *R (Laporte) v Chief Constable of Gloucestershire Constabulary* [2006] UKHL 55 at [29]:

> Every constable, and also every citizen, enjoys the power and is subject to a duty to seek to prevent, by arrest or other action short of arrest, any breach of the peace occurring in his presence, or any breach of the peace which (having occurred) is likely to be renewed, or any breach of the peace which is about to occur.

105 *R v Williams* [1987] 3 All ER 411 at 414: 'acting in self-defence the exercise of any necessary and reasonable force to protect himself from unlawful violence is not unlawful'.

106 This applies where the use of force is needed to prevent an imminent or immediate crime: see *R (Director of Public Prosecutions) v Stratford Magistrates' Court* [2017] EWHC 1794 (Admin).

107 MCA 2005 s5(1)(b). See also MCA 2005 s4.

108 MCA 2005 s6(3).

109 B Hale, *Mental Health Law*, 6th edn, Sweet & Maxwell, 2017, pp231–232.

7.51 Otherwise, although case-law from the 1970s suggests that staff in psychiatric hospitals can use reasonable restraint as part of their powers to control patients, whether or not they are detained under the MHA 1983, the nature and extent of such powers, in particular in relation to informal patients are unclear.[110] In his analysis of the relevant legal provisions, Richard Jones notes that informal patients who have the capacity to make such decision who are not willing to accept the control and discipline deemed necessary, should either be asked to leave or their detention under the MHA 1983 be considered.[111]

Specific issues for adolescents

7.52 In relation to under-18s, the MHA Code states that restrictive interventions 'must only be used with great caution on children and young people who are not detained under the Act' and that in cases where the use of restrictive interventions (particularly physical restraint or seclusion) might become necessary, detention under the MHA 1983 should be considered.[112]

7.53 Having emphasised the need for caution before taking such action, the MHA Code refers to the following as having the potential to authorise restrictive interventions:

- *parental consent:* in relation to under-18s who lack the competence (if aged under 16) or capacity (if aged 16 or 17) to consent to restrictive interventions – 'but only if the decision falls within the 'scope of parental responsibility';[113]
- *the MCA 2005:* in relation to 16- and 17-year-olds who lack capacity to make such decisions (subject to meeting the requirements under MCA 2005 s6 and the action taken not amounting to a deprivation of liberty);[114] or

110 *Pountney v Griffiths* [1976] AC 314, although per Lord Edmund-Davies, 'the nature and duration of control varies with the category to which the patient belongs'.

111 R Jones, *Mental Health Act Manual*, 23rd edn, Sweet & Maxwell, 2020, appendix A. The author notes that 'the powers to control informal patients are clearly far less extensive than those that apply to detained patients'.

112 MHA Code para 26.59.

113 MHA Code para 26.59

114 MHA Code para 26.60. Decision-making under the MCA 2005 is considered in chapter 4.

- *the Children Act (CA) 1989 s3(5)*: which permits those caring for an under-18-year-old to 'do what is reasonable in all the circumstances of the case for the purpose of safeguarding or promoting the child's welfare'. The MHA Code adds:

  Whether an intervention is reasonable or not will depend, among other things, upon the urgency and gravity of what is required. This might allow action to be taken to prevent a child from harming him/herself, however it would not allow restrictive interventions that are not proportionate and would not authorise actions that amounted to a deprivation of liberty.[115]

7.54 The circumstances in which these suggested legal routes would provide the requisite authority for restrictive interventions is not clear – whether they provide for anything more than a response to an emergency situation is debatable[116] – and none permit actions that give rise to a deprivation of liberty.[117]

Local authority responsibilities

Introduction

7.55 Local authorities have a range of duties in respect of adolescents who are receiving in-patient psychiatric care, which apply whether or not the adolescent is detained under the MHA 1983. Local authorities will have responsibilities in relation to adolescents' education. In addition to these, local authorities will have a role in overseeing the care of adolescents during their stay in hospital. The nature of these responsibilities will depend on the adolescent's legal status under the CA 1989 – whether they are a looked after child; a child in need; or an accommodated child for the purpose of CA 1989 s85 or s86. Each of these groups are considered below.

115 MCA Code para 26.61.

116 For example, in relation to medical interventions the court in *R (G) v Nottingham CC* [2008] EWHC 152 (Admin) at [24]–[25] suggested that the powers conferred on hospital staff by CA 1989 s3(5) might justify action being taken in the absence of parental consent, 'in order to preserve the child's life or to protect a child from irreversible harm in circumstances of such urgency that there is not even time to make an urgent telephone application to a judge'.

117 The relationship between deprivation of liberty and parental consent is discussed at paras 3.57–3.58.

Education for adolescents receiving inpatient psychiatric care

7.56 The MHA Code highlights the importance of education for under-18s who have been admitted to hospital.[118] MHA Code para 19.116 notes that that local authorities must make arrangements to provide suitable education for all children of compulsory school age,[119] and makes the following points:

- Suitable education means education suitable to their age, ability and aptitude and to any special educational needs (SEN) they may have. This education must be full-time, unless the local authority determines that, for reasons relating to the physical or mental health of the child, a reduced level of education would be in the child's best interests.
- Children and young people admitted to hospital under the MHA 1983 should have access to education that is on a par with that of mainstream provision, including appropriate support for those with SEN.
- Practitioners and local authorities should work together to minimise any disruption to education; and in order to ensure that local authorities can meet their duty to provide suitable education, when a child or young person is admitted under the Act, they should be notified as soon as possible, ideally in advance of the placement.
- The duty on local authorities to ensure suitable education also applies when a child or young person is receiving treatment in an area where they are not normally resident.

7.57 Where adolescents with an education, health and care (EHC) plan are admitted to hospital, the local authority responsible for maintaining the plan should be informed, so that the local authority can ensure that the provision set out in the plan continues to be

118 See also CQC Brief Guide: education arrangements for children in Tier 4 CAMHS settings, February 2018.

119 See Education Act 1996 ss13–19 for provisions concerning local authorities' responsibilities for education. See also *Ensuring a good education for children who cannot attend school because of health needs: statutory guidance for local authorities*, Department for Education (DfE), January 2013.

provided.[120] It adds that it may be necessary to review and amend the EHC plan 'to ensure it remains appropriate and the child's SEN continue to be met'.[121]

7.58 The *Special educational needs and disability code of practice: 0 to 25 years. Statutory guidance for organisations which work with and support children and young people who have special educational needs or disabilities* (Department for Education (DfE) and Department of Health (DoH), January 2015) ('SEND Code') notes that when in hospital, adolescents with SEN should receive good quality education which prevents them from slipping behind their peers. It adds that the education:

> . . . should involve suitably qualified staff who can help pupils progress and enable them to successfully reintegrate back into school as soon as possible. This includes children and young people admitted to hospital under Section 2 of the Mental Health Act 2007.[122]

7.59 Presumably the SEND Code is referring to MHA 1983 s2 (admission for assessment). It is not clear why the position would be any different for under-18s who are detained in hospital under MHA 1983 s3 given that they too would need support to reintegrate back into school.[123]

7.60 The provision of education will also need to be considered in cases where adolescents are admitted to adult wards (see MHA Code para 19.91).

Looked after children: on-going responsibilities

Introduction

7.61 As noted in chapter 2 above, to meet their duties to safeguard and promote the welfare of under-18s who are looked after by them,[124]

120 *Special educational needs and disability code of practice: 0 to 25 years. Statutory guidance for organisations which work with and support children and young people who have special educational needs or disabilities*, DfE and DoH, January 2015, para 10.49. Whereas MHA Code para 19.118 refers to the local authority being informed when admissions are made under the MHA 1983, the SEND Code refers to any hospital admission.

121 SEND Code para 10.49. See also MHA Code para 19.118.

122 SEND Code para 10.47.

123 As noted in para 6.51 detention under s3 is initially for a period of up to six months and can be renewed, those detained under s3 can be discharged from detention at any point.

124 CA 1989 s22(3). CA 1989 s22(1) defines a 'looked after child', see para 2.46.

local authorities have extensive responsibilities in relation to planning the care arrangements for each 'looked after child' and keeping these under review. These duties are detailed in the DfE's 2015 statutory guidance, *Children Act 1989 guidance and regulations. Volume 2: care planning, placement and case review* ('Care Planning Guidance'). Local authorities will continue to have responsibilities for adolescents who are looked after children and who are admitted to hospital for psychiatric care. Such duties will apply whether or not the adolescent is detained under the MHA 1983.[125]

7.62 The consequences of admission to hospital for looked after children are considered below.

Admission to hospital: case reviews

7.63 Local authorities are required to review the care plan of each looked after child,[126] in order to 'monitor the progress of achieving the outcomes set out in the care plan and to make decisions to amend the plan as necessary in light of changed information and circumstances'.[127] These review meetings are chaired by the looked after child's Independent Review Office (IRO).[128]

7.64 Although there is no requirement to hold a review meeting following a looked after child's admission to hospital, IROs must be informed of the admission.[129] In such cases, the IRO may conclude that a case review is necessary. The *IRO Handbook: Statutory guidance for independent reviewing officers and local authorities on their functions in relation to case management and review for looked after children*, issued by the Department for Children, Schools and Families in 2010, states:

125 This is an area of potential confusion given that the Care Planning Guidance makes no reference to looked after children who have been admitted into hospital for mental health care.

126 Care Planning, Placement and Case Review (England) Regulations 2010 SI No 959 reg 32.

127 Care Planning Guidance para 4.1.

128 CA 1989 ss25A and 25B. IROs: 'have an effective and independent oversight of the child's case to ensure that the care plan represents an effective response to the assessed needs of the child and that progress is being made towards achieving the identified outcomes' (Care Planning Guidance para 2.17; and see chapter 4 which sets out the case review process and the role of the IRO).

129 The Care Planning Guidance (para 4.7) states that the IRO must be informed of any 'significant change/event in the child's life', with 'hospitalisation' being listed as one such change.

> An admission to hospital, whether planned or unplanned, is a significant change for the child and the IRO should be kept informed. In relation to medical admissions, the IRO should be satisfied that there is a plan in place to ensure that the needs of the child are being met. If the hospital stay is likely to be for some considerable time it may be appropriate to hold a review in the hospital.[130]

Detention under the MHA 1983: impact on 'looked after child' status

7.65 Although the legal status of adolescents who are subject to care orders or interim care orders is not affected by their detention under the MHA 1983, the situation of adolescents who were accommodated under CA 1989 s20 prior to their admission to hospital is less clear.[131] The potential adverse consequences of this lack of clarity is illustrated by the case of *Re T (children)* which concerned a 15-year-old (referred to as 'St') who had been accommodated by Lancashire County Council (LCC) under CA 1989 s20.[132]

7.66 *Re T* concerned St's application for a child arrangements order permitting her to see her brothers and sisters. However, during these proceedings, it emerged that LCC had, in accordance with 'internal policy' ended St's status of being a 'looked after child' on her detention under MHA 1983 s3, treating her instead as a 'child in need'.[133] Her Honour Judge Singleton QC was (to use her own words) 'trenchantly critical' of this decision. Given her concern that St had 'fallen between two statutory umbrellas of protection' the judge considered it important to publicise her judgment:

> It seems to me right that the plight of children who are subject to both the Mental Health Act because they are ill and need to be detained for treatment and to the Children Act because they are likely to suffer significant harm attributable to being out of control or by reason of parental default is one that should be brought to the public attention.[134]

130 Para 4.16.

131 *Promoting the health and well-being of looked-after children: statutory guidance for local authorities, clinical commissioning groups and NHS England*, DfE and DoH, January 2015, para 87 confirms that the legal status of under-18s under a care order or interim care order is unaffected by detention under the MHA 1983. However, it makes no reference to those accommodated under CA 1989 s20.

132 *Re T (children)* [2014] Case No BB13P00548 [2014] Lexis Citation 190.

133 *Re T* at [13]–[14]. The judge was concerned that that the local authority had declined to issue care proceedings despite (in the judge's view) the threshold criteria justifying such proceedings being made out.

134 *Re T* at [51].

7.67 The judge's observations underline why local authorities should not adopt a policy that deems an adolescent's 'looked after' status to end upon detention under MHA 1983 s3:[135]

1) *Upholding the general principle of 'parity of esteem':* Noting that when people are admitted to hospital they do not change their residence, the judge questioned whether the local authority would have changed the child's status if her hospital admission was for treatment for a serious or long-term physical illness rather than a mental disorder.[136]
2) *Consideration of impact on the adolescent:* The judge considered that removing the looked after child status from St 'was deleterious to the welfare of the child'. Box 7.4 below sets out paras 26 and 27 of the judgment which provide a helpful (albeit not exhaustive) comparison between the rights of a looked after child as compared to a child in need.
3) *Compliance with the procedural requirements for determining whether to cease looked after child status:* The judge questioned the lawfulness of the decision-making process, noting 'there appears to have been no consultation about this decision either with her [St], with her parents, with her independent reviewing officer or with the clinicians at the hospital where she was being treated'.[137]
This third point is of particular importance given that regulations[138] and the Care Planning Guidance[139] set out extensive procedural requirements to be followed by local authorities before ending an adolescent's looked after child status. Accordingly, it is suggested that blanket policies that hold that the looked after child status ends where an adolescent is detained under MHA 1983 s3, or decisions that are otherwise made without following the required procedures properly, or at all, would be open to legal challenge.

7.68 In any event, local authorities are likely to continue to have responsibilities to adolescents they deem to have ceased to be a looked after child. As in the case of *Re T*, such adolescents are likely to be a child in need.[140] Moreover, local authorities will have responsibilities to

135 By way of comparison, see *R (O) v East Riding of Yorkshire CC* [2011] EWCA Civ 196.

136 *Re T* at [31].

137 *Re T* at [28].

138 Care Planning, Placement and Case Review (England) Regulations 2010 ('Care Planning Regs') SI No 959 – see, for example, regs 33(3)(e) and 39.

139 Chapter 5 ('Ceasing to look after a child').

140 See paras 2.37 and 9.21.

adolescents aged 16 and 17 who were looked after and then become a 'relevant child' for the purpose of the CA 1989.[141]

Box 7.4: Looked after child versus child in need (Extracts from *Re T (children)*)[142]

- [26] By paragraph 15, Schedule 2, of the Children Act 1989, the Local Authority are mandated to endeavour to promote contact so far as is reasonably practicable between a looked after child and her parents and other relatives. Other relatives plainly include her brothers and sisters whether they are full brothers and sisters or half brothers and sisters. Section 22 imposes various other duties on the local authority in respect of looked after children, including the duty of consultation in respect of any decision made in respect of them. That duty is set out in section 22(4). Furthermore, a child who enjoys looked after status is a child whom the local authority must maintain by section 22(b) of the Children Act 1989 and I understand that to mean financially maintain the child. Finally, for St's purposes, a looked after child is subject to the 2010 Care Planning Placement and Case Review regulations, that is SI 2010/959. In particular this means she must have an Independent Reviewing Officer, she must be subject to a looked after child regime and the local authority must prepare written care plans in respect of her.
- [27] Section 17 of the Children Act 1989 requires a local authority to safeguard and promote the welfare of children within their area who are in need. That assistance is subject to the local authority exercising their discretion as to what form it may take. Obviously they have a duty to exercise that discretion reasonably and the provision made could include providing that child with financial assistance or maintaining them. Under s17 there is no duty to promote contact,[143] there is no duty to carry out regular reviews of that child's circumstances, there is no independent reviewing officer and the child has no right to be maintained by the local authority.

141 CA 1989 s23A; Care Leavers (England) Regulations 2010 SI No 2571; and *The Children Act 1989 guidance and regulations Volume 3: planning transition to adulthood for care leavers*, DfE, October 2010, revised January 2015.

142 Case No BB13P00548 [2014] Lexis Citation 190 at [26]–[27].

143 On this point a duty does arise in certain circumstances, see: CA 1989 Sch 2 para 10(1) – see para 7.88.

Local authorities' duties to arrange for visits and to provide support to looked after children

7.69 Both the MHA 1983 and the CA 1989 include duties to arrange for visits and to provide support to looked after children in circumstances that will be relevant to adolescents receiving in-patient psychiatric care, whether or not they are detained under the MHA 1983. These are summarised below.

Adolescents subject to care orders: MHA 1983 s116

7.70 Local authorities must arrange for visits to be made to under-18s who are in their care (by reason of a care order[144]) and to 'take such other steps in relation to the patient while in hospital ... as would be expected to be taken by his parents'.[145] This duty applies to adolescents who are admitted to both NHS hospitals and independent hospitals whether or not they are detained under the MHA 1983.

Looked after children: CA 1989 s23ZA

7.71 Where an adolescent is a looked after child, the local authority responsible for looking after the adolescent ('the responsible authority') must ensure that the adolescent receives visits from its representative.[146] If the adolescent requests this, the responsible authority must also arrange for 'appropriate advice, support and assistance' to be made available to the adolescent.[147] The Care Planning, Placement and Case Review (England) Regulations 2010 ('Care Planning Regs')[148] specify how local authorities are to meet these obligations, with further guidance being provided in the Care Planning Guidance. Box 7.5 below sets out key points concerning these visits.

7.72 Regulation 28 requires local authorities to ensure that visits are made to looked after children 'wherever' they are living.[149] The frequency of visits of looked after children who have been admitted

144 CA 1998 s31. By virtue of CA 1989 s31(11) this will also include an interim care order.

145 Rather oddly, given that the MHA 1983 is concerned with the care and treatment of people with mental disorder, s116 applies to all admissions to hospitals, independent hospitals or care homes 'whether for treatment for mental disorder or for any other reason'. MHA 1983 s116(2).

146 CA 1989 s23ZA(2)(a).

147 CA 1989 s23ZA(2)(b).

148 Care Planning Regs regs 28–31.

149 Care Planning Regs reg 28(1). See also Care Planning Guidance paras 3.230–3.235.

to hospital is not explicitly covered.[150] However, adolescents subject to a care order will fall within reg 28(6) which refers to 'C' (the looked after child) who is 'in the care of the responsible authority but another person is responsible for the arrangements under which C is living for the time being'. To comply with the timescales set out in reg 28(6), the local authority must visit adolescents who are subject to a care order and are admitted to hospital within one week of their admission to hospital (and if transferred elsewhere, within one week of that change) and thereafter every six weeks for the first year and every three months in any subsequent year.[151]

7.73 Whether they are under a care order or accommodated under CA 1989 s20 prior to their admission, local authorities will be under a duty to visit adolescents who have 'reasonably requested' the responsible authority to do so.[152]

7.74 The duty to visit forms part of the responsible authority's arrangements for supervising the looked after child's welfare.[153] The Care Planning Guidance notes that the visits have a number of purposes. Points which would be of particular importance to adolescents receiving in-patient psychiatric care (especially those placed in hospital, a long distance from home), are:

- to 'provide an opportunity to talk to the child and to offer reassurance if s/he feels isolated and vulnerable while away from family and friends'; and
- to 'monitor contact arrangements', which includes 'to identify any additional supports carers may need to support positive contact arrangements'.[154]

7.75 In addition, where adolescents are a looked after child, the local authority responsible for them will be required to ensure that advice, support and assistance are available to the adolescent in between

150 Care Planning Regs reg 28(2)–(6) sets out the frequency of visits, which vary depending on the looked after child's circumstances. It is not clear which of these would apply to adolescents who are looked after by virtue of having been accommodated under CA 1989 s20 given that save for reg 28(6) they concern visits to placements arranged by the local authority. Reg 28(2) requires a visit to be undertaken within one week of a placement and every six weeks for the first year of the placement.

151 See also Care Planning Guidance para 3.238.

152 Care Planning Regs reg 28(7).

153 Care Planning Regs reg 28(1); Care Planning Guidance para 3.230.

154 Care Planning Guidance para 3.230.

visits and that 'so far as practicable', having regard to the adolescent's age and understanding the adolescent knows how to seek this.[155]

Box 7.5: Visits to looked after children – key points

- Save for exceptional circumstances, the local authority's representative should be the looked after child's allocated social worker.[156]
- The social worker must see and speak to the looked after child alone (exceptions to this requirement including where this is not possible because the adolescent has refused this, or where the social worker considers it inappropriate to do so).[157]
- The content and outcome of each visit should be recorded, setting out 'the main issues that were raised during the visit, any issues of concern and how these will be addressed and an overall conclusion'.[158]
- A review of the placement will be required if the social worker considers that it does not adequately safeguard and promote the looked after child's welfare).[159]
- The local authority must ensure that appropriate advice, support and assistance is available to the looked after child in between visits and that, so far as practicable given the looked after child's age and understanding, that the child knows how to seek this.
- Looked after children should be informed by their social worker, at least once a year, of their rights and entitlements[160]
- Support 'must be appropriate, having regard to the child's age and understanding, his/her religious persuasion, racial origin, cultural and linguistic background and any disability s/he may have'.[161]

155 CA 1989 s23ZA(2)(b); Care Planning Regs reg 31; Care Planning Guidance para 3.251.

156 Care Planning Guidance para 3.231. CA 1989 s23ZA(5) states that the local authority 'must satisfy themselves that the person chosen has the necessary skills and experience to perform the functions of a representative'.

157 Care Planning Regs reg 29. See also Care Planning Guidance paras 3.243–3.244.

158 Care Planning Guidance para 3.246.

159 Reg 30; and Care Planning Guidance paras 3.248 and 3.249–3.250.

160 Care Planning Guidance paras 3.251–3.252.

161 Care Planning Guidance para 3.252, referring to Care Planning Regs reg 31(a)(ii).

7.76 It should be noted that the Adoption and Children (Coronavirus) (Amendment) Regulations 2020[162] introduce amendments to reg 28. These provide that visits 'may be conducted by telephone, video-link or other electronic means'[163] and that if the responsible authority's representative is unable to visit the looked after child 'within the timescales set out in this regulation the responsible authority must ensure that R visits C as soon as is reasonably practicable thereafter'.[164]

Independent visitors

7.77 Under CA 1989 s23ZB, local authorities must appoint an independent person to visit a looked after child if 'it appears to them that it would be in the child's interests to do so' (unless the child or young person objects to such an appointment[165]) who must 'visit, advise and befriend the child'.[166] The MHA Code 2015 states that local authorities should arrange such visits if a looked after child has not been regularly visited by their parents.[167]

Local authority duties to adolescents receiving in-patient care for three months or more

Overview

7.78 Under CA 1989 ss85–86A, local authorities are required to arrange for visits and the provision of support to under-18s who are accommodated in NHS hospitals[168] or independent hospitals.[169] Such

162 SI 2020 No 445. These regulations are the subject to legal challenge, see: *R (Article 39) v Secretary of State for Education* [2020] EWHC 2184 (Admin). This decision is subject to appeal. New regulations have been issued, see: Adoption and Children (Coronavirus) (Amendment) (No 2) Regulations 2020 SI No 909 (in force until 31 March 2021)

163 SI 2020 No 445 reg 9(3) amending reg 28 by inserting para (1A).

164 SI 2020 No 445 reg 9(3) amending reg 28 by inserting para (1B).

165 CA 1989 s23ZB(6).

166 CA 1989 s23ZB(2).

167 MHA Code para 19.123.

168 CA 1989 s85. In addition to applying to under-18s accommodated by NHS bodies, this duty applies to under-18s accommodated by local authorities 'in the exercise of education functions'.

169 CA 1989 s86. Sections 85 and 86 also apply to adolescents accommodated in residential schools and care homes. Guidance issued by the DfE and the DoH in 2017, *Statutory visits to children with special educational needs and disabilities or health conditions in long-term residential settings – statutory guidance for local authorities, health bodies and health or educational establishments* ('Statutory Visits Guidance') states (at p4) that these provisions do not apply to looked-after children.

duties apply to adolescents who are receiving in-patient psychiatric care whether or not they are detained under the MHA 1983.

7.79 Where an adolescent's in-patient stay is for a consecutive period of at least three months (or where it is likely to be for this period),[170] the hospital[171] must inform the Director of Children's Services of the relevant local authority (see para 7.86 below).[172] The MHA Code states that hospital managers must have systems in place to ensure that these notifications are made.[173] When notified, the local authority must 'take such steps as are reasonably practicable to enable them to determine' whether the adolescent's 'welfare is adequately safeguarded and promoted' while the adolescent is accommodated and consider what action (if any) it needs to take.[174]

7.80 By virtue of CA 1989 s86A, the local authority must make arrangements for the adolescent to be visited in accordance with Visits to Children in Long-Term Residential Care Regulations 2011 ('Visits Regs').[175] Guidance published by the DfE and the Department of Health, *Statutory visits to children with special educational needs and disabilities or health conditions in long-term residential settings: Statutory guidance for local authorities, health bodies and health or educational establishments* ('Statutory Visits Guidance'),[176] provides further advice on how the duties under this part of the CA 1989 should be implemented.[177]

170 The Statutory Visits Guidance states (at p5) that short breaks away from the accommodation, such as weekend leave, should not be counted when calculating the three-month period.

171 CA 1989 s85(1) refers to NHS bodies such as NHS trusts. CA 1989 s86(1) refers to the independent hospital.

172 CA 1989 ss85(1), (3A) and 86(1).

173 MHA Code para 19.126. See Statutory Visits Guidance p12 which states that for pre-planned long-term residential placements notifications should be made before the placement.

174 CA 1989 ss85(4) and 86(3).

175 Visits to Children in Long-Term Residential Care Regulations 2011 SI No 1010.

176 Statutory Visits Guidance, November 2017, which is issued under Local Authority Social Services Act (LASSA) 1970 s7 (the relevance of this is considered at para 1.10).

177 The Statutory Visits Guidance was issued in response to a recommendation made by a report of Council for Disabled Children, *These are our children – A review by Dame Christine Lenehan Direct, Council or Disabled Children, Commissioned by the Department of Health*, January 2017. Although predominantly concerned with the placement of under-18s with learning disabilities and/or autism and those with special educational needs, this guidance applies to all under-18s falling within the scope of CA 1989 ss85 and 86 which therefore includes under-18s receiving in-patient psychiatric care.

Frequency of visits

7.81 The Visits Regs provide as follows:

- If the adolescent has not had a child in need assessment[178] in the 12 months before the notification was made, the local authority visit must take place within seven working days of that notification.
- If a child in need assessment has been carried out in relation to the adolescent within the 12 months before the notification, the visit must take place within three months of the notification.

7.82 Thereafter, the visits should take place every six months, while additional visits can be made whenever reasonably requested by the adolescent and whenever the local authority considers that it is necessary to do so in order to safeguard the adolescent's welfare.[179] The Statutory Visits Guidance suggests that such visits are linked to other reviews such as EHC plans[180] and CETRs.[181]

Requirements for the visits

7.83 Regulation 3 (frequency of visits) of the Visits Regs provides that local authority's representative (who must have the skills and experience to fulfill the statutory requirements[182]) must:

- speak to the adolescent in private (unless the adolescent refuses to do so or it would be either inappropriate or not possible to do so);[183] and
- provide a report of the visit, which must include: the ascertainable views of the adolescent about the accommodation, an assessment of whether the adolescent's welfare is being adequately protected and safeguarded and what further action is required (such as further visits and services to promote contact between the adolescent and the adolescent's family).[184]

7.84 The regulations also prescribe who must be given a copy of the report, which includes the adolescent (unless inappropriate to do so,

178 Visits Regs reg 3(1).
179 Visits Regs reg 3(3)(b).
180 These are explained at paras 2.54–2.72.
181 Statutory Visits Guidance p8.
182 CA 1989 s86A(6).
183 Visits Regs reg 4.
184 Reg 5. Statutory Visits Guidance (pp15–17) provides details on the skills and suggested qualification of the local authority representative.

having regard to the adolescent's age and understanding); the adolescent's parents; and anyone with parental responsibility (unless to do so would place the adolescent at risk of significant harm).[185]

Advocacy

7.85 The Statutory Visits Guidance notes that some under-18s may have communication needs and 'may require the support of an advocacy service which is skilled in the methods of non-verbal communication'.[186] Furthermore, it states that it would be 'helpful, in maintaining continuity of support, if reports of the local authority visitor indicated whether advocacy support was requested and provided'.[187] As noted in chapter 6, adolescents who are detained under the MHA 1983 will have a right to support from an IMHA.

Relevant local authority

7.86 The identity of the relevant local authority depends on the application of CA 1989 ss85 and 86:

- *CA 1989 s85*: If the adolescent is receiving in-patient care in an NHS hospital, the local authority to be notified is the one 'within whose area the child was ordinarily resident immediately before being accommodated'[188] (unless the adolescent was not ordinarily resident in any local authority, in which case local authority 'within whose area the accommodation is situated' is to be notified.[189])
- *CA 1989 s86:* Where the adolescent is accommodated in an independent hospital, the 'local authority within whose area the establishment is carried on' shall be notified.[190] The Statutory Visits Guidance notes that once notified of the placement that authority should inform the local authority for where the adolescent is ordinarily resident to ensure that the 'home local authority is both aware of the placement and prepared for any subsequent financial responsibilities it may incur for any education element of the placement'.[191]

185 Visits Regs reg 5(3).
186 Statutory Visits Guidance p14.
187 Statutory Visits Guidance p14.
188 CA 1989 s85(3)(a).
189 CA 1989 s85(3)(b).
190 CA 1989 s86(1).
191 DfE, November 2017, p13.

Additional duties to visit and provide support

Introduction

7.87 In addition to the above provisions, local authorities have the following responsibilities in relation to visiting adolescents in hospital and providing them and their families with support.

Promoting contact between adolescents and their families

7.88 The CA 1989 places a duty on local authorities to promote contact between under-18s (who are either children in need or are looked after children) and their families, if they live away from home, and to help them get back together'.[192] Accordingly:

- *Adolescents who are a 'child in need':* Local authorities must 'take such steps as are reasonably practicable' to promote contact between adolescents and their family. This duty applies to local authorities where 'any child within their area who is in need and whom they are not looking after is living apart from his family' and in the local authority's opinion it is necessary to do so in order to safeguard or promote the adolescent's welfare.[193]
- *Adolescents who are a 'looked after child'*: Local authorities must 'unless it is not reasonably practicable or consistent with' their welfare, 'endeavour to promote contact' between adolescents and their parents, anyone else who has parental responsibility and any relative, friend or person connected with them.[194]

Financial support to enable families to visit

7.89 The MHA Code states that local authorities should consider providing financial support to enable families to visit adolescents in hospital 'taking into account their duties to promote contact between children and young people and their families'.[195] The relevant provisions are as follows:

- *Adolescents who are looked after children*: Where visits to, or by, them 'could not otherwise be made without undue financial hardship' and the circumstances warrant such payments to be made,

192 MHA Code para 19.123.
193 CA 1989 Sch 2 para 10(1).
194 CA 1989 Sch 2 para 15(1).
195 MHA Code para 19.122.

local authorities may make payments to cover the costs of such visits.[196]

- *Adolescents falling within the CA 1989 ss85 and 86:* With a view to promoting contact between them and their families, local authorities are required to make provision for 'services necessary to enable the child to visit, or be visited by, members of the family'.[197]

7.90 In addition, the MHA Code states:

> When a patient's carer informs the commissioner of difficulties in visiting the patient because of the distance that they need to travel, the commissioner should consider whether they can provide any assistance to support the patient's carer to visit and maintain contact with the patient. The commissioner should inform the carer that they can request a carer's assessment from the local authority. CCGs should work with the relevant NHS Commissioning Board regional team under these circumstances to seek to move the patient closer to their preferred location[198].

Visits for under-18s where parents' whereabouts is unknown

7.91 In addition to the above duties, the MHA Code highlights the need to alert local authorities if 'the whereabouts of the person with parental responsibility is not known or if that person has not visited the child or young person for a significant period of time'. In such cases, 'the local authority should consider whether visits should be arranged'.[199]

196 CA 1989 Sch 2 para 16(1)–(3).

197 CA 1989 Sch 2 para 8A.

198 MHA Code para 14.85.

199 MHA Code para 19.125. The MHA Code does not identify which local authority would be responsible for arranging such visits. This is likely to depend on the circumstances of the case but it is suggested that the default situation would be the local authority in which the hospital is situated – see CA 1989 s17.

CHAPTER 8

Discharge from detention

continued

Introduction

8.1 The Mental Health Act (MHA) 1983 sets out a range of legal mechanisms by which individuals detained under the Act can be discharged from their detention. This chapter considers how the provisions for discharge relating to individuals detained in hospital under MHA 1983[1] ss2, 3 and 4 apply to children and young people aged under 18 ('adolescents').

8.2 In general, the MHA 1983 provisions for discharge apply to adolescents in the same way as to adults, although there are a few areas where there are differences between adults and under-18s, which are highlighted in the text below.[2] This chapter covers:

- discharge of patients under MHA 1983 s23; and
- discharge of patients by a tribunal.

Powers of discharge: overview

8.3 The powers of discharge for those detained under MHA 1983 ss2, 3 and 4 are as follows:

- *MHA 1983 s23 (discharge of patients):* This section governs the circumstances in which patients' discharge from detention can be ordered by either their responsible clinician (RC),[3] their nearest relative (NR) (see para 5.17) or the hospital managers.[4]
- *MHA 1983 s72 (powers of tribunals):* This section sets out the powers of an independent judicial body (the tribunal) to discharge patients from detention.

8.4 It should be noted that discharge from detention is not necessarily the same as leaving hospital. For example, an adolescent may agree

1 The procedures for discharge from detention under MHA 1983 Part 3 are not covered in this chapter. There are no formal procedures for discharge for individuals held under MHA 1983 s5.

2 See: hospital managers' duty to refer to the tribunal (para 8.32); consideration of capacity to apply to a tribunal (para 8.37–8.40) and instruct a representative (paras 8.41–8.46).

3 For definition of the responsible clinician (RC) see glossary, appendix D.

4 MHA 1983 s23(2)(a) refers to 'the managers' which are defined in MHA 1983 s145(1). These are generally referred to as 'the hospital managers'. See *Mental Health Act 1983: Code of Practice,* Department of Health (DoH), 2015 ('MHA Code') annex A of which describes them as 'The organisation (or individual) responsible for the operation of the Act in a particular hospital'. See also MHA Code paras 37.2–37.6.

to remain in hospital, having been discharged from detention under the MHA 1983, while an adolescent who is given leave from hospital under MHA 1983 s17 remains 'liable to be detained'[5] (meaning that the adolescent can be recalled to hospital and continues to be subject to the compulsory treatment provisions of MHA 1983 Part 4).[6]

8.5 The *Mental Health Act 1983: Code of Practice*[7] ('MHA Code') provides guidance on the powers of discharge: chapter 12 (the tribunal); chapter 32 (powers of discharge by the RC and the NR); and chapter 38 (hospital managers' discharge power).

Powers of discharge under Mental Health Act 1983 s23

Introduction

8.6 The powers of discharge by the RC, the NR and the hospital managers, in relation to individuals detained under MHA 1983 s2, s3 or s4, are set out in MHA 1983 s23(2)(a). Although these provisions apply to individuals of any age, the summary below focuses on their relevance to adolescents.

Powers of discharge by the responsible clinician

8.7 An adolescent's RC can exercise the power of discharge at any time.[8]

8.8 RCs must keep their power of discharge under review and should discharge adolescents from detention if the criteria for detention are not met.[9] An RC will do so by making 'an order for discharge' (which must be sent to the hospital managers 'as soon as practicable',[10] but is effective as soon as it is made).[11]

5 The provisions for leave under MHA 1983 s17 are considered at paras 10.4–10.6.
6 However, MHA Code para 27.25 notes that recall to hospital should be considered if it is necessary to administer treatment without the person's consent.
7 DoH, 2015.
8 MHA 1983 s23(2)(a).
9 MHA Code paras 32.17–32.19.
10 Mental Health (Hospital, Guardianship and Treatment) (England) Regulations 2008 SI No 1184 reg 18(a).
11 DoH *Reference guide to the Mental Health Act 1983* ('MHA Reference Guide'), 2015, para 27.3. See MHA 1983 s133 on duty to give the NR seven days' notice of discharge.

Powers of discharge by nearest relative

8.9 Although adolescents can be discharged by their NR, the NR's power to order discharge is subject to MHA 1983 s25.[12] Under s25(1):

- the adolescent's NR must give the hospital managers no less than 72 hours' written notice that it is the NR's intention to discharge the adolescent;
- the adolescent's RC can block the adolescent's discharge by delivering a report to the hospital managers (often referred to as a 'barring report') within the 72-hour notice period, which certifies that in the RC's opinion 'the patient, if discharged, would be likely to act in a manner dangerous to other persons or to himself'.[13]

8.10 Hospital managers are expected to ensure that the NR is aware of this power of discharge and how to use it, such as providing the NR with a standard letter to complete.[14] The MHA Code provides an illustrative standard letter.[15]

8.11 Although the NR's notice and the discharge order should be two separate documents (the order for discharge being made after the 72-hour notice has expired), hospital managers are advised to treat a discharge order given without prior notice as being both a notice of intention to discharge and the actual order to do so.[16]

8.12 In addition to blocking discharge, the effect of the RC's barring report is that the NR will not be able to make any further order for discharge during the six months beginning with the date of the report.[17] If the adolescent is detained under MHA 1983 s3,[18] the NR

12 In addition, if the adolescent is a ward of the court the NR would require the leave of the court before seeking discharge; see MHA 1983 s33(2).

13 MHA 1983 s25. The report must be issued on Form M, see Mental Health (Hospital) (England) Regulations 2008 reg 25(1)(a). MHA Code para 32.32 states: 'This question focuses on the probability of dangerous acts, such as causing serious physical injury or lasting psychological harm, not merely on the patient's general need for safety and others' general need for protection.'

14 MHA 1983 s132(4). The approved mental health professional (AMHP) must also inform the NR of the power of discharge under MHA 1983 s23(2)(a): see MHA 1983 s11(3).

15 MHA Code p356; see also paras 32.20–32.25 (guidance on the NR's power of discharge).

16 MHA Code para 32.24.

17 MHA 1983 s25(1)(b). MHA 1983 s24 provides that for the purpose of advising the NR on exercising the power of discharge, the NR can authorise a doctor or approved clinician to visit and examine the patient.

18 The NR's power to apply to the tribunal does not apply in relation to patients detained under s2.

may apply to the tribunal for the adolescent's discharge, but must do so within 28 days of the barring report being issued.[19] Furthermore, an application can be made to displace the NR, if the NR has sought to exercise this power of discharge 'without due regard to the welfare of the patient or the interests of the public'.[20] It would therefore be important to ensure that an adolescent's NR is aware of these provisions before seeking to discharge the adolescent.

Powers of discharge by hospital managers

Overview

8.13 Adolescents can be discharged by the 'hospital managers' whose powers of discharge will usually be exercised by a panel of three or more people.[21] Adolescents and their NR should be informed that they can ask to be discharged by the hospital managers and that this is separate, and in addition to, their right to apply to the tribunal.[22]

8.14 MHA Code chapter 38 (hospital managers' discharge power), provides detailed guidance on the constitution and role of this 'managers' panel'.[23] Their application to adolescents is summarised below.

19 MHA 1983 s66(1)(g) and (2)(d).

20 MHA 1983 s29(3)(d).

21 MHA 1983 s23(4), (5) and (6); MHA Code paras 38.3–38.7. MHA Code para 37.5 notes that 'decisions about discharge from detention and CTOs are taken by panels of people (managers' panels) specifically selected for this role'. When ordering discharge from hospital these panels have equal standing to that of a tribunal operating under MHA 1983 s72 (*South Staffordshire and Shropshire Healthcare NHS Foundation Trust v The Hospital Managers of St George's Hospital* [2016] EWHC 1196 (Admin) at [30]).

22 MHA Code para 38.11. Individuals can be legally represented at hospital managers review hearings but unlike the tribunal (see para 8.23) they will not be automatically entitled to legal aid. If an application has been to the tribunal, the person's legal representative may be able to attend the hearing, as part of the preparation for the tribunal but otherwise legal aid will be subject to a means and merits test. For further information on funding see S Johnston, S Miles and Dr C Royston, *Mental health tribunal handbook*, LAG, 2015, chapter 10.

23 For guidance on holding hospital managers hearings during the coronavirus pandemic see NHS (publication approval reference: 001559) *Legal guidance for mental health, learning disability and autism, and specialised commissioning services supporting people of all ages during the coronavirus pandemic*, 19 May 2020, version 2, pp41–42.

When to undertake a review

8.15 Hospital managers:

- must undertake a review of the adolescent's detention when the RC is seeking to renew the adolescent's detention for treatment in accordance with MHA 1983 s20;[24]
- should consider holding a review if requested to do so by the adolescent and also when the RC has issued a barring report blocking the NR's order for discharge (see above);[25]
- may review whether an adolescent should be discharged at any time at their discretion.[26]

Criteria, procedures for review and decision

8.16 Although there are no specific criteria in the MHA 1983, the MHA Code states that the 'essential consideration is whether the grounds for continued detention' are satisfied.[27] It sets out a series of questions to be considered by the managers panel in sequence (paras 38.16 and 38.17 – see box 8.1 below). In essence, these mirror the criteria for detention, with an additional question for cases where the RC has barred the NR's order for discharge (which is set out at para 38.20 of the MHA Code). Its guidance on the procedure for reviewing the detention[28] emphasises the importance of ensuring 'the fundamental legal requirements of fairness, reasonableness and lawfulness', as well as enabling the participation of patients and their NR and/or carers.[29]

8.17 Hospital managers must give reasons for their decisions[30] and 'should ensure that patients are offered an opportunity to discuss the hearing and informed of their rights to be considered for discharge by the Tribunal'.[31]

24 MHA Code paras 38.12 and 38.14. The powers to renew are considered at paras 6.51–6.53.

25 MHA Code paras 38.12 and 38.13.

26 MHA Code para 38.12.

27 MHA Code para 38.15.

28 MHA Code paras 38.24–38.49.

29 MHA Code paras 38.24 and 38.25.

30 MHA Code para 38.47.

31 MHA Code para 38.49.

Box 8.1: Criteria to be applied by hospital managers (MHA Code)

38.16 For patients detained for assessment under sections 2 or 4 of the [MHA 1983]:

- Is the patient still suffering from mental disorder?
- If so, is the disorder of a nature or degree that warrants the continued detention of the patient in hospital?
- Ought the detention to continue in the interests of the patient's health or safety or for the protection of other people?

38.17 For other detained patients:

- Is the patient still suffering from mental disorder?
- If so, is the disorder of a nature or degree that makes treatment in a hospital appropriate?
- Is continued detention for medical treatment necessary for the patient's health or safety or for the protection of other people?
- Is appropriate medical treatment available for the patient?
- Consideration should also be given to whether the Mental Capacity Act 2005 can be used to treat the patient safely and effectively.

38.18 [Criteria for patients on a community treatment order (CTO).]
38.19 If three or more members of the panel (who between them make up a majority) are satisfied from the evidence presented to them that the answer to any of the questions set out above is 'no', the patient should be discharged. If so, where a patient lacks capacity to decide where to live, the hospital managers may request that consideration be given to making a deprivation of liberty authorisation or a deprivation of liberty order.[32]

38.20 Where the answer to all the relevant questions above is 'yes', but the responsible clinician has made a report under section 25 barring a nearest relative's attempt to discharge the patient, the panel should also consider the following question:

- Would the patient, if discharged, be likely to act in a manner that is dangerous to other persons or to themselves?

38.21 This last question provides a more stringent test for continuing the detention or the CTO (see chapter 29).

32 The reference to a deprivation of liberty authorisation is to procedures under MCA 2005 Sch A1, known as Deprivation of Liberty Safeguards (DoLS). These do not apply to under-18s – but as noted in paras 4.53–4.77, when they come into force the Liberty Protection Safeguards, which will replace DoLS, will apply to individuals aged 16 and over.

> 38.22 If three or more members of the panel (being a majority) disagree with the responsible clinician and decide that the answer to this question is 'no', the panel should usually discharge the patient. The hospital managers retain a residual discretion not to discharge in these cases, so panels should always consider whether there are exceptional reasons why the patient should not be discharged.
>
> 38.23 In all cases, hospital managers have discretion to discharge patients even if the criteria for continued detention or a CTO are met. Managers' panels should always consider whether there are other reasons why the patient should be discharged despite the answers to the questions set out above; regard should be had to the principle of least restrictive option and maximising independence (see paragraphs 1.2–1.6).

The tribunal's powers of discharge

Overview

8.18 A significant safeguard for patients detained in hospital under the MHA 1983 is the right to apply to an independent judicial body for their discharge from detention.[33] In England,[34] the application is made to the Mental Health Tribunal ('the tribunal'), which is part of the Health, Education and Social Care (HESC) Chamber of the First-tier Tribunal established under the Tribunals, Courts and Enforcement Act (TCEA) 2007.[35] Its procedures are governed by the Tribunal Procedure (First-tier Tribunal) (Health, Education and Social Care Chamber) Rules 2008 ('Tribunal Procedure Rules').[36] The MHA Code states:

> Children and young people who are detained under the Act have the same rights as other patients to apply to the Tribunal (see chapter 12). It is important that children and young people are informed of their right to apply to the Tribunal and are assisted in obtaining legal representation at an early stage.[37]

33 MHA 1983 s66(1).

34 In Wales, the application is made to the Mental Health Review Tribunal for Wales (MHRT Wales), which is established under MHA 1983 s65 and its procedures are governed by the Mental Health Review Tribunal for Wales Rules 2008 (SI No 2705 (L.17)), which are made under MHA 1983 s78.

35 MHA 1983 s77(2)(2)(a).

36 SI No 2699.

37 MHA Code para 19.107.

8.19 The tribunal provides an independent review as to whether the grounds for detention are met, together with the duty (and in some cases, power) to direct the person's discharge from detention. As such, it performs the role of 'a court' for the purpose of European Convention on Human Rights (ECHR) Article 5(4), which states that everyone who is deprived of their liberty:

> . . . shall be entitled to take proceedings by which the lawfulness of his detention shall be decided speedily by a court and his release ordered if the detention is not lawful.[38]

8.20 The powers of the tribunal are set out in MHA 1983 Part 5 ss72–75. The tribunal reviews the cases of individuals who are detained under MHA 1983 Part 2 and Part 3, as well as cases of individuals who are living in the community and subject to the MHA 1983 (individuals who have been conditionally discharged into the community under Part 3, subject to CTOs or subject to guardianship[39]). Appeals against the decision of the tribunal can be made to the Upper Tribunal on a point of law, with permission of either the tribunal or the Upper Tribunal.[40] The MHT operates in accordance with the Tribunal Procedure Rules (noted above at para 8.18).

8.21 MHA Code chapter 12 and the *Reference Guide to the Mental Health Act 1983*[41] ('MHA Reference Guide') chapter 6 provide information on the role and powers of the tribunal. The Law Society has issued a practice note *Representation before mental health tribunals* (2019) ('Law Society's Practice Note') which provides detailed guidance for practitioners representing clients before the tribunal in England and the Mental Health Review Tribunal in Wales.[42]

8.22 Representation before the tribunal is a highly specialised area and beyond the scope of this book.[43] The following provides a summary

38 A summary of Article 5 ECHR is provided at box 1.2.

39 CTOs and guardianship are considered in chapter 10.

40 Tribunal Courts and Enforcement Act (TCEA) 2007 s11.

41 DoH, 2015.

42 Available on the Law Society website: www.lawsociety.org.uk.

43 For resources specific to this area of law and practice, see for example: S Johnston, S Miles and Dr C Royston, *Mental Health Tribunal Handbook*, LAG, 2015; and P Fennell, P Letts and J Wilson, *Mental Health Review Tribunals: law, policy and practice*, The Law Society, 2013.

of the key issues, and highlights areas that are specific to under-18s who are detained under MHA 1983 Part 2.[44]

Information, advice and legal representation

8.23 Like adults, adolescents who are detained in hospital under MHA 1983 Part 2 s2, s3 or s4 will have the following rights:

- *Right to information*: Right to be given information about their rights (orally and in writing) to apply to a tribunal (hospital managers are under a duty to 'take such steps are as practicable to ensure that the patient understands' such information).[45] In addition, adolescents should also be informed of their entitlement to free legal advice and representation in making their application to the tribunal[46] and unless they request otherwise, this information should be given to their NR.[47]
- *Right to help from an independent mental health advocate (IMHA)*:[48] IMHAs should help adolescents apply to the tribunal, contact a lawyer, understand the role of the tribunal and what to expect at the tribunal hearing.[49] The MHA Code states:

> IMHAs have an important role in ensuring that children and young people understand, and are able to exercise, their rights under the Act. The IMHA's help in relation to applications to Tribunal will be particularly important, such as helping the child or young person contact a lawyer and understanding the role of the Tribunal, and what to expect at the Tribunal hearing.[50]

44 In response to the coronavirus pandemic, temporary changes have been introduced to the tribunal's practice and procedure (such as holding hearings by phone or video) through regulations (Tribunal Procedure (Coronavirus) (Amendment) Rules 2020 SI No 416) and practice directions (eg see *Pilot Practice Direction: health, education and social care chamber of the first-tier tribunal (mental health)* 19/3/20). See also *Guidance from the Chamber President and Deputy Chamber President of HESC regarding the Mental Health jurisdiction* 19/3/2020. For a list of relevant resources, see *Mental health tribunal and coronavirus*, Mental Health Law Online, available at: www.mentalhealthlaw.co.uk/Mental_Health_Tribunal_and_coronavirus.

45 MHA 1983 s132(1)(b); MHA Code paras 4.21–4.22.

46 MHA Code paras 12.6 and 12.26.

47 MHA 1983 s132(4); MHA Code para 12.7.

48 MHA 1983 s130D(2)(a).

49 MHA Code para 19.107. See also *Mental Health Tribunal, Practice Note: Role of the Independent Mental Health Advocate in First-tier Tribunal (Mental Health) Hearings*, May 2011.

50 MHA Code para 19.107.

- *Right to legal representation:* Adolescents will have the right to have legal representation at the tribunal,[51] for which legal aid (non-means tested) is available.[52] A list of accredited mental health lawyers is available from the Law Society's website.[53] This list will usually be kept in the hospital's Mental Health Act Administrator's office.

Applications and referrals to the tribunal

Overview

8.24 Adolescents who have been admitted to hospital under MHA 1983 Part 2 may have their case heard by a tribunal by the one of the following routes:

- application by, or on behalf of,[54] the adolescent;
- application by the adolescent's NR;
- referral by the Secretary of State for Health and Social Care; or
- referral by the hospital managers.

These are summarised in table 8.1, with further explanation provided below. .

Table 8.1: Applications and references to the tribunal

Who	When	Comment	Provision
Adolescents detained under MHA 1983 s2 or s4	Within 14 days of admission.	If MHA 1983 s4 converted to s2, the time starts to run from date of s4 admission. (See para 6.49.)	MHA 1983 s66(1)(a) and (2)(a).
Adolescents detained under MHA 1983 s3	An application can be made any time during each period of detention.	Initial detention is for up to six months, which can be renewed for a further six months and thereafter on an annual basis.[55] (See paras 6.51–6.53.)	MHA 1983 s66(1)(b) and (2)(b); s66(1)(f) and (2)(f).

51 Tribunal Procedures Rules 2008 r11(1A) states that a child or young person may appoint a representative (whether a legal representative or not).

52 MHA Code para 12.6 notes that hospital managers should 'advise patients of their entitlement to free legal advice and representation'.

53 See: www.lawsociety.org.uk/for-the-public/using-a-solicitor/quality-marks/Mental-health/.

54 The application must be in writing and signed by the applicant or the person authorised by the applicant to do so, see Tribunal Procedure Rules r32(1).

55 The provisions for renewal are set out in MHA 1983 s20.

NR (Note: the leave of the court is required for adolescents who are wards of court MHA 1983 s33(2))	Within 28 days of NR being informed that the report barring the adolescent's discharge has been submitted to the hospital managers.	Only applies where RC blocks NR's order to discharge from MHA 1983 s3 detention. (See para 8.9.)	MHA 1983 s66(1)(g) and (2)(d).
Displaced NRs	The application can be made within 12 months beginning with the date of the order and in any subsequent period of 12 months while the order is in force.	Applies if court has displaced the NR under MHA 1983 s29(3)(c) or (d). (See para 8.26.)	MHA 1983 s66(1)(h) and (2)(g).
Secretary of State for Health and Social Care (SoS) may refer an adolescent's case	A reference to the tribunal may be made by the SoS at any time they think fit. Anyone can request that such a referral is made.	See guidance: *Section 67 of the Mental Health Act 1983: References by the Secretary of State for Health and Social Care to the First-tier Tribunal.*[56] (See para 8.28.)	MHA 1983 s67(1).
Hospital managers' duty to refer to the tribunal (1)[58]	Referral must be made on the expiry of six months from the date on which the adolescent was admitted to hospital under the MHA 1983.	Duty arises if during first six months of detention, the tribunal has not considered the adolescent's case (except in relation to MHA 1983 s2 detention). (See para 8.32.)	MHA 1983 s68(2) and (3).[57]
Hospital managers' duty to refer to the tribunal (2)	Hospital managers must make a referral if a year has elapsed since the adolescent's case was last heard by the tribunal.	Duty arises if the tribunal has not considered the adolescent's case for over a year (for adults, this duty is engaged if the person's case has not been heard for three years). (See para 8.32.)	MHA 1983 s68(6).

56 DHSC, updated August 2019.

57 MHA 1983 s68(4) provides that if an application is made but then withdrawn, that person is treated as not having exercised the right to apply to the tribunal. This is particularly important given that only one application per period of detention can be made.

58 This duty will usually apply to individuals detained under MHA 1983 s3. However, it could also apply to cases where s2 detention has been extended pending an application to displace the patient's nearest relative under s29. See MHA 1983 s29(4); MHA Code figure 20 p382.

Hospital managers should consider requesting that SoS makes a reference	Any time individuals are unable to have their case considered speedily by the tribunal (therefore their ECHR Article 5(4) rights are at risk).	This advice is made by the MHA Code in the light of case-law. (See para 8.31.)	MHA Code para 37.45; and MHA Reference Guide para 6.57.

Applications by adolescents

8.25 Adolescents have the right to apply to the tribunal as follows:

- *Adolescents detained under MHA 1983s2 or s4*: The application must be made within 14 days of the adolescent's admission for assessment under the MHA 1983.[59] If the adolescent was initially admitted under section 4, which was then converted to an admission under section 2, the time will start to run on the day on which the adolescent was admitted under section 4.[60]
- *Adolescents detained under MHA 1983 s3:* An application can be made for each period of detention under section 3[61] (the initial detention is for up to six months, which can be renewed for a further six months and thereafter on an annual basis[62]). The application can be made at any time during the adolescent's detention.[63]

Applications by the nearest relative

8.26 An adolescent's NR (or former NR) can make an application to the tribunal in the following circumstances:

- Where the NR's order to discharge the adolescent from detention under MHA 1983 s3 has been blocked by the RC, an application may be made by the NR within 28 days of being informed that the report barring the adolescent's discharge has been submitted to the hospital managers.[64] (The NR has no right to apply in cases where the RC has barred the discharge of an adolescent who has been admitted for assessment under s2.)[65]
- Former NRs can apply to the tribunal where they have been displaced as the NR by an the order of the county court under

59 MHA 1983 s66(1)(a).
60 MHA 1983 s66(2)(a).
61 MHA 1983 s66(1)(b).
62 The provisions for renewal are set out in MHA 1983 s20.
63 See MHA 1983 s66(1)(b) and (f) and (2)(b) and (f).
64 MHA 1983 s66(2)(d)
65 MHA 1983 s66(1)(g).

section 29[66] on the grounds that they unreasonably objected 'to the making of an application for admission for treatment'[67] or that they exercised their power of discharge 'without due regard to the welfare of the patient or the interests of the public'.[68] The application can be made within 12 months beginning with the date of the order and in any subsequent period of 12 months while the order is in force.[69]

8.27 If the adolescent is a ward of court, the NR can only make an application to the tribunal with leave of the court.[70]

References to the tribunal by the secretary of state

8.28 An adolescent's case can be referred to the tribunal by Secretary of State for Health and Social Care, and this may be done at any time the secretary of state thinks fit.[71] Anyone can request a referral, and information on how to do so is provided in the Department of Health and Social Care's (DHSC) guidance *Section 67 of the Mental Health Act 1983: References by the Secretary of State for Health and Social Care to the First-tier Tribunal.*[72]

8.29 Hospital managers should consider making a request at any time there is risk that a patient's rights under ECHR Article 5(4) might be jeopardised.[73]

8.30 In particular, they should normally seek such a reference in any case where:

- a patient's detention under MHA 1983 s2 has been extended under s29 of the Act pending the outcome of an application to the county court for the displacement of their NR;
- the patient lacks capacity to request a reference; or

66 MHA 1983 s66(1)(h).
67 MHA 1983 s29(3)(c).
68 MHA 1983 s29(3)(d).
69 MHA 1983 s66(2)(g).
70 MHA 1983 s33(2).
71 MHA 1983 s67(1).
72 August 2019, available at: www.gov.uk/government/publications/section-67-of-the-mental-health-act/section-67-of-the-mental-health-act-1983-references-by-the-secretary-of-state-for-health-and-social-care-to-the-first-tier-tribunal. Anecdotally, such referrals can be arranged within days if needed.
73 MHA Code para 37.45; and MHA Reference Guide para 6.57. See also *R (MH) v Secretary of State for Health* [2005] UKHL 60; *MH v UK* App No 11577/06 (2013) ECHR 1008; and *R (Modaresi) v Secretary of State for Health* [2011] EWHC 417. These cases are discussed in S Johnston, S Miles and Dr C Royston, *Mental Health Tribunal Handbook*, LAG, 2015, paras 5.19–5.22.

- either the patient's case has never been considered by the tribunal, or a significant period has passed since it was last considered.[74]

8.31 The MHA Code makes specific reference to under-18s, stating that hospital managers should consider asking the secretary of state to refer their case to the tribunal where under-18s 'are unable to have their case considered speedily by the Tribunal'.[75] For example, this could be where the adolescent (for whatever reason) did not apply to the tribunal when detained under MHA 1983 s2 within the 14-day period or where the adolescent lacks the capacity or competence to make the application to the tribunal, or to authorise another person to do so on their behalf.

Hospital managers' duty to refer to the tribunal

8.32 MHA 1983 s68 sets out the circumstances in which hospital managers must refer a patient's case to the tribunal. For adolescents detained under MHA 1983 s2 or s3, the duty to refer will arise in the following two situations:

- *During the first six months of detention the tribunal has not considered the adolescent's case (except in relation to admission for assessment under MHA 1983 s2):* The hospital managers must make a referral if an application to the tribunal (whether by the adolescent, or the adolescent's NR) or a reference by the secretary of state (see above) has not been considered by the tribunal in respect of that adolescent within the first six months of the adolescent's detention.[76] The reference must be made on the expiry of six months from the date on which the adolescent was admitted to hospital under the MHA 1983.[77]

  The duty to make a referral applies even if the adolescent had a tribunal when detained under MHA 1983 s2, following the adolescent's application or a reference by the secretary of state.[78]

  Although the duty to refer will usually arise in relation to patients who are detained under MHA 1983 s3, it would also be applicable to cases where detention under section 2 has been

74 MHA Code para 37.46. See discussion in *SM v Livewell Southwest CIC* [2020] UKUT 191 (ACC) at [88]-[89].

75 MHA Code para 19.110.

76 MHA 1983 s68(1) and (3). MHA 1983 s68(4) makes clear that if an application is made but then withdrawn that person is treated as not having exercised the right to apply to the tribunal.

77 MHA 1983 s68(2).

78 MHA 1983 s68(1) and (3).

extended pending an application to displace the patient's nearest relative under section 29.[79]

- *The tribunal has not considered the adolescent's case for over a year:* The hospital managers must make a referral if a year has elapsed since the adolescent's case was last heard by the tribunal (for adults, this duty is engaged if the person's case has not been heard for three years).[80]

8.33 The MHA Code states that hospital managers should ensure that systems are in place to identify cases requiring referral to a tribunal in accordance with MHA 1983 s68.[81]

Withdrawals of applications

8.34 The Tribunal Procedure Rules provide that applicants may request (either before the hearing in writing, or orally at the hearing) to withdraw their case, but that this is subject to the tribunal's consent.[82] The applicant cannot withdraw a reference made by the hospital managers or the secretary of state.[83]

Proceedings before the tribunal

Applications to the tribunal

8.35 Adolescents wishing to apply to the tribunal must do so in writing and the application must be signed either by them or any person authorised by them to make the application on their behalf.[84] Similarly, in cases where the adolescent's NR has the right to apply to the tribunal, the application must be made in writing and signed either by the NR or a person authorised to do so on the NR's behalf. The HM Courts and Tribunal Services have produced forms for applications and references to the tribunal.[85]

8.36 Ward staff should offer to assist adolescents in making an application to the tribunal as well as providing information on how to contact a suitably qualified legal representative (and provide

79 MHA 1983 s29(4); MHA Code figure 20 p382.

80 MHA 1983 s68(6).

81 MHA Code para 19.110.

82 Tribunal Procedure Rules 2008 r17(1) and (2).

83 Tribunal Procedure Rules 2008 r17(3).

84 Tribunal Procedure Rules r32(1). This would also apply where the NR is the applicant. This rule also sets out additional information that should be included in the application (r32(2)) or reference (r32(3)).

85 See Form T110 (application) and Form T111 (referral): available at: www.gov.uk.

assistance in doing so) or any other organisation which may be able to help the adolescent make the application.[86]

Capacity to bring proceedings

8.37 When considering 'the nature of the capacity required by a patient to bring proceedings before the First-tier Tribunal in its mental health jurisdiction', Upper Tribunal Judge Jacobs decided in *VS v St Andrews Healthcare* that the test is:

> The patient must understand that they are being detained against their wishes and that the First-Tier Tribunal is a body that will be able to decide whether they should be released.[87]

8.38 As noted by Judge Jacobs, this approach accords with Lady Hale's view in *R (MH) v Secretary of State for Health* that most patients admitted under the MHA 1983 'have the very limited capacity required to make an application to a mental health review tribunal or have someone else who can help them to make it', the exceptions being those with 'severe learning disability or severe dementia'.[88]

8.39 Although both the decision in *VS* and Lady Hale's comments in *MH* concerned adults, given its low threshold for capacity to apply to the tribunal, it is suggested that many adolescents, including those aged under 16 will meet the test set by *VS*. However, the principle under the MCA 2005 (individuals are assumed to have capacity unless evidence shows otherwise),[89] does not apply to under 16s.[90] Accordingly, for the avoidance of doubt, representatives for this age group may find it helpful to record that they have assessed that the adolescent has the level of understanding required by *VS*.

8.40 In cases where an adolescent does not meet the *VS* test for the capacity to make an application to the tribunal, the Secretary of State for Health and Social Care can be requested to make a referral to the tribunal on the adolescent's behalf (see para 8.31 above).

86 MHA Code paras 4.22 and 12.26.

87 [2018] UKUT 250 (AAC), [2019] AACR 4 at [2]. See also *SM v Livewell Southwest CIC* [2020] UKUT 191 (ACC) at [88] and Judge Johnston's judgment in which she argues that the test set out in *VS* is too high.

88 *R (MH) v Secretary of State for Health* [2005] UKHL 60, [2006] 1 AC 441 at [4]; see also [26].

89 MCA 2005 s1(2).

90 Save for exceptions (not relevant in this context) the MCA 2005 does not apply to individuals aged under 16 (MCA 2005 s2(5)). The MCA 2005 is considered in chapter 5. Assessment of capacity and competence is considered at paras 3.23–3.37.

Legal representation and capacity to instruct

8.41 Adolescents who wish to challenge their detention before the tribunal have the right to be represented. They can appoint a representative (legal or otherwise) to represent them in the proceedings before the tribunal.[91]

8.42 Where adolescents have not appointed a legal representative, the tribunal may appoint one on their behalf in certain situations. Under Tribunal Procedure Rules r11(7) the tribunal may do so where 'the patient has stated that they do not wish to conduct their own case or that they wish to be represented'[92] or where 'the patient lacks the capacity to appoint a representative, but the tribunal believes that it is in the patient's best interests to be represented'.[93] Anecdotally, it is usual for the tribunal to make such appointments unless there is a reason not to do so.[94] The Law Society's Practice Note notes that once appointed the legal representative has 'a heightened responsibility to identify and then act on the interests of the client'.[95]

8.43 In *PI v West London Mental Health NHS Trust*, Upper Tribunal Judge Knowles QC emphasised the need for all those involved, including the tribunal, to keep under review 'the issue of a patient's capacity to appoint a representative, to give instructions and to participate in proceedings before the tribunal'.[96]

8.44 The Law Society's Practice Note's guidance on taking instructions advises legal representatives that they 'must assume that your client has capacity unless the contrary is established (section 1(2) MCA)'.[97] It also observes:

91 Tribunal Procedure Rules r11(1) and (11A). (Rule 11(1A) was introduced by the Tribunal Procedure (Amendment No 3) Rules 2014 SI No 2128 (L.30)) r21.)

92 Rule 11(7)(a).

93 Rule 11(7) (b). For further discussion on the capacity of patients to appoint, see *YA v Central and North West London NHS Trust* [2015] UKUT 37 (AAC), (in particular at [58]) and *PI v West London Mental Health NHS Trust* [2017] UKUT 0066 (AAC) (both cases related to adults).

94 In *YA v Central and North West London NHS Trust* [2015] UKUT 37 (ACC) Mr Justice Charles noted that for 'sensible pragmatic reasons' such appointments are made by tribunal staff under Tribunal Procedure Rules r11(7). See *Practice statement delegation of functions to registrars, tribunal case workers and authorised tribunal staff on or after 8 July 2016 – First Tier Tribunal Health, Education & Social Care Chamber (Mental Health)*.

95 *Representation before Mental Health Tribunals*, The Law Society, 4.2. The responsibilities of the legal representative appointed by the tribunal was considered in *YA v Central and North West London NHS Trust* [2015] UKUT 37 (ACC) at [13]–[16].

96 [2017] UKUT 0066 (AAC) at [34].

97 *Representation before mental health tribunals*, The Law Society, 4.1.

> The information that a patient is required to understand to instruct a solicitor in the context of an application to a tribunal is not complex and people severely affected by a mental disorder may still be able to provide instructions if you explain matters simply and clearly.[98]

8.45 Although the presumption of capacity under the MCA 2005, cited by the Law Society applies only to individuals aged 16 years and over, adolescents aged under 16 years may be able to give instructions if the issues are explained to them clearly and in age-appropriate language. However, given that there is no presumption of capacity for this age group, legal representatives acting for adolescents aged 15 or younger might find it helpful to record that they have assessed the adolescent's capacity to instruct them and (where that is the case) are satisfied that the adolescent is capable of doing so.[99]

8.46 The Law Society's Practice Note explains that there will be occasions where the legal representative cannot act for a client because that person lacks capacity to give instructions, noting that this might arise where 'the client is profoundly learning disabled and cannot appreciate that they are detained under the MHA 1983'.[100] As there are no age limits to the powers to detain under the MHA 1983, in some cases adolescents might lack the capacity to instruct a legal representative because they are too young to understand the relevant information, such as that they are detained under the MHA 1983. Where such concerns arise, as noted above (para 8.42) the tribunal can appoint a legal representative to act on behalf of the adolescent.[101]

Pre-hearing examination[102]

8.47 Adolescents who have applied to the tribunal when detained under MHA 1983 s2 will be examined by the medical member of the tribunal before the hearing. While such pre-hearing examinations are automatic in relation to MHA 1983 s2 applications, they are not for applications to the tribunal in relation to detention under section 3. Accordingly, where adolescents have made an application in relation to section 3 and it is thought that it will be helpful for them to meet with the medical member prior to the tribunal hearing,

98 *Representation before mental health tribunals,* The Law Society, 4.1.

99 See paras 3.31–3.34 for the assessment of under-16s's ability to make decisions (competence).

100 *Representation before mental health tribunals,* The Law Society, 4.2.

101 See Tribunal Procedure Rules r11(7)(a) and (b). See *VS v St Andrews Healthcare* [2018] UKUT 250 (AAC), [2019] AACR 4 at [1] for list of cases that have considered the capacity of detained patients in relation to different aspects of proceedings before the tribunal.

102 Tribunal Procedure Rules r34.

they or their representative must request the pre-hearing examination 14 days or more before the hearing.[103]

Conduct of the hearing

8.48 The tribunal has powers to determine who can attend the hearing or part of it[104] and will make such decisions within the context of the tribunal's overriding objective of dealing with cases fairly and justly, in particular 'ensuring, so far as practicable, that the parties are able to participate fully in the proceedings'.[105] For example, to make the adolescent feel more at ease, the tribunal may reduce the number of mental health professionals in the room; or if the adolescent is unhappy about their parents being present, the tribunal may ask that they leave the room when the adolescent is giving evidence.

Tribunal powers

Introduction

8.49 The powers of the tribunal that are relevant to adolescents detained in hospital for assessment or treatment under MHA 1983 Part 2 are set out in s72. The circumstances in which the tribunal must discharge an adolescent are set out below. The tribunal also has powers to discharge patients 'in any case',[106] although this power should only be exercised in 'exceptional circumstances'.[107]

103 Tribunal Procedure Rules r34(2)(b). Some adolescents may find a pre-hearing examination (PHE) helpful. It may also be useful given that, anecdotally, some adolescents choose not to attend the hearing and while Tribunal Procedure Rules r39 permits hearings to take place in the party's absence this is subject to certain conditions being met, one of which is that there has been a PHE (unless this is 'impracticable or unnecessary'). For a discussion on PHEs see S Johnston, S Miles and Dr C Royston, *Mental Health Tribunal Handbook,* LAG, 2015, paras 11.119–11.123. However, it should be noted that one of the temporary measures introduced in response to the coronavirus pandemic was that (on a six month 'pilot basis') no PHEs were to be undertaken (see *Pilot Practice Direction: health, education and social care chamber of the first-tier tribunal (mental health)* 19 March 2020).

104 Tribunal Procedure Rules r38(1). One of the temporary measures introduced by SI 2020 No 416 is to make provision for decisions to be made without a hearing if: the matter is urgent; it is not reasonably practicable for there to be a hearing (including a hearing where the proceedings would be conducted wholly or partly as video proceedings or audio proceedings); and it is in the interests of justice to do so (see Tribunal Procedure Rules r5A (as inserted by SI 2020 No 416 r2(2)).

105 Tribunal Procedure Rules r2(1) and (2)(c).

106 MHA 1983 s72(1).

107 *GA v Betsi Cadwaladr University LHB* [2013] UKUT 280 (AAC) (12 June 2013) at [24].

Adolescents liable to be detained under MHA 1983 s2

8.50 MHA 1983 s72(1)(a) will be relevant to adolescents detained under s2. It provides that the tribunal must discharge a patient detained under section 2 if it is not satisfied:

> (i) that he is then suffering from mental disorder or from mental disorder of a nature or degree which warrants his detention in a hospital for assessment (or for assessment followed by medical treatment) for at least a limited period; or
> (ii) that his detention as aforesaid is justified in the interests of his own health or safety, or with a view to the protection of other persons . . .

8.51 If, by the time the adolescent's case comes before the tribunal,[108] the adolescent is detained under MHA 1983 s3, the tribunal will apply the criteria relevant to patients detained under s3 set out below.[109] This will not prevent the adolescent from applying to the tribunal in relation to the period of detention under s3.

Adolescents liable to be detained under MHA 1983 s3

8.52 MHA 1983 s72(1)(b) will be relevant to adolescents detained under s3. It provides that the tribunal must discharge a patient detained under s3 if it is not satisfied:

> (i) that he is then suffering from mental disorder or from mental disorder of a nature or degree which makes it appropriate for

108 Tribunal Procedure Rules r37(1) requires the hearing to be within seven days after the date on which the tribunal received the application notice. However, one of the changes introduced in response to the COVID-19 pandemic is that SI 2020 No 416 reg 2(5)(a) amends this rule to extend the time to 10 days. It adds a further provision that permits the tribunal to decide when to convene the hearing if it 'considers that it is not reasonably practicable' for a hearing to start within the 10-day period (see Tribunal Procedure Rules r37(1A) (as amended by SI 2020/416 reg 2(5)(b)). The rules make no provision for listing of s3 hearings although anecdotally these are heard between four and eight weeks (see *R (C) v London South and South West Region MHRT* [2001] EWCA Civ 1110; and *R (KB) v Mental Health Review Tribunal and Secretary of State for Health* [2002] EWHC 639 (Admin).

109 *R v South Thames Mental Health Review Tribunal ex p M* (unreported) 3 September 1997 (CO/2700/97) cited in P Fennell, *Mental health law and practice*, 3rd edn, Jordans, p308; and R Jones, *Mental Health Act Manual*, 23rd edn, Sweet & Maxwell, 2020, p441. See also *SM v Livewell Southwest CIC* [2020] UKUT 191 (ACC) at [55] and *AD'A v Cornwall Partnership NHS Trust* [2020] UKUT 110 (AAC)

him to be liable to be detained in a hospital for medical treatment; or

(ii) that it is necessary for the health or safety of the patient or for the protection of other persons that he should receive such treatment; or

(iia) that appropriate medical treatment is available for him; . . .

8.53 If the patient has a learning disability, the learning disability qualification (discussed at para 6.10) will apply. This means that where adolescents have a learning disability, if this is to be considered to be a mental disorder for the purpose of MHA 1983 s72, the learning disability must be associated with their 'abnormally aggressive or seriously irresponsible conduct'. [110]

8.54 It should be noted that the tribunal must consider an additional criterion in cases where the patient's NR has made an application to the tribunal after the RC blocked the NR's order to discharge (see above, para 8.9). In such cases, the tribunal must discharge the patient if not satisfied 'that the patient if released would be likely to act in a manner dangerous to other persons or to himself'.[111]

Burden of proof

8.55 In all cases before the tribunal, it will be for those who believe that the person should continue to be detained 'to present the tribunal with sufficient evidence to support continuing liability to detention', with clinical and social reports forming 'the backbone of this evidence'.[112] This is because, as noted above, the tribunal must direct a patient's discharge from detention if it is not satisfied that the criteria set out under MHA 1983 s72 are met. It is therefore for the detaining authority (the hospital managers[113]) to satisfy the tribunal that the relevant criteria are met.[114] The standard of proof applied by the tribunal when determining whether the relevant criteria are met in each case, is the balance of probabilities (meaning more likely than not).[115]

110 MHA 1983 s1(2A) and (2B)(c).

111 MHA 1983 s72(2)(b)(iii).

112 MHA Code para 12.5.

113 Tribunal Procedure Rules r1(3) ('responsible authority'). See also MHA Reference Guide figure 12.

114 *R (N) v Mental Health Review Tribunal (Northern Region)* [2005] EWCA Civ 1605 at [8].

115 *R (N) v Mental Health Review Tribunal (Northern Region)* [2005] EWCA Civ 1605 at [104].

Deferred discharge and recommendations

8.56 Tribunals can defer discharge by directing that it takes place on a specified future date.[116] Delaying discharge in this way may be needed to make the necessary arrangements for the adolescent's care and support on leaving hospital, for example where they are to live. In cases where it decides not to direct a patient's discharge, the tribunal has the power to make recommendations under MHA 1983 s72(3). With a view to facilitating a patient's discharge on a future date, the tribunal may recommend that the patient is 'granted leave of absence or transferred to another hospital or into guardianship' and can consider the patient's case again if its recommendations have not been followed.[117]

8.57 The power to recommend a transfer to another hospital might be helpful in an adolescent's case where that adolescent is placed a long distance from home (as noted at paras 6.97–6.104 this continues to be a concern) if the tribunal considers that being in a hospital closer to home will facilitate the adolescent's discharge.

8.58 In *RB v Nottinghamshire Healthcare NHS Trust,* the Upper Tribunal emphasised the need for careful consideration by the tribunal in deciding whether to make recommendations given that it has no power to enforce them:

> If the tribunal does make a recommendation, it has to take account of the tenuous nature of its control. This makes it essential to consider very carefully the timescale and the directions that the tribunal might give in order (i) to apply its moral pressure on the authority and (ii) to be fully informed by the time it has to decide whether to reconvene. It may, for example, be appropriate for the tribunal to direct that a progress report be provided shortly before a specified date so that it can decide if there is any practical purpose in reconvening. Finally, the tribunal has to decide whether to reconvene. In making that decision, it has to decide what practical value this would serve. It has no power to enforce the recommendation and is not reconvening for that purpose. It has the power to embarrass the authority into explaining its thinking or, possibly, into compliance. But it has to make a judgment on what it can practically achieve, if anything.[118]

8.59 Although the tribunal's recommendations are not binding on them, the MHA Reference Guide states that if the hospital managers or the RC 'do not put the recommendations in place, it is good practice that

116 MHA 1983 s72(3).
117 MHA 1983 s72(3)(b).
118 [2011] UKUT 73 (AAC) at [16].

they put their reasons in writing and explain these to the patient, nearest relative and, if different, carer'.[119]

8.60 The tribunal may also recommend that the RC considers whether to make a CTO 'and may (but need not) further consider the patient's case, if the responsible clinician does not make an order'.[120]

Reports to the tribunal

Overview

8.61 The Tribunal Procedure Rules[121] and the Senior President of Tribunals' 2013 Practice Direction[122] specify the information that the hospital managers (as the 'responsible authority'[123]) must send to the tribunal prior to the hearing date and the timescales for doing so. These are:

- a 'statement of information about the patient';
- the 'responsible clinician's report';
- the 'nursing report'; and
- the 'social circumstances report'.[124]

Timescale for submitting reports

8.62 In cases concerning patients who are detained under MHA 1983 s3, such reports must be sent to the tribunal 'as soon as practicable and in any event within three weeks after the responsible authority made the reference or received a copy of the application or reference'.[125] In cases concerning patients detained under MHA 1983 s2, these reports should be prepared as soon as practicable after receiving a copy of the application or reference and 'must be made available to

119 MHA Reference Guide para 6.74.

120 MHA 1983 s72(3A).

121 Rule 32 ('Procedure in mental health cases').

122 *First-tier Tribunal Health Education and Social Care Chamber Statements and Reports in Mental Health Cases*, Tribunals Judiciary, October 2013.

123 Tribunal Procedure Rules r1(3).

124 Practice Direction 2013 para 7.

125 Tribunal Procedure Rules r32(6); Practice Direction 2013 para 8. In some cases, the tribunal can withhold information from the patient. However this is only permitted if the stringent conditions set out in Tribunal Procedure Rules r14(2) are met (disclosure likely to cause serious harm and non-disclosure is a proportionate measure having regard to the interests of justice). An important practical consideration is the impact of the contents of the report on the adolescent, how such information should be conveyed and what support the adolescent may need, if they find any aspect of the report upsetting, unclear and/or inaccurate.

the Tribunal and the patient's representative at least one hour before the hearing is due to start' (and the reports should state if any of the specified information is omitted because it is not available).[126]

After-care planning and the social circumstances report

8.63 The social circumstances report is expected to contain a range of information, including matters relevant to aftercare planning, such as 'details of any Care Pathway Approach and/or [MHA 1983] Section 117 aftercare plan in full or in embryo'.[127] Annex E of the Practice Direction lists the additional information which is required for the social circumstances reports for under-18s. In doing so, it highlights the wide range of legislation and policy that may be applicable to under-18s, an overview of which is explained in chapter 2 above, with further information in relation to planning for adolescents' after-care being provided in chapter 9 below. As noted in these chapters, this is an area in which there are significant differences between under-18s and adults. The information required by Annex E is considered below (paras 8.67–8.69).

Tribunal panel and under-18s

8.64 Tribunals are heard by three members:

- the legal member (referred to as the tribunal judge, who chairs the hearing);
- the medical member (a psychiatrist); and
- a specialist lay member (who has substantial experience of health or social care matters).[128]

8.65 The tribunal has established a Child and Adolescent Mental Health Services (CAMHS) panel. The purpose of this panel is to ensure that when considering the case of an under 18-year-old, at least one

126 Tribunal Procedure Rules r32(5); Practice Direction 2013 para 9.

127 Practice Direction 2013 paras 7 and 14(i). See also MHA Code para 19.109.

128 *Practice statement composition of tribunals in relation to matters that fall to be decided by the health, education and social care chamber on or after 16 December 2015*, Tribunals Judiciary, December 2015. As a result of the coronavirus pandemic, cases were listed before a single judge, unless considered inappropriate in a particular case (*Pilot Practice Direction: health, education and social care chamber of the first-tier tribunal (mental health)*, 19 March 2020). However, at the time of writing (August 2020) three-member panels are once again in operation.

member of the tribunal has experience of working with this age group.[129]

8.66 The Senior President of Tribunals' Annual Report, 2018 noted that there has been a gradual increase in the numbers of tribunal members on this panel, observing that 'cases, involving young people often placed a considerable distance away from home, demand particular judicial skills and sensitivity'.[130] The 2019 Annual Report notes that the CAMHS panel has worked with YoungMinds(a children and young people's mental health charity), to provide accessible information on tribunals on YoungMinds website.[131]

Social circumstances report: additional information for under-18s

8.67 The MHA Code (para 19.109) states:

> Professionals preparing social circumstances reports for the Tribunal must ensure that such reports include any information required in the Tribunal's Practice Directions.

8.68 As noted above, the Senior President of Tribunals' 2013 Practice Direction[132] sets out the information to be included in the social circumstances report, with Annex E setting out the additional information required for all patients under the age of 18 (para 35.a)–q)). Key points from Annex E are listed below, with cross-references to other chapters in this book for further information.[133]

129 MHA Code para 19.108.

130 Senior President of Tribunals Annual Report 2018, May 2018, p30.

131 Senior President of Tribunals Annual Report 2019, October 2019, p34. YoungMinds has also published *A guide to mental health tribunals for young people*, see: www.youngminds.org.

132 *First-tier Tribunal Health Education and Social Care Chamber Statements and Reports in Mental Health Cases*, Tribunals Judiciary, October 2013.

133 Who is the best person to prepare the social circumstances report and give evidence to the tribunal, is an important consideration given that those working with the adolescent may have a range of differing perspectives and areas of expertise, eg CAMHS professionals (mental health law and policy) and local authority children's services (CA 1989 and related law and policy).

Table 8.2: Social circumstances report – additional information for under 18s

1) Parental responsibility (PR)

Practice Direction (PD)	Comments and cross-references
Identifying those with PR: 'The names and addresses of any people with parental responsibility, and how they acquired parental responsibility' (PD 35.a)).	Acquisition of PR; roles and powers of those with PR. See paras 5.13–5.14.

2) Care orders and interim care orders

Practice Direction (PD)	Comments and cross-references
Care orders and interim care orders: 'if the patient is subject to or has been the subject of a Care Order or an Interim Care Order: • [general information on the order eg: 'date and duration of any such order'; 'identity of the relevant local authority'; 'identity of any person(s) with whom the local authority shares parental responsibility'; and information about any ongoing proceedings including 'the court in which proceedings are taking place and the date of the next hearing']; • whether the patient comes under the Children (Leaving Care) Act 2000; • whether there has been any liaison between, on the one hand, social workers responsible for mental health services to children and adolescents and, on the other hand, those responsible for such services for adults; • the name of the social worker within the relevant local authority who is discharging the function of the Nearest Relative under Section 27 of the [MHA 1983]' (PD 35.j)).	• If there has been a care order or interim care order in place, it will be necessary to ascertain whether this continues to be in place or if it has been discharged. • If in place, the relevant local authority will have parental responsibility (shared with others (see para 5.13)). • The Children (Leaving Care) Act 2000 amends the Children Act (CA) 1989, placing duties on local authorities to provide support for young people leaving care. (See The Children Act 1989 guidance and regulations. Volume 3: planning transition to adulthood for care leavers (Department for Education, January 2015).) • The local authority will be the NR for adolescents subject to a care order or interim care order (MHA 1983 s27 – see table 5.2 for exceptions).

3) Adolescents accommodated under CA 1989 s20

Practice Direction (PD)	Comments and cross-references
• 'if a patient has been or is a looked after child under Section 20 of the Children Act 1989, when the child	• Accommodation under CA 1983 s20 (see paras 9.30–9.35). • CA 1989 Sch 2 para 17 has now been

became looked after, why the child became looked after, what steps have been taken to discharge the obligations of the local authority under Paragraph 17(1) of Schedule 2 of the Children Act 1989, and what steps are being taken (if required) to discharge the obligations of the local authority under Paragraph 10(b) of Schedule 2 of the Children Act 1989' (PD 35.n)).	repealed, but see local authorities' duties to visit CA 1989 s23ZA (see paras 7.69–7.77). • CA 1989 Sch 2 para 15(1) places duties on local authorities to promote contact between looked after children and their families (para 10(b) relates to children in need who are not looked after who are living apart from their families) (see para 7.88).

4) The NR and orders under the CA 1989

Practice Direction (PD)	Comments and cross-references
'whether any other orders under the Children Act 1989 are in existence in respect of the patient and, if so, the details of those orders, together with the date on which such orders were made, and whether they are final or interim orders' (PD 35.m)).	• These might be child arrangement orders (CAOs), guardianship orders (CA 1989 s5), or special guardianship orders (CA 1989 s14A), which will be relevant to who has PR (see table 5.1) and who is the NR (MHA 1983 s28).

5) Wards of court

Practice Direction (PD)	Comments and cross-references
'if the patient is a Ward of Court, when the patient was made a ward of court and what steps have been taken to notify the court that made the order of any significant steps taken, or to be taken, in respect of the patient' (PD 35.l)).	• '. . . although day to day care and control of the ward is given to an individual or to a local authority, no important step can be taken in the child's life without the court's consent'.[134] • MHA 1983 s33 (see paras 5.37–5.38).

6) Secure accommodation: CA 1989 s25

Practice Direction (PD)	Comments and cross-references
'if a patient has been the subject of a secure accommodation order under Section 25 of the Children Act 1989, the date on which the order was made, the reasons it was made, and the date it expired' (PD 35.p)).	• Where an adolescent is detained in hospital under the MHA 1983, CA 1989 s25 cannot be applied.[135] See also para 3.22.

134 Practice Direction 12D – Inherent Jurisdiction (including wardship) proceedings, para 1.3. This 'no important step principle' was reiterated in *Re A (ward of court)* [2017] EWHC 1022 (Fam) para 17.

135 Children (Secure accommodation) Regulations 1991 SI No 1505 reg 5(1). Note, however, that in *Hereford and Worcester CC v S* [1993] 2 FLR 360 the court held that an s25 order could be made in respect an adolescent who was on s17 leave, having been detained under MHA 1983 s2.

7) Accommodated children: CA 1989 ss85–86A

Practice Direction (PD)	Comments and cross-references
'if a patient is a child provided with accommodation under Sections 85 and 86 of the Children Act 1989, what steps have been taken by the accommodating authority or person carrying on the establishment in question to discharge the their notification responsibilities, and what steps have been taken by the local authority to discharge their obligations under Sections 85, 86 and 86A of the Children Act 1989' (PD 35.q)).	• These provisions require the hospital to notify the relevant local authority that an under-18-year-old has been / is expected to be, accommodated in hospital for three months or more. • See paras 7.78–7.86 for notification and local authority's duties once notified.

8) Relevant personnel

Practice Direction (PD)	Comments and cross-references
'the name and contact details of the patient's Care Co-ordinator, Community Psychiatric Nurse, Social Worker/AMHP or Social Supervisor' (PD 35.g)).	• Other useful contact details: the independent review officer (IRO) (if a looked after child) and the 'Personal Advisor' (if an 'eligible child' – see paras 2.52–2.53).

9) Guardianship under MHA 1983 s7

Social circumstances report (SCR)	Comments and cross-references
'if the patient is subject to guardianship under Section 7 of the Act, whether any orders have been made under the Children Act 1989 in respect of the patient, and what consultation there has been with the guardian' (PD 35.k)).	• Although used rarely, guardianship under MHA 1983 s7 can apply to individuals aged 16 and over (see paras 10.72–10.91).

10) Assessment of needs and service provision

Practice Direction (PD)	Comments and cross-references
Assessment of needs: 'whether the patient's needs have been assessed under the Children Act 1989 or the Chronically Sick and Disabled Persons Act 1970 and, if not, the reasons why such an assessment has not been carried out and whether it is proposed to carry out such an assessment' (PD h)).	• Assessments under CA 1989 s17 and Chronically Sick and Disabled Persons Act (CSDPA) 1970 s2 are likely to be relevant to the planning of adolescents' after-care, whether or not they are entitled to services under MHA 1983 s117. • See paras 9.20–9.38.
Findings from assessment of needs: 'if there has been such an assessment, what needs or requirements have been identified and how those needs or requirements will be met' (PD 35.i)).	• On CA 1989 s17 child in need assessments, see paras 9.21–9.25.

Child in need: 'if a patient has been treated by a local authority as a child in need (which includes a child who has a mental disorder) under Section 17(11) of the Children Act 1989, the period or periods for which the child has been so treated, why they were considered to be a child in need, what services were or are being made available to the child by virtue of that status, and details of any assessment of the child' (PD 35.o)).	• For the definition of a child in need, see paras 9.21–9.22.

11) MHA 1983 s117 after-care services

Practice Direction (PD)	Comments and cross-references
Liaison between agencies: 'which public bodies have worked together or need to liaise in relation to after-care services that may be provided under Section 117 of the [MHA 1983]' (PD 35.b)).	• See paras 9.39–9.56 for MHA 1983 s117 after-care planning. • The SCR is expected to cover 'details of any Care Pathway Approach and/or Section 117 aftercare plan in full or in embryo'.[136]
Outcome of liaison: 'the outcome of any liaison that has taken place' (PD 35.c)) **Reasons for lack of liaison:** 'if liaison has not taken place, why not – and when liaison will take place' (PD 35.d)). **Care plan:** 'the details of any multi-agency care plan in place or proposed' (PD 35.e)); **Disputes:** 'whether there are any issues as to funding the care plan and, if so, the date by which those issues will be resolved' (PD 35.f)).	• Not all adolescents will be entitled to MHA 1983 s117 after-care. However, adolescents who are receiving in-patient psychiatric care may be entitled to support under other legislation. An over-view of the relevant legal frameworks is provided in chapter 3 and further considered in relation to after-care in chapter 9.

8.69 The Practice Direction was published in 2013. Since then further legislation and policy has been introduced which form part of the legal framework for the planning of adolescents' discharge from hospital. Reflecting such developments, the table below includes additional questions which it is suggested would need to be

136 Practice Direction First-tier Tribunal Health and Education and Social Care Chamber Statements and Reports in Mental Health Cases, para 7 and see also para 14(i): 'so far as is known, details of the care pathway and Section 117 after-care to be made available to the patient, together with details of the proposed care plan'. See also information on the Care Programme Approach (CPA) (see para 9.9 and box 9.1).

considered as part of the care-planning process, with cross references to other chapters of this book for further information.

Additional Care-planning considerations	**Comments and cross-references**
Support for parents and carers: *Have any assessments been undertaken of parents and other carers' willingness and ability to provide care to the under 18 year old, and if so, with what result?*	• See 'Carers' assessments', chapter 9 paras 9.57–9.65
EHC Plan: if the adolescent has an EHC plan: *When was this put in place, which local authority is responsible for maintaining the EHC plan?* *Has the authority been involved in creating the discharge plan, so that the EHC plan is revised as necessary to continue to reflect the child or young person's*[137] *educational, health and social care needs?* (MHA Code para 19.118)	• See 'Special educational needs and disability', chapter 2, paras 2.54–2.72 • See chapter 9, para 9.9
Transition to Adult Services *If the adolescent is likely to be in need of care and support on becoming 18 has a 'transition assessment' under section 58 of the Care Act 2014 been considered?* *If a transition assessment has been undertaken, what was the outcome?*	• See chapter 9, paras 9.65–9.81 on transition assessments • See also the MHA Code (para 19.119) which states that transition planning should start at least 6 months before the adolescent is due to leave CAMHS
Care Education and Treatment Reviews (CETR): *When was the last CETR review?* *What were the CETR's key findings and recommendations?* *Who has been identified as the person responsible for ensuring that 'the CETR*	• CETRs apply if the adolescent has learning disabilities, autism or both (see chapter 2, paras 2.91–2.95) • Standard 6.3 of the CETR Toolkit (concerning the preparation and dissemination (of the report of the CETR) states that this report 'will always inform the professional's report' to the Tribunal and Hospital Managers'[138] and

137 In this context the young person may be aged between 16 and 25 – see CFA 2014 s83(2).

138 NHS England *Care, Education and Treatment Reviews for children and young people Code and Toolkit: a guide for commissioners, panel members and people who provide support* April 2017 (CETR Toolkit) CETR Toolkit, 6.3.5.

recommendations are embedded in other relevant assessment and planning processes along with clear timescales' (such as EHC assessments/plans, Children in Need plans, Looked After Children plans and risk assessments?).[140]	'should be made available to the adolescent's legal representative.[139]

139 CETR Toolkit 6.3.4.

140 CETR Toolkit, Standard 7.4, p28.

CHAPTER 9

After-care planning

continued

Introduction

9.1 Chapter 19 of the *Mental Health Act 1983: Code of Practice*[1] ('MHA Code') highlights the range of differing legal and policy frameworks that may be relevant when determining the level of after-care support that children and young people aged under 18 ('adolescents') will need on being discharged from hospital:

> Prior to their discharge from hospital all children and young people should have an assessment of their needs, on which a care plan for their after-care is based. Guidance on the duty to provide after-care under section 117 of the Act, is set out in chapter 33. Such guidance is applicable to individuals of all ages, but in relation to children and young people additional factors will need to be considered. This may include ensuring that the after-care integrates with any existing provision made for looked after children and those with special educational needs or disabilities, as well as safeguarding vulnerable children. Whether or not section 117 of the Act applies, a child or young person who has been admitted to hospital for assessment and/or treatment of their mental disorder may be 'a child in need' for the purpose of section 17 of the Children Act 1989.[2]

9.2 This chapter considers the various legal frameworks that will be relevant when determining an adolescent's care and support needs on discharge from hospital. It covers the following areas in relation to after-care:

- an overview of planning adolescents' after-care;
- the involvement of local authority children's services;
- after-care services under Mental Health Act (MHA) 1983 s117;
- carers' assessments;
- transition to adult services;
- identifying the responsible MHA 1983 s117 after-care bodies; and
- ordinary residence.

Planning adolescents' after-care: overview

Introduction

9.3 The 'planning of after-care needs to start as soon as the patient is admitted to hospital'. Clinical commissioning groups (CCGs)

1 DoH, 2015.

2 MHA Code chapter 19 para 19.111.

(see Glossary) and local authorities are expected to take reasonable steps to 'identify appropriate after-care services for patients in good time for their eventual discharge from hospital'.[3] The key points relevant to planning an adolescent's after-care are summarised below.

Assessing needs for services and support following discharge

9.4 The four main provisions governing the assessment of adolescents' needs and the provision of services on their discharge from hospital are as follows:

- *MHA 1983 s117:* Adolescents detained under MHA 1983 s3 are entitled to receive the 'after-care services' they have been assessed to need on their discharge from hospital.[4]
- *Children Act (CA) 1989 s17:* Whether or not they are entitled to aftercare services under MHA 1983 s117, adolescents who have been receiving in-patient psychiatric care are likely to fall within the definition of a 'child in need' under CA 1989 s17.
- *Chronically Sick and Disabled Persons Act (CSDPA) 1970 s2:* Assessments for after-care services under MHA 1983 s117, 'child in need' assessments under CA 1989 s17, as well as education, health and care (EHC) needs under Children and Families Act (CFA) 2014 Part 3, are likely to require consideration of the adolescent's needs as a 'disabled child' under CSDPA 1970 s2.
- *Care Act 2014 ss58 and 59:* Provide for the circumstances in which adolescents are entitled and assessment of their needs for care and support on becoming 18 ('transition assessments').

Core purpose of assessment of adolescents' needs

9.5 Although there is a range of differing legislation and associated policy that provide for adolescents' assessment of needs, their common purpose is to assess each adolescent's individual needs and determine what services and supports are to be provided to meet such needs.[5] HM Government's July 2018 report *Working Together to*

3 MHA Code para 34.17.

4 The application of MHA 1983 s117 to individuals detained under MHA 1983 ss37, 45A, 47 and 48 (Part 3 of the Act) is not covered in this chapter.

5 *Working together* p23 para 38. For further information on *Working together*, see paras 2.30–2.34.

Safeguard Children: A guide to inter-agency working to safeguard and promote the welfare of children ('*Working together*') makes this clear:

> Whatever legislation the child is assessed under, the purpose of the assessment is always:
> - to gather important information about a child and family
> - to analyse their needs and/or the nature and level of any risk and harm being suffered by the child
> - to decide whether the child is a child in need ([CA 1989] section 17) or is suffering or likely to suffer significant harm ([CA 1989] section 47)
> - to provide support to address those needs to improve the child's outcomes and welfare and where necessary to make them safe.[6]

Joint-working and participation

9.6 Two overarching principles are as follows:

- *Joint working:* The process for planning the after-care to be provided on an adolescent's discharge should be underpinned by the joint working provisions identified at para 2.77 and the overarching principles of the MHA Code (para 2.86).
- *Participation:* Legislation and policy guidance emphasise the importance of involving adolescents in the planning of their care.[7] Their parents and other carers should also be involved (unless there are grounds for not doing so).[8]

Preparation for tribunal or hospital managers' hearings

9.7 The MHA Code highlights the importance of considering a person's after-care needs before their case is considered by the Mental Health Tribunal (see chapter 8) or hospital managers:

> When considering relevant patients' cases, the Tribunal and hospital managers will expect to be provided with information from the professionals concerned on what after-care arrangements might be made if they were to be discharged. Some discussion of after-care arrangements involving local authorities, other relevant agencies and families or carers (where appropriate) should take place in advance of the Tribunal hearing.[9]

6 *Working together* p23 para 38.

7 See for example: CA 1989 s20(4) and MHA Code para 19.5.

8 MHA Code paras 19.14–19.16.

9 MHA Code para 33.11.

9.8 Accordingly, if an adolescent has a forthcoming tribunal or hospital managers' hearing, the hospital managers should inform the relevant CCG and local authority of such a hearing. In turn, these bodies should consider what after-care arrangements are needed prior to a tribunal or hospital managers' hearing, particularly if 'there is a strong possibility' that the adolescent will be discharged if appropriate after-care can be arranged.[10]

Integration of relevant legal and policy frameworks

9.9 The after-care planning should integrate any other care planning provisions, including carers' assessments (see paras 9.57–9.64 below). In particular, it should integrate the following matters (explained below):

- looked after children;
- special educational needs (SEN);
- guidance on care-planning;
- Care, Education and Treatment Reviews (CETRs);
- Care Programme Approach (CPA).

Looked after children

9.10 For adolescents who are a 'looked after child' (see paras 9.21–9.25), the responsible local authority's involvement in the planning of their discharge arrangements will be essential. For example, guidance for independent reviewing officers (IROs) states that whether the looked after child is an informal patient or detained under the MHA 1983, 'the IRO will need to be satisfied that the local authority is fulfilling its responsibilities and that appropriate plans to meet the child's needs and planned outcomes are in place before discharge'.[11]

9.11 Regulations set out a range of issues that must be considered in a looked after child's case review, including whether the 'placement continues to be the most appropriate available'.[12] It is suggested therefore that when planning a looked after child's discharge from hospital, an important consideration will be whether the placement

10 MHA Code para 33.12.

11 *IRO Handbook: Statutory guidance for independent reviewing officers and local authorities on their functions in relation to case management and review for looked after children*, Department for Children, Schools and Families, 2010, para 4.17. See also the Care Planning, Placement and Case Review (England) Regulations 2010 SI No 959 reg 32(2).

12 SI 2010 No 959 reg 35 and Sch 7.

prior to that adolescent's admission to hospital is still appropriate and will continue to meet the adolescent's needs.[13]

9.12 Guidance on case reviews is included in chapter 4 of the *Children Act 1989 guidance and regulations. Volume 2: care planning, placement and case review*[14] ('Care Planning Guidance').

Special educational needs

9.13 For adolescents who have an EHC plan, the local authority responsible for maintaining the plan 'should also be involved in creating the discharge plan' so that the EHC plan is revised to reflect the adolescent's needs.[15] In addition to provision for the adolescent's SEN, the EHC plan must include details of the provision of social care and health[16] and these will need to be reviewed in the light of the adolescent's discharge from hospital.

9.14 If adolescents do not have an EHC plan, they (if aged over 16), their parents, or a person acting on behalf of a school or post-16 institution can request an EHC assessment.[17] CCGs and NHS trusts must notify the local authority (having first raised this with the adolescent's parents) where they believe that an adolescent has SEN or a disability.[18]

9.15 Guidance on special educational needs is set out in *Special educational needs and disability code of practice: 0 to 25 years. Statutory guidance for organisations which work with and support children and young people who have special educational needs or disabilities* ('SEND Code').[19]

Guidance on care-planning

9.16 *Working together* notes that assessments should be 'co-ordinated so that the child does not become lost between the different organisational

13 *The Children Act 1989 Volume 2, Care Planning, Placement and Case Review*, June 2015, p119.

14 DfE, June 2015.

15 MHA Code para 19.118.

16 CFA 2014 s37(2).

17 CFA 2014 s36(1). The local authority responsible for undertaking the assessment is determined under CFA 2014 s24 (the adolescent must be 'in the authority's area'). The SEND Code (para 10.8) states that this means the local authority where the child is ordinarily resident. However, see discussion in *R (JG) v Kent CC* [2016] EWHC 1102 (Admin).

18 CFA 2014 s23. See also SEND Code para 9.9.

19 DfE and DoH, January 2015. See also chapter 2 above, which provides an overview of relevant law and policy concerning SEN and disability, with references to further information.

procedures', with 'clear procedures for how these organisations and agencies will communicate with the child and family'.[20] In addition, 'the local protocol for assessment should clarify how organisations and agencies and practitioners undertaking assessments and providing services can make contributions'.[21]

9.17 This point is also made in the guidance on the CPA (see below). Similarly, the SEND Code highlights the importance of co-ordinating social care provision for children in need and looked after children with the assessment and review of EHC plans.[22]

Care, Education and Treatment Reviews

9.18 NHS England's policy on CETRs applies to adolescents with learning disabilities, autism or both. The CETR Code and Toolkit includes discharge standards, such as having a named discharge facilitator, CPA community care co-ordinator, social worker and advocate.[23] Details on CETRs are provided at paras 2.91–2.95.

Care Programme Approach

9.19 Whether or not they are detained under the MHA 1983 or entitled to section 117 after-care services, the support that an adolescent will need on discharge from hospital should be assessed and planned under the CPA.[24] Chapter 34 of the MHA Code provides guidance on the CPA. Annex B of guidance issued by the Department of Health (DoH) in 2008 – *Refocusing the Care Programme Approach: policy and positive practice guidance* ('CPA Guidance') – considers how the CPA can be adapted to apply to Child and Adolescent Mental Health Services (CAMHS) (see appendix C below).[25] Box 9.1 below sets out the core components of the CPA and how it relates to adolescents.

20 *Working together* p24 para 42.

21 *Working together* p24 para 42.

22 SEND Code paras 3.49–3.50 and 10.1–10.12 (looked after children and care leavers).

23 *Care, Education and Treatment Reviews for children and young people: Code and Toolkit – A guide for commissioner, panel members and people who provide support*, NHS England, April 2017, 57.

24 MHA Code para 33.14. As noted at para 2.88, NHS England expects in-patient Tier 4 services to plan under-18s' mental health care in accordance with the CPA.

25 Albeit published over a decade ago, this guidance is still considered to be relevant – see MHA Code 'Related material' p.367.

Box 9.1: The Care Programme Approach and adolescents – key points

Early planning

- After-care planning 'needs to start as soon as the patient is admitted to hospital'.
- CCGs and local authorities 'should take reasonable steps to identify appropriate after-care services for patients in good time for their eventual discharge from hospital'.[26]

Core components of the CPA

Adolescents receiving care through the CPA should have:

- a named individual who is responsible for co-ordinating the preparation, implementation and evaluation of the care plan;[27]
- a comprehensive multi-disciplinary assessment covering the full range of needs and risks (including an assessment of social care needs and consideration of specific needs, such as those arising from learning disability or autism spectrum disorder);[28]
- a comprehensive written care plan (a copy of which should be given to the adolescent) which includes a treatment plan; support provided in relation to social needs, such as housing; details on how the adolescent will be supported in meeting their personal goals; support provided to carers; and guidance on action to be taken in the event of a crisis;[29] and
- a regular review of their care plan.[30]

Involving adolescents

Steps to ensure that the care plan is prepared 'in close partnership'[31] with the adolescent include:

- making the meetings 'young-person friendly' (considering matters such as language used; timing of meetings; location of venues; who is in attendance; and the possible need for interpreters);
- providing information in age-appropriate language; and
- supporting adolescents 'using advocates as necessary'.[32]

26 MHA Code para 34.17.

27 MHA Code para 34.5.

28 MHA Code para 34.19.

29 MHA Code paras 34.3 and 34.4.

30 See MHA Code paras 34.2–34.20.

31 MHA Code 34.10.

32 *Refocusing the Care Programme Approach: policy and positive practice guidance* 2008 ('CPA Guidance') DoH, March 2008, p48.

Advocacy

The CPA Guidance anticipates that advocacy will be made available to those receiving care through the CPA who would like such help[33] and the MHA Code also states that individuals 'should be given to access independent advocacy or other support where this is available'.[34] In addition:

- adolescents detained under MHA 1983 s2 or s3 are entitled to support from an independent mental health advocate (IMHA) (see paras 6.63–6.65);
- (in limited circumstances) 16- and 17-year-olds are entitled to support from an independent mental capacity advocate (IMCA) (see paras 4.45–4.47).[35]

Involving adolescents' parents or other carers

The MHA Code notes that this 'may also be necessary . . . to ensure that they will be ready and able to provide the assistance and support which the patient may need'.[36]

Integrating the CPA with other legal and policy frameworks

- Local protocols between mental health services and other local agencies will be needed so that it is clear on which agency has the overall care for the adolescent. Where 'care is shared across agencies, it must be clear who takes the lead on which areas'.[37]
- The CPA 'needs to be seen in the context of other planning mechanisms for children with complex needs and agreement must be made locally on how to co-ordinate multi-agency care planning'.[38]

Implementing the care plan

An agreed outline of the adolescent's needs and timescale for implementing the various aspects of the plan should be established (in discussion with the adolescent) and all those with specific responsibilities in relation to the adolescent identified.[39]

33 CPA Guidance p16 lists 'Increased need for advocacy support' under 'What the service users should expect'.

34 MHA Code para 34.13.

35 For example, where the adolescent's accommodation is to be provided by a local authority in accordance with MHA 1983 s117: see MCA 2005 s39(1B).

36 MHA Code para 34.20. See also 'carers assessments' below.

37 CPA Guidance pp47–49.

38 CPA Guidance p48.

39 MHA Code para 34.18.

After-care: involvement of local authority children's services

Overview

9.20 Local authority children's services will have a crucial role in planning an adolescent's aftercare. This is because:

- Adolescents detained under MHA 1983 s3 will be planned within the legislative framework of MHA 1983 s117 which entails significant responsibilities for local authorities (see paras 9.39–9.56 below).
- Under CA 1989 Part 3 and CSDPA 1970 s2, local authorities have a range of duties and powers for the provision of services for under-18s. These responsibilities will be particularly important for adolescents who are being discharged from hospital but are not entitled to MHA 1983 s117 after-care services (ie those who were admitted informally, those who were detained under MHA 1983 s2 and the shorter detention sections, such as s4). Such adolescents may be a 'child in need', as well as being a 'disabled child' for the purpose of CSPDA 1970 s2, while some may also have accommodation needs.
- Local authorities may already be involved in the adolescent's care. This might be because the adolescent has SEN, is a looked after child, or both. Alternatively, the adolescent may have been receiving services as a child in need prior to admission, or the local authority may have been providing support to the adolescent during the adolescent's in-patient stay in accordance with CA 1989 ss85–86A.[40]

Children in need: Children Act 1989 s17

9.21 Whether or not MHA 1983 s117 applies, adolescents who have been admitted to hospital for assessment and/or treatment of their mental disorder and are due to be discharged from hospital are likely to be a 'child in need' for the purpose of CA 1989 s17.[41] This is because all under-18s who are 'disabled' are automatically regarded as a child in

40 See paras 7.78–7.86

41 MHA Code para 19.111. The complexities that can arise in relation to adolescents' after-care planning are illustrated by Local Government and Social Care Ombudsman Complaint (15 013 556) against Stoke on Trent, 22 August 2016, which considered a complaint that the local authority had failed to consider possible discharge options for the adolescent. See: https://www.lgo.org.uk/decisions/children-s-care-services/child-protection/15-013-556.

need[42] and the definition of 'disabled' includes having a 'mental disorder of any kind'.[43]

9.22 Alternatively, if the presence of a mental disorder is disputed (for example, if it is argued that because no diagnosis has been given, it is not clear whether the adolescent has a mental disorder[44]), the additional criteria under CA 1989 s17 should be considered. Adolescents will be a child in need if, without the provision of local authority services, they are either 'unlikely to achieve or maintain, or to have the opportunity of achieving or maintaining, a reasonable standard of health or development',[45] or their 'health or development is likely to be significantly impaired, or further impaired'.[46]

9.23 A wide range of services can be provided under CA 1989 s17, such as advice, guidance and counselling; occupational, social, cultural or recreational activities; and home help. In addition, local authorities have powers and duties to provide accommodation to children in need under CA 1989 s20 (see paras 9.30–9.35 below).

9.24 In most cases, the after-care planning will be in anticipation of the adolescent returning home, so the local authority responsible for undertaking the CA 1989 s17 assessment is likely to be the local authority in which the adolescent was living prior to being admitted to hospital. That local authority can investigate and assess the circumstances in the adolescent's home 'and form a view as to their suitability and on that basis form a view as to whether there are needs for services'.[47]

42 For other groups of under-18s it will be for the local authority to determine whether they are 'a child in need'; see *R (C, T, M and U) v Southwark LB* [2016] EWCA Civ 707 at [12].

43 CA 1989 s17(11) uses outdated language, stating: 'a child is disabled if he is blind, deaf or dumb or suffers from mental disorder of any kind or is substantially and permanently handicapped by illness, injury or congenital deformity or such other disability as may be prescribed'.

44 Anecdotally, such arguments are made. However, as S Broach and L Clements, *Disabled children: a legal handbook*, 3rd edn, LAG, 2020 (para 3.18) note, a medical diagnosis is not required prior to an assessment under CA 1989 s17 being undertaken.

45 CA 1989 s17(11) states that '"development" means physical, intellectual, emotional, social or behavioural development; and "health" means physical or mental health'.

46 CA 1989 s17(10) and (11).

47 *R (K) v Manchester CC* [2006] EWHC 3164 (Admin), (2007) 10 CCLR 87 at [42]. See also *R (VC) v Newcastle CC* [2011] EWHC 2673 (Admin) at [35]. See also 'relevant local authority' in box 9.2.

9.25 Guidance on the procedures for undertaking assessments of children in need and determining what services and support are to be provided is included in *Working together*, which 'should be complied with unless exceptional circumstances arise'.[48] Box 9.2 below summarises the key duties placed on local authorities under CA 1989 s17.

Box 9.2: Children Act 1989 s17 – local authorities' key duties to 'children in need'

Local authorities' general duty to children in need

Local authorities are under a general duty to 'safeguard and promote the welfare of children within their area who are in need'[49] and to do so 'by providing a range and level of services appropriate to those children's needs'.[50]

Meaning of 'child in need'

The definition contained in CA 1989 s17(10). The definition is broad, covering under-18s:

- who are 'unlikely to achieve or maintain, or to have the opportunity of achieving or maintaining, a reasonable standard of health or development' without the provision of local authority services;[51]
- whose 'health[52] or development[53] is likely to be significantly impaired, or further impaired' without the provision of such services ('development' means 'physical, intellectual, emotional, social or behavioural development' and 'health' meaning 'physical or mental health');[54]
- who are disabled (defined as 'blind, deaf or dumb or suffers from mental disorder of any kind or is substantially and permanently handicapped by illness, injury or congenital deformity or such other disability as may be prescribed').[55]

48 See *R (C, T, M and U) v Southwark LBC* [2016] EWCA Civ 707 at [16]. See also *Working together* p6; pp7–8 list the legislation under which this guidance is issued.

49 CA 1989 s17(1)(a).

50 CA 1989 s17(1).

51 CA 1989 s17(10)(a).

52 CA 1989 s17(11): ' "health" means physical or mental health'.

53 CA 1989 s17(11): ' "development" means physical, intellectual, emotional, social or behavioural development'.

54 CA 1989 s17(10)(b).

55 CA 1989 s17(10)(c) and (11).

Relevant local authority

- As local authorities' responsibilities under CA 1989 s17 are engaged when under-18s are 'within their area', the courts have held that 'physical presence is both necessary and of itself sufficient to establish that a child is within a local authority's area'.[56]
- This means that it is possible for an adolescent to be physically present in more than one local authority, for example, living in one area but going to school in another.
- In such cases, it will be for the local authorities concerned to resolve how to address this, as required by the duty of co-operation under CA 1989 s27.[57]

Duty to assess a child in need

Although not made explicit, the courts have established that local authorities are under a duty to assess a child in need.[58]

Timeframe for assessment

- The timeframe for assessment 'should be no longer than 45 working days from the point of referral' (which should be acknowledged within one working day).[59]
- If the assessment exceeds this period, the reasons for this should be recorded.[60]

Importance of the wishes and feelings of the child or young person

Before determining what (if any) services to provide to adolescents who are 'a child in need', local authorities must, so far as reasonably practicable, ascertain the adolescent's wishes and feelings regarding the provision of those services; and give 'due consideration' (having regard to the adolescent's age and understanding) to those wishes and feelings, so far as they have been able to ascertain them.[61]

56 *R (BC) v Birmingham CC* [2016] EWHC 3156 (Admin) at [46].

57 *R(S) v Wandsworth LBC* [2001] EWHC 709 (Admin) which emphasised the importance of co-operation between local authorities (at [28]) and noted (at [27]) that the deeming provision of CA 1989 s105(6) concerns ordinary residence and is not relevant to the duties under CA 1989 s17. See also *Suffolk CC v Nottinghamshire CC* [2012] EWCA Civ 1640 at [23] and [31].

58 *R (G) v Barnet LBC* [2003] UKHL 57; *R (J) v Worcestershire CC* [2014] EWCA Civ 1518 at [18].

59 *Working together* p31 para 75.

60 *Working together* p32.

61 CA 1989 s17(4A). See also *Working together* p21.

Duty to provide services

- Although there is no 'absolute' right of under-18s to receive services they are assessed to need,[62] the courts have emphasised that local authorities are required to 'make a rational decision as to what, if any, support is necessary and appropriate to meet the child's needs'.[63]
- While local authorities have a broad discretion to determine how and to what extent they will make provision for the identified needs, this can be challenged by way of judicial review.[64] The question for the court will be whether the local authority has gathered sufficient information to enable it to comply with its duties under the CA 1989 and the Children Act 2004 s11 (duty to make arrangements to safeguard and promote the welfare of children).[65]

Continuation of the provision of services to a 'child in need'

Local authorities have 'the power to provide services for a child in need who they have assessed regardless of the circumstances which have led to that child being no longer physically present in the area of that local authority'.[66]

Local authorities should publish protocols for assessment

- Local authority assessment protocols should 'set out clear arrangements for how cases will be managed once a child is referred into local authority children's social care' and be consistent with the guidance in *Working together*.[67]
- They should also 'reflect where assessments for some children will require particular care' (eg those with EHC plans) and set out the process for challenge by under-18s and their families by publishing the complaints procedures.[68]

62 *R (G) v Barnet LBC* [2003] UKHL 57 at [85].

63 *R (AC and SH (Children)) v Lambeth LBC* [2017] EWHC 1796 (Admin).

64 *R (J) v Worcestershire CC* [2015] EWCA Civ 1518 at [18(ii)] and *R (VC) v Newcastle CC* [2011] EWHC 2673 (Admin) at [26].

65 *R (C, T, M and U) v Southwark LBC* [2016] EWCA Civ 707 at [12]. See also discussion in S Broach and L Clements, *Disabled children: a legal handbook*, 3rd edn, LAG, para 3.53–3.61 on the use of eligibility criteria. The authors note that in addition to having a rational process for deciding which children are eligible for services and which are not', local authorities must also comply with human rights and equality obligations.

66 *R (J) v Worcestershire CC* [2014] EWCA Civ 1518 at [34].

67 *Working together* pp23–24. See also the SEND Code para 10.17.

68 *Working together* p24; CA 1989 s26(3); and Children Act 1989 Representations Procedure (England) Regulations 2006 SI No 1738.

Link to CSPDA 1970 s2

Where adolescents are recognised as being 'disabled', their child in need assessment should also include an assessment of their needs under the CSDPA 1970 (see below).

Welfare services under the Chronically Sick and Disabled Persons Act 1970[69]

9.26 The duty to provide welfare services to disabled children under CSDPA 1970 s2 will be relevant to the after-care planning of adolescents given that, as noted above, they are likely to fall within the definition of a 'disabled child'. This duty is significant because, as *Working together* explains:

> Where a local authority is satisfied that the identified services and assistance can be provided under section 2 of the CSDPA, and it is necessary in order to meet a disabled child's needs, it must arrange to provide that support.[70]

9.27 The range of welfare services falling within this provision are listed under CSDPA 1970 s2(6). They include:

- 'practical assistance in the home' (such as the provision of personal care);
- recreational facilities outside the home;
- home adaptations;
- facilitating holidays; and
- the provision of, or help in obtaining 'wireless, television, library or similar recreational facilities' (which could include a computer, gaming consoles and audio books[71]).

Such services may be of significant benefit to adolescents and their families, such as supporting the adolescent to engage in community life on leaving hospital.

69 See S Broach and L Clements, *Disabled Children: a legal handbook*, 3rd edn, LAG, 2020, paras 3.66–3.78 (services provided under the CSDPA 1970).

70 *Working together* p21 para 28, summarising CSDPA 1970 s2(4):

> Where a local authority have functions under Part 3 of the Children Act 1989 in relation to a disabled child and the child is ordinarily resident in their area, they must, in exercise of those functions, make any arrangements within subsection (6) that they are satisfied it is necessary for them to make in order to meet the needs of the child.

71 S Broach and L Clements, *Disabled Children: a legal handbook*, 3rd edn, LAG, 2020, para 3.61.

9.28 The duty to consider whether an adolescent has needs for services under CSDPA 1970 s2[72] will be relevant to assessments undertaken in relation to:

- a 'child in need' under CA 1989 s17;[73]
- EHC needs under CFA 2014 Part 3 (where an adolescent falls within the definition of 'disabled child');[74] and
- after-care support needs under MHA 1983 s117.[75]

9.29 It should be noted that the duty under CSDPA 1970 s2 applies to the local authority in which 'the child is ordinarily resident'. The concept of ordinary residence and its application to adolescents is considered at paras 9.94–9.104 below.

Adolescents' accommodation needs

Introduction

9.30 An important consideration for an adolescent's after-care is what, if any, accommodation needs they will have. The local authority children's services will be under a duty to provide accommodation to an adolescent who is 'a child in need within their area' if the circumstances set out in CA 1989 s20(1) or (3) are met. They also have powers to accommodate under CA 1989 s20(4) and (5).

Local authorities' duties to accommodate

9.31 Local authorities have duties to accommodate:

- Under CA 1989 s20(1), the local authority must accommodate the adolescent if the adolescent appears to require accommodation either because:
  - there is no one with parental responsibility for the adolescent;
  - the adolescent is lost or abandoned; or

72 See S Broach and L Clements, *Disabled Children: a legal handbook*, 3rd edn, LAG, 2020, paras 3.53–3.61 on the use of eligibility criteria.

73 CSDPA 1970 s2(4) and CA 1989 Sch 2 para 3(a); see also *Working together* p21 para 28.

74 CSDPA 1970 s2(4) and CA 1989 Sch 2 para 3(ba). SEND Code para 3.49 states:

> Where a child or young person has been assessed as having social care needs in relation to their SEN or disabilities social care teams . . . must secure social care provision under the [CSDPA] 1970 which has been assessed as being necessary to support a child or young person's SEN and which is specified in their EHC plan; see also para 9.137.

75 NHS and Community Care Act 1990 s47(2).

  - the person who has been caring for the adolescent is 'prevented (whether or not permanently, and for whatever reason)' from providing the adolescent with suitable accommodation or care.[76]
- Under CA 1989 s20(3) the local authority must provide accommodation if the adolescent is aged 16 or over and the local authority considers that the adolescent's welfare 'is likely to be seriously prejudiced if they do not provide him with accommodation'.

Local authorities' powers to accommodate

9.32 Local authorities also have *powers* to accommodate adolescents:

- Under CA 1989 s20(4) they may provide accommodation to an adolescent where the adolescent is 'within their area (even though a person who has parental responsibility for him is able to provide him with accommodation) if they consider that to do so would safeguard or promote the child's welfare'.
- Under CA 1989 s20(5), they may provide accommodation to an adolescent who has 'reached the age of sixteen but is under twenty-one in any community home which takes children who have reached the age of sixteen if they consider that to do so would safeguard or promote his welfare'.

Seeking the adolescent's views on accommodation

9.33 The adolescent is 'given a voice in the decision, but not a decisive one'.[77] Under CA 1989 s20(6), local authorities are required 'so far as reasonably practicable and consistent with the child's welfare', to seek the child in needs wishes and feelings regarding the accommodation and 'give due consideration (having regard to his age and understanding) to such wishes and feelings of the child as they have been able to ascertain'.[78]

76 See *R (G) v Southwark LBC* [2009] UKHL 26, in which (at [28]) Lady Hale adopted the 'series of judgments, helpfully set out by Ward LJ in *R (A) v Croydon LBC* [2008] EWCA Civ 1445, at para 75' relevant to whether a duty under s20 has arisen.

77 *R (M) v Hammersmith LBC* [2008] UKHL at [17]. However, Lady Hale noted (obiter) at [43]: 'It is most unlikely that section 20 was intended to operate compulsorily against a child who is competent to decide for herself.'

78 CA 1989 s20(6).

Limits to the use of CA 1989 s20 to accommodate children in need

9.34 The limits of local authorities' powers and duties to provide accommodation to children in need under CA 1989 s20 were examined by the Supreme Court in *Williams and another v Hackney LBC*.[79] Lady Hale (giving the leading judgment) endorsed the view expressed in *R (G) v Nottingham City Council*[80] in stating that 'no local authority have the right or the power to remove a child from a parent who is looking after the child and wants to go on doing so without a court order'.[81]

9.35 CA 1989 s20 makes explicit that parents and others with parental responsibility who are willing and able to provide, or arrange the provision of, accommodation for the adolescent may object to the accommodation being provided[82] and may also remove the adolescent from the accommodation provided by the local authority.[83] However, they may not do so if the adolescent is 16 years or over and agrees to being provided with accommodation under CA 1989 s20.[84]

Adolescents who are homeless

9.36 Although it is possible for accommodation to be provided under CA 1989 s17(6), joint guidance issued by the Ministry of Housing, Communities and Local Government and Department for Education (DfE) in 2018 ('Housing Guidance') notes that this 'will almost always concern children needing to be accommodated with their families'.[85]

79 [2018] UKSC 37; see [38]–[50] for a summary of issues on the application of s20.

80 [2008] EWHC 152 (Admin), [2008] 1 FLR 1660 and [2008] EWHC 400, [2008] 1 FLR 1668.

81 [2018] UKSC 37 at [38]. This is subject to the caveat noted at [44].

82 CA 1989 s20(7). In *R (M) v Hammersmith and Fulham LBC* [2008] UKHL Lady Hale noted (at [17]) that the prohibition on a local authority accommodating under 18s if their parents object to this is 'fundamental' to the scheme of the CA 1989.

83 CA 1989 s20(8).

84 CA 1989 s20(11); see also s20(9) and (10). For general overview of use of CA 1989 s20, see J Masson, 'Understanding the current use of s20' *Family Law*, October 2018, Vol 48, 1289.

85 *Prevention of homelessness and provision of accommodation for 16 and 17 year old young people who may be homeless and/or require accommodation. Guidance to children's services authorities and local housing authorities about their duties under Part 3 of the Children Act 1989 and Part 7 of the Housing Act 1996 to secure or provide accommodation for homeless 16 and 17 year old young people*, 2018, para 3.58.

9.37 Where the local authority has a duty to provide accommodation under CA 1989 s20, this is the legal basis on which accommodation is to be provided.[86] This duty takes precedence over both the power to provide accommodation under CA 1989 s17 and the local authority duties under the Housing Act (HA) 1996.[87] The Housing Guidance explains that the only two circumstances in which an adolescent aged 16 or 17 who is homeless should not be accommodated under CA 1989 s20 and may be owed duties under the HA 1996 are:

- where that adolescent is not a child in need; or
- where that adolescent is a child in need but 'having been properly and fully advised of the implications and having the capacity to reach a decision, has decided that they do not want to be accommodated under section 20'.[88]

Children Act 1989 s20: relevance to 'looked after child' provisions

9.38 The question whether the duty to accommodate an adolescent under CA 1989 s20 has been engaged is significant because this will lead to the adolescent becoming a 'looked after child' and therefore entitled to a range of services and support. These are detailed the statutory guidance: the Care Planning Guidance;[89] and *The Children Act 1989 guidance and regulations. Volume 3: planning transition to adulthood for care leavers.*[90] As the Housing Guidance explains:

> As a result of being accommodated by children's services for a continuous period of more than 24 hours the young person will become looked after, and the local authority will owe them the duties that are owed to all looked after children, and once they cease to be looked after, the duties that are owed to care leavers under that Act. Whilst accommodated under section 20 the young person will not be eligible for welfare benefits, including housing benefits or housing costs under universal credit. Children's services will have a duty to maintain them, including meeting the cost of accommodation.[91]

86 *R (G) v Southwark LBC* [2009] UKHL 26.

87 *R (G) v Southwark LBC* [2009] UKHL 26; and *R (M) v Hammersmith and Fulham LBC* [2008] UKHL. See also, the Housing Guidance paras 1.2 and 3.58–3.59.

88 Housing Guidance para 3.13. This reflects (obiter) comments by Lady Hale in *R (M) v Hammersmith and Fulham LBC* [2008] UKHL at [43] (referring to the wishes of an adolescent who is 'fully informed of the consequences of the choices before her'. See paras 3.60–3.61 on the limited circumstances in which the provision of accommodation under s17 might be appropriate.

89 DfE, June 2015.

90 DfE, January 2015.

91 Housing Guidance para 3.12.

After-care services under MHA 1983 s117

Introduction

9.39 MHA 1983 s117 is of major significance for adolescents who are detained under MHA 1983 s3, given that it entitles them to receive the 'after-care services' that they have been assessed to need when they cease to be detained and leave hospital. Section 117(2) provides:

> It shall be the duty of the clinical commissioning group or Local Health Board and of the local social services authority to provide or arrange for the provision of, in co-operation with relevant voluntary agencies, after-care services for any person to whom this section applies until such time as the clinical commissioning group or Local Health Board and the local social services authority are satisfied that the person concerned is no longer in need of such services; but they shall not be so satisfied in the case of a community patient while he remains such a patient.[92]

9.40 Accordingly, where MHA 1983 s117 applies, the relevant NHS body (usually a CCG) and local social service authority are under a joint duty to provide (or arrange for their provision) after-care services to the adolescent until such time as the CCG and the local authority agree that the adolescent no longer needs such services. Local authorities will therefore have a key role to play in the assessment and the care planning process.

9.41 The duty to provide after-care under MHA 1983 s117 is a freestanding duty, in that it operates independently of other provisions relating to the assessment and provision of individuals' health and social care needs. Accordingly, the application of the MHA 1983 s117 after-care duty (who it applies to and when, which NHS bodies and local authorities are subject to it, and how long for) is determined by the provisions set out in section 117 and not by other legislation, such as the CA 1989 or the Care Act 2014.[93] It also means that charges cannot be made for services provided under MHA 1983 s117.[94]

9.42 Like adults, adolescents' after-care planning should start on admission to hospital and should be undertaken within the framework of the CPA.[95] However, the duty to provide MHA 1983 s117 after-care

92 Note that s117 has been amended by virtue of various enactments, including the Care Act 2014. The amendments are not indicated in the text.

93 As noted in *Reference guide to the Mental Health Act 1983* ('MHA Reference Guide'), DoH, 2015 at para 29.7.

94 *R v Manchester City Council ex p Stennett* [2002] UKHL 34.

95 MHA Code 33.10 and chapter 34.

services will continue even if they are no longer receiving mental health care under the CPA.[96] The rules governing which NHS bodies and local authorities are responsible for a person's adolescent's after-care services are considered below (paras 9.82–9.93).

9.43 Guidance on MHA 1983 s117 is provided in chapter 33 of the MHA Code.[97] Box 9.3 below provides an overview of MHA 1983 s117 after-care.

Box 9.3: MHA 1983 s117 after-care – key points

What is the duty to provide after-care under MHA 1983 s117?

- The relevant NHS bodies and local authorities are under an enforceable joint duty to provide, or arrange for the provision of, after-care services for certain categories of patients who have been detained under the MHA 1983 following their discharge from hospital. They are required to do so 'in cooperation with relevant voluntary agencies' (MHA 1983 s117(2)).
- CCGs and local authorities must jointly commission or provide after-care services. CCGs must commission, whereas local authorities may both commission and provide, such services.[98]

Who has the right to MHA 1983 s117 after-care services?

The following have the right to MHA 1983 s117 after-care services:

- individuals of any age who have been detained in hospital under MHA 1983 s3 or detained under certain provisions of Part 3[99] (MHA 1983s117(1)); whereas
- those detained under MHA 1983 s2, 4, 5(2), 5(4), 135 or 136 are *not* covered by s117.

96 See by way of analogy (concerning the difference between eligibility for CPA and eligibility for community care services) *R (HP and KP) v Islington LBC* [2004] EWHC 7 (Admin) at [37]: 'even if Islington was right that Mr P did not meet its CPA eligibility criteria, because he did not have a severe and enduring mental illness, that was not determinative of whether he nonetheless had a need for generic health or social services community care'. See also MHA Code paras 33.20–33.23.

97 See also the MHA Reference Guide chapter 29.

98 See MHA 1983 s117(2D); and MHA Code para 33.7.

99 The duty under MHA 1983 s117 also applies to patients detained under s37 (a hospital order with or without a restriction order), s45A (a hospital direction with or without a limitation direction), s47 and s48 (a transfer direction with or without a restriction direction).

Which NHS bodies and local authorities will be the 'responsible after-care bodies'?

- The after-care duty is placed jointly on the relevant NHS body (usually a CCG in England) and the relevant local authority. In some cases, NHS England may be the relevant NHS body.
- The criteria for identifying the responsible after-care bodies are set out in MHA 1983 s117(3) (see below at paras 9.82–9.93).

When is the MHA 1983 s117 duty triggered?

Although the duty to provide after-care applies on discharge from hospital (when patients 'cease to be detained and (whether or not immediately after so ceasing) leave hospital') (MHA 1983 s117(1)),[100] 'the planning of after-care needs to start as soon as the patient is admitted to hospital'.[101]

When does the duty to provide after-care services end?

- The duty applies until such time as *both* the relevant NHS body and local authority 'are satisfied that the person concerned is no longer in need of such services' (MHA 1983 s117(2)).[102]
- The MHA Code (paras 33.22–33.23) highlights the need for careful consideration before withdrawing after-care services, eg pointing out that MHA 1983 s117 services should not be withdrawn just because the person is no longer receiving care from specialist mental health services.

Community treatment orders and MHA 1983 s117

- After-care services under MHA 1983 s117 cannot be discontinued if the person is subject to a community treatment order (CTO).[103]
- Individuals may continue to need after-care services under MHA 1983 s117 even if they are discharged from the CTO.[104]

100 *R(W) v Doncaster MBC* [2004] EWCA Civ 378 at [51].

101 MHA Code para 33.10. See also *R(W) v Doncaster MBC* [2004] EWCA Civ 378 at [48]–[51].

102 See *R (Mwanza) v Greenwich LBC and Bromley LBC* [2010] EWHC 1462 (Admin) paras 83–88.

103 CTOs are discussed in chapter 10.

104 MHA Code para 33.6.

The meaning of 'after-care services'

9.44 The definition of MHA 1983 s117 after-care services focuses on their purpose, rather than specifying the actual services to be provided. MHA 1983 s117(6) states:

> In this section 'after-care services', in relation to a person, means services which have both of the following purposes–
> (a) meeting a need arising from or related to the person's mental disorder; and
> (b) reducing the risk of a deterioration of the person's mental condition (and accordingly, reducing the risk of the person requiring admission to hospital again for treatment for mental disorder).[105]

9.45 The MHA Code makes the following points on the scope and purpose of after-care services:

- Their 'ultimate aim' 'is to maintain patients in the community, with as few restrictions as are necessary, wherever possible'.[106]
- They can encompass a range of services (health care, social care and employment services, supported accommodation[107] and services) to meet individuals' social, cultural and spiritual needs providing that the 'services meet a need that arises directly from or is related to the particular patient's mental disorder, and help to reduce the risk of a deterioration in the patient's mental condition'.[108]
- They are not just about meeting the person's 'immediate needs for health and social care'; they 'should aim to support them in

105 The provisions concerning 'preference for particular accommodation' (MHA 1983 s117A) do not apply to under-18s; see Care and Support and After-care (Choice of Accommodation) Regulations 2014 SI No 2670 reg 4(2)(a).

106 MHA Code para 33.3.

107 It is unlikely that MHA 1983 s117 covers a person's 'basic' housing needs but will be relevant where the need for accommodation is linked to their mental health needs. See: *R (Afework) v Camden LBC* [2013] EWHC 1637 (Admin); *R (Mwanza) v Greenwich LBC and Bromley LBC* [2010] EWHC 1462 (Admin); and *R (Baisden) v Leicester City Council* [2011] EWHC 3219 (Admin) at [33].

108 MHA Code 2015 para 33.4; see also para 34.19. The definition of 'after-care' under MHA 1983 s117(6) was introduced into the MHA 1983 by the Care Act 2014. For cases preceding this amendment which considered the services and support that could fall within the meaning of 'after-care' see: *Clunis v Camden and Islington Health Authority* (1998) 1 WLR 902; *R (Mwanza) v Greenwich LBC and Bromley LBC* [2010] EWHC 1462 (Admin); and *R (Afework) v Camden LBC* [2013] EWHC 1637 (Admin).

regaining or enhancing their skills, or learning new skills, in order to cope with life outside hospital'.[109]

9.46 Furthermore, after-care services are 'not necessarily limited to the specific disorder, or disorders for which the person was previously detained under the Act'.[110]

9.47 Although in practice, it may not always be clear whether individuals' needs arise from, or are related to, their mental disorder, it should be noted that the MHA Code advises that 'CCGs and local authorities should interpret the definition of after-care services broadly'.[111]

If a case arises in which an adolescent's needs are considered to fall outside the scope of MHA 1983 s117, that adolescent may be entitled to services to meet such additional needs under an alternative statutory framework, for example, CA 1989 s17. For the reasons noted at paras 9.21–9.22 above, adolescents who have been receiving in-patient psychiatric care (whether or not detained under the MHA 1983) are likely to fall within the definition of 'a child in need' for the purpose of CA 1989 s17.

After-care planning under MHA 1983 s117

9.48 Although the duty to provide after-care services under MHA 1983 s117 will only be triggered on the person's discharge from hospital, the relevant CCG and local authority are expected to consider what after-care arrangements will be needed.[112] This is made clear by the MHA Code (para 33.10) which states:

> . . . the planning of after-care needs to start as soon as the patient is admitted to hospital. CCGs and local authorities should take reasonable steps, in consultation with the care programme approach care co-ordinator and other members of the multi-disciplinary team to identify appropriate after-care services for patients in good time for their eventual discharge from hospital or prison.

9.49 The MHA Code expects the responsible clinician to 'ensure that the patient's needs for after-care have been fully assessed, discussed with

109 MHA Code para 33.5.

110 Earl Howe (Parliamentary Under-Secretary of State, DH) House of Lords, Hansard 16 October 2013 Vol 748 No 53 Col 600.

111 MHA Code para 33.4.

112 MHA 1883 s117(1) refers to persons who 'cease to be detained' and 'leave hospital'. See *R (W) v Doncaster MBC* [2004] EWCA Civ 378 at [49]; and *R (K) v Camden and Islington Health Authority* [2001] EWCA Civ 240 at [21].

the patient (and their carers, where appropriate) and addressed in their care plan'.[113]

9.50 Notwithstanding the MHA Code's emphasis on planning after-care within the framework of the CPA[114] (the expectation being that such planning is health led), the duty to provide after-care services is a *joint* duty on the relevant CCG and local authority.[115] This point is made by the Department of Health and Social Care's (DHSC) *Care and support statutory guidance*:[116]

> Section 117 of the MHA places a duty on the NHS and local authorities to provide aftercare and this will usually involve a joint assessment (often under the Care Programme Approach) including an assessment of the person's care and support needs, a care and support or support plan and subsequent review (which may reach a decision that a person is no longer in need of aftercare).[117]

9.51 The local authority therefore has a key role in the assessment of the adolescent's needs under MHA 1983 s117. This is reinforced by the following provisions:

- *Assessments under National Health Service and Community Care Act (NHSCCA) 1990 s47:* Although repealed in other contexts,[118] this provision is still relevant to assessments under MHA 1983 s117.[119] NHSCCA 1990 s47(1) provides that local authorities must undertake an assessment of a person's MHA 1983 s117 after-care needs where it appears to them that the person 'may be in need of any such services' and 'having regard to the results of

113 MHA Code para 33.13. See MHA Code para 34.19 on the range of considerations to be included in the CPA assessment.

114 MHA Code para 33.14. The care planning process under the CPA is summarised at para 9.19 and box 9.1.

115 *R v Ealing District Health Authority ex p Fox* [1993] 3 All ER 170 at 182:

> Thus, the duty is not only a general duty but a specific duty owed to the applicant to provide him with after-care services until such time as the district health authority and local social services authority are satisfied that he is no longer in need of such services.

116 Department for Health and Social Care, updated June 2020, available at: www.gov.uk/government/publications/care-act-statutory-guidance/care-and-support-statutory-guidance.

117 *Care and support statutory guidance* para 7.23.

118 For adult social care, 'community care assessments' has been replaced by 'needs assessments' under Care Act 2014 s9. As noted by R Jones *Mental Health Act Manual* 23rd edn, Sweet & Maxwell, 2020, para 1-1198 and L Clements *Community Care and the Law,* 7th edn, LAG 2019, para 16.63, the eligibility criteria under the Care Act 2014 are not applicable to assessments for MHA 1983 s117 after-care services.

119 NHSCC Act 1990 s47 is set out in appendix A below.

that assessment, shall then decide whether his needs call for the provision by them of any such services'.[120]

- *Local authorities' duty to consider under-18s' needs for welfare services under CSDPA 1970 s2:* Under NHSCCA 1990 s47(2), if at any time during an MHA 1983 s117 after-care assessment, it appears to the local authority that the person they are assessing is 'disabled' and aged under 18, the local authority must decide whether the disabled person's needs call for the provision of the welfare services listed in CSDPA 1970 s2 (these are noted at para 9.27 above).[121] For the reasons noted at para 9.28, this provision is likely to be relevant to adolescents entitled to MHA 1983 s117 aftercare services given that the definition of 'disability' includes an individual who 'suffers from mental disorder of any kind'.[122] There is no need for the adolescent to request such an assessment, but the local authority must inform the adolescent that they are making this assessment.[123]

120 NHSCC Act 1990 s47(3) provides for the co-operation between agencies, requires the local authority to invite the relevant CCG and housing authority if the person appears to have health or housing needs.

121 This is the effect of the convoluted provision: NHSCCA 1990 s47(2) refers to services mentioned in Disabled Persons (Services, Consultation and Representation) Act (DP(SCR)A) 1986 s4, which in turn refers to the duty on the local authority to undertake an assessment under CSDPA 1970 s2 when requested by the disabled person to do so (whereas under NHSCCA 1990 s47 no such request is required).

122 CA 1989 s17(11) (the definition of 'disabled' under the DP(SCR)A 1986 s16(1) refers back to the definition under CA 1989 Part 3).

123 NHSCCA 1990 s47(2)(b). It is suggested that if the adolescent's needs for welfare services are related to their mental health and fall within the definition of 'after-care services' under MHA 1983 s117(6), these will be provided under MHA 1983 s117 and not under CSDPA 1970 s2 (so charges for such services cannot be made). In any event, S Broach and L Clements, *Disabled children: a legal handbook*, 3rd edn, LAG, 2020 state (at para 3.156) that in practice few authorities charge for services under CA 1989 Part 3 or CSDPA 1970 s2.

Joint duty for the provision of after-care services under MHA 1983 s117

9.52 The relevant CCG and local authority must use their best endeavours to ensure that the necessary after-care services are in place.[124] However, the MHA 1983 does not provide how the joint responsibility to provide after-care should be allocated between them. To date, there is a lack of up-to-date guidance on how local authorities and CCGs should meet their joint duty under MHA 1983 s117. Guidance from 2000 highlights the need for local policies to explain how they will implement s117. It states:

> Social services and health authorities should establish jointly agreed local policies on providing section 117 after-care. Policies should set out clearly the criteria for deciding which services fall under section 117 and which authorities should finance them. The section 117 after-care plan should indicate which services are provided as part of the plan.[125]

9.53 Luke Clements notes in *Community care and the law* that despite this advice, 'it appears in practice that this is something that has been neglected'.[126]

Duty to provide after-care and MHA 1983 s17 leave

9.54 The duty to provide after-care under MHA 1983 s117 can apply to patients eligible for such services when they are given leave from hospital under MHA 1983 s17.[127] However, this is limited to individuals who are discharged from hospital (even if only on a

124 *R (W) v Doncaster MBC* [2004] EWCA Civ 378 at [58]–[59] and [67], see in particular [59]: 'Stretched local authorities and health care providers have to make do as best they can with the facilities and resources that are available. Local authorities face especial difficulties when trying to fund a placement outside their own area'. See also *R (K) v Camden and Islington Health Authority* [2001] EWCA Civ 240 at [29]; and *R (IH) v Secretary of State for the Home Department and others* [2003] UKHL 59 at [29].

125 *After-care under the Mental Health Act 1983: section 117 after-care services* HSC 2003/003: LAC (2000) 3, DoH, February 2000, para 3.

126 L Clements, *Community care and the law*, 7th edn, LAG, 2019, para 16.76.

127 *R v Richmond LBC ex p Watson; R v Redcar and Cleveland BC ex p Armstrong; R v Manchester ex p Stennett; Re v Harrow LBC ex p Cobham;* cited with approval in *R (CXF) v Central Bedfordshire Council* [2018] EWCA Civ 2852 at [39]–[41]. MHA Code paras 27.26 and 33.13.

temporary basis). In *R (CXF) v Central Bedfordshire Council*, which considered whether section 117 would apply to escorted day trips from hospital, the Court of Appeal held that the 'inescapable conclusion is that the claimant does not "cease to be detained" or "leave hospital" within the meaning of section 117(1) when he is escorted on day trips and is therefore not a person to whom section 117 applies'.[128]

Direct payments for MHA 1983 s117 after-care services

9.55 MHA 1983 s117(2C) makes provision for direct payments to be made in respect of s117 after-care services, but in relation to under-18s the approach is inconsistent as between health and social care:[129]

- In relation to health, the relevant NHS body (the CCG or NHS England) may make direct payments for after-care services for children aged under 16 years (payments being made to their representative) and individuals aged 16 and over.[130]
- In relation to social care, although provision is made for direct payments for MHA 1983 s117 after-care services to be made to adults, there appears to be no authority to make such payments for under-18s.[131]

128 [2018] EWCA Civ 2852 at [44].

129 As noted in chapter 2 (para 2.43) direct payments can be made in relation to services provided under the CA 1989, the CSDPA 1970 and in relation to EHC plans.

130 National Health Service Act 2006 s12A(4); and National Health Service (Direct Payments) Regulations 2013 SI No 1617, as amended by National Health Service (Direct Payments) (Amendment) Regulations 2013 No 2342 regs 3 and 4. See also *Guidance on direct payments for healthcare: understanding the regulations*, 2014 para 3.1 and the MHA Code para 33.19.

131 MHA 1983 s2C(a) refers to direct payments under the CA 2014 (ss31–33) all of which concern direct payments to adults. In comparison, direct payments for under-18s are covered in ss50–53 of the Social Services and Well-being (Wales) 2014, eg s51.

Carers' assessments[132]

Overview

9.56 Parents and other carers for adolescents with mental health needs have rights to request an assessment of their own needs, arising from their caring responsibilities.[133] The MHA Code states:

> In many instances, especially when a patient is not in hospital, the patient's carers and wider family will provide more care and support than health and social care professionals. It is important for professionals to identify all individuals who provide care and support for patients, to ensure that health and care services assess those carers' needs and, where relevant, provide support to meet them. Local authorities also have duties in the Care Act 2014 to assess adult carers' current and future needs for support and, must meet eligible needs for support. The Children and Families Act 2014 also places a duty on local authorities to assess needs for support of both parent carers of disabled children and young carers.[134]

9.57 Carers' rights to an assessment will be relevant where the adolescents they are caring for have any of the following assessments:

- assessments of needs for MHA 1983 s117 after-care services (see paras 9.49–9.51);
- 'child in need' assessments under CA 1989 s17 (see paras 9.21–9.25); or
- assessments under CSDPA 1970 s2 (see paras 9.26–9.29).

132 The law relating to carers is discussed in S Broach and L Clements, *Disabled children: a legal handbook*, 3rd edn, LAG, 2020, chapter 8. See also *Care and support statutory guidance* chapter 16. Coronavirus Act 2020 s15 Sch 12 makes provision for temporary measures to be introduced in relation to the Care Act 2014, including carers' assessments (para 3(2)). For further details see: *Care Act easements guidance for local authorities* (updated May 2020) available at: www.gov.uk/government/publications/coronavirus-covid-19-changes-to-the-care-act-2014/care-act-easements-guidance-for-local-authorities. Information provided by the CQC states that as at 3 July 2020 no local authority was using easements; see: www.cqc.org.uk/guidance-providers/adult-social-care/care-act-easements-it

133 See *Working together* p21 paras 28 and 29. See also Annex B of *The Care Act and whole-family approaches*, DoH, Local Government Association, ADASS (Directors of Social Services), The Children's Society and Carers Trust, January 2015, available at: www.local.gov.uk/sites/default/files/documents/care-act-and-whole-family-6e1.pdf.

134 MHA Code para 4.42.

It should also be noted that the CA 1989 includes duties to assess 'young carers',[135] as do the provisions to facilitate under-18s' transition to adult social care in the Care Act 2014.[136]

Parent carer's needs assessments

9.58 Provisions for a 'parent carer's needs assessment', which were introduced by the CFA 2014, are set out under CA 1989 s17ZD–17F. They will be relevant where adolescents fall within the CA 1989 s17's definition of a 'disabled child' (which as noted above at para 9.21 includes under-18s who have a 'mental disorder of any kind').

9.59 Local authorities must undertake an assessment of the needs of 'parent carers'[137] of a 'disabled child' to 'assess whether a parent carer within their area has needs for support and, if so, what those needs are'.[138] *Working together* notes:

> If a local authority considers that a parent carer of a disabled child . . . may have support needs, it must carry out an assessment under section 17ZD of the Children Act 1989. The local authority must also carry out such an assessment if a parent carer requests one. Such an assessment must consider whether it is appropriate for the parent carer to provide, or continue to provide, care for the disabled child, in light of the parent carer's needs and wishes.[139]

9.60 Where it has undertaken a parent carer's needs assessment, the local authority will then be required to consider whether the adolescent's parent carer or the adolescent (as a 'disabled child') has needs for support that could be provided under CA 1989 s17, and if so, whether or not to provide services to meet those needs.[140] In addition, the transition provisions under the Care Act 2014 (discussed below at paras 9.65–9.81) include duties on local authorities to carry out 'a child carer's assessment'.

135 CA 1989 ss17ZA–17ZC. A 'young carer' is defined as: 'a person under 18 who provides or intends to provide care for another person' (s17ZA(3) but see the qualifications in s17ZB(3)–(4). The same definition applies under the CA 2014 – see s63(6)–(8).

136 CA 2014 ss63–64. The provisions regarding young carers are explained in S Broach and L Clements, *Disabled children: a legal handbook*, 3rd edn, LAG, 2020, paras 8.27–8.60 and 10.45–10.46.

137 CA 1989 s17ZD(2): 'a person aged 18 or over who provides or intends to provide care for a disabled child for whom the person has parental responsibility'.

138 CA 1989 s17ZD(1).

139 *Working together* p21 para 29. This reflects CA 1989 s17D(3)–(4) and (9).

140 CA 1989 s17F.

Assessments of the needs of carers who do not have parental responsibility

9.61 Carers (Recognition and Services) Act (C(R&S)A) 1995 s1 will be relevant to individuals who are providing or intend 'to provide a substantial amount of care on a regular basis' for an adolescent but do not have parental responsibility (for example, a grandparent who has not taken steps to acquire parental responsibility). They may request a carer's assessment if the adolescent's needs for after-care services under MHA 1983 s117 are being assessed[141] or the adolescent's needs as a disabled child are being assessed under CA 1989 s17 or CSDPA 1970 s2. Where such a request is made, the local authority must carry out the carer's assessment and take this into account before making its decision on whether the adolescent's needs call for the provision of any services.[142]

9.62 Carers can request an assessment of their 'ability to provide and to continue to provide care' for the adolescent and the local authority must inform them of their right to make such a request if it appears that the carer may be entitled to such an assessment.[143]

Transition to adult care and support

9.63 The right to a child carer's assessment under Care Act 2014 s60 will be relevant to an adult,[144] including the adolescent's parent, 'who provides or intends to provide care' for the adolescent.[145] Section 60(1) provides:

> Where it appears to a local authority that a carer of a child is likely to have needs for support after the child becomes 18, the authority must, if satisfied that it would be of significant benefit to the carer to do so, assess–
>
> (a) whether the carer has needs for support and, if so, what those needs are, and

141 This is in accordance with NHSCCA 1990 s47(1).

142 C(R&S)A 1995 s1(1) and (2).

143 C(R&S)A 1995 s2B.

144 Provisions are also made for assessing young carer's needs for care and support (ss63 and 64).

145 Care Act 2014 s60(7), but note Care Act 2014 s60(8) and (9) which provide that those providing care under a contract or as voluntary work are not to be regarded as a carer unless the local authority considers that it would be appropriate to do so.

(b) whether the carer is likely to have needs for support after the child becomes 18 and, if so, what those needs are likely to be.[146]

9.64 Care Act 2014 s61 sets out the requirements for a child carer's assessment, including consideration of the carer's willingness and ability to continue to provide care beyond the child's 18th birthday. Section 62 provides that the local authority may provide services to the carer if it considers it appropriate to do so, having regard to any services provided to the carer under CA 1989 s17. It is expected that such needs 'will usually be met' under CA 1989 s17.[147] Chapter 16 of the DHSC's *Care and support statutory guidance* includes guidance on undertaking a child carer's assessment.

Transition to adult services[148]

Introduction

9.65 The planning for an adolescent's transition from CAMHS should start at least six months before the adolescent is due to leave CAMHS.[149] The Care Act 2014 provisions to facilitate the planning of under-18's transition from children's services to adult social care, which will therefore be of relevance to an adolescent's transition planning from CAMHS, are summarised below. Detailed guidance on these provisions is included in chapter 16 of the DHSC's *Care and support statutory guidance.*

146 Unlike assessments under the C(R&S)A 1995 there is no need for the carer to be providing a substantial amount of support on a regular basis.

147 Explanatory Note, para 379.

148 Coronavirus Act 2020 s15 and Sch 12 makes provision for temporary measures to be introduced in relation to the Care Act 2014, including transition (see paras 2(3) and 15). For further details see: *Care Act easements guidance for local authorities* (updated May 2020) available at: www.gov.uk/government/publications/coronavirus-covid-19-changes-to-the-care-act-2014/care-act-easements-guidance-for-local-authorities. Information provided by the CQC (dated 3 July 2020 states that no local authorities are applying such measures – see: www.cqc.org.uk/guidance-providers/adult-social-care/care-act-easements-it

149 MHA Code para 19.119.

Assessment of needs for care and support

9.66 Care Act 2014 s58 requires local authorities to undertake an assessment of adolescents' needs for care and support (a 'child's needs assessment'[150]) if two conditions are met: the first is that the local authority is 'satisfied that it would be of significant benefit to the child to do so';[151] and the second is that the 'consent condition is met'.

9.67 To meet the 'consent condition' either the adolescent must have consented (having the competence or capacity to do so) or, if the adolescent lacks the competence or capacity to consent to the assessment, 'the local authority is satisfied that carrying out a child's needs assessment would be in the child's best interests'.[152] However, the local authority must carry out the assessment even if the consent requirement is not met 'if the child is experiencing, or is at risk of, abuse or neglect'.[153]

9.68 Adolescents, their parents or anyone providing care for them (which may be 'practical or emotional support'[154]) can request such an assessment.[155] It is not necessary for the adolescent to be receiving children's services, the key issue is whether that adolescent may need adult social care after their 18th birthday.[156] The *Care and support statutory guidance* states that 'young people and young carers receiving Children and Adolescent Mental Health Services (CAMHS) may also require care and support as adults even if they did not receive children's services from the local authority'.[157]

9.69 The 'child's needs assessment' will assess whether the adolescent 'has needs for care and support and, if so, what those needs are' and whether the adolescent 'is likely to have needs for care and support after becoming 18, and if so, what those needs are likely to be'.[158] If

150 The *Care and support statutory guidance* refers to 'transition assessments', using this term to include child's needs assessments, adult carers assessments and young carers assessments under the Care Act 2014 ss58–65.

151 The *Care and support statutory guidance* para 16.10 states that consideration of 'significant benefit' is concerned with the timing of the assessment, which may depend on a range of factors.

152 Care Act 2014 s58(2).

153 Care Act 2014 s58(4).

154 Care Act 2014 s58(8). Section 59 provides more detail on the scope of the assessment and procedures involved.

155 Care Act 2014 s58(5).

156 *Care and support statutory guidance* para 16.8.

157 *Care and support statutory guidance* para 16.18.

158 Care Act 2014 s58(1)(a) and (b). See *Care and support statutory guidance* para 16.9.

adolescents are receiving children's services, local authorities should undertake a child's needs assessment 'so that they have information about what to expect when they become an adult'.[159]

9.70 The requirements for an assessment (what it should cover, who should be involved and action to be taken after the assessment) are set out in Care Act 2014 s59 with further guidance being provided on such assessments in the *Care and support statutory guidance*.[160] Local authorities will be required to provide independent advocates to facilitate adolescents' involvement in the assessment where adolescents 'would experience substantial difficulty' in understanding and using the relevant information or communicating their views and there was nobody appropriate to act on their behalf.[161]

9.71 There is no lower age limit for such assessments which are for adult social care. They are 'not intended to be used to assess needs for children's services'[162] (the adolescent's rights to assessment and support under the CA 1989 are not affected).[163] The assessment must include an indication of whether any of the needs identified are likely to meet the eligibility criteria (and if so, which ones).[164]

9.72 The adolescent's 'child's needs assessment' can be combined with other assessments.[165] For example, the *Care and support statutory guidance* states that for young people with EHC plans, such an assessment 'should be undertaken as part of one of the annual statutory reviews of the EHC plan, and should inform a plan for the transition from children's to adult care and support'[166] while it might be possible to include them in for the statutory Pathway Planning process for care leavers.[167] Accordingly, it is suggested that

159 *Care and support statutory guidance* para 16.9, which also states: 'a young person or carer is "likely to have needs" means they have any likely appearance of any need for care and support as an adult – not just those needs that will be deemed eligible under the adult statute'.

160 *Care and support statutory guidance* paras 16.25–16.40.

161 Care Act 2014 s67. This right to advocacy applies in other cases, such as carer's assessments – see s67(3). See also *Care and support statutory guidance* para 16.40.

162 Care Act 2014, Explanatory Note para 360: 'A child does not have to be receiving services under children's legislation in order to receive or request this assessment. Similarly, there is no restriction on the age of child assessed, or their proximity to their 18th birthday.'

163 Explanatory Note para 358.

164 Care Act 2014 s59(4).

165 Care Act 2014 s65(5).

166 *Care and support statutory guidance* para 6.11.

167 *Care and support statutory guidance* para 6 12.

an adolescent's 'child needs assessment' could be undertaken as part of the adolescent's CPA.

Continuity of services: services for children in need and welfare services

9.73 Although the child's needs assessment, in itself, does not lead to the provision of adult services before an adolescent's 18th birthday, Care Act 2014 s66 introduces important provisions for the 'continuity of services' until the local authority makes a decision as to what services are to be provided under the Care Act 2014.

9.74 The amendments to the CA 1989 (inserting s17ZH 'Section 17 services: transition for children to adult care and support') and the CSDPA 1970 (inserting s2A 'Welfare services: transition for children to adult care and support') introduce similar provisions. CA 1989 s17ZH applies to adolescents who are receiving services as a child in need under section 17 of that Act. CSDPA 1970 s2A applies to adolescents who are receiving welfare services under s2 of that Act.

9.75 In essence, their effect is that where an adolescent has reached their 18th birthday and either has had a child's needs assessment or has requested one and this has not been undertaken, the local authority must continue to provide the services that it had been providing prior to the adolescent becoming 18 until it reaches a conclusion on the adult care services to be provided.[168] This provision should ensure that there is no gap in provision during the transition to adult care and support.[169]

9.76 Given the significance of this provision, it is suggested that a request for a child's needs assessment (and a carer's needs assessment if appropriate) should be made by, or on behalf of, adolescents[170] as part of their transition planning from CAMHS.

Continuity of services: education, health and care plans

9.77 The CA 1989 includes provisions that will be relevant to the transition planning for adolescents with special educational needs and who have EHC plans.[171] Under CA 1989 s17ZG local authorities have the power to continue to provide CA 1989 s17 services to a child in need beyond the adolescent's 18th birthday. Although the local

168 *Care and support statutory guidance* paras 16.67–16.74.

169 *Care and support statutory guidance* paras 16.67 and 16.68. Explanatory Note para 401.

170 Care Act 2014 s58(5).

171 See *Care and support statutory guidance* paras 16.71–16.74.

authority may not do so if the EHC plan ceases to be maintained, this is subject to section 17ZI which states that where the local authority is required to carry out a needs assessment under the Care Act 2014,[172] it must continue to provide section 17 services until it makes a decision about the adult social care services to be provided.

9.78 The MHA Code states that where 'a young person has an EHC plan that includes agreed provision to support mental health then health commissioners must put arrangements in place to secure that provision'. It also notes that 'Commissioners should be aware that where appropriate, local authorities may maintain EHC plans up to the age of 25'.[173]

Care leavers

9.79 The DHSC's *Care and support statutory guidance* refers to the powers of local authorities to extend foster placements beyond the age of 18.[174] It notes:

> All local authorities must have a Staying Put[175] policy to ensure transition from care to independence and adulthood that is similar for care leavers to that which most young people experience, and is based on need and not on age alone.[176]

Advocacy under the Care Act 2014

9.80 Reflecting Care Act 2014 s67, the DHSC's *Care and support guidance* states:

> Those people who do not retain a right to an IMHA, whose care and support needs are being assessed, planned or reviewed should be considered for an advocate under the Care Act, if they have substantial difficulty in being involved and if there is no appropriate person to support their involvement.[177]

172 The threshold for this is low: Care Act 2014 s9(1) states that the local authority must assess an adult who 'may have needs for care and support'.

173 MHA Code para 19.120.

174 CA 1989 s23CZA.

175 For further information on these policies, see HM Government's guidance, *"STAYING PUT" Arrangements for care leavers aged 18 and above to stay on with their former foster carers*, May 2013. See also *Children Act 1989 Guidance and Regulations. Volume 3 (Planning Transition to Adulthood for Care Leavers): Guidance setting out the responsibilities of local authorities towards looked after children and care leavers*, DfE, January 2015; and see SEND Code para 10.12.

176 *Care and support statutory guidance* para 16.70.

177 At para 7.23.

9.81 The main provisions of the Care Act 2014 are concerned with adults. However, Care Act 2014 s67 will apply to adolescents who are receiving a 'transition assessment' under that Act. Although there may be circumstances in which a parent will be an 'appropriate person', the adolescent's parents cannot be regarded as such if the adolescent who has the capacity or competence to make such a decision does not want to be supported by them.[178] In addition, comments in the *Care and support guidance* on when a individuals might not fulfil the 'appropriate person' role would need to be considered:

> . . . the appropriate individual is expected to support and represent the person and to facilitate their involvement in the processes. It is unlikely that some people will be able to fulfil this role easily, for instance a family member who lives at a distance and who only has occasional contact with the person, a spouse who also finds it difficult to understand the local authority processes, a friend who expresses strong opinions of her own prior to finding out those of the individual concerned, or a housebound parent. It is not sufficient to know the person well or to love them deeply; the role of the appropriate individual is to support the person's active involvement with the local authority processes (see chapter 6).[179]

Identifying the responsible MHA 1983 s117 after-care bodies

Introduction

9.82 Where an adolescent is entitled to MHA 1983 s117 after-care services, it will be necessary to identify which NHS body and local authority are responsible for ensuring that such services are provided ('the s117 responsible after-care bodies'). Box 9.4 sets out the relevant provisions under MHA 1983 s117(3).

9.83 However, it is important to note that in relation to NHS bodies, the section 117(3) provisions are subject to regulations as well as guidance issued by NHS England (the latest version of which was published in August 2020 and took effect as from 1 September 2020). Accordingly, section 117(3), as it applies to local authorities is considered first, followed by the rules relevant to NHS bodies.

178 Care Act 2014 s67(5)(a); see also s67(5)(b) which covers cases where the person lacks capacity or competence to make such decision, stating that it will be for the local authority to be 'satisfied that being represented and supported by that person would be in the individual's best interests'.

179 At para 7.35.

Box 9.4: The responsible after-care bodies – MHA 1983 s117(3)

- MHA 1983 s117(3)(a) provides that the responsible s117 bodies will be the local authority and CCG for the area in England in which the person was ordinarily resident 'immediately before being detained'.[180]
- MHA 1983 s117(3)(b) makes a similar provision for individuals ordinarily resident in Wales, save that the relevant NHS body will be the Local Health Board in whose area the person is ordinarily resident.
- MHA 1983 s117(3)(c) provides that 'in any other case', the relevant local authority and NHS body will be 'for the area in which the person concerned is resident or to which he is sent on discharge by the hospital in which he was detained'.[181] Presumably therefore, this section will only apply where the person's 'ordinary residence' cannot be established (likely to be rare) and the regulations concerning NHS bodies (noted below) are not engaged.

Identifying the responsible local authority: Ordinary residence

9.84 The starting point for identifying the local authority responsible for the provision of MHA 1983 s117 after-care services ('the responsible local authority') is by determining where the person was 'ordinarily resident' before being detained.[182] As this term is not defined under the MHA 1983, the person's ordinary residence is determined in accordance with the principles identified by case-law.[183] (Ordinary residence is considered at paras 9.95–9.99 below.)

9.85 Determining the ordinary residence of adolescents who were living with their parent(s) before their admission to hospital, is likely

180 Para (3)(b) makes a similar provision for individuals ordinarily resident in Wales (the NHS body will usually be the relevant Local Health Board (LHB)).

181 Reflecting the original wording of s117(3). See *R (Sunderland City Council) v South Tyneside Council* [2012] EWCA Civ 1232; and discussion at paras xx below.

182 MHA 1983 s117(3)(a) and (b).

183 Care Act 2014 s39 (deeming the person to be ordinarily resident in a particular local authority's area) do not apply to under-18s. Nor do they apply to adults in relation to the MHA 1983 (save for s39(4)) (see *Care and support statutory guidance* paras 19.62–19.68).

to be a question of identifying where the family home is situated. However, not all cases will be as straightforward. For example, uncertainties about an adolescent's ordinary residence may arise where the adolescent's parents have separated and share the care of their child or if the adolescent was not living in the family home prior to being admitted to hospital. Questions may also arise in relation to the ordinary residence of adolescents who are a 'looked after child' and were living in accommodation out of area immediately before being detained in hospital under the MHA 1983[184] (if such disputes arise, the courts have emphasised that local authorities should work together to resolve matters and ensure 'that the child does not "fall between two stools"').[185]

9.86 It is important to note that how to determine the ordinary residence of a person who is receiving s117 after-care services and is then re-admitted under MHA 1983 s3 is currently in a state of flux. In June 2020, the DHSC published a note stating that the *Care and support statutory guidance* 'particularly paragraphs 19.62 to 19.68' no longer represents the Secretary of State's position and will be 'updated in due course'. Currently, para 19.64 (which is considered to be of particular concern) states:

> Under section 117 of the 1983 Act, as amended by the Care Act 2014, if a person is ordinarily resident in local authority area (A) immediately before detention under the 1983 Act, and moves on discharge to local authority area (B) and moves again to local authority area (C), local authority (A) will remain responsible for providing or commissioning their after-care. However, if the patient, having become ordinarily resident after discharge in local authority area (B) or (C), is subsequently detained in hospital for treatment again, the local authority in whose area the person was ordinarily resident immediately before their subsequent admission (local authority (B) or (C)) will be responsible for their after-care when they are discharged from hospital.

184 The 'deeming' provision under CA 1989 s105(6) (see box 9.5 below) is explicitly stated to be 'for any purpose of this Act' (namely the CA 1989), suggesting that it would not apply when determining ordinary residence under the MHA 1983. However, the originating local authority may take the view that as it is responsible for the adolescent as a looked after child it is appropriate to accept s117 responsibilities. See also *R (Cornwall Council) v Secretary of State for Health* [2015] UKSC 46.

185 *R (AM) v Havering LB and Tower Hamlets LB* [2015] EWHC 1004 Admin at [34]–[35]. See also *R (G) v Southwark LBC* [2009] UKHL 57 at [28(3)]: 'But there should be no more passing the child from pillar to post while the authorities argue about where he comes from.' See paras 9.100–9.103 below for disputes in relation to ordinary residence for the purpose of s117.

The Secretary of State's repudiation of paras 19.62–19.68 of the *Care and support statutory guidance* follows eight determinations of disputes between local authorities on this issue (undertaken by the Secretary of State, in accordance with the Care Act s40 (see paras 9.100–9.103 below)). One of these determinations, (*R (Worcestershire County Council) v Secretary of State for Health and Social Care and Swindon Borough Council*) is subject to judicial review proceedings.[186] It is expected that new guidance will be issued following the outcome of this case.

Identifying the responsible NHS after-care body: NHS regulations and guidance

9.87 Although MHA 1983 s117(3) provides that the CCG responsible for a person's s117 after-care will be the CCG in which that person was ordinarily resident 'immediately before being detained', this is not the basis on which the NHS responsible body is to be determined. As noted above, regulations and NHS England guidance govern this matter. These are:

- National Health Service Commissioning Board and Clinical Commissioning Groups (Responsibilities and Standing Rules) Regulations 2012 (as amended)[187] ('NHS Regs'). The two relevant regulations are:
  - reg 14: 'Circumstances in which duty may be imposed on another CCG'; and
  - reg 15: 'Circumstances in which duty may be imposed on [NHS England]'.
- *Who Pays? Determining which NHS commissioner is responsible for making payment to a provider*, NHS England August 2020 (*Who Pays?* 2020).[188] This guidance 'clarifies responsibilities for funding

186 See: Review of the Secretary of State's determination of ordinary residence in the case of X arising from the dispute between Council A and Council B (Ordinary Residence 7:2020) which found that the guidance, in particular para 19.64 was not a correct interpretation of the law (both in relation to the meaning of s117 application of the Supreme Court's decision in *R (Cornwall Council) v Secretary of State for Health* (discussed below at paras 9.97–9.98). See: www.gov.uk/government/publications/ordinary-residence-anonymised-determinations-2020/ordinary-residence-7-2020.

187 SI 2012 No 2996; amended by the National Health Service Commissioning Board and Clinical Commissioning Groups (Responsibilities and Standing Rules) (Amendment) Regulations 2016 SI No 293. These regulations are issued under MHA 1983 s117(2E).

188 Available at: https://www.england.nhs.uk/publication/who-pays-determining-responsibility-for-nhs-payments-to-providers/

care on discharge from hospital (para 1.2) and aims to provide 'certainty on responsibility for commissioning and payment' (para 5.9).

9.88 The NHS regulations are complex and not well understood. This has not been helped by the fact that NHS England's guidance, *Who Pays? Determining responsibility for payments to providers* (revised in 2016),[189] was not updated to reflect the changes to the NHS regulations. Whereas reg14(2)(a) had provided that the responsible CCG for s117 after-care was to be determined by identifying which GP the person is registered with (this being the general rule for identifying the responsible CCG, namely the CCG of which the GP practice is a member),[190] this was repealed in 2016.[191]

Noting the confusion in this area, *Who Pays? 2020* states that it 'provides a clear position' on 'responsibilities for commissioning and payment' (para 1.2) in relation to section 117 after-care services (albeit this is pending any new legislation or guidance (para 18.1)). Guidance on identifying the responsible NHS bodies for the purpose of MHA 1983 s117 is set out in paras 18.1-18.9 of *Who Pays? 2020*. Such guidance introduces a significant change to the rules governing how the responsible CCG is to be determined for the purpose of section 117.[192] This is summarised below.

Identifying the responsible CCG

9.89 As noted by *Who Pays? 2020*, under MHA 1983 s117, the responsible NHS commissioner for individuals receiving s117 after-care services 'is the CCG in whose area the patient was ordinarily resident,

189 NHS England, April 2013. The 2016 revision to paras 33 and 34 of the *Who Pays?* guidance, entitled '2.10 "Who Pays" amendment to the section on "persons detained under the Mental Health Act 1983"' is available as a separate document at: www.england.nhs.uk/who-pays/.

190 This is explained at para 10.2 of *Who Pays 2020*. The exceptions to this are explained in Section D of this guidance, which includes 'Out of area placements of children' (paras 15.1-15.13) and 'Detention under the Mental Health Act and section 117 aftercare' (paras 18.1-18.19).

191 National Health Service Commissioning Board and Clinical Commissioning Groups (Responsibilities and Standing Rules) (Amendment) Regulations 2016 SI No 293 reg 2. This point is made by R Jones, *Mental Health Act Manual* 23rd edn, Sweet & Maxwell, 2020, see 1-1222, in particular p546.

192 *Who Pays? 2020* makes a distinction as between responsibility for payment of services and responsibility for commissioning of services (para 18.5). It is not clear how this distinction will work in practice. The guidance states (at para 18.5) 'we do not seek to describe how mental health services should be commissioned or how CCGs should work together to ensure that patients receive the care that is appropriate to their needs. . .'.

immediately prior to being detained in hospital under the Act' (para 18.3). However, exercising its powers under NHS Act 2006 s14Z7 to issue binding guidance[193] 'to state that the rules for determining responsibility are to be different from the legal position on responsibility for commissioning' (para 18.4),[194] NHS England sets out in para 18.6 of *Who Pays? 2020,* how the rules for payment responsibility will apply. In relation to s117 after-care, this means that the general rule for identifying the responsible CCG (linked to GP registration see para 9.88 above), applies. This will identify the 'originating CCG' at the point of the initial detention under the MHA 1983 (which includes under MHA 1983 s2). Furthermore:

> This originating CCG will then retain responsibility for payment throughout the initial detention (including any period of informal admission following detention, during which the patient is no longer detained but remains in hospital voluntarily), for the whole period for which any s117 aftercare is provided and for any subsequent repeat detentions or voluntary admissions from aftercare, until such point as the patient is finally discharged from s117 aftercare – regardless of where the patient is treated or placed, where he or she lives or which GP practice he or she is registered with (para 18.6).[195]

9.90 In addition, the NHS Regs reg 14 specifies cases in which the duty to arrange for the provision of after-care under MHA 1983 s117 is placed on a different CCG to the one that would be determined under s117(3).[196] These provisions cover under-18s who have been placed out of the CCG's area in residential accommodation[197] and who are (or who have been) a looked after child, who are receiving services under an EHC plan; or who have continuing care needs.[198] Additional

193 NHS Act 2006 s14Z7(2).

194 See paras 4.3 – 4.5 of *Who Pays? 2020* for further explanation of these powers.

195 *Who Pays 2020,* further clarification of the application of these rules is given at para 18.7. The reasons for NHS England's approach is given at 18.4. These new rules are not retrospective. *Who Pays 2020* (para 18.10) sets out 'mandatory transitional requirements'.

196 SI 2012 No 2996 (as amended by SI 2016 No 293 reg 2) reg 14(2)(b), which refers to four cases set out in Sch 1 para 2 of these regulations: paras (c), (g), (h), (i) and (j).

197 *Who Pays? 2020* (para 15.3) states that this can include an independent hospital.

198 *Who Pays? 2020* explains when these exceptions will apply (para 15.5), the effect of which is that the responsible CCG will be the CCG in whose area the adolescent was living prior to being moved out of area, paras 15.8 –15.12 provide illustrative scenarios Scenario 7 at para 18.18 provides an example of how these exceptions apply to an adolescent who is detained under the MHA 1983.

provisions apply to individuals (of any age) who have been granted MHA 1983 s17 leave[199] and cases where the person is not resident in England.[200] The relevant provisions are set out in appendix A below.

NHS England as the responsible after-care body

9.91 NHS Regs reg 15 provides that NHS England will be the responsible after-care body under MHA 1983 s117 if the after-care services to be provided fall within the range of services that NHS England, rather than a CCG, has a duty to arrange. It is possible that cases arise in which this provision is relevant to adolescents. This is because NHS England is required to arrange, 'Child and adolescent mental health services – Tier 4',[201] which may include community-based services, such as 'home treatment, step-down care and other alternatives to admission when delivered as part of a provider network'.[202]

MHA 1983 117(3)(c)

9.92 MHA 1983 s117(3)(c) applies 'in any other case', which presumably means when neither the rules under MHA 117(3)(a) and (b), nor (in the case of NHS bodies) the NHS Regs and *Who Pays? 2020* guidance apply. In relation to local authorities, this will be where it is not possible to ascertain the person's ordinary residence.[203] This provision sets out two possible grounds for determining the responsible after-care bodies:

- 'the area in which the person concerned is resident'; or
- the area 'to which he is sent on discharge by the hospital in which he was detained'.[204]

199 SI 2012 No 2996 (as amended by SI 2016 No 293 reg 2) reg 14(2)(b), Sch 1 para 2(j). As noted at para 9.54, MHA 1983 s117 can apply where MHA 1983 s17 leave is granted. The effect of this provision is that the responsible CCG will be the one in which the hospital is situated.

200 SI 2012 No 2996 (as amended by SI 2016 No 293 reg 2) reg 14(2)(b), Sch 1 para 2(h) and (i).

201 SI 2012 No 2996 reg 11; Sch 4 para 33: 'Child and adolescent mental health services – Tier 4.'

202 See *Child and Adolescent Mental Health Services (CAMHS) Tier 4: General adolescent services including specialist eating disorder services*, para 1.3.1.

203 See DHSC *Care and support statutory guidance* (updated June 2020) para 19.65. It should be noted that para is included in group of paragraphs that are pending revision (see para 9.86 above).

204 These were the criteria applied prior to the Care Act 2014's amendments which introduced ss117(3)(a) and (b).

However, the second ground is likely to be rare given that it is to 'cater for the situation where a patient does not have a current place of residence'[205] and such a finding is 'a last resort . . . an ultimate default position, which should not be held to apply except in extreme and clear circumstances'.[206]

9.93 In relation to identifying where the person 'is resident', in *R (Sunderland City Council) v South Tyneside Council,* which considered this provision, the court identified the key factors as being physical presence (where the person eats and sleeps) as well as the extent to which the person's presence there is voluntary.[207] Individuals can still be resident in a place even if absent, for example, having to spend time in hospital or a period of imprisonment following a criminal conviction.[208] While individuals cannot be considered to be resident in a hospital in which they are detained,[209] they can be resident in a hospital if they are there on a voluntary basis and have no other place of residence, for example because their tenancy was terminated after they were admitted into hospital.[210]

Ordinary residence

Introduction

9.94 As noted above, in some cases – for example, for the purpose of MHA 1983 s117 after-care and services under CSDPA 1970 – it will be necessary to ascertain where adolescents are 'ordinarily resident' to identify which local authority, or CCG, has responsibilities for them.

The meaning of 'ordinary residence' is not defined in either the MHA 1983 or the CSDPA 1970 and must therefore be determined in accordance with relevant case-law. For adults, *R v Barnet LBC ex p*

205 *R v Mental Health Review Tribunal ex p Hall* [1999] 3 All ER 132, 143, (1999) 2 CCLR 361; approved in *R (Hertfordshire CC v Hammersmith & Fulham LBC and JM* [2011] EWCA Civ 77 at [22].

206 *R (Sunderland City Council) v South Tyneside Council* [2012] EWCA Civ 1232 at [46]. See also *Care and support statutory guidance* para 19.65.

207 *R (Sunderland City Council) v South Tyneside Council* [2012] EWCA Civ 1232 at [31].

208 *R (Sunderland City Council) v South Tyneside Council* [2012] EWCA Civ 1232 at [31].

209 *R (Hertfordshire CC) v Hammersmith & Fulham LBC and JM* [2011] EWCA Civ 77.

210 *R (Sunderland City Council) v South Tyneside Council* [2012] EWCA Civ 1232. See also *R (Worcestershire CC) v Essex CC* [2014] EWHC 3557 (Admin).

Shah[211] is the leading case on ordinary residence, which is considered in the *Care and support statutory guidance*[212] under 'How to determine ordinary residence'. The '*Shah* test' focuses on whether the place the person is living has been 'adopted for voluntary and settled purposes as part of the regular order of his life for the time being, whether of short or long duration'.[213]

9.95 Following the Supreme Court's decision in *R (Cornwall Council) v Secretary of State for Health*[214] the *Care and support statutory guidance* provides guidance on how to determine the ordinary residence of an adult who lacks capacity to make decisions about where to live. Noting that they will not be able to voluntarily adopt a place as they have no capacity to do so, the guidance advises that in such cases, all the facts should be considered:

> . . . such as the place of the person's physical presence,[215] their purpose for living there, the person's connection with the area, their duration of residence there and the person's views, wishes and feelings (insofar as these are ascertainable and relevant) to establish whether the purpose of the residence has a sufficient degree of continuity to be described as settled, whether of long or short duration.[216]

9.96 As noted in box 9.5 below, the decision in *Cornwall* may also be relevant to adolescents due to transition to adult social care.

9.97 *Cornwall* concerned a dispute between local authorities as to which one was responsible for the care of a young disabled adult (PH), who when aged under 18 had been accommodated under the CA 1989 and on becoming an adult was provided with accommodation under the National Assistance Act (NAA) 1948. Both the CA 1989[217] and the NAA 1948[218] include provisions to the effect that where the person concerned has been placed by a local authority in accommodation situated in the area of another local authority, that

211 [1983] 2 AC 309, HL.

212 See paras 19.12–19.16.

213 [1983] 2 AC 309, HL at 343G.

214 [2015] UKSC 46.

215 *Care and support statutory guidance* notes (at para 19.33) that although that physical presence is a starting point, it does not equate to ordinary residence.

216 At para 19.32.

217 CA 1989 s105(6) – see box 9.5.

218 National Assistance Act (NAA) 1948, s24(5):

> Where a person is provided with residential accommodation under this Part of this Act, he shall be deemed for the purposes of this Act to continue to be ordinarily resident in the area in which he was ordinarily resident immediately before the residential accommodation was provided for him.

person will be deemed to be ordinarily resident in the originating local authority. In the Supreme Court's view, the underlying purpose of these provisions is that 'an authority should not be able to export its responsibility for providing the necessary accommodation by exporting the person who is in need of it'.[219]

9.98 The Supreme Court held that PH's ordinary residence did not change on his transition to adult care when he became eighteen so that the local authority that had been responsible for his care under the CA 1989 continued to have responsibility for his care under adult social care legislation. The *Care and support statutory guidance* explains this point as follows:

> . . . a looked after child who had been placed in foster care in local authority A by local authority B under the 1989 Act and who was ordinarily resident in local authority B for the purposes of the 1989 Act, continued to be ordinarily resident in local authority B when he reached 18 for the purposes of deeming provisions in the 1948 Act.[220]

9.99 Box 9.5 below highlights points that may be of relevance when determining under-18s' ordinary residence.

Box 9.5: Ordinary residence and under-18s

Ordinary residence and the Children Act 1989

CA 1989 s105(6) of the may be relevant when determining an adolescent's ordinary residence. It states:

(6) In determining the 'ordinary residence' of a child for any purpose of this Act, there shall disregarded any period in which he lives in any place–

- (a) which is a school or other institution;
- (b) in accordance with the requirements of a supervision order under this Act
- (ba) in accordance with the requirements of a youth rehabilitation order under Part 1 of the Criminal Justice and Immigration Act 2008; or
- (c) while he is being provided with accommodation by or on behalf of a local authority.

This means that where a local authority places an adolescent in accommodation (for example, a children's home) which is situated outside the local authority's area, the adolescent will not acquire

219 *R (Cornwall Council) v Secretary of State for Health* [2015] UKSC 46 at [54].

220 *Care and support statutory guidance* paras 19.37–19.39.

ordinary residence in the area in which the adolescent is living. As a result, the adolescent will continue to be ordinary resident in the local authority that made the placement. (See below in relation to adolescents due to transition to adult social care.)

Adolescents aged under 16

Based on case-law dating from the 1960s (*Re P (GE) (an infant)*,[221] it is generally assumed that under-16s' ordinary residence will be that of their parents.[222] However, *Re P* referred to 'a child of tender years who cannot decide for himself where to live' and although suggesting that this would be under 16, gave no fixed aged limit.[223] This raises the question whether, in certain cases, the *Shah* test might be relevant to under 16s. Although in most cases children aged under 16 will have little choice on where they live 'and no settled purpose, other than survival, in living there',[224] situations may arise where their choices are relevant, for example, where a child is living with other relatives, and is adamant that she does not wish to live her parents.[225]

Adolescents aged 16 and 17

Adolescents aged 16 and 17 can choose to live away from their parents at the age of sixteen.[226] In *Re D (a child)*, notwithstanding that the local authority maintained parental responsibility for a 17-year-old who was subject to a care order, the Court of Appeal applied the *Shah* test in determining that she was ordinarily resident in Kent on the basis that she 'was well able' to voluntarily adopt Kent as her abode and 'to demonstrate that she lives there for settled purposes as part of the regular order of her life for the time being'.[227]

221 *Re P (GE) (an infant)* [1964] 3 All ER 977, CA.

222 This continues to be the starting point for babies and young children: see *Re D (a child)* [2012] EWCA Civ 627; *C (a child) v Plymouth CC* [2000] 1 FLR 875, 879H. However, drawing from cases on 'habitual residence', the Court of Appeal found that for a baby to acquire his mother's ordinarily ordinary residence it was necessary for him to be physically present at that place: *Re S (a child)* [2017] EWCA Civ 2695.

223 *Re P (GE) (an infant)* [1964] 3 All ER 977 at 982, HL.

224 *Re A (children) (jurisdiction: return of child)* [2013 UKSC 60 at [38].

225 Ideally this should be formalised, eg through a special guardianship order.

226 See, for example, CA 1989 s20(3), (5) and (11) in relation to duties and powers of local authorities to provide accommodation to adolescents aged over 16.

227 *Re D (a child)* [2012] EWCA Civ 627 at [39].

Guidance in the *Care and support statutory guidance* on cases where a person lacks capacity to decide where to live may be of assistance in cases where 16- or 17-year-olds lack the capacity to make decisions about where to live and their ordinary residence is unclear.[228]

Ordinary residence and 'looked after children transitioning to adult social care services'[229]

The *Care and support statutory guidance* provides guidance on the situation of such adolescents in the light of the *Cornwall* decision (see para 9.96).[230] Where the relevant deeming provisions apply,[231] individuals who were placed out of area as a looked after child under the CA 1989 and then require accommodation under the Care Act 2014[232] after becoming 18 will continue to be regarded as ordinarily resident in the local authority in which they were ordinarily resident under the CA 1989.[233]

Where the deeming provisions of the Care Act 2014 (or the NAA 1948) are not applicable, there is a rebuttable presumption that the adolescent remains ordinarily resident in the originating local authority.[234]

MHA 1983 s117: disputes over ordinary residence

9.100 MHA 1983 s117(4) sets out how disputes between local authorities over where a person was ordinarily resident before being detained under the MHA 1983 are to be resolved.[235] However, the process for resolving disputes between local authorities in England appears to cover adults but not under-18s: MHA 1983 s117(4)(a) provides that

228 *Care and support statutory guidance* paras 19.23–19.34.

229 *Care and support statutory guidance* paras 19.37; see also paras 19.38–19.39.

230 Although the decision in *Cornwall* concerned the deeming provisions of the NAA 1948, the Care Act 2014, which is now the main legislation governing adult social care, has similar deeming provisions.

231 This depends on the type of accommodation to be provided (Care and Support (Ordinary Residence) (Specified Accommodation) Regulations 2014 SI No 2828.

232 The circumstances in which accommodation is provided under the NAA 1948 are outlined in the *Care and support statutory guidance* fn59.

233 *Care and support statutory guidance* paras 19.37–19.39.

234 *Care and support statutory guidance* paras 19.40 – 19.41.

235 Introduced by Care Act 2014 s75.

the dispute is to be determined in accordance with Care Act 2014 s40 which concerns 'disputes about where an adult is ordinarily resident'.

9.101 For adults, such disputes will be determined by the secretary of state (or appointed person) if it cannot be resolved locally.[236] Regulations provide that authorities in dispute 'must not allow the existence of the dispute to prevent, delay, interrupt or otherwise adversely affect the meeting of the needs of the adult or carer to whom the dispute relates'.[237] Presumably a similar approach would be taken where a dispute between local authorities arise in relation to an adolescent's ordinary residence given that this is the mechanism for dealing with disputes about ordinary residence under the CA 1989.[238]

9.102 As required under MHA 1983 s117(5), the DoH in England and the Welsh Government have published arrangements for resolving disputes over ordinary residence between local authorities in England and local authorities in Wales.[239]

9.103 Disputes between NHS bodies are not covered by MHA 1983 s117. However, *Who Pays?* (Appendix 1) provides guidance on new arrangements for dispute resolution.[240]

236 See the *Care and Support (Disputes Between Local Authorities) Regulations* 2014 SI No 2829.

237 2014 SI 2829 reg 2. See also *Care and support statutory guidance* para 19.77.

238 CA 1989 s30(2).

239 DoH (England) and the Welsh Government, March 2015: https://assets.publishing.service.gov.uk/government/uploads/system/uploads/attachment_data/file/416555/MH_aftercare.pdf.

240 *Who Pays? Determining responsibility for payments to providers*, August 2013, revised in 2016, p8.

CHAPTER 10

Powers in the community

continued

Introduction

10.1 There are three ways in which children and young people aged under 18 ('adolescents') may be subject to compulsory powers under Mental Health Act (MHA)1983 Part 2 while living in the community:

- leave of absence (under MHA 1983 s17);
- community treatment orders (CTOs); and
- guardianship.

10.2 This chapter considers the circumstances in which these community powers arise and when they might be applicable to adolescents. The *Mental Health Act 1983: Code of Practice*[1] ('MHA Code') provides guidance on these powers:

- 'Leave of absence' (chapter 27);
- 'Community treatment orders' (chapter 29); and
- 'Guardianship' (chapter 30).

Further guidance is provided in chapter 31 ('Guardianship, leave of absence or CTO?') and chapter 32 ('Detention and CTO: renewal, extension and discharge').

10.3 In addition to the matters listed above, this chapter provides:

- a summary of police powers under MHA 1983 ss135(1) and 136 and the Children Act (CA) 1989 s46.

Leave of absence

10.4 Where they are detained in hospital under the MHA 1983, individuals (of whatever age) can only leave hospital, even temporarily, if they are given leave of absence by their responsible clinician (RC) under MHA 1983 s17.[2] Only the RC has the power to grant leave and this cannot be delegated to anyone else.[3] Such leave can be subject to conditions that the RC 'considers necessary in the interests of the patient, or for the protection of other persons'.[4]

1 Department of Health (DoH), 2015.

2 This does not include those detained under the holding powers of MHA 1983 s5(2) and (4) – this is because they do not have a responsible clinician (RC); see MHA 1983 s34(1) for definition of the RC.

3 MHA Code para 27.8 points out that if the usual RC is absent (eg on leave) permission for s17 leave can only be granted by an approved clinician who is acting as the temporary RC.

4 MHA 1983 s17(1).

10.5 Individuals who are on leave under MHA 1983 s17 qualify for the assistance of an independent mental health advocate (IMHA).[5]

10.6 The provision of leave can be an important part of the adolescent's care plan – for example, weekend home leave may be a significant step for both the adolescent and the adolescent's family in preparing for discharge from hospital. Box 10.1 below sets out further key points in relation to MHA 1983 s17 leave.

Box 10.1: Mental Health Act 1983 s17 leave – key points

- *Short-term leave:* This might cover going to the local shops with a member of staff; or leave for a specific occasion – for example, attending a funeral.
- *Longer-term leave:* For example, weekend home leave, or a more extended time out of hospital, for the purpose of assessing the adolescent's suitability for discharge. Leave can be extended while the adolescent is on leave.[6]
- *Leave under MHA 1983 s17 or CTO?:* The RC must consider the suitability of a CTO before granting leave of absence for more than seven consecutive days, or extending leave so that the total period is more than seven consecutive days.[7] Although not prevented from using longer-term leave, the RC 'will need to be able to show that both options have been duly considered'.[8]
- *Planning for leave:* Before granting leave, the RC is expected to consider a range of factors such as: what, if any, conditions to attach to the leave; what support the adolescent will need (and whether it can be provided); as well as ensuring that any community services that will need to provide support during the leave are involved in the planning of the leave and are aware of the leave arrangements.[9]
- *Escorted leave:* If the RC considers this to be in the adolescent's interests or for the protection of others, the RC may direct that

5 MHA 1983 s130C(1).

6 MHA 1983 s17(2). See MHA Code paras 27.8–27.14; para 31.5 states that longer term leave should not normally be for longer than one month.

7 MHA 1983 s17(2A) and (2B). See also MHA Code para 27.11.

8 MHA Code para 27.12.

9 MHA Code para 27.10.

the adolescent remains in the custody of a member of staff (or any other authorised person) while on leave.[10]

- *After-care:* The duty to provide after-care services under MHA 1983 s117 will apply for those detained under section 3,[11] albeit as discussed at para 9.55 this duty does not cover all types of s17 leave, for example it does not extend to day trips from hospital.[12]
- *Treatment under MHA 1983 Part 4:* Although MHA 1983 Part 4 applies to individuals on section 17 leave, the MHA Code advises that if it becomes necessary to give treatment without consent 'consideration should be given to whether it would be more appropriate to recall the patient to hospital'.[13]
- *Family and carers:* Subject to the duty of confidentiality 'carers and other relevant people should be consulted before leave is granted (especially where the patient is to reside with them)'.[14] In cases where adolescents do not wish their parents to be consulted, their RC's 'should reconsider whether or not it is safe and appropriate to grant leave'.[15]
- *Revocation of leave:* The RC can revoke MHA 1983 s17 leave at any time if the RC considers it 'necessary so to do in the interests of the patient's health or safety, or for the protection of other persons'.[16] Refusal to take medication would not in itself be a reason for revoking the leave, 'although it would almost always be

10 MHA 1983 s17(3). In such cases patients will be in 'legal custody' (s137) and if they escape from the authorised person's custody, that person can retake the adolescent (s138) or others can do so under the powers of s18 (return and readmission of patients absent without leave). The MHA Code describes this as 'escorted leave' (MHA Code para 27.27). In contrast, where patients are granted 'accompanied leave' (para 27.28) their friends or relatives have agreed to accompany them on leave, but do not have the legal responsibility for keeping them in custody.

11 MHA Code para 27.26.

12 *R (CXF) v Central Bedfordshire Council* [2018] EWCA Civ 2852.

13 MHA Code para 27.25.

14 MHA Code para 27.18.

15 MHA Code para 27.19.

16 MHA s17(4). Recall is put into effect by serving a written notice on the patient. MHA Code para 27.36 highlights the importance of taking into account the views of carers:

> It is essential that carers (especially where the patient is residing with them while on leave) and professionals who support the patient while on leave should have easy access to the patient's responsible clinician if they feel consideration should be given to return of the patient before their leave is due to end.

a reason to consider revocation'.[17] If they are recalled from leave, the reason for this decision should be explained to the adolescent.[18]

Community treatment orders

Introduction

10.7 The scope, purpose and application of CTOs will be a relevant consideration when planning the aftercare of individuals of any age, who are detained in hospital under MHA 1983 s3. CTOs were introduced in 2008, and their purpose is:

> . . . to allow suitable patients to be safely treated in the community rather than under detention in hospital, and to provide a way to help prevent relapse and any harm – to the patient or to others – that this might cause. It is intended to help patients to maintain stable mental health outside hospital and to promote recovery.[19]

10.8 Whether CTOs have achieved this purpose is debatable. The independent review of the MHA 1983, *Modernising the Mental Health Act: Increasing choice, reducing compulsion*,[20] noted that CTOs are controversial. Concerns about CTOs include that they 'are being used far more extensively than had been anticipated when they were introduced in 2007'[21] (with about 5,000 being subject to CTOs) and of the individuals subject to their powers, there is a significant overrepresentation of ethnic minority groups.[22] Although deciding against recommending their abolition, the review set out proposals to reduce the numbers of people subject to CTOs (referred to as 'community patients' under the MHA 1983) and enhance the safeguards for those subject to these powers. It also stressed that more research on

17 MHA Code para 27.32; para 27.34 states: 'The reasons for recall should be fully explained to the patient and a record of the explanation recorded in the patient's notes.'

18 MHA Code para 27.34.

19 MHA Code para 29.5.

20 *Modernising the Mental Health Act: Increasing choice, reducing compulsion, Final report of the Independent Review of the Mental Health Act 1983*, (MHA Review), December 2018.

21 Mental Health Act (MHA) 2007 s32(2) amended the MHA 1983 by inserting ss17A–17G. CTOs came into force in November 2008.

22 MHA Review p28.

their efficacy is needed and the question whether CTOs should be abolished revisited within five years.[23]

10.9 As there is no lower age limit for a CTO, it is possible for adolescents who are detained under MHA 1983 s3 to then be placed on a CTO on their discharge from hospital. The MHA Code advises:

> The number of children and young people whose clinical and family circumstances make them suitable to move from being detained to being a community patient is likely to be small, but it should be used where appropriate.[24]

10.10 As suggested by the MHA Code, the numbers of under-18s on CTOs are low. Data from NHS Digital shows that for the period 2018/19, out of 4,840 individuals on CTOs, 41 of them were aged under 18 (15 aged under 16 years; and 26 aged 16 or 17).[25]

CTOs: overview

10.11 The provisions for CTOs are set out in MHA 1983 ss17A–17G. A central feature of the CTO is the power that it gives to the RC to recall the 'community patient' (the term given to those subject to a CTO) back to hospital for treatment for mental disorder. The power of recall to hospital is set out in MHA 1983 s17E (see paras 10.47–10.49 below). Community patients are entitled to after-care services under MHA 1983 s117 which must be provided for the duration of the CTO.[26] Individuals who are placed on a CTO (s17A) qualify for the assistance of an IMHA.[27]

10.12 MHA 1983 Part 4A governs the treatment of community patients who have not been recalled to hospital. It provides powers to treat community patients who lack the capacity or competence to consent

23 MHA Review p135.

24 MHA Code para 19.113.

25 See: https://digital.nhs.uk/data-and-information/publications/statistical/mental-health-act-statistics-annual-figures/2018-19-annual-figures. NHS Digital figures for previous years show that the number of under-18s on CTOs are as follows: 2017/18: 53 (11 aged under 16 years and 42 aged 16 or 17) and 2016/17: 33 (five aged under 16; and 28 aged 16 or 17 years). See: https://digital.nhs.uk/data-and-information/publications/statistical/mental-health-act-statistics-annual-figures/2017-18-annual-figures; https://digital.nhs.uk/data-and-information/publications/statistical/mental-health-act-statistics-annual-figures/mental-health-act-statistics-annual-figures-2016-17-experimental-statistics.

26 MHA 1983 s117(2). See also MHA Code para 29.21.

27 MHA s130C(1).

to their treatment for mental disorder.[28] Significantly, Part 4A does not include the power to treat community patients who have the capacity or competence to make decisions about their treatment and refuse such treatment. However, community patients can be recalled to hospital and will then become subject to MHA 1983 Part 4.

10.13 The Mental Health Tribunal (see chapter 8) has no power to order a CTO, but it can recommend that the RC considers a CTO for a detained patient, in which case the RC should assess whether a CTO would be appropriate.[29] A 'discharge CPA [Care Programme Approach]' meeting should be held before a person is discharged from hospital onto a CTO.[30]

Determining whether a CTO should be made

Overview

10.14 CTOs apply to individuals who have been detained under MHA 1983 s3 or who are unrestricted patients under MHA 1983 Part 3. Adolescents who are detained under MHA 1983 s2 or have been admitted to hospital informally cannot be placed on a CTO. As noted above (box 10.1), before granting indefinite leave, or leave for seven consecutive days or more, under MHA 1983 s17, the RC must consider whether a CTO should be used instead.[31]

10.15 Adolescents who are detained under MHA 1983 s3 can be placed on a CTO if their RC considers that the criteria for a CTO are met and an approved mental health professional (AMHP)[32] both agrees with the RC that the criteria for a CTO are met and considers that it is appropriate for the CTO to be made.[33] The AMHP should meet with the adolescent before making this decision.[34] The RC must give reasons for concluding that the grounds for the CTO are met, as well as specifying the date on which the CTO is to commence (which may be a date after the forms are signed so as to allow time for the necessary discharge arrangements to be put in place).[35]

28 MHA 1983 s64D, 64F and 64G.

29 MHA 1983 s72(3A)(a); and MHA Code para 29.19.

30 MHA Code para 29.33; see also paras 34.13–34.14 and 34.19.

31 MHA 1983 s17(2A) and (2B). See also MHA Code chapter 31.

32 See MHA Code paras 29.22–29.25 for the role of the AMHP.

33 MHA 1983 s4. The RC and the AMHP must complete CTO1 (Mental Health (Hospital) (England) Regulations 2008 SI No 1184 reg 6(1)(a), (b) and (2)(a)).

34 MHA Code para 29.22.

35 MHA Code para 29.26.

CTO criteria

10.16 The criteria for a CTO are set out in MHA 1983 s17A(5):

(a) the patient is suffering from mental disorder of a nature or degree which makes it appropriate for him to receive medical treatment;
(b) it is necessary for his health or safety or for the protection of other persons that he should receive such treatment;
(c) subject to his being liable to be recalled as mentioned in paragraph (d) below, such treatment can be provided without his continuing to be detained in a hospital;
(d) it is necessary that the responsible clinician should be able to exercise the power under section 17E(1) below to recall the patient to hospital; and
(e) appropriate medical treatment is available for him.

Importance of the power of recall

10.17 MHA 1983 s17A(6) requires the RC to give specific consideration to whether it is necessary to exercise the power of recall (which is set out in s17E(1) – see paras 10.47–10.49 below).

10.18 Accordingly, as for adults, when determining whether a CTO is suitable for an adolescent, the RC must consider what risk there would be of the adolescent's condition deteriorating after discharge – for example, as a result of 'refusing or neglecting to receive the treatment he requires for his mental disorder'.[36] In assessing this risk, the RC should take into consideration the adolescent's history of mental disorder and other relevant factors such as previous experience of contact with services and engagement with treatment.

10.19 A 'tendency to fail to follow a treatment plan or to discontinue medication in the community, and then relapsing may suggest a risk justifying use of a CTO rather than discharge into community care'.[37] However, the RC 'must be satisfied that the risk of harm arising from the patient's disorder is sufficiently serious to justify having the power to recall the patient to hospital for treatment'.[38] Other relevant factors are likely to include the adolescent's current mental state, ability to make care and treatment decisions, attitude to treatment and risk of relapse, and importantly 'the willingness and ability of

36 MHA 1983 s17A(6).
37 MHA Code para 29.13.
38 MHA Code para 29.16.

family and/or carers to provide support (especially where aspects of the care plan depend on them)'.[39]

10.20 The MHA Code also states that 'CTOs should only be used when there is reasonable evidence to suggest that there will be benefits to the individual', such as 'clear evidence that there is a positive response to medication without an undue burden of side effects' and 'evidence that recall may be necessary (rather than informal admission or reassessment under the Act').[40]

Conditions attached to a CTO

Mandatory and discretionary conditions

10.21 MHA 1983 s17B sets out conditions to be attached to a CTO. These fall into two categories: mandatory and discretionary.

Mandatory conditions

10.22 For all CTOs, community patients will be required to make themselves available for a medical examination in two circumstances:

- where the RC is required under MHA 1983 s20A to examine the community patient to decide whether to extend the CTO (see below at paras 10.45–10.46); and
- if a second opinion approved doctor (SOAD) is required under MHA 1983 Part 4A to consider whether to issue a certificate authorising treatment (see below at paras 10.40–10.41).

10.23 The RC has no discretion on whether or not to impose these conditions.

Discretionary conditions

10.24 In addition to the mandatory conditions that apply to all community patients, RCs can impose conditions that they consider to be 'necessary or appropriate'. It is therefore likely that adolescents who are subject to a CTO will be required to comply with additional conditions set by the RC.

10.25 MHA 1983 s17B(2) provides that conditions may be specified if the RC (with the agreement of the AMHP) considers them to be:

> . . . necessary or appropriate for one or more of the following purposes–
> (a) ensuring that the patient receives medical treatment;

39 MHA Code para 29.14.

40 MHA Code para 29.16.

(b) preventing risk of harm to the patient's health or safety;
(c) protecting other persons.

10.26 The MHA Code advises that the conditions should be 'kept to a minimum number consistent with achieving their purpose' and 'restrict the patient's liberty as little as possible while being consistent with their care plan and recovery goal'. They should also 'have a clear rationale' which is linked to one or more of the purposes set out under MHA 1983 s17(2B)(2)(a)–(c) (see para 10.25 above) and 'be clearly and precisely expressed, so that the patient can readily understand what is expected'.[41] The MHA Code goes on to state that the 'nature of the conditions will depend on the patient's individual circumstances' and the conditions 'should be stated clearly having regard to the least restriction principle'.[42]

10.27 Accordingly, adolescents subject to a CTO might have to comply with conditions on when and where they are to receive treatment, where they are to live, as well as other conditions being imposed on them to avoid known risk factors or high-risk situations that are relevant to the adolescent's mental disorder.[43] The reasons for the conditions imposed should be explained to the adolescent and, if appropriate,[44] others concerned for the adolescent, such as those with parental responsibility and the adolescent's IMHA.

CTO conditions and deprivation of liberty

10.28 The MHA Code's statement that 'the conditions imposed on a community patient must not deprive the patient of their liberty'[45] has been confirmed by the Supreme Court in *Welsh Ministers v PJ*.[46] Giving judgment for the court, Lady Hale concluded:

> . . . that the MHA does not give the RC power to impose conditions which have the concrete effect of depriving a community patient of his liberty within the meaning of article 5 of the European Convention.[47]

41 MHA Code para 29.31.

42 MHA Code paras 29.31 and 29.32.

43 MHA Code para 29.32.

44 There may be cases in which the adolescent does not want others, including their parents, to be given information. See points below (paras 10.31–10.33) if it is expected that the parents are to provide support to the adolescent in the community.

45 MHA Code para 29.31.

46 [2018] UKSC 66.

47 [2018] UKSC 66 para 29. See box 1.2 for information on Article 5.

10.29 In a subsequent (unreported) case, Hayden J stated that there was nothing to prevent the Court of Protection from making an order to authorise the deprivation of liberty of individuals subject to a CTO and who lack 'the material decision-making capacity' provided that the CTO 'does not contain conditions that on their face give rise to the confinement of the individual'.[48]

CTO conditions and the AMHP's agreement

10.30 Although the AMHP's agreement to the discretionary conditions is required when the CTO is made, the RC can at a later date vary or suspend the conditions without needing to seek the AMHPs agreement.[49] However, the MHA Code comments that it would not be good practice to do so when the conditions had only recently been agreed, without discussing this with the AMHP.[50]

Seeking the views of the adolescent and those with parental responsibility

10.31 Although there is no requirement that an individual consents to being made subject to a CTO, the MHA Code emphasises the importance of involving patients in the relevant decisions, such as the conditions to be attached to the CTO, any proposed changes to such conditions and the consideration of what changes to the care plan might be needed following a recall to hospital.[51] The MHA Code also highlights the importance of keeping carers and parents informed,[52] as well as noting that it will be helpful for families to

48 The full recital of the order is included in 39 Essex Chambers' *Mental Capacity Report: Compendium*, July 2019, pp27–28 (the report states that Hayden J, Vice President of the Court of Protection gave permission for this to be published). Although this case concerned an adult, presumably the Court of Protection could exercise such powers in relation to a young person (where the MCA 2005 applies) and similarly there would be no bar to the High Court authorising the deprivation of liberty of under-18s subject to a CTO if deemed appropriate to do so. See also *Birmingham City Council v SR* [2019] EWCOP 28, which took a similar approach in relation to patients subject to hospital orders with restrictions (MHA 1983 Part 3 ss37/41) in the light of the Supreme Court's decision in *MM v Secretary of State for Justice* [2018] UKSC 60. The Mental Capacity (Amendment) Act 2019 anticipates that the Liberty Protection Safeguards can authorise a deprivation of liberty where the arrangements are made in accordance with a CTO; see Sch 1 para 57(1)(c).

49 MHA 1983 s17B(4) and (5).

50 MHA Code para 29.40.

51 MHA Code paras 29.10. 29.30, 29.43 and 29.62.

52 MHA Code paras 29.10, 29.33, 29.35 and 29.43.

'have access to support so they can help the patient to comply'.[53] These points apply just as much to adolescents as adults.

10.32 Subject to patient confidentiality,[54] the adolescent's parents (or others with parental responsibility) should be consulted about relevant decisions concerning the CTO, such as changes made to the conditions imposed.[55] The MHA Code also notes that 'prompt attention should be paid to carers when they raise a concern that the patient is not complying with the conditions or that the patient's mental health appears to be deteriorating', which may lead to a review of how the CTO is working.[56]

10.33 Chapter 19 of the MHA Code ('Children and young people under the age of 18') considers the role of parents when their child is subject to a CTO:

> Parents (or other people with parental responsibility) cannot consent (or refuse consent) to treatment for mental disorder on a child or young person's behalf while the child or young person is on a CTO. If community patients under the age of 18 are living with one or both parents, the responsible clinician should consult with the parent(s) about the particular treatment (subject to the normal considerations of patient confidentiality). This dialogue should continue throughout the period of the CTO. If a parent is unhappy with the particular treatment or conditions attached to the CTO, and the child is not competent to consent (or young person lacks capacity to consent), a review by the child or young person's team should take place. This will be to consider whether the treatment and care plan, and CTO in general, are still appropriate for them.[57]

Provision of information

10.34 Community patients must be given information about their rights under a CTO, including the right to apply to a tribunal and to receive assistance from an IMHA.[58] They should also be given a copy of the care plan before being discharged from hospital onto the CTO.[59]

53 MHA Code para 29.33.
54 This is discussed in paras 2.96–2.103.
55 MHA Code para 29.30.
56 MHA Code para 29.44.
57 MHA Code para 19.114.
58 MHA 1983 s132A; see also ss20A(5) and 130D. MHA Code paras 4.13–4.19, 29.17, 29.34–29.35.
59 MHA Code para 29.33.

Treatment under CTOs

Overview

10.35 The treatment for mental disorder of all community patients, including under-18s, is governed by MHA 1983 Part 4A, unless they are recalled to hospital[60] (in which case, Part 4 of the Act will apply (see paras 10.51–10.53)).[61]

10.36 Part 4A distinguishes between two age groups: it refers to 'adult community patients' (individuals aged 16 and over); and 'child community patients' (individuals aged under 16 years). Within these two age groups, specific provisions are included for those who are unable to make treatment decisions for themselves: 'Adult community patients lacking capacity' will include adolescents aged 16 and over who lack capacity to make treatment decisions and 'child community patients lacking competence' cover adolescents aged under 16 who lack competence to make treatment decisions.

Assessments of 'capacity' and 'competence'

10.37 The provisions concerning 'adult community patients lacking capacity' will apply to adolescents aged 16 and over if they are assessed to lack capacity to make the relevant treatment decision within the meaning of the Mental Capacity Act (MCA) 2005.[62]

10.38 The provisions concerning 'child community patients lacking competence' will apply to adolescents aged under 16 who are assessed to lack the competence to make the relevant treatment decision. No definition of 'competence' is given in the MHA 1983. However, the MHA Code provides guidance on assessing competence which is considered at para 3.33, together with recent case-law on assessing Gillick competence (see paras 3.31–3.34).

10.39 The provisions under MHA 1983 Part 4A (ss64A–64K) are lengthy, complex and potentially confusing. Guidance on the treatment of community patients is provided in chapters 24 ('Medical

60 MHA 1983 Part 4A will continue to apply to individuals who are in hospital without having been recalled, eg they have been admitted to hospital voluntarily (see MHA Code para 24.14).

61 MHA 1983 Part 4A does not cover treatment under s57; see MHA 1983 s64A(b).

62 MHA 1983 s64K(1) and (2). See paras 4.20–4.33 for assessment of capacity under the MCA 2005.

treatment') and 25 ('Treatments subject to special rules and procedures') of the MHA Code.[63]

Summary of MHA 1983 Part 4A

10.40 A summary of how MHA 1983 Part 4A will apply to under-18s who are community patients is set out in box 10.2 below.[64] The term 'decisional capacity' is used in this summary to describe a person's ability to make the decision in question, whether this has been determined in accordance with the test of capacity under the MCA 2005 (applied to 16- and 17-year-olds) or Gillick competence (applied under-16s).

Box 10.2: CTOs and treatment under MHA 1983 Part 4A – key points

Refusal of treatment

Treatment for mental disorder *cannot* be given to community patients without their consent if they have the decisional capacity to make the treatment decision.

MHA 1983 Part 4A makes no exceptions to this rule, even in emergencies.[65]

Accordingly, under the CTO framework, where an adolescent has the capacity (aged 16 and over) or competence (aged under 16) and refuses the proposed treatment, treatment can only be given if the adolescent is recalled to hospital and treatment is authorised under MHA 1983 Part 4.[66]

Parents

MHA 1983 Part 4A makes no provision for decisions by parents. This means: 'Parents (or other people with parental responsibility) cannot consent to (or refuse) treatment for mental disorder on behalf of a child or young person's behalf which the child or young person is on a CTO'.[67]

63 See also Department of Health, *Reference Guide to the Mental Health Act 1983* (MHA Reference Guide) 2015, chapter 24,

64 MHA Reference Guide chapter 24 provides detailed guidance on the application of Part 4A.

65 MHA Code para 24.17.

66 MHA Code para 19.71 refers to the provision of life-saving treatment (see paras 3.95–3.97).

67 MHA Code para 19.114. See also MHA Reference Guide para 24.21.

However, where adolescents are living with their parents, the CTO care plan should be discussed with the parents and the dialogue continue throughout the CTO.[68]

Two key requirements: 'authority' and 'certification'

Whereas MHA 1983 Part 4A sets out circumstances in which certification is not required, there *must always* be authority for the treatment.

- *Authority requirement:* In all cases, the person giving the treatment must have the authority to do so. The authority for giving treatment under MHA 1983 Part 4A depends on whether the community patient has decisional capacity. For example, where an adolescent has the capacity (if aged 16 or 17) or is competent (if aged under 16) to make the relevant treatment decision, the authority for the treatment can only be provided by that adolescent's consent.
- *Certification requirement:* This applies to two categories of treatment.[69] The first is medication for mental disorder, after a specified period has elapsed (such treatment is referred to in MHA 1983 Part 4A as 'section 58 type treatment').[70] The second category is electro-convulsive treatment (ECT), which is referred to in Part 4A as 'section 58A type treatment'.[71] (As noted in para 7.7, ECT is rarely given to under-18s.) The certification requirement does not apply to emergency treatment (where treatment is 'immediately necessary' – see below).

Adolescents with decisional capacity

16- and 17-year olds with capacity to make treatment decisions, and under-16s who are competent to do so, can be given treatment under MHA 1983 Part 4A in the following circumstances:

- *Authority requirement is met:* treatment can only be given if the adolescent consents;[72]

68 MHA Code para 19.114.

69 MHA 1983 ss64B(2)(b) and 64E(2)(b).

70 MHA 1983 s64C(3) explains that this term is used to describe treatments that would have fallen under s58 if the person had been detained under the MHA 1983. Section 58 type treatment is medication that is given beyond the initial three-month period (see para 7.17 which explains this rule for the purpose of MHA 1983 s58). In addition, the certificate requirement does not apply to the administration of medication for the first month of the CTO – see ss64B(4) and 64E(4).

71 MHA 1983 s64C(3).

72 MHA 1983 ss64C(2)(a) and 64E(6)(a).

- *Certification requirement (if any) is met:* this will depend on what treatment is proposed:
  - *MHA 1983 s58 type treatment (medication):* the approved clinician in charge of the treatment must certify in writing that the adolescent has the capacity or competence to consent to the treatment and has consented to it;[73]
  - *MHA 1983 s58A type treatment (ECT):* a SOAD must certify in writing that the adolescent has the capacity or competence to consent to the treatment and has consented to it;[74]
  - *MHA 1983 emergency treatment:* the certification requirement does not apply where the treatment is 'immediately necessary' (but the adolescent *must* consent to such treatment).[75]

Adolescents aged 16 or 17 who lack capacity

Adolescents aged 16 or 17 who lack capacity (within the meaning of the MCA 2005) can be given treatment under MHA 1983 Part 4A in the following circumstances:

- *Authority requirement is met:* authority for the proposed treatment can be provided as follows:
  - a deputy (appointed by the Court of Protection) or the Court of Protection consents to the treatment on the adolescent's behalf;[76] or
  - the treatment is given by, or under the direction of, the approved clinician in charge of the treatment who has no reason to believe that the adolescent objects to the treatment or, if the adolescent does object, it is not necessary to use force against the adolescent to give the treatment.[77] In addition, giving the treatment must not conflict with a decision made by a deputy (appointed by the Court of Protection[78]) or the Court of Protection[79]); or

73 MHA 1983 s64C(4) and (4A); MHA Code para 25.29.

74 MHA 1983 ss64C(4), (4B) and 64E(7)(a); see also MHA Code para 19.82.

75 MHA 1983 ss64B(3)(b) and 64E(3)(b). MHA 1983 s64C(5)–(9) sets out the circumstances in which the treatment is 'immediately necessary' (see box 10.2 below). See also SI 2008 No 1184 reg 28(2).

76 MHA 1983 s64C(2)(b).

77 MHA 1983 s64D. See also MHA 1983 s64J ('Factors to be considered in determining whether patient objects to treatment'); and MHA Code paras 24.20–24.22 for guidance on objection and use of force.

78 MCA 2005 s19.

79 MHA 1983 s64D(6)(b). Reference to advance decisions and decisions by a donee (referring to a done of a 'lasting power of attorney' – see s64K(4)) are not relevant to adolescents as they can only be made by individuals aged 18 and over (see MCA 2005 s9(2)(c) and s24(1)).

- the treatment falls within MHA 1983 s64G ('Emergency treatment for patients lacking capacity or competence'): this provides the authority for treatment to be given if it is 'immediately necessary'.[80]
- *Certification requirement (if any) is met:* This is will depend on what treatment is proposed:
  - *MHA 1983 s58 type treatment (medication) and s58A type treatment (ECT):* the certificate requirement is met where a SOAD certifies in writing that it is appropriate for the treatment to be given.[81] The SOAD can also specify conditions that must be met before the treatment can be given;[82]
  - *emergency treatment under MHA 1983 s64G:* the certification requirement does not apply.[83]

Adolescents aged under 16 who lack competence

For adolescents aged under 16 who lack competence, the following rules apply:

- *Authority requirement is met:* authority for the proposed treatment can be provided as follows:
  - the treatment is given by, or under the direction of, the approved clinician in charge of the treatment who has no reason to believe that the adolescent objects to the treatment or, if the adolescent does object, it is not necessary to use force against the adolescent to give the treatment;[84] or
  - the treatment falls within MHA 1983 s64G ('Emergency treatment for patients lacking capacity or competence'): this provides the authority for treatment to be given if it is 'immediately necessary'.[85]
- *Certification requirement (if any) is met:*
  - *MHA 1983 s58 type treatment (medication) and s58A type treatment (ECT):* the certificate requirement is met where a

80 MHA 1983 s64C(2)(c). See box 10.2 below for details on treatment that is 'immediately necessary'.

81 MHA 1983 s64C(4). MHA 1983 s64H sets out who the SOAD must consult before determining whether to approve the treatment.

82 MHA 1983 s64C(4)); see also MHA Code para 25.32.

83 MHA 1983 s64B(3)(a).

84 MHA 1983 s64F. See also MHA 1983 s64J ('Factors to be considered in determining whether patient objects to treatment') and MHA Code paras 24.20–24.22 for guidance on objection and use of force.

85 MHA 1983 s64(5) provides that the treatment will be 'immediately necessary'.

SOAD certifies in writing that it is appropriate for the treatment to be given.[86] The SOAD can also specify conditions that must be met before the treatment can be given;[87]
- *emergency treatment under MHA 1983 s64G:* the certification requirement does not apply.[88]

Emergency treatment

MHA 1983 s64G: ('Emergency treatment for patients lacking capacity or competence') provides the authority for treatment to be given if it is 'immediately necessary':[89]

- *Immediately necessary:* Treatment is 'immediately necessary' if it is immediately necessary to:
  a) save the patient's life;
  b) prevent a serious deterioration of the patient's condition and is not irreversible;
  c) alleviate serious suffering by the patient and is not irreversible or hazardous; or
  d) represents the minimum interference necessary to prevent the patient from behaving violently to themself or others and is not irreversible or hazardous.[90]

However, if the treatment is ECT (or medication administered as part of ECT) only categories a) and b) apply.[91]

- *Use of force:* This is only permitted where 'the treatment needs to be given to prevent harm to the patient' and 'the use of such force is a proportionate response to the likelihood of the patient's suffering harm and the seriousness of that harm'.[92]
- *Conflicts with decision-makers:* The effect of MHA 1983 s64G is that emergency treatment can be given even if it conflicts with the decision of someone appointed under the MCA 2005 to make decisions on behalf of the community patient (in a 16- or 17-year-old's case, this would be a deputy appointed by the Court of Protection).[93]

86 MHA 1983 ss64E(7) and 64C(4). MHA 1983 s64H sets out who the SOAD must consult before determining whether to approve the treatment.

87 MHA 1983 ss64C(4) and 64E(7); see also MHA Code para 25.32.

88 MHA 1983 s64E(3)(a).

89 See MHA Code paras 25.38–25.42.

90 MHA 1983 s64C(5)–(9); and SI 2008 No 1184 reg 28(3).

91 MHA 1983 s64G(6).

92 MHA 1983 s64G(4).

93 See MHA Reference Guide para 24.14.

10.41 It is important to note that the above provisions do not apply to community patients who are recalled to hospital (paras 10.47–10.49 below) and for those whose CTO is revoked (paras 10.50 below). The treatment provisions governing such situations are considered at paras 10.51–10.53 below.

CTOs and the nearest relative

10.42 Unlike the provisions for admission under MHA 9183 s3, there is no requirement to consult with the person's nearest relative (NR) before making a CTO. However, the MHA 1983 requires that the community patient's NR be provided with certain information.[94] Unless adolescents request that such information is not be disclosed,[95] if they are placed on a CTO, their NR has the right to be given information (in writing) about the adolescent's rights, such as the right to apply to the tribunal to be discharged from the CTO[96] and if the adolescent's CTO has been renewed under MHA 1983 s20A (see below).[97]

10.43 In addition, the adolescent's NR must be informed when the adolescent is to be discharged from hospital as well as when the adolescent is to be discharged from the CTO. In both cases the information is to be given, 'if practicable', at least seven days before the date of the discharge[98] unless either the NR or the adolescent has requested that this information should not be given.[99]

10.44 The NR's rights in relation to seek the community patient's discharge are explained below (paras 10.57–10.59).

Duration and renewal of the CTO

10.45 A CTO applies for an initial period of 6 months but can be extended under MHA 1983 s20A for another six-month period and thereafter on an annual basis.[100]

94 MHA 1983 s132A. See also SI 2008 No 1184 reg 26.
95 MHA 1983 s132A(3).
96 MHA 1983 s132A(1) and (2). See also MHA Code paras 4.31–4.36.
97 MHA 1983 s20A(5); and SI 2008 No 1184 reg 26(e). See also reg 26(f), (g) and (h).
98 MHA 1983 s133(1), (1A) and (1B).
99 MHA 1983 s133(2). See also MHA Code para 4.36 on the need to consider the implications for Article 8 of the European Convention on Human Rights (ECHR) when disclosing information without consent.
100 MHA 1983 s20A(3).

10.46 If the adolescent's RC considers that the adolescent's CTO should be extended the RC must examine the adolescent within the two-month period prior to the expiry of the adolescent's CTO in order to decide whether the conditions for renewal are met. The criteria for renewal under s20A(6) mirror the conditions for making a CTO – see para 10.16 above),[101] save that para (c) refers to 'continuing to be liable to be recalled' and para (d) requires that it is necessary that the RC should continue to be able to exercise the power of recall.[102] If the RC considers that these conditions are met and an AMHP agrees with this opinion and that it is appropriate to extend the CTO,[103] the RC must submit a report to that effect to the hospital managers, giving reasons for this opinion.[104] Before doing so, however, the RC must consult one or more other people who have been professionally concerned with the adolescent.[105]

Recall and revocation

Overview

10.47 Adolescents who are subject to CTOs may be recalled to hospital by their RC[106] in one of the two following circumstances:

1) the adolescent has failed to comply with one of the mandatory conditions (as noted above at para 10.22, these require community patients to make themselves available for medical examinations in relation to the CTO);[107] or
2) the RC considers that the adolescent requires treatment for their mental disorder and there would be a risk of harm to the adolescent's health or safety or to others if the adolescent is not recalled to hospital.[108]

101 They are set out MHA 1983 s20A(6). See also s20A(7) which mirrors s17A(6). Guidance on extending a CTO is provided in MHA Code chapter 31, see in particular paras 32.11–32.16.

102 MHA 1983 s20(4)(c) and (d).

103 MHA 1983 s20A(8).

104 Form CTO7 in Mental Health (Hospital) England Regulations 2008 reg 13(6)(a) and (b).

105 MHA 1983 s20A(9).

106 This is by a serving a notice in writing on the patient (MHA 1983 s17E(5) and (6)). See MHA Code paras 29.52–29.60 for the procedure for recall.

107 MHA 1983 s17E(2). MHA Code states (para 29.47) that the RC should consider whether the patient had a valid reason for not complying with the condition.

108 MHA 1983 s17E(1).

10.48 Although the RC would not need to interview or examine the adolescent before deciding whether to exercise this power of recall, the MHA Code advises that the action taken should be proportionate to the level of risk and that the RC 'should consider in each case whether recalling the patient is justified in all the circumstances'.[109]

10.49 Adolescents who are recalled to hospital may be detained there for up to 72 hours, during which time the treatment provisions under Part 4 apply (as explained at paras 10.51–10.52 below). During this time, the adolescent's care team will decide on the next steps. Possible options are that:

- the adolescent is discharged from hospital and remains on the CTO (with perhaps a change in the care plan and discretionary conditions);
- the adolescent agrees to stay in hospital beyond the 72 hours on an informal basis; or
- the CTO is revoked.

10.50 The RC can revoke the CTO if the grounds for detention under MHA 1983 s3(2) are met (see para 6.14) and an AMHP agrees with the RC's opinion and that it is appropriate to revoke the order.[110] The effect of the revocation is that the adolescent will once again be detained under MHA 1983 s3 (the date of the detention starting from the date of the revocation of the CTO).[111] The hospital managers must refer the adolescent's case to the tribunal 'as soon as possible after the order is revoked'[112] and should notify the adolescent (and where appropriate), the adolescent's NR when they have done so.[113]

Treatment provisions on recall to hospital and revocation of the CTO

10.51 The treatment of community patients who are recalled to hospital and for those whose CTO is revoked is governed by MHA 1983 Part 4 (discussed at paras 7.7–7.36) rather than Part 4A. As explained at paras 7.19–7.22, under MHA 1983 Part 4, section 58 governs the provision of medication for mental disorder beyond the initial three-month period while section 58A governs the provision of ECT

109 MHA Code paras 29.47–29.49.

110 MHA 1983 s17F. The RC and the AMHP must complete CTO5 (SI 2008 No 1206 reg 8).

111 MHA 1983 s17G(5).

112 MHA 1983 s68(7).

113 MHA Code para 29.68.

whenever it is proposed. Given that ECT is rarely given to under-18s, the following points focus on the application of s58 (the provision of medication).

10.52 In cases where MHA 1983 s58 applies (because the 'three-month rule'[114] is met), the effect of an adolescent's recall to hospital is that unless that adolescent consents to the medication (having the capacity or competence to do so), a SOAD must certify that it is appropriate to be given.[115] However, MHA 1983 s62A sets out the circumstances in which it will not be necessary to obtain a SOAD's approval for such treatment.[116] The exceptions under s62A are as follows:

- the SOAD certification requirement does not apply because it is less than one month since the adolescent became a community patient;[117]
- the SOAD certification requirement does not apply because it is treatment that is 'immediately necessary' under MHA 1983 s62 (urgent treatment);[118]
- if an adolescent was receiving medication while a community patient which had been approved by a SOAD in accordance with MHA 1983 Part 4A (see box 10.2 above), that treatment can continue to be given on the adolescent's recall to hospital provided that the SOAD's certificate expressly states that it is appropriate to do so;[119]
- treatment can be continued on the adolescent's recall to hospital, while steps are being taken to seek a SOAD certificate, if the approved clinician in charge of the treatment considers that withdrawing the treatment would cause serious suffering to the adolescent.[120]

114 Explained at para 7.17.

115 MHA 1983 s58(3)(b).

116 See MHA Code (paras 25.33–25.36). The MHA Reference Guide provides more detailed guidance (paras 24.32–24.43) and figure 74.

117 MHA 1983 s62(3)(b).

118 See paras 7.23–7.28.

119 MHA 1983 s62A(5)(a). The SOAD can include conditions to this, such as the treatment can only be given if the adolescent has the capacity (aged 16 and over) or competence (aged under 16) to make decision and consents to the treatment – see MHA Code para 25.34 and MHA Reference Guide para 24.36.

120 MHA 1983 s62A(6) and (6A).

10.53 These exceptions will also apply if the adolescent's CTO is revoked while steps are being taken to seek a SOAD certificate in accordance with MHA 1983 s58.[121]

Discharge from a CTO

Introduction

10.54 Community patients may be discharged from their CTO via the same routes as those who are detained under MHA 1983 Part 2[122] – namely:

- their RC;
- their NR;[123]
- the hospital managers;[124] or
- the tribunal.[125]

Such powers provide important safeguards for all individuals who are subject to CTOs.

10.55 The powers of discharge for RCs, NRs and hospital managers are set out in MHA 1983 s23. The tribunal's powers of discharge are set out in MHA 1983 s72.[126] These powers of discharge from CTOs and how they apply to adolescents are summarised below.[127]

The responsible clinician

10.56 Adolescents can be discharged from their CTO by their RC at any time.[128] The MHA Code states that RCs must discharge a community patient if the criteria for a CTO are no longer met and that CTOs 'should not simply be allowed to lapse'.[129] Reviews of CTOs should be included in CPA reviews and if the criteria for the CTO are no longer met, it 'must be discharged without delay'.[130]

121 MHA 1983 s62A(1)(b) and (7).
122 See chapter 6.
123 MHA 1983 s23(1A) and (2)(c).
124 MHA 1983 s23(1A) and (2)(c).
125 MHA 1983 s72(2).
126 MHA 1983 s72(2).
127 The discharge of the CTO will also discharge the suspended s3 (MHA 1983 s23(1A)).
128 MHA 1983 s23(1A) and (2)(c); and SI 2008 No 1184 reg 18.
129 MHA Code para 29.76. Paragraph 29.75 sets out a series of questions to be considered to ascertain whether the CTO continues to be necessary.
130 MHA Code para 29.74.

The nearest relative

10.57 The adolescent's NR can seek to discharge the adolescent from a CTO,[131] but this can be blocked by the adolescent's RC.[132]

10.58 To discharge a community patient from a CTO, the NR must give the managers of the 'responsible hospital'[133] not less than 72 hours' notice in writing.[134] The RC can prevent discharge by issuing a report (often referred to as a 'barring report'[135]) within the 72 hours' notice period which certifies that in the RC's opinion 'the patient, if discharged, would be likely to act in a manner dangerous to other persons or to himself'.[136]

10.59 If a barring report is issued, the NR will be prevented from ordering the adolescent's discharge during the six months beginning with the date of the report.[137] However, the NR may apply to the tribunal for the adolescent's discharge, but must do so within 28 days of the barring report being issued.[138]

Hospital managers

10.60 The hospital managers of the 'responsible hospital'[139] can order an adolescent's discharge from a CTO.[140]

131 MHA 1983 s23(1A).

132 MHA 1983 s25(1A).

133 MHA 1983 s17A(7) and s145(1): responsible hospital means 'the hospital in which [the community patient] was liable to be detained immediately before the community order was made, subject to section 19A below' (under s19A regulations provide for the transfer of responsibility from one hospital to another – see SI 2008 No 1184 reg 17).

134 MHA 1983 s25.

135 Issued in accordance with SI 2008 No 1184 reg 25.

136 MHA 1983 s25(1).

137 MHA 1983 s25(1)(b).

138 MHA 1983 s66(1)(g) and (2)(d).

139 See MHA Code annex A, which states that this term means: 'The hospital whose managers are responsible for a community patient.' Reflecting MHA s17A(7), it adds: 'To begin with, at least, this is the hospital in which the patient was detained before being discharged onto a community treatment order.' However, this responsibility can be assigned to another hospital, see MHA 1983 s19(A).

140 Advice on conducting hospital managers' hearings during the coronavirus pandemic is given in NHS guidance, (Publications approval reference: 001559) *Legal guidance for mental health, learning disability and autism, and specialised commissioning services supporting people of all ages during the coronavirus pandemic* 19 May 2020 version 2 ('COVID-19 Legal Guidance') pp41–42.

10.61 As noted at para 8.13, the hospital managers' power of discharge is usually exercised by a panel of three or more individuals. Detailed guidance on how these powers are exercised is set out in chapter 38 of the MHA Code. In relation to CTOs, hospital managers may review the CTO at any time and must review where the CTO has been extended under MHA 1983 s20A (paras 10.45–10.46 above). They should also consider holding a review both where this has been requested by, or on behalf of, a community patient and where the RC has barred the NR's order for the community patient's CTO to be discharged. Reasons must be documented if the hospital managers decide not to review the case.[141]

10.62 In the absence of statutory criteria for the hospital managers to apply when determining whether to discharge community patients from their CTO, the MHA Code advises that the 'essential consideration is whether the grounds for . . . continued CTO under the Act are satisfied'.[142] It sets out a series of questions to be considered in sequence and which essentially mirror the criteria for making a CTO.[143] Where three or more members of the panel of hospital managers (who between them make up a majority) 'are satisfied from the evidence presented to them' that the answer to any one of the questions is 'no', the community patient should be discharged from the CTO.[144] However, in all cases the hospital managers have the discretion to discharge.[145]

10.63 In cases where the RC has made a report barring the NR from discharging the community patient's CTO, the hospital managers should also consider whether they agree with the RC's view that if discharged the community patient is likely to act in a manner that is 'dangerous to other persons or to themselves'.[146] Usually, they should discharge if they disagree with the RC's opinion but 'should always consider whether there are exceptional reasons' for not doing so.[147]

141 MHA Code paras 38.12 and 38.13.

142 MHA Code para 38.15.

143 MHA Code para 38.18; and see MHA 1983 s17A(5).

144 MHA Code para 38.19.

145 MHA Code para 38.23.

146 MHA Code para 38.22.

147 MHA Code para 38.22.

The tribunal

10.64 Adolescents, like other community patients, can be discharged by the tribunal,[148] which has the power to discharge community patients from their CTO 'at any time as it sees fit'[149] but also must discharge in the cases noted below (paras 10.66–10.68).

10.65 Adolescents who are subject to CTOs may have their case heard by the tribunal following their application (made by them or their representative on their behalf).[150] Their NR may in certain cases apply to the tribunal, for example where the RC has blocked the NR's order for discharge (see above at para 10.58).[151] Hospital managers are also under a duty to make referrals in the circumstances set out in MHA 1983 s68, which include where an under-18's case has not been heard by the tribunal for a year.[152] It will be for those considering that the adolescent needs to continue to be on a CTO to prove their case, not for the adolescent to disprove it.[153]

10.66 The tribunal must discharge a community patient from the CTO if it is not satisfied that the following criteria (set out in MHA 1983 s72(1)(c)) are met:

(i) that he is then suffering from mental disorder or mental disorder of a nature or degree which makes it appropriate for him to receive medical treatment; or
(ii) that it is necessary for his health or safety or for the protection of other persons that he should receive such treatment; or
(iii) that it is necessary that the responsible clinician should be able to exercise the power under section 17E(1) above to recall the patient to hospital; or
(iv) that appropriate medical treatment is available for him.

10.67 The tribunal must discharge if any one of the above conditions are not met. When considering point (iii), which concerns the need for the RC's power of recall, the tribunal must

> . . . in particular, consider, having regard to the patient's history of mental disorder and any other relevant factors, what risk there would

148 See MHA Code chapter 12; and MHA Reference Guide chapter 6, for information on the tribunal. See also S Johnston, S Miles and Dr C Royston, *Mental Health Tribunal Handbook*, LAG, 2015.

149 MHA Reference Guide para 6.75. The discretion to discharge is set out in MHA 1983 s72(1).

150 MHA 1983 s66(1).

151 MHA 1983 s66(1)(g) and s66(1)(ii). See also s66(1)(h) and s66(1)(ii).

152 MHA 1983 s68(6).

153 MHA Code para 12.5.

be of a deterioration of the patient's condition if he were to continue not to be detained in a hospital (as a result, for example, of his refusing or neglecting to receive the medical treatment he requires for his mental disorder).[154]

10.68 In cases where the NR has made an application to the tribunal following the decision of the RC to bar the NR's order for discharge (see para 10.58 above), the tribunal must also consider whether 'the patient, if discharged, would be likely to act in a manner dangerous to other persons or to himself'.[155]

Information on discharge

10.69 Where adolescents are discharged from a CTO, the reasons for this should be explained to them. As noted above (para 10.42) unless the adolescent has requested that such information should not be given, the hospital must, if practicable, give the adolescent's NR seven days' notice of the adolescent's discharge from a CTO.[156]

10.70 The MHA Code advises that 'any concerns on the part of the patient, the NR or any carer (and in the case of children and young people, those with parental responsibility) should be considered and dealt with as far as possible'.[157]

After-care services

10.71 Adolescents who are placed on CTOs will be entitled to MHA 1983 s117 after-care services for the duration of the CTO and following their discharge from the CTO until such time as the NHS body and local authority responsible for the adolescent's after-care are satisfied that the adolescent is no longer in need of after-care services.[158] Their care team should ensure that the after-care services the adolescent

154 MHA 1983 s72(1A). See *LW v Cornwall NHS Trust, SE v Devon Partnership Trust and TS v Birmingham & Solihull MH Trust* [2018] UKUT 408 (AAC) for discussion on the approach to be taken by the tribunal when considering CTO cases, in particular the 'likelihood of relapse if a patient, once free of the CTO, does not take his or her medication and the possible consequences if such a relapse were to occur' and holding that 'the authorities do not establish as a matter of law that likely relapse must be "soon", "in the near future" or within the permitted duration of a CTO for discharge to be lawfully refused' (para 49).

155 MHA 1983 s72(1)(c)(v).

156 See MHA Code para 4.36 on the need to consider the implications for ECHR Article 8 when disclosing information without consent.

157 MHA Code para 29.77.

158 MHA 1983 s117(2).

continues to need will be available.[159] Further information on after-care is provided in chapter 9.

Guardianship[160]

Introduction

10.72 The powers of guardianship under the MHA 1983 (not to be confused with guardianship under the CA 1989[161]) can be used in relation to individuals aged 16 and over. The purpose of guardianship under the MHA 1983 (ss7–10) is to enable individuals aged 16 and over 'to receive care outside hospital where it cannot be provided without the use of compulsory powers'.[162] These powers are used very rarely – as at 31 March 2018, only 300 people were subject to guardianship in England.[163] NHS Digital suggests that the continuing decline in the use of guardianship may be due to the introduction of CTOs (in November 2008) and Deprivation of Liberty Safeguards (DoLS) (in April 2009).[164]

10.73 The potential application of guardianship for adolescents is considered first, followed by a summary of the key provisions of guardianship under the MHA 1983.

Guardianship and adolescents

Overview

10.74 As the age of people subject to guardianship is not recorded, it is not known how many, if any, 16- and 17-year-olds are subject to these powers. While in theory, adolescents aged 16 and 17 can be made subject to guardianship,[165] its use for this age group is probably rare.

159 MHA Code para 29.77.

160 Save that the government should review whether such powers should continue to be included in the MHA 1983 (pp138–139), the 2018 MHA Review made no specific recommendations on guardianship.

161 See CA 1989 s5 (Appointment of Guardians).

162 MHA Code para 30.2.

163 *Guardianship under the Mental Health Act 1983, England, 2016-17 and 2017–18,* National Statistics, 20 November 2018.

164 NHS Digital, *Guardianship under the Mental Health Act 1983 England 2016–17 and 2017–18,* 20 November 2018.

165 MHA 1983 s7(1). MHA Code para 19.115 (although stating that these powers may be appropriate for under-18s, the Code gives no examples of when guardianship could be usefully applied to under-18s).

Given that the purpose of guardianship is to provide care and protection for individuals, rather than ensuring that they receive treatment for mental disorder, powers under the CA 1989 are likely to be a more appropriate vehicle for protecting the welfare of adolescents living in the community. However, there may be circumstances – for example, where the adolescent is aged 17 (so a care order cannot be made) – in which guardianship may be a viable option.

The Mental Capacity Act 2005 and guardianship

10.75 MCA 2005 s5 ('Acts in connection with care or treatment') may provide the necessary authority for the care and living arrangements of adolescents who lack the capacity to make such decisions. If these arrangements give rise to a deprivation of liberty, an application for its authorisation can be made to the Court of Protection.[166] In addition, when in force, the Liberty Protection Safeguards (which will apply to 16- and 17-year-olds as well as adults) will provide an administrative scheme for authorising a deprivation of liberty. However, the MHA Code notes that guardianship may still be appropriate in such cases, for example if 'there is a particular need to have explicit statutory authority for the patient to be returned to the place where the patient is to live should they go absent'.[167]

Alternatives to guardianship under the Children Act 1989

10.76 Another factor against the use of guardianship in relation to young people aged 16 and 17 is the availability of more 'child-centred'[168] provisions.

10.77 For adolescents who require some form of supervision in the community, powers under the CA 1989, such as a care order[169] or supervision order[170] may be considered more appropriate than guardianship (if the threshold for these orders are met).[171] However, where the adolescent is 17 (or aged 16 and married), so that neither a care order nor a supervision order can be made,[172] guardianship might be considered a suitable option.

10.78 Another potential option is that of wardship.

166 MHA Code para 30.12.
167 MHA Code para 30.13.
168 *Re F (Mental Health Act: guardianship)* [2000] 1 FLR 192, 199.
169 CA 1989 s31.
170 CA 1989 s31, s35 and Sch 3.
171 CA 1989 s31(2).
172 CA 1989 s31(3).

Wardship versus guardianship

10.79 Adolescents who are wards of court cannot be placed under guardianship.[173] However, the question may arise as to which of the two – wardship or guardianship – is the more appropriate mechanism for overseeing an adolescent's care.

10.80 In *Re F (Mental Health Act: guardianship)*, the Court of Appeal considered that the first instance judge had been wrong to reject wardship as more an appropriate alternative to guardianship in relation to 'T', a seventeen year old with learning disabilities.[174] However, the availability of wardship in such cases may be more limited than *Re F* suggests given the restrictions placed on the use of wardship under CA 1989 s100(2), in particular s100(2)(b) which prohibits the use of the inherent jurisdiction 'so as to require a child to be accommodated by or on behalf of a local authority'.[175]

10.81 This limitation on the use of wardship was not considered in *Re F* even though the local authority's decision to use guardianship for T was in response to the decision of her parents to withdraw their agreement to T's placement in a specialist children's home.[176] However, this has since been highlighted by the courts. In *Re E (a child)*, Thorpe LJ noted that CA 1989 s100(2) prevents the court from making a wardship order that has the effect of 'requiring a child to be placed in care or under the supervision of a local authority'.[177] In *Re M (jurisdiction: wardship)*, McFarlane LJ noted that the court cannot 'grant authority to the local authority to provide care for a child where the local authority would not otherwise have the power to do so under

173 MHA 1983 s33(3).

174 *Re F (Mental Health Act: guardianship)* [2000] 1 FLR 192. The Court of Appeal also considered that guardianship was not applicable in this case. Taking a 'restrictive construction' of the MHA 1983, the court considered that the young woman's wish to return to live with her parents, despite the risks that the local authority thought this would entail, did not amount to 'seriously irresponsible conduct' and therefore she did not have a 'mental impairment'. Although amendments introduced by the MHA 2007 mean that 'mental impairment' no longer forms part of the criteria for guardianship under the MHA 1983, such considerations remain relevant given that the 'learning disability qualification' discussed in para 6.10 applies to guardianship. See MHA 1983 s1(2A) and (2B).

175 *A City Council v LS and others (secure accommodation: inherent jurisdiction)* [2019] EWHC 1384 (Fam); and *Re K (a child) (post adoption placement breakdown)* [2012] EWHC 4148 (Fam).

176 As noted in *Re K (a child) (post adoption placement breakdown)* [2012] EWHC 4148 (Fam) at [169] it is therefore unclear how this restriction on the use of wardship was overcome.

177 *Re E (a child)* [2012] EWCA Civ 1773 at [16].

the statutory scheme'.[178] However, s100(2) does not preclude the court 'from making an order in wardship where the child is not required to be accommodated, but is voluntarily accommodated'.[179]

Guardianship under the MHA 1983: key provisions

10.82 The key provisions relating to guardianship under the MHA 1983 are set out below.

Applications for guardianship (MHA 1983 s7)

10.83 MHA 1983 s7(2) provides that a guardianship application can be made in relation to individuals aged 16 and over who:

- are 'suffering from mental disorder'[180] of a nature or degree which warrants their reception into guardianship under section 7; and
- it is necessary in the interests of their 'welfare' or 'for the protection of other persons' that they should be received into guardianship.

10.84 The application is made by either an AMHP or the person's NR[181] and is founded on two medical recommendations which must confirm that the above conditions for guardianship are met.[182] The application must include the age of the person or (if the age is not known) a statement that the person is believed to be over 16 years of age.[183]

10.85 Guardianship is for an initial period of six months; it can be renewed for another six months and thereafter on an annual basis.[184] Individuals who are subject to guardianship under section 7 qualify for the assistance of an IMHA.[185]

178 [2016] EWCA Civ 937 at [39].

179 *Re E (a child)* [2012] EWCA Civ 1773 at [16]. For an example of a recent case on the use of wardship see: *A London Borough v X and Others* [2019] EWHC B16 (Fam).

180 Note that the 'learning disability qualification' under MHA 1983 s1(2A) and (2B) (discussed at para 6.10) applies.

181 As with applications for detention in hospital under the MHA 1983, although the adolescent's NR has the power to make an application for guardianship, it is rare for such applications to be made (see MHA Reference Guide para 28.26).

182 MHA 1983 s7(3). An application for guardianship cannot be made in respect of an adolescent who is a ward of court (MHA 1983 s33(3)).

183 MHA 1983 s7(4).

184 MHA 1983 s20(2).

185 MHA 1983 s130C(1) and (2)(b).

Powers of the guardian

10.86 The guardian (usually an officer of the local authority)[186] has three key powers 'to the exclusion of any other person':[187]

- *residence*: to require the person to reside in a specified place;[188]
- *attendance*: to require the person to attend places at specified times for the purpose of 'medical treatment, occupation, education or training; and
- *access:* to require that access is given to any place the person is residing to a doctor, AMHP or any other specified person.

10.87 The powers of the guardian are limited in that guardianship 'must not be used to impose restrictions that amount to a deprivation of liberty', nor does it 'give anyone the right to treat the patient without their permission or to consent to treatment on their behalf'.[189] However, authority for a deprivation of liberty or treatment without consent might be provided by an alternative legal route, for example, acting in accordance with the MCA 2005.[190]

Powers of discharge

10.88 Individuals can be discharged from guardianship at any time by their RC, the local authority[191] or their NR.[192] They can also apply to the tribunal for discharge from guardianship during each period of

186 MHA 1983 s7(5). Although a private individual who is willing to act as the guardian can undertake this role if approved by the local authority, this is rare. NHS Digital, *Guardianship under the Mental Health Act 1983 England 2016–17 and 2017–18* (20 November 2018) notes (under figure 2) that in 99 per cent of all new and continuing cases, the guardian was the local authority. The MHA Reference Guide (paras 28.21–28.22) notes that with the exception of the powers of discharge, local authorities may delegate their functions in relation to guardianship 'to any committee, officer or other body or person to whom they can normally delegate functions under the Local Government Act 2000, or the Local Government Act 1972, if relevant'.

187 MHA 1983 s8(1). This includes the Court of Protection, see: *C v Blackburn and Darwen BC* [2011] EWHC 3321 (Admin) at [39] and [40].

188 Under MHA 1983 s18(3), individuals subject to guardianship can be returned to the place they are required to reside if they have left that residence without the guardian's permission.

189 MHA Code paras 30.4 and 30.5. The compulsory treatment provisions of Part 4 do not apply to people subject to guardianship.

190 See MHA Code para 30.32.

191 This power can be exercised on behalf of the local authority by a committee of at least three individuals; see MHA 1983 s23(4).

192 MHA 1983 s23(2)(b).

guardianship.[193] The person who was their NR can apply to the tribunal if that person has been displaced as the NR under MHA 1983 s29(3)(c) (unreasonable objection to the making of a guardianship application).[194]

10.89 The tribunal must direct that the person be discharged from guardianship if it is satisfied either that the person 'is not then suffering from a mental disorder' or 'that it is not necessary for that person's welfare or the protection of others, that the person remain under guardianship.[195]

Rights of the nearest relative

10.90 If it is proposed to place an adolescent under guardianship, the adolescent's NR will have a range of rights under the MHA 1983. These include:

- *Consultation about the guardianship application:* The AMHP must consult the adolescent's NR before making an application for guardianship.[196] If the NR objects, the application cannot go ahead unless the NR is displaced by the court under MHA 1983 s29.[197]
- *Information:* The information to be given includes the NR's right to apply for the adolescent to be discharged from guardianship[198] as well as (unless the adolescent requests otherwise) the adolescent's rights to apply to the tribunal[199] and the role of IMHAs.[200]
- *Order the adolescent's discharge from guardianship:* The NR can do so at any time.[201] Unlike detention in hospital and CTOs (see above), there is no need to give 72 hours' notice and the RC has no power to bar the discharge.[202]

193 MHA 1983 s66(1)(c) and (f).
194 MHA 1983 s66(1)(h) and s66(1)(ii).
195 MHA 1983 s72(4).
196 MHA 1983 s11(4) (the duty to consult is subject to circumstances in which it is 'not reasonably practicable or would involve unreasonable delay'). See MHA Code paras 4.36 and 14.57–14.65.
197 MHA 1983 s29(3)(c).
198 MHA 1983 s23.
199 MHA 1983 s66; SI 2008 No 1184 reg 26(3) and (4).
200 MHA 1983 s130D(5).
201 See MHA 1983 s24 (visits and examinations by doctors for the purpose of advising the nearest relatives on the exercise of their power of discharge).
202 MHA 1983 s23(2).

Visits to those subject to guardianship

10.91 The local authority responsible for the guardianship must arrange for someone to visit the person subject to guardianship on the local authority's behalf at least every three months and by either an MHA 1983 s12 approved doctor or approved clinician at least once a year.[203]

Police powers

Overview

10.92 Both the MHA 1983 (ss135(1) and 136) and the CA 1989 (s46) provide the police with powers which will be relevant to adolescents with complex mental health needs.[204]

10.93 In relation to police powers under the MHA 1983, guidance is provided in chapter 16 of the MHA Code. However, it is important to note that such guidance precedes the amendments to s135 and s136 which were introduced by the Policing and Crime Act 2017 ss80–83. These amendments are explained in the Department of Health (DoH) and Home Office's *Guidance for the implementation of changes to police powers and places of safety provisions in the Mental Health Act 1983* ('Police Powers Guidance').[205]

Power of entry to remove a person to a 'place of safety'

10.94 MHA 1983 s135(1) provides for the circumstances in which an AMHP can obtain a warrant which authorises a police officer to enter (using force if necessary) the premises specified in the warrant and remove the person to a 'place of safety' with a view to making an application for the person's admission to hospital under the MHA 1983 'or of other arrangements for his treatment or care' (such as informal admission or the provision of support in the community). When executing the warrant, the police officer must be accompanied by an AMHP and a doctor.[206]

203 SI 2008 No 1184 reg 23. See also MHA 1983 s116 if the adolescent is admitted to hospital.

204 The role of the police under the MHA 1983 is not limited to these powers; see for example s18 (return and admission of patients absent without leave) and s135(2).

205 This joint guidance was published in October 2017.

206 MHA 1983 s135(4). MHA Code para 16.4 notes that it would be 'helpful' if the doctor is approved for the purpose of MHA 1983 s12(2) (see para 6.21).

10.95 The criteria for obtaining such a warrant are that:

> . . . there is reasonable cause to suspect that a person believed to be suffering from mental disorder–
> (a) has been, or is being, ill-treated, neglected or kept otherwise than under proper control, in any place within the jurisdiction of the justice, or
> (b) being unable to care for himself, is living alone in any such place.

10.96 Key points concerning a 'place of safety', which is defined under the MHA 1983 (s135(6) and (7)), are set out in box 10.3 below.

10.97 MHA 1983 s135(1A) provides that if the premises specified in the warrant are a place of safety, the person can be kept there rather than being removed to another place of safety. However, for private premises to be a 'place of safety' they must be both considered to be 'suitable' (which 'will involve evaluation of a number of inter-related factors including for example, the physical environment, the condition and behaviour of the person, and potentially any relationship between the person and that place'[207]) and the agreement of the relevant people obtained.[208] Whose agreement will be required depends on the circumstances. For example, if a MHA 1983 s135(1) warrant is executed at the adolescent's family home, both the adolescent and one of the other occupiers, such as one of the adolescent's parents, would need to agree to the home being used as a place of safety.[209]

Box 10.3: Places of safety under the Mental Health Act 1983 – key points

- MHA 1983 s135(6) specifies premises that are a place of safety, such as a hospital. It also refers to 'any other suitable place'.
- Rather than defining a 'suitable place', MHA 1983 s135(7) provides that 'a house, flat or room where a person is living' cannot be regarded as suitable unless certain individuals agree to the premises being used as a place of safety. Whose agreement is required depends on the circumstances but in all cases 'the person believed to be suffering from a mental disorder' must

207 *Guidance for the implementation of changes to police powers and places of safety provisions in the Mental Health Act 1983* p13 para 3.4.

208 MHA 1983 s135(7).

209 MHA 1983 s135(7)(a)(ii). See also box 10.3 below.

agree.[210] Other places can only be a place of safety if 'a person who appears to the constable exercising powers under this section to be responsible for the management of the place agrees to its use as a place of safety'.[211]

- The period of detention in a place of safety is up to 24 hours.[212] This can be extended for up to another 12 hours but only in limited circumstances.[213]
- Police stations cannot be used as a place of safety for under-18s.[214]
- The MHA Code states that under-18s should be taken to an appropriate place of safety and be assessed either by a CAMHS consultant or an AMHP with experience of working with this age group.[215] The Police Powers Guidance states that 'local protocols should set out clearly the provision made for places of safety appropriate for children and or young persons aged under 18 years' and 'where such places are in short supply, partners may wish to explore the feasibility of cross boundary co-operation with neighbouring areas'.[216]

210 MHA 1983 s135(7)(a). See MHA 1983 s135(7)(b) in. See also *Guidance for the implementation of changes to police powers and places of safety provisions in the Mental Health Act 1983* ('Police Powers Guidance'), DoH and the Home Office, October 2017, paras 3.3–3.14.

211 MHA 1983 s135(7)(b) concerns premises that are not occupied by the person subject to s135(1) or s136 powers. See police powers under the MHA Reference Guide paras 3.3–3.17.

212 MHA 1983 ss135(3ZA) and 136 (2A). Policing and Crime Act 2017 s82(3) amended the MHA 1983 by reducing the permitted period of detention from 72 hours to 24. The Coronavirus Act 2020 Sch 8 para 10 makes provision for the period of 24 hours to be extended to 36. At the time of writing (September 2020) this provision is not in force.

213 MHA 1983 s136B. During this period of detention, a person can be transferred to another place of safety (s135(3A) and (3B)). The time starts to run when the person arrives at the place of safety. If the person is kept at a place of safety, the time starts to run when the police officer decides to keep the person there (MHA 1983 ss135(3ZA) and 136(2A)).

214 MHA 1983 ss135(8) and 136A(1). They can only be used as a place of safety for adults in limited circumstances: see Mental Health Act 1983 (Places of Safety) Regulations 2017 SI No 1036.

215 MHA Code 16.49.

216 Police Powers Guidance p16 para 3.9.

Power to remove to, or keep a person in, a 'place of safety'

10.98 Under MHA 1983 s136, if it appears to a police officer that a person (of any age) is 'suffering from mental disorder and in immediate need of care or control' and that it is necessary to do so in the person's interests or for the protection of other people, the police officer may remove the person to a 'place of safety' (see box 10.3), or if the person is already in a place of safety, keep the person there, or remove the person to another place of safety.

10.99 The police can exercise such powers in any place other than a private dwelling (including any outside space that is used in connection with that private dwelling and is not shared with other properties)[217] and can enter by force if necessary.[218] Individuals can be detained in a place of safety to enable them to be examined by a doctor and interviewed by an AMHP and for 'making any necessary arrangements' for their treatment or care.[219]

Police protection and the Children Act 1989 (CA 1989 s46 'Removal and accommodation by the police in cases of emergency')

10.100 Under the CA 1989 s46 ('Removal and accommodation by the police in cases of emergency) a 'child' (defined as a person under the age of 18[220]) can be taken into 'police protection'[221] for up to 72 hours. A police officer who has 'reasonable cause to believe that a child who would otherwise be likely to suffer significant harm' can either 'remove the child to suitable accommodation and keep him there' or 'take such steps as are reasonable to ensure that the child's removal from any hospital, or other place, in which he is then being accommodated is prevented'.[222] However, s46 'should be used only in exceptional circumstances where there is insufficient time to seek an EPO

217 MHA 1983 s136(1A).

218 MHA 1983 s136(1B). Before deciding to remove the person to, or keep a person in, a place of safety, a police officer must consult, 'if practicable to do so' one of the professionals listed under the Act and regulations, such as a doctor, nurse or AMHP (MHA 1983 s136(1C)).

219 MHA 1983 s136(2).

220 CA 1989 s105.

221 This is the term used when the police exercise this power, see CA 1989 s46(2).

222 CA 1989 s46(1).

[emergency protection order][223] or for reasons relating to the immediate safety of the child'.[224]

10.101 Although the police do not acquire parental responsibility when they exercise powers under CA 1989 s46, if an adolescent is taken into police protection, the police must do what is reasonable in the circumstances to safeguard or promote that adolescent's welfare.[225] Both the police and the relevant local authority[226] will be required to undertake enquiries to establish whether further action is needed to safeguard the adolescent.[227]

223 A summary of EPOs is given at box 5.2

224 HM Government, *Working Together to Safeguard Children: A guide to inter-agency working to safeguard and promote the welfare of children*, 2018, p33. See also *Langley v Liverpool City Council* [2005] EWCA Civ 1173, [2006] 2 All ER 202, [2006] 1 FLR 342.

225 CA 1989 s46(9).

226 CA 1989 s46(3) states that as soon as reasonably practicable, the police are required to a) 'inform the local authority within whose area the child was found of the steps that have been, and are proposed to be, taken with respect to the child under this section and the reasons for taking them' and b) 'give details to the authority within whose area the child is ordinarily resident ("the appropriate authority") of the place at which the child is being accommodated'. See also CA 1989 s47(1) and (12).

227 The action to be taken by the police is set out in CA 1989 s46(3)–(10). See also HM Government, *Working Together to Safeguard Children: A guide to inter-agency working to safeguard and promote the welfare of children*, 2018p33; and *Court orders and pre-proceedings: for local authorities*, Department for Education (DfE), April 2014, pp40–41.

APPENDICES

APPENDIX A

Extracts from legislation[1]

Statutes

Regulations

CARE ACT 2014 ss1, 58, 59

Part 1 Care and Support

General responsibilities of local authorities

Promoting individual well-being

1 (1) The general duty of a local authority, in exercising a function under this Part in the case of an individual, is to promote that individual's well-being.

(2) 'Well-being', in relation to an individual, means that individual's well-being so far as relating to any of the following–

(a) personal dignity (including treatment of the individual with respect);

(b) physical and mental health and emotional well-being;

(c) protection from abuse and neglect;

(d) control by the individual over day-to-day life (including over care and support, or support, provided to the individual and the way in which it is provided);

(e) participation in work, education, training or recreation;

(f) social and economic well-being;

(g) domestic, family and personal relationships;

(h) suitability of living accommodation;

(i) the individual's contribution to society.

(3) In exercising a function under this Part in the case of an individual, a local authority must have regard to the following matters in particular–

(a) the importance of beginning with the assumption that the individual is best-placed to judge the individual's well-being;

(b) the individual's views, wishes, feelings and beliefs;

(c) the importance of preventing or delaying the development of needs for care and support or needs for support and the importance of reducing needs of either kind that already exist;

(d) the need to ensure that decisions about the individual are made having regard to all the individual's circumstances (and are not based only on the individual's age or appearance or any condition of the individual's or aspect of the individual's behaviour which might lead others to make unjustified assumptions about the individual's well-being);

(e) the importance of the individual participating as fully as possible in decisions relating to the exercise of the function concerned and being provided with the information and support necessary to enable the individual to participate;

(f) the importance of achieving a balance between the individual's well-being and that of any friends or relatives who are involved in caring for the individual;

(g) the need to protect people from abuse and neglect;

(h) the need to ensure that any restriction on the individual's rights or freedom of action that is involved in the exercise of the function is kept to the minimum necessary for achieving the purpose for which the function is being exercised.

(4) 'Local authority' means–

(a) a county council in England,

(b) a district council for an area in England for which there is no county council,

(c) a London borough council, or

(d) the Common Council of the City of London.

. . .

Assessment of a child's needs for care and support

58 (1) Where it appears to a local authority that a child is likely to have needs for care and support after becoming 18, the authority must, if it is satisfied that it would be of significant benefit to the child to do so and if the consent condition is met, assess–

(a) whether the child has needs for care and support and, if so, what those needs are, and

(b) whether the child is likely to have needs for care and support after becoming 18 and, if so, what those needs are likely to be.

(2) An assessment under subsection (1) is referred to in this Part as a *'child's needs assessment'*.

(3) The consent condition is met if–

(a) the child has capacity or is competent to consent to a child's needs assessment being carried out and the child does so consent, or

(b) the child lacks capacity or is not competent so to consent but the authority is satisfied that carrying out a child's needs assessment would be in the child's best interests.

(4) Where a child refuses a child's needs assessment and the consent condition is accordingly not met, the local authority must nonetheless carry out the assessment if the child is experiencing, or is at risk of, abuse or neglect.

(5) Where a local authority, having received a request to carry out a child's assessment from the child concerned or a parent or carer of the child, decides not to comply with the request, it must give the person who made the request–

(a) written reasons for its decision, and

(b) information and advice about what can be done to prevent or delay the development by the child of needs for care and support in the future.

(6) *'Parent'*, in relation to a child, includes–

(a) a parent of the child who does not have parental responsibility for the child, and

(b) a person who is not a parent of the child but who has parental responsibility for the child.

(7) *'Carer'*, in relation to a child, means a person, other than a parent, who is providing care for the child, whether or not under or by virtue of a contract or as voluntary work.

(8) The reference to providing care includes a reference to providing practical or emotional support.

Child's needs assessment: requirements etc

59 (1) A child's needs assessment must include an assessment of–

(a) the impact on the matters specified in section 1(2) of what the child's needs for care and support are likely to be after the child becomes 18,

(b) the outcomes that the child wishes to achieve in day-to-day life, and

(c) whether, and if so to what extent, the provision of care and support could contribute to the achievement of those outcomes.

(2) A local authority, in carrying out a child's needs assessment, must involve–

(a) the child,

(b) the child's parents and any carer that the child has, and

(c) any person whom the child or a parent or carer of the child requests the local authority to involve.

(3) When carrying out a child's needs assessment, a local authority must also consider whether, and if so to what extent, matters other than the provision of care and support could contribute to the achievement of the outcomes that the child wishes to achieve in day-to-day life.

(4) Having carried out a child's needs assessment, a local authority must give the child–

(a) an indication as to whether any of the needs for care and support which it thinks the child is likely to have after becoming 18 are likely to meet the eligibility criteria (and, if so, which ones are likely to do so), and

(b) advice and information about–

(i) what can be done to meet or reduce the needs which it thinks the child is likely to have after becoming 18;

(ii) what can be done to prevent or delay the development by the child of needs for care and support in the future.

(5) But in a case where the child is not competent or lacks capacity to understand the things which the local authority is required to give under subsection (4), that subsection is to have effect as if for 'must give the child' there were substituted 'must give the child's parents'.

(6) Where a person to whom a child's needs assessment relates becomes 18, the local authority must decide whether to treat the assessment as a needs assessment; and if the authority decides to do so, this Part applies to the child's needs assessment as if it were a needs assessment that had been carried out after the person had become 18.

(7) In considering what to decide under subsection (6), a local authority must have regard to–

(a) when the child's needs assessment was carried out, and
(b) whether it appears to the authority that the circumstances of the person to whom the child's needs assessment relates have changed in a way that might affect the assessment.

(8) *'Carer'* has the same meaning as in section 58.

CHILDREN ACT 1989 (EXTRACTS)

Provision of services for children and their families

Provision of services for children in need, their families and others

17 (1) It shall be the general duty of every local authority (in addition to the other duties imposed on them by this Part)–

(a) to safeguard and promote the welfare of children within their area who are in need; and

(b) so far as is consistent with that duty, to promote the upbringing of such children by their families,

by providing a range and level of services appropriate to those children's needs.

(2) For the purpose principally of facilitating the discharge of their general duty under this section, every local authority shall have the specific duties and powers set out in Part 1 of Schedule 2.

(3) Any service provided by an authority in the exercise of functions conferred on them by this section may be provided for the family of a particular child in need or for any member of his family, if it is provided with a view to safeguarding or promoting the child's welfare.

(4) The Secretary of State may by order amend any provision of Part I of Schedule 2 or add any further duty or power to those for the time being mentioned there.

(4A) Before determining what (if any) services to provide for a particular child in need in the exercise of functions conferred on them by this section, a local authority shall, so far as is reasonably practicable and consistent with the child's welfare–

(a) ascertain the child's wishes and feelings regarding the provision of those services; and

(b) give due consideration (having regard to his age and understanding) to such wishes and feelings of the child as they have been able to ascertain.

(5) Every local authority–

(a) shall facilitate the provision by others (including in particular voluntary organisations) of services which it is a function of the authority to provide by virtue of this section, or section 18, 20, 22A to 22C, 23B to 23D, 24A or 24B; and

(b) may make such arrangements as they see fit for any person to act on their behalf in the provision of any such service.

(6) The services provided by a local authority in the exercise of functions conferred on them by this section may include providing accommodation and giving assistance in kind or in cash.

(7) Assistance may be unconditional or subject to conditions as to the repayment of the assistance or of its value (in whole or in part).

(8) Before giving any assistance or imposing any conditions, a local authority shall have regard to the means of the child concerned and of each of his parents.

(9) No person shall be liable to make any repayment of assistance or of its value at any time when he is in receipt of universal credit (except in such circumstances as may be prescribed)[, [of income support under Part VII of the Social Security Contributions and Benefits Act 1992,][2] of any element of child tax credit other than the family element, of working tax credit, of an income-based jobseeker's allowance or of an income-related employment and support allowance][3].

(10) For the purposes of this Part a child shall be taken to be in need if–

(a) he is unlikely to achieve or maintain, or to have the opportunity of achieving or maintaining, a reasonable standard of health or development without the provision for him of services by a local authority under this Part;

(b) his health or development is likely to be significantly impaired, or further impaired, without the provision for him of such services; or

(c) he is disabled,

and *'family'*, in relation to such a child, includes any person who has parental responsibility for the child and any other person with whom he has been living.

(11) For the purposes of this Part, a child is disabled if he is blind, deaf or dumb or suffers from mental disorder of any kind or is substantially and permanently handicapped by illness, injury or congenital deformity or such other disability as may be prescribed; and in this Part–

'development' means physical, intellectual, emotional, social or behavioural development; and

'health' means physical or mental health.

[(12) The Treasury may by regulations prescribe circumstances in which a person is to be treated for the purposes of this Part (or for such of those purposes as are prescribed) as in receipt of any element of child tax credit other than the family element or of working tax credit.][4]

(13) The duties imposed on a local authority by virtue of this section do not apply in relation to a child in the authority's area who is being looked after by a local authority in Wales in accordance with Part 6 of the Social Services and Well-being (Wales) Act 2014.

2 Words repealed by Welfare Reform Act 2009 Sch 7(1) para 1. Not yet in force.

3 Words repealed by Welfare Reform Act 2012 Sch 14(1) para 1. Not yet in force.

4 Repealed by Welfare Reform Act 2012 Sch 14(1) para 1. Not yet in force.

Young carers' needs assessments

17ZA (1) A local authority must assess whether a young carer within their area has needs for support and, if so, what those needs are, if–

(a) it appears to the authority that the young carer may have needs for support, or

(b) the authority receive a request from the young carer or a parent of the young carer to assess the young carer's needs for support.

(2) An assessment under subsection (1) is referred to in this Part as a *'young carer's needs assessment'*.

(3) In this Part *'young carer'* means a person under 18 who provides or intends to provide care for another person (but this is qualified by section 17ZB(3)).

(4) Subsection (1) does not apply in relation to a young carer if the local authority have previously carried out a care-related assessment of the young carer in relation to the same person cared for.

(5) But subsection (1) does apply (and so a young carer's needs assessment must be carried out) if it appears to the authority that the needs or circumstances of the young carer or the person cared for have changed since the last care-related assessment.

(6) *'Care-related assessment'* means–

(a) a young carer's needs assessment;

(b) an assessment under any of the following–

(i) section 1 of the Carers (Recognition and Services) Act 1995;

(ii) section 1 of the Carers and Disabled Children Act 2000;

(iii) section 4(3) of the Community Care (Delayed Discharges) Act 2003;

(iv) Part 1 of the Care Act 2014.

(7) A young carer's needs assessment must include an assessment of whether it is appropriate for the young carer to provide, or continue to provide, care for the person in question, in the light of the young carer's needs for support, other needs and wishes.

(8) A local authority, in carrying out a young carer's needs assessment, must have regard to–

(a) the extent to which the young carer is participating in or wishes to participate in education, training or recreation, and

(b) the extent to which the young carer works or wishes to work.

(9) A local authority, in carrying out a young carer's needs assessment, must involve–

(a) the young carer,

(b) the young carer's parents, and

(c) any person who the young carer or a parent of the young carer requests the authority to involve.

(10) A local authority that have carried out a young carer's needs assessment must give a written record of the assessment to–
   (a) the young carer,
   (b) the young carer's parents, and
   (c) any person to whom the young carer or a parent of the young carer requests the authority to give a copy.

(11) Where the person cared for is under 18, the written record must state whether the local authority consider him or her to be a child in need.

(12) A local authority must take reasonable steps to identify the extent to which there are young carers within their area who have needs for support.

Young carers' needs assessments: supplementary

17ZB (1) This section applies for the purposes of section 17ZA.

(2) *'Parent'*, in relation to a young carer, includes–
   (a) a parent of the young carer who does not have parental responsibility for the young carer, and
   (b) a person who is not a parent of the young carer but who has parental responsibility for the young carer.

(3) A person is not a young carer if the person provides or intends to provide care–
   (a) under or by virtue of a contract, or
   (b) as voluntary work.

(4) But in a case where the local authority consider that the relationship between the person cared for and the person under 18 providing or intending to provide care is such that it would be appropriate for the person under 18 to be regarded as a young carer, that person is to be regarded as such (and subsection (3) is therefore to be ignored in that case).

(5) The references in section 17ZA and this section to providing care include a reference to providing practical or emotional support.

(6) Where a local authority–
   (a) are required to carry out a young carer's needs assessment, and
   (b) are required or have decided to carry out some other assessment of the young carer or of the person cared for;

   the local authority may, subject to subsection (7), combine the assessments.

(7) A young carer's needs assessment may be combined with an assessment of the person cared for only if the young carer and the person cared for agree.

(8) The Secretary of State may by regulations make further provision about carrying out a young carer's needs assessment; the regulations may, in particular–
   (a) specify matters to which a local authority is to have regard in carrying out a young carer's needs assessment;

(b) specify matters which a local authority is to determine in carrying out a young carer's needs assessment;
(c) make provision about the manner in which a young carer's needs assessment is to be carried out;
(d) make provision about the form a young carer's needs assessment is to take.

(9) The Secretary of State may by regulations amend the list in section 17ZA(6)
(b) so as to–
(a) add an entry,
(b) remove an entry, or
(c) vary an entry.

Consideration of young carers' needs assessments

17ZC A local authority that carry out a young carer's needs assessment must consider the assessment and decide–
(a) whether the young carer has needs for support in relation to the care which he or she provides or intends to provide;
(b) if so, whether those needs could be satisfied (wholly or partly) by services which the authority may provide under section 17; and
(c) if they could be so satisfied, whether or not to provide any such services in relation to the young carer.

Parent carers' needs assessments

17ZD(1) A local authority must, if the conditions in subsections (3) and (4) are met, assess whether a parent carer within their area has needs for support and, if so, what those needs are.

(2) In this Part *'parent carer'* means a person aged 18 or over who provides or intends to provide care for a disabled child for whom the person has parental responsibility.

(3) The first condition is that–
(a) it appears to the authority that the parent carer may have needs for support, or
(b) the authority receive a request from the parent carer to assess the parent carer's needs for support.

(4) The second condition is that the local authority are satisfied that the disabled child cared for and the disabled child's family are persons for whom they may provide or arrange for the provision of services under section 17.

(5) An assessment under subsection (1) is referred to in this Part as a *'parent carer's needs assessment'*.

(6) Subsection (1) does not apply in relation to a parent carer if the local authority have previously carried out a care-related assessment of the parent carer in relation to the same disabled child cared for.

(7) But subsection (1) does apply (and so a parent carer's needs assessment must be carried out) if it appears to the authority that the needs or circumstances

of the parent carer or the disabled child cared for have changed since the last care-related assessment.

(8) *'Care-related assessment'* means–

(a) a parent carer's needs assessment;

(b) an assessment under any of the following–

(i) section 1 of the Carers (Recognition and Services) Act 1995;

(ii) section 6 of the Carers and Disabled Children Act 2000;

(iii) section 4(3) of the Community Care (Delayed Discharges) Act 2003;

(iv) Part 1 of the Care Act 2014.

(9) A parent carer's needs assessment must include an assessment of whether it is appropriate for the parent carer to provide, or continue to provide, care for the disabled child, in the light of the parent carer's needs for support, other needs and wishes.

(10) A local authority in carrying out a parent carer's needs assessment must have regard to–

(a) the well-being of the parent carer, and

(b) the need to safeguard and promote the welfare of the disabled child cared for and any other child for whom the parent carer has parental responsibility.

(11) In subsection (10) *'well-being'* has the same meaning as in Part 1 of the Care Act 2014.

(12) A local authority, in carrying out a parent carer's needs assessment, must involve–

(a) the parent carer,

(b) any child for whom the parent carer has parental responsibility, and

(c) any person who the parent carer requests the authority to involve.

(13) A local authority that have carried out a parent carer's needs assessment must give a written record of the assessment to–

(a) the parent carer, and

(b) any person to whom the parent carer requests the authority to give a copy.

(14) A local authority must take reasonable steps to identify the extent to which there are parent carers within their area who have needs for support.

Parent carers' needs assessments: supplementary

17ZE (1) This section applies for the purposes of section 17ZD.

(2) The references in section 17ZD to providing care include a reference to providing practical or emotional support.

(3) Where a local authority–

(a) are required to carry out a parent carer's needs assessment, and

(b) are required or have decided to carry out some other assessment of the parent carer or of the disabled child cared for, the local authority may combine the assessments.

(4) The Secretary of State may by regulations make further provision about carrying out a parent carer's needs assessment; the regulations may, in particular–

(a) specify matters to which a local authority is to have regard in carrying out a parent carer's needs assessment;

(b) specify matters which a local authority is to determine in carrying out a parent carer's needs assessment;

(c) make provision about the manner in which a parent carer's needs assessment is to be carried out;

(d) make provision about the form a parent carer's needs assessment is to take.

(5) The Secretary of State may by regulations amend the list in section 17ZD(8)(b) so as to–

(a) add an entry,

(b) remove an entry, or

(c) vary an entry.

Consideration of parent carers' needs assessments

17ZFA local authority that carry out a parent carer's needs assessment must consider the assessment and decide–

(a) whether the parent carer has needs for support in relation to the care which he or she provides or intends to provide;

(b) whether the disabled child cared for has needs for support;

(c) if paragraph (a) or (b) applies, whether those needs could be satisfied (wholly or partly) by services which the authority may provide under section 17; and

(d) if they could be so satisfied, whether or not to provide any such services in relation to the parent carer or the disabled child cared for.

Section 17 services: continued provision where EHC plan maintained

17G (1) This section applies where, immediately before a child in need reaches the age of 18–

(a) a local authority is providing services for the child in the exercise of functions conferred by section 17, and

(b) an EHC plan is maintained for the child.

(2) The local authority may continue to provide services for the child in the exercise of those functions after the child reaches the age of 18, but may not continue to do so after the EHC plan has ceased to be maintained, except in so far as the authority is required to do so under section 17ZH or 17ZI.

(3) In this section *'EHC plan'* means a plan within section 37(2) of the Children and Families Act 2014.

Section 17 services: transition for children to adult care and support

17ZH (1) Subsections (2) to (4) apply where a local authority providing services for a child in need in the exercise of functions conferred by section 17–

(a) are required by section 58(1) or 63(1) of the Care Act 2014 to carry out a child's needs assessment or young carer's assessment in relation to the child, or

(b) are required by section 60(1) of that Act to carry out a child's carer's assessment in relation to a carer of the child.

(2) If the local authority carry out the assessment before the child reaches the age of 18 and decide to treat it as a needs or carer's assessment in accordance with section 59(6), 61(6) or 64(7) of the Care Act 2014 (with Part 1 of that Act applying to the assessment as a result), the authority must continue to comply with section 17 after the child reaches the age of 18 until they reach a conclusion in his case.

(3) If the local authority carry out the assessment before the child reaches the age of 18 but decide not to treat it as a needs or carer's assessment in accordance with section 59(6), 61(6) or 64(7) of the Care Act 2014–

(a) they must carry out a needs or carer's assessment (as the case may be) after the child reaches the age of 18, and

(b) they must continue to comply with section 17 after he reaches that age until they reach a conclusion in his case.

(4) If the local authority do not carry out the assessment before the child reaches the age of 18, they must continue to comply with section 17 after he reaches that age until–

(a) they decide that the duty under section 9 or 10 of the Care Act 2014 (needs or carer's assessment) does not apply, or

(b) having decided that the duty applies and having discharged it, they reach a conclusion in his case.

(5) Subsection (6) applies where a local authority providing services for a child in need in the exercise of functions conferred by section 17–

(a) receive a request for a child's needs assessment or young carer's assessment to be carried out in relation to the child or for a child's carer's assessment to be carried out in relation to a carer of the child, but

(b) have yet to be required by section 58(1), 60(1) or 63(1) of the Care Act 2014 to carry out the assessment.

(6) If the local authority do not decide, before the child reaches the age of 18, whether or not to comply with the request, they must continue to comply with section 17 after he reaches that age until–

(a) they decide that the duty under section 9 or 10 of the Care Act 2014 does not apply, or

(b) having decided that the duty applies and having discharged it, they reach a conclusion in his case.

(7) A local authority reach a conclusion in a person's case when–

(a) they conclude that he does not have needs for care and support or for support (as the case may be), or

(b) having concluded that he has such needs and that they are going to meet some or all of them, they begin to do so, or

(c) having concluded that he has such needs, they conclude that they are not going to meet any of those needs (whether because those needs do not meet the eligibility criteria or for some other reason).

(8) In this section, *'child's needs assessment'*, *'child's carer's assessment'*, *'young carer's assessment'*, *'needs assessment'*, *'carer's assessment'* and *'eligibility criteria'* each have the same meaning as in Part 1 of the Care Act 2014.

Section 17 services: provision after EHC plan no longer maintained

17ZI (1) This section applies where a local authority providing services for a person in the exercise, by virtue of section 17ZG, of functions conferred by section 17 are required to carry out a needs assessment in that person's case.

(2) If the EHC plan for the person ceases to be maintained before the local authority reach a conclusion in the person's case, they must continue to comply with section 17 until they do reach a conclusion in his case.

(3) The references to the local authority reaching a conclusion in a person's case are to be read with section 17ZH(7).

(4) In this section, *'needs assessment'* has the same meaning as in Part 1 of the Care Act 2014.

Direct payments

17A (1)The Secretary of State may by regulations make provision for and in connection with requiring or authorising the responsible authority in the case of a person of a prescribed description who falls within subsection (2) to make, with that person's consent, such payments to him as they may determine in accordance with the regulations in respect of his securing the provision of the service mentioned in that subsection.

(2) A person falls within this subsection if he is–

(a) a person with parental responsibility for a disabled child,

(b) a disabled person with parental responsibility for a child, or

(c) a disabled child aged 16 or 17,

and a local authority ('the responsible authority') have decided for the purposes of section 17 that the child's needs (or, if he is such a disabled child, his needs) call for the provision by them of a service in exercise of functions conferred on them under that section.

(3) Regulations under this section may, in particular, make provision–

(a) specifying circumstances in which the responsible authority are not required or authorised to make any payments under the regulations to a person, whether those circumstances relate to the person in question or to the particular service mentioned in subsection (2);

(b) for any payments required or authorised by the regulations to be made to a person by the responsible authority ('direct payments') to be made to that person ('the payee') as gross payments or alternatively as net payments;

(c) for the responsible authority to make for the purposes of subsection (3A) or (3B) such determination as to–

(i) the payee's means, and

(ii) the amount (if any) which it would be reasonably practicable for the payee to pay to the authority by way of reimbursement or contribution,

as may be prescribed;

(d) as to the conditions falling to be complied with by the payee which must or may be imposed by the responsible authority in relation to the direct payments (and any conditions which may not be so imposed);

(e) specifying circumstances in which the responsible authority–

(i) may or must terminate the making of direct payments,

(ii) may require repayment (whether by the payee or otherwise) of the whole or part of the direct payments;

(f) for any sum falling to be paid or repaid to the responsible authority by virtue of any condition or other requirement imposed in pursuance of the regulations to be recoverable as a debt due to the authority;

(g) displacing functions or obligations of the responsible authority with respect to the provision of the service mentioned in subsection (2) only to such extent, and subject to such conditions, as may be prescribed;

(h) authorising direct payments to be made to any prescribed person on behalf of the payee;

(j) as to matters to which the responsible authority must, or may, have regard when making a decision for the purposes of a provision of the regulations;

(k) as to steps which the responsible authority must, or may, take before, or after, the authority makes a decision for the purposes of a provision of the regulations;

(l) specifying circumstances in which a person who has fallen within subsection (3D) but no longer does so (whether because of fluctuating capacity, or regaining or gaining of capacity) is to be treated, or may be treated, as falling within subsection (3D) for purposes of this section or for purposes of regulations under this section.

[(3A) For the purposes of subsection (3)(b) *'gross payments'* means payments–

(a) which are made at such a rate as the authority estimate to be equivalent to the reasonable cost of securing the provision of the service concerned; but

(b) which may be made subject to the condition that the payee pays to the responsible authority, by way of reimbursement, an amount or amounts determined under the regulations.][5]

(3B) For the purposes of subsection (3)(b) *'net payments'* means payments–

(a) which are made on the basis that the payee will pay an amount or amounts determined under the regulations by way of contribution towards the cost of securing the provision of the service concerned; and

(b) which are accordingly made at such a rate below that mentioned in subsection (3A)(a) as reflects any such contribution by the payee.

(3C) Regulations made for the purposes of subsection (3)(a) may provide that direct payments shall not be made in respect of the provision of residential accommodation for any person for a period in excess of a prescribed period.

(3D) A person falls within this subsection if the person lacks capacity, within the meaning of the Mental Capacity Act 2005, to consent to the making of direct payments.

(4) Regulations under this section shall provide that, where payments are made under the regulations to a person falling within subsection (5)–

(a) the payments shall be made at the rate mentioned in subsection (3A)(a); and

(b) subsection (3A)(b) shall not apply.

(5) A person falls within this subsection if he is–

(a) a person falling within subsection (2)(a) or (b) and the child in question is aged 16 or 17, or

(b) a person who is in receipt of universal credit (except in such circumstances as may be prescribed)[, [of income support under Part 7 of the Social Security Contributions and Benefits Act 1992,][6] of any element of child tax credit other than the family element, of working tax credit of an income-based jobseeker's allowance or of an income-related employment and support allowance.][7]

(6) In this section–

'disabled' in relation to an adult has the same meaning as that given by section 17(11) in relation to a child;

'prescribed' means specified in or determined in accordance with regulations under this section.

Provision of accommodation for children: general

20 (1) Every local authority shall provide accommodation for any child in need within their area who appears to them to require accommodation as a result of–

5 Added by Health and Social Care Act 2008 Sch 14 para 1. Not yet in force: insertion cannot take effect as Health and Social Care Act 2008 Sch 14 para 1 never came into force.

6 Words repealed by Welfare Reform Act 2009 Sch 7(1) para 1. Not yet in force.

7 Words repealed by Welfare Reform Act 2012 Sch 14(1) para 1. Not yet in force.

(a) there being no person who has parental responsibility for him;
(b) his being lost or having been abandoned; or
(c) the person who has been caring for him being prevented (whether or not permanently, and for whatever reason) from providing him with suitable accommodation or care.

(2) Where a local authority provide accommodation under subsection (1) for a child who is ordinarily resident in the area of another local authority, that other local authority may take over the provision of accommodation for the child within–
(a) three months of being notified in writing that the child is being provided with accommodation; or
(b) such other longer period as may be prescribed in regulations made by the Secretary of State.

(2A) Where a local authority in Wales provide accommodation under section 76(1) of the Social Services and Well-being (Wales) Act 2014 (accommodation for children without parents or who are lost or abandoned etc) for a child who is ordinarily resident in the area of a local authority in England, that local authority in England may take over the provision of accommodation for the child within–
(a) three months of being notified in writing that the child is being provided with accommodation; or
(b) such other longer period as may be prescribed in regulations made by the Secretary of State.

(3) Every local authority shall provide accommodation for any child in need within their area who has reached the age of sixteen and whose welfare the authority consider is likely to be seriously prejudiced if they do not provide him with accommodation.

(4) A local authority may provide accommodation for any child within their area (even though a person who has parental responsibility for him is able to provide him with accommodation) if they consider that to do so would safeguard or promote the child's welfare.

(5) A local authority may provide accommodation for any person who has reached the age of sixteen but is under twenty-one in any community home which takes children who have reached the age of sixteen if they consider that to do so would safeguard or promote his welfare.

(6) Before providing accommodation under this section, a local authority shall, so far as is reasonably practicable and consistent with the child's welfare–
(a) ascertain the child's wishes and feelings regarding the provision of accommodation; and
(b) give due consideration (having regard to his age and understanding) to such wishes and feelings of the child as they have been able to ascertain.

(7) A local authority may not provide accommodation under this section for any child if any person who–
   (a) has parental responsibility for him; and
   (b) is willing and able to–
      (i) provide accommodation for him; or
      (ii) arrange for accommodation to be provided for him,
   objects.

(8) Any person who has parental responsibility for a child may at any time remove the child from accommodation provided by or on behalf of the local authority under this section.

(9) Subsections (7) and (8) do not apply while any person–
   (a) who is named in a child arrangements order as a person with whom the child is to live;
   (aa) who is a special guardian of the child; or
   (b) who has care of the child by virtue of an order made in the exercise of the High Court's inherent jurisdiction with respect to children,
   agrees to the child being looked after in accommodation provided by or on behalf of the local authority.

(10) Where there is more than one such person as is mentioned in subsection (9), all of them must agree.

(11) Subsections (7) and (8) do not apply where a child who has reached the age of sixteen agrees to being provided with accommodation under this section.

Duties of local authorities in relation to children looked after by them

General duty of local authority in relation to children looked after by them

22 (1) In this section, any reference to a child who is looked after by a local authority is a reference to a child who is–
   (a) in their care; or
   (b) provided with accommodation by the authority in the exercise of any functions (in particular those under this Act) which are social services functions within the meaning of the Local Authority Social Services Act 1970, apart from functions under sections 17, 23B and 24B.

(2) In subsection (1) 'accommodation' means accommodation which is provided for a continuous period of more than 24 hours.

(3) It shall be the duty of a local authority looking after any child–
   (a) to safeguard and promote his welfare; and
   (b) to make such use of services available for children cared for by their own parents as appears to the authority reasonable in his case.

(3A) The duty of a local authority under subsection (3)(a) to safeguard and promote the welfare of a child looked after by them includes in particular a duty to promote the child's educational achievement.

(3B) A local authority must appoint at least one person for the purpose of discharging the duty imposed by virtue of subsection (3A).

(3C) A person appointed by a local authority under subsection (3B) must be an officer employed by that authority or another local authority.

(4) Before making any decision with respect to a child whom they are looking after, or proposing to look after, a local authority shall, so far as is reasonably practicable, ascertain the wishes and feelings of–

(a) the child;

(b) his parents;

(c) any person who is not a parent of his but who has parental responsibility for him; and

(d) any other person whose wishes and feelings the authority consider to be relevant,

regarding the matter to be decided.

(5) In making any such decision a local authority shall give due consideration–

(a) having regard to his age and understanding, to such wishes and feelings of the child as they have been able to ascertain;

(b) to such wishes and feelings of any person mentioned in subsection (4)(b) to (d) as they have been able to ascertain; and

(c) to the child's religious persuasion, racial origin and cultural and linguistic background.

(6) If it appears to a local authority that it is necessary, for the purpose of protecting members of the public from serious injury, to exercise their powers with respect to a child whom they are looking after in a manner which may not be consistent with their duties under this section, they may do so.

(7) If the Secretary of State considers it necessary, for the purpose of protecting members of the public from serious injury, to give directions to a local authority with respect to the exercise of their powers with respect to a child whom they are looking after, the Secretary of State may give such directions to the authority.

(8) Where any such directions are given to an authority they shall comply with them even though doing so is inconsistent with their duties under this section.

Provision of accommodation for children in care

22A When a child is in the care of a local authority, it is their duty to provide the child with accommodation.

Maintenance of looked after children

22B It is the duty of a local authority to maintain a child they are looking after in other respects apart from the provision of accommodation.

Ways in which looked after children are to be accommodated and maintained

22C (1) This section applies where a local authority are looking after a child ('C').

(2) The local authority must make arrangements for C to live with a person who falls within subsection (3) (but subject to subsection (4)).

(3) A person ('P') falls within this subsection if–
  (a) P is a parent of C;
  (b) P is not a parent of C but has parental responsibility for C; or
  (c) in a case where C is in the care of the local authority and there was a child arrangements order in force with respect to C immediately before the care order was made, P was a person named in the child arrangements order as a person with whom C was to live.

(4) Subsection (2) does not require the local authority to make arrangements of the kind mentioned in that subsection if doing so–
  (a) would not be consistent with C's welfare; or
  (b) would not be reasonably practicable.

(5) If the local authority are unable to make arrangements under subsection (2), they must place C in the placement which is, in their opinion, the most appropriate placement available.

(6) In subsection (5) *'placement'* means–
  (a) placement with an individual who is a relative, friend or other person connected with C and who is also a local authority foster parent;
  (b) placement with a local authority foster parent who does not fall within paragraph (a);
  (c) placement in a children's home in respect of which a person is registered under Part 2 of the Care Standards Act 2000 or Part 1 of the Regulation and Inspection of Social Care (Wales) Act 2016 (anaw 2); or
  (d) subject to section 22D, placement in accordance with other arrangements which comply with any regulations made for the purposes of this section.

(7) In determining the most appropriate placement for C, the local authority must, subject to subsection (9B) and the other provisions of this Part (in particular, to their duties under section 22)–
  (a) give preference to a placement falling within paragraph (a) of subsection (6) over placements falling within the other paragraphs of that subsection;
  (b) comply, so far as is reasonably practicable in all the circumstances of C's case, with the requirements of subsection (8); and
  (c) comply with subsection (9) unless that is not reasonably practicable.

(8) The local authority must ensure that the placement is such that–
  (a) it allows C to live near C's home;
  (b) it does not disrupt C's education or training;
  (c) if C has a sibling for whom the local authority are also providing accommodation, it enables C and the sibling to live together;
  (d) if C is disabled, the accommodation provided is suitable to C's particular needs.

(9) The placement must be such that C is provided with accommodation within the local authority's area.

(9A) Subsection (9B) applies (subject to subsection (9C)) where the local authority–

(a) are considering adoption for C, or

(b) are satisfied that C ought to be placed for adoption but are not authorised under section 19 of the Adoption and Children Act 2002 (placement with parental consent) or by virtue of section 21 of that Act (placement orders) to place C for adoption.

(9B) Where this subsection applies–

(a) subsections (7) to (9) do not apply to the local authority,

(b) the local authority must consider placing C with an individual within subsection (6)(a), and

(c) where the local authority decide that a placement with such an individual is not the most appropriate placement for C, the local authority must consider placing C with a local authority foster parent who has been approved as a prospective adopter.

(9C) Subsection (9B) does not apply where the local authority have applied for a placement order under section 21 of the Adoption and Children Act 2002 in respect of C and the application has been refused.

(10) The local authority may determine–

(a) the terms of any arrangements they make under subsection (2) in relation to C (including terms as to payment); and

(b) the terms on which they place C with a local authority foster parent (including terms as to payment but subject to any order made under section 49 of the Children Act 2004).

(11) The Secretary of State may make regulations for, and in connection with, the purposes of this section.

(12) For the meaning of *'local authority foster parent'* see section 105(1).

Review of child's case before making alternative arrangements for accommodation

22D (1) Where a local authority are providing accommodation for a child ('C') other than by arrangements under section 22C(6)(d), they must not make such arrangements for C unless they have decided to do so in consequence of a review of C's case carried out in accordance with regulations made under section 26.

(2) But subsection (1) does not prevent a local authority making arrangements for C under section 22C(6)(d) if they are satisfied that in order to safeguard C's welfare it is necessary–

(a) to make such arrangements; and

(b) to do so as a matter of urgency.

Children's homes provided by Secretary of State or Welsh Ministers

22E Where a local authority place a child they are looking after in a children's home provided, equipped and maintained by the Secretary of State or the Welsh Ministers under section 82(5), they must do so on such terms as the Secretary of State or the Welsh Ministers (as the case may be) may from time to time determine.

Regulations as to children looked after by local authorities

22F Part 2 of Schedule 2 has effect for the purposes of making further provision as to children looked after by local authorities and in particular as to the regulations which may be made under section 22C(11).

General duty of local authority to secure sufficient accommodation for looked after children

22G (1) It is the general duty of a local authority to take steps that secure, so far as reasonably practicable, the outcome in subsection (2).

(2) The outcome is that the local authority are able to provide the children mentioned in subsection (3) with accommodation that–

(a) is within the authority's area; and

(b) meets the needs of those children.

(3) The children referred to in subsection (2) are those–

(a) that the local authority are looking after,

(b) in respect of whom the authority are unable to make arrangements under section 22C(2), and

(c) whose circumstances are such that it would be consistent with their welfare for them to be provided with accommodation that is in the authority's area.

(4) In taking steps to secure the outcome in subsection (2), the local authority must have regard to the benefit of having–

(a) a number of accommodation providers in their area that is, in their opinion, sufficient to secure that outcome; and

(b) a range of accommodation in their area capable of meeting different needs that is, in their opinion, sufficient to secure that outcome.

(5) In this section *'accommodation providers'* means–

local authority foster parents; and

children's homes in respect of which a person is registered under Part 2 of the Care Standards Act 2000.

Information and advice for promoting educational achievement

23ZZA (1) A local authority in England must make advice and information available in accordance with this section for the purpose of promoting the educational achievement of each relevant child educated in their area.

(2) The advice and information must be made available to–

(a) any person who has parental responsibility for the child,

(b) the member of staff at the child's school designated under section 20A of the Children and Young Persons Act 2008 or by virtue of section 2E of the Academies Act 2010, and

(c) any other person that the local authority consider appropriate.

(3) A local authority in England may do anything else that they consider appropriate with a view to promoting the educational achievement of relevant children educated in their area.

(4) A local authority in England must appoint at least one person for the purpose of discharging the duty imposed by subsection (1).

(5) The person appointed for that purpose must be an officer employed by the authority or another local authority in England.

(6) In this section–

'relevant child' means–

(a) a child who was looked after by the local authority or another local authority in England or Wales but ceased to be so looked after as a result of–

(i) a child arrangements order which includes arrangements relating to with whom the child is to live, or when the child is to live with any person,

(ii) a special guardianship order, or

(iii) an adoption order within the meaning given by section 72(1) of the Adoption Act 1976 or section 46(1) of the Adoption and Children Act 2002, or

(b) a child who appears to the local authority–

(i) to have been in state care in a place outside England and Wales because he or she would not otherwise have been cared for adequately, and

(ii) to have ceased to be in that state care as a result of being adopted.

(7) For the purposes of this section a child is educated in a local authority's area if–

(a) the child is receiving early years provision secured by the local authority under section 7(1) of the Childcare Act 2006, or

(b) the child is of compulsory school age and–

(i) the child attends a school in the local authority's area, or

(ii) if the child does not attend school, the child receives all or most of his or her education in the local authority's area.

(8) For the purposes of this section a child is in 'state care' if he or she is in the care of, or accommodated by–

(a) a public authority,

(b) a religious organisation, or

(c) any other organisation the sole or main purpose of which is to benefit society.

Visiting

Duty of local authority to ensure visits to, and contact with, looked after children and others

23ZA (1) This section applies to–

(a) a child looked after by a local authority;

(b) a child who was looked after by a local authority but who has ceased to be looked after by them as a result of prescribed circumstances.

(2) It is the duty of the local authority–

(a) to ensure that a person to whom this section applies is visited by a representative of the authority ('a representative');

(b) to arrange for appropriate advice, support and assistance to be available to a person to whom this section applies who seeks it from them.

(3) The duties imposed by subsection (2)–

(a) are to be discharged in accordance with any regulations made for the purposes of this section by the Secretary of State;

(b) are subject to any requirement imposed by or under an enactment applicable to the place in which the person to whom this section applies is accommodated.

(4) Regulations under this section for the purposes of subsection (3)(a) may make provision about–

(a) the frequency of visits;

(b) circumstances in which a person to whom this section applies must be visited by a representative; and

(c) the functions of a representative.

(5) In choosing a representative a local authority must satisfy themselves that the person chosen has the necessary skills and experience to perform the functions of a representative.

Independent visitors for children looked after by a local authority

23ZB (1) A local authority looking after a child must appoint an independent person to be the child's visitor if–

(a) the child falls within a description prescribed in regulations made by the Secretary of State; or

(b) in any other case, it appears to them that it would be in the child's interests to do so.

(2) A person appointed under this section must visit, befriend and advise the child.

(3) A person appointed under this section is entitled to recover from the appointing authority any reasonable expenses incurred by that person for the purposes of that person's functions under this section.

(4) A person's appointment as a visitor in pursuance of this section comes to an end if–

(a) the child ceases to be looked after by the local authority;
(b) the person resigns the appointment by giving notice in writing to the appointing authority; or
(c) the authority give him notice in writing that they have terminated it.

(5) The ending of such an appointment does not affect any duty under this section to make a further appointment.

(6) Where a local authority propose to appoint a visitor for a child under this section, the appointment shall not be made if–
(a) the child objects to it; and
(b) the authority are satisfied that the child has sufficient understanding to make an informed decision.

(7) Where a visitor has been appointed for a child under this section, the local authority shall terminate the appointment if–
(a) the child objects to its continuing; and
(b) the authority are satisfied that the child has sufficient understanding to make an informed decision.

(8) If the local authority give effect to a child's objection under subsection (6) or (7) and the objection is to having anyone as the child's visitor, the authority does not have to propose to appoint another person under subsection (1) until the objection is withdrawn.

(9) The Secretary of State may make regulations as to the circumstances in which a person is to be regarded for the purposes of this section as independent of the appointing authority.

Secure accommodation

Use of accommodation for restricting liberty

25 (1) Subject to the following provisions of this section, a child who is being looked after by a local authority in England or Wales may not be placed, and, if placed, may not be kept, in accommodation in England or Scotland provided for the purpose of restricting liberty (*'secure accommodation'*) unless it appears–
(a) that–
(i) he has a history of absconding and is likely to abscond from any other description of accommodation; and
(ii) if he absconds, he is likely to suffer significant harm; or
(b) that if he is kept in any other description of accommodation he is likely to injure himself or other persons.

(2) The Secretary of State may by regulations–
(a) specify a maximum period–
(i) beyond which a child may not be kept in secure accommodation in England or Scotland without the authority of the court; and
(ii) for which the court may authorise a child to be kept in secure accommodation in England or Scotland;

(b) empower the court from time to time to authorise a child to be kept in secure accommodation in England or Scotland for such further period as the regulations may specify; and
(c) provide that applications to the court under this section shall be made only by local authorities in England or Wales.

(3) It shall be the duty of a court hearing an application under this section to determine whether any relevant criteria for keeping a child in secure accommodation are satisfied in his case.

(4) If a court determines that any such criteria are satisfied, it shall make an order authorising the child to be kept in secure accommodation and specifying the maximum period for which he may be so kept.

(5) On any adjournment of the hearing of an application under this section, a court may make an interim order permitting the child to be kept during the period of the adjournment in secure accommodation.

(5A) Where a local authority in England or Wales are authorised under this section to keep a child in secure accommodation in Scotland, the person in charge of the accommodation may restrict the child's liberty to the extent that the person considers appropriate, having regard to the terms of any order made by a court under this section.

(6) No court shall exercise the powers conferred by this section in respect of a child who is not legally represented in that court unless, having been informed of his right to apply for the provision of representation under Part 1 of the Legal Aid, Sentencing and Punishment of Offenders Act 2012 and having had the opportunity to do so, he refused or failed to apply.

(7) The Secretary of State may by regulations provide that–
(a) this section shall or shall not apply to any description of children specified in the regulations;
(b) this section shall have effect in relation to children of a description specified in the regulations subject to such modifications as may be so specified;
(c) such other provisions as may be so specified shall have effect for the purpose of determining whether a child of a description specified in the regulations may be placed or kept in secure accommodation in England or Scotland;
(d) a child may only be placed in secure accommodation that is of a description specified in the regulations (and the description may in particular be framed by reference to whether the accommodation, or the person providing it, has been approved by the Secretary of State or the Scottish Ministers).

(8) The giving of an authorisation under this section shall not prejudice any power of any court in England and Wales or Scotland to give directions relating to the child to whom the authorisation relates.

(8A) Sections 168 and 169(1) to (4) of the Children's Hearings (Scotland) Act 2011 (asp 1) (enforcement and absconding) apply in relation to an order under subsection (4) above as they apply in relation to the orders mentioned in section 168(3) or 169(1)(a) of that Act.

(9) This section is subject to section 20(8).

Independent reviewing officers

25A Appointment of independent reviewing officer

(1) If a local authority are looking after a child, they must appoint an individual as the independent reviewing officer for that child's case.

(2) The initial appointment under subsection (1) must be made before the child's case is first reviewed in accordance with regulations made under section 26.

(3) If a vacancy arises in respect of a child's case, the local authority must make another appointment under subsection (1) as soon as is practicable.

(4) An appointee must be of a description prescribed in regulations made by the Secretary of State.

25B Functions of the independent reviewing officer

(1) The independent reviewing officer must–

(a) monitor the performance by the local authority of their functions in relation to the child's case;

(b) participate, in accordance with regulations made by the Secretary of State, in any review of the child's case;

(c) ensure that any ascertained wishes and feelings of the child concerning the case are given due consideration by the local authority;

(d) perform any other function which is prescribed in regulations made by the Secretary of State.

(2) An independent reviewing officer's functions must be performed–

(a) in such manner (if any) as may be prescribed in regulations made by the Secretary of State; and

(b) having regard to such guidance as that authority may issue in relation to the discharge of those functions.

(3) If the independent reviewing officer considers it appropriate to do so, the child's case may be referred by that officer to–

(a) an officer of the Children and Family Court Advisory and Support Service.

(b) [Repealed.]

(4) If the independent reviewing officer is not an officer of the local authority, it is the duty of the authority–

(a) to co-operate with that individual; and

(b) to take all such reasonable steps as that individual may require of them to enable that individual's functions under this section to be performed satisfactorily.

Care and Supervision – general

Care and supervision orders

31 (1) On the application of any local authority or authorised person, the court may make an order–

(a) placing the child with respect to whom the application is made in the care of a designated local authority; or

(b) putting him under the supervision of a designated local authority.

(2) A court may only make a care order or supervision order if it is satisfied–

(a) that the child concerned is suffering, or is likely to suffer, significant harm; and

(b) that the harm, or likelihood of harm, is attributable to–

(i) the care given to the child, or likely to be given to him if the order were not made, not being what it would be reasonable to expect a parent to give to him; or

(ii) the child's being beyond parental control.

(3) No care order or supervision order may be made with respect to a child who has reached the age of seventeen (or sixteen, in the case of a child who is married).

(3A) A court deciding whether to make a care order–

(a) is required to consider the permanence provisions of the section 31A plan for the child concerned, but

(b) is not required to consider the remainder of the section 31A plan, subject to section 34(11).

(3B) For the purposes of subsection (3A), the permanence provisions of a section 31A plan are–

(a) such of the plan's provisions setting out the long-term plan for the upbringing of the child concerned as provide for any of the following–

(i) the child to live with any parent of the child's or with any other member of, or any friend of, the child's family;

(ii) adoption;

(iii) long-term care not within sub-paragraph (i) or (ii);

(b) such of the plan's provisions as set out any of the following–

(i) the impact on the child concerned of any harm that he or she suffered or was likely to suffer;

(ii) the current and future needs of the child (including needs arising out of that impact);

(iii) the way in which the long-term plan for the upbringing of the child would meet those current and future needs.

(3C) The Secretary of State may by regulations amend this section for the purpose of altering what for the purposes of subsection (3A) are the permanence provisions of a section 31A plan.

(4) An application under this section may be made on its own or in any other family proceedings.

(5) The court may–

(a) on an application for a care order, make a supervision order;

(b) on an application for a supervision order, make a care order.

(6) Where an authorised person proposes to make an application under this section he shall–

(a) if it is reasonably practicable to do so; and

(b) before making the application,

consult the local authority appearing to him to be the authority in whose area the child concerned is ordinarily resident.

(7) An application made by an authorised person shall not be entertained by the court if, at the time when it is made, the child concerned is–

(a) the subject of an earlier application for a care order, or supervision order, which has not been disposed of; or

(b) subject to–

(i) a care order or supervision order;

(ii) a youth rehabilitation order within the meaning of Part 1 of the Criminal Justice and Immigration Act 2008; or

(iii) a compulsory supervision order or interim compulsory supervision order as defined by sections 83 and 86 of the Children's Hearings (Scotland) Act 2011.

(8) The local authority designated in a care order must be–

(a) the authority within whose area the child is ordinarily resident; or

(b) where the child does not reside in the area of a local authority, the authority within whose area any circumstances arose in consequence of which the order is being made.

(9) In this section–

'authorised person' means –

(a) the National Society for the Prevention of Cruelty to Children and any of its officers; and

(b) any person authorised by order of the Secretary of State to bring proceedings under this section and any officer of a body which is so authorised;

'harm' means ill-treatment or the impairment of health or development including, for example, impairment suffered from seeing or hearing the ill-treatment of another;

'development' means physical, intellectual, emotional, social or behavioural development;

'health' means physical or mental health; and

'ill-treatment' includes sexual abuse and forms of ill-treatment which are not physical.

(10) Where the question of whether harm suffered by a child is significant turns on the child's health or development, his health or development shall be compared with that which could reasonably be expected of a similar child.

(11) In this Act–

'a care order' means (subject to section 105(1)) an order under subsection (1)(a) and (except where express provision to the contrary is made) includes an interim care order made under section 38; and

'a supervision order' means an order under subsection (1)(b) and (except where express provision to the contrary is made) includes an interim supervision order made under section 38.

Care orders: care plans

31A (1) Where an application is made on which a care order might be made with respect to a child, the appropriate local authority must, within such time as *the court may direct* [may be prescribed], prepare a plan ('a care plan') for the future care of the child.

(2) While the application is pending, the authority must keep any care plan prepared by them under review and, if they are of the opinion some change is required, revise the plan, or make a new plan, accordingly.

(3) A care plan must give any prescribed information and do so in the prescribed manner.

(4) For the purposes of this section, the appropriate local authority, in relation to a child in respect of whom a care order might be made, is the local authority proposed to be designated in the order.

[(4A) In this section 'prescribed'–

(a) in relation to a care plan whose preparation is the responsibility of a local authority for an area in England, means prescribed by the Secretary of State; and

(b) in relation to a care plan whose preparation is the responsibility of a local authority in Wales, means prescribed by the Welsh Ministers].[8]

(5) In section 31(3A) and this section, references to a care order do not include an interim care order.

(6) A plan prepared, or treated as prepared, under this section is referred to in this Act as a 'section 31A plan'.

Care orders

Effect of care order

33 (1) Where a care order is made with respect to a child it shall be the duty of the local authority designated by the order to receive the child into their care and to keep him in their care while the order remains in force.

8 Words in square brackets in subs (1) and (4A) were inserted by the Children and Families Act 2014. Not yet in force

(2) Where–

(a) a care order has been made with respect to a child on the application of an authorised person; but

(b) the local authority designated by the order was not informed that that person proposed to make the application,

the child may be kept in the care of that person until received into the care of the authority.

(3) While a care order is in force with respect to a child, the local authority designated by the order shall–

(a) have parental responsibility for the child; and

(b) have the power (subject to the following provisions of this section) to determine the extent to which–

(i) a parent, guardian or special guardian of the child; or

(ii) a person who by virtue of section 4A has parental responsibility for the child,

may meet his parental responsibility for him.

(4) The authority may not exercise the power in subsection (3)(b) unless they are satisfied that it is necessary to do so in order to safeguard or promote the child's welfare.

(5) Nothing in subsection (3)(b) shall prevent a person mentioned in that provision who has care of the child from doing what is reasonable in all the circumstances of the case for the purpose of safeguarding or promoting his welfare.

(6) While a care order is in force with respect to a child, the local authority designated by the order shall not–

(a) cause the child to be brought up in any religious persuasion other than that in which he would have been brought up if the order had not been made; or

(b) have the right–

(i) [Repealed].

(ii) to agree or refuse to agree to the making of an adoption order, or an order under section 84 of the Adoption and Children Act 2002, with respect to the child; or

(iii) to appoint a guardian for the child.

(7) While a care order is in force with respect to a child, no person may–

(a) cause the child to be known by a new surname; or

(b) remove him from the United Kingdom,

without either the written consent of every person who has parental responsibility for the child or the leave of the court.

(8) Subsection (7)(b) does not–

(a) prevent the removal of such a child, for a period of less than one month, by the authority in whose care he is; or

(b) apply to arrangements for such a child to live outside England and Wales (which are governed by paragraph 19 of Schedule 2 in England, and section 124 of the Social Services and Well-being (Wales) Act 2014 in Wales).

(9) The power in subsection (3)(b) is subject (in addition to being subject to the provisions of this section) to any right, duty, power, responsibility or authority which a person mentioned in that provision has in relation to the child and his property by virtue of any other enactment.

Notification of children accommodated in certain establishments

Children accommodated by health authorities and local education authorities

85 (1) Where a child is provided with accommodation in England by any Special Health Authority, National Health Service trust or NHS foundation trust or by a local authority in England in the exercise of education functions (*'the accommodating authority'*)–

(a) for a consecutive period of at least three months; or

(b) with the intention, on the part of that authority, of accommodating him for such a period,

the accommodating authority shall notify the appropriate officer of the responsible authority.

(2) Where subsection (1) applies with respect to a child, the accommodating authority shall also notify the appropriate officer of the responsible authority when they cease to accommodate the child.

(2ZA) Where a child is provided with accommodation–

(a) by a body which is not mentioned in subsection (1), and

(b) pursuant to arrangements made by the Secretary of State, the National Health Service Commissioning Board or a clinical commissioning group under the National Health Service Act 2006,

subsections (1) and (2) apply in relation to the Secretary of State, the Board or (as the case may be) the clinical commissioning group as if it were the accommodating authority.

(2A) In a case where the child is provided with accommodation in England by a local authority in England in the exercise of education functions, subsections (1) and (2) apply only if the local authority providing the accommodation is different from the responsible authority.

(3) In this section *'the responsible authority'* means –

(a) the local authority appearing to the accommodating authority to be the authority within whose area the child was ordinarily resident immediately before being accommodated; or

(b) where it appears to the accommodating authority that a child was not ordinarily resident within the area of any local authority, the local authority within whose area the accommodation is situated.

(3A) In this section and sections 86 and 86A *'the appropriate officer'* means–
(a) in relation to a local authority in England, their director of children's services; and
(b) in relation to a local authority in Wales, their director of social services.

(4) Where the appropriate officer of a local authority in England has been notified under this section, or under section 120 of the Social Services and Well-being (Wales) Act 2014 (assessment of children accommodated by health authorities and education authorities), the local authority shall–
(a) take such steps as are reasonably practicable to enable them to determine whether the child's welfare is adequately safeguarded and promoted while he is accommodated by the accommodating authority; and
(b) consider the extent to which (if at all) they should exercise any of their functions under this Act with respect to the child.

(5) For the purposes of subsection (4)(b), if the child is not in the area of the local authority, they must treat him as if he were in that area.

Children accommodated in care homes or independent hospitals

86 (1) Where a child is provided with accommodation in England in any care home or independent hospital–
(a) for a consecutive period of at least three months; or
(b) with the intention, on the part of the person taking the decision to accommodate him, of accommodating him for such period,

the person carrying on the establishment in question shall notify the appropriate officer of the local authority within whose area the establishment is carried on.

(2) Where subsection (1) applies with respect to a child, the person carrying on the establishment shall also notify the appropriate officer of that authority when he ceases to accommodate the child in the establishment.

(3) Where the appropriate officer of a local authority has been notified under this section, the local authority shall–
(a) take such steps as are reasonably practicable to enable them to determine whether the child's welfare is adequately safeguarded and promoted while he is accommodated in the establishment in question; and
(b) consider the extent to which (if at all) they should exercise any of their functions under this Act with respect to the child.

(4) If the person carrying on any care home or independent hospital fails, without reasonable excuse, to comply with this section he shall be guilty of an offence.

(5) A person authorised by a local authority in England may enter any care home or independent hospital within the authority's area for the purpose of establishing whether the requirements of this section have been complied with.

(6) Any person who intentionally obstructs another in the exercise of the power of entry shall be guilty of an offence.

(7) Any person exercising the power of entry shall, if so required, produce some duly authenticated document showing his authority to do so.

(8) Any person committing an offence under this section shall be liable on summary conviction to a fine not exceeding level 3 on the standard scale.

Visitors for children notified to local authority

86A(1) This section applies if the appropriate officer of a local authority in England–

(a) has been notified with respect to a child under section 85(1) or 86(1), or under section 120(2)(a) of the Social Services and Well-being (Wales) Act 2014; and

(b) has not been notified with respect to that child under section 85(2), 86(2) or under section 120(2)(b) of the Social Services and Well-being (Wales) Act 2014, as the case may be.

(2) The local authority must, in accordance with regulations made under this section, make arrangements for the child to be visited by a representative of the authority ('a representative').

(3) It is the function of a representative to provide advice and assistance to the local authority on the performance of their duties under section 85(4) or, as the case may be, 86(3).

(4) Regulations under this section may make provision about–

(a) the frequency of visits under visiting arrangements;

(b) circumstances in which visiting arrangements must require a child to be visited; and

(c) additional functions of a representative.

(5) Regulations under this section are to be made by the Secretary of State.

(6) In choosing a representative a local authority must satisfy themselves that the person chosen has the necessary skills and experience to perform the functions of a representative.

(7) In this section *'visiting arrangements'* means arrangements made under subsection (2).

SCHEDULE 2: SUPPORT FOR CHILDREN AND FAMILIES PROVIDED BY LOCAL AUTHORITIES IN ENGLAND

Sections 17, 23, 29

Part I: Provision of Services for Families

Application to local authorities in England

A1 (1) This Schedule applies only in relation to local authorities in England.

(2) Accordingly, unless the contrary intention appears, a reference in this Schedule to a local authority means a local authority in England.

Identification of children in need and provision of information

1(1) Every local authority shall take reasonable steps to identify the extent to which there are children in need within their area.

(2) Every local authority shall–

(a) publish information–

(i) about services provided by them under sections 17, 18, 20 and 23D; and

(ii) where they consider it appropriate, about the provision by others (including, in particular, voluntary organisations) of services which the authority have power to provide under those sections; and

(b) take such steps as are reasonably practicable to ensure that those who might benefit from the services receive the information relevant to them.

Children's services plans

1A [Repealed.]

Maintenance of a register of disabled children

2 (1) Every local authority shall open and maintain a register of disabled children within their area.

(2) The register may be kept by means of a computer.

Assessment of children's needs

3 Where it appears to a local authority that a child within their area is in need, the authority may assess his needs for the purposes of this Act at the same time as any assessment of his needs is made under–

(a) the Chronically Sick and Disabled Persons Act 1970;

(b) Part IV of the Education Act 1996;

(ba) Part 3 of the Children and Families Act 2014;

(c) the Disabled Persons (Services, Consultation and Representation) Act 1986; or

(d) any other enactment.

Prevention of neglect and abuse

4(1) Every local authority shall take reasonable steps, through the provision of services under Part III of this Act, to prevent children within their area suffering ill-treatment or neglect.

(2) Where a local authority believe that a child who is at any time within their area–

(a) is likely to suffer harm; but

(b) lives or proposes to live in the area of another local authority or in the area of a local authority in Wales

they shall inform that other local authority or the local authority in Wales, as the case may be.

(3) When informing that other local authority or the local authority in Wales they shall specify–

(a) the harm that they believe he is likely to suffer; and

(b) (if they can) where the child lives or proposes to live.

Provision of accommodation in order to protect child

5 (1) Where–

(a) it appears to a local authority that a child who is living on particular premises is suffering, or is likely to suffer, ill treatment at the hands of another person who is living on those premises; and

(b) that other person proposes to move from the premises,

the authority may assist that other person to obtain alternative accommodation.

(2) Assistance given under this paragraph may be in cash.

(3) Subsections (7) to (9) of section 17 shall apply in relation to assistance given under this paragraph as they apply in relation to assistance given under that section.

Provision for disabled children

6(1) Every local authority shall provide services designed–

(a) to minimise the effect on disabled children within their area of their disabilities;

(b) to give such children the opportunity to lead lives which are as normal as possible; and

(c) to assist individuals who provide care for such children to continue to do so, or to do so more effectively, by giving them breaks from caring.

(2) The duty imposed by sub-paragraph (1)(c) shall be performed in accordance with regulations made by the Secretary of State.

Provision to reduce need for care proceedings etc

7 Every local authority shall take reasonable steps designed–

(a) to reduce the need to bring–

(i) proceedings for care or supervision orders with respect to children within their area;

(ii) criminal proceedings against such children;

(iii) any family or other proceedings with respect to such children which might lead to them being placed in the authority's care; or

(iv) proceedings under the inherent jurisdiction of the High Court with respect to children;

(b) to encourage children within their area not to commit criminal offences; and

(c) to avoid the need for children within their area to be placed in secure accommodation within the meaning given in section 25 and in section 119 of the Social Services and Well-being (Wales) Act 2014.

Provision for children living with their families

8 Every local authority shall make such provision as they consider appropriate for the following services to be available with respect to children in need within their area while they are living with their families–

(a) advice, guidance and counselling;

(b) occupational, social, cultural or recreational activities;

(c) home help (which may include laundry facilities);

(d) facilities for, or assistance with, travelling to and from home for the purpose of taking advantage of any other service provided under this Act or of any similar service;

(e) assistance to enable the child concerned and his family to have a holiday.

Provision for accommodated children

8A (1) Every local authority shall make provision for such services as they consider appropriate to be available with respect to accommodated children.

(2) 'Accommodated children' are those children in respect of whose accommodation the local authority have been notified under section 85 or 86 or under section 120 of the Social Services and Well-being (Wales) Act 2014 (assessment of children accommodated by health authorities and education authorities).

(3) The services shall be provided with a view to promoting contact between each accommodated child and that child's family.

(4) The services may, in particular, include–

(a) advice, guidance and counselling;

(b) services necessary to enable the child to visit, or to be visited by, members of the family;

(c) assistance to enable the child and members of the family to have a holiday together.

(5) Nothing in this paragraph affects the duty imposed by paragraph 10.

Family centres

9(1) Every local authority shall provide such family centres as they consider appropriate in relation to children within their area.

(2) *'Family centre'* means a centre at which any of the persons mentioned in sub-paragraph (3) may–

(a) attend for occupational, social, cultural or recreational activities;

(b) attend for advice, guidance or counselling; or

(c) be provided with accommodation while he is receiving advice, guidance or counselling.

(3) The persons are–

(a) a child;

(b) his parents;

(c) any person who is not a parent of his but who has parental responsibility for him;

(d) any other person who is looking after him.

Maintenance of the family home

10 Every local authority shall take such steps as are reasonably practicable, where any child within their area who is in need and whom they are not looking after is living apart from his family–

(a) to enable him to live with his family; or

(b) to promote contact between him and his family,

if, in their opinion, it is necessary to do so in order to safeguard or promote his welfare.

Duty to consider racial groups to which children in need belong

11 Every local authority shall, in making any arrangements–

(a) for the provision of day care within their area; or

(b) designed to encourage persons to act as local authority foster parents,

have regard to the different racial groups to which children within their area who are in need belong.

CHILDREN AND FAMILIES ACT 2014

Part 3: Children and young people in England with special educational needs or disabilities

Local authority functions: general principles

Local authority functions: supporting and involving children and young people

19 In exercising a function under this Part in the case of a child or young person, a local authority in England must have regard to the following matters in particular–

(a) the views, wishes and feelings of the child and his or her parent, or the young person;

(b) the importance of the child and his or her parent, or the young person, participating as fully as possible in decisions relating to the exercise of the function concerned;

(c) the importance of the child and his or her parent, or the young person, being provided with the information and support necessary to enable participation in those decisions;

(d) the need to support the child and his or her parent, or the young person, in order to facilitate the development of the child or young person and to help him or her achieve the best possible educational and other outcomes.

Special educational needs etc

When a child or young person has special educational needs

20 (1) A child or young person has special educational needs if he or she has a learning difficulty or disability which calls for special educational provision to be made for him or her.

(2) A child of compulsory school age or a young person has a learning difficulty or disability if he or she–

(a) has a significantly greater difficulty in learning than the majority of others of the same age, or

(b) has a disability which prevents or hinders him or her from making use of facilities of a kind generally provided for others of the same age in mainstream schools or mainstream post-16 institutions.

(3) A child under compulsory school age has a learning difficulty or disability if he or she is likely to be within subsection (2) when of compulsory school age (or would be likely, if no special educational provision were made).

(4) A child or young person does not have a learning difficulty or disability solely because the language (or form of language) in which he or she is or will be taught is different from a language (or form of language) which is or has been spoken at home.

(5) This section applies for the purposes of this Part.

Special educational provision, health care provision and social care provision

21 (1) *'Special educational provision'*, for a child aged two or more or a young person, means educational or training provision that is additional to, or different from, that made generally for others of the same age in–
(a) mainstream schools in England,
(b) maintained nursery schools in England,
(c) mainstream post-16 institutions in England, or
(d) places in England at which relevant early years education is provided.

(2) *'Special educational provision'*, for a child aged under two, means educational provision of any kind.

(3) *'Health care provision'* means the provision of health care services as part of the comprehensive health service in England continued under section 1(1) of the National Health Service Act 2006.

(4) *'Social care provision'* means the provision made by a local authority in the exercise of its social services functions.

(5) Health care provision or social care provision which educates or trains a child or young person is to be treated as special educational provision (instead of health care provision or social care provision).

(6) This section applies for the purposes of this Part.

Identifying children and young people with special educational needs and disabilities

Identifying children and young people with special educational needs and disabilities

22 A local authority in England must exercise its functions with a view to securing that it identifies–
(a) all the children and young people in its area who have or may have special educational needs, and
(b) all the children and young people in its area who have a disability.

Duty of health bodies to bring certain children to local authority's attention

23 (1) This section applies where, in the course of exercising functions in relation to a child who is under compulsory school age, a clinical commissioning group, NHS trust or NHS foundation trust form the opinion that the child has (or probably has) special educational needs or a disability.

(2) The group or trust must–
(a) inform the child's parent of their opinion and of their duty under subsection (3), and
(b) give the child's parent an opportunity to discuss their opinion with an officer of the group or trust.

(3) The group or trust must then bring their opinion to the attention of the appropriate local authority in England.

(4) If the group or trust think a particular voluntary organisation is likely to be able to give the parent advice or assistance in connection with any special educational needs or disability the child may have, they must inform the parent of that.

Children and young people for whom a local authority is responsible

When a local authority is responsible for a child or young person

24 (1) A local authority in England is responsible for a child or young person if he or she is in the authority's area and has been–

(a) identified by the authority as someone who has or may have special educational needs, or

(b) brought to the authority's attention by any person as someone who has or may have special educational needs.

(2) This section applies for the purposes of this Part.

Education, health and care provision: integration and joint commissioning

Promoting integration

25 (1) A local authority in England must exercise its functions under this Part with a view to ensuring the integration of educational provision and training provision with health care provision and social care provision, where it thinks that this would–

(a) promote the well-being of children or young people in its area who have special educational needs or a disability, or

(b) improve the quality of special educational provision–

(i) made in its area for children or young people who have special educational needs, or

(ii) made outside its area for children or young people for whom it is responsible who have special educational needs.

(2) The reference in subsection (1) to the well-being of children and young people is to their well-being so far as relating to–

(a) physical and mental health and emotional well-being;

(b) protection from abuse and neglect;

(c) control by them over their day-to-day lives;

(d) participation in education, training or recreation;

(e) social and economic well-being;

(f) domestic, family and personal relationships;

(g) the contribution made by them to society.

Assessment

Assessment of education, health and care needs

36 (1) A request for a local authority in England to secure an EHC needs assessment for a child or young person may be made to the authority by the child's parent, the young person or a person acting on behalf of a school or post-16 institution.

(2) An '*EHC needs assessment*' is an assessment of the educational, health care and social care needs of a child or young person.

(3) When a request is made to a local authority under subsection (1), or a local authority otherwise becomes responsible for a child or young person, the authority must determine whether it may be necessary for special educational provision to be made for the child or young person in accordance with an EHC plan.

(4) In making a determination under subsection (3), the local authority must consult the child's parent or the young person.

(5) Where the local authority determines that it is not necessary for special educational provision to be made for the child or young person in accordance with an EHC plan it must notify the child's parent or the young person–

(a) of the reasons for that determination, and

(b) that accordingly it has decided not to secure an EHC needs assessment for the child or young person.

(6) Subsection (7) applies where–

(a) no EHC plan is maintained for the child or young person,

(b) the child or young person has not been assessed under this section or section 71 during the previous six months, and

(c) the local authority determines that it may be necessary for special educational provision to be made for the child or young person in accordance with an EHC plan.

(7) The authority must notify the child's parent or the young person–

(a) that it is considering securing an EHC needs assessment for the child or young person, and

(b) that the parent or young person has the right to–

(i) express views to the authority (orally or in writing), and

(ii) submit evidence to the authority.

(8) The local authority must secure an EHC needs assessment for the child or young person if, after having regard to any views expressed and evidence submitted under subsection (7), the authority is of the opinion that–

(a) the child or young person has or may have special educational needs, and

(b) it may be necessary for special educational provision to be made for the child or young person in accordance with an EHC plan.

(9) After an EHC needs assessment has been carried out, the local authority must notify the child's parent or the young person of–

(a) the outcome of the assessment,

(b) whether it proposes to secure that an EHC plan is prepared for the child or young person, and

(c) the reasons for that decision.

(10) In making a determination or forming an opinion for the purposes of this section in relation to a young person aged over 18, a local authority must consider whether he or she requires additional time, in comparison to the majority of others of the same age who do not have special educational needs, to complete his or her education or training.

(11) Regulations may make provision about EHC needs assessments, in particular–

(a) about requests under subsection (1);

(b) imposing time limits in relation to consultation under subsection (4);

(c) about giving notice;

(d) about expressing views and submitting evidence under subsection (7);

(e) about how assessments are to be conducted;

(f) about advice to be obtained in connection with an assessment;

(g) about combining an EHC needs assessment with other assessments;

(h) about the use for the purposes of an EHC needs assessment of information obtained as a result of other assessments;

(i) about the use of information obtained as a result of an EHC needs assessment, including the use of that information for the purposes of other assessments;

(j) about the provision of information, advice and support in connection with an EHC needs assessment.

Education, health and care plans

Education, health and care plans

37 (1) Where, in the light of an EHC needs assessment, it is necessary for special educational provision to be made for a child or young person in accordance with an EHC plan–

(a) the local authority must secure that an EHC plan is prepared for the child or young person, and

(b) once an EHC plan has been prepared, it must maintain the plan.

(2) For the purposes of this Part, an EHC plan is a plan specifying–

(a) the child's or young person's special educational needs;

(b) the outcomes sought for him or her;

(c) the special educational provision required by him or her;

(d) any health care provision reasonably required by the learning difficulties

and disabilities which result in him or her having special educational needs;
(e) in the case of a child or a young person aged under 18, any social care provision which must be made for him or her by the local authority as a result of section 2 of the Chronically Sick and Disabled Persons Act 1970;
(f) any social care provision reasonably required by the learning difficulties and disabilities which result in the child or young person having special educational needs, to the extent that the provision is not already specified in the plan under paragraph (e).

(3) An EHC plan may also specify other health care and social care provision reasonably required by the child or young person.

(4) Regulations may make provision about the preparation, content, maintenance, amendment and disclosure of EHC plans.

(5) Regulations under subsection (4) about amendments of EHC plans must include provision applying section 33 (mainstream education for children and young people with EHC plans) to a case where an EHC plan is to be amended under those regulations.

Preparation of EHC plans: draft plan

38 (1) Where a local authority is required to secure that an EHC plan is prepared for a child or young person, it must consult the child's parent or the young person about the content of the plan during the preparation of a draft of the plan.

(2) The local authority must then–
(a) send the draft plan to the child's parent or the young person, and
(b) give the parent or young person notice of his or her right to–
(i) make representations about the content of the draft plan, and
(ii) request the authority to secure that a particular school or other institution within subsection (3) is named in the plan.

(3) A school or other institution is within this subsection if it is–
(a) a maintained school;
(b) a maintained nursery school;
(c) an Academy;
(d) an institution within the further education sector in England;
(e) a non-maintained special school;
(f) an institution approved by the Secretary of State under section 41 (independent special schools and special post-16 institutions: approval).

(4) A notice under subsection (2)(b) must specify a period before the end of which any representations or requests must be made.

(5) The draft EHC plan sent to the child's parent or the young person must not–
(a) name a school or other institution, or
(b) specify a type of school or other institution.

Finalising EHC plans: request for particular school or other institution

39(1) This section applies where, before the end of the period specified in a notice under section 38(2)(b), a request is made to a local authority to secure that a particular school or other institution is named in an EHC plan.

(2) The local authority must consult–

(a) the governing body, proprietor or principal of the school or other institution,

(b) the governing body, proprietor or principal of any other school or other institution the authority is considering having named in the plan, and

(c) if a school or other institution is within paragraph (a) or (b) and is maintained by another local authority, that authority.

(3) The local authority must secure that the EHC plan names the school or other institution specified in the request, unless subsection (4) applies.

(4) This subsection applies where–

(a) the school or other institution requested is unsuitable for the age, ability, aptitude or special educational needs of the child or young person concerned, or

(b) the attendance of the child or young person at the requested school or other institution would be incompatible with–

(i) the provision of efficient education for others, or

(ii) the efficient use of resources.

(5) Where subsection (4) applies, the local authority must secure that the plan–

(a) names a school or other institution which the local authority thinks would be appropriate for the child or young person, or

(b) specifies the type of school or other institution which the local authority thinks would be appropriate for the child or young person.

(6) Before securing that the plan names a school or other institution under subsection (5)(a), the local authority must (if it has not already done so) consult–

(a) the governing body, proprietor or principal of any school or other institution the authority is considering having named in the plan, and

(b) if that school or other institution is maintained by another local authority, that authority.

(7) The local authority must, at the end of the period specified in the notice under section 38(2)(b), secure that any changes it thinks necessary are made to the draft EHC plan.

(8) The local authority must send a copy of the finalised EHC plan to–

(a) the child's parent or the young person, and

(b) the governing body, proprietor or principal of any school or other institution named in the plan.

Finalising EHC plans: no request for particular school or other institution

40 (1) This section applies where no request is made to a local authority before the end of the period specified in a notice under section 38(2)(b) to secure that a particular school or other institution is named in an EHC plan.

(2) The local authority must secure that the plan–

(a) names a school or other institution which the local authority thinks would be appropriate for the child or young person concerned, or

(b) specifies the type of school or other institution which the local authority thinks would be appropriate for the child or young person.

(3) Before securing that the plan names a school or other institution under subsection (2)(a), the local authority must consult–

(a) the governing body, proprietor or principal of any school or other institution the authority is considering having named in the plan, and

(b) if that school or other institution is maintained by another local authority, that authority.

(4) The local authority must also secure that any changes it thinks necessary are made to the draft EHC plan.

(5) The local authority must send a copy of the finalised EHC plan to–

(a) the child's parent or the young person, and

(b) the governing body, proprietor or principal of any school or other institution named in the plan.

Independent special schools and special post-16 institutions: approval

41 (1) The Secretary of State may approve an institution within subsection (2) for the purpose of enabling the institution to be the subject of a request for it to be named in an EHC plan.

(2) An institution is within this subsection if it is–

(a) an independent educational institution (within the meaning of Chapter 1 of Part 4 of ESA 2008)–

(i) which has been entered on the register of independent educational institutions in England (kept under section 95 of that Act), and

(ii) which is specially organised to make special educational provision for students with special educational needs,

(b) an independent school–

(i) which has been entered on the register of independent schools in Wales (kept under section 158 of the Education Act 2002), and

(ii) which is specially organised to make special educational provision for pupils with special educational needs, or

(c) a special post-16 institution which is not an institution within the further education sector or a 16 to 19 Academy.

(3) The Secretary of State may approve an institution under subsection (1) only if its proprietor consents.

(4) The Secretary of State may withdraw approval given under subsection (1).

(5) Regulations may make provision about giving and withdrawing approval under this section, in particular–

(a) about the types of special post-16 institutions which may be approved under subsection (1);

(b) specifying criteria which an institution must meet before it can be approved under subsection (1);

(c) about the matters which may or must be taken into account in deciding to give or withdraw approval;

(d) about the publication of a list of all institutions who are approved under this section.

Duty to secure special educational provision and health care provision in accordance with EHC Plan

42 (1) This section applies where a local authority maintains an EHC plan for a child or young person.

(2) The local authority must secure the specified special educational provision for the child or young person.

(3) If the plan specifies health care provision, the responsible commissioning body must arrange the specified health care provision for the child or young person.

(4) *'The responsible commissioning body'*, in relation to any specified health care provision, means the body (or each body) that is under a duty to arrange health care provision of that kind in respect of the child or young person.

(5) Subsections (2) and (3) do not apply if the child's parent or the young person has made suitable alternative arrangements.

(6) *'Specified'*, in relation to an EHC plan, means specified in the plan.

Schools and other institutions named in EHC plan: duty to admit

43 (1) Subsection (2) applies if one of the following is named in an EHC plan–

(a) a maintained school in England;

(b) a maintained nursery school in England;

(c) an Academy;

(d) an institution within the further education sector in England;

(e) a non-maintained special school in England;

(f) an institution approved by the Secretary of State under section 41.

(2) The governing body, proprietor or principal of the school or other institution must admit the child or young person for whom the plan is maintained.

(3) Subsection (2) has effect regardless of any duty imposed on the governing body of a school by section 1(6) of SSFA 1998.

(4) Subsection (2) does not affect any power to exclude a pupil or student from a school or other institution.

Reviews and re-assessments

44 (1) A local authority must review an EHC plan that it maintains–

(a) in the period of 12 months starting with the date on which the plan was first made, and

(b) in each subsequent period of 12 months starting with the date on which the plan was last reviewed under this section.

(2) A local authority must secure a re-assessment of the educational, health care and social care needs of a child or young person for whom it maintains an EHC plan if a request is made to it by–

(a) the child's parent or the young person, or

(b) the governing body, proprietor or principal of the school, post-16 institution or other institution which the child or young person attends.

(3) A local authority may also secure a re-assessment of those needs at any other time if it thinks it necessary.

(4) Subsections (1) and (2) are subject to any contrary provision in regulations made under subsection (7)(b).

(5) In reviewing an EHC plan maintained for a young person aged over 18, or deciding whether to secure a re-assessment of the needs of such a young person, a local authority must have regard to whether the educational or training outcomes specified in the plan have been achieved.

(6) During a review or re-assessment, a local authority must consult the parent of the child, or the young person, for whom it maintains the EHC plan.

(7) Regulations may make provision about reviews and re-assessments, in particular–

(a) about other circumstances in which a local authority must or may review an EHC plan or secure a re-assessment (including before the end of a specified phase of a child's or young person's education);

(b) about circumstances in which it is not necessary for a local authority to review an EHC plan or secure a re-assessment;

(c) about amending or replacing an EHC plan following a review or reassessment.

(8) Regulations under subsection (7) about re-assessments may in particular apply provisions of or made under this Part that are applicable to EHC needs assessments, with or without modifications.

(9) Regulations under subsection (7)(c) must include provision applying section

33 (mainstream education for children and young people with EHC plans) to a case where an EHC plan is to be amended following a review.

Ceasing to maintain an EHC plan

45 (1) A local authority may cease to maintain an EHC plan for a child or young person only if–

(a) the authority is no longer responsible for the child or young person, or

(b) the authority determines that it is no longer necessary for the plan to be maintained.

(2) The circumstances in which it is no longer necessary for an EHC plan to be maintained for a child or young person include where the child or young person no longer requires the special educational provision specified in the plan.

(3) When determining whether a young person aged over 18 no longer requires the special educational provision specified in his or her EHC plan, a local authority must have regard to whether the educational or training outcomes specified in the plan have been achieved.

(4) A local authority may not cease to maintain an EHC plan for a child or young person until–

(a) after the end of the period allowed for bringing an appeal under section 51 against its decision to cease to maintain the plan, where no such appeal is brought before the end of that period;

(b) after the appeal has been finally determined, where such an appeal is brought before the end of that period.

(5) Regulations may make provision about ceasing to maintain an EHC plan, in particular about–

(a) other circumstances in which it is no longer necessary for an EHC plan to be maintained;

(b) circumstances in which a local authority may not determine that it is no longer necessary for an EHC plan to be maintained;

(c) the procedure to be followed by a local authority when determining whether to cease to maintain an EHC plan.

Maintaining an EHC plan after young person's 25th birthday

46 (1) A local authority may continue to maintain an EHC plan for a young person until the end of the academic year during which the young person attains the age of 25.

(2) *'Academic year'* means the period of twelve months ending on the prescribed date.

Transfer of EHC plans

47 (1) Regulations may make provision for an EHC plan maintained for a child or young person by one local authority to be transferred to another local authority in England, where the other authority becomes responsible for the child or young person.

(2) The regulations may in particular–
  (a) impose a duty on the other authority to maintain the plan;
  (b) treat the plan as if originally prepared by the other authority;
  (c) treat things done by the transferring authority in relation to the plan as done by the other authority.

Release of child or young person for whom EHC plan previously maintained

48 (1) This section applies where–
  (a) a child or young person who has been subject to a detention order (within the meaning of section 562(1A)(a) of EA 1996) is released,
  (b) on the release date, a local authority in England becomes responsible for him or her, and
  (c) an EHC plan was–
    (i) maintained for him or her immediately before the start of the detention, or
    (ii) kept for him or her under section 74 during the detention.

(2) The local authority must–
  (a) maintain the plan, and
  (b) review the plan as soon as reasonably practicable after the release date.

(3) Subsection (2)(b) is subject to any contrary provision in regulations under section 44(7)(b).

Personal budgets and direct payments

49 (1) A local authority that maintains an EHC plan, or is securing the preparation of an EHC plan, for a child or young person must prepare a personal budget for him or her if asked to do so by the child's parent or the young person.

(2) The authority prepares a 'personal budget' for the child or young person if it identifies an amount as available to secure particular provision that is specified, or proposed to be specified, in the EHC plan, with a view to the child's parent or the young person being involved in securing the provision.

(3) Regulations may make provision about personal budgets, in particular–
  (a) about requests for personal budgets;
  (b) about the amount of a personal budget;
  (c) about the sources of the funds making up a personal budget;
  (d) for payments ('direct payments') representing all or part of a personal budget to be made to a child's parent or a young person, or a person of a prescribed description in prescribed circumstances, in order to secure provision to which the budget relates;
  (e) about the description of provision to which personal budgets and direct payments may (and may not) relate;

(f) for a personal budget or direct payment to cover the agreed cost of the provision to which the budget or payment relates;
(g) about when, how, to whom and on what conditions direct payments may (and may not) be made;
(h) about when direct payments may be required to be repaid and the recovery of unpaid sums;
(i) about conditions with which a person or body making direct payments must comply before, after or at the time of making a direct payment;
(j) about arrangements for providing information, advice or support in connection with personal budgets and direct payments.

(4) If the regulations include provision authorising direct payments, they must–
(a) require the consent of a child's parent or a young person, or a person of a prescribed description in prescribed circumstances, to be obtained before direct payments are made;
(b) require the authority to stop making direct payments where the required consent is withdrawn.

(5) Special educational provision acquired by means of a direct payment made by a local authority is to be treated as having been secured by the authority in pursuance of its duty under section 42(2), subject to any prescribed conditions or exceptions.

(6) Subsection (7) applies if–
(a) an EHC plan is maintained for a child or young person, and
(b) health care provision specified in the plan is acquired for him or her by means of a payment made by a commissioning body under section 12A(1) of the National Health Service Act 2006 (direct payments for health care).

(7) The health care provision is to be treated as having been arranged by the commissioning body in pursuance of its duty under section 42(3) of this Act, subject to any prescribed conditions or exceptions.

(8) *'Commissioning body'*, in relation to any specified health care provision, means a body that is under a duty to arrange health care provision of that kind in respect of the child or young person.

CHRONICALLY SICK AND DISABLED PERSONS ACT 1970 ss2, 2A

Provision of welfare services

2 (1) [Repealed.]

(1A) [Repealed.]

(2) [Repealed.]

(3) Subsections (4) to (6) apply to local authorities in England.

(4) Where a local authority have functions under Part 3 of the Children Act 1989 in relation to a disabled child and the child is ordinarily resident in their area, they must, in exercise of those functions, make any arrangements within subsection (6) that they are satisfied it is necessary for them to make in order to meet the needs of the child.

(5) Subsection (4) is subject to sections 7(1) and 7A of the Local Authority Social Services Act 1970 (exercise of social services functions subject to guidance or directions of the Secretary of State).

(6) The arrangements mentioned in subsection (4) are arrangements for any of the following–

(a) the provision of practical assistance for the child in the child's home;

(b) the provision of wireless, television, library or similar recreational facilities for the child, or assistance to the child in obtaining them;

(c) the provision for the child of lectures, games, outings or other recreational facilities outside the home or assistance to the child in taking advantage of available educational facilities;

(d) the provision for the child of facilities for, or assistance in, travelling to and from home for the purpose of participating in any services provided under arrangements made by the authority under Part 3 of the Children Act 1989 or, with the approval of the authority, in any services, provided otherwise than under arrangements under that Part, which are similar to services which could be provided under such arrangements;

(e) the provision of assistance for the child in arranging for the carrying out of any works of adaptation in the child's home or the provision of any additional facilities designed to secure greater safety, comfort or convenience for the child;

(f) facilitating the taking of holidays by the child, whether at holiday homes or otherwise and whether provided under arrangements made by the authority or otherwise;

(g) the provision of meals for the child whether at home or elsewhere;

(h) the provision of a telephone for the child, or of special equipment necessary for the child to use one, or assistance to the child in obtaining any of those things.

(7) Any question arising under this section as to a person's ordinary residence in

an area in England or Wales is to be determined by the Secretary of State or by the Welsh Ministers.

(8) The Secretary of State and the Welsh Ministers must make and publish arrangements for determining which cases are to be dealt with by the Secretary of State and which are to be dealt with by the Welsh Ministers.

(9) Those arrangements may include provision for the Secretary of State and the Welsh Ministers to agree, in relation to any question that has arisen, which of them is to deal with the case.

Welfare services: transition for children to adult care and support

2A (1) Subsections (2) to (4) apply where a local authority in England making arrangements for a disabled child under section 2 are required by section 58(1) of the Care Act 2014 to carry out a child's needs assessment in relation to the child.

(2) If the local authority carry out the assessment before the child reaches the age of 18 and decide to treat it as a needs assessment in accordance with section 59(6) of the Care Act 2014 (with Part 1 of that Act applying to the assessment as a result), the authority must continue to comply with section 2 after the child reaches the age of 18 until they reach a conclusion in his case.

(3) If the local authority carry out the assessment before the child reaches the age of 18 but decide not to treat it as a needs assessment in accordance with section 59(6) of that Act–

(a) they must carry out a needs assessment after the child reaches the age of 18, and

(b) they must continue to comply with section 2 after he reaches that age until they reach a conclusion in his case.

(4) If the local authority do not carry out the assessment before the child reaches the age of 18, they must continue to comply with section 2 after he reaches that age until–

(a) they decide that the duty under section 9 of the Care Act 2014 (needs assessment) does not apply, or

(b) having decided that the duty applies and having discharged it, they reach a conclusion in his case.

(5) Subsection (6) applies where a local authority in England making arrangements for a disabled child under section 2–

(a) receive a request for a child's needs assessment to be carried out in relation to the child, but

(b) have yet to be required by section 58(1) of the Care Act 2014 to carry out the assessment.

(6) If the local authority do not decide, before the child reaches the age of

18, whether or not to comply with the request, they must continue to comply with section 2 after he reaches that age until–

(a) they decide that the duty under section 9 of the Care Act 2014 does not apply, or

(b) having decided that the duty applies and having discharged it, they reach a conclusion in his case.

(7) A local authority reach a conclusion in a person's case when–

(a) they conclude that he does not have needs for care and support,

(b) having concluded that he has such needs and that they are going to meet some or all of them, they begin to do so, or

(c) having concluded that he has such needs, they conclude that they are not going to meet any of those needs (whether because those needs do not meet the eligibility criteria or for some other reason).

(8) In this section, *'child's needs assessment'*, *'needs assessment'* and *'eligibility criteria'* each have the same meaning as in Part 1 of the Care Act 2014.

EQUALITY ACT 2010 ss4, 6, 13-15, 19-22, 149, SCHEDULE 1

Part 2: Equality: Key Concepts

Chapter 1: Protected Characteristics

The protected characteristics

4 The following characteristics are protected characteristics–

age;
disability;
gender reassignment;
marriage and civil partnership;
pregnancy and maternity;
race;
religion or belief;
sex;
sexual orientation.

Disability

6 (1) A person (P) has a disability if–

(a) P has a physical or mental impairment, and

(b) the impairment has a substantial and long-term adverse effect on P's ability to carry out normal day-to-day activities.

(2) A reference to a disabled person is a reference to a person who has a disability.

(3) In relation to the protected characteristic of disability–

(a) a reference to a person who has a particular protected characteristic is a reference to a person who has a particular disability;

(b) a reference to persons who share a protected characteristic is a reference to persons who have the same disability.

(4) This Act (except Part 12 and section 190) applies in relation to a person who has had a disability as it applies in relation to a person who has the disability; accordingly (except in that Part and that section)–

(a) a reference (however expressed) to a person who has a disability includes a reference to a person who has had the disability, and

(b) a reference (however expressed) to a person who does not have a disability includes a reference to a person who has not had the disability.

(5) A Minister of the Crown may issue guidance about matters to be taken into account in deciding any question for the purposes of subsection (1).

(6) Schedule 1 (disability: supplementary provision) has effect.

Chapter 2: Prohibited Conduct

Discrimination

Direct discrimination

13 (1) A person (A) discriminates against another (B) if, because of a protected characteristic, A treats B less favourably than A treats or would treat others.

(2) If the protected characteristic is age, A does not discriminate against B if A can show A's treatment of B to be a proportionate means of achieving a legitimate aim.

(3) If the protected characteristic is disability, and B is not a disabled person, A does not discriminate against B only because A treats or would treat disabled persons more favourably than A treats B.

(4) If the protected characteristic is marriage and civil partnership, this section applies to a contravention of Part 5 (work) only if the treatment is because it is B who is married or a civil partner.

(5) If the protected characteristic is race, less favourable treatment includes segregating B from others.

(6) If the protected characteristic is sex–

(a) less favourable treatment of a woman includes less favourable treatment of her because she is breast-feeding;

(b) in a case where B is a man, no account is to be taken of special treatment afforded to a woman in connection with pregnancy or childbirth.

(7) Subsection (6)(a) does not apply for the purposes of Part 5 (work).

(8) This section is subject to sections 17(6) and 18(7).

Combined discrimination: dual characteristics

14 (1) A person (A) discriminates against another (B) if, because of a combination of two relevant protected characteristics, A treats B less favourably than A treats or would treat a person who does not share either of those characteristics.

(2) The relevant protected characteristics are–

(a) age;

(b) disability;

(c) gender reassignment;

(d) race

(e) religion or belief;

(f) sex;

(g) sexual orientation.

(3) For the purposes of establishing a contravention of this Act by virtue of subsection (1), B need not show that A's treatment of B is direct discrimination because of each of the characteristics in the combination (taken separately).

(4) But B cannot establish a contravention of this Act by virtue of subsection (1) if, in reliance on another provision of this Act or any other enactment, A

shows that A's treatment of B is not direct discrimination because of either or both of the characteristics in the combination.

(5) Subsection (1) does not apply to a combination of characteristics that includes disability in circumstances where, if a claim of direct discrimination because of disability were to be brought, it would come within section 116 (special educational needs).

(6) A Minister of the Crown may by order amend this section so as to–

(a) make further provision about circumstances in which B can, or in which B cannot, establish a contravention of this Act by virtue of subsection (1);

(b) specify other circumstances in which subsection (1) does not apply.

(7) The references to direct discrimination are to a contravention of this Act by virtue of section 13.

Discrimination arising from disability

15 (1) A person (A) discriminates against a disabled person (B) if–

(a) A treats B unfavourably because of something arising in consequence of B's disability, and

(b) A cannot show that the treatment is a proportionate means of achieving a legitimate aim.

(2) Subsection (1) does not apply if A shows that A did not know, and could not reasonably have been expected to know, that B had the disability.

Indirect discrimination

19 (1) A person (A) discriminates against another (B) if A applies to B a provision, criterion or practice which is discriminatory in relation to a relevant protected characteristic of B's.

(2) For the purposes of subsection (1), a provision, criterion or practice is discriminatory in relation to a relevant protected characteristic of B's if–

(a) A applies, or would apply, it to persons with whom B does not share the characteristic,

(b) it puts, or would put, persons with whom B shares the characteristic at a particular disadvantage when compared with persons with whom B does not share it,

(c) it puts, or would put, B at that disadvantage, and

(d) A cannot show it to be a proportionate means of achieving a legitimate aim.

(3) The relevant protected characteristics are–

age;
disability;
gender reassignment;
marriage and civil partnership;
race;
religion or belief;

sex;
sexual orientation.

Adjustments for disabled persons

Duty to make adjustments

20 (1) Where this Act imposes a duty to make reasonable adjustments on a person, this section, sections 21 and 22 and the applicable Schedule apply; and for those purposes, a person on whom the duty is imposed is referred to as A.

(2) The duty comprises the following three requirements.

(3) The first requirement is a requirement, where a provision, criterion or practice of A's puts a disabled person at a substantial disadvantage in relation to a relevant matter in comparison with persons who are not disabled, to take such steps as it is reasonable to have to take to avoid the disadvantage.

(4) The second requirement is a requirement, where a physical feature puts a disabled person at a substantial disadvantage in relation to a relevant matter in comparison with persons who are not disabled, to take such steps as it is reasonable to have to take to avoid the disadvantage.

(5) The third requirement is a requirement, where a disabled person would, but for the provision of an auxiliary aid, be put at a substantial disadvantage in relation to a relevant matter in comparison with persons who are not disabled, to take such steps as it is reasonable to have to take to provide the auxiliary aid.

(6) Where the first or third requirement relates to the provision of information, the steps which it is reasonable for A to have to take include steps for ensuring that in the circumstances concerned the information is provided in an accessible format.

(7) A person (A) who is subject to a duty to make reasonable adjustments is not (subject to express provision to the contrary) entitled to require a disabled person, in relation to whom A is required to comply with the duty, to pay to any extent A's costs of complying with the duty.

(8) A reference in section 21 or 22 or an applicable Schedule to the first, second or third requirement is to be construed in accordance with this section.

(9) In relation to the second requirement, a reference in this section or an applicable Schedule to avoiding a substantial disadvantage includes a reference to–

(a) removing the physical feature in question,
(b) altering it, or
(c) providing a reasonable means of avoiding it.

(10) A reference in this section, section 21 or 22 or an applicable Schedule (apart from paragraphs 2 to 4 of Schedule 4) to a physical feature is a reference to–

(a) a feature arising from the design or construction of a building,
(b) a feature of an approach to, exit from or access to a building,

(c) a fixture or fitting, or furniture furnishings, materials, equipment or other chattels, in or on premises, or
(d) any other physical element or quality.

(11) A reference in this section, section 21 or 22 or an applicable Schedule to an auxiliary aid includes a reference to an auxiliary service.

(12) A reference in this section or an applicable Schedule to chattels is to be read, in relation to Scotland, as a reference to moveable property.

(13) The applicable Schedule is, in relation to the Part of this Act specified in the first column of the Table, the Schedule specified in the second column.

Part of this Act	*Applicable Schedule*
Part 3 (services and public functions)	Schedule 2
Part 4 (premises)	Schedule 4
Part 5 (work)	Schedule 8
Part 6 (education)	Schedule 13
Part 7 (associations)	Schedule 15
Each of the Parts mentioned above	Schedule 21

Failure to comply with duty

21 (1) A failure to comply with the first, second or third requirement is a failure to comply with a duty to make reasonable adjustments.

(2) A discriminates against a disabled person if A fails to comply with that duty in relation to that person.

(3) A provision of an applicable Schedule which imposes a duty to comply with the first, second or third requirement applies only for the purpose of establishing whether A has contravened this Act by virtue of subsection (2); a failure to comply is, accordingly, not actionable by virtue of another provision of this Act or otherwise.

Regulations

22 (1) Regulations may prescribe–

(a) matters to be taken into account in deciding whether it is reasonable for A to take a step for the purposes of a prescribed provision of an applicable Schedule;
(b) descriptions of persons to whom the first, second or third requirement does not apply.

(2) Regulations may make provision as to–

(a) circumstances in which it is, or in which it is not, reasonable for a person of a prescribed description to have to take steps of a prescribed description;
(b) what is, or what is not, a provision, criterion or practice;
(c) things which are, or which are not, to be treated as physical features;

(d) things which are, or which are not, to be treated as alterations of physical features;

(e) things which are, or which are not, to be treated as auxiliary aids.

(3) Provision made by virtue of this section may amend an applicable Schedule.

Part 11: Advancement of Equality

Chapter 1: Public Sector Equality Duty

Public sector equality duty

149 (1) A public authority must, in the exercise of its functions, have due regard to the need to–

(a) eliminate discrimination, harassment, victimisation and any other conduct that is prohibited by or under this Act;

(b) advance equality of opportunity between persons who share a relevant protected characteristic and persons who do not share it;

(c) foster good relations between persons who share a relevant protected characteristic and persons who do not share it.

(2) A person who is not a public authority but who exercises public functions must, in the exercise of those functions, have due regard to the matters mentioned in subsection (1).

(3) Having due regard to the need to advance equality of opportunity between persons who share a relevant protected characteristic and persons who do not share it involves having due regard, in particular, to the need to–

(a) remove or minimise disadvantages suffered by persons who share a relevant protected characteristic that are connected to that characteristic;

(b) take steps to meet the needs of persons who share a relevant protected characteristic that are different from the needs of persons who do not share it;

(c) encourage persons who share a relevant protected characteristic to participate in public life or in any other activity in which participation by such persons is disproportionately low.

(4) The steps involved in meeting the needs of disabled persons that are different from the needs of persons who are not disabled include, in particular, steps to take account of disabled persons' disabilities.

(5) Having due regard to the need to foster good relations between persons who share a relevant protected characteristic and persons who do not share it involves having due regard, in particular, to the need to–

(a) tackle prejudice, and

(b) promote understanding.

(6) Compliance with the duties in this section may involve treating some persons more favourably than others; but that is not to be taken as permitting conduct that would otherwise be prohibited by or under this Act.

(7) The relevant protected characteristics are–

age;
disability;
gender reassignment;
pregnancy and maternity;
race;
religion or belief;
sex;
sexual orientation.

(8) A reference to conduct that is prohibited by or under this Act includes a reference to–
  (a) a breach of an equality clause or rule;
  (b) a breach of a non-discrimination rule.

(9) Schedule 18 (exceptions) has effect.

Chapter 2: Positive Action

Positive action: general

158 (1) This section applies if a person (P) reasonably thinks that–
  (a) persons who share a protected characteristic suffer a disadvantage connected to the characteristic,
  (b) persons who share a protected characteristic have needs that are different from the needs of persons who do not share it, or
  (c) participation in an activity by persons who share a protected characteristic is disproportionately low.

(2) This Act does not prohibit P from taking any action which is a proportionate means of achieving the aim of–
  (a) enabling or encouraging persons who share the protected characteristic to overcome or minimise that disadvantage,
  (b) meeting those needs, or
  (c) enabling or encouraging persons who share the protected characteristic to participate in that activity.

(3) Regulations may specify action, or descriptions of action, to which subsection (2) does not apply.

(4) This section does not apply to–
  (a) action within section 159(3), or
  (b) anything that is permitted by virtue of section 104.

(5) If section 104(7) is repealed by virtue of section 105, this section will not apply to anything that would have been so permitted but for the repeal.

(6) This section does not enable P to do anything that is prohibited by or under an enactment other than this Act.

SCHEDULE 1

Disability: Supplementary Provision

Section 6

Part 1: Determination of Disability

Impairment

1 Regulations may make provision for a condition of a prescribed description to be, or not to be, an impairment.

Long-term effects

2 (1) The effect of an impairment is long-term if–

(a) it has lasted for at least 12 months,

(b) it is likely to last for at least 12 months, or

(c) it is likely to last for the rest of the life of the person affected.

(2) If an impairment ceases to have a substantial adverse effect on a person's ability to carry out normal day-to-day activities, it is to be treated as continuing to have that effect if that effect is likely to recur.

(3) For the purposes of sub-paragraph (2), the likelihood of an effect recurring is to be disregarded in such circumstances as may be prescribed.

(4) Regulations may prescribe circumstances in which, despite sub-paragraph (1), an effect is to be treated as being, or as not being, long-term.

Severe disfigurement

3 (1) An impairment which consists of a severe disfigurement is to be treated as having a substantial adverse effect on the ability of the person concerned to carry out normal day-to-day activities.

(2) Regulations may provide that in prescribed circumstances a severe disfigurement is not to be treated as having that effect.

(3) The regulations may, in particular, make provision in relation to deliberately acquired disfigurement.

Substantial adverse effects

4 Regulations may make provision for an effect of a prescribed description on the ability of a person to carry out normal day-to-day activities to be treated as being, or as not being, a substantial adverse effect.

Effect of medical treatment

5 (1) An impairment is to be treated as having a substantial adverse effect on the ability of the person concerned to carry out normal day-to-day activities if–

(a) measures are being taken to treat or correct it, and

(b) but for that, it would be likely to have that effect.

(2) 'Measures' includes, in particular, medical treatment and the use of a prosthesis or other aid.

(3) Sub-paragraph (1) does not apply–

(a) in relation to the impairment of a person's sight, to the extent that the impairment is, in the person's case, correctable by spectacles or contact lenses or in such other ways as may be prescribed;

(b) in relation to such other impairments as may be prescribed, in such circumstances as are prescribed.

Certain medical conditions

6(1) Cancer, HIV infection and multiple sclerosis are each a disability.

(2) HIV infection is infection by a virus capable of causing the Acquired Immune Deficiency Syndrome.

Deemed disability

7 (1) Regulations may provide for persons of prescribed descriptions to be treated as having disabilities.

(2) The regulations may prescribe circumstances in which a person who has a disability is to be treated as no longer having the disability.

(3) This paragraph does not affect the other provisions of this Schedule.

Progressive conditions

8 (1) This paragraph applies to a person (P) if–

(a) P has a progressive condition,

(b) as a result of that condition P has an impairment which has (or had) an effect on P's ability to carry out normal day-to-day activities, but

(c) the effect is not (or was not) a substantial adverse effect.

(2) P is to be taken to have an impairment which has a substantial adverse effect if the condition is likely to result in P having such an impairment.

(3) Regulations may make provision for a condition of a prescribed description to be treated as being, or as not being, progressive.

Past disabilities

9 (1)A question as to whether a person had a disability at a particular time ('the relevant time') is to be determined, for the purposes of section 6, as if the provisions of, or made under, this Act were in force when the act complained of was done had been in force at the relevant time.

(2) The relevant time may be a time before the coming into force of the provision of this Act to which the question relates.

Part 2: Guidance

Preliminary

10 This Part of this Schedule applies in relation to guidance referred to in section 6(5).

Examples

11 The guidance may give examples of–

(a) effects which it would, or would not, be reasonable, in relation to particular activities, to regard as substantial adverse effects;

(b) substantial adverse effects which it would, or would not, be reasonable to regard as long-term.

Adjudicating bodies

12(1) In determining whether a person is a disabled person, an adjudicating body must take account of such guidance as it thinks is relevant.

(2) An adjudicating body is–

(a) a court;

(b) a tribunal;

(c) a person (other than a court or tribunal) who may decide a claim relating to a contravention of Part 6 (education).

Representations

13 Before issuing the guidance, the Minister must–

(a) publish a draft of it;

(b) consider any representations made to the Minister about the draft;

(c) make such modifications as the Minister thinks appropriate in the light of the representations.

Parliamentary procedure

14 (1) If the Minister decides to proceed with proposed guidance, a draft of it must be laid before Parliament.

(2) If, before the end of the 40-day period, either House resolves not to approve the draft, the Minister must take no further steps in relation to the proposed guidance.

(3) If no such resolution is made before the end of that period, the Minister must issue the guidance in the form of the draft.

(4) Sub-paragraph (2) does not prevent a new draft of proposed guidance being laid before Parliament.

(5) The 40-day period–

(a) begins on the date on which the draft is laid before both Houses (or, if laid before each House on a different date, on the later date);

(b) does not include a period during which Parliament is prorogued or dissolved;

(c) does not include a period during which both Houses are adjourned for more than 4 days.

Commencement

15 The guidance comes into force on the day appointed by order by the Minister.

Revision and revocation

16 (1) The Minister may–

(a) revise the whole or part of guidance and re-issue it;

(b) by order revoke guidance.

(2) A reference to guidance includes a reference to guidance which has been revised and re-issued.

HUMAN RIGHTS ACT 1998 ss3, 6, 7, 8, SCHEDULE 1

Legislation

Interpretation of legislation

3 (1) So far as it is possible to do so, primary legislation and subordinate legislation must be read and given effect in a way which is compatible with the Convention rights.

(2) This section–

(a) applies to primary legislation and subordinate legislation whenever enacted;

(b) does not affect the validity, continuing operation or enforcement of any incompatible primary legislation; and

(c) does not affect the validity, continuing operation or enforcement of any incompatible subordinate legislation if (disregarding any possibility of revocation) primary legislation prevents removal of the incompatibility.

. . .

Public authorities

Acts of public authorities

6 (1) It is unlawful for a public authority to act in a way which is incompatible with a Convention right.

(2) Subsection (1) does not apply to an act if–

(a) as the result of one or more provisions of primary legislation, the authority could not have acted differently; or

(b) in the case of one or more provisions of, or made under, primary legislation which cannot be read or given effect in a way which is compatible with the Convention rights, the authority was acting so as to give effect to or enforce those provisions.

(3) In this section 'public authority' includes–

(a) a court or tribunal, and

(b) any person certain of whose functions are functions of a public nature,

but does not include either House of Parliament or a person exercising functions in connection with proceedings in Parliament.

(4) [Repealed.]

(5) In relation to a particular act, a person is not a public authority by virtue only of subsection (3)(b) if the nature of the act is private.

(6) 'An act' includes a failure to act but does not include a failure to–

(a) introduce in, or lay before, Parliament a proposal for legislation; or

(b) make any primary legislation or remedial order.

Proceedings

7 (1) A person who claims that a public authority has acted (or proposes to act) in a way which is made unlawful by section 6(1) may–

(a) bring proceedings against the authority under this Act in the appropriate court or tribunal, or

(b) rely on the Convention right or rights concerned in any legal proceedings, but only if he is (or would be) a victim of the unlawful act.

(2) In subsection (1)(a) 'appropriate court or tribunal' means such court or tribunal as may be determined in accordance with rules; and proceedings against an authority include a counterclaim or similar proceeding.

(3) If the proceedings are brought on an application for judicial review, the applicant is to be taken to have a sufficient interest in relation to the unlawful act only if he is, or would be, a victim of that act.

(4) If the proceedings are made by way of a petition for judicial review in Scotland, the applicant shall be taken to have title and interest to sue in relation to the unlawful act only if he is, or would be, a victim of that act.

(5) Proceedings under subsection (1)(a) must be brought before the end of–

(a) the period of one year beginning with the date on which the act complained of took place; or

(b) such longer period as the court or tribunal considers equitable having regard to all the circumstances,

but that is subject to any rule imposing a stricter time limit in relation to the procedure in question.

(6) In subsection (1)(b) 'legal proceedings' includes–

(a) proceedings brought by or at the instigation of a public authority; and

(b) an appeal against the decision of a court or tribunal.

(7) For the purposes of this section, a person is a victim of an unlawful act only if he would be a victim for the purposes of Article 34 of the Convention if proceedings were brought in the European Court of Human Rights in respect of that act.

(8) Nothing in this Act creates a criminal offence.

(9) In this section 'rules' means–

(a) in relation to proceedings before a court or tribunal outside Scotland, rules made by the Lord Chancellor or the Secretary of State for the purposes of this section or rules of court,

(b) in relation to proceedings before a court or tribunal in Scotland, rules made by the Secretary of State for those purposes,

(c) in relation to proceedings before a tribunal in Northern Ireland–

(i) which deals with transferred matters; and

(ii) for which no rules made under paragraph (a) are in force,

rules made by a Northern Ireland department for those purposes,

and includes provision made by order under section 1 of the Courts and Legal Services Act 1990.

(10) In making rules, regard must be had to section 9.

(11) The Minister who has power to make rules in relation to a particular tribunal may, to the extent he considers it necessary to ensure that the tribunal can provide an appropriate remedy in relation to an act (or proposed act) of a public authority which is (or would be) unlawful as a result of section 6(1), by order add to–

(a) the relief or remedies which the tribunal may grant; or

(b) the grounds on which it may grant any of them.

(12) An order made under subsection (11) may contain such incidental, supplemental, consequential or transitional provision as the Minister making it considers appropriate.

(13) 'The Minister' includes the Northern Ireland department concerned.

Judicial remedies

8 (1) In relation to any act (or proposed act) of a public authority which the court finds is (or would be) unlawful, it may grant such relief or remedy, or make such order, within its powers as it considers just and appropriate.

(2) But damages may be awarded only by a court which has power to award damages, or to order the payment of compensation, in civil proceedings.

(3) No award of damages is to be made unless, taking account of all the circumstances of the case, including–

(a) any other relief or remedy granted, or order made, in relation to the act in question (by that or any other court), and

(b) the consequences of any decision (of that or any other court) in respect of that act,

the court is satisfied that the award is necessary to afford just satisfaction to the person in whose favour it is made.

(4) In determining–

(a) whether to award damages, or

(b) the amount of an award,

the court must take into account the principles applied by the European Court of Human Rights in relation to the award of compensation under Article 41 of the Convention.

(5) A public authority against which damages are awarded is to be treated–

(a) in Scotland, for the purposes of section 3 of the Law Reform (Miscellaneous Provisions) (Scotland) Act 1940 as if the award were made in an action of damages in which the authority has been found liable in respect of loss or damage to the person to whom the award is made;

(b) for the purposes of the Civil Liability (Contribution) Act 1978 as liable in respect of damage suffered by the person to whom the award is made.

(6) In this section–

'court' includes a tribunal;

'damages' means damages for an unlawful act of a public authority; and

'unlawful' means unlawful under section 6(1).

. . .

SCHEDULE 1: THE ARTICLES

Part I: The Convention

Rights and Freedoms

Article 2: Right to life

1 Everyone's right to life shall be protected by law. No one shall be deprived of his life intentionally save in the execution of a sentence of a court following his conviction of a crime for which this penalty is provided by law.

2 Deprivation of life shall not be regarded as inflicted in contravention of this Article when it results from the use of force which is no more than absolutely necessary:

(a) in defence of any person from unlawful violence;

(b) in order to effect a lawful arrest or to prevent the escape of a person lawfully detained;

(c) in action lawfully taken for the purpose of quelling a riot or insurrection.

Article 3: Prohibition of torture

No one shall be subjected to torture or to inhuman or degrading treatment or punishment.

Article 4: Prohibition of slavery and forced labour

1 No one shall be held in slavery or servitude.

2 No one shall be required to perform forced or compulsory labour.

3 For the purpose of this Article the term 'forced or compulsory labour' shall not include:

(a) any work required to be done in the ordinary course of detention imposed according to the provisions of Article 5 of this Convention or during conditional release from such detention;

(b) any service of a military character or, in case of conscientious objectors in countries where they are recognised, service exacted instead of compulsory military service;

(c) any service exacted in case of an emergency or calamity threatening the life or well'being of the community;

(d) any work or service which forms part of normal civic obligations.

Article 5: Right to liberty and security

1 Everyone has the right to liberty and security of person. No one shall be deprived of his liberty save in the following cases and in accordance with a procedure prescribed by law:

(a) the lawful detention of a person after conviction by a competent court;

(b) the lawful arrest or detention of a person for non'compliance with the lawful order of a court or in order to secure the fulfilment of any obligation prescribed by law;

(c) the lawful arrest or detention of a person effected for the purpose of bringing him before the competent legal authority on reasonable suspicion of having committed an offence or when it is reasonably considered necessary to prevent his committing an offence or fleeing after having done so;
(d) the detention of a minor by lawful order for the purpose of educational supervision or his lawful detention for the purpose of bringing him before the competent legal authority;
(e) the lawful detention of persons for the prevention of the spreading of infectious diseases, of persons of unsound mind, alcoholics or drug addicts or vagrants;
(f) the lawful arrest or detention of a person to prevent his effecting an unauthorised entry into the country or of a person against whom action is being taken with a view to deportation or extradition.

2 Everyone who is arrested shall be informed promptly, in a language which he understands, of the reasons for his arrest and of any charge against him.

3 Everyone arrested or detained in accordance with the provisions of paragraph 1(c) of this Article shall be brought promptly before a judge or other officer authorised by law to exercise judicial power and shall be entitled to trial within a reasonable time or to release pending trial. Release may be conditioned by guarantees to appear for trial.

4 Everyone who is deprived of his liberty by arrest or detention shall be entitled to take proceedings by which the lawfulness of his detention shall be decided speedily by a court and his release ordered if the detention is not lawful.

5 Everyone who has been the victim of arrest or detention in contravention of the provisions of this Article shall have an enforceable right to compensation.

Article 6: Right to a fair trial

1 In the determination of his civil rights and obligations or of any criminal charge against him, everyone is entitled to a fair and public hearing within a reasonable time by an independent and impartial tribunal established by law. Judgment shall be pronounced publicly but the press and public may be excluded from all or part of the trial in the interest of morals, public order or national security in a democratic society, where the interests of juveniles or the protection of the private life of the parties so require, or to the extent strictly necessary in the opinion of the court in special circumstances where publicity would prejudice the interests of justice.

2 Everyone charged with a criminal offence shall be presumed innocent until proved guilty according to law.

3 Everyone charged with a criminal offence has the following minimum rights:
(a) to be informed promptly, in a language which he understands and in detail, of the nature and cause of the accusation against him;
(b) to have adequate time and facilities for the preparation of his defence;

(c) to defend himself in person or through legal assistance of his own choosing or, if he has not sufficient means to pay for legal assistance, to be given it free when the interests of justice so require;
(d) to examine or have examined witnesses against him and to obtain the attendance and examination of witnesses on his behalf under the same conditions as witnesses against him;
(e) to have the free assistance of an interpreter if he cannot understand or speak the language used in court.

Article 7: No punishment without law

1 No one shall be held guilty of any criminal offence on account of any act or omission which did not constitute a criminal offence under national or international law at the time when it was committed. Nor shall a heavier penalty be imposed than the one that was applicable at the time the criminal offence was committed.

2 This Article shall not prejudice the trial and punishment of any person for any act or omission which, at the time when it was committed, was criminal according to the general principles of law recognised by civilised nations.

Article 8: Right to respect for private and family life

1 Everyone has the right to respect for his private and family life, his home and his correspondence.

2 There shall be no interference by a public authority with the exercise of this right except such as is in accordance with the law and is necessary in a democratic society in the interests of national security, public safety or the economic well'being of the country, for the prevention of disorder or crime, for the protection of health or morals, or for the protection of the rights and freedoms of others.

Article 9: Freedom of thought, conscience and religion

1 Everyone has the right to freedom of thought, conscience and religion; this right includes freedom to change his religion or belief and freedom, either alone or in community with others and in public or private, to manifest his religion or belief, in worship, teaching, practice and observance.

2 Freedom to manifest one's religion or beliefs shall be subject only to such limitations as are prescribed by law and are necessary in a democratic society in the interests of public safety, for the protection of public order, health or morals, or for the protection of the rights and freedoms of others.

Article 10: Freedom of expression

1 Everyone has the right to freedom of expression. This right shall include freedom to hold opinions and to receive and impart information and ideas without interference by public authority and regardless of frontiers. This Article shall not prevent States from requiring the licensing of broadcasting, television or cinema enterprises.

2 The exercise of these freedoms, since it carries with it duties and responsibilities, may be subject to such formalities, conditions, restrictions or penalties as are prescribed by law and are necessary in a democratic society, in the interests of national security, territorial integrity or public safety, for the prevention of disorder or crime, for the protection of health or morals, for the protection of the reputation or rights of others, for preventing the disclosure of information received in confidence, or for maintaining the authority and impartiality of the judiciary.

Article 11: Freedom of assembly and association

1 Everyone has the right to freedom of peaceful assembly and to freedom of association with others, including the right to form and to join trade unions for the protection of his interests.

2 No restrictions shall be placed on the exercise of these rights other than such as are prescribed by law and are necessary in a democratic society in the interests of national security or public safety, for the prevention of disorder or crime, for the protection of health or morals or for the protection of the rights and freedoms of others. This Article shall not prevent the imposition of lawful restrictions on the exercise of these rights by members of the armed forces, of the police or of the administration of the State.

Article 12: Right to marry

Men and women of marriageable age have the right to marry and to found a family, according to the national laws governing the exercise of this right.

Article 14: Prohibition of discrimination

The enjoyment of the rights and freedoms set forth in this Convention shall be secured without discrimination on any ground such as sex, race, colour, language, religion, political or other opinion, national or social origin, association with a national minority, property, birth or other status.

Article 16: Restrictions on political activity of aliens

Nothing in Articles 10, 11 and 14 shall be regarded as preventing the High Contracting Parties from imposing restrictions on the political activity of aliens.

Article 17: Prohibition of abuse of rights

Nothing in this Convention may be interpreted as implying for any State, group or person any right to engage in any activity or perform any act aimed at the destruction of any of the rights and freedoms set forth herein or at their limitation to a greater extent than is provided for in the Convention.

Article 18: Limitation on use of restrictions on rights

The restrictions permitted under this Convention to the said rights and freedoms shall not be applied for any purpose other than those for which they have been prescribed.

Part II: The First Protocol

Article 1: Protection of property

Every natural or legal person is entitled to the peaceful enjoyment of his possessions. No one shall be deprived of his possessions except in the public interest and subject to the conditions provided for by law and by the general principles of international law.

The preceding provisions shall not, however, in any way impair the right of a State to enforce such laws as it deems necessary to control the use of property in accordance with the general interest or to secure the payment of taxes or other contributions or penalties.

Article 2: Right to education

No person shall be denied the right to education. In the exercise of any functions which it assumes in relation to education and to teaching, the State shall respect the right of parents to ensure such education and teaching in conformity with their own religious and philosophical convictions.

Article 3: Right to free elections

The High Contracting Parties undertake to hold free elections at reasonable intervals by secret ballot, under conditions which will ensure the free expression of the opinion of the people in the choice of the legislature.

Part III: Article 1 of the Thirteenth Protocol

Article 1: Abolition of the death penalty

The death penalty shall be abolished. No one shall be condemned to such penalty or executed.

LOCAL AUTHORITY SOCIAL SERVICES ACT 1970 s7

Local authorities to exercise social services functions under guidance of Secretary of State

7 (1) Local authorities shall, in the exercise of their social services functions, including the exercise of any discretion conferred by any relevant enactment, act under the general guidance of the Secretary of State.

(1A) Section 78 of the Care Act 2014 applies instead of this section in relation to functions given by Part 1 of that Act or by regulations under that Part.

(2) [Repealed.]

(3) [Repealed.]

NATIONAL HEALTH SERVICE AND COMMUNITY CARE ACT 1990 s47

Assessment of needs for community care services

47 (1) Subject to subsections (5) and (6) below, where it appears to a local authority that any person for whom they may provide or arrange for the provision of services under section 117 of the Mental Health Act 1983 may be in need of any such services, the authority–

(a) shall carry out an assessment of his needs for those services; and

(b) having regard to the results of that assessment, shall then decide whether his needs call for the provision by them of any such services.

(2) If at any time during the assessment of the needs of any person under subsection (1)(a) above it appears to a local authority in England that he is a disabled person (and, that he is under 18), the authority–

(a) shall proceed to make such a decision as to the services he requires as is mentioned in section 4 of the Disabled Persons (Services, Consultation and Representation) Act 1986 without his requesting them to do so under that section; and

(b) shall inform him that they will be doing so and of his rights under that Act.

(3) If at any time during the assessment of the needs of any person under subsection (1)(a) above, it appears to a local authority–

(za) that there may be a need for the provision to that person, pursuant to arrangements made under the National Health Service Act 2006 by such clinical commissioning group as may be determined in accordance with regulations, of any services (including services that may be provided pursuant to such arrangements by virtue of section 7A of that Act),

(a) that there may be a need for the provision to that person by such Health Authority as may be determined in accordance with regulations of any services under the National Health Service (Wales) Act 2006, or

(b) that there may be a need for the provision to him of any services which fall within the functions of a local housing authority (within the meaning of the Housing Act 1985) which is not the local authority carrying out the assessment,

the local authority shall notify that clinical commissioning group, Health Authority or local housing authority and invite them to assist, to such extent as is reasonable in the circumstances, in the making of the assessment; and, in making their decision as to the provision of the services needed for the person in question, the local authority shall take into account any services which are likely to be made available for him by that clinical commissioning group, Health Authority or local housing authority.

(4) The Secretary of State may give directions as to the manner in which an assessment under this section is to be carried out or the form it is to take

but, subject to any such directions and to subsection (7) below, it shall be carried out in such manner and take such form as the local authority consider appropriate.

(5) Nothing in this section shall prevent a local authority from temporarily providing or arranging for the provision of services mentioned in subsection (1) for any person without carrying out a prior assessment of his needs in accordance with the preceding provisions of this section if, in the opinion of the authority, the condition of that person is such that he requires those services as a matter of urgency.

(6) If, by virtue of subsection (5) above, services have been provided temporarily for any person as a matter of urgency, then, as soon as practicable thereafter, an assessment of his needs shall be made in accordance with the preceding provisions of this section.

(7) [Repealed.]

(8) In this section–

'disabled person' has the same meaning as in that Act; and

'local authority' means a county council in England, a district council for an area in England for which there is no county council, the council of a county or county borough in Wales, a London borough council or the Common Council of the City of London.

NATIONAL HEALTH SERVICE COMMISSIONING BOARD AND CLINICAL COMMISSIONING GROUPS (RESPONSIBILITIES AND STANDING RULES) REGULATIONS 2012 REGS 4, 14, 15 AND SCHEDULE 1 (EXTRACTS)

Additional persons for whom a CCG has responsibility

4 (1) Subject to paragraphs (2) to (4), for the purposes of sections 3 and 3A of the 2006 Act (which relate respectively to a CCG's duty to commission services and its power to do so), a CCG has responsibility for the persons listed in paragraph 2 of Schedule 1 (in addition to those mentioned in section 3(1A) of that Act).

(2) In the case of a person listed in paragraph 2(a), (b), (d), (e) or (f) of Schedule 1, a CCG has responsibility only in relation to the provision of accommodation or services specified in the sub-paragraph of paragraph 2 which relates to that person.

(3) The responsibility for a person listed in paragraph 2(c), (g), (h), (i) or (j) of Schedule 1, does not apply in relation to the provision of ambulance services or accident and emergency services, whether provided at a hospital accident and emergency department, a minor injuries unit, a walk-in centre or elsewhere (but excluding any services provided after the person has been accepted as an in-patient, or at an out-patient appointment).

(4) The responsibility for persons listed in paragraph 2(b) to (j) of Schedule 1 does not apply where the person is detained in—

(a) an immigration removal centre;

(b) a secure training centre; or

(c) a young offender institution.

Circumstances in which duty may be imposed on another CCG

14 (1) The duty imposed by subsection (2) of section 117 of the 1983 Act on a CCG (CCG A) to arrange for the provision of after-care services for a person (P) to whom section 117 applies is to be imposed instead on another CCG (CCG B) in the circumstances below.

(2) These circumstances are where CCG B has responsibility for P by virtue of—

(a) [Repealed.]

(b) regulation 4 of, and sub-paragraph (c), (g), (h), (i) or (j) of paragraph 2 of Schedule 1 to these Regulations.

Circumstances in which duty may be imposed on the Board

15 (1) The duty imposed by subsection (2) of section 117 of the 1983 Act on a CCG to arrange for the provision of after-care services for a person (P) to whom section 117 of the 1983 Act applies is to be imposed instead on the Board in the circumstances below.

(2) These circumstances are where P is receiving an after-care service under section 117 which, if it were being provided under the 2006 Act, would be a service whose provision the Board had a duty to arrange.

. . .

SCHEDULE 1: ADDITIONAL PERSONS FOR WHOM A CCG HAS RESPONSIBILITY

2 The list of persons referred to in regulation 4(1) is as follows—

(a) every person present in the CCG's area, in relation to the provision of ambulance services or accident and emergency services, whether provided at a hospital accident and emergency department, a minor injuries unit, a walk-in centre or elsewhere (but excluding any services provided after the person has been accepted as an in-patient, or at an out-patient appointment);

. . .

(c) every child who falls within paragraph 4;

. . .

(g) every child who falls within paragraph 8;

(h) every person present in the CCG's area who is resident outside the United Kingdom and not provided with primary medical services by a member of any CCG;

(i) every person resident in Scotland, Wales or Northern Ireland and present in the CCG's area who is a qualifying patient within the meaning of section 130C of the 1983 Act (section 130A:supplemental), and not provided with primary medical services by a member of any CCG;

(j) every person who is a qualifying patient within the meaning of section 130C of the 1983 Act and liable to be detained under that Act in a hospital or registered establishment (within the meaning of that Act) in the CCG's area.

. . .

4 (1) A child falls within this paragraph if both of sub-paragraphs (2) and (3) apply to the child.

(2) This sub-paragraph applies to a child if any of the following is the case—

(a) the child is looked after by a local authority within the meaning of section 22 of the Children Act 1989 (general duty of local authority in relation to children looked after by them), other than by way of being accommodated in a secure children's home in respect of which the National Health Service Commissioning Board must arrange for the provision of services to children detained there;

(b) the child is a relevant child within the meaning of section 23A of that Act (the responsible authority and relevant children);

(c) the child is a person to whom section 24(1A) or (1B) of that Act (persons qualifying for advice and assistance) applies;

(d) the child is provided with accommodation at a school to which he or she is admitted in accordance with an EHC plan made under section 37 of the Children and Families Act 2014; or

(e) the child requires accommodation in a care home, a children's home or an independent hospital to meet the child's continuing care needs.

(3) This sub-paragraph applies to a child if—

(a) the child is provided with—

(i) services which consist of or include the provision of accommodation situated in the area of another CCG or of a Local Health Board, under arrangements made by the CCG in the exercise of its commissioning functions (by itself or jointly with a local authority), or

(ii) such services under arrangements made by the local authority and immediately before those arrangements were made the CCG was responsible for the child under section 3(1A) of the 2006 Act; and

(b) the child is both—

(i) resident in that accommodation, and

(ii) would not be a person for whom the CCG is responsible under section 3(1A)(a) of the 2006 Act.

. . .

8 (1) A child falls within this paragraph if—

(a) a local authority has made an arrangement before the relevant date by virtue of which the child is provided with accommodation at a school in the area of another CCG or a Local Health Board, to which the child is admitted in accordance with an EHC plan made under section 37 of the 2014 Act;

(b) immediately before the child was accommodated at that school the child was either—

(i) provided with primary medical services by a person who is now a member of the CCG; or

(ii) usually resident in the area of the CCG and not provided with primary medical services by a person who is now a member of the CCG; and

(c) the child would not be a person for whom the CCG is responsible under section 3(1A)(a) of the 2006 Act.

APPENDIX B

International conventions

UNITED NATIONS CONVENTION ON THE RIGHTS OF PERSONS WITH DISABILITIES 2006

Article 3

General Principles

The principles of the present Convention shall be:

(*a*) Respect for inherent dignity, individual autonomy including the freedom to make one's own choices, and independence of persons;

(*b*) Non-discrimination;

(*c*) Full and effective participation and inclusion in society;

(*d*) Respect for difference and acceptance of persons with disabilities as part of human diversity and humanity;

(*e*) Equality of opportunity;

(*f*) Accessibility;

(*g*) Equality between men and women;

(*h*) Respect for the evolving capacities of children with disabilities and respect for the right of children with disabilities to preserve their identities.

Article 7

Children with Disabilities

1. States Parties shall take all necessary measures to ensure the full enjoyment by children with disabilities of all human rights and fundamental freedoms on an equal basis with other children.
2. In all actions concerning children with disabilities, the best interests of the child shall be a primary consideration.
3. States Parties shall ensure that children with disabilities have the right to express their views freely on all matters affecting them, their views being given due weight in accordance with their age and maturity, on an equal basis with other children, and to be provided with disability and age-appropriate assistance to realize that right.

Article 12

Equal Recognition before the Law

1. States Parties reaffirm that persons with disabilities have the right to recognition everywhere as persons before the law.
2. States Parties shall recognize that persons with disabilities enjoy legal capacity on an equal basis with others in all aspects of life.
3. States Parties shall take appropriate measures to provide access by persons with disabilities to the support they may require in exercising their legal capacity.

4. States Parties shall ensure that all measures that relate to the exercise of legal capacity provide for appropriate and effective safeguards to prevent abuse in accordance with international human rights law. Such safeguards shall ensure that measures relating to the exercise of legal capacity respect the rights, will and preferences of the person, are free of conflict of interest and undue influence, are proportional and tailored to the person's circumstances, apply for the shortest time possible and are subject to regular review by a competent, independent and impartial authority or judicial body. The safeguards shall be proportional to the degree to which such measures affect the person's rights and interests.
5. Subject to the provisions of this article, States Parties shall take all appropriate and effective measures to ensure the equal right of persons with disabilities to own or inherit property, to control their own financial affairs and to have equal access to bank loans, mortgages and other forms of financial credit, and shall ensure that persons with disabilities are not arbitrarily deprived of their property.

Article 14

Liberty and Security of Person

1. States Parties shall ensure that persons with disabilities, on an equal basis with others:
   (*a*) Enjoy the right to liberty and security of person;
   (*b*) Are not deprived of their liberty unlawfully or arbitrarily, and that any deprivation of liberty is in conformity with the law, and that the existence of a disability shall in no case justify a deprivation of liberty.
2. States Parties shall ensure that if persons with disabilities are deprived of their liberty through any process, they are, on an equal basis with others, entitled to guarantees in accordance with international human rights law and shall be treated in compliance with the objectives and principles of the present Convention, including by provision of reasonable accommodation.

Article 16

Freedom from Exploitation, Violence and Abuse

1. States Parties shall take all appropriate legislative, administrative, social, educational and other measures to protect persons with disabilities, both within and outside the home, from all forms of exploitation, violence and abuse, including their gender-based aspects.
2. States Parties shall also take all appropriate measures to prevent all forms of exploitation, violence and abuse by ensuring, inter alia, appropriate forms of gender- and age-sensitive assistance and support for persons with disabilities and their families and caregivers, including through the

provision of information and education on how to avoid, recognize and report instances of exploitation, violence and abuse. States Parties shall ensure that protection services are age-, gender- and disability-sensitive.

3. In order to prevent the occurrence of all forms of exploitation, violence and abuse, States Parties shall ensure that all facilities and programmes designed to serve persons with disabilities are effectively monitored by independent authorities.
4. States Parties shall take all appropriate measures to promote the physical, cognitive and psychological recovery, rehabilitation and social reintegration of persons with disabilities who become victims of any form of exploitation, violence or abuse, including through the provision of protection services. Such recovery and reintegration shall take place in an environment that fosters the health, welfare, self-respect, dignity and autonomy of the person and takes into account gender- and age-specific needs.
5. States Parties shall put in place effective legislation and policies, including women- and child-focused legislation and policies, to ensure that instances of exploitation, violence and abuse against persons with disabilities are identified, investigated and, where appropriate, prosecuted.

Article 17

Protecting the Integrity of the Person

Every person with disabilities has a right to respect for his or her physical and mental integrity on an equal basis with others.

Article 19

Living independently and being included in the community

States Parties to the present Convention recognize the equal right of all persons with disabilities to live in the community, with choices equal to others, and shall take effective and appropriate measures to facilitate full enjoyment by persons with disabilities of this right and their full inclusion and participation in the community, including by ensuring that:

a) Persons with disabilities have the opportunity to choose their place of residence and where and with whom they live on an equal basis with others and are not obliged to live in a particular living arrangement;

b) Persons with disabilities have access to a range of in-home, residential and other community support services, including personal assistance necessary to support living and inclusion in the community, and to prevent isolation or segregation from the community;

c) Community services and facilities for the general population are available on an equal basis to persons with disabilities and are responsive to their needs.

Article 23

Respect for Home and the Family

1. States Parties shall take effective and appropriate measures to eliminate discrimination against persons with disabilities in all matters relating to marriage, family, parenthood and relationships, on an equal basis with others, so as to ensure that:
   (*a*) The right of all persons with disabilities who are of marriageable age to marry and to found a family on the basis of free and full consent of the intending spouses is recognized;
   (*b*) The rights of persons with disabilities to decide freely and responsibly on the number and spacing of their children and to have access to age-appropriate information, reproductive and family planning education are recognized, and the means necessary to enable them to exercise these rights are provided;
   (*c*) Persons with disabilities, including children, retain their fertility on an equal basis with others.
2. States Parties shall ensure the rights and responsibilities of persons with disabilities, with regard to guardianship, wardship, trusteeship, adoption of children or similar institutions, where these concepts exist in national legislation; in all cases the best interests of the child shall be paramount. States Parties shall render appropriate assistance to persons with disabilities in the performance of their child-rearing responsibilities.
3. States Parties shall ensure that children with disabilities have equal rights with respect to family life. With a view to realizing these rights, and to prevent concealment, abandonment, neglect and segregation of children with disabilities, States Parties shall undertake to provide early and comprehensive information, services and support to children with disabilities and their families.
4. States Parties shall ensure that a child shall not be separated from his or her parents against their will, except when competent authorities subject to judicial review determine, in accordance with applicable law and procedures, that such separation is necessary for the best interests of the child. In no case shall a child be separated from parents on the basis of a disability of either the child or one or both of the parents.
5. States Parties shall, where the immediate family is unable to care for a child with disabilities, undertake every effort to provide alternative care within the wider family, and failing that, within the community in a family setting.

Article 25

Health

States Parties recognize that persons with disabilities have the right to the enjoyment of the highest attainable standard of health without discrimination on the basis of disability. States Parties shall take all appropriate measures to ensure access for persons with disabilities to health services that are gender-sensitive, including health-related rehabilitation. In particular, States Parties shall:

(*a*) Provide persons with disabilities with the same range, quality and standard of free or affordable health care and programmes as provided to other persons, including in the area of sexual and reproductive health and population-based public health programmes;

(*b*) Provide those health services needed by persons with disabilities specifically because of their disabilities, including early identification and intervention as appropriate, and services designed to minimize and prevent further disabilities, including among children and older persons;

(*c*) Provide these health services as close as possible to people's own communities, including in rural areas;

(*d*) Require health professionals to provide care of the same quality to persons with disabilities as to others, including on the basis of free and informed consent by, inter alia, raising awareness of the human rights, dignity, autonomy and needs of persons with disabilities through training and the promulgation of ethical standards for public and private health care;

(*e*) Prohibit discrimination against persons with disabilities in the provision of health insurance, and life insurance where such insurance is permitted by national law, which shall be provided in a fair and reasonable manner;

(*f*) Prevent discriminatory denial of health care or health services or food and fluids on the basis of disability.

UNITED NATIONS CONVENTION ON THE RIGHTS OF THE CHILD 1989

Article 2

1. States Parties shall respect and ensure the rights set forth in the present Convention to each child within their jurisdiction without discrimination of any kind, irrespective of the child's or his or her parent's or legal guardian's race, colour, sex, language, religion, political or other opinion, national, ethnic or social origin, property, disability, birth or other status.
2. States Parties shall take all appropriate measures to ensure that the child is protected against all forms of discrimination or punishment on the basis of the status, activities, expressed opinions, or beliefs of the child's parents, legal guardians, or family members.

Article 3

1. In all actions concerning children, whether undertaken by public or private social welfare institutions, courts of law, administrative authorities or legislative bodies, the best interests of the child shall be a primary consideration.
2. States Parties undertake to ensure the child such protection and care as is necessary for his or her well-being, taking into account the rights and duties of his or her parents, legal guardians, or other individuals legally responsible for him or her, and, to this end, shall take all appropriate legislative and administrative measures.
3. States Parties shall ensure that the institutions, services and facilities responsible for the care or protection of children shall conform with the standards established by competent authorities, particularly in the areas of safety, health, in the number and suitability of their staff, as well as competent supervision.

Article 4

States Parties shall undertake all appropriate legislative, administrative, and other measures for the implementation of the rights recognized in the present Convention. With regard to economic, social and cultural rights, States Parties shall undertake such measures to the maximum extent of their available resources and, where needed, within the framework of international co-operation.

Article 5

States Parties shall respect the responsibilities, rights and duties of parents or, where applicable, the members of the extended family or community as provided for by local custom, legal guardians or other persons legally responsible for the child, to provide, in a manner consistent with the evolving capacities of the child, appropriate direction and guidance in the exercise by the child of the rights recognized in the present Convention.

Article 12

1. States Parties shall assure to the child who is capable of forming his or her own views the right to express those views freely in all matters affecting the child, the views of the child being given due weight in accordance with the age and maturity of the child.
2. For this purpose, the child shall in particular be provided the opportunity to be heard in any judicial and administrative proceedings affecting the child, either directly, or through a representative or an appropriate body, in a manner consistent with the procedural rules of national law.

Article 20

1. A child temporarily or permanently deprived of his or her family environment, or in whose own best interests cannot be allowed to remain in that environment, shall be entitled to special protection and assistance provided by the State.
2. States Parties shall in accordance with their national laws ensure alternative care for such a child.
3. Such care could include, inter alia, foster placement, kafalah of Islamic law, adoption or if necessary placement in suitable institutions for the care of children. When considering solutions, due regard shall be paid to the desirability of continuity in a child's upbringing and to the child's ethnic, religious, cultural and linguistic background.

Article 23

1. States Parties recognize that a mentally or physically disabled child should enjoy a full and decent life, in conditions which ensure dignity, promote self-reliance and facilitate the child's active participation in the community.
2. States Parties recognize the right of the disabled child to special care and shall encourage and ensure the extension, subject to available resources, to the eligible child and those responsible for his or her care, of assistance for which application is made and which is appropriate to the child's condition and to the circumstances of the parents or others caring for the child.
3. Recognizing the special needs of a disabled child, assistance extended in accordance with paragraph 2 of the present article shall be provided free of charge, whenever possible, taking into account the financial resources of the parents or others caring for the child, and shall be designed to ensure that the disabled child has effective access to and receives education, training, health care services, rehabilitation services, preparation for employment and recreation opportunities in a manner conducive to the child's achieving the fullest possible social integration and individual development, including his or her cultural and spiritual development
4. States Parties shall promote, in the spirit of international cooperation, the exchange of appropriate information in the field of preventive health care

and of medical, psychological and functional treatment of disabled children, including dissemination of and access to information concerning methods of rehabilitation, education and vocational services, with the aim of enabling States Parties to improve their capabilities and skills and to widen their experience in these areas. In this regard, particular account shall be taken of the needs of developing countries.

Article 24

1. States Parties recognize the right of the child to the enjoyment of the highest attainable standard of health and to facilities for the treatment of illness and rehabilitation of health. States Parties shall strive to ensure that no child is deprived of his or her right of access to such health care services.
2. States Parties shall pursue full implementation of this right and, in particular, shall take appropriate measures:
   (a) To diminish infant and child mortality;
   (b) To ensure the provision of necessary medical assistance and health care to all children with emphasis on the development of primary health care;
   (c) To combat disease and malnutrition, including within the framework of primary health care, through, inter alia, the application of readily available technology and through the provision of adequate nutritious foods and clean drinking-water, taking into consideration the dangers and risks of environmental pollution;
   (d) To ensure appropriate pre-natal and post-natal health care for mothers;
   (e) To ensure that all segments of society, in particular parents and children, are informed, have access to education and are supported in the use of basic knowledge of child health and nutrition, the advantages of breastfeeding, hygiene and environmental sanitation and the prevention of accidents;
   (f) To develop preventive health care, guidance for parents and family planning education and services.
3. States Parties shall take all effective and appropriate measures with a view to abolishing traditional practices prejudicial to the health of children.
4. States Parties undertake to promote and encourage international co-operation with a view to achieving progressively the full realization of the right recognized in the present article. In this regard, particular account shall be taken of the needs of developing countries.

Article 25

States Parties recognize the right of a child who has been placed by the competent authorities for the purposes of care, protection or treatment of his or her physical or mental health, to a periodic review of the treatment provided to the child and all other circumstances relevant to his or her placement.

Article 37

States Parties shall ensure that:

(a) No child shall be subjected to torture or other cruel, inhuman or degrading treatment or punishment. Neither capital punishment nor life imprisonment without possibility of release shall be imposed for offences committed by persons below eighteen years of age;

(b) No child shall be deprived of his or her liberty unlawfully or arbitrarily. The arrest, detention or imprisonment of a child shall be in conformity with the law and shall be used only as a measure of last resort and for the shortest appropriate period of time;

(c) Every child deprived of liberty shall be treated with humanity and respect for the inherent dignity of the human person, and in a manner which takes into account the needs of persons of his or her age. In particular, every child deprived of liberty shall be separated from adults unless it is considered in the child's best interest not to do so and shall have the right to maintain contact with his or her family through correspondence and visits, save in exceptional circumstances;

(d) Every child deprived of his or her liberty shall have the right to prompt access to legal and other appropriate assistance, as well as the right to challenge the legality of the deprivation of his or her liberty before a court or other competent, independent and impartial authority, and to a prompt decision on any such action.

APPENDIX C

Policy

REFOCUSING THE CARE PROGRAMME APPROACH: POLICY AND POSITIVE PRACTICE GUIDANCE

Annex B: CPA and Child and Adolescent Mental Health Services

An approach such as CPA can particularly add value for those children and young people with more complex needs, such as those which need help from specialist multi-disciplinary Child and Adolescent Mental Health Services (CAMHS). The value of CPA in enabling transparency of care and treatment and promoting accountability of clinicians needs to be enhanced by linking with other planning and assessment frameworks (see below). Teams and individuals working in a given locality will need to be clear about where the threshold lies for use of CPA. If a criterion of complexity of need is applied, there should arguably be no lower age limit for the use of CPA.

It is vital that local protocols are used to agree which system, co-ordinator, or person is in the lead in the overall care of a child or young person. Where care is shared across agencies it must be clear who takes the lead on which areas. This is especially important for children and young people who may have a Lead Professional appointed across agencies. The risk, if this is not clarified and agreed, is that professionals might assume that others are taking responsibility e.g. for child protection or mental health, when they are not.

Adapting CPA for CAMHS

When using CPA for children and young people, health professionals need to take appropriate account of:

- The fact that the needs of children and young people vary and change over time to a possibly greater extent than adults. The environment experienced by a child or young person may be changing, for example, because of progress through the educational system or changes in fostering arrangements for those children in care. CPA will be particularly important when a child or young person is in a secure setting or leaving a secure setting. Reviews may need to be more frequent for children and young people compared to adults.
- The more complex inter-agency issues that often affect the care management and planning for children and young people. For example, a child or young person in contact with the Youth Justice System.
- The need to ensure that the child or young person's family are involved in the care plan decision making process and have a good quality relationship with the care co-ordinator. CAMHS typically works from a family centred orientation rather than a person centred approach and care must be taken to ensure all relevant family members are included, as appropriate to the child or young person's age, developmental level and taking into account their choice.

> The educational needs of children and young people.

Children, more than adults, are likely to be subject to multiple care plans and review mechanisms from multiple agencies e.g. Looked After Child Reviews, Special Educational Needs reviews, (children's) Common Assessment Framework (CAF). All professionals and agencies need to work together to ensure minimum duplication of information, meetings and clarity of roles (especially who is leading) to avoid confusion and risk. CPA needs to be seen in the context of other planning mechanisms for children with complex needs and agreement must be made locally on how to co-ordinate multi-agency care planning.

To ensure continuity of care the care coordinator should follow the transition protocols at their Trust for CAMHS to adult services.

Children and Young People's Involvement

Young people's involvement brings advantages in terms of promoting user empowerment and choice. However, to make young people's involvement in CPA a reality rather than an aspiration careful attention needs to be paid to, for example, the design of paperwork so that service users do not feel excluded. Children and young people need communication to be tailored to them, to recognise their process of cognitive development and, for those under 16, the extent of their competence to give consent.

Key issues in relation to the involvement of young people are that:

> The review and other meetings should be young-person friendly (including the language used, timing of meetings, location of venues, who is in attendance, the possible need for interpreters); information leaflets and paperwork should be age-appropriate; staff should be competent in managing meetings in such a way as to ensure young people's views are heard and taken into account.
> Young people should be supported in this process, using advocates as necessary, and assisted in developing skills to voice their views; the views of their parents and carers should also be incorporated, and where appropriate, distinguished from those of the young person.
> Agencies in a given locality need to have protocols for working together in this process, for example in the duty to cooperate, and information sharing processes.

Local teams are likely to have experience of cross-agency meetings for Looked After Children (LAC) and family group conferences and should draw upon this expertise in developing care plans for children and young people.

CAMHS CPA and other Planning/Assessment Frameworks

As CPA is not the only care planning method for children and young people, its use needs to be coordinated with the other systems e.g. the (children's) CAF, and any local systems for Looked After Children. Practitioners need to be clear about which approach to use in a given situation and how the (children's) CAF would capture issues about the psychological wellbeing of children and young people who were not subject to CPA. It will be important that young people are not overloaded with assessment and review meetings. In addition, there is a need to consider the interplay between the CPA care co-ordinator role and that of the (children's) Lead Professional.

It will be important to minimise different approaches, to avoid duplication and to work towards a situation where there are clear and agreed links between the different frameworks.

CPA should be modified for children and young people at a local level and decisions on what framework to use should be decided across agencies on a case by case basis. Issues to be considered locally between mental health services and partner agencies when developing CPA for children include:

- how CPA can facilitate the management of those young people in out-of-area placements, including those with long-term needs;
- the extent to which IT systems are compatible with those partner agencies;
- the extent the (children's) CAF is being implemented locally;
- how consent will be given for information sharing;
- clarity about the respective roles of the CPA care co-ordinator and (children's) Lead Professional, and who has ultimate responsibility;
- clarity about which young people CPA should be used for, consideration of any risks inherent in using CPA must be considered and minimised;
- how to ensure user involvement in CPA;
- clarity about how CPA works alongside other planning and assessment frameworks.

APPENDIX D

Glossary[1]

Approved Clinician (AC)*: 'A mental health professional approved by the Secretary of State or a person or body exercising the approval function of the Secretary of State, or by the Welsh Ministers to act as an approved clinician for the purposes of the Act. Some decisions under the Act can only be taken by people who are approved clinicians. All responsible clinicians must be approved clinicians.'

Approved mental health professional (AMHP)*: 'A social worker or other professional approved by a local authority to carry out a variety of functions under the Act.'

Care Programme Approach (CPA)*: 'A system of care and support for individuals with complex needs which includes an assessment, a care plan and a care coordinator. It is used mainly for adults in England who receive specialist mental healthcare and in some CAMHS services.'

Care Quality Commission (CQC)*: 'The regulator established by the Health and Social Care Act 2008 of all providers of regulated health and social care. This includes care provided under the Mental Health Act 1983.'

Child and adolescent mental health services (CAMHS)*: 'Specialist mental health services for children and adolescents. CAMHS covers all types of provision and intervention from mental health promotion and primary prevention, specialist community-based services through to very specialist care as provided by in-patient units for children and young people with mental illness. It is mainly composed of a multi-disciplinary workforce with specialist training in child and adolescent mental health.'

Child and young people's services (CYPMHS): see child and adolescent mental health services (CAMHS).

Child in need: 'is defined under the Children Act 1989 as a child who is unlikely to achieve or maintain a reasonable level of health or development, or whose health and development is likely to be significantly or further impaired, without the provision of services; or a child who is disabled. Children in need may be assessed under section 17 of the Children Act 1989 by a social worker'. (HM Government, *Working Together to Safeguard Children A guide to inter-agency working to safeguard and promote the welfare of children,* ('*Working* Together'), 2018, p20).

Child arrangements order: 'an order regulating arrangements concerning with whom a child is to live, spend time or otherwise have contact and when a child is to live, spend time or otherwise have contact with any person. From 22 April 2014, existing contact orders and residence orders are deemed to be child arrangements orders. They will remain valid, and any allowances or other entitlements which are linked to them are not therefore affected by the change.' (DfE, *Court orders and pre-proceedings for local authorities* April 2014, p7)

Child protection plan: plan which sets out how a child (under 18 years) is to be safeguarded. The aim of such plans are to: a) ensure the child is safe from harm and prevent them from suffering further harm; b) promote the child's health and development and c) support the family and wider family members to safeguard and promote the welfare of their child, provided it is in the best interests of the child (see *Working Together* p48).

Clinical Commissioning Groups (CCGs)*: 'The NHS body responsible for commissioning (arranging) NHS services for a particular part of England from NHS trusts, NHS foundation trusts and independent sector providers. CCGs replaced primary care trusts from 1 April 2013. CCGs' commissioning plans are reviewed by the NHS Commissioning Board (NHS England). CCGs are generally responsible for commissioning mental healthcare, except for specialist care commissioned by the NHS Commissioning Board.'

Community Treatment Orders (CTOs)*: 'The legal authority for the discharge of a patient from detention in hospital, subject to the possibility of recall to hospital for further medical treatment if necessary. Community patients are expected to comply with the conditions specified in the community treatment order.'

Court of Protection*: 'The specialist court set up under the Mental Capacity Act to deal with issues relating to people who lack capacity to take decisions for themselves.'

Department for Education (DfE): 'is responsible for children's services and education, including early years, schools, higher and further education policy, apprenticeships and wider skills in England' (see: www.gov.uk/government/organisations/department-for-education).

Department of Health and Social Care: (formerly Department of Health (DoH) 'supports ministers in leading the nation's health and social care to help people live more independent, healthier lives for longer' (see: www.gov.uk/government/organisations/department-of-health-and-social-care).

Deputy (or Court-appointed deputy)*: 'A person (aged 18 or over) appointed by the Court of Protection under section 16 of the Mental Capacity Act to take specified decisions on behalf of someone who lacks capacity to take those decisions themselves. This is not the same thing as the nominated deputy sometimes appointed by the doctor or approved clinician in charge of a patient's treatment.'

Doctor approved under section 12*: 'A doctor who has been approved under the Act by the Secretary of State for Health as having special experience in the diagnosis or treatment of mental disorder, or by a body which the Secretary of State has authorised to exercise the approval function under the Act, or by Welsh Ministers. Some medical recommendations and medical evidence to courts under the Act can only be made by a doctor who is approved under section 12.' (Doctors who are approved clinicians are automatically treated as though they have been approved under section 12.)'

Donees of lasting power of attorney*: 'An attorney appointed under the Mental Capacity Act to make decisions in relation to the welfare, property or affairs of a person subject to the Act who lacks capacity.

Education, Health and Care plan (EHC plan): 'An EHC plan details the education, health and social care support that is to be provided to a child or young person who has SEN or a disability. It is drawn up by the local authority after an EHC needs assessment of the child or young person has determined that an EHC plan is necessary, and after consultation with relevant partner agencies.' (DfE and DoH, *Special educational needs and disability code of practice: 0 to 25 years Statutory guidance for organisations which work with and support children and young people who have special educational needs or disabilities* January 2015, ('SEND Code') Glossary of terms.)

European Convention on Human Rights (ECHR)*: 'The European Convention for the Protection of Human Rights and Fundamental Freedoms. The substantive rights it guarantees are largely incorporated into UK law by the Human Rights Act 1998.'

Hospital managers*: 'The organisation (or individual) responsible for the operation of the Act in a particular hospital (eg an NHS trust, an NHS foundation trust or the owners of an independent hospital). Hospital managers have various functions under the Act, which include the power to discharge a patient. In practice, most of the hospital managers' decisions are taken on their behalf by individuals (or groups of individuals) authorised by the hospital managers to do so. This can include clinical staff. Hospital managers' decisions about discharge are normally delegated to a 'managers' panel' of three or more people.'

Independent hospital*: 'A hospital which is not managed by the NHS.'

Independent Mental Capacity Advocate (IMCA)*: 'An advocate able to offer help to patients who lack capacity under arrangements which are specifically required to be made under the Mental Capacity Act 2005.'

Independent Mental Health Advocate (IMHA)*: 'An advocate available to offer help to patients under arrangements which are specifically required to be made under the Act.'

Independent Reviewing Officer (IRO): 'The appointment of an IRO is a statutory requirement for local authorities under the Adoption and Children Act 2002. IROs make an important contribution to the goal of significantly improving outcomes for looked after children. Their primary focus is to quality assure the care planning process for each child, and to ensure that his or her current wishes and feelings are given full consideration.' (SEND Code Glossary of terms).

Information, Advice and Support Services: 'Information, Advice and Support Services provide advice and information to children with SEN or disabilities, their parents, and young people with SEN or disabilities. They provide neutral and factual support on the special educational needs system to help the children, their parents and young people to play an active and informed role in their education and care. Although funded by local authorities, Information, Advice and Support Services are run either at arm's length from the local authority or by a voluntary organisation to ensure children, their parents and young people have confidence in them.' (SEND Code Glossary of terms).

Lasting power of attorney attorneys*: see Donees of lasting power of attorney

Learning disability qualification*: 'the rule which says that certain parts of the Act only apply to a learning disability if the learning disability is associated with abnormally aggressive or seriously irresponsible behaviour on the part of the person concerned.'

Leave of absence*: 'Permission for a patient who is detained in hospital to be absent from the hospital for short periods eg to go to the shops or spend a weekend at home, or for much longer periods. Patients remain under the powers of the Act when they are on leave and can be recalled to hospital if necessary in the interest of the patient's health or safety or for the protection of other people.'

Local Offer: 'Local authorities in England are required to set out in their Local Offer information about provision they expect to be available across education, health and social care for children and young people in their area who have SEN or are disabled, including those who do not have Education, Health and Care (EHC) plans. Local authorities must consult locally on what provision the Local Offer should contain.' (SEND Code Glossary of terms).

Looked after child (LAC): 'A child is looked after by a local authority if s/he is in their care by reason of a care order or is being provided with accommodation under section 20 of the 1989 Act for more than 24 hours with the agreement of the parents, or of the child if s/he is aged 16 or over (section 22(1) and (2) of the 1989 Act).' (DfE, *The Children Act 1989 guidance and regulations Volume 2: care planning, placement and case review* June 2015 para 1.21).

Managers' panel*: 'A panel of three or more people appointed to take decisions on behalf of hospital managers about the discharge of patients from detention or community treatment order.'

Mental disorder*: 'Any disorder or disability of the mind. As well as mental illnesses, it includes conditions like personality disorders, autistic spectrum disorders and learning disabilities.'

Nearest relative*: 'A person defined by section 26 of the Act (and in relation to children and young people, sections 27 and 28) who has certain rights and powers under the Act in respect of a patient for whom they are the nearest relative.'

NHS Commissioners*: 'Clinical commissioning groups (CCGs) and the NHS Commissioning Board (NHS England) are responsible for commissioning NHS treatment and care under the Act.'

NHS Commissioning Board (NHS England)*: 'The NHS Commissioning Board (also known as NHS England) reviews the commissioning plans of CCGs and assures the Secretary of State that the plans will deliver a comprehensive health service. The NHS Commissioning Board took over most of the functions of Strategic Health Authorities from 1 April 2013.'

NHS England: see NHS Commissioning Board.

NHS trust and NHS foundation trust*: 'Types of NHS body responsible for providing NHS services in a local area.'

NHS trust: 'NHS trusts are public sector bodies that provide community health, hospital, mental health and ambulance services on behalf of the NHS in England and Wales. Each trust is headed by a board consisting of executive and nonexecutive directors, and is chaired by a non-executive director.' (SEND Code Glossary of terms).

Personal Education Plan: 'An element of a Care Plan maintained by a local authority in respect of a looked after child, which sets out the education needs of the child. If a looked after child has an EHC plan, the regular reviews of the EHC plan should, where possible, coincide with reviews of the Personal Education Plan.' (SEND Code Glossary of terms).

Place of safety*: 'A place in which people may be temporarily detained under section 135 or 136 of the Act, as defined in section 135(6).'

Special Educational Needs (SEN): 'A child or young person has SEN if they have a learning difficulty or disability which calls for special educational provision to be made for him or her. A child of compulsory school age or a young person has a learning difficulty or disability if he or she has a significantly greater difficulty in learning than the majority of others of the same age, or has a disability which prevents or hinders him or her from making use of educational facilities of a kind generally provided for others of the same age in mainstream schools or mainstream post-16 institutions.' (SEND Code Glossary of terms).

Responsible Clinician (RC)*: 'The approved clinician with overall responsibility for a patient's case. Certain decisions (such as renewing a patient's detention or placing a patient on a community treatment order) can only be taken by the responsible clinician.'

Second Opinion Appointed Doctor (SOAD)*: 'An independent doctor appointed by the Care Quality Commission who gives a second opinion on whether certain types of medical treatment for mental disorder should be given without the patient's consent.'

Special guardianship orders (SGOs): are orders by which a person(s) (who must be 18 and over and cannot be the child's parents) is appointed to be the child's special guardian and who will have parental responsibility for the child. 'Subject to any later order, the special guardian may exercise parental responsibility to the exclusion of all others with parental responsibility, apart from another special guardian. An exception applies in circumstances where the law provides that the consent of more than one person with parental responsibility is required (for example, the sterilisation of a child). The intention is that the special guardian will have clear responsibility for all the day to day decisions about caring for the child or young person and his upbringing.' (DfE, *Special guardianship guidance Statutory guidance for local authorities on the Special Guardianship Regulations 2005 (as amended by the Special Guardianship (Amendment) Regulations 2016)* January 2017)

Tribunal*: 'The First-tier Tribunal (Mental Health) called in the Code 'the Tribunal' was established under the Tribunals, Courts and Enforcement Act 2007. This is a judicial body which has the power to discharge patients from detention, community treatment orders, guardianship and conditional discharge.'

Index